The Composition of Everyday Life

A Guide to Writing

SECOND EDITION

John Mauk
Northwestern Michigan College

John Metz

THOMSON

WADSWORTH

Australia • Brazil • Canada • Mexico • Singapore • Spain • United Kingdom • United States

THOMSON

WADSWORTH

The Composition of Everyday Life:
A Guide to Writing, **Second Edition**
Mauk/Metz

Publisher: Michael Rosenberg
Senior Acquisitions Editor: Dickson Musslewhite
Development Editor: Karen R. Smith
Editorial Assistant: Jonelle Lonergan
Technology Project Manager: Tim Smith
Managing Marketing Manager: Mandee Eckersley
Marketing Assistant: Dawn Giovanniello
Associate MarCom Manager: Patrick Rooney
Senior Project Manager, Editorial Production: Samantha Ross
Senior Art Director: Bruce Bond
Manufacturing Manager: Marcia Locke
Senior Permissions Editor: Isabel Alves

Permissions Editor: Tracey Douglas
Production Service: Laura Horowitz, Hearthside Publishing
  Services
Text/Cover Designer: Steve Mockensturm, Madhouse Creative
Photo Manager: Sheri Blaney
Photo Researcher: Marcy Lunetta
Cover Printer: CTPS
Interior Design and Compositon: Greg Johnson, Art Directions
Printer: CTPS
Cover Photos: *Clockwise:* © Gilbert Tremblay/Stock.Xchng;
  © Andy Lim/www.andylim.com; *both* © Xavier Ruiz/
  Stock.Xchng

Printed in China
4 5 6 7 09 08 07

Library of Congress Control Number: 2005936479
ISBN-13: 978-1-4130-1849-3
ISBN-10: 1-4130-1849-1

Thomson Higher Education
25 Thomson Place
Boston, MA 02210-1202
USA

For more information about our products, contact us at:
Thomson Learning Academic Resource Center
1-800-423-0563

For permission to use material from this text or product,
submit a request online at **http://www.thomsonrights.com**
Any additional questions about permissions can be submitted
by e-mail to **thomsonrights@thomson.com**

BRIEF CONTENTS

CONTENTS

Chapter 5 Analyzing Images   188

Chapter 6 Making Arguments   244

Chapter 8 Evaluating   358

Chapter 12 Thinking Radically: Re-Seeing the World   560

Using CEL as a Thematic Reader

Readings throughout this book can be grouped thematically—according to subject matter. Here we suggest how readings from different chapters might be grouped together thematically. As you explore a particular subject (education and learning, for example), you might focus on a particular rhetorical aim (such as evaluating or proposing a solution). Or you might explore a subject area without a particular aim in mind, eventually discovering not only a writing topic but also the rhetorical aim into which it falls.

Education and Learning

How do people view education in both formal and informal settings? What is the role of education in our lives, and how might we view that role differently? A variety of readings explore education and learning from a variety of viewpoints. Through reading, writing, and discussion, you might explore education and learning to the extent that you come to think differently about it and can participate in an ongoing dialogue about its role in people's lives. You might discover an important point about education by exploring a memory, identifying a less-usual relationship, making sense out of an observation, redefining a key term, and so on.

> "The Grapes of Mrs. Rath," *Steve Mockensturm*
> "A *Beat* Education," *Leonard Kress*
> "What the Honey Meant," *Cindy Bosley*
> "Have It Your Way," *Simon Benlow*
> "In Search of . . . Something," *Skye Bass*
> "Why We No Longer Use the 'H' Word," *Dan Wilkins*
> "Why a Great Books Education Is the Most Practical!" *David Crabtree*
> "Entitlement Education," *Daniel Bruno*
> "When Bright Girls Decide That Math Is a 'Waste of Time,'" *Susan Jacoby*
> "How to Say Nothing in 500 Words," *Paul Roberts*
> "Television: Destroying Childhood," *Rose Bachtel*
> "The Menstrual Cycle," *Christiane Northrup, M.D.*
> "Group Minds," *Doris Lessing*

Justice and Equality

A quick survey of the readings about justice and equality listed below suggests a range of areas: Native American rights, body type, legal drugs, the mentally and physically challenged, wildlife, and so on. These readings can help you identify and explain a relationship, analyze a concept (such as "justice" or "equality"), respond to an argument, identify a cause, or propose a solution. What is justice, and how might exploring the concept of justice in today's world be of value? What interesting idea about justice and equality might you discover and share with others?

"Why We No Longer Use the 'H' Word," *Dan Wilkins*
"Crimes Against Humanity," *Ward Churchill*
"Cruelty, Civility, and Other Weighty Matters," *Ann Marie Paulin*
"Beware of Drug Sales," *Therese Cherry*
"The Tyranny of the Majority," *Lani Guinier*
"Is Hunting Ethical?" *Ann F. Causey*
"A Uterus Is No Substitute for a Conscience," *Barbara Ehrenreich*
"The New Politics of Consumption," *Juliet Schor*
"Why Doesn't GM Sell Crack?" *Michael Moore*
"The Menstrual Cycle," *Christiane Northrup, M.D.*
"An Apology to Future Generations," *Simon Benlow*

Environment and Animals

These readings, which offer different ways of looking at environment and animals, encourage you to explore ideas beyond your initial thoughts and beyond conventional beliefs. What is your relationship to the land? To the air? To the animals? How might you think differently about that relationship? And what might be the consequence of your new way of thinking?

"Americans and the Land," *John Steinbeck*
"Living Like Weasels," *Annie Dillard*
"Planting a Tree," *Edward Abbey*
"Gombe," *Jane Goodall*
"The Front Porch," *Chester McCovey*
"Is Hunting Ethical?" *Ann F. Causey*
"The New Politics of Consumption," *Juliet Schor*
"The Obligation to Endure," *Rachel Carson*
"Technology, Movement, and Sound," *Ed Bell*
"The Parting Breath of the Now Perfect Woman," *Chester McCovey*
"Farming and the Global Economy," *Wendell Berry*
"The Menstrual Cycle," *Christiane Northrup, M.D.*
"An Apology to Future Generations," *Simon Benlow*

Consumerism and Economy

Several readings in this book encourage you to think about yourself as a consumer. What and how do you consume? And what, if anything, do you produce by consuming? As with other subjects in CEL, you might spend an entire semester exploring this one subject area, or you might explore it for just one assignment. Perhaps it would be of great value to spend an entire semester exploring just this question: What does it mean to be a consumer?

"The Front Porch," *Chester McCovey*
"Have It Your Way," *Simon Benlow*

"We Love Them. We Hate Them. We Take Them." *Abigail Zuger*

"Addiction as a Relationship," *Jean Kilbourne*

"Rise of the Image Culture: Re-Imagining the American Dream," *Elizabeth Thoman*

"The Mighty Image," *Cameron Johnson*

"Response to Juliet Schor," *Betsy Taylor*

"Entitlement Education," *Daniel Bruno*

"Whales R Us," *Jayme Stayer*

"Rethinking Divorce," *Barbara Dafoe Whitehead*

"The New Politics of Consumption," *Juliet Schor*

"Sex, Lies, and Conversation: Why Is It So Hard for Men and Women to Talk to Each Other?" *Deborah Tannen*

"Technology, Movement, and Sound," *Ed Bell*

"Television: Destroying Childhood," *Rose Batchel*

"Farming and the Global Economy," *Wendell Berry*

"An Apology to Future Generations," *Simon Benlow*

America

These readings deal with America and being American. They allow you to explore the relationship between yourself and your country. (International students may find this subject to be especially interesting as they bring a unique perspective.) To what degree do the two—individual and country—influence each other? You can make observations, evaluate, identify causes, propose solutions, and so on. And, you can explore how America communicates with you.

"The Grapes of Mrs. Rath," *Steve Mockensturm*

"Americans and the Land," *John Steinbeck*

"Planting a Tree," *Edward Abbey*

"We Love Them. We Hate Them. We Take Them." *Abigail Zuger*

"In Search of . . . Something," *Skye Bass*

"Rise of the Image Culture: Re-Imagining the American Dream," *Elizabeth Thoman*

"Cartoons 'n Comics: Communication to the Quick," *Joy Clough*

"The Mighty Image," *Cameron Johnson*

"Revealing the Ugly Cartoonish Truth: *The Simpsons*," Simon Benlow

"Crimes Against Humanity," *Ward Churchill*

"Cruelty, Civility, and Other Weighty Matters," *Ann Marie Paulin*

"The Tyranny of the Majority," *Lani Guinier*

"Whales R Us," *Jayme Stayer*

"The New Politics of Consumption," *Juliet Schor*

"The Plight of High-Status Women," *Barbara Dafoe Whitehead*

"Hip-Hop: A Roadblock or Pathway to Black Empowerment?" *Geoffrey Bennett*

"Why Doesn't GM Sell Crack?" *Michael Moore*

"Group Minds," *Doris Lessing*

The World

This book encourages you to look outward—from self, to tribe, to nation, to world. The readings below allow you to think about your role in the world. How do your actions impact the world, and what is the world's impact on you? From "Planting a Tree" to "An Apology to Future Generations" you can read about and discuss a very interesting relationship—the one you have with the world.

"Planting a Tree," *Edward Abbey*
"Gombe," *Jane Goodall*
"The New Politics of Consumption," *Juliet Schor*
"When Bright Girls Decide That Math Is a 'Waste of Time,'" *Susan Jacoby*
"Farming and the Global Economy," *Wendell Berry*
"Why Doesn't GM Sell Crack?" *Michael Moore*
"The Menstrual Cycle," *Christiane Northrup, M.D.*
"An Apology to Future Generations," *Simon Benlow*

Self

Looking at self can be fascinating and worthwhile. The readings in this book encourage you to explore your own life in a way you have perhaps not done before. These readings about self go beyond mere expressive writing. They encourage you to connect with others, even though—or perhaps *especially when*—you are looking inward at yourself. You can explore how these readings, your own writing, and focused discussion with others helps you to see differently—to learn something about yourself and connect it to the world around you.

"How I Lost the Junior Miss Pageant," *Cindy Bosley*
"The Greatest Gift," *Samantha Tengelitsch*
"A *Beat* Education," *Leonard Kress*
"Thrill of Victory . . . The Agony of Parents," *Jennifer Schwind-Pawlak*
"What the Honey Meant," *Cindy Bosley*
"Friend or Foe?," *Dean A. Meek*
"What It Means to be Creative," *S.I. Hayakawa*
"In Search of . . . Something," *Skye Bass*
"Addiction as a Relationship," *Jean Kilbourne*
"Cruelty, Civility, and Other Weighty Matters," *Ann Marie Paulin*
"*The Andy Griffith Show:* Return to Normal," *Ed Bell*
"Rethinking Divorce," *Barbara Dafoe Whitehead*
"The New Politics of Consumption," *Juliet Schor*
"Throwing Up Childhood," *Leonard Kress*
"In Bed," *Joan Didion*
"Knuckle Down," *Ani DiFranco*
"The Plight of High-Status Women," *Barbara Dafoe Whitehead*
"The Menstrual Cycle," *Christiane Northrup, M.D.*
"Group Minds," *Doris Lessing*

Others (Community)

Can we look at ourselves without looking at our community? Both subjects (self and others) explore relationships between the individual and his or her surroundings. What is community? How is community created? These readings will help you to explore what we commonly call *community,* to consider how it works, and to examine your place in it. An entire writing course might be an exploration of one very important question: What is the relationship between community and communication?

"The Greatest Gift," *Samantha Tengelitsch*
"Dog-Tied," *David Hawes*
"Living Like Weasels," *Annie Dillard*
"Cruelty, Civility, and Other Weighty Matters," *Ann Marie Paulin*
"Is Hunting Ethical?" *Ann F. Causey*
"Rethinking Divorce," *Barbara Dafoe Whitehead*
"Technology, Movement, and Sound," *Ed Bell*
"Television: Destroying Childhood," *Rose Bachtel*
"The Parting Breath of the Now Perfect Woman," *Chester McCovey*
"Hip-Hop: A Roadblock or Pathway to Black Empowerment?" *Geoffrey Bennett*
"Farming and the Global Economy," *Wendell Berry*
"Why Doesn't GM Sell Crack?" *Michael Moore*
"An Apology to Future Generations," *Simon Benlow*
"Group Minds," *Doris Lessing*

Language and Culture

How is language important in culture? How is language important in the way a person thinks? These readings deal with the relationship between language and culture—between words and ideas. For example, "handicapped" is a word, but it is also a concept—a very important one. These readings and others will help you step back and explore the relationship between words, ideas, and actions. Through exploration of this subject, you might discover that your college writing class is something more than you had originally imagined it to be.

"The Grapes of Mrs. Rath," *Steve Mockensturm*
"In Praise of the Humble Comma," *Pico Iyer*
"Why We No Longer Use the 'H' Word," *Dan Wilkins*
"Rise of the Image Culture: Re-Imagining the American Dream," *Elizabeth Thoman*
"Cartoons 'n Comics: Communication to the Quick," *Joy Clough*
"The Mighty Image," *Cameron Johnson*
"Crimes Against Humanity," *Ward Churchill*
"Why a Great Books Education Is the Most Practical!" *David Crabtree*
"Whales R Us," *Jayme Stayer*
"Rethinking Divorce," *Barbara Dafoe Whitehead*
"Sex, Lies, and Conversation: Why Is It So Hard for Men and Women to Talk to Each Other?" *Deborah Tannen*
"When Bright Girls Decide That Math Is a 'Waste of Time,'" *Susan Jacoby*
"The Plight of High-Status Women," *Barbara Dafoe Whitehead*

"Hip-Hop: A Roadblock or Pathway to Black Empowerment?" *Geoffrey Bennett*
"Why Doesn't GM Sell Crack?" *Michael Moore*
"The Menstrual Cycle," *Christiane Northrup, M.D.*

Gender and Identity

What role does gender play in our lives? What does it mean to be male or female? How does gender affect our identities? And what influence can we have on issues of gender and identity? This group of readings can be used in combination with other reading groups—from America or pop culture, for example. Instead of exploring just gender and identity, you might narrow your focus to readings that relate to gender and identity and pop culture.

"How I Lost the Junior Miss Pageant," *Cindy Bosley*
"The Greatest Gift," *Samantha Tengelitsch*
"The Thrill of Victory . . . The Agony of Parents," *Jennifer Schwind-Pawlak*
"Cruelty, Civility, and Other Weighty Matters," *Ann Marie Paulin*
"Rethinking Divorce," *Barbara Dafoe Whitehead*
"Throwing Up Childhood," *Leonard Kress*
"Sex, Lies, and Conversation: Why Is It So Hard for Men and Women to Talk
    to Each Other?'" *Deborah Tannen*
"When Bright Girls Decide That Math Is a 'Waste of Time,'" *Susan Jacoby*
"In Bed," *Joan Didion*
"A Uterus Is No Substitute for a Conscience," *Barbara Ehrenreich*
"The Plight of High-Status Women," *Barbara Dafoe Whitehead*
"The Menstrual Cycle," *Christiane Northrup, M.D.*

Parents and Family

What role do our parents play in our lives? Such a question might be explored endlessly with interesting results for both writer and reader. You might spend an entire semester exploring issues about parents and family. Such a simple subject area can prove to be far more complicated—and interesting—than you first imagined. What might be the value of thinking analytically and finding public resonance regarding the subject of parents and family?

"How I Lost the Junior Miss Pageant," *Cindy Bosley*
"The Greatest Gift," *Samantha Tengelitsch*
"The Thrill of Victory . . . The Agony of Parents," *Jennifer Schwind-Pawlak*
"What the Honey Meant," *Cindy Bosley*
"Friend or Foe?" *Dean A. Meek*
"Gombe," *Jane Goodall*
"The Front Porch," *Chester McCovey*
"*The Andy Griffith Show:* Return to Normal," *Ed Bell*
"Rethinking Divorce," *Barbara Dafoe Whitehead*
"Throwing Up Childhood," *Leonard Kress*
"An Apology to Future Generations," *Simon Benlow*

Popular Culture

What is the relationship between the individual and his or her pop culture? In what ways are we products of our own popular culture? From beauty pageants to hopping trains, the readings dealing with popular culture allow you to consider the world that surrounds you from a fresh perspective. You can explore the *why* of your own behavior, considering how you and others are influenced by pressures of which you are both very aware and barely aware.

"How I Lost the Junior Miss Pageant," *Cindy Bosley*
"A *Beat* Education," *Leonard Kress*
"The Front Porch," *Chester McCovey*
"Onward, Gamers, Onward!" *Royce Flores*
"Have It Your Way," *Simon Benlow*
"Addiction as a Relationship," *Jean Kilbourne*
"Rise of the Image Culture: Re-Imagining the American Dream," *Elizabeth Thoman*
"Cartoons 'n Comics: Communication to the Quick," *Joy Clough*
"The Mighty Image," *Cameron Johnson*
"Revealing the Ugly Cartoonish Truth: *The Simpsons*," *Simon Benlow*
"Crimes Against Humanity," *Ward Churchill*
"Cruelty, Civility, and Other Weighty Matters," *Ann Marie Paulin*
"Entitlement Education," *Daniel Bruno*
"Is Hunting Ethical?" *Ann F. Causey*
"*Star Wars*," *Roger Ebert*
"Whales R Us," *Jayme Stayer*
"*The Andy Griffith Show:* Return to Normal," *Ed Bell*
"Rethinking Divorce," *Barbara Dafoe Whitehead*
"The New Politics of Consumption," *Juliet Schor*
"Sex, Lies, and Conversation: Why Is It So Hard for Men and Women to Talk to Each Other?" *Deborah Tannen*
"Television: Destroying Childhood," *Rose Bachtel*
"The Plight of High-Status Women," *Barbara Dafoe Whitehead*
"The Parting Breath of the Now Perfect Woman," *Chester McCovey*
"Hip-Hop: A Roadblock or Pathway to Black Empowerment?" *Geoffrey Bennett*

Technology

We cannot overlook technology. How does it influence the way we live? Through reading, writing, and discussion, you can explore beyond your initial thoughts and perceptions. You can consider the complex relationship in today's world between the individual and technology—or between one individual and another *because of technology.* What idea about technology might you discover and share with others, helping them to think or act differently?

"Americans and the Land," *John Steinbeck*
"We Love Them. We Hate Them. We Take Them." *Abigail Zuger*
"Planting a Tree," *Edward Abbey*
"The Front Porch," *Chester McCovey*

"Rise of the Image Culture: Re-Imagining the American Dream," *Elizabeth Thoman*

"Cruelty, Civility, and Other Weighty Matters," *Ann Marie Paulin*

"Beware of Drug Sales," *Therese Cherry*

"Whales R Us," *Jayme Stayer*

"*The Andy Griffith Show:* Return to Normal," *Ed Bell*

"The New Politics of Consumption," *Juliet Schor*

"Technology, Movement, and Sound," *Ed Bell*

"Television: Destroying Childhood," *Rose Bachtel*

"The Parting Breath of the Now Perfect Woman," *Chester McCovey*

"Farming and the Global Economy," *Wendell Berry*

"Why Doesn't GM Sell Crack?" *Michael Moore*

"The Menstrual Cycle," *Christiane Northrup, M.D.*

"An Apology to Future Generations," *Simon Benlow*

Acknowledgments

Book projects rely on people who can transcend job descriptions, conjure possibilities, and fix what might otherwise seem unbroken. The individuals involved make books that are more than mechanical reiterations. We have been fortunate to work with the best in the field, and we offer our humble gratitude: To our development editor, Karen R. Smith, for contributing her intensive focus and sophisticated perspective; to our production editor, Samantha Ross, for giving us constant attention (peeled eyeballs) and savvy advice; to Dickson Musslewhite for maintaining the institutional support behind and in front of the project; to Steve Mockensturm for shaping the textual landscape, charting out ideas, and fueling our aesthetic; to Janet McCartney for adjusting and vitalizing our prose; to Laura Horowitz for adeptly managing conversations, edits, and re-revisions; to Greg Johnson for carefully composing each page; to the marketing crew at Thomson Wadsworth who keep sounding the word about our projects; to the intensive sales folks throughout the country who give arms and legs to our books; and to Michael Rosenberg for consistent emphasis and affirmation.

Thanks also to our students and colleagues who graciously stumble along with us in our efforts to transcend *what is* and to invent *what could be.* Thanks to our families and friends for enduring yet another project—who have stopped saying, "I thought you were done."

Any textbook project requires hearty professionals who give up their time and energy to help steer the pedagogy in valuable directions. We relied heavily on the insights of our reviewers and were often humbled at their prowess. We are indebted to the following teachers, theorists, rhetoricians, and scholars:

Sarah Abts, *University of Toledo*

Russ Bodi, *Owens Community College*

Loretta Brister, *Tarleton State University*

Sharon Buzzard, *Quincy University*

Tom Carey, *Scottsdale Community College*

Jennifer Pooler Courtney, *The University of North Carolina at Charlotte*

Meoghan Byrne Cronin, *Saint Anselm College*

Susan M. Cruea, *Bowling Green State University*

Jim Dervin, *Winston-Salem State University*

Chitralekha Duttagupta, *Arizona State University*

Doug Eisner, *Fullerton College*

Diana Fox, *Western Michigan University*

Todd Fox, *California State University, Long Beach*

Darryl E. Haley, *East Tennessee State University*

A. Harper, *Scottsdale Community College*

Hershman John, *Phoenix College*

Emory D. Jones, *Northeast Mississippi Community College*

Paula J. Lambert, *Bowling Green State University*

Gary Leising, *Northern Kentucky University*

Lindsay Lewan, *Arapahoe Community College*

William Losinger, *Adirondack Community College*

Cameron MacElvee, *Scottsdale Community College*

Michael Mackey, *Community College of Denver*

Vincent Marianiello, *Bemidji State University*

Melissa McCaughan, *Northern Kentucky University*

Kate Mohler, *Mesa Community College*

Susan Moore, *Scottsdale Community College*

Marilee Motto, *Owens Community College*

Barb Nelson, *Bemidji State University*

Carol S. O'Shea, *Bowling Green State University*

Carole Pfeffer, *Bellarmine University*

Larry Roderer, *J. Sargeant Reynolds Community College*

Danielle Saad, *Alvernia College*

Donald R. Stinson, *Northern Oklahoma College*

Shirley Turner, *Scottsdale Community College*

Linda van der Wal, *Scottsdale Community College*

Karol L. Walchak, *Alpena Community College*

Note to Students

The first and most important principle of this book is that writing is deeply connected to everyday life. A writer develops ideas and revises thoughts simply by living life. If we see writing as something that only occurs during a few short hours before a deadline, we shrink all the intellectual processes and layers into a single isolated act. Granted, some isolated typing, drafting, and editing is necessary for academic writing. But such work is only a portion of the real-life activities of a writer. Writing occurs long before the computer is turned on or the pen is in hand. In short, writing is an extension of living and being curious.

Secondly, writing is not merely for communicating or expressing an idea. It is not the performance of something we know; rather, *it is the act of inventing, developing, and re-inventing what can be known.* In this sense, writing is an intellectual tool. The act of writing is not simply a one-way flow of information from the brain to the hand. Quite the opposite — it actually produces new thoughts; changes everyday life; and changes the individual consciousness of the writer, the reader(s), and the people who interact with both of them.

The act of writing is an intellectual struggle—to shape thoughts and make connections that seem, at first, totally impossible. Writers do not look for the easy topics; they understand that valuable ideas are not those that simply fall out of the brain and onto the page. And in the most difficult moments, they remember that difficulty is an essential part of the process. Because the human brain is not a *linear* machine (it does not necessarily produce thoughts that go from left to right and then down a page), writers understand that their ideas have to be formed and re-formed. And in that long, and sometimes exhausting, process, they turn frustration to inquiry. They hope to find the most valuable insights in the moments of uncertainty.

> The writer is an intellectual excavator, loosening the ground, and re-shaping the terrain.

As you begin *The Composition of Everyday Life,* remember that a writer engages everyday life, but also stops consistently amidst the hustle and bustle to discover meaning. While participating in the daily chaos, the writer also goes beneath the surface, looks behind the wall, digs up personal biases. The writer is an intellectual excavator: looking to discover what would otherwise be overlooked, left behind, or discarded. From this point on, when you are working or socializing, when you are steeped in everyday life, consider yourself a writer.

How to Use **The Composition of Everyday Life**

CHAPTER READINGS

The essays in this book were written for fellow scientists, philosophers, economists, business leaders, politicians, family members, students, and public citizens. They show the real writing that gets done in the public sphere—how real people talk to their colleagues and to the public.

Despite their discipline or career field, the writers all seek to communicate a point that involves and impacts the world around them. And while writing techniques and personal styles differ, some qualities are constant: valuable insights, well-supported ideas, and engaging voices.

In academia, we read for particular reasons: To re-think issues, to discover positions we had not previously imagined, to revise common perceptions. To fulfill such goals, we cannot breeze through paragraphs. We must expect to work through ideas, even struggle at times. And most importantly, we must expect to be surprised, to have our comfortable mental rooms messed up occasionally. Reading in academia means being intellectually adventurous and expecting something new or radically different. It also means reading actively: always analyzing and re-figuring ideas as they develop throughout a text.

To help you read actively and critically, each reading is followed by Writing Strategies and Exploring Ideas questions. Also, each chapter features an *annotated* essay (an essay with comments and analysis in the margins). These annotations show a reader stopping at certain places, noticing particular claims, and speaking back to ideas.

WRITING TOPICS

The Composition of Everyday Life offers several possibilities for inventing and developing writing topics. Students can (1) read the essays in a designated chapter and then use the Ideas for Writing after one or more of the essays; (2) use the Point of Contact section, which will help generate topics from everyday life; or (3) read several content-related essays, according to the Thematic Reader table of contents (on pages xxv–xxxii), and then develop topics that emerge from the readings. For all three options, the Invention sections of each chapter can be used to develop writing projects.

> The only reason to write an essay is to invite yourself and your readers into a new way of thinking.

INVENTION

Have you ever wondered why some writers draw you in with new ideas and others seem like they are merely rehearsing their thoughts? What causes the difference? You might be inclined to believe that some people are simply better writers than others; however, good writing comes as a result of particular strategies, not innate mental capacity, and there is no more important writing strategy than *invention*.

> "Invention is the mother of necessities."
>
> —Marshall McLuhan

Invention is the process of discovering some idea you are not presently thinking and developing that idea through focused exploration. It is the activity of developing points and thinking through potential topics. Often it is associated with only a particular activity: coming up with an idea to write about. However, invention is a complex activity that extends far beyond the initial topic idea. It involves committing to an idea, exploring it in depth, and discovering its worth. When writers take the time to explore topics, they discover what is beyond their own biases or preconceptions—and even beyond the common beliefs of their potential audiences. They discover something worth telling, something that is not already floating around in everyone's minds. In short, invention makes all the difference between powerful, engaging writing that introduces new ideas and dull, lifeless writing that offers nothing but a writer's attempt to fulfill an assignment.

The following sections, which appear in each chapter, are designed to help you through the invention process:

- **Point of Contact** will help you discover a topic from everyday life.
- **Analysis** will launch you beyond initial thoughts and help you explore the topic.
- **Public Resonance** will help you extend the topic outward, to make the topic relevant to a community of readers.
- **Thesis** will help you focus your thinking and develop a revelatory point.
- **Rhetorical Tools** will help you support your point with a variety of common strategies.

The questions in each section are not meant to be answered directly in a final essay. But answering them during the invention stage of the writing process will help you discover ideas.

Point of Contact

The Point of Contact section, after the essays in each chapter, invites the writer to slow down, to stop, to notice common and not-too-common aspects of life. The *point of contact* refers to the intersection of the writer's perspective and the real world. It is where the writer's vision collides with issues, events, situations, behaviors, and people. The idea in this section is that writing begins with a discovery—a realization about something that might otherwise go unnoticed. Therefore, writers have to be ready; their radar has to be on.

As you go through the Point of Contact sections, you will notice lists of questions that are designed to generate possibilities for writing topics. Think of the questions as exploration tools; they raise possible points of interest for writing. However, the lists are by no means exhaustive; they are simply examples of what can be asked. Follow up (in peer groups or alone) to generate more questions. (And if you are outside of an academic setting, it is certainly fair play to borrow a family member or friend to help with the invention process.)

Analysis

We are all familiar with analysis. We participate in it constantly. We see auto mechanics analyze our cars to discover the cause of the knocking sound. We see our doctors analyze conditions to understand why we feel sick. Basically put, such analysis is a process of discovering *why* and/or *how* something occurs. But analysis also involves discovering meaning. Writers are not content to simply see a person or situation or object. They explore the *significance*; that is, they imagine what ideas a thing might suggest. For instance, a writer sees an empty storefront in a strip mall and imagines that it suggests corporate irresponsibility or a declining economic system or even the end of an era when businesses lasted for several years before leaving a community. In other words, the storefront has potential meaning when analyzed (and often that analysis, as we will make clear in the next section, can make a topic relevant to a broader community).

> Revealing complexity is at the heart of college writing.

Analysis leads to the complexities of issues, and revealing those complexities, rather than avoiding them, is at the heart of college writing. The Invention questions in each Analysis section are designed to help you reveal the complexities of your topic. As in all the invention sections, the goal of the questions is to help generate some idea that is distinct, surprising . . . even weird.

Public Resonance

Perhaps the most important feature of writing is that it matters to a reader. This may sound obvious, but topics are not necessarily, in and of themselves, relevant to people's lives. They need to be *made* relevant. They need to be expressed in a way that involves readers. Consider capital punishment: It is not, in itself, a relevant topic to the average college student—or even the average American citizen. Most people have not had a personal experience with the death penalty, but many people still have much to say about it. Why? The answer is rather simple: Capital punishment has been *made* relevant. Human rights activists, civil liberties groups, and religious groups have spoken or written the relevance of capital punishment into being. They have made the life of a death row inmate in Texas relevant to a suburban schoolteacher in Minnesota or a biology major at UCLA.

Good writers can make an issue resonate with the feelings, thoughts, and situations of readers. They can make personal situations resonate with readers. They can transform a bad day at the office into an important efficiency issue for all workers. Or they can make a seemingly distant event, like the deforestation of rainforests or the death of a prison inmate, real and immediate. They make a connection between two things: (1) what they see, know, do, believe, and feel and (2) how that matters to other people. It may not matter to every other person, but generally it *resonates* with the public. It speaks to and engages the members of a community who, like the writer, are able to look beyond themselves (beyond the "me") and into the public arena (the "we").

The assumption behind public resonance is that we are deeply connected to others in our communities—and even beyond those communities. Our very identities are bound to a complex system of relationships that extend into all different realms of social life. We are tied by economic, social, institutional, political, familial, religious, and even physiological connections. We share laws, fears, dreams, and hopes. And when writers tap into those connections, when they make topics part of that large social network, they achieve public resonance.

Thesis

A thesis statement is more than a one-sentence summary of an essay. It represents an essay's most pointed and thick idea—the one that gives everything else in the essay purpose. Whether the essay project is observing, arguing, or problem solving, thesis statements focus writer and reader on an intensive claim—one that reveals some new insight or way of seeing.

Thesis statements do not emerge out of thin air. They come from an intensive evolution, in which writers develop ideas with hard questions, focused dialogue, and reflective writing. Therefore,

> **Revelatory thesis statements show the writer and reader how to re-see the topic. They reveal something new, which is the goal of college writing.**

each chapter of *The Composition of Everyday Life* includes a thesis section with prompts, sample thesis statements, and common thesis problems. Each section also shows the Evolution of a Thesis, the gradual development of one writer's idea.

Rhetorical Tools

A *rhetorical tool* is a persuasion technique, a strategy for making people believe or accept an idea. Throughout the book, we will often refer to writers' rhetorical strategies—the techniques they use to convey their ideas and attempt to convince others to accept their positions. Good writers use good rhetorical tools. They come in many different forms:

Narration is the act of storytelling. Stories are often used to persuade people, to help them appreciate the value of an idea.

Description involves giving specific details to the reader. Sensory details (sounds, smells, sights, tastes, touches) prompt a reader to experience a topic—and so accept the ideas the writer offers.

Illustration is the graphic depiction of an idea. While illustration certainly suggests pictures and charts, it can also be accomplished with words.

Allusions are references to some bit of public knowledge—such as an historical event, a news event, a popular culture icon, or a literary text.

> The term *rhetoric* comes from ancient Greece, where philosophers such as Aristotle studied the acts of persuasion and the role of language in public affairs.

Scenarios are hypothetical situations.

Testimony is an eyewitness account of a particular scene or situation.

The Rhetorical Tools section in each chapter explains the strategies that are most applicable and appropriate to that writing situation. However, no strategy is exclusive to any particular kind of writing. (The tools depend on the task at hand—the purpose, the audience, the topic.) The strategies introduced throughout the book can be used for unlimited writing situations. In Chapter 6, Making Arguments, the rhetorical tools become a bit more complicated. They involve *appeals, counter-arguments,* and *concessions.* As you will see, the latter chapters of the book (from Chapter 6 on) all involve argumentative rhetorical tools; however, those introduced earlier in the book (such as narration, allusion, and so on) can also apply to argumentative writing. As you move through the book, think of your collection of rhetorical tools growing.

> "If school sucks, it's because all the invention has been removed, and students do little else besides practice and perform."
>
> —Justin James

Organizational Strategies

Writers must decide when and where they will use different rhetorical tools. Whether narrating an event, describing a scene, offering evidence, or making an allusion, writers can arrange rhetorical tools in an unlimited number of ways. If a writer has succeeded, a completed text should read like a coherent journey: The reader begins with some sense of direction (a good introduction), passes through various locations and over different terrain (in separate paragraphs), which are all connected with road signs (transitions). And finally, having traveled an intellectual route, the reader should feel as though he or she has arrived somewhere unique and valuable (a good conclusion).

The Organizational Strategies sections suggest various possible ways ideas might be arranged. They present common (and sometimes not-so-common) options for shaping essays, ordering points, and connecting ideas.

Writer's Voice

When we talk, we project a character or mood, not only by choosing certain words, but also by changing the sound, pitch, and pace of our voices. (Some people talk with dramatic ups and downs; others blab at us in a single-note dirge.) Also, when we talk, we have the added tool of physical gestures. We can swing our hands around wildly or bow our heads, or open our eyes very wide—all at different moments of a sentence—simply to project an attitude. As writers, we have just as many strategies at our disposal. We may not be able to use our hands and eyeballs to gesture to the reader, but we have plenty of *writerly* strategies.

Every writer, for each writing event, creates a voice—the character that is projected by the language and style of the essay. Writers use a vast array of techniques to create voices. Sometimes those voices are very sober and formal. Other voices are comedic, even hilarious. This does not mean that the topic itself is funny; it means that the writer's presentation of ideas is humorous. Some of the best writers can make a potentially dull topic feel quirky, or a light topic have depth and profound significance. Of course, most writers fall somewhere in the middle—between serious and comic, between utterly stiff and totally untamed.

Ultimately, you will create a voice whether you know it or not. That is, by simply writing a sentence, in some small way, you create a voice. And since a writerly voice will emerge from your essays, it's certainly better to be crafty; otherwise, your voice might very well come off as . . . well . . . boring.

The Writer's Voice section in each chapter will help you to shape an appropriate voice or to explore different voices. While it is valuable to develop a personal voice (a style that feels unique or somehow genuinely more *you*), it is more valuable to experiment with voices. Because we often have to write in various different contexts, for various different audiences, and on various different occasions, we need to be flexible, able to fit into audiences' conventions and expectations. (A radically informal, knee-slappin' voice would not go over well in a formal report to a government agency, nor would an overly somber voice be appropriate for a public invitation to a community event.) Learning how to stylize voice according to the audience and situation is one of the most valuable skills for a writer.

> You will create a voice . . . whether you know it or not.

Vitality

Vitalized writing is lively. It yanks on readers' awareness. Vitality sometimes calls for winding sentence patterns that bring the reader through important intellectual curves and into nuanced, layered thoughts. And it sometimes calls for brief statements—short pops to the brain. The important principle is that sentences are the only interaction between a reader and writer. If the sentences are full of empty phrases, stiffened by repetitious patterns, or slowed by jumbled clauses, the reading experience will be lifeless.

Creating vitality in writing requires close attention to sentence patterns—and a commitment to shaping and reshaping the language. To that end, each chapter in *The Composition of Everyday Life* includes a section that explains and illustrates particular vitality strategies. Like the rhetorical tools, vitality strategies are not exclusive to any one chapter or writing situation. They can be applied across the board—according to the writer's discretion.

> Vitalized sentences propel readers into and through ideas.

Revision and Peer Review

Revision is about re-approaching ideas. As academic writers work, they are constantly re-thinking their original ideas. To some degree, revision is fused into every act of the writing process. Writers are constantly asking questions: "Is this the best way to do this?" "Is there a better way to engage my reader?" Writers also benefit from a *holistic* re-reading of their work: a process that involves first stepping away from the text for a period of time, and then re-examining everything (the main ideas, the supporting points, the organization, and even the voice). This probably sounds intimidating—re-thinking everything after a significant amount of work has already gone into a draft. But revision is where a writer can make a text function as a whole—by making important connections and adding necessary detail. Often, it is only through revision that a text comes to life. And then, after a holistic, or global, re-reading of the text, writers go on to editing, making smaller, sentence-level changes.

Each chapter provides a variety of revision prompts. They appear throughout the Invention sections and invite you to stop, re-focus on the ideas you've created, to investigate the value and complexity of those ideas—with the hope that everything can be more intense, more focused, more engaging. Each chapter also includes a Peer Review section so that writers can share their projects with others and receive focused and helpful feedback.

Delivery

One look at history tells us that writing changes the world. It provokes people to think differently and ultimately to act differently. Consider, for example, the Declaration of Independence: Jefferson's declaration helped a group of diverse colonies imagine themselves as a unified people against a tyrannical king. Or consider Mary Wollstonecraft's *Vindication on the Rights of Women,* which prompted increasingly more public debate about the role of women in everyday life. And beyond these momentous historical texts, everyday writing, the kind that gets done in offices and homes and schools, also changes the world. Memos about office meetings or new policies directly impact people's behaviors. Letters (or e-mails) to friends and relatives can profoundly influence their behaviors and their attitudes. Advertising changes how we think about ourselves and the world around us: The constant presence of particular words and slogans eventually prompts us to think (even desire!) in certain ways. And we all use written instructions to get us through complicated tasks (like hooking up the stereo).

But on a deeper level, beyond hooking up an FM receiver, academia depends on the idea that writing affects how people think. The academic community works on the assumption that writing can motivate people to re-consider ideas or even consider something totally novel. The practice of writing, then, is deeply connected to the act of influencing thought.

At the end of each chapter in *The Composition of Everyday Life,* the Delivery section contains questions about the consequences of your writing. The goal is to see the relationship between your work (your thinking, your typing, your revising) and the world that surrounds you. The Delivery sections also invite you to go "Beyond the Essay"—to take your ideas from the chapter and re-cast them in some other format: a poster, a cartoon, and so on. As you explore the various possibilities of writing, speech, action, and visual rhetoric, see Chapter 14, Everyday Rhetoric, for examples and guidelines. This chapter explores various possibilities for interacting with the world.

A Final Note

As you work through the chapters, remember that writing is not merely a tool for expressing opinions; rather, it is a tool for making new ideas, and for adding new dimensions to old ideas. Our purpose in writing is not merely to express what we think, but to shape what can be known. We are hoping to explore intellectual possibilities. In this light, the college essay can be seen as a record of intellectual exploration—a writer's attempt and invitation to figure out something new.

Our purpose: to explore and shape what can be known.

THE COMPOSITION
OF EVERYDAY LIFE

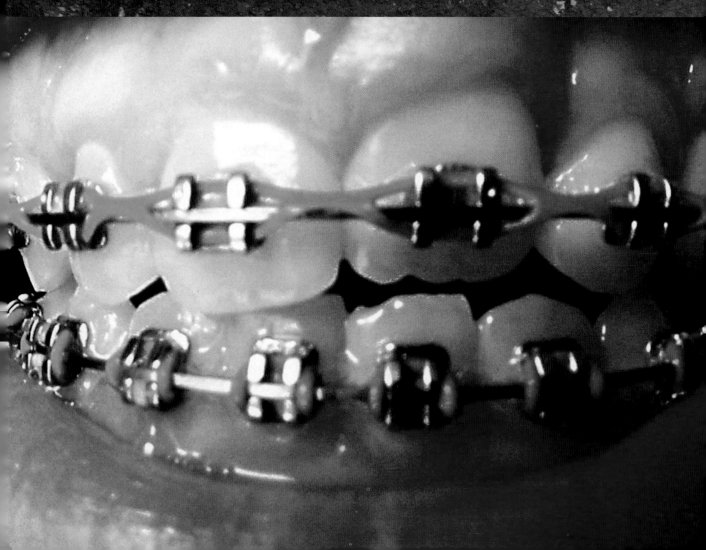

Chapter Contents

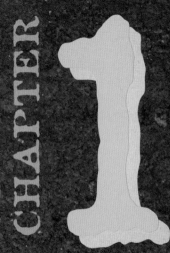

CHAPTER 1

"Those who fail to learn the lessons of history are doomed to repeat them."

—George Santayana

You have probably heard this famous statement—perhaps when someone in a history class asked plaintively, "Why do we have to learn this stuff?" Santayana's point, of course, is that the past is filled with situations that teach us about ourselves, and that ignoring the past results in blindness to the present and future. While Santayana's statement is most often applied to a collective history (e.g., American or world history), it also suggests something for the individual. In the same way that countries learn from their pasts, individuals come to new insights because of their own experiences. Obviously, we learn basic *dos* and *don'ts* from experience (not to ride a bike over the icy patch in the driveway, not to talk during math class, not to indulge too much the night before an exam). But our pasts are filled with more opportunity for insight beyond simple I'll-never-do-that-again situations. A vast array of moments lurks in the past, moments that may mean far more than what we have always assumed.

Writers looking into their pasts attempt to learn something new, to understand the importance of some moment, or to understand the significance of a situation. They are retrieving an event or situation, uncovering a moment, and examining it from their present perspective. The hope is that the writer will see more about the situation than he or she possibly could have seen in the past. Imagine an adult writer looking back at a childhood baseball game: As a child, he fretted over striking out in the last inning. But as an adult, he can see how important that moment of failure was to his life, to his intellectual and spiritual growth. The present (adult) writer is able to see this because the elapsed time has allowed him emotional and intellectual distance.

In academia, writers often look to the past for insight:

- In a sociology course, students recall their childhood communities; they pay close attention to the institutions (churches and schools) they attended and include their memories in a theory about institutional affiliation.

- A psychology professor prompts students to recall their early experiences with non-parental authority (such as teachers, extended family, and babysitters) and form a theory of authority based on those experiences.

- In a Western Civilization course, students recall their early experiences with organized religion. They include their experiences in their collective examination of religious principles.

Memories do not, in themselves, teach us anything. We must create the lesson. We must look back at the past with a certain perspective: one of curiosity and possibility. Although we have lived through the past, we must entirely rediscover it if we are to learn.

This chapter will help you rediscover a specific situation or event from your past, explore it in depth, develop a particular point about it, and communicate your ideas in writing. The following essays will provide insight to various writing strategies. After you read the essays, you can find a topic in one of two ways:

1. Go to the **Point of Contact** section to find a topic from your everyday life.
2. Choose one of the **Ideas for Writing** that follow the essays.

After you find a topic, go to the **Analysis** section to begin developing your ideas.

Each essay in this chapter takes the reader back in time to a particular event or set of events from the writer's life. However, the essays are not merely memories; rather, they are reflections on the past that give way to new insights about family, education, growing up, even America. In each, the past is used to learn something and to share new insights with readers. In Bosley's essay, for example, the writer goes back into the past to find meaning and to dig up the origin of her own feelings in the present. Mockensturm's essay seems to exist at the intersection of his past and his daughters' present, where he rediscovers dimensions of his life. All the authors use their own experiences to show us some point that is bigger and more public than their own lives. That point, the idea that can be extracted from the personal and delivered to the public, is most often the main idea of these essays.

How I Lost the Junior Miss Pageant

Cindy Bosley

Most people have never participated in a beauty pageant. But nearly everyone has experienced the angst associated with the quiet pageantry of everyday life—the constant pressure to perform well in public, to look the part of a happy, stable, well-to-do member of society. Cindy Bosley, a teacher and published poet, is brave enough to share her early attempts at dealing with this pressure. On one hand, this essay is an examination of beauty pageants and the awkward system of values and beliefs that surround them; on the other, it is an intimate look at a mother/daughter relationship that is defined by the social goings-on of a small city in the middle of America. (Cindy Bosley's writing also appears in Chapter 2.)

Every evening of the annual broadcast of the Miss America Pageant, I, from the age of seven or so, carefully laid out an elaborate chart so that I might also participate as an independent judge of the most important beauty contest in the world. From my viewing seat on a green striped couch in my parents' smoky living room where the carpet, a collage of white, brown, and black mixed-shag, contrasted so loudly with the cheap 70s furnishings that it threatened my attention to the television set, I sat with popcorn and soda, pen in hand, thrilled at the oncoming parade of the most beautiful women in the world.

In the hours before the show began, I'd carefully written out in ink, sometimes over and over, names of all 50 states, Washington, D.C., and Puerto Rico along the y axis of my paper. And my categories of evaluation of the contestants ribbed themselves along the x axis—beauty, poise, swimsuit, evening gown—plus categories of my own—hair, likability, teeth. Over the years, an increasingly complex system of points and penalties evolved: an extra point for being tan, a loss of points for sucking up, more points for breasts, more points for unpainted nails, fewer points for big noses, fewer points for skinny lips, an extra point for smartness, subtraction of a point for playing the piano. Who wants to hear a sonata? Dance for me, bounce your bootie.

My mother had secret hopes. Finally divorced for the second time from the same man, my father, she sat with me and gave her own running commentary about who was cute, who smiled too much, who would find a handsome husband. My mother, having always been a little to a lot overweight, excelled at swimming, and she told me much later that she chose swimming because she didn't feel fat in the water. Her sister was the cheerleader, but she was a swimmer, too heavy for a short skirt of her own, she said. My mother's secret was that she wanted the winner to be her daughter. Sitting with me on the couch at 137 North Willard Street, she already knew I wasn't tall enough or pretty enough in the way of models and movie stars to ever stand a chance, but her real fear, which I only became aware of as an older teen, was that I would always be too chubby and too backward and too different and too poor, for which she blamed herself, to win a beauty pageant. Still, there were always those surprises of the contests—Miss Utah? She was no good! Why did she win? What were those judges thinking! It should have been Miss Alabama, anyone can see that. Who would have guessed Miss Utah, with that mole on her shoulder?

After my mother's never-subtle hints that if I'd just lose 20 pounds boys would like me and I might even win a beauty contest, it was my friend Bridget who wanted us to enter the Ottumwa (pronounced Uh-TUM-wuh) Junior Miss Pageant together. I secretly believed that I stood a better chance than Bridget did, though she had the right name and the right body, though she wore the right clothes and was more magazine-beautiful than I. I had *some* hope for the contest: I had *some* talents and a kind of baby-cute innocence complete with blond hair and blue eyes that I was sure the judges would find "charming and fresh." Yeah, okay, so I was already engaged to be married—so what—I was still on my way to college, and Bridget was not. And Judy was funny but

had a flat face. Marcy was smart but had no breasts or hips. Carol was pretty but totally uncoordinated and her knees came together when she jumped. Desirea had enviable boobs, almost as nice as mine and probably firmer, but her chin did weird things when she smiled and her eyes were brown.

5   We practiced, all of us together, several times a week with a lithe woman—somebody's mom with good hair and body—getting us into form for the stage. This was the era of *Flashdance,* so we all wore our own leg warmers and torn sweatclothes and fancy headband scarves. If you were one of the north-side girls (that meant your daddy was a businessman or doctor), you had gotten your leg warmers from Marshall Fields in Chicago. If you were Bridget, your dad worked at John Deere like mine but was in management and not out in the factory threading bolts on a greasy, noisy machine, so you got your leg warmers from the mall in Des Moines. If you were me, with a factory dad who didn't even live in the same house, you got your leg warmers from Kmart down the road because Target was all the way across town and too expensive, and Wal-Mart hadn't yet been born as far as we knew. The fancy mom-lady made sure everyone had a brochure about her charm school (this is small-town Iowa, mind you, so anyone operating a charm school and modeling agency in this town was kidding themselves. But making lots of money.).

So 14 of us, nervous, jealous, ears ringing with Mirror-Mirror-on-the-Wall, met daily for two weeks prior to the pageant to go over our choreographed group fitness routine to be performed, not in swimsuits, but in short-shorts and white T-shirts, Hooters-style (also not invented yet as far as we knew), and to discuss such techniques as Vaseline along the teeth and gum lines to promote smooth smiles, lest our lips dry out and get stuck in a grin during discussions with the judges of the agonies of world hunger. We were each responsible for our own talent routines and props, and each one of us had to provide a 5×7 black-and-white photo for the spread in the town paper.

The photographs were a problem. My father did not believe in such things for girls as shoes, clothes, haircuts, college, or photographs for Junior Miss, and so there was no way he was going to give a penny for a pageant-worthy dress or a professional photographer's 10-minutes-plus-proofs. I believe my mother even humiliated herself enough to ask. This was hard for her, since he'd admitted before leaving to a five-year affair with a woman who looked surprisingly like my mother but heavier. So Mom and I tried some Polaroid head-shots against the side of the house, but me dressed up in my prettiest sailor blouse couldn't counteract the hospital green of the aluminum siding. We moved up to our only other option, which was my mother's flash camera with Instamatic film, and still nothing suitable (I could have agreed on one of the Polaroid shots, but my mother knew it would knock me out of the contest for sure even before the night itself).

I don't know who she borrowed the money from or what she did to get the favor, but my mother had me down at Lee's Photography the very next afternoon, and he took one shot and offered us the one proof. Abracadabra, there was my face among all the other faces as a contestant in the Uh-TUM-wuh Junior Miss Pageant. From the layout in the paper, it looked to me, and to my flushed mother, as though I had as good a shot as any.

The contest night went quickly: my foot, couched, pinched, and Band-Aided uncomfortably in a neighbor's hand-me-down high heels, slipped (hear the auditorium's quick and loud intake of breath in horror!) as I walked forward to say my name with a strong, vibrant hello just like I'd been coached by the fancy-mom; my dress was last year's prom dress, which earned me no cool points with my peers but didn't lose me any either since I had none to subtract; I managed not to land on my bottom (as I had in every practice before the contest) in my gymnastics routine, self-choreographed with my own robot-style moves to the synthesizer-heavy tune "Electricity," by a band that was popular in Sacramento, California, in that year, 1985, but not yet in my hometown. (The cassette tape had been given to me by my Hispanic, juvenile delinquent, just-released-from-young-boy-prison-in-California ex-boyfriend Jim.)

10   My exercise routine went off very well in front of the crowd, and I don't think anyone could even tell that my shorts were soaking wet from having been dropped by me into the toilet just an hour before as I arranged my items for quick-change. My mother and fiancé were actually sitting together, their mutual hatred of each other squeezed like a child between them. I'd even kept myself from leaving my mother behind when, backstage after the contest as I hugged and cried in joy for the co-winners and out of desperate relief that it was over now, my mother, beside herself with embarrassment for me and disappointment for herself, and misunderstanding my tears, hissed loudly enough for the benefit of everyone, "STOP your crying, they'll think you're not a nice LOSER!"

So I had done it: I had been a contestant in the Junior Miss Pageant and my mother had the snapshots to prove it.

I'd lost the contest because I didn't yet know how to tell people what they wanted to hear. The small girl that boys secretly liked but wouldn't date doesn't win Miss America. The girl hiding in her room reading and writing poetry doesn't win Miss America. The girl playing violin despite her mother's anxiousness that other people will think she's weird doesn't win Miss America. The girl on Willard Street doesn't ever win Miss America.

But the truth is that I'd lost the contest when I told the judges, when they asked, that my most personal concern was my mother's loneliness, and if I could change anything at all, I would give her something—a man, God, anything to free her from that loneliness.

Clearly, I lacked the save-the-whales-and-rainforest civic-mindedness required not only of Miss America, but of Junior Miss America, too. Even, although one wouldn't think it, in Ottumwa, Iowa, where my mother would go on to work in a bathtub factory, and then a glue factory, and then an electrical connectors factory (the factory worker's version of upward mobility), and finally, a watch factory where they shipped and received not just watches but cocaine in our town that at that time had more FBI agents in it than railroad engineers.

And even in this town where my sister would go to work the kill floor of the pork plant where, for fun, the workers shot inspection dye at each other and threatened each other's throats with hack-knives. And even in this town where my cousin, age 13, would bring a bomb to seventh grade for show-and-tell, and get caught and evacuated, and be given community service to do because the public-school-as-terrorist-ground phenomena hadn't yet been born. And even in this town where if you want to go to college, you better know someone who knows how to get you there because otherwise it's too far away and too much money and too much trouble and way, way, way beyond your own intellect and sense of self to do it alone. How scary (get married). How wasteful (get married). How expensive (get married). How strange (get married). How pretentious (get married). How escapist (get married).

15   If your parents are crazy and poor, and if you can't win the Junior Miss Pageant, and if it's the kind of town where you stay or they don't ever want you coming back, you get married, you move to Texas where your husband sells drugs, you hide away from the world until your self grows enough to break you out, and then you leave and you pray for your mother's loneliness and you spend your life learning to come to terms with your own, and you are smart and willful and strong, and you don't ever have to draw another chart before the pageant begins.

My mother told me later that she was just sure I would have won the Junior Miss contest if I hadn't made that awful mistake in my gymnastics routine (I don't know what mistake she was talking about—it was the least flawed part of the evening), but I knew the truth about why I'd lost, and I knew I'd lost even before the contest or the practices began. I'd lost this contest at birth, probably, to be born to my father who had a date that night, and to my mother who believed some girls—girls like me, and girls like her—had to try very hard to catch and keep a boy's attention. I'd lost the contest in borrowed shoes and an out-of-date dress. I'd lost the contest with the engagement ring on my seventeen-year-old finger. I'd lost the contest with wet shorts and too funky music. I'd lost the contest with a bargain photograph and Kmart leg warmers. I'd lost the contest with an orange Honda Express moped parked between the other girls' cars. I'd lost the contest in a falling-down green house. I'd lost the contest in the grease on my father's hands and hair and the taste of grease in his lunchbox leftovers. I'd lost the contest in my growingly cynical evaluation of Miss America as I'd gotten older— "chubby thighs touching, minus five points," "big hair, minus three points," "too small nipples, minus two," "flabby arms, minus five," and subtract and subtract and subtract. It's a contest no one should want to win. Our mothers should not have such dreams for us. Our mothers should not have such loneliness.

Writing Strategies

1. Bosley provides details throughout her essay. Which ones work best for you? Select several details and compare them to the ones your classmates selected. Attempt to explain why certain details made the essay more engaging to you.

2. What is the public resonance of Bosley's essay? That is, how does it matter to others? How does it matter to someone who doesn't care at all about such pageants?

3. If workshopping Bosley's essay, how would you complete the following statements: What I like most about your essay is _____. The main suggestion I have about your essay is _____.

4. Bosley's title suggests that she will tell us how she lost the Junior Miss Pageant. Does she deliver? What is the point of her essay? How did she lose the pageant?

Exploring Ideas

1. Interview several classmates to find out how they view beauty pageants (or interview several people outside of class to find out their views). Record their responses, and then explain in writing what viewpoints seemed to be the most common, most unusual, most interesting, most thought-provoking.

2. How does Bosley's point about beauty pageants speak to larger (more general) issues, such as competition, class, tradition, media, and so on?

3. With others or alone, explore the past, identifying experiences that speak to the angst associated with the quiet pageantry of everyday life—the constant pressure to perform well in public, to look the part of a happy, stable, well-to-do member of society. What experiences of your own provide an intimate look at some relationship that is defined by social goings-on?

4. Do research to learn more about the history of the Miss America Pageant—its origins, its popularity, and how it has changed over the years. How has the pageant tried to stay in step with cultural trends? Why has the pageant, and American culture, changed?

5. Consider your responses to #4 above. How have other American traditions, besides the Miss America Pageant, changed with the culture?

Ideas for Writing

1. Discover the significance of an experience or activity you participated in with disappointing results. Perhaps it was sitting on the bench for an entire season in a sport, running for student council and not winning, pursuing a certain girl or boy without luck, or something else altogether.

2. Recall an experience or activity at which you exceeded your own expectations. What, now, is the significance of that experience to you?

If responding to one of these ideas, go to the **Analysis** section of this chapter to begin developing ideas for your essay.

"Our mothers should not have such dreams for us."

A *Beat* Education

Leonard Kress

It's easy to list the things we know. But it's impossible to list the things we do not know. Occasionally, people get a direct glimpse of the gaps in their learning and come face to face with the huge, dangerous, unruly reality beyond their knowing. For Leonard Kress, a poet and professor at Owens Community College in Toledo, Ohio, this moment came on a hobo-like trip to Chicago. As you read this essay, notice his allusion to the Beats—a group of influential writers and thinkers from the mid-twentieth century who lived hard and traveled throughout America, who dramatized freedom and intellectual revolution. Like Kress, many writers, musicians, artists, and scholars were influenced by the Beats and the world they imagined. (Kress's writing also appears in Chapter 9.)

At 20 I was convinced that the single most important experience, without which my education would remain shamefully incomplete, was that of hopping a freight. Doubtless, my sense of education at that time (as well as my sense of what constituted good writing) was more than mildly seasoned by huge doses of the Beats—Allen Ginsberg, Gregory Corso, William Burroughs, Kenneth Patchen, LeRoi Jones, and, of course, Jack Kerouac. That these writers were at the time considered non-scholarly, marginal, and were all but vilified by my literature teachers made them, I'm sure, that much more irresistible. I would merely open a page at random—a short story, say Kerouac's "Railroad Earth"—and find myself filled with wonder and admiration and conviction: this was sacramental:

> Remembering my wonder at the slow grinding movement and squee of gigantic boxcars and flats and gons rolling by with that overpowering steel and dust clenching closh and clack of steel on steel, the shudder of the whole steely proposition, a car going by . . . the frightening fog nights in California when you can see thru the mists the monsters slowly passing . . . when those wheels go over your leg they don't care about you.

I did manage, once at least, to imitate the Beats. I was staying with some friends in Grand Rapids, Michigan, when I decided, receiving little or no discouragement from them, to seek out the local freight yard. I figured I would ride the rails in whichever direction they took me—unconcerned as I was with notions of destination and arrival. Unable to summon up any practical or procedural advice on how to begin from Kerouac's disjointed and out-of-control prose, I simply searched for a site full of boxcars and cabooses and lanes upon lanes of tracks.

It was early morning and the yard seemed deserted, so I brazenly set forth. I had no fear of the dreaded railway dicks, no sense of the danger of heavy machinery, but I did carry with me a bright blue rucksack, a sense that all would go well if I only abandoned myself to the open road. As hoped for and expected, a figure appeared out of nowhere. I assumed he was something of a tramp or hobo—I had the sense at least not to ask him about his vocation—and he quickly took me under his grimy wing. With no exchange of words, we managed to cross over several tracks, duck out of sight of the hollering switchers, and second-guess the direction of cars clanking over shuntings. He knew which trains were already made up and ready to pull out, and which might sit for hours filling up with unbearable heat from the morning sun. He led me to one, sitting on the outer tracks, mostly a string of lime-dusty hoppers interspersed with empty boxcars—doors flung invitingly wide open! I rushed in front of him, tossed my rucksack in, and was about to hoist myself inside, when he grabbed my leg and tackled me down to the rails. I was too shocked to resist; he pinned me to the railroad ties and moved his head in real close to mine. Just when I was sure that he was about to slit my throat, he released his grip and delivered what seemed to be a prepared speech about hopping freights. "Don't never board a still train," I remember him saying, "they shut them doors when the train's pulling out. You get stuck in there, you roast, you just roast, that's all there is to it."

Although I was a bit chastened from the stern warning, which at the time didn't seem to be warranted, and covered with brush and gravel burns from the take-down, I felt that I had just participated in some arcane initiation rite and passed through it successfully, the bearer of some sort of *tramp-gnosis.* If I were to characterize it now, I might say that it seemed to be a particular mix of the medieval Franciscan ideal, International Workers of the World notions of brotherhood and solidarity . . . and my own middle class suburban naïveté.

5   We strode together—in some sort of unacknowledged sync—farther down the line, to a spot beyond the cluster of workers' shacks and railroad paraphernalia. Ducking in a trackside ravine almost as if we were kids playing backyard war, we waited until the freight began its slow grinding movement, almost overwhelmed by what Kerouac called that *overpowering steel dust and clenching closh and clack of steel on steel, the shudder of the whole steely proposition. . . .* We waited, nodding as each car rolled past, until a boxcar with unshut doors presented itself to us. Then we sprung up, tossed our packs inside and scissor-jumped our way in.

While I was making myself comfortable, shifting around on a sift of rust and pebbles, dangling my legs over the side, my companion leaped off, barely losing his footing, and rushed off. I didn't know why he left. I thought at first that he had forgotten something, later that he was trying to set me up—for what, though, I couldn't imagine. He just disappeared, and though the train was barely snailing along, I was afraid to jump down after him. As it picked up speed, however, I regretted not taking that chance, as my dangling legs were almost sheared off by a switching signal the boxcar curved past.

The ride itself was unbelievably jittery and uncomfortable. I couldn't open the can of beans I'd brought along, and the slices of bread I'd stuffed into my rucksack fell onto the floor and coated themselves in rust-flecked grease. The freight did, however, grant me a spectacular view of the setting sun as it ambled ever so slowly along the banks of Lake Michigan. And it did ease through innumerable small town backyards where children ran alongside, not easily winded, cheering both the train and me on. Even young mothers waved shyly while they pinned banner-like sheets onto their clotheslines.

Almost half a day later, around midnight, the train crunched into Chicago, where I hopped off, exhausted and exhilarated. As my shaky train-legs hit the gravel of the roadbed, I thought I heard a threatening shout, so I ran, tripped mostly, over the 50 or so tracks and platforms and switchings, down a steep embankment. Right into the middle of some rundown neon-shod shopping strip near 95th Street on the South Side— bars and liquor stores and boarded-up groceries, card readers, barber colleges, and storefront churches, groups of men hanging on the corners drinking from passed-around rumpled paper bags. Here was a whole gallery of street life like nothing I'd ever seen. Somehow the rickety freight ride and all that drama and lure of the past two days quickly dissipated, replaced by an urgent sense of new gaps in my learning, of new educational possibilities.

"Don't never board a still train," I remember him saying, "they shut them doors when the train's pulling out. You get stuck in there, you roast, you just roast, that's all there is to it."

Writing Strategies

1. Through his use of vivid language, Kress shows himself riding the rails. Identify several fresh expressions that appealed to you. Was it "shifting around on a sift of rust and pebbles" (¶ 6) or "he grabbed my leg and tackled me down to the rails" (¶ 3)? Explain how several expressions helped bring his experience to life for you.

2. How else might Kress have vividly described his experience for the reader? Write two or three additional sentences of description, and explain why each one is successful at describing the scene.

3. Describe Kress's voice as a writer. What does he sound like? Provide several examples from the essay (particular word choices, for example) that support your description. How is, or isn't, Kress's voice appropriate for an essay about hopping a freight train?

4. If workshopping Kress's essay, how would you answer the following questions: What do you like most about the essay? What do you like the least about it? What suggestion do you have for the writer?

5. Kress refers (or alludes) to several poets and writers in the essay. Explain the effect of these allusions: how they help to illustrate a point, how they influenced you as you read.

Exploring Ideas

1. How does the way Kress talks about education invite the reader to think differently about the subject?

2. How is Kress's essay part of a larger discussion? What is the general subject matter—or issue—of that larger discussion?

3. What educational experiences can you remember that might help you think further, and differently, about this topic?

4. Interview several people about an important learning experience of their own. How many people's experiences included formal education settings? How many didn't? How were others' experiences similar to or different from yours or Kress's? How might these responses help you better understand and write about an educational experience of your own?

Ideas for Writing

1. Have you had an experience without which your education would be shamefully incomplete?

2. Kress's train ride leaves him ready to learn. Recall an experience from your own life that had a positive impact on your education—not just because you learned something, but because your overall attitude about learning changed. Of course, a certain teacher might come to mind. If so, try to focus not on the teacher but on the experience (the train ride)—a very specific moment, perhaps—that left you ready to learn.

3. How might you respond to Kress's essay and thus take part in that ongoing discussion? What memories of your own can you use to illustrate your main idea?

If responding to one of these ideas, go to the **Analysis** section of this chapter to begin developing ideas for your essay.

The Thrill of Victory . . .
The Agony of Parents

Jennifer Schwind-Pawlak

We often get caught up in the moment. As children—and as adults—we first react to situations one way, and then later make better sense of what happened. Jennifer Schwind-Pawlak, who wrote the following essay for a college writing course, explores one of these moments from her past. As you read the essay, notice how Schwind-Pawlak uses her own particular experience to tap into a more universal one. From a new perspective, allowed for by the distance of time, she finds the positive value of what appeared back then to be a negative experience. In this essay, she stands back and talks about the experience, engaging the reader with key details, a mature writer's voice, and an important lesson.

Writing Strategies

Exploring Ideas

Worth writing about?

Trying to convey?

My own experiences?

Parents—one word that can strike many emotions in children when said aloud. Some children will smile and think about how silly their dad looked when he put carrot sticks up his nose that very morning, while others will cringe when they think about how their mother picked them up from school last week wearing orange polyester pants and a green shirt, oblivious to the hard work that some fellow went through to create the color wheel. My own emotional state of mind seemed to run the gamut throughout childhood. I chose to blame my parents for all of the traumatic events that unfolded but took pride in my obvious independence during the successes. One of the most heinous crimes that my parents committed was "the soccer foul." If I could have ejected them from the game of life at that point, I would have.

Ironically, I was not particularly fond of soccer. Being the youngest of four children, I often chose to run around the field with friends while my brothers and sisters performed feats of soccer, the likes of which had only been seen during the World Cup. I would happily contort my fingers into chubby pretzels while singing "The Itsy Bitsy Spider" as the game's events were recounted on the drives home. Still, whether by guilt or by the need to belong, I joined the team when I became of age.

The team that I played on was designed to turn the young and awkward into the swans of the soccer field. My father (a one-time soccer coach) explained several times that this was the time that I would learn the rules and workings of the game and that I shouldn't

Introduces general subject matter leading up to the main idea: Parent/child dynamics.

Develops essay through narration and description.

expect much more than that. Since it was a child's league, learning and the team experience were the focuses. Winning was a pleasant bonus but should not be achieved at the cost of the main objectives. This litany was taken and stored somewhere in the recesses of my brain. For me, however, the main objective was looking cool while running down the field chasing a spotted ball. Everything else seemed secondary.

Due to the family history, I attended every Tuesday and Thursday practice and managed to make each a social occasion while going through the motions of the game. I succeeded in understanding the game and, though not the most skilled of players, began to enjoy the half game of playing time that was required by the league for each player. Though I was far from a star player, I felt that my contribution mattered to the overall outcomes of the games, all of which had been lost to this point.

5 Sunday, the morning of the fifth game of the season, came with no warning. I got up, went to church with the family, then came home to suit up for the game. Upon arrival at the field, I was greeted by the coach and went to take my place along the sidelines with the rest of my team. There was a buzz of excitement that left me with the feeling that I would get when my brother would poke me with his fingertip after dragging his stocking feet across the carpet. The team that we were playing had a record identical to ours. We could win this game. I didn't care what the parents said. Winning would be a blast.

The coach kept me on the sidelines the entire first half of the game, which my pre-adolescent mind attributed to my obviously increasing skill at the game. He was saving his trump card, me, for the last half of the game. I knew this was rare, but I was sure that his reason was to bedazzle the crowd and the other team with my pure firepower on the field. The other players, except one other girl, continued to cycle in and out of the game. While I was excited because we were winning the game, I was concerned that the coach had forgotten about me. I inched, ever so slowly, toward him and started mindless conversation to let him know that I was there. He spoke to me, so I knew that he could not have forgotten about me. As the game was winding down, I was sure that he must have decided to put me in for the last play of the game.

The game ended.

I was horrified to realize that I had not played one moment of the first win of the season. After all of that practice and the ugly uniform, I was deemed such a poor player that I was not even good

---

Details are carefully selected: Father's explanation becomes key later in the essay.

We have all participated in these childhood activities that were supposed to teach us lessons, about sportsmanship, teamwork, etc.

We all—most of us—have not gotten to play at some point: Common experience?

Three-word paragraph has dramatic effect.

enough to play one moment of that game. How would I ever live this down at school? How would I face all of my classmates on Monday? My stomach began to churn, the way that it does when you are going down the first hill of any great roller coaster. I looked to my parents for support, which only added to the horror of that day.

Joann (the name I call my mother when she does something embarrassing) was screaming at the coach. In a voice so screeching that it rivaled fingernails on a blackboard, she told him that he was a disgraceful coach and that he should be ashamed of himself. She continued to point out the error of his ways by reminding him that I had not played at all in the game. How could she do this to me? My mother had managed to enlighten the few people that hadn't noticed on their own that I had not played at all. What was she thinking? She might as well have rented billboard space saying, "So what if Jeni sucks at soccer? The coach wouldn't let her play." My only thought was, "I don't want to go to school tomorrow!"

10   Looking back, I realize that it wasn't so bad the next day at school. I walked out to recess and talked about how nuts my mother was and everyone seemed to agree, sympathize, and get on with the important task of freeze tag. At that moment I wasn't sure that I would ever be able to forgive my mother for what happened that day, but, as far as I can recall, I began loving her again within the week. I am sure that she either cooked my favorite dinner, told a corny joke, or told me how much she loved me to make that lump of anger fade away.

I never went to soccer again. As a matter of fact, I never played another organized sport again. Maybe it was the fear of rejection. Maybe it was the uncertainty of my talent. Maybe I was just too busy with other things. I never really felt the urge to compete on that level after that day.

The relationship that I have with my parents has changed very much throughout the years. The polyester pants don't bother me anymore, but the carrot sticks still make me laugh. While their "soccer foul" embarrassed and angered me at the time, I understand and appreciate it now. My mother was angry <u>FOR</u> me. She was hurt <u>FOR</u> me. Through the pages of time, I can look back and see that, more often than not, I embarrassed her. She never stopped feeling for me, loving me, or protecting me. I have grown enough to realize that, though I often pointed out my parents' fouls, they scored countless goals that I didn't even notice.

Reflects on her experience: What "looking back" means.

Mentions possible impact of this experience.

Finds meaning through reflection.

Worth writing about: Because it's a common feeling growing up?

We have all, I guess, been embarrassed by our parents, though maybe not in this way.

Worth writing about because she sees the experience differently now. Sometimes—many times—we see differently when something's happening than we do later on.

She might want us to see this: Parents do things FOR us even though we not only don't appreciate it, but are embarrassed. My experiences:

1. my own flipping out and yelling at umpire in Little League.
2. my father's short pants.
3. Dad asking basketball referee after the game why he threw me out, then taking the referee's side.
4. Mom working at the gas station.

Writing Strategies

1. Describe Schwind-Pawlak's opening strategy. Does it work for you? Do you want to read on? How else might Schwind-Pawlak have begun her essay?

2. Why does Schwind-Pawlak tell us that her father "explained several times that this was the time that [she] would learn the rules and workings of the game and that [she] shouldn't expect much more than that" (¶ 3)? Why does she place this information in her third paragraph? Where else might she have placed this information, and how would that placement affect her essay?

3. Describe the tone of this essay. Is it funny, serious, pensive, silly? Describe it with your own one-word description and then refer to three sentences that support your decision.

4. Explain the effect of Schwind-Pawlak's one-sentence paragraph: "The game ended." (¶ 7)

5. Schwind-Pawlak writes, "My mother was angry <u>FOR</u> me. She was hurt <u>FOR</u> me." (¶ 12) Why do you think she decides to both underline and all-cap the word "for"?

Exploring Ideas

1. Describe a particular childhood experience that you view differently now that you are older. You might, like Schwind-Pawlak, remember an experience involving a parent and yourself in a public setting.

   - How do you view the experience differently now?

   - Why are you able to view the experience differently now?

   - How might your new way of viewing the experience help you to view present or future experiences differently?

2. In groups, discuss a film or novel in which one of the characters comes to learn a valuable lesson from a childhood or other past experience.

3. Read Cindy Bosley's essay "How I Lost the Junior Miss Pageant" (earlier in this chapter) and compare Bosley's experience to Schwind-Pawlak's. Specifically, how do the two essays explore the angst and pressure involved in being a member of society?

Ideas for Writing

1. What is the significance of a big game or event from your past?

2. What emotional or intellectual experience has prevented you from ever doing something again? How has the experience influenced your later decisions?

If responding to one of these ideas, go to the **Analysis** section of this chapter to begin developing ideas for your essay.

The Grapes of Mrs. Rath

Steve Mockensturm

We are often invited to think about the past as something that is behind us—something to forget about, something that can no longer influence who we are, how we think, what we value. But Steve Mockensturm, an artist, musician, and graphic designer, reminds us that the past looms all around us. The places we drive by, swing into, and rarely notice have absorbed the past and offer it back to us constantly. The buildings where we learned and lived have been defined by our own lives and the social events that swirl around them. And, more importantly for Mockensturm, these places have worked their way into our lives, into our understanding of ourselves and the world we inhabit.

I wonder if Mrs. Hulda Rath ever realized how much she affected my life. Probably not. It's funny how a teacher gets stuck in your head and you find yourself referencing that for the rest of your life.

Mrs. Rath taught English at DeVilbiss High School in 1975—my junior year. I say taught, but she didn't really teach. Didn't even talk that much, just gave us a lot of stories to read. She said they were classic, important books, but I'd never heard of any of them: *Animal Farm, Lord of the Flies, 1984, The Crucible, Cry the Beloved Country.*

DeVilbiss was a rough and rowdy school (inner city, a thousand kids, half black, half white) with a lot of distractions. During the '40s and '50s it was THE high school to attend, very academic, but by the mid-'70s it was starting to run down, perhaps stigmatized by a few race riots in '68.

Mrs. Rath had an ability to recognize the kids that actually wanted to read and learn and, often times, would send a few of us down to the library where it was quiet and we could have some sanctuary from the usual classroom shenanigans. Looking back, I realize how amazing and grand this school library was. It was bigger than the local public branch and very church-like with its vaulted ceiling and tall windows. Everything was made of wood—the chairs, the tables, the shelves, the big librarian's station in the middle—and it was always full of light, the windows exposed to the south and west. Three sets of large mahogany doors would clang and creak, echoing down the hall, up around the stairwell, and into our classroom.

5   It was in this environment that I was introduced to the work of John Steinbeck. Two of the books assigned were *The Grapes of Wrath* and *Of Mice and Men.* I was smitten with these masterpieces and savored Steinbeck's work like a rich meal. Reading these stories in the great, holy library of my young life is one of the happiest memories I have. These were stories about my country and my people. Flawed yet beautiful people in tough situations in an imperfect land. I was discovering America. I suddenly wanted to read everything Steinbeck had ever written.

I checked out *Tortilla Flat* and *The Wayward Bus* from the library and asked Mrs. Rath what else he wrote and where I could get it. She loaned me her copy of "In Dubious Battle." Soon, I wanted to own all of Steinbeck's books. I scoured the bookstores to complete the collection, a collection that has traveled with me for 25 years.

The city sadly closed down DeVilbiss High School a few years after I graduated. It was too big and too expensive to maintain. Thankfully, they never tore it down and trimmed only a few trees from the large oak grove lining the front walkway. For years it sat empty,

"Sometimes I'll stand in the doorway and picture the room as it was back in '75, gazing around, putting old friends in their seats."

the massive entrance looking out on Upton Avenue with no expression.

Then, a few years ago, some parts of it reopened for special programs and the industrial skills center was transformed into a technology academy. My children were enrolled in the Horizons program at the old school. From time to time, during open house, I'll wander the halls and conjure up old voices. Many areas of the building are unsafe; the library is almost unrecognizable. It's a massive storage room now, crap piled to the ceiling, desks and shelves torn out and not a book in sight.

The girls have Russian language lessons in Mrs. Rath's old room at the top of the stairwell. Sometimes I'll stand in the doorway and picture the room as it was back in '75, gazing around, putting old friends in their seats. Whenever I'm reading Steinbeck, my memory goes back to this classroom, the library, and Mrs. Hulda Rath's quiet ways and I get the urge to plop down and read *Cannery Row.*

Writing Strategies

1. Describe Mockensturm's voice as a writer. That is, how does he come across to the reader? Refer to three specific passages to support your description.

2. If workshopping Mockensturm's essay, how would you answer the following questions: What do you like most about the essay? What suggestion do you have for the writer?

3. What would you say is Mockensturm's main idea? How does he convey it to the reader?

4. Identify the most effective uses of narration (storytelling) and description in Mockensturm's essay, and explain why they work.

Exploring Ideas

1. In groups, discuss how Mockensturm sees high school English differently from the way you see it. (Some may see it the same as he does.) What values, beliefs, or assumptions underlie the different ways people view high school English?

2. Visit your old school, an old playground, a park, or some other place from your past, and write down any memories that come to mind. What experience there influenced your identity—or still influences you today?

3. Consider the people from your past. Explain how their behaviors (even the very subtle ones) influenced your outlook on life.

Ideas for Writing

1. What high school experience do you view differently—for example, as more valuable or less valuable—than most of your peers do?

2. What individual influenced you growing up and may not realize it?

If responding to one of these ideas, go to the **Analysis** section of this chapter to begin developing ideas for your essay.

The Greatest Gift

Samantha Tengelitsch

Emotions have a way of hiding in the past and conceal-ing the complexities of life from ourselves and others. But writing can break open the past, unravel the truth, and show us what we're made of. Samantha Tengelitsch, who bravely wrote this essay for her first-semester Eng-lish course at Northwestern Michigan College, cracks open the past. She finds insight about motherhood in an odd place: a puppy. As you read this essay, consider the intellectual risks the writer takes and how she uncovers big emotions in little places. Tengelitsch reminds us of something that is easy to forget: Every event in our lives impacts every other event in our lives.

Let me say first, I am flexible. In birth, I stretched for the little being who unfolded from within me. In the months preceding her birth, I read every book on babies, pregnancy, on labor, breastfeeding, bonding and diapering; if it had been written, I had read it, prepar-ing to stretch further, in my thinking, in my way of being. Curiously, I can't recall a single true-to-the-topic book on motherhood. And after the birth of our daugh-ter, there all at once appeared an obvious and enormous gap in my education.

Immediately following the birth, I was bombarded by family and friends, armed with cameras and Hall-mark cards, all anxious to see the new baby. Even the strange relations who only appear at weddings and at funerals came from all around, smothering me with noisy talk when what I wanted most in the whole world was to curl up into myself and discover who I had become.

I was nothing like the women I saw on television or in magazines. Never were they caught in their paja-mas in the afternoon, or in milk-stained t-shirts, eyes the color red, dark splotches below. I had stretch marks in places I hadn't realized stretch marks would appear. I loved my child with a fierceness unlike anything I had ever experienced before, but in this, I felt lost. When my husband returned to work and the busy distraction of family finally petered out, I found myself alone for the first time. Suddenly, I could stretch no further. I felt isolated and vulnerable. While images surrounding me in the media were of happy, bubbling mothers and babies, I sat alone on the couch in despair, waiting for my husband to return home from work day after day; writhing with envy at the fun my single or child-free friends seemed to be having without me. I was starving for adult conversation, but with family and friends scat-tered across the country, I didn't feel like I could call back the troops. *Bring your damn cameras,* I thought, anything to relieve me from this monotony someone tricked me into believing was supposed to be bliss.

It was then I abandoned my worldly ambitions and fell into a dull routine that consisted of playing with baby, changing diapers, preparing food, cleaning house, and watching television. I began studying *Martha Stew-art.* This woman was legendary in her perfection. I watched her make birthday cakes, pull together aston-ishing flower arrangements from her impeccable gar-dens and make every evening special with an elaborate table setting. I, like many women, both envied and hated her for this.

5　My neighbor was a Martha. She, too, had recently given birth to a healthy baby girl, but somehow she sur-vived unscathed. I watched from my living room win-dow as she carefully tucked her baby into the car seat and went out for groceries each day. Her house was immaculate, dinner was on the table every night by five and she even had time to garden. I couldn't see then through the veil of expectations placed upon me by Martha and others before her, that this woman was older, wiser, and far more emotionally and financially prepared for motherhood.

So, while the country sat glued to their televisions following the attacks of September 11th, I sat glued to mine, searching for some answer as to who I was sup-posed to be. What is a mother after all?

I can now say with certainty that motherhood is a progressive transition, an evolution of acceptance of self. We immerse ourselves in images of perfection: women who can do no wrong, who require no help, who never ask for help. We are not taught to ask for help. I remember that the case of the woman in Texas who killed her children was in the news at this time and I hated myself because I *empathized* with the woman. How could I feel that way? What kind of horrible person was I to empathize with what the papers labeled a *monster*? I knew I wasn't sick and that my child was not in danger, but I felt her isolation, her desperation and I wanted to reach out to her, but it was too late.

My husband never once ignored my growing vulnerability. He was desperate to help. That winter, a few weeks before the holiday, he brought home a special gift. He carried it through the door, under his arm like the morning paper. It was a puppy, wrapped carefully in a big green bow. I know he saw me in my depressed heap on the couch and wanted, like me, to do anything to help me surface from the sea of hormones and emotions, the complexity of which frightened even him. This snuggly, black and white puppy, he hoped, would end my depression.

I was elated at first to have a dog in the house, but soon the cold Michigan winter won over my countless potty-training attempts. (The dog obviously preferred the warmth of our house when relieving herself.) I awoke suddenly to the realization that my problems were now compounded by the puppy. It was then, while mopping up pee in our kitchen that I made my first decision, not as the girl who wanted to keep her Christmas puppy, but as a woman *and* mother. The dog would have to go. I picked up my daughter and held her close, for the first time savoring the sweet smell of her breath and the way her little body fit so perfectly into mine. She snuggled down and fell blissfully asleep, her head resting on my shoulder. The change was almost undetectable, but she felt it too. Her body relaxed as did mine for the first time in months. I glowed, now face to face with my new identity as a mother and, for the first time, accepting this as such.

10 A few years later, Martha Stewart was arrested for committing securities violations. I noticed many people seemed elated with the news of her arrest: Their enthu-

siasm was the result of witnessing this image of perfection finally topple. It was like watching the people of the former Soviet Union tear down the busts and statues of Stalin and Lenin. Martha Stewart, guilty as charged by the imperfect women of America for aiding the real criminal, the media, in its unyielding and misleading representation of women and motherhood. And there were others before her: June Cleaver, guilty; Carol Brady, guilty; Barbie, guilty; NBC, CBS, ABC, guilty, guilty, guilty.

If only I had realized earlier how unfair it was to compare myself and my baby to these fictional characters, I would have saved myself the agony of unwarranted expectations and the feeling of stubborn independence that blocked me from asking others for help. This is my experience—only I can claim it. *All of it,* the imperfections and the beautiful wisdom born out of the sacred transition of woman to mother. If only I could have realized then that the real perfection exists not in the glamour-hungry media but in our own imperfection; in our uniqueness as women and as mothers.

Show me motherhood as it really exists. Why simplify such a diverse and powerful, womanly transition? Show me the midnight feedings, talk to me about sore nipples, breastfeeding, sleeplessness. Let us honor the restless abandonment of ourselves for our new identities as mothers. Let us recognize the wisdom of our elders and pass it on to the next generation of women through the simple act of putting down the camera and doing a load of laundry, or by holding the baby while a mother takes a long-deserved shower or nap. Let us ask for help and surround ourselves with other women, mothers. Let us be comfortable enough in our womanly bodies to embrace motherhood.

The real gift I received that holiday was not the little puppy, but what my experience inspired: growth, wisdom, the ability to stretch further than ever before, to be swallowed whole, to surrender, evolve, and accept my new role as a mother. This wisdom alone was the greatest of all gifts.

"Show me motherhood as it really exists. Why simplify such a diverse and powerful, womanly transition?"

Writing Strategies

1. How do certain details of Tengelitsch's introduction set up the main idea that comes later in her essay?

2. How does Tengelitsch use cultural references (to Martha Stewart, to "the woman in Texas") to develop her main idea?

3. How is the essay's title a unifying device throughout the essay?

4. If workshopping this essay, what major strength would you point out? What suggestion would you make for improving the essay, and why?

Exploring Ideas

1. In groups, explore how the puppy impacted Tengelitsch's thinking.

2. Tegelitsch says, "I was nothing like the women I saw on television or in magazines." (¶ 3) In addition to the specific examples she mentions, what specific media images can you think of that Tengelitsch, and other mothers, should not compare themselves to? What media images may be helpful to new mothers?

3. What other roles, in addition to motherhood, are a "progressive transition, an evolution of acceptance of self" (¶ 7)?

Ideas for Writing

1. Try to pinpoint the moment a major change occurred in your thinking.

2. How have you (and others like you) had to overcome a media-created image?

If responding to one of these ideas, go to the **Analysis** section of this chapter to begin developing ideas for your essay.

Outside Reading

Find a written text about a memory, and print it out or make a photocopy. In journals or magazines, these texts are often called *memoirs.* You might find a memoir in a general readership publication (such as *Time, Newsweek, Reader's Digest,* or the *New York Times*). Some publications feature writers who tell their own stories. Enthusiast magazines (about specific hobbies and travel) often feature personal memoirs as well. (Check the table of contents for story titles with the first-person pronouns *I* or *my.*) To conduct an electronic search of journals and magazines, go to your library's periodical database or to InfoTrac® College Edition (http://infotrac.galegroup.com/itweb/). In your library's database, perform a keyword search, or go to the main search box for InfoTrac College Edition and click on "keywords." Enter word combinations that interest you, such as *memoir and Jewish and women, memoir and Japan and war, memoir and soccer, memoir and punk rock.* (When performing keyword searches, avoid using the phrases or articles *a, an, the;* instead, use nouns separated by *and.*) The search results will yield lists of journal and magazine articles.

You can also search the Internet. Try the search engine Altavista.com. Like most Internet search engines, Altavista.com combines words using *and.* In the search box, try various combinations, such as those above.

The purpose of this assignment is to broaden the range of possibilities; that is, to help you discover more strategies for writing about the past. As you are probably discovering, this kind of writing varies widely in organization, voice, and even length. As you read through this chapter and begin your own writing, keep the memoir you have discovered close by and notice the elements and strategies the writer uses. Depending on your instructor's suggestions, do one or more of the following:

1. Notice how the writer applies various strategies from this chapter. On the hard copy or photocopy:

   - Highlight the thesis (or main idea about the memory) if it is stated. If the thesis is implied, write it in your own words.

   - Highlight the most descriptive or detailed passage(s).

   - Highlight any passages that suggest a connection between the writer's memory and the reader's (your) life. In the margin, write "public resonance."

2. Analyze the strategies employed by the writer. The following questions may be helpful:

   - How does the writer's approach differ from the readings in this chapter?

   - How does the writer connect his or her own experience to potential readers?

   - Who is the audience for this text?

   - How does the audience impact the kinds of things said in the memoir?

3. Write at least three "Writing Strategies" questions for the text you found.

4. Write at least three "Exploring Ideas" questions for the text you found.

5. Write two "Ideas for Writing" questions, such as the ones following the essays in this book, for the text you found.

INVENTION

"I'm digging in the dirt / To find the places I got hurt /
To open up the places I got hurt."

—"Digging in the Dirt," Peter Gabriel

Invention is not simply about finding a topic. It also involves exploring and analyzing that topic, examining your thoughts, and developing points. For a remembering essay, the process will be self-reflective. It will begin with a personal exploration, but the broader goal is to discover something that others can share. The following three sections are designed to help you through invention: specifically, to discover a particular topic, situation, or event from your past (in **Point of Contact**), to develop points about the topic (in **Analysis**), and to make it relevant to a community of readers (in **Public Resonance**). The Invention questions in each section are not meant to be answered directly in your final written assignment. But using them to explore ideas will help you begin writing and keep intensive ideas flowing.

POINT OF CONTACT

Remembering is a process of digging up the past, unearthing moments that have been buried. You should begin by looking back and trying to find a specific situation, event, or set of events from your life. Throughout this chapter, you will analyze and develop the situation or event you choose for your topic. Use the suggestions and questions that follow for your exploration.

You might think that nothing interesting has ever happened to you. But even if you have lived in one place your whole life, never won the lottery, never wrestled an alligator, never written a top ten song, or never been on a first date, your life is still filled with thousands of situations and moments that can reveal something to you and to your audience.

Some of the most interesting and valuable memories linger quietly.

Recall an event from your past life:

School

Did I ever get beat up? Did I ever beat up someone else? Was I ever embarrassed by a teacher or classmate? Did I ever win or lose a big sporting event? Was I popular, unpopular, or normal? Was I one of the "smart" kids? Was I one of the "normal" kids? Did I fit into a particular clique (jocks, hoods, hippies, punks, nerds, etc.)? Did I come out of my shell a particular year?

Work

What was my first job? Did I like or dislike it? Why did I leave? How did I get along with my peers? My boss? Did the job put me in any weird situations?

Answering "no" to any of these questions is as interesting as answering "yes."

Social life

When and with whom was my first date? When did I first stay out late? Did I have a lot of friends? No friends? What situation led to my first friendship? When did I first learn about the differences between girls and boys? Was I ever asked to drink or try drugs? (Did I?) When did I first drive a car (illegally or legally)? Did I ever change my hair or image drastically?

Family life

Did I experience a sibling being born? Have I experienced a child of my own being born? Did we have a pet? (Did it pass away?) Did we take any family vacations? Have I ever embarrassed my family? (Has my family ever embarrassed me?) What did we do on weekends? Did we eat dinner, watch television, or attend religious services together?

Visit a place from your past (a schoolyard, a house, an apartment building, an old neighborhood, a workplace, etc.). Once there, ask yourself the following: What memories or feelings are most prominent? How have my feelings about the place changed?

REMEMBER
TIME CHANGES
OCT 30

Look through a photo album or yearbook. Find photographs from your life that seem distant, that seem to belong to another lifetime.

CALL OR WRITE SOMEONE FROM YOUR PAST. ASK HIM OR HER ABOUT YOUR SHARED HISTORY. WHAT DO YOU REMEMBER MOST ABOUT OUR LIVES BACK THEN? WHAT WAS THE BEST PART OF OUR LIVES? THE WORST? HOW HAVE WE BOTH CHANGED SINCE THEN? WHY DID WE CHANGE? WHAT FORCES, FEELINGS, SITUATIONS KEPT US TOGETHER?

Do something that you have not done for many years: go fishing, play baseball, listen to a particular song, reread a particular book, do nothing. Afterwards, consider the following: How was the activity different from the past?

ACTIVITY

These questions only hint at the many possible topics. In a group or alone, generate more questions until one has triggered something for you.

ANALYSIS

Analysis is an art and a science. It involves intellectual freedom and careful, deliberate probing. Good analysis calls for writers to venture into possibilities and also to monitor their thinking. This is difficult intellectual work, but it yields insight and meaning. As you examine a particular event or situation from your past, try to find the *significance* (why something is important for both the writer and the reader).

Use the following questions to find the significance of your topic:

- How did I change? (Who was I before and after the situation?)
- Why did the event or situation occur? What forces were at work?
- Did I realize the significance of the event at the time? Why or why not?
- What do I see now that I didn't see then? What did that younger person not understand?
- Why was the event or situation important to me?
  - Did it help me to understand myself as a man or woman?
  - Did it help me to grow intellectually? Spiritually? Socially?
  - Did it help me to see myself in a different way?

Significance = why something is important for the writer and reader

INVENTION WRITING

As you analyze your project, remember that the goal is not simply to tell a story about your past, but to discover something meaningful—something that can be shared with and valued by others. Avoid moving too quickly through your thoughts. Imagine a writer, Jack, who visited his old elementary school:

> **What do I see now that I didn't see then?**
> I see that school is important, and back then I didn't.

Jack answers the question and *begins* walking the path of analysis, but his brief answer does not go far enough. It does not reveal the real complexity of his experience. He says that "school is important," but such a phrase is broad and hollow. What particular aspect of school, we might ask, is important? What specific moments or situations are valuable to a growing individual? Struggling through impossibly difficult classes? The reward of a good grade? Being prompted to read material one would otherwise ignore? Or maybe what's important is the slow and charted evolution of one's identity through various classes, teachers, friends, and hallways. Jack's answer blankets such rich possibilities, covering them up with a broad, sweeping phrase.

Another writer, Diana, goes further in her thinking:

> **What do I see now that I didn't see then?**
> When I was younger, I didn't see the big picture, how my life in school connected to anything outside of school. I went, did the work, and came home, but mostly daydreamed about the time I'd spend away from schoolwork. For me, and probably most of my friends, life was separate from schoolwork. Every day, the goal was to get it done so we could be away from it. I remember the feeling of freedom in running out the door after school or during recess, but what I was running toward was a bunch of silly games, posing, and meaningless searches for excitement. I never thought, maybe I was never taught, that learning is really

what makes life worth anything, that an intellectual challenge is real excitement. When I was a teenager, I was
focused on the surface—the shallow giddiness of thrills
and "parties." I thought school was a drag—and I looked
for every possible excuse to be bored. I actually *convinced*
myself to be bored. But now that I am older, I realize that
school is the only place where people actually care about
your mind—where they want you to grow, imagine, and
experience new ideas. These are the things that make life
outside of school worth living. I see that now.

All the jobs I had after high school just wanted me to
perform a certain duty. No one wanted me to explore my
intellectual potential. And unfortunately, I see a lot of
younger college students still thinking the way I did in high
school. They moan at challenging assignments; they just
want to duck out of everything. Today, a boy said to me,
"Can you believe how long that reading took?" as though
the goal was to get through it. What's that about? Well, I
know what it's about—blindness to the big picture.

Diana's thoughts are beginning to develop here: She is making powerful and specific distinctions between her present
and her past understanding. In the past, she did not think to
evaluate, to question, her own boredom and apathy. But
now, in the present, she has distance from her old self and
can see false assumptions and misplaced values.

THINKING FURTHER

Although Diana has already analyzed further than Jack did,
she should not stop yet. Through analysis she has unearthed
some interesting new ideas. Now Diana can review her
invention writing and identify her best ideas, using them
not as final conclusions but as springboards into even greater
exploration. Now she can seek out some insight that lurks
even further below the surface of her previous discoveries.

For example, if Diana's goal is to share the significance
of a memory, she could say that she realized *school is where
people care about your mind—where they want you to grow,*
imagine, and experience new ideas—and that these are the
things that make life outside of school worth living. And she
could illustrate her thesis by discussing how certain teachers
encouraged her to grow and imagine while she scorned their
encouragement. But what if Diana sought out the underlying reasons for her childhood behavior? She could quickly
claim that she was a wild and typical adolescent. Or, she
could think past that assumption, returning to the Invention
questions on the previous page.

Now that she has generated some new thinking, the
same questions (and new ones that Diana comes up with on
her own) can lead to even further insights. For example,

Why did the event or situation occur? What forces were at work?

Why didn't I see the big picture? Who or what is to blame?
It isn't as if everybody in high school failed to take advantage of it. Many students were highly motivated. (Although
even students who seemed motivated might have had misplaced priorities.) Still, had I known then what I know now,
I might have worked harder and learned more, perhaps
gone to a better college, and excelled in all kinds of ways.
Perhaps my parents should have forced me to study harder,
or helped me to better understand the importance of high
school. Perhaps—probably—they didn't understand it
themselves. But couldn't my teachers have gotten through
to me? So many of them seemed disinterested. Others
tried, but what could they do? And what about the media,
pop culture, sports, the mall? All these factors competed
and, in my case, won out over education.

By analyzing further, Diana is getting closer to the root of a
complex issue: She is discovering that her attitude toward
high school was impacted by competing factors, such as the
media, pop culture, sports, and the mall. However, the writing above does not provide final answers. Diana has even
more exploring to do, which might include additional
invention writing, discussion with others, and secondary
research.

To go further with your own thinking, focus on a key issue in your invention writing. Then return to the Invention questions on page 28, and create probing questions on your own. Use them to reveal something deeper, more hidden, more complex, about the behaviors or about the situation. For example:

- What other forces were at play?
- Why were they hidden from my view back then?
- What makes people blind to such forces in their lives?

In her response to the Invention questions on page 28, Cindy Bosley hones in and finds meaning in a "small moment." Bosley's notes are exploratory. They are not simple answers to questions. Much of the language in her response does not appear in her final essay, but she is willing to explore and stretch her reasoning:

> **Why did the event or situation occur?**
>
> If I isolate the event or situation as the gulf between my own grasp of fun and happiness and my mother's severe disappointment and embarrassment, her concern that others would think I was not a "nice loser" in that small moment, I think it clearly speaks so much more about my mother—as though I saw her, her disappointments and worries about image and desirability in herself through me. She was no stage mother, not at all, but she must have had these fears about how people in the town looked at her, and at us, her three children, because of my father to a certain extent, but also just because she herself was a woman who'd grown up to some degree "unacceptable" in her and her family's eyes because she was heavy, or because she liked lots of boys, or because she got pregnant and married, or because she moved so far away. My mother was and is a creative, talented, vibrant woman and she worked very hard, and very successfully, sacrificing so much for herself so my sister, brother, and I could have the things that we wanted like the other kids, things that might help us break out of our own family's economic situation. Things like acrobat lessons, and cheerleading camp, and swimming lessons, and overnight birthday parties. I have absolutely no idea how she pulled all those things off.

Bosley does not focus only on the beauty pageant but on the layers of emotions beneath it—those tied to her mother. She discovers a fresh perspective about the pageant by looking closely at the life that led up to and surrounded it. And from these notes, the ideas evolve in her essay:

> But the truth is that I'd lost the contest when I told the judges, when they asked, that my most personal concern was my mother's loneliness, and if I could change anything at all, I would give her something—a man, God, anything to free her from that loneliness. (8)

The goal is to *reveal* some new idea that is hiding in the past—to offer a *revelatory* insight to readers.

ANALYSIS IN CHAPTER READINGS

Discovering the significance of the past can be tricky because it is not obvious. In fact, the most significant events might be those that seem totally normal or insignificant. For example, a single soccer game spent standing on the sidelines would seem to have no meaning, other than frustration, for the younger Schwind-Pawlak; but to the older writer looking back, the game reveals something about her relationship with her parents:

> The relationship that I have with my parents has changed very much throughout the years. The polyester pants don't bother me anymore, but the carrot sticks still make me laugh. While their "soccer foul" embarrassed and angered me at the time, I understand and appreciate it now. My mother was angry <u>FOR</u> me. She was hurt <u>FOR</u> me. Through the pages of time, I can look back and see that, more often than not, I embarrassed her. She never stopped feeling for me, loving me, or protecting me. I have grown enough to realize that, though I often pointed out my parents' fouls, they scored countless goals that I didn't even notice. (16)

For her, the significance lies in the difference between her past and present perspectives. Her present perspective allows her to see the soccer game differently than her childhood self did. This realization is valuable because it shows the stark differences between childhood and adult perspectives.

REVISION

Are you stuck? Have you hit a wall? Go back to the Invention questions on page 28, the engines for new ideas. As you look back, ask yourself: *What could I now tell that younger version of me?* Then go further with the idea. Once you develop an answer to the question, ask yourself: *What hidden forces were at work? Why didn't I understand things differently back then?* Remember that the goal of this project (and all academic writing) is to reveal something new, to shed light on some complexity that would otherwise remain in the dark, hiding in the past.

The best topics never reveal their significance easily or quickly.

PUBLIC RESONANCE

Even though this writing assignment focuses primarily on your past, the ideas should also have meaning for others. What you discover should suggest something for the lives of your readers. Dealing with public resonance is simply a process of addressing the connection between your particular memory and its relation to a public or shared issue.

You may have already found public resonance by answering the Invention questions. But closely consider your response to the following:

- What public issue is related to my memory?
- What does my memory reveal or show about the nature of _____? (Childhood? Teenagers? Towns? Families? Schools? Teachers? Religious institutions? Education? Parenthood? Growing up? Failing? Succeeding? Suffering? Dying? Healing?)
- Who else, what type of person, might relate to my memory?

If you cannot imagine the public resonance of your experience, ask others: *How does my experience relate to you or to people you know?*

INVENTION WRITING

In this excerpt from Cindy Bosley's invention notes, she does not merely reinforce her early feelings of confusion; she discovers "the truth of" her confusion:

What public issue is related to my memory?

This isn't about my mother so much as it is about women more generally, and the images we're given through history at birth and before and never ever really break. I always felt shame after what I told the judges about wanting my mother to not have to be so lonely—how narrow of me, how far I missed the point—and yet, now I feel the truth of it, and I hope if I could go back, I'd still tell them that's the one thing I'd want to be able to change—for my mother to be able to feel beautiful and free and lovely and bright, overweight or not, advanced education or not, and with or without a man.

I remember my joy in graduate school when my friend Karen hosted a Miss America party the night of the pageant, and maybe my essay began to grow here. It was that night that I discovered I wasn't the ONLY little girl making up my own score sheets for the contest, hoping to predict who would win, and always imagining, because we thought it was the thing to wish for, that we could someday be Miss America. And all the usual stuff about women's narrow, "perfected" images in the media, Barbie dolls, fairy tales, all of it comes to bear here. There's such a feeling of shame and degradation (I don't think it is too big a word to describe it) in allowing oneself to be judged in this way, whether literally in a contest, or even just by agreeing to play, which we all do, by all the ancient rules of "fitting in" whether you're male or female. And there seems to be this desperate hole of loneliness and fear that seems anchored to it all. We often recognize it first in other people.

PUBLIC RESONANCE IN CHAPTER READINGS

As in the Analysis section, your answers to the Invention questions may not appear directly in your final writing. However, they may generate focused thinking about your topic that, eventually, may find its way into your final draft. For example, in Bosley's conclusion, her initial thoughts show up. They do not come word-for-word from her notes, but it is easy to see the connection. In her notes, she understands that her situation (and her mother's loneliness) is not unique. And in the conclusion of her essay, she makes this evident by changing the personal pronoun from *I* to *our,* thereby including others in her thinking. She attempts to link her realization about beauty pageants and mother/daughter relationships to others, so that her essay is not simply about herself, but about people who grew up in similar conditions. Bosley shows us how an unusual memory can resonate with readers: The importance and meaning of the memory translates into something beyond her personal feelings.

In her essay, Samantha Tengelitsch extends her own exploration of motherhood outward. Her personal memory is not simply a revelation about her own life; she is inviting other women to share the concept emerging from her essay:

> So, while the country sat glued to their televisions following the attacks of September 11th, I sat glued to mine searching for some answer as to who I was supposed to be. What is a mother after all?

> I can now say with certainty that motherhood is a progressive transition, an evolution of acceptance of self. We immerse ourselves in images of perfection: Women who can do no wrong, who require no help, who never ask for help. We are not taught to ask for help. (21)

The public resonance in Mockensturm's writing is a bit subtler. Early in the essay, he describes the social world around him. While the following details seem only incidental, they show a connection between the individual experience and broader societal experience:

> DeVilbiss was a rough and rowdy school (inner city, a thousand kids, half black, half white) with a lot of distractions. During the '40s and '50s it was THE high school to attend, very academic, but by the mid-'70s it was starting to run down, perhaps stigmatized by a few race riots in '68. (18)

Later in the essay, Mockensturm makes a direct connection between himself and the world around him:

> I was smitten with these masterpieces and savored Steinbeck's work like a rich meal. Reading these stories in the great, holy library of my young life is one of the happiest memories I have. These were stories about my country and my people. Flawed yet beautiful people in tough situations in an imperfect land. I was discovering America. (18)

ACTIVITY

Discuss the public resonance of the other essays in this chapter.

THESIS

Like any essay, one that is based on a personal experience should have a main point or *thesis*. And that point should reveal something to the writer and reader. It may be tempting to offer an overly broad statement about life, but more valuable statements will narrow in on a particular quality, situation, relationship, or layer of everyday life. The first broad statement in each set can be developed into more revelatory possibilities:

1. People are deeply influenced by their friends.
   - Friends develop our sense of ambition—what we want for ourselves.
   - Friends create the intellectual terrain of our past and present.
   - Friends mirror our own worldviews back to us.

2. Family is all that matters.
   - Our early struggles with brothers and sisters create the limitations we place on ourselves later in life.
   - As we grow into adulthood, our siblings keep alive the memory of our childhood selves.
   - Fathers create a sense of place, a sense of location that looms throughout our lives, even when we are spinning far out of control.

3. Teenage years are wild.
   - During adolescence, the world makes sense, even though that sense is a complete illusion.
   - A fourteen-year-old boy can barely contain all the energy coursing through his veins. He spends most of his time struggling to tame instincts that he cannot even name.
   - Before leaving our formative years, we might glimpse the best and worst habits we have acquired from our families . . . if we are lucky.

So how does someone go from a broad, flat statement to a revelatory idea? Intensive analysis! More intensive analysis always (not sometimes, but *always*!) leads to more intensive and focused statements. But when writers have difficulty expressing an intensive single statement, they can re-tool the specific words—the key verbs and nouns. Notice how the more intensive and revelatory statements often avoid linking verbs (*is, am, are, was, were,* and so on). Instead, they rely on active verbs *(develop, create, mirror, keep, glimpse)* to pull the reader's mind through ideas. So changing the verb in a sentence can actually prompt the writer to think differently, in more intensive ways.

ACTIVITY

With a small group of peers, create a broad, flat sentence, something that offers very little new insight. Then, from that sentence, develop three or more intense, focused, and insightful statements. In these more insightful statements, try to reveal something that normally goes ignored or that rarely gets considered. To create more insightful statements, try: 1) replacing broad nouns with more specific nouns; 2) replacing linking verbs with active verbs. Use adventurous or unusual verbs . . . and see where your mind goes.

EVOLUTION OF A THESIS

The thesis of a remembering essay suggests the *significance of the memory.* Notice how the following statement evolves from a description of what happened to an explanation of its significance.

- I remember as a kid sitting in my grandparents' back-yard listening to them and my parents tell boring family stories.

- I realize now that I learned a lot about my family history from sitting around as a kid listening to my grandparents and parents tell family stories.

- We learn important things about who we are and where we came from by listening to family stories.

- Though we might prefer not to hear them, we can better understand who we are and why by taking in family stories as children.

A thesis that is stated directly in the essay is *explicit;* an *implied* thesis is suggested by the details of the text but is not directly stated. Having an implied thesis does not mean a writer can simply wander through many different ideas. The details throughout the essay must be focused and coherent enough to suggest a main point, both for the writer and the reader.

Because you have already explored the significance and public resonance of your memory, you may already have a thesis. Ask yourself: *What is the most important point about this memory that should be communicated?* Try to express that point in one statement. (Even if you have an implied thesis, stating the main idea will help you develop the essay.)

COMMON THESIS PROBLEMS

When it comes time to craft a focused statement, writers also should avoid the temptation to flatten out their experiences into an overused, worn-out phrase or *cliché.* Clichés have a comfortable ring to them, but they rarely prompt new insight or reveal complexities in life. In fact, clichés like the following often *cover up* complexities because they are applied as blanket statements to many different situations:

- You don't know what you've got until it's gone.
- Blood is thicker than water.
- What doesn't kill you only makes you stronger.
- Home is where the heart is.

Such statements may be entirely true and worth considering, but academic writing seeks to go beyond common considerations and to prompt hard thinking. (Clichés are substitutes for hard thinking!) Clichés may also *sound* profound, but that profundity is misleading.

Clichés are substitutes for hard thinking!

RHETORICAL TOOLS

The writing for this chapter, more than any other, is personal in nature. However, such personal writing needs to involve an audience. It needs to extend beyond the personal and to develop into a point that connects to the public. And to do this, writers can explore various tools.

> "Quite often you want to tell somebody your dream, your nightmare. Well, nobody wants to hear about someone else's dream, good or bad; nobody wants to walk around with it. The writer is always tricking the reader into listening to the dream."
>
> —Joan Didion

Narration

Narration is a retelling of events, or a story. As Joan Didion argues, we must do more than tell a story. We must trick the reader into listening to the story and accepting its significance. The art of storytelling involves pace, or the movement of events. At important points in a narrative, the amount of detail tends to increase, and so the reader slows down and experiences each moment. But good storytellers move quickly through unimportant events. It might be helpful to think of this strategy as it works in movies: At the climax of an adventure movie, the events slow down (we see the lead character's hand grasping for the light saber; we hear each breath of the character as she runs down the hallway and toward the open window), but during less important moments, an entire day or week can flash by in a second.

In her narrative, Jennifer Schwind-Pawlak moves quickly through unimportant events. She quickly relates the pregame events (going to church and suiting up) because they do not have a significant impact on the main idea of the essay:

> Sunday, the morning of the fifth game of the season, came with no warning. I got up, went to church with the family, then came home to suit up for the game. Upon arrival at the field, I was greeted by the coach and went to take my place along the sidelines with the rest of my team. (15)

However, the narrative slows down (and offers more details) at important moments:

> Joann (the name I call my mother when she does something embarrassing) was screaming at the coach. In a voice so screeching that it rivaled fingernails on a blackboard, she told him that he was a disgraceful coach and that he should be ashamed of himself. She continued to point out the error of his ways by reminding him that I had not played at all in the game. How could she do this to me? My mother had managed to enlighten the few people that hadn't noticed on their own that I had not played at all. What was she thinking? She might as well have rented billboard space saying, "So what if Jeni sucks at soccer? The coach wouldn't let her play." My only thought was, "I don't want to go to school tomorrow!" (16)

As you consider your own narrative, slow the pace when relaying events that are directly related to your main idea.

Allusions

Allusions are references to some public bit of knowledge (such as a historical event, a political situation, or a popular culture figure). An allusion can give a personal essay a more public and broader feeling; that is, it can make the ideas and events of a personal situation relate to the reader through a shared culture. Mockensturm's brief allusion to the race riots of the 1960s, for instance, helps create public resonance.

And Leonard Kress relates his personal experience to us by pointing to the Beat writers, Kerouac specifically. By alluding to these writers, he reinforces the intensity of the experience. In simply mentioning Kerouac, Kress turns the train ride into an important educational moment, one that relates to travel and experience. In other words, the allusion expands the meaning of Kress's narrative.

In considering your essay, ask yourself: Does my situation relate to any historical situations, figures, or events? Any popular culture figures or fictional characters?

Dialogue

Dialogue is discussion between two or more people. Portraying dialogue in an essay can make an event or memory more real and engaging to the reader. Dialogue is most valuable when it is used to emphasize a main point in an essay, rather than simply to convey events. Conveying general events is better left to narration. But dialogue is useful when a particular exchange of words shows something significant.

Formatting for dialogue involves several steps:

- Use quotation marks before and after the actual spoken words.
- Put end punctuation (such as a period) inside the end quotation marks.
- Indent when a new speaker begins.

Integrating a speaker's words can be accomplished in several ways:

- Use a comma between the quotation and the speaking verb (*explained, asked, said, yelled, proclaimed,* etc.).

  Louisa asked, "What are we going to do now?"

- Use a colon before the speaker's words. In this case, the narrator usually forecasts the ideas or mood of the speaker in the sentence preceding the colon.

  I was clearly agitated by her accusation: "What the heck are you talking about?"

- Work the speaker's words directly into the grammar of your sentence.

  But Louisa was convinced that our decision would "hurt us either way."

See all of these rules operating in the following exchange:

"Come on in," Mr. Smith said.

"Hey, something smells great," I said as I walked into his lamp-lit living room. The small terrier looked up out of its lazy place on the sofa as Mr. Smith reached to get his wallet.

"Yep, I've been cookin' my chili again. It's Max's favorite." He gestured at the complacent blurry-eyed dog. "So, is the price of papers still the same?"

"Well, as far as I know, it's still $4.25 for the month." And then without considering the consequences, I asked the wrong question: "How have you been, Mr. Smith?" It took him 45 minutes to explain his "return to normal" after a long spell of stomach flu.

In this example, notice how attributive phrases (such as *he said*), which give ownership to the spoken words, are absent after the second indentation. Generally, after the dialogue pattern is established and the reader can easily tell who is speaking at each indentation, attributive phrases are unnecessary.

If you are considering dialogue for your essay, ask yourself: *How does the dialogue help to show something in support of the main idea?*

ORGANIZATIONAL STRATEGIES

What Details Should I Include?

Sometimes when we tell stories (especially our own), they take over, and we wander through irrelevant details. If this happens, you might consider two primary strategies: (1) leave out irrelevant details that distract the reader, and (2) emphasize those details that help illustrate your main idea. For instance, in Mockensturm's essay, we are not told about the antics of his school buddies or the long walk to school in the mornings. But we do hear about the library:

> Looking back, I realize how amazing and grand this school library was. It was bigger than the local public branch and very church-like with its vaulted ceiling and tall windows. Everything was made of wood—the chairs, the tables, the shelves, the big librarian's station in the middle—and it was always full of light, the windows exposed to the south and west. Three sets of large mahogany doors would clang and creak, echoing down the hall, up around the stairwell, and into our classroom. (18)

Such details convey Mockensturm's feelings of awe as he looks back. The elaborate description helps portray the environment in which he encountered literature and America. In Kress's essay, the writer does not tell us about the day before his journey; he even excludes how he made it home from Chicago. But he uses details strategically to show us all the "gaps" in his learning:

> He led me to one, sitting on the outer tracks, mostly a string of lime-dusty hoppers interspersed with empty boxcars—doors flung invitingly wide open! I rushed in front of him, tossed my rucksack in, and was about to hoist myself inside, when he grabbed my leg and tackled me down to the rails. I was too shocked to resist; he pinned me to the railroad ties and moved his head in real close to mine. Just when I was sure that he was about to slit my throat, he released his grip and delivered what seemed to be a prepared speech about hop-

ping freights. "Don't never board a still train," I remember him saying, "they shut them doors when the train's pulling out. You get stuck in there, you roast, you just roast, that's all there is to it." (11–12)

These details ultimately link to Kress's main point about the gaps in his learning. The dramatic scene here illustrates the first of several educational moments that lead to his final point. And because the scene helps the reader witness the main idea, Kress includes minute details (such as the closeness of the stranger's head). Like a good filmmaker, Kress slows down time and brings the memory into sharp focus:

> The ride itself was unbelievably jittery and uncomfortable. I couldn't open the can of beans I'd brought along, and the slices of bread I'd stuffed into my rucksack fell onto the floor and coated themselves in rust-flecked grease. The freight did, however, grant me a spectacular view of the setting sun as it ambled ever so slowly along the banks of Lake Michigan. (12)

If anything illustrates Kress's gaps in learning, it is certainly the image of his bread slices lying on the rusty floor of a train car, coated in goo!

As in these essays, details should add up to the main point. That is, as readers work through the text, gathering details along the way, they should be led to the main idea; they should, in fact, experience the deep complexity of living in a particular moment. And without those details, the reader will merely experience being told something about a distant time and place. As you consider your own narrative, think of the details that can help illustrate your point. If the moment is important, do not hold any detail back. If you were sitting in an alley, for instance, explain the color of the empty bottles and the smell of the damp brick. If you were standing in a classroom at the end of a day, explain the placement of the desks and the dying fern by the window. If you were swimming in a pond, explain how the weeds waved back and forth from the impact of your movements. But only focus on such particulars when they help get your reader closer to the main idea.

Ask yourself: What details from the past will help the reader to fully understand my point?

How Should I Begin?

As with any essay, introduction strategies are limitless. A favorite strategy among writers (especially those in this chapter) is to begin in the past, taking the readers back in time from the first sentence. Some of the writers in this chapter (such as Kress) not only start in the past, but also give the reader a general statement about the past:

> At 20 I was convinced that the single most important experience, without which my education would remain shamefully incomplete, was that of hopping a freight. Doubtless, my sense of education at that time (as well as my sense of what constituted good writing) was more than mildly seasoned by huge doses of the Beats—Allen Ginsberg, Gregory Corso, William Burroughs, Kenneth Patchen, LeRoi Jones, and, of course, Jack Kerouac. That these writers were at the time considered non-scholarly, marginal, and were all but vilified by my literature teachers made them, I'm sure, that much more irresistible. (11)

Other writers (such as Bosley) begin narrating and wait to characterize or give meaning to the events until later in their essays. Still another option is to make a general statement about the subject, and then begin narrating events. Notice Schwind-Pawlak's strategy:

> Parents—one word that can strike many emotions in children when said aloud. Some children will smile and think about how silly their dad looked when he put carrot sticks up his nose that very morning, while others will cringe when they think about how their mother picked them up from school last week wearing orange polyester pants and a green shirt, oblivious to the hard work that some fellow went through to create the color wheel. My own emotional state of mind seemed to run the gamut throughout childhood. I chose to blame my parents for all of the traumatic events that unfolded but took pride in my obvious independence during the successes. One of the most heinous crimes that my parents committed was "the soccer foul." If I could have ejected them from the game of life at that point, I would have. (14)

She begins with a statement that has public resonance; that is, she makes a point that readers can immediately share, and then integrates her own particular experience.

ACTIVITY

After writing an introduction for your essay, share it with two classmates (either in class or by e-mail). Each classmate should write an alternative introduction, using an entirely different strategy. Do the same for each classmate. After each writer has seen the others' alternatives to his or her introduction, discuss the strategies and decide if they might inspire changes. (Do not be afraid to borrow ideas from your peers. The best writers take inspiration from others: J. R. R. Tolkien, author of *The Lord of the Rings*, consistently took advice from his friend C. S. Lewis, author of many books, including *The Chronicles of Narnia*.)

How Should I Conclude?

Perhaps the most popular strategy for concluding a remembering essay is to explain the significance and/or public resonance in the last paragraph. All the writers in this chapter end their essays by explaining the importance of their memory, and some writers, such as Bosley, even suggest that others can share the personal significance:

> It's a contest no one should want to win. Our mothers should not have such dreams for us. Our mothers should not have such loneliness. (9)

Schwind-Pawlak explains the significance of her memory in her conclusion:

> The relationship that I have with my parents has changed very much throughout the years. The polyester pants don't bother me anymore, but the carrot sticks still make me laugh. While their "soccer foul" embarrassed and angered me at the time, I understand and appreciate it now. My mother was angry <u>FOR</u> me. She was hurt <u>FOR</u> me. Through the pages of time, I can look back and see that, more often than not, I embarrassed her. She never stopped feeling for me, loving me, or protecting me. I have grown enough to realize that, though I often pointed out my parent's fouls, they scored countless goals that I didn't even notice. (16)

Most of the conclusions in the chapter readings work similarly. In some way, they all communicate the main idea, the significance of their memories. For example, in Mockensturm's essay, the conclusion brings together his own memories and his daughters' education:

> The girls have Russian language lessons in Mrs. Rath's old room at the top of the stairwell. Sometimes I'll stand in the doorway and picture the room as it was back in '75, gazing around, putting old friends in their seats. Whenever I'm reading Steinbeck, my memory goes back to this classroom, the library, and Mrs. Hulda Rath's quiet ways and I get the urge to plop down and read *Cannery Row*. (19)

Kress's conclusion follows suit, but is perhaps more subtle than the others. Notice that he does not explain specifically what he learned, nor does he draw attention to his present perspective ("Looking back, I now realize . . ."). Instead, he leaves his readers in the past, alone in Chicago:

> Almost half a day later, around midnight, the train crunched into Chicago, where I hopped off, exhausted and exhilarated. As my shaky train-legs hit the gravel of the roadbed, I thought I heard a threatening shout, so I ran, tripped mostly, over the 50 or so tracks and platforms and switchings, down a steep embankment. Right into the middle of some run-down neon-shod shopping strip near 95th Street on the South Side— bars and liquor stores and boarded-up groceries, card readers, barber colleges, and storefront churches, groups of men hanging on the corners drinking from passed-around rumpled paper bags. Here was a whole gallery of street life like nothing I'd ever seen. Somehow the rickety freight ride and all that drama and lure of the past two days quickly dissipated, replaced by an urgent sense of new gaps in my learning, of new educational possibilities. (12)

The conclusion actually dramatizes his main point: Along with the younger, more naïve Kress, we are left in the gaps of his learning.

> . . . they all communicate the main idea, the significance of their memories.

A conclusion is the final
moment of a relationship,
the final opportunity for
writers to give their readers
a particular and unique
insight to carry back into
the world beyond the text.

WRITER'S VOICE

A writer's voice characterizes the ideas in a text. It creates the mood in which the reader will approach the ideas. Imagine walking into a party and the host greets you at the door: "Hey! Look what the cat dragged in!" Her interaction would prompt you to assume that the party is fairly informal and festive. But the host could also greet you more soberly: "Hello. Please come in. May I take your coat?" In this case, her voice would lend formality to the affair. In other words, the host creates a particular mood for the incoming guests. Likewise, a writer creates the mood in which readers will enter the text. And this can be accomplished in a variety of ways.

Using Figurative Language

Figurative language is non-literal. It goes beyond words' basic definitions and uses them to suggest imaginative connections between ideas. Consider the following four strategies:

Metaphor A comparison of one thing to another in which one thing is made to share the characteristics of another: Her home was a sanctuary, where we felt healed spiritually and psychologically.

Simile A comparison of two seemingly unrelated things using *like* or *as:* Life is like a box of chocolates.

Similes and metaphors help create voice. For example, Forrest Gump's simile, above, fits with his uncomplicated and easy-going character. A box of chocolates is a simple, pleasant surprise, and so it equates with his character. (It certainly would not be fitting for Gump to say, "Life is like a raging volcanic explosion bursting forth from the fires of the earth.")

Jennifer Schwind-Pawlak's metaphors help create her voice:

> At that moment I wasn't sure that I would ever be able to forgive my mother for what happened that day, but, as far as I can recall, I began loving her again within the week. I am sure that she either cooked my favorite dinner, told a corny joke, or told me how much she loved me to make that lump of anger fade away. (16)

Her anger is "a lump," not a mountain or a raging river. The smaller, more manageable, lump fits the mood of a child. We get the sense from her language that she is effectively over her childhood emotions.

Understatement A claim that is deliberately less forceful or dramatic than reality: Hurricanes tend to create a little wind.

Hyperbole A deliberate exaggeration: I'm so hungry, I could eat a horse.

These strategies lend a certain layer of informality to writing. That is, writers who are attempting to lay low, to remain seemingly invisible, or to write formally usually refrain from hyperbole and understatement.

Choosing Details

The details one chooses help create voice. Both Bosley and Schwind-Pawlak focus on their mothers, but they give different details. While Schwind-Pawlak's details are comedic and light, Bosley's details are serious. The details alone make the reader experience the memories and the writers differently:

Schwind-Pawlak:
Some children will smile and think about how silly their dad looked when he put carrot sticks up his nose that very morning, while others will cringe when they think about how their mother picked them up from school last week wearing orange polyester pants and a green shirt, oblivious to the hard work that some fellow went through to create the color wheel. (14)

Bosley:

My mother had secret hopes. Finally divorced for the second time from the same man, my father, she sat with me and gave her own running commentary about who was cute, who smiled too much, who would find a handsome husband. My mother, having always been a little to a lot overweight, excelled at swimming, and she told me much later that she chose swimming because she didn't feel fat in the water. Her sister was the cheerleader, but she was a swimmer, too heavy for a short skirt of her own, she said. (7)

In your own writing, how do you want to appear to the reader: darkly reflective, comfortable, learned, free-spirited? Your decision will influence what details you mention and what moments you emphasize. The details will affect how the reader understands you (as a writer) and the ideas you communicate. (This is a powerful lesson about writing: It not only conveys ideas but also shapes how people feel about those ideas.)

Using Sentence Length

Sentence structure is perhaps the most powerful, yet most invisible, tool a writer has for creating voice. Sentence length, specifically, can create a wide variety of different effects, depending on the context (or material surrounding the sentence). Long, winding sentences, which travel in and out of various ideas before returning the reader to the original path, can create a self-reflective and sophisticated voice, one that considers complexities. Short sentences can create a determined voice. Notice the difference between the following:

Childhood was a gas.

Childhood was a raucous journey of twists and turns in which each moment was its own forever and every day a monument.

While the metaphors help create distinct voices, the sentence length also helps characterize the writers.

Although sentence length alone does not automatically create voice, it figures into the process. Notice, again, Bosley's passage to the left and how the sentence length tugs and pulls at the reader. The first sentence is short—and because of the content, it is almost a whisper. The second, longer sentence takes the reader further into the idea. Both sentences, working together, create the sensation of a living person telling a story. The movement, the back and forth between long and short sentences, helps conjure the sense of a real human telling a real story. And the content of those sentences helps communicate the feelings and emotional complexities of that human.

> A writer's voice characterizes the idea in a text. It creates the mood in which the reader will approach the ideas.

VITALITY

Vitality is life. Writing that has vitality keeps readers' minds awake and moving. Vitalized writing does not draw attention to itself with overly elaborate structures, but it does move the reader into and through ideas. When readers encounter vitalized writing, they may not know exactly what's happening, but they find themselves easily gliding along—almost disappearing into the text.

There are many strategies for sentence vitality, but applying even the three listed below can make a dramatic difference between flat, exhausted sentences and intensive, lively writing.

Vitality (vi-tal-i-te) (n) The characteristic, principle, or force that distinguishes living things from nonliving things.

Combine Sentences

Sentences cue the reader. A period says, "Stop." A new sentence says, "Go." This stopping and starting helps create life. (Readers, like all humans, are drawn to pulsating movement.) But too many starts and stops keep readers from settling into ideas, so writers should combine sentences to keep readers gliding along.

Sentences can be combined with *coordination* (adding together clauses of equal importance):

> My father did not believe in such things for girls as shoes, clothes, haircuts, college, or photographs for Junior Miss, **and** so there was no way he was going to give a penny for a pageant-worthy dress or a professional photographer's 10-minutes-plus-proofs. (7–8)

> I was starving for adult conversation, **but** with family and friends scattered across the country, I didn't feel like I could call back the troops. (20)

> Mrs. Rath had an ability to recognize the kids that actually wanted to read and learn and, often times, would send a few of us down to the library where it was quiet **and** we could have some sanctuary from the usual classroom shenanigans. (18)

The highlighted conjunctions in these sentences show where the writers joined ideas together. Information before and after the conjunctions is equal; the grammar cues the reader to give them equal intellectual weight.

Sentences also can be combined with *subordination* (making an idea less important than the main part of a sentence). Subordination involves tucking some ideas into others, creating the critical overlapping quality of good writing:

> For years <u>it sat empty</u>, the massive entrance looking out on Upton Avenue with no expression. (18)

> As hoped for and expected, <u>a figure appeared out of nowhere</u>. (11)

> Almost half a day later, around midnight, <u>the train crunched into Chicago</u>, where I hopped off, exhausted and exhilarated. (12)

These examples of subordination show a variety of possibilities. Each sentence has a main clause (underlined), and other parts attached to it. Notice how the third sentence, from Kress's essay, would read differently if the ideas were separated into full sentences:

> Almost half a day later, around midnight, the train crunched into Chicago. I hopped off, and I felt exhausted and exhilarated.

Invention
Vitality

Although the difference is small, this version creates more stops and starts for the reader. Those shorter separated ideas sometimes are valuable, but good writers subordinate less important information. Hopping off the train is necessary information for Kress's narrative, but it is not something readers need at the front of their minds. Kress thus subordinates the fact to other details.

Repeat Structures

Although readers need a variety of patterns, a constant change in length and structure, vitalized writing sometimes repeats key phrases or clauses. It is the writerly equivalent of pounding on a podium, driving a set of ideas at the audience:

> I never went to soccer again. As a matter of fact, I never played another organized sport again. Maybe it was the fear of rejection. Maybe it was the uncertainty of my talent. Maybe I was just too busy with other things. (16)

> Let us honor the restless abandonment of ourselves for our new identities as mothers. Let us recognize the wisdom of our elders and pass it on to the next generation of women through the simple act of putting down the camera and doing a load of laundry, or by holding the baby while a mother takes a long-deserved shower or nap. Let us ask for help and surround ourselves with other women, mothers. Let us be comfortable enough in our womanly bodies to embrace motherhood. (21)

The repeating patterns here create a cyclical feel, making the reader return to the same feeling established at the start of each passage.

Intensify Verbs

Readers like intense verbs, those that create specific images of movement. It is easy to use weaker verbs, such as *is, was, are, were,* and so on. But such verbs do little to propel the reader's mind through ideas. Notice the following verb use:

> I couldn't open the can of beans I'd brought along, and the slices of bread I'd <u>stuffed</u> into my rucksack <u>fell</u> onto the floor and <u>coated</u> themselves in rust-flecked grease. The freight did, however, <u>grant</u> me a spectacular view of the setting sun as it <u>ambled</u> ever so slowly along the banks of Lake Michigan. (12)

> I would happily <u>contort</u> my fingers into chubby pretzels while singing "The Itsy Bitsy Spider" as the game's events <u>were recounted</u> on the drives home. (14)

> Three sets of large mahogany doors would <u>clang</u> and <u>creak</u>, echoing down the hall, up around the stairwell, and into our classroom. (18)

The verbs in these sentences do more than point out the action of the world. They portray that action—a necessary quality of vital writing.

Vital writing does not merely describe action. It portrays the movement of the world.

PEER REVIEW

Your instructor may arrange for someone else to read your essay and for you to read someone else's. Or it may be up to you to arrange this on your own. Any interested person can provide helpful feedback, but working with a conscientious classmate may be especially helpful—to both of you. Peer review can be done in various ways. Your instructor may provide specific guidelines and, of course, you are always free to try different approaches outside the classroom. Some general advice, however, can be given to ensure that you work efficiently and get positive results.

The writer should

- Provide the reader with a readable copy of the rough draft.
- Help to focus the reader by asking questions about several major concerns you have. Write down your questions, wording them carefully.

The reader should

- Carefully read the draft at least twice, and then respond in writing (not just verbally) to the writer's main concerns.
- Be specific. In addition to saying what you think, say why you think it.
- Be encouraging *and* honest. Providing only praise will not help the writer, yet phrasing your comments in too negative terms might be discouraging.

1. Write down your overall impression of the essay.
2. Write down a summary of the writer's main points. (For example, instead of saying, "I understood what you were saying," say, "I think you were saying. . . ." Then, if the writer was not trying to say that at all, he or she knows that in this case the point was not successfully communicated.)
3. Write down specific responses to the writer's questions about the essay.
4. Write down any major concerns that you feel the writer should have raised but didn't.

The writer should

- Not defend your essay, but instead view it as a work in progress.
- Listen carefully, ask questions only to clarify what the reviewer means, take notes on *all* verbal comments for later reference, and thank the reader for his or her help.
- Later, carefully consider all comments and make only the changes that you consider to be appropriate.

You might do peer review face to face, discussing the papers as you go; or you might read and write comments without any verbal discussion between writer and reader. You might even do peer review over the Internet. If you are pressed for time, or if you have difficulty staying focused on the work at hand, exchanging written comments without discussion can be an efficient peer review strategy.

PEER REVIEW TRUISMS

- **The process can make writers think differently about their own work.** Humans are great modelers. We model our behavior after others, and we make all kinds of subtle changes to our thinking when we read others' work. As modelers, peer reviewers can discover new approaches to an assignment, new writerly moves, new patterns of thinking, or new strategies for creating an engaging voice. (Reviewers can also discover qualities that they want to avoid in their own writing. They might discover some sentence or organization patterns and try to avoid them!)

- **Even the most inexperienced writer can offer valuable comments.** Some people believe that they have little to offer: "I'm not the teacher!" they'll announce. However, peer review is not about pointing out wrongs and rights. It's about reading closely and responding as a thoughtful human in a shared situation. If you can read and focus your attention, you can be a valuable reviewer. In fact, fellow students may even have more to offer one another because they're in a similar situation—faced with a similar task, experiencing the same pressures, at the same moment, in the same place.

- **Chat is the great enemy of good analysis.** Some instructors may set up sessions so that writers can converse about their drafts. Such sessions can be valuable and engaging—even intense and animated. But the danger is that they can devolve into chat sessions about the topics (or something else!). While chatting about one's topic is helpful (and can be worked into a class), a focused and intensive peer review session has its own kind of value.

- **Peer review can be the most valuable component of a writing class.** Writing in college is a social occasion. An academic essay (or any writing assignment) is an intersection of writers, instructors, and students. Peer review brings that to life. It makes the interaction of thinkers real and dramatic. When reviewers take the process seriously, it increases the value of the experience.

- **All writers need help.** Even the best of the best writers rely on the insights and assistance of others. Name a great writer from the past or the present (Steinbeck? Tolkien? Morrison? Dillard?). Each used the ideas and thoughts of others to help shape their projects and even their sentences.

- **Done carelessly, peer review can be a terrible thing.** If peer reviewers read drafts quickly and only point to small, surface-level issues, they waste their partners' time. It is a similar waste if they read for "agreement" and "disagreement"—simply looking for passages they agree or disagree with—and then announce their approval or disapproval of certain points.

After you exchange drafts with another writer, use the following questions to guide your review:

1. How does the essay prompt you to think differently? (For instance, do you see something with more complexity, more beauty, more ugliness, or more intensity than you did before reading? Explain, specifically, what the essay helps you to see differently. If you have a difficult time answering this question, perhaps the essay has not yet gone far enough.)

2. Point to any clichés (or statements that you've heard many times) that the writer can rethink.

3. Which details best illustrate the main idea? (Which details make you picture something specific and reinforce the main idea?)

4. Which details could be added to illustrate the main idea? (What particular behaviors or events could be more dramatized with details?) For instance, the essay probably has a focused moment—a specific event that holds intense meaning. Could that moment use more detail?

5. Which details do not seem related to the thesis of the essay? Why not?

6. How could the writer create more public resonance? (Refer to the Public Resonance section of this chapter.)

7. Are the paragraphs *coherent*? Or do you get the sense that a paragraph is merely wandering through the past, giving details that seem to hold more meaning for the writer than for the point of the essay?

8. How could the writer begin the essay with more intensity? (For instance, if the writer begins with a broad statement about children, such as *Children are curious creatures,* the writer could instead begin with his or her narrative or with a more surprising and focused statement.)

9. Describe the writer's voice. Is it consistent and appropriate? Could the writer use details or metaphors that are more fitting (more comedic or sobering)? What about sentence length? Where do you feel the voice flatten out (get boring!) because of overly consistent sentence length?

10. Focus on sentence vitality. Point to sentences that could be rewritten to create more vitality. Use the following to help guide your attention:

    - Where can the writer combine sentences with coordination?

    - Where can the writer combine with subordination?

    - Help the writer intensify the action with more sensory verbs.

    - Help the writer avoid common grammatical errors: comma splices, sentence fragments, or pronoun/antecedent agreement.

DELIVERY

Any act of writing is an act of creation. And the act of creation, say many philosophers, is the greatest act of humanity, the single act that announces to the world that an individual exists . . . here, in this place, in this time. An academic essay is no different. It is a record of intellectual life within a particular culture.

Consider Cindy Bosley's essay. While it recounts the details of a beauty pageant in Ottumwa, it also chronicles the nature of working-class life in the Great Plains during the late 20th century. It shows what people at the time valued, how they imagined themselves, how they treated others in their community, how they yearned to be different, how they celebrated what they might be. Beyond the narrow focus of Bosley's essay, in the margins of the narrative, we learn about a type of desperation running through the city. Behind the pageantry of civil life is a bigger, less made-up human drama, involving cocaine, factory work, isolation, distinct social classes, and the desperate attempts at concealing it all. This is the hidden, quiet, unperformed life that surrounds Bosley's memory.

Consider other essays in the chapter:

- What does Mockensturm's essay reveal about the relationship between formal schooling and social crisis? What does it say about the state of education in the late 20th century?

- From Tengelitsch's essay, what can we conclude about popular culture in mainstream society and how it affects our lives?

- What does Kress's experience reveal about human curiosity? How does that relate to other stories in American culture?

- Based on Schwind-Pawlak's essay, what are children supposed to believe about themselves?

Now that you have spent many hours generating an essay, crafting your ideas for a particular audience, what does your essay say about you—as an individual human being living in a particular society within the giant wash of history? How is your essay an artifact of its time? What does it reveal about American life in the late 20th/early 21st century? Look beyond the essay's main idea, at the particulars layered throughout the essay.

Beyond the Essay

An *autobiography* is an account of a person's life, told by that person. A *biography* is an account of a person's life told by someone else. While we generally think of biographies as written works, films or television shows can also be *biographical*. For example, each weeknight the television series "Biography" on A&E gives an account of a series of events making up a person's life. Films, too, such as *Ali* or *Ray,* tell a person's life story by relating a series of events.

Biographies and autobiographies are like remembering essays in that they do not merely report what happened. Instead, they present certain events in a particular light so as to tell a story or make a point. For example, two different biographies of Muhammad Ali might present him quite differently. One might show him as a great American hero by focusing on his role as an activist or humanitarian. The other might show him as a great heavyweight boxer, focusing on his career as a fighter. Both biographies could be accurate and interesting, yet quite different. The selection and arrangement of details would present two different Alis.

- Consider one biography or autobiography you have read. How did it make a particular point by presenting certain events or details of a person's life?

- Consider one biographical or autobiographical television show or movie you have seen. How did it make a particular point by presenting certain events or details of a person's life?

"Well, what is creativity but another name for Spirit?"

—Ken Wilber

EXPLAINING RELATIONSHIPS

Chapter Contents

CHAPTER 2

"The human beings depended on the aid and charity of the animals. Only through interdependence could the human beings survive. Families belonged to clans, and it was by the clan that the human being joined with the animal and plant world. Life on the high arid plateau became viable when the human beings were able to imagine themselves as sisters and brothers to the badger, antelope, clay, yucca, and sun. Not until they could find a viable relationship to the terrain, the landscape they found themselves in, could they emerge."

—Leslie Marmon Silko

In the above passage, from "Landscape, History, and the Pueblo Imagination," Silko explains the conceptual and physical relationship between the pueblo Native Americans and their surrounding landscape. It was a subtle and complex relationship, one that went far beyond harvesting crops and extracting resources. The land, for the Pueblo people, helped them to know who they were; it helped them to have a particular identity and culture. Silko's explanation sheds light on this particular relationship.

Explaining relationships is common daily work: People on city councils explore the relationship between neighborhoods to help their cities better understand ethnic diversity; corpo-rate executives constantly try to understand the nature of the relationship between their own companies and their competitors; and certainly, everyone is aware of the ongoing attempts by political leaders to explain the relationships between countries or regions. In a shrinking world in which people of vastly different value systems attempt to coexist, explaining relationships is more than an exercise—it is an act of survival. It might even be argued that the greatest philosophical and scientific discoveries have involved the discovery of relationships—between, for example, atomic elements, religious practices, geological events, historical figures, or heavenly bodies.

In all academic disciplines, people work to understand and communicate the nature of relationships:

- In a computer technology course, students study the relationship between an individual computer and a network of computers, or between a group of users and the Internet.
- In an anthropology course, students explore the relationship between a particular waterway and the ruins of a past civilization.
- In a biology course, students and faculty work to see the relationship between two forms of bacteria.
- In an interior design course, students examine the relationship between a large interior office space and a front entrance to a particular building.

This chapter explores relationships—between places, things, events, people, even ideas. The goal here is to investigate, to seek out some of the hidden dynamics of relationships, to discover the nature of a relationship, or to discover a relationship where one is not necessarily seen.

This chapter will help you discover a topic (a particular relationship), explore that relationship in depth, and explain the nature of the relationship in writing. The following essays will provide valuable insight and necessary strategies for exploring relationships. After reading the essays, you can begin looking for a particular relationship in one of two ways:

1. Go to the **Point of Contact** section to find a relationship from everyday life.
2. Choose one of the **Ideas for Writing** that follow the essays.

After finding a topic, go to the **Analysis** section to begin developing the evaluation.

In the following essays, the authors deal with various possible relationships. While their ideas and stylistic strategies vary, these essays also share some features. Notice, for instance, that the writers offer very specific details about the relationship—sometimes through narrative, sometimes through description. Some writers, such as Meek and Zuger, use dialogue to emphasize key moments and better illustrate the nature of the relationship. All the writers do more than simply relay details about a relationship; instead, they use particular details to make an interesting point that the reader can carry away from the essay, a point that has public resonance. In other words, each writer makes a point about relationships that is bigger than any one particular detail—or any one relationship. In some essays, such as Steinbeck's, that point is obvious. In others, such as Zuger's, it is subtle, hidden inside the details of the essay.

Americans and the Land

John Steinbeck

In John Steinbeck's novels, such as *The Grapes of Wrath* and *Of Mice and Men,* the setting is a vital element of the stories. Steinbeck often draws attention to the ways in which the land influences people's lives. In this essay, from *America and Americans,* Steinbeck focuses on the American settlers' impact on the land. Notice that the land, here, is not something to simply live *on* or even *from.* Instead, it is something to live *with*—or, in the case of many early Americans, to live *against.* As with so many of his novels and stories, this essay invites readers to see in a new light the relationship that people cultivate with the world around them.

I have often wondered at the savagery and thoughtlessness with which our early settlers approached this rich continent. They came at it as though it were an enemy, which of course it was. They burned the forests and changed the rainfall; they swept the buffalo from the plains, blasted the streams, set fire to the grass, and ran a reckless scythe through the virgin and noble timber. Perhaps they felt that it was limitless and could never be exhausted and that a man could move on to new wonders endlessly. Certainly there are many examples to the contrary, but to a large extent the early people pillaged the country as though they hated it, as though they held it temporarily and might be driven off at any time.

This tendency toward irresponsibility persists in very many of us today; our rivers are poisoned by reckless dumping of sewage and toxic industrial wastes, the air of our cities is filthy and dangerous to breathe from the belching of uncontrolled products from combustion of coal, coke, oil, and gasoline. Our towns are girdled with wreckage and the debris of our toys—our automobiles and our packaged pleasures. Through uninhibited spraying against one enemy we have destroyed the natural balances our survival requires. All these evils can and must be overcome if America and Americans are to survive; but many of us still conduct ourselves as our ancestors did, stealing from the future for our clear and present profit.

Since the river-polluters and the air-poisoners are not criminal or even bad people, we must presume that they are heirs to the early conviction that sky and water are unowned and that they are limitless. In the light of our practices here at home it is very interesting to me to read of the care taken with the carriers of our probes into space, to make utterly sure that they are free of pollution of any kind. We would not think of doing to the moon what we do every day to our own dear country.

When the first settlers came to America and dug in on the coast, they huddled in defending villages hemmed in by the sea on one side and by endless forests on the other, by Red Indians and, most frightening, the mystery of an unknown land extending nobody knew how far. And for a time very few cared or dared to find out. Our first Americans organized themselves and lived in a state of military alertness; every community built its blockhouse for defense. By law the men went armed and were required to keep their weapons ready and available. Many of them wore armor, made here or imported; on the East Coast, they wore the cuirass and helmet, and the Spaniards on the West Coast wore both steel armor and heavy leather to turn arrows.

5   On the East Coast, and particularly in New England, the colonists farmed meager lands close to their communities and to safety. Every man was permanently on duty for the defense of his family and his village; even the hunting parties went into the forest in force, rather like raiders than hunters, and their subsequent quarrels with the Indians, resulting in forays and even massacres, remind us that the danger was very real. A man took his gun along when he worked the land, and the women stayed close to their thick-walled houses and listened day and night for the signal of alarm. The towns they settled were permanent, and most of them exist today with their records of Indian raids, of slaughter, of scalpings, and of punitive counter-raids. The military leader of the community became the chief authority in time of trouble, and it was a long time before danger receded and the mystery could be explored.

After a time, however, brave and forest-wise men drifted westward to hunt, to trap, and eventually to bargain for the furs which were the first precious negotiable wealth America produced for trade and export. Then trading posts were set up as centers of collection and the exploring men moved up and down the rivers and crossed the mountains, made friends for mutual profit with the Indians, learned the wilderness techniques, so that these explorer-traders soon dressed, ate, and generally acted like the indigenous people around them. Suspicion lasted a long time, and was fed by clashes sometimes amounting to full-fledged warfare; but by now these Americans attacked and defended as the Indians did.

For a goodly time the Americans were travelers, moving about the country collecting its valuables, but with little idea of permanence; their roots and their hearts were in the towns and the growing cities along the eastern edge. The few who stayed, who lived among the Indians, adopted their customs and some took Indian wives and were regarded as strange and somehow treasonable creatures. As for their half-breed children, while the tribe sometimes adopted them they were unacceptable as equals in the eastern settlements.

Then the trickle of immigrants became a stream, and the population began to move westward—not to grab and leave but to settle and live, they thought. The newcomers were of peasant stock, and they had their roots in a Europe where they had been landless, for the possession of land was the requirement and the proof of a higher social class than they had known. In America they found beautiful and boundless land for the taking—and they took it.

It is little wonder that they went land-mad, because there was so much of it. They cut and burned the forests to make room for crops; they abandoned their knowledge of kindness to the land in order to maintain its usefulness. When they had cropped out a piece they moved on, raping the country like invaders. The topsoil, held by roots and freshened by leaf-fall, was left helpless to the spring freshets, stripped and eroded with the naked bones of clay and rock exposed.

The destruction of the forests changed the rainfall, for the searching clouds could find no green and beckoning woods to draw them on and milk them. The merciless nineteenth century was like a hostile expedition for loot that seemed limitless. Uncountable buffalo were killed, stripped of their hides, and left to rot, a reservoir of permanent food supply eliminated. More than that, the land of the Great Plains was robbed of the manure of the herds. Then the plows went in and ripped off the protection of the buffalo grass and opened the helpless soil to quick water and slow drought and the mischievous winds that roamed through the Great Central Plains. There has always been more than enough desert in America; the new settlers, like overindulged children, created even more.

10   The railroads brought new hordes of land-crazy people, and the new Americans moved like locusts across the continent until the western sea put a boundary to their movements. Coal and copper and gold drew them on; they savaged the land, gold-dredged the rivers to skeletons of pebbles and debris. An aroused and fearful government made laws for the distribution of public lands—a quarter section, one hundred and sixty acres, per person—and a claim had to be proved and improved; but there were ways of getting around this, and legally. My own grandfather proved out a quarter section for himself, one for his wife, one for each of his children, and, I suspect, acreage for children he hoped and expected to have. Marginal lands, of course, suitable only for grazing, went in larger pieces. One of the largest land-holding families in California took its richest holdings by a trick: By law a man could take up all the swamp or water-covered land he wanted. The founder of this great holding mounted a scow on wheels and drove his horses over thousands of acres of the best bottomland, then reported that he had explored it in a boat, which was true, and confirmed his title. I need not mention his name; his descendants will remember.

Another joker with a name still remembered in the West worked out a scheme copied many times in after years. Proving a quarter section required a year of residence and some kind of improvement—a fence, a shack—but once the land was proved the owner was free to sell it. This particular princely character went to the stews and skid rows of the towns and found a small army of hopeless alcoholics who lived for whisky and nothing else. He put these men on land he wanted to own, grubstaked them and kept them in cheap liquor until the acreage was proved, then went through the motions of buying it from his protégés and moved them and their one-room shacks on sled runners on to new quarter sections. Bums of strong constitution might prove out five or six homesteads for this acquisitive hero before they died of drunkenness.

It was full late when we began to realize that the continent did not stretch out to infinity; that there were limits to the indignities to which we could subject it. Engines and heavy mechanical equipment were allowing us to ravage it even more effectively than we had with fire, dynamite, and gang plows. Conservation came to us slowly, and much of it hasn't arrived yet. Having killed the whales and wiped out the sea otters and most of the beavers, the market hunters went to work on game birds; ducks and quail were decimated, and the passenger pigeon eliminated. In my youth I remember seeing a market hunter's gun, a three-gauge shotgun bolted to a frame and loaded to the muzzle with shingle nails. Aimed at a lake and the trigger pulled with a string, it slaughtered every living thing on the lake. The Pacific Coast pilchards were once the raw material for a great and continuing industry. We hunted them with aircraft far at sea until they were gone and the canneries had to be closed. In some of the valleys of the West, where the climate makes several crops a year available, which the water supply will not justify, wells were driven deeper and deeper for irrigation, so that in one great valley a million acre feet more of water was taken out than rain and melting snow could replace, and the water table went down and a few more years may give us a new desert.

The great redwood forests of the western mountains early attracted attention. These ancient trees, which once grew everywhere, now exist only where the last Ice Age did not wipe them out. And they were found to have value. The Sempervirens and the Gigantea, the two remaining species, make soft, straight-grained timber. They are easy to split into planks, shakes, fenceposts, and railroad ties, and they have a unique virtue: they resist decay, both wet and dry rot, and an inherent acid in them repels termites. The loggers went through the great groves like a barrage, toppling the trees—some of which were two thousand years old—and leaving no maidens, no seedlings or saplings on the denuded hills.

Quite a few years ago when I was living in my little town on the coast of California a stranger came in and bought a small valley where the Sempervirens redwoods grew, some of them three hundred feet high. We used to walk among these trees, and the light colored as though the great glass of the Cathedral at Chartres had strained and sanctified the sunlight. The emotion we felt in this grove was one of awe and humility and joy; and then one day it was gone, slaughtered, and the sad wreckage of boughs and broken saplings left like nonsensical spoilage of the battle-ruined countryside. And I remember that after our rage there was sadness, and when we passed the man who had done this we looked away, because we were ashamed for him.

15 From early times we were impressed and awed by the fantastic accidents of nature, like the Grand Canyon and Yosemite and Yellowstone Park. The Indians had revered them as holy places, visited by the gods, and all of us came to have somewhat the same feeling about them. Thus we set aside many areas of astonishment as publicly owned parks; and though this may to a certain extent have been because there was no other way to use them, as the feelings of preciousness of the things we had been destroying grew in Americans, more and more areas were set aside as national and state parks, to be looked at but not injured. Many people loved and were in awe of the redwoods; societies and individuals bought groves of these wonderful trees and presented them to the state for preservation.

No longer do we Americans want to destroy wantonly, but our new-found sources of power—to take the burden of work from our shoulders, to warm us, and cool us, and give us light, to transport us quickly, and to make the things we use and wear and eat—these power sources spew pollution on our country, so that the rivers and streams are becoming poisonous and lifeless. The birds die for the lack of food; a noxious cloud hangs over our cities that burns our lungs and reddens our eyes. Our ability to conserve has not grown with our power to create, but this slow and sullen poisoning is no longer ignored or justified. Almost daily, the pressure of outrage among Americans grows. We are no longer content to destroy our beloved country. We are slow to learn; but we learn. When a super-highway was proposed in California which would trample the redwood trees in its path, an outcry arose all over the land, so strident and fierce that the plan was put aside. And we no longer believe that a man, by owning a piece of America, is free to outrage it.

But we are an exuberant people, careless and destructive as active children. We make strong and potent tools and then have to use them to prove that they exist. Under the pressure of war we finally made the atom bomb, and for reasons which seemed justifiable at the time we dropped it on two Japanese cities— and I think we finally frightened ourselves. In such things, one must consult himself because there is no other point of reference. I did not know about the bomb, and certainly I had nothing to do with its use, but I am horrified and ashamed; and nearly everyone I know feels the same thing. And those who loudly and angrily justify Hiroshima and Nagasaki—why, they must be the most ashamed of all.

Writing Strategies

1. Evaluate Steinbeck's opening paragraph. How does it function? Does it state or imply the main idea? Does it establish tone? Does it invite the reader into the essay? If so, how?

2. Study Steinbeck's use of subjects and verbs. Write down at least ten lively action verbs Steinbeck uses. Then go through an old piece of your own writing, redrafting sentences with livelier action verbs.

3. In paragraph 10, Steinbeck describes the people that the railroad brought west as "land-crazy" and says they moved "like locusts." Identify other expressions he uses to describe the people. Which expressions are especially effective? Think of several appropriate expressions that Steinbeck might have used, but didn't.

4. Describe Steinbeck's tone. Is his essay inviting to the reader, or does it put the reader off? Support your response with specific references to the text.

5. Describe Steinbeck's conclusion. Where does he end up—that is, where does he ultimately take the reader? Is his conclusion effective or not? What seems to be his concluding strategy?

Exploring Ideas

1. What does Steinbeck say about Americans and the land? What is he trying to accomplish in this essay?

2. What does your response to the reading tell you about the way that you view "the land" or "the environment"?

3. What is your relationship with the land? What everyday actions of your own have a positive impact on the land? What everyday actions of your own have a negative impact on the land?

4. Observe the way land is used in your community. Take field notes. Then organize the data you have collected into two categories: observations that support what Steinbeck says, and observations that refute what he says.

Ideas for Writing

1. What is the relationship between Americans and the land today?

2. Describe your relationship with your immediate surroundings (your house, bedroom, apartment, dorm, etc.). How is it typical (or not typical) of your broader attitude concerning the relationship of humans to the land?

3. Discuss your observations (Exploring Ideas #4) with others, looking for ways that you might participate in Steinbeck's discussion of Americans and the land. How might you contribute to this discussion? What idea, for example, could use further explanation or clarification?

If responding to one of these ideas, go to the **Analysis** section of this chapter to begin developing ideas for your essay.

We Love Them. We Hate Them. We Take Them.

Abigail Zuger

In all occupations, relationships are mysterious, troubling, and controversial. And professionals in all walks of life find themselves stumped by the relationships that seem most common and mundane. In this essay, published in the *New York Times* in December 2004, Abigail Zuger, a physician, explores the relationship among doctors, patients, and the pills that bind them.

There were eight of us crowded into the exam room as an exasperated patient and I tried to figure out why he was feeling weak and tired and itchy and nauseated and almost fainted in the subway Thursday night.

Two of us, the patient and I, were human beings. The rest had no voices, bodies or personalities in the ordinary sense of the word, but they played a role in the discussion that was just as vigorous and important as if they did.

They were, of course, my patient's pills. Or rather, they were my pills: the pills I gave him. Or rather, they were Merck's pills and Pfizer's and GlaxoSmithKline's and a couple of generic manufacturers'. They were the Food and Drug Administration's pills, too, released into our little sphere only with that agency's blessing.

But mostly, the pills were the patient's and mine, and we tussled over them with all the wishful thinking and hidden agenda of estranged parents haggling over the kids. The blue capsule? He'd been taking it for years, with good results. It seemed unlikely to be causing problems now. The new white capsule I gave him last month, the one I figured was making him sick?

5 "I love it," he said. "Makes me feel like myself. Can't live without it."

The big white tablet from last spring?

"I just look at one and I feel sick," he said. "I hate them and I'm not taking them anymore. The end."

"You'll wind up in the hospital without them," I said for the sixth time in six months. "Please, bear with them. There's nothing else to use."

But I knew perfectly well he had probably stopped taking them regularly months ago, and would never swallow one again.

10 When he left the room, I gazed for a few moments at the single prescription he had left sitting on the desk. The big white tablet. Such a good pill. Cheap, safe and effective, if a little hard on the stomach. How I loved that modest, hardworking pill. Of course, I had never put one into my mouth, but it was still one of my favorites. How could he reject it, reject me, out of hand like that?

The nation's use of prescription drugs is soaring, a government report said this month, and the relationships we all have with those little pieces of matter, our pills, are becoming ridiculously tangled.

Medical anthropologists have written at length about how medications "commodify" health, fostering the illusion that it is something bought and sold at market. In doctors' offices and in medicine cabinets, though, a reverse process takes place: We all anthropomorphize pills right back from commodities to willful agents of good or evil. For patients, they can be saviors, or assassins. For doctors, the voodoo is even stronger. Medicines are our prosthetics, at once utterly foreign (we are unlikely to take them ourselves, and may not even know what they look like) yet so much a part of us that we can barely function without them.

For those of us in specialties without scalpels or scopes, they are our only tools (if you don't count all the good advice). Inevitably, we evolve idiosyncratic patterns of prescribing, favorite combinations, pills we love or hate. The pills become our friends, our servants, our agents, ourselves.

Of course, that artistry and control is all an illusion. We flex our dosing muscles at a remove too far from the actual ingestion to be in control of anything, and we are in turn controlled by forces we never see.

One moment we are signing for Vioxx, confident and enthusiastic; the next moment, it disappears, and we are left to explain why. One moment we are prescribing a patient's big white tablet, happy that we are practicing medicine of the highest quality by protecting him from bad things. The next, we discover once again that little known fact: There is a placebo effect for doctors, too.

15   Pity the doctor who thinks that prescribing a drug is the same thing as treating a patient, and the patient who agrees. Some never learn otherwise. The rest of us slowly wake up to the fact that the prescription is just the beginning, sometimes not even that. Without constant discussion and re-evaluation, we might as well all be writing poetry on those prescription forms.

After a month without the big white pills my patient said he felt a lot better. I, of course, was no longer practicing quality medicine, and felt a lot worse. His stomach talked to him. The statistics of what would happen to him without the pills talked to me. The pills, for once, were silent. Perhaps the best we could do, under the circumstances, was keep talking to each other.

Writing Strategies

1. How is Zuger's opening strategy ("There were eight of us crowded into the exam room . . .") important to the rest of her essay?

2. Zuger begins her essay with a narrative. At what point does she leave the narrative, and why?

3. What conclusions does Zuger come to at the end of her essay? What would she like her reader to consider?

4. Zuger's essay was published in the *New York Times*, a daily newspaper with a general readership. How might Zuger have presented her ideas differently if her essay were

   • written for an academic journal?
   • written for a college writing course?
   • an advertisement?

Exploring Ideas

1. In groups, explore the following:

   Medical anthropologists have written at length about how medications "commodify" health, fostering the illusion that it is something bought and sold at the market. (¶ 12)

   What evidence can you provide to support the statement?

2. Why do Americans take so many pills? Generate as many reasons or possibilities as you can. Then explore them further through discussion. Which reasons are most valid or least valid? Are any just the tip of the iceberg?

3. In paragraph 14, Zuger says doctors are "controlled by forces we never see." What does she mean? How much are, or aren't, doctors in control?

Ideas for Writing

1. Further research the popularity of prescription drugs in the United States, and try to uncover more about the relationship between prescription drugs and people's lives.

2. What else, besides medications, have Americans come to see as a commodity—an article of trade or commerce? Show how viewing the thing as a commodity creates a particular relationship.

3. Share some insight about the relationship between doctor and patient, focusing on how some unseen force(s) impacts the relationship.

If responding to one of these ideas, go to the **Analysis** section of this chapter to begin developing ideas for your essay.

What the Honey Meant

Cindy Bosley

It is easy to see ourselves moving steadily ahead in time. But Cindy Bosley, poet, novelist, and writing teacher, invites us to see how the past circles up into our lives—and how the people from our past linger in the present. In this essay, Bosley's present relationship with her husband involves her past relationship with her father. While the essay is highly narrative, it is also highly analytical, making intense connections between single moments throughout Bosley's life. And these connections help to reveal significant meaning in a simple honeycomb. (Bosley's writing also appears in Chapter 1.)

Writing Strategies

Exploring Ideas

My husband disappeared out the back door with an empty bowl in his hand. I did not see him leave, but a few moments later, he came back in and asked me to shut my eyes. I did as he asked. When I opened them, he stood in front of me holding out a bowl of fresh honey and a piece of the comb which had been pulled away from the hive and was still running with the buttery sweet liquid of all my best memories. My husband might as well have gone out just then and shoved his hand, in brown bear fashion, through the stinging, angry bees to release this small brick of honeycomb for all the love and gratitude I felt toward him at that moment. He stood there holding out to me a bowl filled with my life as it should have been, and I wept.

Begins with an anecdote.

The metaphor sets up the rest of the essay.

When I think of honeycomb, I think of my father. I first tried a small bite, and then more and more by the spoonful, the day before my father left. He had brought the honey home from a guy at work, he said, and so he set the brick in its jar onto the counter, and found a spoon for himself, plunged the spoon into the hexagon cells and pulled it away with a *suck*. And then he went back for more. I stood over the jar of honeycomb marveling at it—the many sections of honey, the yellowish layer of beeswax sealing the liquid in, the small brown and black flecks of flower remnant, or bee poop, I guessed. My father said nothing to me, and he did not offer me his spoon, but when I got off my chair to get one from the drawer, I stood over the honey jar again waiting for permission, and he said, "Wanna try it?" with surprise and, I think, a little joy, as if it hadn't occurred to him before to offer some to others. That was the way he was. And I ate and ate and ate. I loved the wax like gum,

Honeycomb is the link to understanding her relationship with her father.

We're gaining insight into his character. He seems the opposite of the husband, who brings her the honey without notice.

The degree and level of detail suggest that this is an important situation.

how it stayed behind in my mouth long after the honey part was gone, swallowed, tasted, and replaced with another spoonful.

The honey is related to sharing.

When my father left that night, I was sleeping and he did not say good-bye. In the years to come as he came and went, moving in and out like a college boy from a dormitory, I would learn that this was how he did things. That first morning, though, I did not know anything had happened, but like a too bulky winter coat a kid inherits from an older sibling, that morning when I woke, the house just *felt* different—a little bigger, a little old. The rooms were quieter. It's hard to believe that was possible, the new quiet, since my father was a too quiet man to begin with, but it was *quiet*. And the browns and golds of our '70s decor were browner, and deeper gold. And my mother was in her bedroom on the phone trying to muffle hard crying. And my younger sister was watching *Land of the Lost,* while my brother played with his Tinker Toys. Something had happened, and I didn't have to ask anyone what that was. The sun was a sawblade in the sky.

She uses paragraph changes as shifts in time.

The allusions to popular culture give the essay a context—help the reader to experience the situation in time.

The metaphor of the sun creates a feeling of hardness—cutting.

Another painful or hard metaphor.

Life changes here. The father is gone. This is the beginning of something—a "new quiet."

I didn't quite know what to feel about this. Part of what I felt was certainly excitement. *Wow. Our dad's gone. Wow.* I also felt a puncture, very small like a needle, that I couldn't locate inside me. And I was, I think now, terrified at the new development that no one had yet explained to me though it was nearing lunch time, though it was time for someone to talk.

5   I finally had to ask the obvious question, but I didn't know how these things were supposed to go—I had imagined other families, more loving families, sitting down together to talk over the coming changes with the children well before they happened, or maybe even a day before they happened. I had imagined other families dealing with it in other ways—the father kissing the children a special goodnight when he knew he would not be there the next day when they woke up, or maybe he would not save the trauma for the night or morning, but ease out in the smooth part of the afternoon, lots of hugs and tears, but at least the witnessing of leave-taking. And then I remembered the honeycomb.

The honey is about hope—a hope for sharing in something meaningful?

And if I say: I went to the kitchen to look for something. Like a small and pitiful gesture of his helplessness and regret, there on the counter was a spoon he'd left beside the jar of honey, and I knew he meant it for me.

It feels one way.

But if I say: I went to the kitchen to look for the jar of honey. When I saw the counter, I saw there was nothing there, and I suppose I expected that. He must have taken it with him.

She tends to use short sentences to shift the reader back into her reflections.

The one-sentence paragraphs slow everything down. They make this section feel very reflective—almost meditative.

The situation has different possible meanings. Every event has different possible outcomes. The outcome of this event creates a particular reality—and set of relationships.

That feels another way.

10   But what really happened is that I did not have to ask my obvious question, "What happened with Dad?" And I did not have to bother looking for the honey because, yes, he left it—it simply wasn't that important to him. And no, there was no symbolic spoon or other invitation, *Eldest Daughter, please eat,* nearby. What happened was that I took a bite of honey and then I joined my sister and brother, two and ten years younger, watching Saturday morning cartoons together on the black, brown, white carpet, patterned in such a wild way that it was quickly making my head ache.

I heard my mother tell the story five or six times that morning, with different details and emphasis, to the people she talked to most easily. She had moved from the heavy weight of the red and black paisley bedroom to the dimness of the kitchen, a room the sun rarely ventured into, like all the dark rooms of our house. She told Aunt Edith that he better damn well get his stereo cabinet out of this house today. She moaned her money fears to Patty, and there was a hitch in my heart when I heard her mention my violin lessons. While she talked to Marlene, I heard several female names come flying, and with Darla, I understood more clearly that there was somehow another woman involved. What had happened I never did learn exactly, but my father had moved out overnight. Everything felt brand new. And there was a jar half-full of honey in the kitchen that no one but me wanted to eat.

When my husband brought his bowl of honeycomb to me that bright, grown-up day in the kitchen, I did not think *Father.* I did not think *Childhood.* I did not think *Old Pain.* But my husband knows my stories well enough to understand what it might mean to me, and when he heard our neighbor at the door that morning telling him to come get some of this amazing honey someone had given him, my husband knew enough to grab a bowl and bring me some.

Everyone I know has aches so deep that small triggers bring tears to their eyes. The honey gift was clearly that trigger for me. I like to think I cried because seeing that bowl of honey made me miss my father. Or maybe I cried because I don't yet understand all that happened in my life back then, or why people can do the things they do to each other. Maybe I cried because my husband loves me that much, enough to know what the honey would mean. But I do know one thing: I sure do like honey. I wept to see that honey just for me.

Same as the honey jar in the kitchen: Situations have different psychological layers, and they come out in different tellings—or stories.

The facts aren't important. The psychological consequences are. (They impact her future.)

The short, almost poem-like, sentences bring the reader into her feelings. (The brevity = intimate realizations.)

Here's the public resonance.

She's returning to the original scene.

Again, the various possibilities create complexity. Her emotions emerge from a long complex history, and we cannot pin down, exactly, what makes her (us?) feel a certain way.

Writing Strategies

1. In paragraph 3, Bosley offers the reader details about physical goings-on:

   And the browns and golds of our '70s decor were browner, and deeper gold. And my mother was in her bedroom on the phone trying to muffle hard crying. And my younger sister was watching *Land of the Lost,* while my brother played with his Tinker Toys. Something had happened, and I didn't have to ask anyone what that was. The sun was a sawblade in the sky.

   What purpose do these details serve? What point, if any, might they communicate to the reader?

2. Notice how Bosley uses her introduction and conclusion (about honey) to frame her essay. Is her framing technique effective? What are such a technique's effects on the reader? Can you think of any situations in which this framing technique would be ineffective?

3. Paragraphs 7 and 9 are very short—one sentence each. What effect does their brevity have on the reading of the essay? Why does she offer these particular ideas in one-sentence paragraphs?

4. How does Bosley develop her main idea—with narration (story telling), description, or both? In what other ways does she develop it?

5. Identify at least one use of figurative language such as hyperbole, metaphor, understatement, or allusion and explain why it is effective.

Exploring Ideas

1. In a paragraph, explain what the honey means to Bosley. Include in your explanation how the honey comes to have the meaning for her that it does.

2. Revise the paragraph you wrote for #1 and share it with several classmates. Discuss the differences between your paragraphs.

3. How does Bosley's essay encourage the reader to think about everyday things, such as honey?

4. In what ways might you respond to Bosley's essay? What kinds of responses does it invite? List several possibilities and discuss them with your peers.

5. Talk to old friends and relatives and visit places from your past (a playground, old school, church, and so on). Through writing, explore the memories or emotions you experience.

Ideas for Writing

1. Bosley begins her second paragraph, "When I think of honeycomb, I think of my father." What relationship are you reminded of by honeycomb or some other thing?

2. What have you figured out about a relationship you had with a parent, grandparent, or significant adult figure growing up?

If responding to one of these ideas, go to the **Analysis** section of this chapter to begin developing ideas for your essay.

Dog-Tied

David Hawes

We are surrounded by interesting, complex, and puzzling relationships—which we rarely examine closely. In "Dog-Tied," David Hawes explores the relationship he has with his dog, Logan. His essay prompts the rest of us to consider similar relationships. Hawes's essay demonstrates the curious mind at work, looking not just from the owner's point of view but from the pet's as well.

I realize this is an odd paraphrase of the Beatles, but it certainly seems fitting: I have a dog, or should I say, my dog has me? Often it seems unclear which of us is in charge in this arrangement. As I once explained to a non-dog owner, "Logan and I have a symbiotic relationship: I feed him, walk him, bathe him, take him to the vet, give him his heartworm and flea-and-tick medicines, buy him treats, pet him, and play with him. And what does he do? He lets me." This past summer I even bought him a kiddie pool to lay in when he got too hot. He is, after all, a retriever, so he likes water. Not to mention that he has this hairy coat on all the time that he can't take off when he's too warm. Do I spoil him? Of course I do. Isn't that the whole point of having a dog?

On the other hand, I realize some people don't see things the way I do. Just this morning I saw a man walking his dog past the front of my house. In a loud and commanding voice he kept saying, "Heel! Heel!" Obviously he wanted his dog to make no mistake about who was in charge. However, I did notice that the man kept up his commands all the way down the street. Maybe the dog's name is "Heel." I think most people, though, have a tendency to spoil their dogs. Just go to any pet store and look at the vast array of foods, toys, beds, and treats, not to mention the shampoos and skin treatments.

It wasn't always this way, of course. Dogs were originally domesticated so they could help with the work. And some dogs are still workers, helping herd the sheep or bring in the cattle. But I have to believe these true "working dogs" are a small minority. I think most dogs these days, at least in this country, lead a fairly pampered life, so it certainly gives a different meaning to the old sayings about "a dog's life" and "working like a dog." Personally, I'd love to work as much as my dog does.

Sometimes, though, I have to wonder about him liking his pampered life. Sometimes when he's in a really deep sleep, his legs jerk violently, like he's running. Is he dreaming about retrieving ducks and quail? When fall comes, do those longing looks he gives me mean he's wondering when I'm going to get the shotgun out so he can do what he was bred to do? When he lies down with his head between his paws and heaves one of the heavy dog sighs, is he wishing he could be running through a field somewhere, sniffing out the game? Does he feel like something is missing from his life, but he's not sure what it is? And worst of all, does he blame me for what's missing?

5   I worry about these things sometimes, but not too much, I guess, because when I leave for work in the morning and he looks very sad, or when I get home from work and he wiggles all over the place in his happiness to see me, or when he comes into the bedroom and lies beside me first thing in the morning waiting for his wake-me-up belly rub, it seems like maybe this relationship is working out OK.

Writing Strategies

1. How does Hawes convey his main idea? Does he state it explicitly or imply it? Does he develop it through narration, description, explanation, or a combination of the three?

2. Hawes describes his relationship with Logan as "symbiotic." Is this a good word choice? Explain. If it is not, what one word would you use to describe their relationship?

3. Is Hawes's essay engaging—that is, do you as a reader become interested and want to read on? If so, carefully consider why. If not, why not?

4. If workshopping Hawes's essay, how would you answer the following questions: What is the essay's biggest strength? What is the essay's biggest weakness? What one recommendation would you make?

5. Write a new introduction and conclusion for Hawes's essay, and then compare it with one a classmate wrote. Discuss the different strategies you chose and the advantages and disadvantages of both.

Exploring Ideas

1. Describe the relationship between Hawes and his dog.

2. Describe the relationship you have with a dog, another pet, a stray or wild animal, or some other life form, such as your prize orchids, herb garden, and so on.

3. To further explore people's relationships with other life, interview at least five people about their relationship with any nonhuman life form.

   a. Begin by considering what you want to know. For example, you might ask them to describe the relationship in general, explain what they find rewarding about it, explain what they find frustrating about it, and so on. In groups or alone, compose several clear and purposeful questions that will encourage informative responses.

   b. Conduct the interviews, being certain to accurately record the responses. Then look for interesting ideas that help you to learn something new about people's relationships with other life. Write down the two or three most interesting ideas you discovered, and explain what you think is interesting about them.

4. How might you respond to Hawes's essay without writing about dogs or pets? What relationships can you use to illustrate your main idea?

Ideas for Writing

1. What relationship of your own is symbiotic, though it may not appear so to others?

2. Using Hawes's essay for inspiration, what else is interesting about human/animal relationships in general?

If responding to one of these ideas, go to the **Analysis** section of this chapter to begin developing ideas for your essay.

Friend or Foe?

Dean A. Meek

In "Friend or Foe?" Dean Meek explores his relationship with alcohol and with addiction. Meek not only analyzes how his addiction began, how it ended, and how it impacted his life; by casting his addiction as a relation-ship, he helps us to open our minds and perhaps look at the broader subject—*addiction*—differently. As you read, notice how Meek provides relevant narrative details to shed light on the relationship.

As a boy growing up in suburban Indiana, I still remember the feelings of loneliness and alienation. I was always bigger than the other children in my class and they often made fun of my husky build. This was a feeling that I would carry with me through my teenage years, a feeling of not fitting in and being ashamed of the way I looked. However, this would all change once I was introduced to that great healer of all, the one thing that could right all wrongs and change my life forever. From the moment I took my first drink of alco-hol, it was obvious we were meant to be together. We were akin to the likes of Steve Yzerman and Brendan Shanahan or Terry Bradshaw and Lynn Swann. Togeth-er we were unstoppable and feared nothing.

It all started on a lovely fall day my freshman year of high school. Although this day started no different than all the previous, it would drastically change all the days to come. Prior to school I was standing outside and was approached by Cool Jim. Cool Jim was a very popular kid in school; he was happy-go-lucky and very outgoing. He wasn't afraid of anyone or anything and really had a way with the ladies.

"Would you like to buy a bottle of wine?" said Cool Jim.

"No, I'm not into that," I replied, while leaning against the building and smoking a cigarette.

5   "That's cool," commented Jim as he made his way down the side of the school.

Finishing my smoke, I watched Jim stop and talk to all the people; he had so many friends. On the way to my first class, I still recall thinking to myself how lucky Cool Jim was to have so many friends and such self-esteem. "If I could only be more like him, life would be great!"

Later that morning, I passed Jim in the hall between periods.

"Still got that wine!" Jim said.

Before I could respond, a thought came over me: "If I want to be more like Jim, then maybe this is one way to get started."

10   "How much?" I replied.

"Five dollars, it's top shelf," said Jim.

"I'll take it!"

During lunch, I went for a walk with my new-found friend, a bottle of Mad Dog 20/20. As I opened that classy metal cap, it was as if I had transformed into manhood. At first the taste was quite bitter but the more I indulged, the better the flavor became. Walking back to school, my face seemed to become numb and that numbness continued throughout my entire body. "That's it!" I thought. This is what I had been searching for all my life. This new comrade of mine would shel-ter me from those unbearable feelings of loneliness and disgust.

That evening while lying in bed, I had a strange feeling come over me. In a matter of seconds it was obvious to me that my new friend would revisit me. In the bathroom praying at the porcelain altar, I somehow had the crazy notion this was all worthwhile. This phys-ical pain was nothing compared to the emotional tur-moil I endured. Kindly, I would trade an upset stomach for the feeling of fearlessness.

15   Through the years we stuck together and were completely inseparable. Occasionally we would find ourselves in a sticky situation but nonetheless we were best of friends.

Then came the day that would begin an unexpect-ed metamorphosis. It was Sunday morning and I bowled on a league at 11:00 a.m.. As with every Sunday, soon as the clock hit 12:00 noon, it was party time. The bar would start selling alcohol and more importantly, I would begin coming out of my shell. By the middle of the second game, I was back on top and feeling good. Sure, my bowling would suffer but who cares? It was just for fun and lots of it. Then after bowling, we headed into the bar and continued throwing down the suds. Shortly after that, I have no memory of what was to come.

The next morning as I opened my eyes, the glare of bright lights blinded me. The glare magnified the pounding in my head, which had become as certain as the rising of the morning sun. While rubbing my eyes, I noticed a shadow hanging over me. Startled by the image, I fought to gain my faculties. As my eyes began to focus, the image became clear. It was that of a rather large police officer. Overwhelmed by the fear and confusion of not knowing what had happened, I visually scanned the room for answers. I was in a hospital room and at the foot of my bed stood my parents: they were clearly upset and on edge. Placing her hand on my leg, Mom said: "Just relax. You are going to be all right." I tried to speak but could not. It felt as if my heart was pounding in my throat and I was trembling in fear. Then the officer said: "The charges are DUI and leaving the scene of an accident."

"DUI, for what?" I exclaimed.

"Just keep your mouth shut," replied my mother forcefully.

20 After the officer had left the room, my parents informed me that I had hit three cars in the parking lot of the bowling alley. Then, I had continued on to hit two more parked cars and a telephone pole: Thankfully no one was hurt. This was where the police and EMTs had found me. Furthermore, the 1965 Mustang that I had cherished was totaled and I was facing some very serious legal issues. "How could this be?" I thought.

The one thing that had removed my emotional turbulence was now the cause of all this. Well, that thought was short-lived. Maybe I overdid it a little and needed to exercise some control, but quitting was definitely out of the question!

Several months had passed and I lay awake in bed suffering from an anxiety attack. Feelings of loneliness and disgust flowed through me like the Maumee River through Toledo, Ohio. How could I be lonely? After all, I had a wife and four daughters. How could anyone be lonely? Nevertheless, I was and the one true friend that could always be counted on was failing me. Those same emotions of that teenage schoolboy came rushing back. Where drinking once removed them, it now magnified those demons. I could run no more. Those emotions now compounded with alcoholism would be the end of me. I only had two choices left: I would either get help or commit suicide and there were no other options. Thankfully, I chose treatment and, with the help of my wife, was admitted to a program that same day.

That was a few 24 hours ago and life is much better today. That once shy high school boy has matured into a recovering alcoholic. After giving up the alcohol, I again faced those evil emotions but this time I faced them head-on. You see, nothing external could mend this torn soul. It had to be fixed internally. As for my old friend, he is now my foe. I see him around but only from a distance. Sometimes, I think he would like us to rekindle those burning desires we once shared but I refuse. As for those schoolboy feelings of loneliness and shamefulness, gratitude and pride have since replaced them and the yearning to be a part of the crowd is no more.

Writing Strategies

1. Describe Meek's voice, and identify several passages to support your description. How does his voice influence your response to the essay?

2. In your own words, write down what you think Meek's main idea is, and then discuss what you wrote down with several classmates. How were your understandings of the main idea similar or different?

3. Identify several passages in which Meek personifies (gives human characteristics to) his foe. What is the effect of these passages? How are they, or aren't they, successful?

4. How else might Meek have begun and ended his essay? Discuss different approaches with a group of classmates, considering the advantages and disadvantages of each.

Exploring Ideas

1. Briefly summarize Meek's relationship with alcohol, including how/why it began, the nature of the relationship, and its current status.

2. How does Meek's essay encourage the reader to think about alcohol?

3. What "friend or foe" relationships have you had or do you have? Consider, but do not limit yourself to, substances, activities, habits, people, thoughts, and so on. You might discover less-obvious relationships through discussion with relatives, friends, classmates, and co-workers, or by looking through personal belongings.

4. How might writing about one of your "friend or foe" relationships (#3) help you or others? What might be the consequence of such an essay?

Ideas for Writing

1. What "friend or foe" relationship have you experienced yourself, or seen others experience?

2. What "friend or foe" relationship can you think of that doesn't involve humans?

If responding to one of these ideas, go to the **Analysis** section of this chapter to begin developing ideas for your essay.

Outside Reading

Find a written text that explains or points out an un-usual relationship. Go to a library database or search engine and experiment by typing in combinations of words (joined by *and*). To conduct an electronic search through journals and magazines, go to your library's periodical database or to InfoTrac College Edition (http://infotrac.galegroup.com/itweb/). For your library database, perform a keyword search, or for InfoTrac College Edition, go to the main search box and click on "keywords." In the search box, enter word combinations, such as *water and politics, lakes and engineering, nursing and chemistry.* (When performing keyword searches, avoid using phrases or articles *(a, an, the);* instead, use nouns separated by *and.*) The search results will yield lists of journal and magazine articles. The same strategy can be used with an Internet search. Try Google.com and enter various word combinations. Once you find an interesting text, print it out.

The purpose of this assignment is to explore a broad spectrum of possible relationships and to discover more about explanatory writing. You may discover relationships you never imagined, and will probably witness a variety of writing strategies. As you read through this chapter, keep the document you have discovered close by and notice the elements and strategies the writer uses. Depending on your instructor's suggestions, do one or more of the following:

1. Notice how the writer applies various strategies from this chapter. On the hard copy:
   - Highlight the thesis (main point about the relationship) if it is stated. If the thesis is implied, write it in your own words.
   - Identify the major rhetorical tools (narrative, description, allusion).
   - Identify any passages that show public resonance (in which the writer makes the relationship a public issue or concern).

2. Analyze the strategies employed by the writer. The following questions may be helpful:
   - How is the writer's voice different from the essays in this chapter?
   - How does the writer support or illustrate his or her thesis?
   - Who is the audience for this text?
   - How does the audience impact the kinds of things said in the text?

3. Write at least three "Writing Strategies" questions for the text you found.

4. Write at least three "Exploring Ideas" questions for the text you found.

5. Write two "Ideas for Writing," such as the ones following the essays in this book, for the text you found.

INVENTION

Invention is the activity of discovering ideas, developing points, and thinking through a topic. For academic writers, it is a necessary activity, one that leads to vital and valuable ideas. In this chapter, the process will involve focusing on a particular relationship and exploring its possible meaning. The following sections are designed to help you through the invention process: specifically, to discover a topic (in **Point of Contact**), to develop particular points about the topic (in **Analysis**), to make it relevant to a community of readers (in **Public Resonance**), to develop a focus (in **Thesis**), and to generate support (in **Rhetorical Tools**). The Invention questions in each section are not meant to be answered directly in your final written assignment. Rather, they are meant to help you develop increasingly intense ideas for your project.

POINT OF CONTACT

When you hear the word *relationship,* you may imagine an intimate personal bond between significant others, family members, or friends. But consider the relationships that are less obvious, those that surround or define us but remain hidden by the patterns of everyday life. Imagine the intense, but also subtle, relationships that define life as we know it: between an old man and his backyard, among people in a large corporate office, between a lake and a local economy, between pigeons and people in a park. When we examine such relationships, we are apt to discover some hidden workings and ideas—which is often the purpose of writing in academia.

As you explore possible topics, ask yourself: "What is the nature of this relationship?" Don't be discouraged if nothing falls from the sky and says, "Hey! I'm a great topic!" That rarely happens. Use these suggestions and questions to find and develop a topic:

- **Visit a Public Place**
  —How do the people interact or depend on each other?
  —How do the people relate to their surroundings? To objects? To buildings? To nature?
  —How do the objects (buildings, tools, products, shops) relate?
  —How do people or objects influence each other?

No topic is inherently interesting. The process of developing the topic will make it interesting.

- **Examine a Job Site**
  —How do workers relate to their tools or equipment?
  —How must the people relate to each other? (How must they influence or depend on each other?)
  —How do workers relate to their environment?
  —How do workers relate to the public?

- **Examine Everyday Civic Bonds** Between a customer and a sales clerk, a customer and a mail carrier, the public and a city police force, a politician and her constituents, or an artist and the public.

- **Imagine Human/Object Relationships** Between a person and a computer, a person and a musical instrument, a person and a car; or between two objects, such as a college course and a textbook, a book and computer, an old car and a new one, a road and a house.

- **Examine Relationships in Your Academic Major**
  —Between the professionals in your field of study and the public (such as nurses and their patients, or business marketing professionals and potential consumers).
  —Between two things in your field of study. Students of criminal justice, for instance, can explore how one case (or one kind of case) relates to another; environmental scientists can explore the relationship between waterways and surrounding land or between trees and animal life.
  —Between your field of study and another field. Most academic disciplines and professional fields define themselves in conjunction with other fields. For instance, biology explores its relationship with ethics, computer technologies involve visual or graphic design, and political science involves religious studies.

INSERT MONEY

Selection

A B C D
E F G H
K I J

Coin Return

Coin Insert

Change Returned Below

ACTIVITY

Now go beyond these suggestions. Imagine more relationships in your life and the world around you. If you can work in groups, each group should generate a list of possible relationships—those that people overlook in their everyday lives. Each group member should keep a record of the possible topic ideas.

ANALYSIS

Analysis is the process of inspecting how or why something works, but analysis also involves discovering connections and meaning. In this chapter, analysis involves investigating all the possible ways two entities relate to each other. It means going beyond the obvious relationship and exploring the hidden or abstract connections.

Use the following questions to explore deep layers of the relationship that you will explain in your essay:

- Is the relationship difficult? Why?
- What keeps it going?
- How does the presence of one entity (person or thing) influence the other? In what hidden or indirect ways do they influence one another?
- What would occur to one if the other were gone?
- What qualities or characteristics do they share?

Important Questions for Exploring a Human Relationship If you examine an intimate personal relationship, try to go beyond the initial common thoughts ("it is supportive"; "it is difficult"; "it has ups and downs"; "it is loving") and find some hidden complexity. Cindy Bosley, for instance, goes way beyond the first layer of her relationship with her husband and discovers that its significance is tied to her relationship with her father. She finds a particular and interesting emotional complexity: that the past is always potentially intermingling with the present.

Use the following to explore the complexities of a human relationship:

- In what ways do I communicate with this person?
- To what degree do I share in his or her personal crises?
- Do I ever feel obligated to do, think, or say something for this person?

- What do each of us expect from the other?
- What are the consequences of not meeting each other's personal needs?
- What kinds of disagreements arise in the relationship?
- Do they become sources of debate and tension, or do they fade away?

INVENTION WRITING

As you work through these Invention questions, use them to develop ideas. For example, Dean Meek's invention writing (excerpted below) helped him to discover the insights he shares in his essay. In his responses to the Invention questions, we can see how important concepts emerge and lay the groundwork for his essay. For example, his notes uncover his low self-esteem, the description of himself as a drinker, and the manner in which alcohol manipulated his sense of identity:

> **What qualities/characteristics does one give the other?**
> The relationship that I have/had with alcohol was one that initially started out as what I perceived to be a positive one. In my mind alcohol allowed me to be everything I wasn't. Alcohol allowed me to be fun-loving, outgoing, personable, and an all-around better person, or so I thought. Alcohol took me places where I would never go sober and introduced me to many people. Because of alcohol I was able to be the life of the party and was a real ladies' man. It was all these thoughts and feelings that were actually preying on my poor self-esteem. By initially attacking my self-esteem the alcohol was eventually able to consume the rest of my being. It was only at the point that alcohol caused me enormous pain and confusion that I would even half-heartedly look at it as a problem. Yet it still took more pain for me to realize that not only was it a problem, it was the problem.

Now imagine a different topic and writer. Marcus is using the Invention questions on page 74 to explore the relationship between a police department and the surrounding community. Notice how Marcus's response to the last question below (Why are you in this relationship?) takes him further into his own thinking. Although the question seems unrelated to his topic, it actually prompts him to see an essential point: *People can be in a relationship without consciously thinking about it.*

Is the relationship difficult?

Yes. My father is a police officer, and he is constantly stressed about the work. Patrolling in some neighborhoods is hard work—and dangerous. And even though many officers face dangerous situations, they are expected by people in the community to be totally passive. It's nearly impossible work.

What keeps it going?

People stay in the job for obvious reasons: They need money, they have the training, they get some satisfaction out of the job (most of them still assume that they are "protecting and serving"). But the real question is: What keeps the tension going? And that's a mixture of things: On one side, economic problems in the city create bad neighborhoods where people are desperate. On the other side, every time the news reports anything involving the police, it's going to be bad, so people learn to associate police cars and uniforms with negative feelings.

Why are you in this relationship?

Technically, I'm not in it. Or maybe I am. I am "the community." But I guess most people probably don't think they are in the relationship until they see the flashing lights behind them. That's also part of the reason that the tension keeps going. People in the community don't see themselves as part of the relationship—maybe they don't even see a relationship.

In this chapter, analysis involves investigating all the possible ways two entities relate to each other. It means going beyond the obvious relationship and exploring the hidden or abstract connections.

THINKING FURTHER

After responding to the Invention questions on page 74, Marcus must explore his initial writing to discover areas worth pursuing even further. While these areas of potential will sometimes jump out at a writer, they usually sit quietly, going unnoticed, until a careful thinker discovers them.

How to Identify Potentially Interesting Ideas Uncertainty can help writers identify worthy ideas. If you are uncertain how to answer a question, or you can answer it several different ways, explore further. (The uncertainty is a sign of complexity!) For example, Marcus writes, "Technically, I'm not in it. Or maybe I am." As Marcus reviews his notes, he should notice this uncertainty.

Also, occasionally you might see a topic differently than most other people. Because writers are looking for a fresh perspective, such realizations are vital. For example, when Marcus writes "the tension keeps going" because "people in the community don't see themselves as part of the relationship," he has discovered an important idea worth pursuing further. The idea is important because (1) people don't normally see it and (2) it creates tension.

How to Pursue Ideas Even Further To go beyond common thinking, Marcus can explore his initial discoveries further by using the original Invention questions and by developing additional Invention questions of his own.

Explore your own invention notes to identify ideas worth pursuing further.

Marcus might explore further by responding to the following questions:

"Technically, I'm not in it. Or maybe I am."

- Am I in the relationship or not? What is the nature of the relationship?
- Can I ever get out of the relationship? What would happen if I did?
- How does the relationship influence me in hidden ways? How does it influence law enforcement?
- And so on

"That's also part of the reason that the tension keeps going. People in the community don't see themselves as part of the relationship—maybe they don't even see a relationship."

- Why don't people in the community see the relationship? How is their not seeing helpful or harmful?
- Who does see the relationship? How do people who see the relationship act differently?
- If more people saw the relationship, would it be less difficult? Would people be influenced differently?
- And so on

ACTIVITY

What might Marcus write in response to the Invention questions? What other questions might Marcus ask?

INVENTION WORKSHOP

Meet with at least one other writer and use one of the Invention questions (on page 74) to initiate a focused discussion on your topic. Briefly explain your topic to the other writer(s), and then ask one of the Invention questions. Try to stay focused on that question until you've reached some new insight about the relationship. For example, in the following discussion, Diana and Linda are exploring the relationship between a coffee shop and its customers, who are primarily students. Their conversation transforms a simple idea into a more sophisticated one. Notice the following excerpt:

Diana: What would happen to students if we didn't have this coffee house? Or, what would happen to the coffee house if it didn't have the students?

Linda: Well . . . *the coffee shop wouldn't get very much business, and the students wouldn't have their favorite coffee.*

Diana: OK . . . but I wonder what else the coffee shop does for the students. I mean, maybe the coffee shop provides something besides coffee and a place to go.

Linda: It also provides a place to study, doesn't it? A lot of students go there to read. And a few people even bring laptops and write.

Diana: And last semester, in psychology, we had group projects, and our group met there twice to work out our presentation.

Linda: I guess people go there to study and be seen, to do some work, but also to get out a little. Students can go with their books and not feel weird about it. They can do some reading and feel like they're surrounded by college activity.

Diana: Maybe that's important, too. Maybe going to the coffee shop gives students something, the feeling of *being* students. They come here to think and act and talk like college students—and that's pretty important.

Linda: Yeah . . . I think you're right. When I go there, I actually feel more like a college student, and I'm able to concentrate on things and feel more intellectual. *It's odd how a building can actually change how people approach their work.* The coffee shop actually makes many of us more able to focus, and in the big picture take studying more seriously.

Initially, Linda sees only the surface of the relationship: The coffee shop wouldn't get very much business, and the students wouldn't have their favorite coffee. But through discussion, Linda and Diana go beyond this first response. They discover a subtler layer to the relationship: *It's odd how a building can actually change how people approach their work.*

As you develop your own topic, go beyond what you have always assumed and what most people overlook about the nature of the relationship. Look into the deep connections of present and past; look at the consequences of actions; consider the effects of attitudes.

ANALYSIS IN CHAPTER READINGS

Analysis is key to the introduction of John Steinbeck's essay (see page 54). In analyzing the relationship between early American settlers and the North American continent, Steinbeck discovers a particular kind of relationship, one of aggression:

> I have often wondered at the savagery and thoughtlessness with which our early settlers approached this rich continent. They came at it as though it were an enemy, which of course it was. They burned the forests and changed the rainfall; they swept the buffalo from the plains, blasted the streams, set fire to the grass, and ran a reckless scythe through the virgin and noble timber. (54)

Later in the essay, Steinbeck's analysis is even more apparent:

> The merciless nineteenth century was like a hostile expedition for loot that seemed limitless. Uncountable buffalo were killed, stripped of their hides, and left to rot, a reservoir of permanent food supply eliminated. More than that, the land of the Great Plains was robbed of the manure of the herds. Then the plows went in and ripped off the protection of the buffalo grass and opened the helpless soil to quick water and slow drought and the mischievous winds that roamed through the Great Central Plains. There has always been more than enough desert in America; the new settlers, like overindulged children, created even more. (56)

Whether the reader agrees with the analysis or not, Steinbeck has investigated a topic: He has sought out some of the hidden dynamics of the relationship between Americans and the land.

PUBLIC RESONANCE

Remember that you are not writing entirely for yourself. You are writing to explain something for others. The particular relationship you are explaining may be specific and narrow (perhaps between two people), but it may suggest something beyond the particular—something that is relevant or important to your readers.

As you consider your own topic, ask the following questions:

- Does the relationship reveal something about people's strengths or weaknesses?

- Why is it important that people see the meaning of the relationship?

- Is there something unusual about this relationship? (Why is it so unusual?)

- Is there something usual about this relationship? (Why is it so usual? Why do most relationships seem to function this way?)

- Does this relationship show how difficult or easy human relationships can be?

- Does this relationship show how rewarding or valuable a particular kind of relationship can be?

INVENTION WRITING

Exploring public resonance can be hard work. But the process takes writers somewhere important, even vital: to new insights. In his project, Dean Meek stretches his thinking beyond his own struggle with alcohol and makes that struggle resonate with other problems. In the following excerpt from his notes, Meek does not merely say that people deflect blame for their problems—a common idea. Instead, he describes a deeper and more complex struggle: How we come to terms with the true nature of our problems.

Does the relationship reveal something about people's strengths or weaknesses?

I feel this relationship does because it is my belief that people in general would rather look at others or at circumstances as the cause of their problems. None of us want to

look within ourselves and admit that the answer to our problems is within our own being. This is a confusing and sometimes painful process of soul-searching that even the toughest of us will avoid if possible. We will blame others, blame circumstances, blame our parents or our upbringing. But not once will we think that the problem is in our own emotions, personality, and fears.

I also feel that ultimately most of us come to a dead end. At this dead end we are alone and have no one or thing left to blame. It is at this point that we have only two choices left. One, we give up and live the rest of our lives in pain and turmoil, or two, we ask someone for help, seek treatment, and honestly make a decision to fix the real problem. This is true whether it be with alcohol or spiritual, social or economic concerns. Our concerns and issues may vary, and some of us may be better off than others. But none of us are superhuman and all need a little help from time to time living life on its terms.

PUBLIC RESONANCE IN CHAPTER READINGS

In her essay, Cindy Bosley's very personal discoveries extend outward to others. In her final paragraph, Bosley makes a simple but powerful gesture to include others:

> Everyone I know has aches so deep that small triggers bring tears to their eyes. The honey gift was clearly that trigger for me. I like to think I cried because seeing that bowl of honey made me miss my father. Or maybe I cried because I don't yet understand all that happened in my life back then, or why people can do the things they do to each other. Maybe I cried because my husband loves me that much, enough to know what the honey would mean. But I do know one thing: I sure do like honey. I wept to see that honey just for me. (63)

Her point is not simply *honey reminds me of my father.* It is far richer and more complex; it is about the painful memories that are folded quietly away into our histories and how they sometimes emerge. With only one sentence, Bosley extends the explanation of her own relationships to others.

In her essay, Abigail Zuger makes a subtler move. Although she writes from a specialized position (as a doctor), she explains the relationship with pills in broader terms. Zuger includes both doctors and patients in a collective process—of personalizing pills in one way or another:

> Medical anthropologists have written at length about how medications "commodify" health, fostering the illusion that it is something bought and sold at market. In doctors' offices and in medicine cabinets, though, a reverse process takes place: We all anthropomorphize pills right back from commodities to willful agents of good or evil. For patients, they can be saviors, or assassins. For doctors, the voodoo is even stronger. Medicines are our prosthetics, at once utterly foreign (we are unlikely to take them ourselves, and may not even know what they look like) yet so much a part of us that we can barely function without them. (59)

And even when Zuger focuses specifically on doctors and their role, she is actually disclosing attitudes that would otherwise remain hidden from public view:

> For those of us in specialties without scalpels or scopes, they are our only tools (if you don't count all the good advice). Inevitably, we evolve idiosyncratic patterns of prescribing, favorite combinations, pills we love or hate. The pills become our friends, our servants, our agents, ourselves. (59)

Like all good essays, Zuger's gives voice to a particular, nuanced, and otherwise silent set of beliefs or actions. She is, literally, *public-izing* an element in a relationship! This gets to an important aspect of public resonance: A particular topic may not resonate with potential readers, but the nature or essence of that topic will. In other words, a particular relationship (for instance, between a doctor and her pills) is not necessarily a public issue; however, prescription drugs concern many people. When a writer discovers the nature of an issue (such as the core of a relationship crisis), he or she discovers the quality that may resonate with others.

RESEARCH

Discuss your topic with a friend or family member. Ask about his or her take on the topic: "Have you ever thought about the relationship between ____ and ____?" Record the responses, which may show common thinking about your topic.

You can also explore your topic in secondary sources. To find out what else has been said about your topic, do an Internet or online database search. For specific guidance, see Research & Writing, pages 624–634.

Remember that you are not writing entirely for yourself. You are writing to explain something for others.

THESIS

As you focus your topic, you will also be narrowing in on a thesis statement or main idea. Like many writers, you may write your way to a thesis, or you may try to focus the idea before drafting. Either way, you need to have a single statement that not only gives focus to your topic but also gives your particular insight on that topic. Your project might do one of the following:

- Explain the significant qualities of a particular kind of relationship.
- Explain what is sometimes hidden in a particular kind of relationship.
- Explain the difficulties or problems of being a child, friend, parent, or significant other.
- Explain how a particular relationship (say, with a pet) is much like something else (say, an accidental fall down a mountainside).
- Explain how a particular relationship reveals something important about a subject.

Before moving on, try to articulate your main point (your take on the nature of the relationship).

FOCUS

As in any essay, the narrower and more particular your thesis, the more engaging the paper is for the writer and the reader. On the other hand, an essay that attempts to explain an overly broad subject is likely to lose readers. Notice the difference among the following:

General	Specific	More Specific
Students	Third-grade girls	The attitudes of third-grade girls
Employees	Retail sales associates	Retail sales associates' energy
Campus	The new buildings	The look of the new buildings

The more specific subjects help readers (and writers!) focus on more specific insights. They help readers and writers tune in to intricacies and intimacies. (They actually help sharpen the consciousness!)

In considering the focus of your project, examine the nouns you use. Can they be more specific?

REVELATION

If nouns (or subjects in sentences) help create focus, then verbs can help create *revelation*. A revelatory thesis statement shows something new—a commonly overlooked layer, connection, or idea. Notice the following statements:

- The attitudes of third-grade girls <u>depend</u> upon the number of close friends.
- Retail sales associates' energy <u>relies</u> on the number and nature of customers.
- The flat, corporate look of the new buildings on campus <u>competes</u> with the traditional stone giants and illustrates the clash between the old academic tradition and the new corporate designs on education.

In these statements, the verbs *(depend, relies, competes)* are active and intensive. They help show how two things or groups of people relate.

A revelatory thesis shows something new.

EVOLUTION OF A THESIS

Writers should allow their initial ideas to become increasingly more focused and revelatory. Notice how a broad statement can become more intense and sophisticated as it becomes more focused:

- Biology is connected to many fields.
- Stem cell research has changed the way biologists think about law.

The first statement is broad and uninteresting because it does not rediscover or recharacterize a relationship. The second statement offers a more particular point. The subject of the second sentence (stem cell research) is narrower than the initial subject (biology). The verbs also convey something more specific: The first verb merely says two things are connected, while the second says one has changed the other.

Now, the writer can think even more specifically. For example, what the writer asserts about stem cell research can be more specific. The thesis statements below are only two examples of the many statements a writer might develop about stem cell research and its relationship to something else.

- As stem cell research continues to develop, biologists and lawyers will both need to develop an understanding of the other's field.
- Stem cell research has prompted a complex marriage of law and biology that will continue to impact careers in both fields.

These more focused and revelatory thesis statements are bound to generate more specific and interesting support. (Ultimately, then, more focused ideas yield more focused supporting ideas!)

ACTIVITY

1. What other thesis statements might evolve from *Stem cell research has prompted a complex marriage of law and biology that will continue to impact careers in both fields*? Remember, to develop a thesis statement, try to make the subject (stem cell research) and/or the assertion about that subject (has prompted a complex marriage of law and biology . . .) more specific. For help, return to the Invention questions on pages 74 and 78.

2. What thesis statements might evolve from *Biology is connected to many fields*? As you develop the thesis, replace the general subject and assertion with something more specific. For example: What's more specific than biology?

dissecting frogs	nutrition in 21st-century America
evolution	the immune system
DNA testing	stem cell research

Next, make a specific assertion about the more specific subject, and then try to evolve your thesis further.

REVISION

A key part of writing is developing an intellectual rearview mirror: a habit of looking back and redirecting your course. Apply the following questions:

- In my thesis, what nouns could be narrower, more specific?
- In my thesis, what verbs could be intensified to reveal more about the relationship?
- How does the statement offer something beyond a commonsense or simplistic assumption? How is it revelatory?

Other writers can help you with this process. Try exchanging your initial ideas with others and using the above questions for peer evaluation.

RHETORICAL TOOLS

The next step is to develop and support ideas. Remember that a potential reader already knows about relationships in general. (He or she is certainly mired in several.) But in your essay you have the opportunity to shed light, to go beyond ordinary thinking, and to reveal something that most people do not necessarily consider.

Using Narration

Narration, or storytelling, is appropriate for many kinds of writing. It is not simply relegated to remembering events. You might consider beginning your essay with a brief retelling of a situation regarding the relationship, or using a brief account to illustrate something about the relationship. (For example, Dean Meek's essay depends almost entirely on narration, and Cindy Bosley's uses narration at important points.)

If you decide to use narration, make good choices:

1. Start the narrative at an appropriate place. That is, limit your story to include only relevant parts of the situation.

2. Focus on only the relevant details of the events.

3. Use consistent verb tense. (In most cases, past or present tense can work in retelling a story. However, you must be consistent throughout the narrative.)

4. At some point, make sure to explain the significance or relevance of the narrative to the reader.

5. Refer to Chapter 1 (page 36) for other valuable narrative strategies.

An essay is an invitation to discover a new way of thinking.

Using Description

Readers like details. The more detailed the images, the more intensely the reader will experience them. In this essay, you might decide to describe the people involved in the relationship—their particular postures, facial expressions, and gestures. Or you might need to detail more abstract qualities—their imaginations, their appetites, their pride, their esteem, their effect on strangers. In her essay about a coffee shop and its customers, Linda might describe the relationship broadly:

> The coffee shop makes them feel more academic. It is more than a location to do homework and drink caffeine. It is a place where students totally surround themselves in college work.

These are valuable statements, but they remain abstract and general. They would come to life more with details:

> The coffee shop is more than a location for doing homework. It is like a satellite campus where students and professors alike work, talk, reflect. On any given day, several tables will be pushed together while a group of students work together on a project, their papers and notebooks scattered between coffee cups and half-eaten bagels. Invariably, a professor, graduate student, or staff member from the college will sit in one of the corner tables reading a newspaper. Several students will be perched on the windowsill, their backs against the outside world as they read through textbook chapters.

You might need to describe a particular situation in detail. In that case, narration and description will work together. For instance, in Bosley's essay, she narrates a past event while delivering very particular details. This is how she captures her readers, how she draws us in:

> When I think of honeycomb, I think of my father. I first tried a small bite, and then more and more by the spoonful, the day before my father left. He had brought the honey home from a guy at work, he said, and so he set the brick in its jar onto the counter, and found a spoon for himself, plunged the spoon into the hexagon cells and pulled it away with a *suck*. And then

he went back for more. I stood over the jar of honeycomb marveling at it—the many sections of honey,
the yellowish layer of beeswax sealing the liquid in, the
small brown and black flecks of flower remnant, or
bee poop, I guessed. (61)

Using Figurative Language

Any explanatory essay can benefit from figurative language,
which is any language that goes beyond words' basic definitions and uses them to suggest imaginative connections
between ideas.

Metaphor A metaphor is a comparison in which one thing
is made to share the characteristics of another. Cindy Bosley
uses a metaphor of the sun to help convey the gravity of the
situation:

> And the browns and golds of our '70s decor were
> browner, and deeper gold. And my mother was in her
> bedroom on the phone trying to muffle hard crying.
> And my younger sister was watching *Land of the Lost,*
> while my brother played with his Tinker Toys. Some-
> thing had happened, and I didn't have to ask anyone
> what that was. The sun was a sawblade in the sky. (62)

Simile A simile is a comparison that uses *like* or *as*. Notice
John Steinbeck's similes. They help characterize the nature
of the relationship between American settlers and the land:

> I have often wondered at the savagery and thought-
> lessness with which our early settlers approached this
> rich continent. They came at it as though it were an
> enemy, which of course it was. (54)

> There has always been more than enough desert in
> America; the new settlers, like overindulged children,
> created even more. (56)

Metaphors and similes can help to characterize situations; in
this case, they can lend a quality to a relationship.

**As you consider your own topic, create metaphors and
similes if they help to develop a key point. (But
remember that too much figurative language can distract the reader.) The following questions can help:**

- Can I compare the relationship (or the entities in the
  relationship) to an animal? A thing? A place? A person?
- What purpose would this comparison serve?

REVISION

As with all academic essays, the supporting
material should lead the reader to a focused main
idea—hopefully, to the idea the writer intends. You
might think of the essay as an elegant equation:

Rhetorical Tools (narration + description +
figurative language + other variables) = Thesis

Consider your supporting material. What
information does not lead the reader toward the
thesis? What elements might have to be deleted
from this equation? What information would better
lead the reader to your thesis?

ORGANIZATIONAL STRATEGIES

How Should I Begin?

As we will suggest throughout this book, the possibilities for introductions are boundless. For this particular paper, you might:

- Begin with a general statement about the relationship. Steinbeck begins with a general statement about American settlers and the land:

  > I have often wondered at the savagery and thoughtlessness with which our early settlers approached this rich continent. They came at it as though it were an enemy, which of course it was. They burned the forests and changed the rainfall; they swept the buffalo from the plains, blasted the streams, set fire to the grass, and ran a reckless scythe through the virgin and noble timber. (54)

- Begin with a brief story or anecdote about the relationship. Cindy Bosley and Abigail Zuger both begin with stories that they develop throughout their essays. (But also notice that the stories eventually give way to some analysis, some explanation of the meaning in the events.)

- Begin with a typical belief or stereotype about the relationship, and then turn to your particular insight. Imagine a writer focusing on the relationship between the police and the surrounding community:

> Most people assume they have no relationship with their local police departments. Other than an emergency situation, most are even reluctant to acknowledge police officers. They often treat them as uniformed specters lurking on the roads of their towns. But the police of any community are deeply connected to the everyday patterns of life. They are serving their communities and participating in daily routines at all levels.

- Begin with a fictional account, or scenario, of a relationship. Imagine the same topic about police and communities beginning differently:

> Imagine a community in which the police only appeared for emergencies, in which people had to make a 911 call simply to get a police car to visit the area. Imagine the streets of a crowded city without the occasional police cruiser. Imagine the downtown stores without the presence of a city officer.

Where Should My Thesis or Main Point Go?

Remember that a thesis can be either explicitly stated or *implied* (suggested by the content but not stated in the essay). Of course, even if a thesis is implied, the author needs to know the main idea. A thesis for this essay might go:

- At the very beginning—the first sentence of the first paragraph
- At the end of the first paragraph
- In the conclusion
- After a brief account that illustrates the main idea

When to Write the Introduction

If a good introduction comes to mind, by all means, write it down. But if one doesn't, don't worry. Go ahead and write the essay without an introduction. Once you have a draft (without the introduction), you'll have a better idea what you are introducing; thus, the introduction should be easier to write.

What Should I Include?

This essay bases itself on personal insights about a particular relationship. In addition to details about that relationship, consider using the following:

- Particular anecdotes or narratives. This strategy is the most common in the chapter readings. Bosley, for instance, focuses her entire essay on a particular anecdote. Meek uses two primary anecdotes of his relationship with alcohol to illustrate his point.

- Details about similar relationships. Although you are focusing on a particular relationship, other relationships from the past or present can help round out your ideas. Bosley's point depends on her use of the past. Hawes refers briefly to another dog/human relationship to illustrate his point.

Remember that the information throughout the essay should work to support a main idea. Consider Meek's essay. Because the main point of his essay involves his relationship with alcohol, we learn primarily of his feelings and behaviors associated with drinking. We do not, however, see details about his mother or the furniture in his home. Such information would not be important to his point.

Reexamine the chapter readings. What are the most intensive details? What situations or behaviors receive the most detailed attention?

When Should I Change Paragraphs?

Remember that paragraphs are tools for focusing and refocusing your readers' attention. Paragraph breaks stop readers and signal them to refocus their attention. Particularly for this paper, you might change paragraphs:

- When beginning a scenario or narrative
- When offering a memory
- When changing scenes or time in the middle of a longer narrative
- When offering a detailed allusion

How Should I Make Transitions?

You might think of paragraph transitions in two ways. Sometimes making paragraph transitions is as easy as choosing the right information to come next—that is, as choosing the most appropriate information to begin the paragraph. In these cases, the content of the paragraphs works to bridge the gap between them. (See Steinbeck ¶ 7–9. The content of each paragraph follows logically from the preceding paragraph. Steinbeck uses a time sequence to move from one point to the next, so explicit transitions are unnecessary.)

Often, however, the writer needs to create a phrase, sentence, or sentences at the beginning of the new paragraph so that the relationship between the old and the new is clear. This sentence or phrase helps to bridge the gap between points. Notice how Hawes bridges his gaps. Here, both paragraphs begin with statements showing the logical shift from the preceding paragraphs:

> On the other hand, I realize some people don't see things the way I do. Just this morning I saw a man walking his dog past the front of my house. In a loud and commanding voice he kept saying, "Heel! Heel!"

Obviously he wanted his dog to make no mistake about who was in charge. However, I did notice that the man kept up his commands all the way down the street. Maybe the dog's name is "Heel." I think most people, though, have a tendency to spoil their dogs. Just go to any pet store and look at the vast array of foods, toys, beds, and treats, not to mention the shampoos and skin treatments.

It wasn't always this way, of course. Dogs were originally domesticated so they could help with the work. And some dogs are still workers, helping herd the sheep or bring in the cattle. But I have to believe these true "working dogs" are a small minority. I think most dogs these days, at least in this country, lead a fairly pampered life, so it certainly gives a different meaning to the old sayings about "a dog's life" and "working like a dog." Personally, I'd love to work as much as my dog does. (65)

How Should I Conclude?

As with introductions, the possibilities for conclusions are limitless. Short explanatory essays (such as those under 1,000 words) usually do not need to summarize main points. Instead, writers often use conclusions to suggest the significance of the ideas expressed in the body of the essay. For this essay, you might consider concluding with:

- The overall statement on, and particular meaning of, the relationship (the thesis). Notice Bosley's conclusion:

  Everyone I know has aches so deep that small triggers bring tears to their eyes. The honey gift was clearly that trigger for me. I like to think I cried because seeing that bowl of honey made me miss my father. Or maybe I cried because I don't yet understand all that happened in my life back then, or why people can do the things they do to each other. Maybe I cried because my husband loves me that much, enough to know what the honey would mean. But I do know one thing: I sure do like honey. I wept to see that honey just for me. (63)

- An allusion that best illustrates your points about the relationship. An allusion can be a powerful conclusion strategy because it projects the point of the essay onto some other subject or idea. It extends the essay's reach outward. Notice Steinbeck's use of a historical allusion:

  But we are an exuberant people, careless and destructive as active children. We make strong and potent tools and then have to use them to prove that they exist. Under the pressure of war we finally made the atom bomb, and for reasons which seemed justifiable at the time we dropped it on two Japanese cities—and I think we finally frightened ourselves. In such things, one must consult himself because there is no other point of reference. I did not know about the bomb, and certainly I had nothing to do with its use, but I am horrified and ashamed; and nearly everyone I know feels the same thing. And those who loudly and angrily justify Hiroshima and Nagasaki—why, they must be the most ashamed of all. (57)

- A return to an introductory image or scene that reveals something significant about that image. This strategy is often called "framing" (as in Cindy Bosley's conclusion). In her conclusion, Abigail Zuger returns to the patient she described in her introduction:

  After a month without the big white pills my patient said he felt a lot better. I, of course, was no longer practicing quality medicine, and felt a lot worse. His stomach talked to him. The statistics of what would happen to him without the pills talked to me. The pills, for once, were silent. Perhaps the best we could do, under the circumstances, was keep talking to each other. (60)

Having gone through the complexities of the essay, we now know why Zuger is "no longer practicing quality medicine." We understand, as readers, a new poignancy—a new sticking point—in this relationship.

> **Examine the sample essays in this chapter. Can you discover other phrases or sentences that function as transitions?**

Rather than summarizing the essay, a conclusion can emphasize the new poignancy, the new understanding, the sticking point of the relationship.

WRITER'S VOICE

Some writers create very serious, sober voices. They offer claims with the utmost formality. Sentences may be consistent in length and structure. Slang words and contractions are often absent, as in this passage from John Steinbeck's essay:

> This tendency toward irresponsibility persists in very many of us today; our rivers are poisoned by reckless dumping of sewage and toxic industrial wastes, the air of our cities is filthy and dangerous to breathe from the belching of uncontrolled products from combustion of coal, coke, oil, and gasoline. (54)

Other writers create more relaxed or even humorous voices; they offer asides (in parenthetical statements) and fun metaphors. Their allusions also might be informal, such as David Hawes's allusion to the Beatles:

> I realize this is an odd paraphrase of the Beatles, but it certainly seems fitting: I have a dog, or should I say, my dog has me? Often it seems unclear which of us is in charge in this arrangement. (65)

As you write, decide how you want to come off to the reader, how you want to posture yourself. The following strategies can be used for various kinds of voices, whether formal, comedic, or somewhere in between. These strategies help make any voice more engaging.

> ## As you write, decide how you want to come off to the reader, how you want to posture yourself.

Writerly Whispers
(Ways to Draw Readers in Closer)

- Parenthetical statements can offer gentle asides, as in Jennifer Schwind-Pawlak's essay in Chapter 1:

  > Joann (the name I call my mother when she does something embarrassing) was screaming at the coach. In a voice so screeching that it rivaled fingernails on a blackboard, she told him that he was a disgraceful coach and that he should be ashamed of himself. (16)

- Or in Abigail Zuger's article:

  > Medicines are our prosthetics, at once utterly foreign (we are unlikely to take them ourselves, and may not even know what they look like) yet so much a part of us that we can barely function without them.
  >
  > For those of us in specialties without scalpels or scopes, they are our only tools (if you don't count all the good advice). (59)

- Longer sentences with long phrases can create a sense of delicacy and can bring the reader into the subtleties of a thought. Notice in Cindy Bosley's opening paragraph the intricacy of the final two sentences and the corresponding intimacy of the ideas:

  > When I opened them, he stood in front of me holding out a bowl of fresh honey and a piece of the comb which had been pulled away from the hive and was still running with the buttery sweet liquid of all my best memories. My husband might as well have gone out just then and shoved his hand, in brown bear fashion, through the stinging, angry bees to release this small brick of honeycomb for all the love and gratitude I felt toward him at that moment. He stood there holding out to me a bowl filled with my life as it should have been, and I wept. (61)

Writerly Yells
(Ways to Give Emphasis)

- Interrupting the natural flow of a sentence with a phrase or clause can draw attention to an idea. This does not mean that the writer is angry or shouting at the reader; rather, it allows the writer to guide the reader's attention to particular ideas. This is often done, as in Cindy Bosley essay, with appositive phrases, set off by commas—or even dashes:

  That first morning, though, I did not know anything had happened, but like a too bulky winter coat a kid inherits from an older sibling, that morning when I woke, the house just felt different—a little bigger, a little old. (62)

- Repeating words, phrases, or clauses can highlight an idea. John Steinbeck repeats *us* to highlight the collective nature of the issue:

  No longer do we Americans want to destroy wantonly, but our new-found sources of power—to take the burden of work from our shoulders, to warm us, and cool us, and give us light, to transport us quickly, and to make the things we use and wear and eat—these power sources spew pollution on our country, so that the rivers and streams are becoming poisonous and lifeless. (57)

- Very short, even one-sentence, paragraphs can highlight an important point. Cindy Bosley uses two one-sentence paragraphs:

  And if I say: I went to the kitchen to look for something. Like a small and pitiful gesture of his helplessness and regret, there on the counter was a spoon he'd left beside the jar of honey, and I knew he meant it for me.

  It feels one way.

  But if I say: I went to the kitchen to look for the jar of honey. When I saw the counter, I saw there was nothing there, and I suppose I expected that. He must have taken it with him.

  That feels another way. (62–63)

- Short sentences can work many ways. Paradoxically, they can work as whispers or as yells, depending on the content and the context. They sometimes create emphasis because of their placement after longer sentences or after questions, such as in David Hawes's essay:

  Do I spoil him? Of course I do. Isn't that the whole point of having a dog? (65)

- Exclamation points . . . of course!

Writerly Pace
(Ways to Control Speed and Time)

- Having more details slows down time for the reader. Like in a film, time slows down when a writer (or producer) focuses in on many particular details. Steinbeck uses details throughout his essay to focus on particular moments in history:

  Quite a few years ago when I was living in my little town on the coast of California a stranger came in and bought a small valley where the Sempervirens redwoods grew, some of them three hundred feet high. We used to walk among these trees, and the light colored as though the great glass of the Cathedral at Chartres had strained and sanctified the sunlight. The emotion we felt in this grove was one of awe and humility and joy; and then one day it was gone, slaughtered, and the sad wreckage of boughs and broken saplings left like nonsensical spoilage of the battle-ruined countryside. (57)

- Having fewer details speeds up time for the reader. The fewer details a reader gets, the more quickly he or she moves through the events or thoughts in a text. Certainly, it is important to decide which ideas you want the reader to slow down for—and which ideas you want the reader to move quickly through. For example, Bosley moves slowly through key events (such as tasting honey for the first time or finding out about her father's departure). However, she moves quickly through less important events (such as her neighbor being given some honey).

VITALITY

The delete key is perhaps the most underused key in college writing (and college textbooks!). Deleting anything often seems like a burden, like working against our own goals as writers. But good writers face their own sentences and willingly cast away clauses and phrases that dull the ideas, slow down the reader, and lessen the intensity.

Avoid *Be* Verbs When Possible

Be verbs are also called linking verbs: *is, am, are, was, were, being, been,* etc. They link the subject of a sentence to a quality or other noun.

> The kittens are cute.
> The government is out of control.
> Sentences are cues for the reader.

Although such verbs are often necessary and valuable, they are often overused—hanging around in a sentence that would benefit from a more active verb. Notice the small, but important, change to the final example sentence above. We can make the verb active—and shorten the sentence:

> Sentences cue the reader.

This may not mean much for one sentence, but changing *be* verbs to active verbs throughout an essay can have dramatic effects.

Turn Clauses to Phrases

Clauses (elements that include both a subject and verb) can often be shortened to phrases so that sentences become more concise and concentrated. The following sentences (variations on a passage from Cindy Bosley's essay) are not concise. Notice the underlined clauses, which slow down movement of the reader:

> She had moved from the bedroom, <u>which was heavy with red and black paisley</u>, to the kitchen, <u>which was dim</u>. Here, the sun rarely ventured; <u>it was like all the dark rooms of our house</u>.

In Cindy Bosley's actual passage, she avoids unnecessary clauses. Rather than slow down the ideas (by using a "which was . . ." construction), her sentences move along more quickly in more concentrated sentences:

> She had moved from the heavy weight of the red and black paisley bedroom to the dimness of the kitchen, a room the sun rarely ventured into, like all the dark rooms of our house. (63)

Turn Phrases to Words

The same principle can be applied to phrases; they can often be boiled down into single words. Consider the following (a variation on Cindy Bosley's essay):

> When my husband brought his bowl of honeycomb to me that bright, grown-up day in the kitchen, I did not think <u>about my father</u>. I did not think <u>about my childhood</u>. I did not think <u>about old pain</u>.

While the above sentence is entirely correct and readable, Bosley's strategy is more intense. Bosley creates more concise and punctuated ideas by turning "about" phrases into single words:

> When my husband brought his bowl of honeycomb to me that bright, grown-up day in the kitchen, I did not think *Father*. I did not think *Childhood*. I did not think *Old Pain*. (63)

Consider another example:

> She moaned her <u>fears about money</u> to Patty, and there was a hitch in my heart when I heard her mention my violin lessons. While she talked to Marlene, I heard <u>the names of several women</u> come flying . . .

Bosley intensifies the sentences by turning the prepositional phrases (underlined above) into words:

> She moaned her money fears to Patty, and there was a hitch in my heart when I heard her mention my violin lessons. While she talked to Marlene, I heard several female names come flying . . . (63)

Although the differences are slight, such small transformations can build up throughout an essay, creating the difference between slower, droopier writing and intensive, vitalized writing.

PEER REVIEW

Exchange drafts with at least one other writer. Before passing your draft to others, underline the thesis, or write it on the top of your essay. This way, reviewers will get traction as they read.

As a reviewer, use the following questions to guide your response.

1. Point out any phrases in the thesis that could be more specific. (See the Thesis section for more guidance.)

2. Where can the writer do more analysis and reveal more about the relationship? (Point to passages that seem most obvious to you.) As you read, look for claims that anyone could immediately offer without intensive analysis. Beside these passages, write: "More analysis?" If you can suggest an interesting idea, explain it on the back of the writer's draft.

3. Help the writer illustrate his or her claims with details. As you read, look for broad characterizations. If you see phrases such as "influence one another" or "depend on one another," ask yourself: Could this be more specific? Can we *really* see the influence or dependence? In the margin, write "more details" where the writer could more intensely show the points.

4. Offer some figurative language to help characterize the relationship. After you have read the entire draft, offer your own metaphor or simile about the relationship. Give your suggestion on the back of the draft. Make sure it is something that fits the writer's voice—something that he or she could use.

5. Are the paragraphs coherent? Do you ever get the sense that a paragraph is wandering—giving you details that seem unrelated to one another or unrelated to the point of the essay? In the margin, write: "check paragraph coherence."

6. Help the writer kick-start the essay. The writer might begin with a broad statement about the relationship— or about something even broader. But the most focused statement possible often makes for a better introduction. Suggest a surprisingly focused opening statement.

7. Consider the writer's voice. Where could the writer employ a whisper (see page 88) or a yell (see page 89) to better engage the reader?

8. Point to particular sentences and phrases that could gain vitality and intensity. Use the following questions:

   - Where can the writer change *be* verbs to active verbs?

   - Look for clauses (especially those that begin with *which are, which is, that are, that is,* etc.). Suggest a strategy for boiling down the clause to a phrase.

   - Look for phrases (especially prepositional phrases that begin with *about* or *of*). Suggest a strategy for boiling down the phrase to a word.

   - Consider vitality strategies from the previous chapter:
     —Combine sentences
     —Repeat structures
     —Intensify verbs
     —Help the writer avoid common grammatical errors: comma splices, sentence fragments, or pronoun/ antecedent agreement.

Avoid telling writers what they already know. Offer new ideas about their work.

Questions for Research

If the writer used outside sources,
- Where must he or she include in-text citations? (See page 650.)
- Are quotations blended smoothly into the argument and punctuated correctly? (See pages 642–648.)
- Where could more direct textual cues or transitions help the reader? (See pages 641–643.)
- Is the Works Cited page formatted properly? (See pages 652–674.)

DELIVERY

Throughout the country, colleges and universities require one, two, even three semesters of college writing for every academic major. In those courses, most students write personal essays. But once they enter their job fields, many students may never be asked to write a formal essay again. Apparently, the academic world (and the business, governmental, and civic organizations that evaluate, fund, and support it) puts a great deal of stock in a student's ability to write essays. There must be something about an essay, besides the form, that offers something to writers and readers. What is it?

- What do you think the academic community values about the essay and the essay-writing process?

- Why are essay-writing classes required?

- Consider each of the essays in this chapter. What value does each have within this broader academic tradition?

- What about your own essay? How is your essay a compliment to this entire belief system? How does your essay give hope to all the interests involved?

Beyond the Essay

The ideas generated in writing courses do not belong exclusively to essays. Those ideas can take many forms or extend to various media. Find an image that relates to your essay. If you can't find one, or if you prefer, create an original image: a drawing, painting, photograph, sculpture, and so on.

1. After you have found or created an image, explain how the image reveals something about the nature of the relationship. How does it, for instance, reveal some complexity in the relationship between dogs and people, between alcohol and people, between prescription drugs and people, between people and the land they inhabit?

2. Present the image to others in your class. Explain how the image reinforces ideas in your essay. Also explain how the image and essay differ: What complexities does the image suggest beyond your essay? What does your essay reveal that the image conceals? Does your essay go further than the image? How?

3. In groups, discuss the image on the next page. How does it reveal something about a relationship?

OBSERVING

Chapter Contents

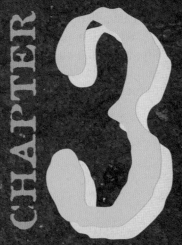

CHAPTER 3

"As I sat there I felt the expectant thrill that, for me, always precedes a day with the chimpanzees, a day roaming the forests and mountains of Gombe, a day for new discoveries, new insights."

—Jane Goodall

Jane Goodall, world-renowned ethologist, has made a life of observing. She has shown the academic community what can be learned through close attention to the living world. As Goodall suggests in the passage above, observing is about discovery—about finding something unique and particular about a subject. It involves more than simple description. Careful observers go beyond the casual glance; they study their subjects and learn something by seeing them in a particular way. In some ways, then, learning how to observe involves learning how to see things, how to notice what is beneath the surface. We casually observe our daily lives constantly.

We watch our communities carrying on with life; we watch our coworkers, friends, children, and families. Occasionally, we take time to study, to focus on subjects and take in something beyond surface meanings: At those times we go beyond what something means to us and discover something outside of our expectations and biases. We see, for instance, how a man sitting on a street corner means something to the city that surrounds him; we suddenly see the systematic design in the movements of a seemingly chaotic crowd of people. Such seeing involves more than open eyes; it involves an open consciousness.

Observation is an essential strategy in academic life:

- Child psychology students observe the behaviors of young teens at a video arcade.
- Education students observe the interaction between high school teachers and their students.

- Biology students study the growth of bacteria over a 24-hour period.
- Chemistry students observe the effects of mixing different compounds.
- Sociology graduate students and faculty observe the language habits of a small island town.

Observers find the hidden meaning, the significant issues, and the important aspects of a particular subject. They point out how and why a particular subject is of interest to a broader public. We experience this kind of observing and reporting when we watch documentaries or nature specials. Writers and researchers for such programs first make general observations. Then they focus their perspective on a particular issue or subject. They analyze that issue or subject to find the most important or valuable thing to say. Throughout this process, the observing writer is always looking to discover, to find and communicate a fresh and interesting idea.

This chapter will help you choose a subject to observe, discover something particular about that subject, and develop a focused essay about your discovery. The following essays will provide insight to various strategies for observing. After reading the essays, you can find a topic in one of two ways:

1. Go to the **Point of Contact** section to find a topic from everyday life.
2. Choose one of the **Ideas for Writing** that follow each essay.

After you find a topic, go to the **Analysis** section to begin developing your observation.

The readings in this chapter all go beyond the quick glance, even beyond commonsense perspectives. Each offers a new way to see a subject, whether a weasel or a porch. It is almost as if each essay calls on us to re-see the subject by asking us: Have you ever thought about weasels (or front porches) this way? Notice that these essays are not mere laundry lists of details. Instead, they each offer a particular point about the subject at hand and use extensive details to support that point. In other words, each essay is a unified whole: Unnecessary details (those that do not support the main point) are minimized or absent altogether.

Living Like Weasels

Annie Dillard

It is easy to imagine weasels as nothing more than wild animals and to see them as entirely divorced from human affairs. After all, we are civilized. Weasels live in holes and eat mice. But in this essay, Annie Dillard, a Pulitzer Prize-winning author, invites us to rethink weasels and our own everyday lives. She insists that something can be learned behind the stare of a simple animal, something essential about life's purpose. After a brief encounter with a weasel, Dillard goes beyond the first glimpse and creates important meaning for herself and others. "Living like Weasels" first appeared in Dillard's book *Teaching a Stone to Talk* (1982).

A weasel is wild. Who knows what he thinks? He sleeps in his underground den, his tail draped over his nose. Sometimes he lives in his den for two days without leaving. Outside, he stalks rabbits, mice, muskrats, and birds, killing more bodies than he can eat warm, and often dragging the carcasses home. Obedient to instinct, he bites his prey at the neck, either splitting the jugular vein at the throat or crunching the brain at the base of the skull, and he does not let go. One natu-ralist refused to kill a weasel who was socketed into his hand deeply as a rattlesnake. The man could in no way pry the tiny weasel off, and he had to walk half a mile to water, the weasel dangling from his palm, and soak him off like a stubborn label.

And once, says Ernest Thompson Seton—once, a man shot an eagle out of the sky. He examined the eagle and found the dry skull of a weasel fixed by the jaws to his throat. The supposition is that the eagle had pounced on the weasel and the weasel swiveled and bit as instinct taught him, tooth to neck, and nearly won. I would like to have seen that eagle from the air a few weeks or months before he was shot: was the whole weasel still attached to his feathered throat, a fur pen-dant? Or did the eagle eat what he could reach, gutting the living weasel with his talons before his breast, bend-ing his beak, cleaning the beautiful airborne bones?

I have been reading about weasels because I saw one last week. I startled a weasel who startled me, and we exchanged a long glance.

Twenty minutes from my house, through the woods by the quarry and across the highway, is Hollins Pond, a remarkable piece of shallowness, where I like to go at sunset and sit on a tree trunk. Hollins Pond is also called Murray's Pond; it covers two acres of bottomland near Tinker Creek with six inches of water and six thousand lily pads. In winter, brown-and-white steers stand in the middle of it, merely dampening their hooves; from the distant shore they look like miracle itself, complete with miracle's nonchalance. Now, in summer, the steers are gone. The water lilies have blossomed and spread to a green horizontal plane that is terra firma to plodding blackbirds, and tremulous ceiling to black leeches, crayfish, and carp.

5   This is, mind you, suburbia. It is a five-minute walk in three directions to rows of houses, though none is visible here. There's a 55 mph highway at one end of the pond, and a nesting pair of wood ducks at the other. Under every bush is a muskrat hole or a beer can. The far end is an alternating series of fields and woods, fields and woods, threaded everywhere with motorcycle tracks—in whose bare clay wild turtles lay eggs.

So. I had crossed the highway, stepped over two low barbed-wire fences, and traced the motorcycle path in all gratitude through the wild rose and poison ivy of the pond's shoreline up into high grassy fields. Then I cut down through the woods to the mossy fallen tree where I sit. This tree is excellent. It makes a dry, upholstered bench at the upper, marshy end of the pond, a plush jetty raised from the thorny shore between a shallow blue body of water and a deep blue body of sky.

The sun had just set. I was relaxed on the tree trunk, ensconced in the lap of lichen, watching the lily pads at my feet tremble and part dreamily over the thrusting path of a carp. A yellow bird appeared to my right and flew behind me. It caught my eye; I swiveled around—and the next instant, inexplicably, I was looking down at a weasel, who was looking up at me.

Weasel! I'd never seen one wild before. He was ten inches long, thin as a curve, a muscled ribbon, brown as fruitwood, soft-furred, alert. His face was fierce, small and pointed as a lizard's; he would have made a good arrowhead. There was just a dot of chin, maybe two brown hairs' worth, and then the pure white fur began

that spread down his underside. He had two black eyes I didn't see, any more than you see a window.

The weasel was stunned into stillness as he was emerging from beneath an enormous shaggy wild rose bush four feet away. I was stunned into stillness twisted backward on the tree trunk. Our eyes locked, and someone threw away the key.

10   Our look was as if two lovers, or deadly enemies, met unexpectedly on an overgrown path when each had been thinking of something else: a clearing blow to the gut. It was also a bright blow to the brain, or a sudden beating of brains, with all the charge and intimate grate of rubbed balloons. It emptied our lungs. It felled the forest, moved the fields, and drained the pond; the world dismantled and tumbled into that black hole of eyes. If you and I looked at each other that way, our skulls would split and drop to our shoulders. But we don't. We keep our skulls. So.

"If you and I looked at each other that way, our skulls would split and drop to our shoulders."

He disappeared. This was only last week, and already I don't remember what shattered the enchantment. I think I blinked, I think I retrieved my brain from the weasel's brain, and tried to memorize what I was seeing, and the weasel felt the yank of separation, the careening splashdown into real life and the urgent current of instinct. He vanished under the wild rose. I waited motionless, my mind suddenly full of data and my spirit with pleadings, but he didn't return.

Please do not tell me about "approach-avoidance conflicts." I tell you I've been in that weasel's brain for sixty seconds, and he was in mine. Brains are private places, muttering through unique and secret tapes— but the weasel and I both plugged into another tape simultaneously, for a sweet and shocking time. Can I help it if it was a blank?

What goes on in his brain the rest of the time? What does a weasel think about? He won't say. His journal is tracks in clay, a spray of feathers, mouse blood and bone: uncollected, unconnected, loose-leaf, and blown.

I would like to learn, or remember, how to live. I come to Hollins Pond not so much to learn how to live as, frankly, to forget about it. That is, I don't think I can learn from a wild animal how to live in particular—shall I suck warm blood, hold my tail high, walk with my footprints precisely over the prints of my hands?—but I might learn something of mindlessness, something of the purity of living in the physical senses and the dignity of living without bias or motive. The weasel lives in necessity and we live in choice, hating necessity and dying at the last ignobly in its talons. I would like to live as I should, as the weasel lives as he should. And I suspect that for me the way is like the weasel's: open to time and death painlessly, noticing everything, remembering nothing, choosing the given with a fierce and pointed will.

15 I missed my chance. I should have gone for the throat. I should have lunged for that streak of white under the weasel's chin and held on, held on through mud and into the wild rose, held on for a dearer life. We could live under the wild rose wild as weasels, mute and uncomprehending. I could very calmly go wild. I could live two days in the den, curled, leaning on mouse fur, sniffing bird bones, blinking, licking, breathing musk, my hair tangled in the roots of grasses. Down is a good place to go, where the mind is single. Down is out, out of your ever-loving mind and back to your careless senses. I remember muteness as a prolonged and giddy fast, where every moment is a feast of utterance received. Time and events are merely poured, unremarked, and ingested directly, like blood pulsed into my gut through a jugular vein. Could two live that way? Could two live under the wild rose, and explore by the pond, so that the smooth mind of each is as everywhere present to the other, and as received and as unchallenged, as falling snow?

We could, you know. We can live any way we want. People take vows of poverty, chastity, and obedience—even of silence—by choice. The thing is to stalk your calling in a certain skilled and supple way, to locate the most tender and live spot and plug into that pulse. This is yielding, not fighting. A weasel doesn't "attack" anything; a weasel lives as he's meant to, yielding at every moment to the perfect freedom of single necessity.

I think it would be well, and proper, and obedient, and pure, to grasp your one necessity and not let it go, to dangle from it limp wherever it takes you. Then even death, where you're going no matter how you live, cannot you part. Seize it and let it seize you up aloft even, till your eyes burn out and drop; let your musky flesh fall off in shreds, and let your very bones unhinge and scatter, loosened over fields, over fields and woods, lightly, thoughtless, from any height at all, from as high as eagles.

Writing Strategies

1. What might Dillard be trying to achieve with her introduction? Does she achieve it? Does her introduction make you want to read on? Why or why not?

2. How did you react when Dillard addressed you directly in paragraph 8? ("He had two black eyes I didn't see, any more than you see a window.") Were you startled? Did you know what she meant? When you write, do you sometimes speak more directly to the reader than at other times? Provide a few examples of how the writing situation influences how directly you speak to the reader.

3. Dillard describes the weasel's face as "fierce." Is this a good description? What are the characteristics of a fierce-looking face? Did her description, or word choice, help you get a better mental image of a weasel? How else might she have described the weasel?

4. What point is Dillard making in her concluding paragraph? How might she have stated her main point in a less poetic essay?

Exploring Ideas

1. What is Dillard trying to accomplish in this essay?

2. What change does Dillard's essay call for? How does she ask the reader to think or live differently?

3. Dillard's experience with the weasel affected her strongly, prompting her to explore her thoughts on how she lives. What similar personal experiences have prompted you to think differently about how you, and others, live?

4. Interview others, asking them what small experiences made them think differently about their lives. Ask them to describe the experience and how it influenced their thinking.

5. Discuss your interview responses from #4 above with classmates. Which responses were most common? Which were most unusual? Which would make for the most interesting essay and why?

Ideas for Writing

1. What person, place, or thing can you describe as a way of making an interesting point?

2. Have you interacted with an animal in the way Dillard has, or in some other thought-provoking way?

If responding to one of these ideas, go to the **Analysis** section of this chapter to begin developing ideas for your essay.

Planting a Tree

Edward Abbey

Edward Abbey, author of *Desert Solitaire* (1968) and other books, is a careful observer. In "Planting a Tree," Abbey shares his observations *and* his insights. The observational details he shares go beyond merely reporting. Instead, he analyzes his observations, and puts forth ideas about what they mean, or might mean. Abbey's thoughtful observation prompts him to plant a tree, and to share the experience with the reader.

My wife and I and my daughter live (for the moment) in a little house near the bright, doomed city of Tucson, Arizona. We like it here. Most of the time. Our back-yard includes a portion of the Sonoran Desert, extend-ing from here to the California border and down into Mexico. Mesquite trees grow nearby, enough to supply fuel for the Franklin stove when the nights are cold, enough to cook the occasional pork chop, or toast the tortilla, on the grill under the decaying Chinese elm.

Out back is the dry creekbed, full of sand, called a "wash" in this country, winding through the trees and cactus toward the Tucson Mountains five miles away. We'll climb those hills yet, maybe. Rattlesnakes live in the rocky grottoes along the wash. Sometimes they come to the house for a social call. We found one coiled on the Welcome mat by the front door Sunday evening. Our cat has disappeared.

There are still a few bands of javelina—wild semi-pigs—out there. They come by at night, driving the dogs into hysterics of outrage, which the javelinas ignore. Coyotes howl at us when they feel like it, usu-ally in the mornings and again around sundown, when I rile them some with my flute—they seem partial to "Greensleeves," played on the upper register. We have an elf owl living in a hole in the big saguaro cactus by the driveway, and three pygmy owls, bobbing and weaving like boxers, up in the palm at evening. There are packrats in the woodpile and scorpions under the bark of the logs; I usually find one when I'm splitting firewood.

So it's pretty nice here. We'd like to stay for a while, a lifetime or two, before trying something else. But we probably won't. We came down here from Utah four years ago, for practical reasons, now satisfied. We are free to leave whenever we wish.

5   The city remains at a comfortable distance. We hear the murmur of it by day, when the wind is from the east, and see its campfires glow by night—those dying embers. The police helicopters circle like fireflies above Tucson, Arizona, all night long, maintaining order. The homicide rate hangs steady at 3.2 per diem per 1,000,000, including lowriders, dope peddlers, and defenseless winos. All is well. Eighteen Titan missile bases ring the city, guarding us from their enemies. The life expectancy of the average Tucsonan, therefore, is thirty minutes—or whatever it takes for an ICBM to shuttle from there to here. Everything is A-OK. We sleep good.

Still, the city creeps closer, day by day. While the two great contemporary empires are dying—one in Afghanistan and Poland, the other in Vietnam, Iran, Nicaragua, El Salvador. And though I welcome their defeat, their pain and fear make them more dangerous than ever. Like mortally wounded tyrannosaurs, they thrash about in frenzy, seeking enemies, destroying thousands of innocent lives with each blind spasm of reaction. And still the city creeps closer. I find a corre-lation in these movements. I foresee the day when we shall be obliged to strike camp, once again.

Where to this time? Home to Utah? Back to Appa-lachia? On to Australia? Down the river of eternal recur-rence? It doesn't matter too much. There is no final escape, merely a series of tactical retreats, until we find the stone wall at our backs, bedrock beneath our feet.

Ah well, enough of this skulking rhetoric. Before we go we will plant a tree. I cleared away some ragweed yesterday, dug a thigh-deep hole this morning, and planted a young budding cottonwood this afternoon. We soaked the hole with well water, mixed in the peat moss and the carefully set-aside topsoil, and lowered the root ball of the sapling into its new home. The tree shivered as I packed the earth around its base. A shiver of pleasure. A good omen. A few weeks of warm weather and the little green leaves will be trembling in the sunlight. A few good years and the tree will be shading the front porch and then the roof of the house. If the house is still here. If someone, or something, as I hope, is still enjoying this house, this place, this garden of rock and sand and paloverde, of sunshine and delight.

We ourselves may never see this cottonwood reach maturity, probably will never take pleasure in its shade or birds or witness the pale gold of its autumn leaves. But somebody will. Something will. In fifty years Tucson will have shrunk back to what it once was, a town of adobe huts by the trickling Santa Cruz, a happier place than it is now, and our tree will be here, with or without us. In that anticipation I find satisfaction enough.

Writing Strategies

1. How does Abbey convey his main idea? Does he state it explicitly or imply it? In your own words, write a thesis statement (a statement of the main idea) for "Planting a Tree."

2. Notice Abbey's use of concrete language ("Tucson, Arizona"; "mesquite trees"; "Franklin stove"; "pork chop"; "tortilla"; "decaying Chinese elm"). Identify specific language that you found to be effective or ineffective in his essay. Explain why you think the specific language did or did not work.

3. Abbey describes his own rhetoric as "skulking." What does he mean? What, if anything, does the writer's own commentary about his rhetoric tell you about the writer?

4. Abbey uses figurative language throughout his essay; for example, he compares the city lights to campfires glowing and police helicopters to fireflies. How are these comparisons consistent with the overall content and tone of "Planting a Tree"?

Exploring Ideas

1. In one paragraph, summarize what Abbey is saying in this essay.

2. How is the way that you see "the city" similar to or different from the way Abbey sees it?

3. How is the way you see "planting a tree" similar to or different from the way Abbey sees it?

4. What does your response to this essay tell you about the way you see things? That is, whether you agree with Abbey, disagree, or have some other response, what does that response tell you about your own outlook on the world?

Ideas for Writing

1. Recall the details of a place you once lived or still live. Pay special attention to the tone of your essay, including details and using language that helps to develop, or support, the purpose of your description.

2. Observe a specific tree—one you have long been familiar with or one you have not noticed until now. Observe it carefully, and also research to learn more about that type of tree.

3. Get reactions to Abbey's essay from several classmates, friends, or relatives. Which reaction do you find to be most interesting? Why? Why would that reaction be worth pursuing in an essay?

If responding to one of these ideas, go to the **Analysis** section of this chapter to begin developing ideas for your essay.

Gombe

Jane Goodall

Jane Goodall is known for her pioneering work in prima-
tology—the study of primates. She has written a number of books about her experiences with chimpanzees;
"Gombe" was originally published in *Through a Window*
(1990). Goodall, like other writers in this chapter, carefully selects certain details to help the reader understand the larger point of her essay. As you read, notice
how Goodall's description of the chimpanzees paves the
way for general points that she will make in the essay's
last seven paragraphs.

I rolled over and looked at the time—5.44 a.m. Long
years of early rising have led to an ability to wake just
before the unpleasant clamour of an alarm clock. Soon
I was sitting on the steps of my house looking out over
Lake Tanganyika. The waning moon, in her last quarter, was suspended above the horizon, where the moun-
tainous shoreline of Zaire fringed Lake Tanganyika. It
was a still night, and the moon's path danced and
sparkled towards me across the gently moving water.
My breakfast—a banana and a cup of coffee from the
thermos flask—was soon finished, and ten minutes
later I was climbing the steep slope behind the house,
my miniature binoculars and camera stuffed into my
pockets along with notebook, pencil stubs, a handful of
raisins for my lunch, and plastic bags in which to put
everything should it rain. The faint light from the
moon, shining on the dew-laden grass, enabled me to
find my way without difficulty and presently I arrived
at the place where, the evening before, I had watched
eighteen chimpanzees settle down for the night. I sat to
wait until they woke.

All around, the trees were still shrouded with the
last mysteries of the night's dreaming. It was very quiet,
utterly peaceful. The only sounds were the occasional
chirp of a cricket, and the soft murmur where the lake
caressed the shingle, way below. As I sat there I felt the
expectant thrill that, for me, always precedes a day
with the chimpanzees, a day roaming the forests and

mountains of Gombe, a day of new discoveries, new
insights.

Then came a sudden burst of song, the duet of a
pair of robin chats, hauntingly beautiful. I realized that
the intensity of light had changed: dawn had crept
upon me unawares. The coming brightness of the sun
had all but vanquished the silvery, indefinite illumina-
tion of its own radiance reflected by the moon. The
chimpanzees still slept.

Five minutes later came a rustling of leaves above.
I looked up and saw branches moving against the light-
ening sky. That was where Goblin, top-ranking male of
the community, had made his nest. Then stillness again.
He must have turned over, then settled down for a last
snooze. Soon after this there was movement from
another nest to my right, then from one behind me,
further up the slope. Rustlings of leaves, the cracking of
a little twig. The group was waking up. Peering through
my binoculars into the tree where Fifi had made a nest
for herself and her infant Flossi, I saw the silhouette of
her foot. A moment later Fanni, her eight-year-old
daughter, climbed up from her nest nearby and sat just
above her mother, a small dark shape against the sky.
Fifi's other two offspring, adult Freud and adolescent
Frodo, had nested further up the slope.

5   Nine minutes after he had first moved, Goblin
abruptly sat up and, almost at once, left his nest and
began to leap wildly through the tree, vigorously swaying the branches. Instant pandemonium broke out. The
chimpanzees closest to Goblin left their nests and
rushed out of his way. Others sat up to watch, tense and
ready for flight. The early morning peace was shattered
by frenzied grunts and screams as Goblin's subordinates
voiced their respect or fear. A few moments later, the
arboreal part of his display over, Goblin leapt down and
charged past me, slapping and stamping on the wet
ground, rearing up and shaking the vegetation, picking
up and hurling a rock, an old piece of wood, another
rock. Then he sat, hair bristling, some fifteen feet away.
He was breathing heavily. My own heart was beating
fast. As he swung down, I had stood up and held onto
a tree, praying that he would not pound on me as he

sometimes does. But, to my relief, he had ignored me, and I sat down again.

With soft, panting grunts Goblin's young brother Gimble climbed down and came to greet the alpha or top-ranking male, touching his face with his lips. Then, as another adult male approached Goblin, Gimble moved hastily out of the way. This was my old friend Evered. As he approached, with loud, submissive grunts, Goblin slowly raised one arm in salutation and Evered rushed forward. The two males embraced, grinning widely in the excitement of this morning reunion so that their teeth flashed white in the semi-darkness. For a few moments they groomed each other and then, calmed, Evered moved away and sat quietly nearby.

The only other adult who climbed down then was Fifi, with Flossi clinging to her belly. She avoided Goblin, but approached Evered, grunting softly, reached out her hand and touched his arm. Then she began to groom him. Flossi climbed into Evered's lap and looked up into his face. He glanced at her, groomed her head intently for a few moments, then turned to reciprocate Fifi's attentions. Flossi moved halfway towards where Goblin sat—but his hair was still bristling, and she thought better of it and, instead, climbed a tree near Fifi. Soon she began to play with Fanni, her sister.

Once again peace returned to the morning, though not the silence of dawn. Up in the trees the other chimpanzees of the group were moving about, getting ready for the new day. Some began to feed, and I heard the occasional soft thud as skins and seeds of figs were dropped to the ground. I sat, utterly content to be back at Gombe after an unusually long time away—almost three months of lectures, meetings, and lobbying in the USA and Europe. This would be my first day with the chimps and I planned to enjoy it to the full, just getting reacquainted with my old friends, taking pictures, getting my climbing legs back.

It was Evered who led off, thirty minutes later, twice pausing and looking back to make sure that Goblin was coming too. Fifi followed, Flossi perched on her back like a small jockey, Fanni close behind. Now the other chimps climbed down and wandered after us. Freud and

Frodo, adult males Atlas and Beethoven, the magnificent adolescent Wilkie, and two females, Patti and Kidevu, with their infants. There were others, but they were travelling higher up the slope, and I didn't see them then. We headed north, parallel with the beach below, then plunged down into Kasakela Valley and, with frequent pauses for feeding, made our way up the opposite slope. The eastern sky grew bright, but not until 8.30 a.m. did the sun itself finally peep over the peaks of the rift escarpment. By this time we were high above the lake. The chimpanzees stopped and groomed for a while, enjoying the warmth of the morning sunshine.

10 About twenty minutes later there was a sudden outbreak of chimpanzee calls ahead—a mixture of pant-hoots, as we call the loud distance calls, and screams. I could hear the distinctive voice of the large, sterile female Gigi among a medley of females and youngsters. Goblin and Evered stopped grooming and all the chimps stared towards the sounds. Then, with Goblin now in the lead, most of the group moved off in that direction.

Fifi, however, stayed behind and continued to groom Fanni while Flossi played by herself, dangling from a low branch near her mother and elder sister. I decided to stay too, delighted that Frodo had moved on with the others for he so often pesters me. He wants me to play, and, because I will not, he becomes aggressive. At twelve years of age he is much stronger than I am, and this behavior is dangerous. Once he stamped so hard on my head that my neck was nearly broken. And on another occasion he pushed me down a steep slope. I can only hope that, as he matures and leaves childhood behind him, he will grow out of these irritating habits.

I spent the rest of the morning wandering peacefully with Fifi and her daughters, moving from one food tree to the next. The chimps fed on several different kinds of fruit and once on some young shoots. For about forty-five minutes they pulled apart the leaves of low shrubs which had been rolled into tubes held closely by sticky threads, then munched on the caterpillars that wriggled inside. Once we passed another female—Gremlin and her infant, little Galahad. Fanni and Flossi ran over to greet them, but Fifi barely glanced in their direction.

All the time we were climbing higher and higher. Presently, on an open grassy ridge we came upon another small group of chimps: the adult male Prof, his young brother Pax, and two rather shy females with their infants. They were feeding on the leaves of a massive *mbula* tree. There were a few quiet grunts of greeting as Fifi and her youngsters joined the group, then they also began to feed. Presently the others moved on, Fanni with them. But Fifi made herself a nest and stretched out for a midday siesta. Flossi stayed too, climbing about, swinging, amusing herself near her mother. And then she joined Fifi in her nest, lay close and suckled.

From where I sat, below Fifi, I could look out over the Kasakela Valley. Opposite, to the south, was the Peak. A surge of warm memories flooded through me as I saw it, a rounded shoulder perched above the long grassy ridge that separates Kasakela from the home valley, Kakombe. In the early days of the study at Gombe, in 1960 and 1961, I had spent day after day watching the chimpanzees, through my binoculars, from the superb vantage point. I had taken a little tin trunk up to the Peak, with a kettle, some coffee and sugar, and a blanket. Sometimes, when the chimps had slept nearby, I had stayed up there with them, wrapped in my blanket against the chill of the night air. Gradually I had pieced together something of their daily life, learned about their feeding habits and travel routes, and begun to understand their unique social structure—small groups joining to form larger ones, large groups splitting into smaller ones, single chimpanzees roaming, for a while, on their own.

15   From the Peak I had seen, for the first time, a chimpanzee eating meat: David Greybeard. I had watched him leap up into a tree clutching the carcass of an infant bushpig, which he shared with a female while the adult pigs charged about below. And only about a hundred yards from the Peak, on a never-to-be-forgotten day in October, 1960, I had watched David Greybeard, along with his close friend Goliath, fishing for termites with stems of grass. Thinking back to that far-off time I re-lived the thrill I had felt when I saw David reach out, pick a wide blade of grass and trim it carefully so that it could more easily be poked into the narrow passage in the termite mound. Not only was he using the grass as a tool—he was, by modifying it to suit a special purpose, actually showing the crude beginnings of tool-*making*. What excited telegrams I had sent off to Louis Leakey, that far-sighted genius who had instigated the research at Gombe. Humans were not, after all, the *only* tool-making animals. Nor were chimpanzees the placid vegetarians that people had supposed.

That was just after my mother, Vanne, had left to return to her other responsibilities in England. During her four-month stay she had made an invaluable contribution to the success of the project: she had set up a clinic—four poles and a thatched roof—where she had provided medicines to the local people, mostly fishermen and their families. Although her remedies had been simple—aspirin, Epsom salts, iodine, Band-Aids and so on—her concern and patience had been unlimited, and her cures often worked. Much later we learned that many people had thought that she possessed magic powers for healing. Thus she had secured for me the goodwill of the local human population.

Above me, Fifi stirred, cradling little Flossi more comfortably as she suckled. Then her eyes closed again. The infant nursed for a few more minutes, then the nipple slipped from her mouth as she too slept. I continued to daydream, re-living in my mind some of the more memorable events of the past.

I remembered the day when David Greybeard had first visited my camp by the lakeshore. He had come to feed on the ripe fruits of an oil-nut palm that grew there, spied some bananas on the table outside my tent, and taken them off to eat in the bush. Once he had discovered bananas he had returned for more and gradually other chimpanzees had followed him to my camp.

One of the females who became a regular visitor in 1963 was Fifi's mother, old Flo of the ragged ears and bulbous nose. What an exciting day when, after five years of maternal preoccupation with her infant daughter, Flo had become sexually attractive again. Flaunting her shell-pink sexual swelling she had attracted a whole retinue of suitors. Many of them had never been to camp, but they had followed Flo there, sexual passions overriding natural caution. And, once they had discovered bananas, they had joined the rapidly growing group of regular camp visitors. And so I had become more and more familiar with the whole host of unforgettable chimpanzee characters who are described in my first book, *In the Shadow of Man.*

20 Fifi, lying so peacefully above me now, was one of the few survivors of those early days. She had been an infant when first I knew her in 1961. She had weathered the terrible polio epidemic that had swept through the population—chimpanzee and human alike—in 1966. Ten of the chimpanzees of the study group had died or vanished. Another five had been crippled, including her eldest brother, Faben, who had lost the use of one arm.

At the time of that epidemic the Gombe Stream Research Centre was in its infancy. The first two research assistants were helping to collect and type out notes on chimp behavior. Some twenty-five chimpanzees were regularly visiting camp by then, and so there had been more than enough work for all of us. After watching the chimps all day we had often transcribed notes from our tape recorders until late at night.

My mother Vanne had made two other visits to Gombe during the sixties. One of those had been when the National Geographic Society sent Hugo van Lawick to film the study—which, by then, they were financing. Louis Leakey had wangled Vanne's fare and expenses, insisting that it would not be right for me to be alone in the bush with a young man. How different the moral standards of a quarter of a century ago! Hugo and I had married anyway, and Vanne's third visit, in 1967, had been to share with me, for a couple of months, the task of raising my son, Grub (his real name is Hugo Eric Louis) in the bush.

There was a slight movement from Fifi's nest and I saw that she had turned and was looking down at me. What was she thinking? How much of the past did she

remember? Did she ever think of her old mother, Flo? Had she followed the desperate struggle of her brother, Figan, to rise to the top-ranking, alpha position? Had she even been aware of the grim years when the males of her community, often led by Figan, had waged a sort of primitive war against their neighbours, assaulting them, one after the other, with shocking brutality? Had she known about the gruesome cannibalistic attacks made by Passion and her adult daughter Pom on newborn infants of the community?

Again my attention was jerked back to the present, this time by the sound of a chimpanzee crying. I smiled. That would be Fanni. She had reached the adventurous age when a young female often moves away from her mother to travel with the adults. Then, suddenly, she wants mother desperately, leaves the group, and sets off to search for her. The crying grew louder and soon Fanni came into sight. Fifi paid no attention, but Flossi jumped out of the nest and scrambled down to embrace her elder sister. And Fanni, finding Fifi where she had left her, stopped her childish crying.

25 Clearly Fifi had been waiting for Fanni—now she climbed down and set off, and the children followed after, playing as they went. The family moved rapidly down the steep slope to the south. As I scrambled after them, every branch seemed to catch in my hair or my shirt. Frantically I crawled and wriggled through a terrible tangle of undergrowth. Ahead of me the chimpanzees, fluid black shadows, moved effortlessly. The distance between us increased. The vines curled around the buckles of my shoes and the strap of my camera, the thorns caught in the flesh of my arms, my eyes smarted till the tears flowed as I yanked my hair from the snags that reached out from all around. After ten minutes I was drenched in sweat, my shirt was torn, my knees bruised from crawling on the stony ground—and the chimps had vanished. I kept quite still, trying to listen above the pounding of my heart, peering in all directions through the thicket around me. But I heard nothing.

For the next thirty-five minutes I wandered along the rocky bed of the Kasakela Stream, pausing to listen, to scan the branches above me. I passed below a troop of red colobus monkeys, leaping through the tree tops, uttering their strange, high-pitched, twittering calls. I encountered some baboons of D troop, including old Fred with his one blind eye and the double kink in his tail. And then, as I was wondering where to go next, I heard the scream of a young chimp further up the valley. Ten minutes later I had joined Gremlin with little Galahad, Gigi and two of Gombe's youngest and most recent orphans, Mel and Darbee, both of whom had lost their mothers when they were only just over three years old. Gigi, as she so often does these days, was 'auntying' them both. They were all feeding in a tall tree above the almost dry stream and I stretched out on the rocks to watch them. During my scramble after Fifi the sun had vanished, and now, as I looked up through the canopy, I could see the sky, grey and heavy with rain. With a growing darkness came the stillness, the hush, that so often precedes hard rain. Only the rumbling of the thunder, moving ever closer, broke this stillness; the thunder and the rustling movements of the chimpanzees.

When the rain began Galahad, who had been dangling and patting at his toes near his mother, quickly climbed to the shelter of her arms. And the two orphans hurried to sit, close together, near Gigi. But Gimble started leaping about in the tree tops, swinging vigorously from one branch to the next, climbing up then jumping down to catch himself on a bough below. As the rain got heavier, as more and more drops found their way through the dense canopy, so his leaps became wilder and ever more daring, his swaying of the branches more vigorous. This behaviour would, when he was older, express itself in the magnificent rain display, or rain dance, of the adult male.

Suddenly, just after three o'clock, heralded by a blinding flash of lightning and a thunderclap that shook the mountains and growled on and on, bouncing from peak to peak, the grey-black clouds let loose such torrential rain that sky and earth seemed joined by moving water. Gimble stopped playing then, and he, like the others, sat hunched and still, close to the trunk of the tree. I pressed myself against a palm, sheltering as

best I could under its overhanging fronds. As the rain poured down endlessly I got colder and colder. Soon, turned in upon myself, I lost all track of time. I was no longer recording—there was nothing to record except silent, patient and uncomplaining endurance.

It must have taken about an hour before the rain began to ease off as the heart of the storm swept away to the south. At 4.30 the chimps climbed down, and moved off through the soaked, dripping vegetation. I followed, walking awkwardly, my wet clothes hindering movement. We travelled along the stream bed then up the other side of the valley, heading south. Presently we arrived on a grassy ridge overlooking the lake. A pale, watery sun had appeared and its light caught the raindrops so that the world seemed hung with diamonds, sparkling on every leaf, every blade of grass. I crouched low to avoid destroying a jewelled spider's web that stretched, exquisite and fragile, across the trail.

30   The chimpanzees climbed into a low tree to feed on fresh young leaves. I moved to a place where I could stand and watch as they enjoyed their last meal of the day. The scene was breathtaking in its beauty. The leaves were brilliant, a pale, vivid green in the soft sunlight; the wet trunk and branches were like ebony; the black coats of the chimps were shot with flashes of coppery-brown. And behind this vivid tableau was the dramatic backcloth of the indigo-black sky where the lightning still flickered and flashed, and the distant thunder rumbled.

There are many windows through which we can look out into the world, searching for meaning. There are those opened up by science, their panes polished by a succession of brilliant, penetrating minds. Through these we can see ever further, ever more clearly, into areas that once lay beyond human knowledge. Gazing through such a window I have, over the years, learned much about chimpanzee behaviour and their place in the nature of things. And this, in turn, has helped us to understand a little better some aspects of human behaviour, our own place in nature.

But there are other windows; windows that have been unshuttered by the logic of philosophers; windows through which the mystics seek their visions of the truth; windows from which the leaders of the great religions have peered as they searched for purpose not only in the wondrous beauty of the world, but also in its darkness and ugliness. Most of us, when we ponder on the mystery of our existence, peer through but one of these windows onto the world. And even that one is often misted over by the breath of our finite humanity. We clear a tiny peephole and stare through. No wonder we are confused by the tiny fraction of a whole that we see. It is, after all, like trying to comprehend the panorama of the desert or the sea through a rolled-up newspaper.

As I stood quietly in the pale sunshine, so much a part of the rain-washed forests and the creatures that lived there, I saw for a brief moment through another window and with other vision. It is an experience that comes, unbidden, to some of us who spend time alone in nature. The air was filled with a feathered symphony, the evensong of birds. I heard new frequencies in their music and, too, in the singing of insect voices, notes so high and sweet that I was amazed. I was intensely aware of the shape, the colour, of individual leaves, the varied patterns of the veins that made each one unique. Scents were clear, easily identifiable—fermenting, over-ripe fruit; water-logged earth; cold, wet bark; the damp odour of chimpanzee hair and, yes, my own too. And the aromatic scent of young, crushed leaves was almost overpowering. I sensed the presence of a bushbuck, then saw him, quietly browsing upwind, his spiralled horns dark with rain. And I was utterly filled with that peace "which passeth all understanding."

Then came far-off pant-hoots from a group of chimpanzees to the north. The trance-like mood was shattered. Gigi and Gremlin replied, uttering their distinctive pant-hoots. Mel, Darbee and little Galahad joined in the chorus.

35   I stayed with the chimps until they nested—early, after the rain. And when they had settled down, Galahad cosy beside his mother, Mel and Darbi each in their own small nests close to the big one of auntie Gigi, I left them and walked back along the forest trail to the lakeshore. I passed the D troop baboons again. They were gathered around their sleeping trees, squabbling, playing, grooming together, in the soft light of evening. My walking feet crunched the shingle of the beach, and the sun was a huge red orb above the lake. As it lit the clouds for yet another magnificent display, the water became golden, shot with gleaming ripples of violet and red below the flaming sky.

Later, as I crouched over my little wood fire outside the house, where I had cooked, then eaten, beans and tomatoes and an egg, I was still lost in the wonder of my experience that afternoon. It was, I thought, as though I had looked onto the world through such a window as a chimpanzee might know. I dreamed, by the flickering flames. If only we could, however briefly, see the world through the eyes of a chimpanzee, what a lot we should learn.

A last cup of coffee and then I would go inside, light the hurricane lamp, and write out my notes of the day, the wonderful day. For, since we cannot know with the mind of a chimpanzee we must proceed laboriously, meticulously, as I have for thirty years. We must continue to collect anecdotes and, slowly, compile life histories. We must continue, over the years, to observe, record and interpret. We have, already, learned much. Gradually, as knowledge accumulates, as more and more people work together and pool their information, we are raising the blind of the window through which, one day, we shall be able to see even more clearly into the mind of the chimpanzee.

Writing Strategies

1. Carefully read Goodall's introduction several times. How does it function in her essay? Does it set the tone, establish her voice, suggest her thesis, state her thesis? What else does it do?

2. Find at least one example of each sense (taste, touch, sight, sound, smell) that Goodall appeals to.

3. How does Goodall convey her main idea to the reader?

4. Provide an example of good narration (storytelling) and good description in Goodall's essay. How does each example relate to or support Goodall's main idea?

5. What is Goodall's concluding strategy? What is she hoping to achieve in her conclusion? Is she successful?

Exploring Ideas

1. What is Goodall trying to accomplish by sharing her observation with others?

2. How does Goodall's essay invite you to think differently?

3. Is observing chimpanzees a worthwhile way to spend one's time? Consider various ways in which people spend their time (observing chimpanzees, playing basketball, writing songs, selling cars, waiting tables, and so on). What determines your answer to the question?

4. How might you participate in Goodall's discussion? Ask yourself what you think is most important and/or interesting about it and how you might contribute some worthwhile thought.

Ideas for Writing

1. What is the value of an activity to which you have dedicated yourself (a sport, a hobby, a profession, and so on)? How might you illustrate the value of that activity through purposeful description?

2. What interesting point can you make by describing a quiet scene that becomes chaotic (a party just getting started and then in full swing; a course that begins well but then deteriorates; Thanksgiving before and during dinner; and so on)?

3. In your own words, summarize Goodall's point. Then ask a variety of people what they think about it. Record and examine their responses, looking for ideas that can be explored through further thinking, writing, and discussion.

If responding to one of these ideas, go to the **Analysis** section of this chapter to begin developing ideas for your essay.

Onward, Gamers, Onward!

Royce Flores

We have built-up stereotypes, prejudices, and presuppositions about the types of people we encounter on a daily basis. We *think* we know the people we encounter. But close observation reveals more. In this essay, Royce Flores presents a group of young gamers. In the beginning of the essay, he shows us the most obvious dimension of their public identities. But then he shows us the subtle interactions and nuances of the gamers' culture. His up-close examination of the gamers illustrates a key move in observation: The writer should, at some point, take readers beyond their prejudices and presuppositions.

In the margins of this essay, a reader's comments point to key ideas and writing strategies. As you read the essay, consider how the comments might influence your own reading and writing.

Writing Strategies

The introduction gets immediately to the main focus.

The specific details help us to see the point: This is more than a game. It's a community of people. The details help us to visualize the subjects.

An important detail that shows the intensity and involvement of the gamers.

The figurative language helps illustrate the points and creates a particular flair to the writer's voice.

Exploring Ideas

Gives us a general understanding of the group—they are outcasts.

Details the quirks of the sub-culture.

Like a camera for an investigative report, the paragraph takes us into the center of the gamers' interaction.

Within the white, poster-covered walls of "The Fun Factory" is the bantering, bartering, and competing of young minds. Here, young men (and the occasional girl, but this occurrence is as rare as a funny April fools' joke) gather, sit around, chat, and play the occasional card game. The gamers that hang out in the shop are distinct from other kids their age. They are the outcasts of their age group; the kids who do not fit the average profile set by their peers. In every town, in every state, and worldwide, collectable card games have created a sub-culture for these kids to call home and weekly tournaments give them an opportunity to compete. Often, they can be seen dressed in shirts with sayings only they and other gamers can understand, such as "ALL YOUR BASE ARE BELONG TO US." Their pockets are stuffed with moderate sums of saved lunch money eagerly waiting to be spent for three or four packs of the newest Magic the Gathering set. To accompany the players (and their shirts) are black "Ultra Pro" cases that carry the personalized arsenal of decks for ensuing card games. These decks are gamers' most valued possessions—often the product of years worth of patient building, trading, and purchasing.

"The Fun Factory" is a long, white, rectangle-shaped room with overhead florescent lighting that the owner, Dave, has stated (on numerous occasions) will be removed for track lighting. White plastic tables lay suffocated in bags, drinks, cards, and most importantly "Ultra Pro" cases. Despite the clutter on top of them, the tables manage to remain in neat rows and columns. The shop reeks, a cocktail mix of young male perspiration and nacho cheese Doritos. The entire shop is glued together by the classic tunes of Double

Rock KLT. On the rare occasion, a true classic like Ozzy Osbourne's "Crazy Train" catches the ear of the gamers, prompting outbursts of group singing and occasional air guitar performances.

Yet it is not just for camaraderie that the gamers come here. It is the tournaments, the contests of mental champions, that attract them to this place.

Before a tournament the gamers are lively, eagerly greeting all other participants that enter the store. When players who have not been in a tournament for a while arrive, he (or occasionally she) is met with group hugs, and, "Hey, Ryan, where in the hell have you been?!" Ryan, or whoever the returnee may be, tells a tale of parental strife and how he JUST made it.

5   Next the group of gamers slips into the second pre-tournament phase, which closely resembles that of the New York stock exchange. Gamers call out for all to hear, "Does anyone have three *Diabolic Edicts?*" If the gamer is lucky, someone will look up and reply, "Yes, but, I need four *Chain Lightenings,* so what else would you be willing to toss in?" This chaotic event is driven by loud requests, denials, and even some begging. As tournament time nears, gamers run from table to table, frantically trying to get that last element added to their decks. The chaos can often last over an hour.

Once it is time for the names to be taken, the store grows silent. Players' faces grow worrisome. Then, one at a time, names get called off, and tournament pairings are made—when officials select opponents. (An occasional sigh or "Fu^%!" pops out when a poor player gets matched up with a superior gamer.)

Contrary to the demeanor at the start of the day, the players now act as if they do not know each other. Their once smiling faces are stern, overthrown by the gamers' will to succeed. The entire atmosphere is thick with the mildew of concentration and brainpower. The friendly conversations have transformed into staccato formalities, announcing the players' turns.

As players are eliminated, via best of three duels, they begin to gather around the better players to watch their games. This process resembles a sort of teacher/student relationship, in which gamers learn from better players on how to improve their games. No one says anything. They just stand intently and watch.

Margin notes (left):

Allusions to pop culture help characterize the group of gamers.

Transition paragraph helps us make the shift to another dimension of the subculture.

The details support the point that this is a subculture.

The writer uses new paragraphs to shift our attention from one phase of a tournament to another. (Paragraphs help divide both space and time.)

The writer draws attention to the shift—so that we can clearly see the type of interaction we might otherwise miss.

Sentence brevity helps convey the tension.

Margin notes (right):

The group has its own set of practices and coded language.

We've gone from camaraderie to worry.

It's not simply a game. There are many nuances to be learned and mimicked.

As the tournament winds down, and the final match approaches, the less astute players filter away and the truly intense gamers stay, assured by the fact that if they walk away from watching the final, they'll miss a great play, the huge turn-around victory, or just an absent-minded folly on one of the finalists' part. And this is where the gaming is great. It is the evolution of the mind, a leap from "dorkdom," air guitar, silly tee-shirts, and big public hugs to deep thinking, highly intuitive, focused individuals.

10   In a society where all information is thrown at the mind in sixty-second intervals, these kids can manage to sit down for two to three hours and play a game that draws so much on concentration and intuition. It is this display of intellect that sets these kids apart from their peers. This respect for the fortitude of thought makes these kids deeper thinkers, able to appreciate when the mind does amazing things through cunning, ingenuity, and knowledge. We see this in their eyes, how one good move lights up the group. There are no fireworks, no dazzling effects, just a mere playing of a card to make onlooking faces smile and nod. By each flop of a card, a gamer's mind is opened up to new possibilities, a chance for victory or to hold out on a loss for one more turn. The watchers of the finals see and respect this; it is why they play, why they watch, why they spend the money to acquire the cards. It is not just a bunch of dorks with nothing to do; this IS what they do.

Here's the thesis: Point that focuses all the details.

Here's a direct move for public resonance. The writer broadens his lens and looks at this group as part of a society.

These details support the main idea.

There are some subtle intellectual complexities going on in these tournaments—behaviors that seem increasingly absent in popular culture.

These kids have created an intensive intellectual space for themselves.

Writing Strategies

1. How does Flores encourage the reader to think differently about gaming?

2. What details help to engage the reader? Are any details unnecessary?

3. How do details from the essay support the assertions put forth in the concluding paragraph?

4. If workshopping Flores's essay, what additional details would you suggest he might use?

5. How does Flores take the reader from the common view of gamers to a more accurate view?

Exploring Ideas

1. Based on this essay, what does Flores value? How does Flores appeal to readers' values?

2. Flores writes, "It is this display of intellect that sets these kids apart from their peers." What other activities besides gaming include a "display of intellect" that can go unnoticed by people outside the activity?

3. Interview several gamers or research Magic the Gathering online: How does your research support or refute Flores's position on gaming?

Ideas for Writing

1. Examine a particular group of people that the general public dismisses or ignores. What important point or quality does the general public not recognize?

2. Observe an event or activity, identifying the moment when the mood or tone changes (when people become more focused or more intense, for example). What can you learn from the shift in mood or tone?

If responding to one of these ideas, go to the **Analysis** section of this chapter to begin developing ideas for your essay.

"There are no fireworks, no dazzling effects, just a mere playing of a card . . . "

The Front Porch

Chester McCovey

Chester McCovey's observing essay illustrates how one can use an observation as a point of contact and then, through analysis, explore why the observation matters. McCovey makes a simple observation: That people don't sit out on their front porches like they did when he was a kid. Then he explores and determines that the loss of the front porch equals a loss of community. Through analysis, he goes from a specific observation (about garages and porches) to a general insight (about a loss of community).

If you walk through my neighborhood, you won't see many porches, at least not the kind people sit on in the evenings. Those days are gone where I live, and likely where you live, too.

The front porch has been replaced—by the two-car garage. Both sets of my grandparents, who lived in the same small town, had big front porches, and summer visits often meant sitting on the porch, talking, and watching cars and people out walking. After a while someone might have suggested getting some ice cream. The adult conversation was often dull, sometimes painfully so for a child, but sometimes it was interesting. The everyday people a child sees in church or at the Little League field in a small town have a few years behind them, and what person who has lived a little doesn't have a story to tell—or a story to be told about them? Sometimes those stories would come out and bring to life a previously uninteresting Frank or Gretchen. Small towns are full of life's everyday dramas. A child hears and figures out many things on a place like a front porch on a thing like a warm summer night.

My grandparents' garages were small, just enough for one car and a few tools—not much of a garage for today's homeowner. In those days the garage kept a car and a small lawnmower, some rakes, and so on. The garage today must keep much more. One can see, then, how the exchange occurred. Like an old-fashioned trade in baseball, gone is the home team's beloved front porch, replaced by a big, new garage. Of course the trade is much more interesting than that. And a look at how it occurred enlightens us a little about the world in which we live. More importantly, it tells us not so much about how life is now but about how it came to be. And, I would argue, it shows us the way in which things will continue to change.

Back then, our own garage held two cars, a riding lawnmower, a push mower, bicycles, and lots of tools. We had a front porch and sat on it, but mostly just when we had company. Our house, then, represents the transition between two generations: my grandparents' generation that traveled less, received only three television stations (*sans* remote control), and didn't have air conditioning and my own generation that is more likely to be on the go (driving from one place to another) or sitting inside, on the computer or watching TV.

5   The front porch fell victim to its two natural enemies: the internal-combustion engine (automobiles) and electricity (air conditioning, lights, and TV). Now, instead of gathering on our front porch as our grandparents did, we are either gone somewhere thanks to our transportation or we are at home but indoors.

> how life must have splashed
> out of the cup
> on warm summer nights
> before the cool air
> of electricity
> urged us all to relax
> in the fluttering glow
> of color tv

We have traded sitting on the front porch for sitting in traffic, or to be more positive about it, for sitting in our automobile as we speed along to some very important place to be. The shift from porch to garage is beautifully simple. It goes like this: I need a place to park my transportation machine (car, truck, SUV) and I don't need a large, outdoor room for sitting. The reasoning (the reality of the situation) is just as simple: There's not as much action on the sidewalk as there once was (the neighbors are indoors or driving somewhere) and I don't need to sit outdoors to stay cool on muggy nights (the air conditioning indoors takes care of that). So, a need or desire—to stay cool, to be entertained, to keep up with what's going on—is replaced not by a different need or desire but instead by a new way of meeting it.

> Need or Desire—To Stay Cool
> Previously met by evening breeze; now met by air conditioning
>
> Need or Desire—To Be Entertained
> Previously met by conversation with neighbors; now met by TV, computer, shopping at the mall, conversation with friends who we drive to see
>
> Need or Desire—To Keep Up with What's Going On
> Previously met by discussion with neighbors and friends; now met through national media (TV and Internet)

I am not saying there are no front porches. Obviously there are. And I am not saying everyone has a two-car garage instead. In my neighborhood, small garages not connected to the house still reign. But obviously, their days are numbered. The new houses sometimes look as much like a house attached to a garage as a garage attached to a house. Today's garage often dominates the house.

Finally, the careful reader is insisting that I deal with the backyard patio deck. What about it? When we do sit outdoors, we choose to do it out back, away from the rest of the world. This is interesting. We need a break, I would suggest, from the hustle and bustle of daily life, so we retreat to our own backyard to be left alone with our families. But that hustle and bustle is mostly the hustle and bustle of traffic, radio, television, and a few quick transactions with total strangers. Of course another reason for opting to relax in the backyard is that, as previously mentioned, there just isn't that much going on out front these days. (If there were, I wonder if we would sit on the front porch and watch it . . . *and* contribute to it.) I am arguing that we lose something very basic—very fundamental—when we lose the front porch culture.

On Sunday drives through the country, I see big new houses with big new porches. As Americans we can have it all—the house with the big front porch *and* the big garage. But I never (I am tempted to qualify this statement and say "almost never" or "rarely" but I have been thinking about it and I do mean "never")—I never see anyone out sitting on those porches. I am not prepared here to argue that we are a civilization in deep trouble because of this, though it does seem to me appropriate that we should lament, at least a little, the loss of the front porch.

Imagine: Being entertained by sitting on a porch and talking.

Writing Strategies

1. Why might McCovey address his reader directly in his first paragraph? Is this strategy effective? What effect does it have on you?

2. McCovey uses the first-person "I" in his essay, referring to his grandparents' houses, his own childhood house, and the houses in his neighborhood today. How might his essay be different had he avoided using "I"? Would it be better? Worse? No different?

3. McCovey deals in his second-to-last paragraph with the backyard deck. Why? Is this an essential part of his essay? What else might he have dealt with?

4. Identify McCovey's use of one metaphor or simile (comparing two unlike things: *The clerk was a bear* [metaphor]; *The clerk was like a bear* [simile]). Think of a metaphor or simile of your own that might work well in this essay.

5. Imagine that you are helping McCovey revise his essay and he is not happy with his conclusion. What suggestions would you make?

Exploring Ideas

1. Based on this essay, what does McCovey value? To what degree do you value the same thing?

2. In your own words, summarize McCovey's main idea. Then share your summary with several classmates who have also read the essay. Discuss your understanding of McCovey's main idea, and then reread his essay and revise your summary as necessary.

3. To further explore this issue, share your summary (via e-mail or in person) with people of various age groups, asking them to respond to McCovey's ideas. Describe how their views are similar to or different from McCovey's.

Ideas for Writing

1. Besides the move from *porch* to *garage,* what other change has taken place? How has that change impacted everyday life?

2. Observe some difference in a way of living, whether it be the result of time (your grandparents and you, for example) or location (southern Californians and midwesterners). Do not be afraid to generalize, as long as you do it thoughtfully and are mindful of exceptions.

If responding to one of these ideas, go to the **Analysis** section of this chapter to begin developing ideas for your essay.

Outside Reading

Find a written observation and print it out or make a photocopy. You might find observing essays in nature or travel periodicals (such as *National Geographic*), or you might find an observation related to your major or a major that you are considering. In that case, explore a professional journal such as *Journal of Clinical Psychology in Medical Settings, Soil Biology & Biochemistry*, or *American Architect and Engineer*. You might also explore your library's electronic database or InfoTrac College Edition (http://infotrac.galegroup.com/itweb), an electronic database of journal and magazine articles. If you are using your library's database, go to "periodicals" or "articles" and then do a keyword search. If you are using InfoTrac College Edition, go to the main search box and click on "keywords." Type in *observing* or *observation* with other words that interest you, using *and* between them, such as *observing and animals, observing and wildlife, observation and city and life, observing and everyday life*. The search results will yield lists of articles in academic journals and magazines.

You might also use the Internet to find websites or articles that feature observations. Try a meta-search engine (a search engine that scans several other search engines) such as Webcrawler.com. As with the above searches, type in *observing* or *observation* and combinations of words that interest you. (Be wary of websites that are selling merchandise.)

The purpose of this assignment is to further your understanding of observation and to introduce a broad range of writing strategies. As you can see by the essays in this chapter, any imaginable subject can be rediscovered through close observation. As you read through this chapter, keep the observation you have discovered close by and notice the strategies the writer uses. Depending on your instructor's suggestions, do one or more of the following:

1. Notice how the writer applies various strategies from this chapter. On the hard copy or photocopy:
   - Highlight the thesis if it is stated. If the thesis is implied, write it in your own words.
   - Highlight any passages that suggest the public resonance of the subject. Write "pr" in the margin.
   - Identify any narrative passages (those that tell a story). Write "narrative" in the margin.

2. Analyze the strategies employed by the writer. The following questions may be helpful:
   - How is this observation different from the observations in this chapter?
   - How does the writer support his or her thesis?
   - Who is the audience for this argument?
   - How does the audience impact the content of the observation?

3. Write at least three "Writing Strategies" questions for the observation.

4. Write at least three "Exploring Ideas" questions for the observation.

5. Write two "Ideas for Writing," such as the ones following the essays in this book, for the observation.

INVENTION

Observation requires a good deal of analysis and planning. It goes far beyond simply choosing a subject and writing down details. Writers usually go through a cyclical invention process, in which they return repeatedly to their original notes to find patterns and significant points. The following sections are designed to help you through this process: specifically, to discover a topic (in **Point of Contact**), develop particular points about the topic (in **Analysis**), make it relevant to a community of readers (in **Public Resonance**), focus your ideas (in **Thesis**), and develop them into an essay (in **Rhetorical Tools**). The Invention questions in each section are not meant to be answered directly in your final written assignment. They are designed to help generate ideas— to guide you through an intellectual process.

POINT OF CONTACT

The goal here is to see something in a new way, to see beyond the casual glance. You may choose to visit places and do things you have never done before, or you may visit the usual places—but with focused attention. Use the following as possible starting points for your observation.

Observing a Place Job site, family restaurant, factory, office, break room, playground, park, movie theater, shopping mall, video arcade, college hall, college club, campground, woods. Gather details about the place. In addition to obvious details, consider the less obvious:

- What subtle behavior patterns do you detect?
- Is there a hidden competition or collaboration going on?
- What mood might the creatures (people, animals, plants) share? How do they unknowingly maintain that mood?
- Are people free to do as they please, or does something restrain them? (Do they know that something is restraining them?)
- What is the unstated, normal mode of behavior?
- Does anyone or anything break out of the norm? What are the hidden consequences?
- What is missing?

Observing People Supervisor, manager, line worker, server, religious leader, teacher or professor, principal, athlete, bingo player, student. Use notes, audio and video recorders, and/or photographs to gather details about the person. You might also interview the subject. (See the section on interviews in Chapter 13.)

Remember that a person's own words cannot reveal everything. In fact, you might find that your own observations reveal much more about this person than what his or her own perspective allows.

- In what hidden ways is the subject working with or against the surroundings?
- Does the subject reinforce or work against rules?
- How do others treat the subject (with quiet respect, hidden disdain, total indifference)?

- If the subject is a group, how do the individuals maintain harmony or unity? How do they conflict?
- What explicit or hidden rules do they follow?

Observing an Animal Family pet, friend's or neighborhood pet, stray cat or dog, birds, animals at a park or zoo, wild animals, farm animals. Observing an animal (or animals) may take significant patience. They are often unpredictable, so it may take some time to collect information. Also, animals may act in more subtle ways than people. They might show anger, happiness, or other feelings with particularly small gestures. Gather basic information about the animal's behavior, but also look beyond the simple glance:

- What does it know?
- What secrets does it have?
- How does it signal its mood?
- Does it have dramatic mood changes?
- How does it get along with humans? With the world around it?
- What habits does it have?
- Is it a public or private creature?
- Does it compromise or alter its behavior to accommodate others?

Observing a Person or Event Involved in Your Major Use any or all of the questions in this section to help gather information, but also develop more questions to help you gain insight to the particular subject. By observing a particular person or event, what can you discover about the nature of your major?

Try to abandon your prejudices about the subject. See it in a new way.

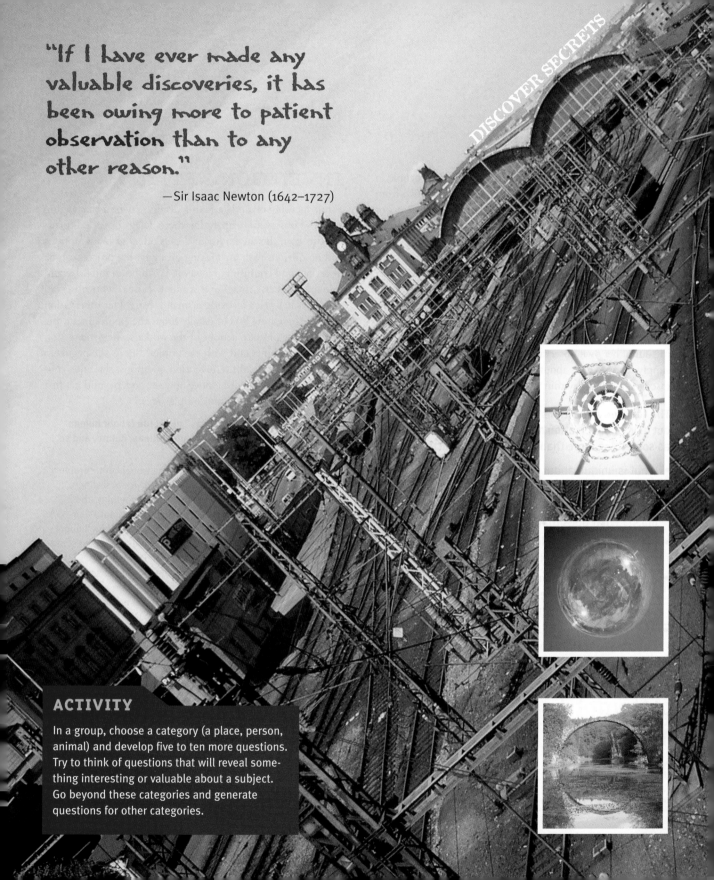

"If I have ever made any valuable discoveries, it has been owing more to patient observation than to any other reason."

—Sir Isaac Newton (1642–1727)

ACTIVITY

In a group, choose a category (a place, person, animal) and develop five to ten more questions. Try to think of questions that will reveal something interesting or valuable about a subject. Go beyond these categories and generate questions for other categories.

ANALYSIS

Details do not have their own meaning. It is up to people to *make* meaning from details. As we analyze, we move from observation notes to focused ideas, from a collection of potentially unrelated details to a set of particular points. Analysis prompts us to see patterns, connections, and paths within the particulars. Jane Goodall, for example, has studied chimpanzees for years, observing minute details of their daily existence. And from her observations, she has made discoveries about chimp behavior. Goodall had to see the connections in her observational notes; she had to discover meaning behind the habits of the chimps and make meaning out of her own observations. In her writing, she does not simply report details about chimp behavior; she analyzes and discovers meaning within the details.

The following questions can help you to make meaning out of your observation notes, and to look at the subject as something more than its physical characteristics:

- What is unique about the subject?
- What is ordinary about this subject? (How are its qualities common to other places, people, or animals?) What does that quality show?
- Is this subject symbolic of something? (Does it stand for some idea or ideal?)
- Does the subject seem different after the observation (more complicated, less intimidating, more human, less human, more predictable, and so on)?
- What does the subject "say" about life (about human interaction, social behavior, institutions, nature, and so on) in this place and time?

Attempt to gain insight beyond the simple glance, beyond the drive-by appearance of things.

INVENTION WRITING

While focusing on and gathering details may be a challenging aspect of observation, analyzing those details poses a difficulty of its own. Because a list of details offers so many options and no obvious path for making meaning, the process can be uncertain and confusing. However, it can be an intensive and valuable process. Imagine a student, Linda, who observed people at her place of work, a small factory. Her observation notes include long lists of details about the environment, the lighting, the physical actions of the workers, their interaction with the machines and with each other. But as she begins to analyze, using one of the Invention questions, she finds connections in those details. Notice how she goes beyond her first simplistic answer to a more complex idea:

> **What does the subject "say" about life (about human interaction, social behavior, institutions, nature, and so on) in this place and time?**
>
> At first, I thought that my coworkers were just miserable people at a job. They work at their individual stations, occasionally interact to communicate something about a machine part or materials, and then go to breaks—or home. But outside of that, I couldn't see anything important. But the more I looked over my notes, I realized something was going on in those small and infrequent interactions between people. While they might seem miserable and disconnected at times (maybe even most of the time), they all offer some support to one another: a small glance, a shared roll of the eyes when the supervisor inspects one person's work, the way Rob, the oldest in the shop, actually runs over to someone who needs help with something, the extra cup of coffee Bob got Maria because she didn't have time during break. All these things mean something—the underground, almost secretive, strategies to keep each other afloat in their shared situation. After I realized this, I went back over all my notes, and remembered things I had not written down. The days are actually filled with these little gestures; they happen at all times: at breaks, on the way into the shop in the morning, while the machines are operating.

Linda could then go on to develop this point in her writing. In fact, the idea may even develop into a thesis statement. This would mean that many other details (about physical structure, about the machines themselves) might be abandoned, unless they have some significance for worker interaction. In this way, Linda's observation goes from a list of seemingly unrelated details to a focused idea.

ACTIVITY

Observe the activities in your classroom. Consider actions and behaviors among work groups, among demographic groups, before the instructor arrives, or as the class ends. As a class or in a group, discuss the possible meaning or significance of particular events, behaviors, or interactions.

In Chester McCovey's invention notes, he explores the possible meaning of the garage—not simply what it does for people (store their cars) but how it works in their lives, how it says something about the way people live.

Is this subject symbolic of something? (Does it stand for some idea or ideal?)

It is, perhaps. These big garages are obviously a necessity for today's homeowner. I mean, most of these homes are not within walking distance of where the owner works. Many, I suspect, can only be afforded if both husband and wife work—two cars! Now, fill the garage up with all the other machinery you need to maintain the yard. The garage quite simply says "go," "drive," "automobile," "transportation." I am at home, but not for long. No doubt the cars have air conditioning as does the house. One need never be hot (or cold). The garage has replaced the porch. You pull into the garage and go inside and stay inside the house. Then get in the air-conditioned space bubble car when you want to leave. Of course there is recreation, but recreation is getting away from life and not a part of it. Let's take a break in our day and burn some calories, not let's burn some calories in the natural course of our day. The garage symbolizes driving, moving, loss of neighborhood, community, wealth, poverty . . .

THINKING FURTHER

Reread McCovey's invention writing. Notice that he explores possibilities and ultimately decides that the garage symbolizes six ideas: "driving, moving, loss of neighborhood, community, wealth, poverty." This list is an indication that McCovey is not yet done thinking about the symbolism of the garage.

Activity A For practice, pick up where McCovey's invention writing leaves off, taking his thinking even further. Consider the following questions:

- Which of the six ideas, if any, can be eliminated from the list, and why?
- What other items might be added, and why?
- How can the big garage symbolize both wealth and poverty?

For help, explore ideas further through discussion with classmates or with others outside of class.

Activity B Now consider your own invention writing, as you considered McCovey's above. For help, explore ideas further through discussion with classmates or with others outside of class.

- What new way of thinking (what insight, what revelation) did you discover?
- How might you explore the complexities of that idea further? For example:

—How might that thinking be wrong?

—How might that thinking be more complex than you presently imagine?

—What apparent contradictions or inconsistencies must be explained?

PUBLIC RESONANCE

Writers do more than focus on a subject: They also make the subject resonate with the lives of others. When we read Annie Dillard or Jane Goodall, for instance, they prompt us to consider our connection to the natural world and the essence of our own lives. When we read Edward Abbey or Chester McCovey, we consider how the world around us is changing, and the effects those changes have on our lives. Royce Flores makes us see into a part of culture that we might otherwise ignore.

The following questions will help broaden your subject's perspective and make it resonate with a potential audience:

- Why is this subject important to people? (Why is its uniqueness important?)
- Why should your peers know about this subject?
- What do people normally experience, understand, or assume about the subject?
- Does the presence or action of this subject teach people something—about themselves, about life, about work, about happiness, about materialism, about sincerity, about identity, about relationships, about the past, about the future, about death?

Even the most intimate observations can have public resonance.

PUBLIC RESONANCE IN CHAPTER READINGS

Some subjects seem to have public resonance automatically. The initial steps of analysis involve making connections to broader cultural trends. For instance, McCovey's focus on porches is a public trend. Some subjects, perhaps most, need to be *made* relevant to the audience, and it is up to a writer or speaker to make the connection. Consider Jane Goodall's strategies. She extends her personal observations into a broader intellectual world:

> There are many windows through which we can look out into the world, searching for meaning. There are those opened up by science, their panes polished by a succession of brilliant, penetrating minds. Through these we can see ever further, ever more clearly, into areas that once lay beyond human knowledge. Gazing through such a window I have, over the years, learned much about chimpanzee behaviour and their place in the nature of things. (109)

Annie Dillard makes a similar move in her essay. The stare of a weasel, one might think, has nothing whatsoever to do with the life of humans (or, specifically, the life of Dillard's readers), but she makes a connection. She prompts the readers to compare their own ordered and calculated lives to the pure moment-by-moment life of the weasel. As Dillard shows, even the most personal observations can have public resonance; even the stare between one woman and one weasel can be connected to the lives of others:

> We could, you know. We can live any way we want. People take vows of poverty, chastity, and obedience— even of silence—by choice. The thing is to stalk your calling in a certain skilled and supple way, to locate the most tender and live spot and plug into that pulse. This is yielding, not fighting. A weasel doesn't "attack" anything; a weasel lives as he's meant to, yielding at every moment to the perfect freedom of single necessity. (100)

Edward Abbey focuses on the connection between his own backyard and the looming city beyond it:

> My wife and I and my daughter live (for the moment) in a little house near the bright, doomed city of Tucson, Arizona. We like it here. Most of the time. (102)

He then goes on to explain the constant intrusion of the city (and its attendant qualities) into intimate and serene life. But he also takes an extra step to show the connection to others:

> Still, the city creeps closer, day by day. While the two great contemporary empires are dying—one in Afghanistan and Poland, the other in Vietnam, Iran, Nicaragua, El Salvador. And though I welcome their defeat, their pain and fear make them more dangerous than ever. Like mortally wounded tyrannosaurs, they thrash about in frenzy, seeking enemies, destroying thousands of innocent lives with each blind spasm of reaction. And still the city creeps closer. I find a correlation in these movements. I foresee the day when we shall be obliged to strike camp, once again. (102)

With this correlation, he suggests that his retreat from Tucson is like that of many people throughout the world who are running from the oppression of massive civilizations.

INVENTION WRITING

Notice how Chester McCovey explores the breadth of his subject—how the question helps him to see the broad implications of porches and garages. Also notice how the initial question leads McCovey to more questions:

Does the presence or action of this subject teach people something—about themselves, about life, about work, about happiness, about materialism, about sincerity, about identity, about relationships, about the past, about the future, about death?

What we see is a loss of community. The big garage shows us we're leaving our own neighborhood a lot. The fact that the garage is connected to the living space shows us that we go from our living area directly, by pushing a button that opens the door, into the street and to another community far enough away that we drive to it. We don't interact with our neighbors (we might not even know their names).

We drive past them with our windows rolled up. We maybe don't even smell or feel our neighborhood (I guess that's an exaggeration, but there's something there). Remember, we're not talking about all houses. We're talking about the ones built today. Is loss of neighborhood a loss to the people who live in those neighborhoods? Does big garage/no front porch mean loss of neighborliness? Yes, these relationships—or ones like them—can exist outside one's own neighborhood. But what is the effect of this? What is a neighbor anymore?

INVENTION WORKSHOP

Remember that an essay does not simply relay information. Rather, it invites readers (and the writer) to re-see something, to think differently. To that end, form a group with one or two other writers. Each writer should explain his or her observation to the others and read his or her initial responses to the Invention questions on pages 122 and 126. Then, the others should address the following:

1. Help the writer go further by applying McCovey's strategy in the previous passage. That is, try to discover what the subject shows about the way people live, about the way people see the world around them.

2. Return to the Invention questions in this section and collectively offer responses for the writer's subject.

Make certain to spend equal time on each writer's observations. The goal is to develop new insights for each project.

THESIS

The thesis of an essay offers a writer's specific insight on the subject. Remember that a thesis can be *explicit* (stated directly) or *implied* (unstated but suggested by the details). And either way, a writer benefits from having a single focused statement to guide the process. For this project, the main idea should reveal a new insight about a subject. The more narrow the insight, the more focused and intensive the writing will be. Although it is easy to offer a first-glance statement, try to narrow in on a particular quality. Notice how the following bulleted statements offer broad and even predictable ideas. But the violet statements reveal something unique and specific:

- The people at the local tavern keep to themselves.

    In the dark, smoky quiet of Timothy's Pub, the regulars face straight ahead but share intimate crises in their quick coded exchanges.

- The neighborhood is a quiet place.

    The disappearing porches in the neighborhood signal a shift to a more disconnected, isolating, but technologically advanced time.

- The Fun Factory has a spirit of competition.

    Once the games begin at The Fun Factory, the players shift radically: from unfocused adolescent "dorks" to focused competitive intellectuals.

Notice how the more specific theses focus on more particular subjects:

> people vs. regulars
> neighborhood vs. disappearing porches
> Fun Factory vs. players

The sentences bring the reader up close. (We can even imagine a television camera literally zooming in to the more particular subjects.) Also, the purple sentences have stronger verbs:

> *keep* vs. *face/share*
> *is* vs. *signal*
> *has* vs. *shift*

The stronger verbs do more than create action in the sentences. They actually enrich the content—making the nouns work harder. As a result, the sentences push the reader's (and writer's) consciousness through the sentence with more energy.

ACTIVITY

In small groups, present your thesis statements. (If possible, write the statements on a board.) The group should analyze each statement and try to create more focus. Apply the following:

1. For each noun, suggest a more specific word.
2. Suggest stronger verbs.

EVOLUTION OF A THESIS

Imagine a writer is observing students at a community college. She notices many things about the students: their clothes, their ages, and so on. But she decides to focus on a particular point: *The students at Beach Community College spend their time coming and going primarily alone.* Such a statement offers a particular idea about the college students. The essay, then, would focus on the solitary nature of the students. The point might grow and develop layers throughout the invention process:

Point of Contact:

- The majority of the students coming in and out of the buildings are alone; they do not talk together or in groups. If people are talking, they are talking on cell phones.

Analysis:

- Although I have always associated college with social life, the students at Beach Community College show that college is often a solitary experience.

Public Resonance:

- When most people talk about college, they inevitably bring up campus life: the parties, the Greek system, the study groups, etc. They think of all the movies and stories about those crazy college years, but the reality may be fundamentally different for many students.

Working Thesis:

- Despite the popular notions of social life on college campuses, the students at Beach Community College show that higher education can be a solitary experience.

Use the Invention questions on pages 122 and 126 to help develop the thesis of your essay. Or you might examine your notes and find one common idea or thread of details, which can lead to a general statement about the subject.

REVISION

Develop a chart that shows the evolution of your thesis. Try to represent the way your thesis gains focus and depth. You might refer to your field notes and specific Invention questions that help generate and focus your ideas. Then ask yourself: *What words or phrases are too broad? Can I make the subject more specific? Can I strengthen the verbs?*

RHETORICAL TOOLS

An observing essay seeks to show a reader something new about a particular subject and to lead a reader to an insightful conclusion about that subject. That insight, the writer's particular understanding about the subject, is the value for the reader—the thing he or she will carry away from the essay. So an observing essay goes far beyond offering details; it offers a unique awareness about a subject and its significance, an awareness that the writer has gained through careful study and examination.

Using Details

Remember that the details of the essay should lead the reader to the same conclusion that the writer makes. Refer to your notes from the Point of Contact section and find all the specific details to support your main point. Your essay should be generated *only* from the details that help to show that point. Unrelated details may be left behind. For example, consider Annie Dillard's observation of a weasel. Her main point focuses on the weasel's "purity of living." She gives us details and images that communicate that idea. You can imagine many other details (such as where the weasel went after the encounter or general information about weasel life), but such information would not support her main idea. The essay includes details that show the contrast between Dillard's life of motive and the weasel's life of purity.

Edward Abbey's essay is filled with many details that might seem disconnected outside of his framework. We might, for instance, wonder how an elf owl and police helicopters are related. At first glance, they might seem like rambling details, but Abbey's point depends on them. Because he is explaining the way the city creeps outward into the surrounding serenity, he uses details that illustrate the distinction between the chaotic city and the peaceful natural world.

Using Narrative

Many writers choose to narrate the events of an observation—to explain the events leading up to a particular moment of discovery. Such narration can help to place the observation in time and help to situate the reader. Dillard uses narration particularly well at the beginning of her essay. She takes the reader through several paragraphs that lead up to the moment of her encounter with the weasel. Here, Dillard uses narration to narrow her focus from a broader view of the natural surroundings to a particular animal:

> The sun had just set. I was relaxed on the tree trunk, ensconced in the lap of lichen, watching the lily pads at my feet tremble and part dreamily over the thrusting path of a carp. A yellow bird appeared to my right and flew behind me. It caught my eye; I swiveled around—and the next instant, inexplicably, I was looking down at a weasel, who was looking up at me. (99)

The narration creates a powerful contrast between the nonchalant, relaxed feeling of the surroundings and the weasel's intense stare. (Also notice Jane Goodall's use of narrative throughout her essay. She uses narrative to explain her own preparation for the chimpanzees. See page 104.)

If you are considering using narration in your writing, ask yourself the following questions:

- Would narrating the events leading up to the observation help engage the reader?
- Would narrating part of the observation help to engage the reader?

Caution: Using narrative can make an observation less formal. Instructors in some disciplines may want you to avoid narration. Always consider your audience when planning such strategies. You might even ask your instructor. For more on narration, see Chapter 2, page 82.

Using Allusions

Allusions are references to bits of public knowledge, things, events, or people outside of the main subject being observed. Writers use allusions to help illustrate a point or create a feeling. For instance, in Edward Abbey's essay, the main focus is the natural area around his home in Arizona, but he alludes to a global political crisis from the 1980s in which the Soviet Union and the United States (two "empires") persistently wreak havoc on people of the world:

> Still, the city creeps closer, day by day. While the two great contemporary empires are dying—one in Afghanistan and Poland, the other in Vietnam, Iran, Nicaragua, El Salvador. And though I welcome their defeat, their pain and fear make them more dangerous than ever. Like mortally wounded tyrannosaurs, they thrash about in frenzy, seeking enemies, destroying thousands of innocent lives with each blind spasm of reaction. And still the city creeps closer. I find a correlation in these movements. I foresee the day when we shall be obliged to strike camp, once again. (102)

His allusion helps to create a point: That the serene beauty of his natural surroundings is jeopardized by the looming presence of an expanding city, one without knowledge or concern of its destructive power.

The following questions will help you develop allusions for your own writing:

- Does my subject relate to any political event or situation?

- Does my subject relate to any social or cultural event or situation?

- Does my subject relate to any person or event in history? In literature? In popular culture (movies, television, music)?

Using Simile and Metaphor

Similes and metaphors are comparisons that point out or create similarities between two or more seemingly different things. (A simile uses "like" or "as.") Writers use them to help create pictures for readers, to make points more engaging and intense. Jane Goodall uses the window metaphor in her essay to explain how human perception is framed. The metaphor helps make a potentially abstract point very tangible. (See page 109.) Likewise, Edward Abbey uses a simile to characterize the behavior of two countries, comparing two empires to wounded dinosaurs. While Abbey could have simply characterized the empires as "destructive," the simile adds an important notion: that the empires are living, breathing organisms, huge, monstrous, and even helpless:

> Like mortally wounded tyrannosaurs, they thrash about in frenzy, seeking enemies, destroying thousands of innocent lives with each blind spasm of reaction. (102)

As you consider your own writing, remember that figurative language such as similes and metaphors should be used to direct the reader's perception toward your main ideas. Such figurative language should be used sparingly.

The following questions will help you develop similes and metaphors for your own writing:

- Can I compare my subject to an animal? A thing? A place? A person?

- What purpose would this comparison serve?

ACTIVITY

Find other similes or metaphors in the chapter readings and explain how they help extend the writer's thinking or support the writer's points.

ORGANIZATIONAL STRATEGIES

How Should I Deal with Public Resonance?

The questions relating to public resonance might simply help the writer develop a sense of mission. However, writers sometimes choose to make a direct appeal to the audience; that is, they invite the reader directly into the issue at hand. Annie Dillard's essay makes a direct appeal to her readers:

> We could, you know. We can live any way we want. People take vows of poverty, chastity, and obedience—even of silence—by choice. The thing is to stalk your calling in a certain skilled and supple way, to locate the most tender and live spot and plug into that pulse. This is yielding, not fighting. A weasel doesn't "attack" anything; a weasel lives as he's meant to, yielding at every moment to the perfect freedom of single necessity. (100)

Chester McCovey extends his observation to the reader's situation. This is an explicit strategy to make the subject relate to the reader:

> If you walk through my neighborhood, you won't see many porches, at least not the kind people sit on in the evenings. Those days are gone where I live, and likely where you live, too. (115)

As his essay develops, McCovey makes his observation a public concern, and by the concluding paragraph, suggests something about the nature of American public life:

> On Sunday drives through the country, I see big new houses with big new porches. As Americans we can have it all—the house with the big front porch *and* the big garage. But I never (I am tempted to qualify this statement and say "almost never" or "rarely" but I have been thinking about it and I do mean "never")—I never see anyone out sitting on those porches. I am not prepared here to argue that we are as a civilization in deep trouble because of this, though it does seem to me appropriate that we should lament, at least a little, the loss of the front porch. (116)

In Edward Abbey's essay (page 102), the main focus, the landscape surrounding his own home, does not necessarily have public resonance, but his essay expands slowly as it progresses: beginning in his yard, opening up to include the looming city of Tucson, and even going beyond the United States to include international politics. The essay, then, becomes increasingly more public, and more political, as it progresses.

In her essay, Jane Goodall develops the public resonance in two particular paragraphs. While much of her essay focuses on specific events of her observation (specific behaviors of the chimps), these paragraphs take a broader look—and help bring more public meaning to her observation:

There are many windows through which we can look out into the world, searching for meaning. There are those opened up by science, their panes polished by a succession of brilliant, penetrating minds. Through these we can see ever further, ever more clearly, into areas that once lay beyond human knowledge. Gazing through such a window I have, over the years, learned much about chimpanzee behaviour and their place in the nature of things. And this, in turn, has helped us to understand a little better some aspects of human behaviour, our own place in nature.

But there are other windows; windows that have been unshuttered by the logic of philosophers; windows through which the mystics seek their visions of the truth; windows from which the leaders of the great religions have peered as they searched for purpose not only in the wondrous beauty of the world, but also in its darkness and ugliness. Most of us, when we ponder on the mystery of our existence, peer through but one of these windows onto the world. And even that one is often misted over by the breath of our finite humanity. We clear a tiny peephole and stare through. No wonder we are confused by the tiny fraction of a whole that we see. It is, after all, like trying to comprehend the panorama of the desert or the sea through a rolled-up newspaper. (109)

How Should I Arrange Details?

Of course, arrangement depends upon the subject to some degree, but writers make deliberate choices about the placement of details. You might decide on a *chronological* strategy (presenting details through time), as Dillard and Goodall use. This strategy depends on narrative. But notice that both Dillard's and Goodall's essays do not depend entirely on narrative. For instance, Dillard begins with general reflections and a related account about weasels before offering a brief narrative. After the narrative, she explains the meaning and significance of her observation. The narrative is only a strategy to relay the details of her observation. You might also arrange the details *spatially*. Abbey, for example, organizes the first three paragraphs of his essay by discussing the spatial layout of his yard. As the essay develops, he uses paragraphs to shift from the rural setting to the city.

But chronological and spatial organization do not work for all topics. Chester McCovey's essay illustrates another set of strategies for arranging details. Like Dillard, McCovey devotes much of his essay to the significance or meaning of his observation. But where Dillard gives a narrative of her observation, McCovey shrinks the observation into a short introductory paragraph. (In other words, we do not witness McCovey encountering porches the way we witness Dillard encountering the weasel.) Because McCovey's point involves history (front porches are no longer central to our way of life), he moves to the past in the second paragraph. His essay, then, is arranged to illustrate the difference between the past and the present.

When Should I Change Paragraphs?

You might think of paragraph changes as camera shifts. That is, if you have a subject that allows spatial arrangement, change paragraphs whenever you want to create a new field of vision—whenever you want the reader to "see" a new thing or imagine a new scene. For example, Annie Dillard uses paragraph breaks to shift focus: from a tree to a whole span of the scene and then to a weasel. (Notice, also, the extra space that Dillard inserts before the paragraph about the weasel. Some writers do this occasionally to create a more emphatic break in the action.)

> Then I cut down through the woods to the mossy fall-en tree where I sit. This tree is excellent. It makes a dry, upholstered bench at the upper, marshy end of the pond, a plush jetty raised from the thorny shore between a shallow blue body of water and a deep blue body of sky.
>
> The sun had just set. I was relaxed on the tree trunk, ensconced in the lap of lichen, watching the lily pads at my feet tremble and part dreamily over the thrusting path of a carp. A yellow bird appeared to my right and flew behind me. It caught my eye; I swiveled around—and the next instant, inexplicably, I was looking down at a weasel, who was looking up at me.
>
> Weasel! I'd never seen one wild before. He was ten inches long, thin as a curve, a muscled ribbon, brown as fruitwood, soft-furred, alert. (99)

In his essay, Royce Flores's paragraphs help to shift spatial attention and to move from one span of time to another. Following are the first sentences of six consecutive paragraphs in Flores's essay:

> Before a tournament the gamers are lively, eagerly greeting all other participants that enter the store.
>
> Next the group of gamers slips into the second pre-tournament phase, which closely resembles that of the New York stock exchange.
>
> Once it is time for the names to be taken, the store grows silent.
>
> Contrary to the demeanor at the start of the day, the players now act as if they do not know each other.
>
> As players are eliminated, via best of three duels, they begin to gather around the better players to watch their games.
>
> As the tournament winds down, and the final match approaches, the less astute players filter away and the truly intense gamers stay, assured by the fact that if they walk away from watching the final, they'll miss a great play, the huge turn-around victory, or just an absent-minded folly on one of the finalists' part. (112–113)

Change paragraphs when you want to create a new field of vision.

WRITER'S VOICE

The Present "I"

Some writers choose to make themselves visible in the text. They refer to themselves and their interactions with the subject. Dillard, Goodall, Abbey, and McCovey all include themselves in their observations and refer to their own presence in the scenes or situations. But they do not simply inject the "I" without good cause. Goodall draws attention to her own presence because the essay is as much about the processes of observation as about the chimpanzees themselves. The presence of the writerly "I" illustrates her point about seeing "through a window." McCovey's presence helps to show the lack of front porches in a particular area, but his personal history (recollections of his grandparents) helps to make a point about changes that have occurred in American society. His use of the personal and of the present "I" gives support to his more general claims.

The present "I" can also be used to illustrate important human responses to a situation. The actual encounter between Dillard and the weasel is vital to the point of her essay. The stare between them provides insight into the weasel's life, and into Dillard's connection to such a life. Abbey uses the "I" to show the real human role in the retreat from civilization. Both Abbey and Dillard attempt to show the deep connection between human life and life beyond us. Without the "I" in these essays, the natural world (the world of the weasel and the desert) would seem more disconnected to their readers.

ACTIVITY

Rewrite the opening paragraph of either Abbey's or Dillard's essay without using the "I." Try to convey the information without attention to the writer. Then discuss how the change might influence how the essay is read.

The Invisible "I"

In observation, the writer is sometimes invisible. That is, the writerly "I" never appears; instead, the text focuses entirely on the subject. In John Steinbeck's "Americans and the Land" (in Chapter 2, Explaining Relationships), the "I" is present only periodically. It surfaces to present a remembered observation, but much of the text offers information without drawing attention to the personal observer. This does not mean the essay lacks a voice or that the essay is not based on Steinbeck's perspective.

Like Steinbeck, Royce Flores remains invisible in his observation. Flores's passage reminds us that writing without the "I" does not mean writing without an interesting voice and a personal feel. Although "I" is absent, the sentences still project a voice and attract the reader. Even though Flores does not draw attention to his own feelings and thoughts (by inserting phrases such as "I think"), an individual writer making personal choices is behind each sentence:

> White plastic tables lay suffocated in bags, drinks, cards, and most importantly "Ultra Pro" cases. Despite the clutter on top of them, the tables manage to remain in neat rows and columns. The shop reeks, a cocktail mix of young male perspiration and nacho cheese Doritos. The entire shop is glued together by the classic tunes of Double Rock KLT. On the rare occasion, a true classic like Ozzy Osbourne's "Crazy Train" catches the ear of the gamers, prompting outbursts of group singing and occasional air guitar performances. (111–112)

You might ask your instructor if he or she finds the writerly "I" valuable, but every writer should also ask some basic questions:

- Should I put myself in the observation?
- If "I" am in the observation, what purpose does it serve?

Level of Formality

Formality is the adherence to an established convention. A formal text is one that closely follows expectations and avoids slipping out of conventional language and organizational patterns. A business memo, for instance, has certain conventions or guidelines, and memo writers rarely deviate from them. This is because of *context*, the situation in which they are written and received. (Readers of memos in professional situations do not expect to follow a writer outside of the conventions.) Scientific reports also have specific conventions, depending on the discipline. The scientist follows the discipline's conventions so that the writing does not interfere with the ideas being communicated. A text that strictly follows conventions is usually considered formal, while a text that deviates is considered informal.

Because essays are used in a number of situations and academic disciplines, the conventions vary, and so does the expected level of formality. Generally, writing that draws no attention to the writer's presence or writing style is considered more formal, while writing that draws attention to the writer's presence and style is considered less formal. (Of course, this is a general rule, and it does not apply to all writing situations.)

In her essay, Dillard illustrates a variety of informal strategies. For instance, she makes explicit her own reflective state of mind. Here, Dillard constructs an elaborate metaphor and speaks directly to the reader (usually a more informal strategy). She draws attention to herself and her particular style with unconventional sentence structure. (Notice the one-word sentence, "So."):

> If you and I looked at each other that way, our skulls would split and drop to our shoulders. But we don't. We keep our skulls. So. (99)

Much of Dillard's essay, in fact, is a study in breaking conventions of formality:

> I would like to learn, or remember, how to live. I come to Hollins Pond not so much to learn how to live as, frankly, to forget about it. That is, I don't think I can learn from a wild animal how to live in particular—shall I suck warm blood, hold my tail high, walk with my footprints precisely over the prints of my hands?—but I might learn something of mindlessness, something of the purity of living in the physical senses and the dignity of living without bias or motive. (100)

In showing us the details of a weasel's life, Dillard goes beyond simply informing us. She does not say, "Weasels live in the purity of physical senses. They suck their prey's warm blood." Instead, she imagines herself in that purity ("Shall I suck warm blood?") and puts herself in the center of those details. Her sentence structure, which varies from very short, one-word sentences, to long, multi-layered musings, draws further attention to the writer's presence. In other words, as we read Dillard, we experience her particular style, her writerly strategies and intimate thoughts, as part of the essay. "Annie Dillard" is not simply a name inscribed at the top of the page. It is an identity competing for our attention and sharing her meditations on the essence of life.

ACTIVITY

Try to rewrite any paragraph in Dillard's essay using a very formal style that does not draw attention to the presence of the writer or the sentence structure. How does the level of formality affect the meaning?

Chester McCovey also uses unconventional strategies to communicate his ideas and, in doing so, draws attention to his own thought processes. Notice how McCovey breaks entirely from essay conventions and inserts a poetic stanza:

> how life must have splashed
> out of the cup
> on warm summer nights
> before the cool air
> of electricity
> urged us all to relax
> in the fluttering glow
> of color tv (115)

The move characterizes the essay's informality, but as with Dillard's informality, the essay's sophistication and complexity do not suffer. In fact, the informal or unconventional moves promote sophisticated ideas. McCovey goes on to draw attention to his relationship with the readers. McCovey's and Dillard's unconventional strategies are purposeful. They are not breaking rules for the sake of breaking rules.

As you consider your own writing, ask yourself:

- Should I break some academic conventions? What might be the consequences?
- Should I appear formal? Why? What good will it do?
- Should I put myself in the observation?
- Will my presence help communicate the main idea or distract the reader from experiencing the subject?

Formal: Adheres to conventions; avoids drawing attention to the writer.

Informal: Breaks or plays with conventions; may draw attention to the writer.

VITALITY

Sentences are the writer's only connection to readers. Engaging sentences lead to engaged readers. Flat, safe, unvaried sentences lead to disinterested readers. In short, sentence structure can make all the difference. Consider the following strategies:

Experiment with Length

If writers aren't careful, they can slip into monotone, in which every sentence has generally the same number of words, the same number of clauses, and the same types of phrases. Just as good speakers vary the sound of their voices, good writers vary the length of sentences. Notice this sentence from Jane Goodall's essay:

> A few moments later, the arboreal part of his display over, Goblin leapt down and charged past me, slapping and stamping on the wet ground, rearing up and shaking the vegetation, picking up and hurling a rock, an old piece of wood, another rock. (104)

Here, the sentence keeps us in the action. We follow the chimpanzee through the twists and turns of his movement. (Likewise, long sentences can keep readers focused on the twists and turns and nuances of an idea!) Of course, the danger with lengthy sentences is committing a run-on error. Goodall's might seem like a run-on sentence because it is so long, but gramatically, it is correct.

> Just as good speakers vary the sound of their voices, good writers vary the length of sentences.

Likewise, Bosley's stylistic sentence (from Chapter 1) is correct:

> So 14 of us, nervous, jealous, ears ringing with Mirror-Mirror-on-the-Wall, met daily for two weeks prior to the pageant to go over our choreographed group fitness routine to be performed, not in swimsuits, but in short-shorts and white T-shirts, Hooters-style (also not invented yet as far as we knew), and to discuss such techniques as Vaseline along the teeth and gum lines to promote smooth smiles, lest our lips dry out and get stuck in a grin during discussions with the judges of the agonies of world hunger. (7)

Such extreme moves are perilous, adventurous, and powerful. They take control of the reader's mind and demand a commitment.

Experiment with Brevity

Short sentences keep readers alert and moving—but only when they are interspersed with longer sentences. Notice how Goodall immediately follows her lengthy sentence with several short sentences:

> A few moments later, the arboreal part of his display over, Goblin leapt down and charged past me, slapping and stamping on the wet ground, rearing up and shaking the vegetation, picking up and hurling a rock, an old piece of wood, another rock. Then he sat, hair bristling, some fifteen feet away. He was breathing heavily. My own heart was beating fast. (104)

The change from long to short helps to create the drama, the life, of Goodall's observation. But short sentences can also help dramatize thought, as in this passage from McCovey:

> I am not saying there are no front porches. Obviously there are. And I am not saying everyone has a two-car garage instead. In my neighborhood, small garages not connected to the house still reign. (116)

Or notice the nuances that Dillard brings out with her short/long/short pattern:

> I missed my chance. I should have gone for the throat. I should have lunged for that streak of white under the weasel's chin and held on, held on through mud and into the wild rose, held on for a dearer life. We could live under the wild rose wild as weasels, mute and uncomprehending. I could very calmly go wild. (100)

In another passage, Dillard goes further with brevity—even breaking the rules of sentence construction:

> It felled the forest, moved the fields, and drained the pond; the world dismantled and tumbled into that black hole of eyes. If you and I looked at each other that way, our skulls would split and drop to our shoulders. But we don't. We keep our skulls. So. (99)

For information on stylistic fragments, see the Vitality section of Chapter 12 on page 606.

Change Out Vague Nouns

Vague nouns refer to nothing in particular: *people, society, things, everyone,* and so on. It is often tempting to rely on vague nouns to float ideas past readers. But vague nouns have at least two negative effects: (1) They keep the reader from focusing, and (2) they signal that the writer has not committed to a statement. Notice the difference between the two passages:

> Animals are wild. They do wild things that we humans cannot imagine.

> A weasel is wild. Who knows what he thinks? He sleeps in his underground den, his tail draped over his nose. (98)

The first sentence starts with a vague noun: *animals.* (That means all animals, everywhere!) And because the subject of the first sentence is so vague, the second sentence (equally vague) seems okay. The vague nouns lull the writer and reader into a relaxed state—in which broad, ill-defined statements seem fine. But Dillard demands more of her nouns, more of herself, and more of her readers. She starts with a more specific noun—a sharper focus. From there, she maintains that focus—and as readers, we follow her into a weasel's den!

Frankly, vague nouns plague college writing (and instructors everywhere dislike them). While they are not inherently evil (sometimes writers need to use words such as *things* and *people*), they generally make for vague statements.

Vital sentences demand the reader's commitment.

PEER REVIEW

Exchange drafts with at least one other writer. Before passing your draft to others, underline the thesis, or write it above your essay. This way, reviewers will get traction as they read.

As a reviewer, use the following questions to guide your response.

1. Point out any words or phrases in the thesis that could be more specific. (See the Thesis section for more guidance.)

2. Where can the writer do more analysis and reveal more about the subject in the observation? (Point to passages that seem most obvious to you. As you read, look for claims that anyone could immediately offer without intensive analysis. Beside these passages, write: "More analysis?" If you can suggest an interesting idea, explain it on the back of the writer's draft.)

3. Help the writer to illustrate his or her claims with details. As you read, look for broad characterizations—those that anyone could imagine without a close observation. Ask yourself: Could this be more specific? Can we *really* see the particular nuances of the subject? In the margin, write "more details" where the writer could more intensely show the points.

4. Offer some figurative language to help characterize the relationship. After you have read the entire draft, offer your own metaphor or simile about the relationship. Give your suggestion on the back of the draft. Make sure it is something that fits the writer's voice, something that he or she could use.

5. If the writer uses narrative, does it help support the main idea of the observation? How? (If you have difficulty explaining how it supports the main point, perhaps the writer should rethink its use in the essay!)

6. Are the paragraphs coherent? Do you ever get the sense that a paragraph is wandering—giving you details that seem unrelated to one another or unrelated to the point of the essay? If so, write in the margin: "check paragraph coherence."

7. The most focused statement possible often makes for a better introduction. Suggest a surprisingly focused opening statement. (The writer might decide to use it.)

8. Consider the writer's voice.
   - If the writer is present (using "I"), is this necessary? Explain how the presence of the writer helps make the point of the observation.
   - If the writer is invisible (no "I"), how is that beneficial?
   - Where could the writer be more informal (breaking some conventions) or more formal?

9. Point to particular sentences and phrases that could gain vitality and intensity. Use the following questions:
   - Help the writer experiment with length and brevity: Take one paragraph and rewrite its sentences. Combine some sentences, weaving together several interconnected ideas. Shorten other sentences so that the passage tugs and pulls, varying long and short sentences for a dramatic effect.
   - Change out vague nouns. Underline vague nouns (such as *people, society, things,* etc.) and suggest more specific words.
   - Consider vitality strategies from other chapters:
     —Change *be* verbs to active verbs.
     —Change clauses to phrases.
     —Change phrases to words.
     —Combine sentences.
     —Repeat structures.
     —Intensify verbs.

10. Help the reader avoid common grammatical errors: comma splices, sentence fragments, or pronoun/antecedent agreement.

Peer Review Truisms

- The process can make writers think differently about their own work.
- Even the most inexperienced writer can offer valuable comments.
- Chat is the great enemy of good analysis.
- Peer review can be the most valuable component of a writing class.
- All writers need help.
- Done carelessly, peer review can be a terrible thing.

For more explanation, see Chapter 1, pages 46–47.

DELIVERY

What we value dictates how we see. What we believe in controls the conclusions we make about the world. For example, someone looking at a car lot full of shiny SUVs might see ridiculous and costly waste, while someone else might see opportunity and signs of success.

Person A

- Values moderation, health, conserving resources, family comfort.
- Believes that people should tread carefully upon the Earth.
- Believes most people are victims of materialist propaganda.
- Hopes for a future with cleaner air, better health, less poverty, and less international strife.
- Sees a lot full of SUVs as a shiny, attractive waste of resources, a nicely structured delusion about the present and the future.

Person B

- Values financial success, health, nice neighborhoods, family comfort
- Believes that people should reap the benefits of their hard work, that human desire is good for the economy, that material things support the pursuit of happiness.
- Believes most people do not work hard enough for what they want.
- Hopes for a future of more economic stability, upward mobility, and less international strife.
- Sees a lot full of SUVs as a sign of America's economic success and people's individual hopes for a more stable and secure life.

Now that you have written an observing essay—and have come to your own conclusions—answer the following questions:

- What values lie beneath my conclusions?
- What beliefs (about people, the past, the present, the future, comfort, animals, cities, etc.) lie beneath my conclusions?
- What hopes for myself, for the future, for all people might have influenced the way I see the subject of the observation?
- More than anything else, what value or belief controlled the way I saw the subject?

Beyond the Essay: An Illustration

Sophisticated ideas can be embodied in various kinds of texts, not just essays. Many writers like to draw their ideas, illustrating them with images and symbols. In this rendering, Chester McCovey illustrates the main distinctions between the porch of the past and the garage of the present:

Consider your own observation. What is the main idea? What new insight do you offer? What important notion do you reveal? What hidden meaning do you dig up and share with readers? How can you illustrate those ideas?

Front Porch

- Sunlight
- Cool Breeze
- Visiting with Neighbors
- Simplicity
- Community

Big Garage

- Electricity
- Air Conditioning
- Sitting in Traffic
- High-Tech Machines

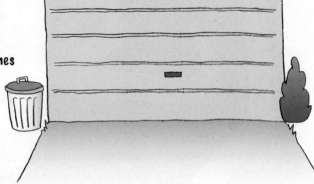

Try your hand at illustrating the main point of your observation.

ANALYZING CONCEPTS

Chapter Contents

CHAPTER

"Concepts have no 'real' definitions; instead, they have uses. They are our ways of coming to understand the world and deciding how to behave within it."

—Susan R. Horton

Concepts are ideas or abstract formulations. They are generalized notions beyond specifics. For example, we have concepts of *college, marriage, friendship,* or *technology* that go beyond any particular college, spouse, friend, or piece of equipment. And when our colleges, spouses, friends, and machines do not measure up to our concepts, we get frustrated, and we may even alter our concepts.

Within a particular culture, concepts change, sometimes drastically. Consider how the concept of *president* has changed for many people. Before the Watergate scandal (involving President Nixon), the Iran Contra scandal (involving President Reagan), and the Monica Lewinsky scandal (involving President Clinton), most Americans' concept of *president* probably did not include scandal. But in the wake of such events, the concept has changed. Or consider how the idea of *America* changed after September 11, 2001. Before that date, most Americans probably did not consider how their country related to the concerns of people in the Middle East; however, after the terrorist attacks, Americans' concept shifted to accommodate our role in global politics.

Of course, people do not always agree on concepts. A dispute over a concept is often the catalyst for major conflict between people, cultures, and countries. Think about the intense and extended battles brought on by differing notions of *God* or of the political struggles brought on by differing concepts of *woman, man, family,* or *life*. Analyzing concepts turns out to be a rather important and sticky business.

In academia, students and professors are mired in the process of analyzing, discussing, and arguing about concepts. Consider, for example, *sex:*

- In a biology course, students discuss sex as reproduction. The concept in biology involves the study of hormones and reproductive systems (egg, sperm, gestation periods, embryo, and so on).

- In psychology, sex might be understood as a complex of drives. Students explore it using Freud's understanding of sexual development, repression, and parental affiliation.

- In sociology, students might approach sex as socially patterned behavior. A sociological understanding of sex may involve the study of social customs (such as dancing, clothing, dating, and marriage).

These concepts of sex are obviously different; in fact, many people claim that a discipline's take on a concept partly defines that discipline. (In other words, part of what defines a sociologist is how he or she understands *sex* or *community* or *family*.) Disciplines also focus on and develop their own concepts (*ego*, for instance, is a concept developed by psychology). And much of your college career will involve exploring and analyzing the main concepts of different disciplines and in your chosen field.

This chapter will help you analyze a particular concept, develop focused explanation, and communicate your ideas in writing. The following essays will provide valuable insight into various analytical strategies. After reading the essays, you can find a concept in one of two ways:

1. Go to the **Point of Contact** section to find a topic from everyday life.
2. Choose one of the **Ideas for Writing** that follow the essays.

After finding a subject, go to the **Analysis** section to begin developing the evaluation.

The authors in this chapter analyze concepts (such as *college, student, and creativity*). But notice that each has a purpose beyond mere analysis. That is, each author offers the analysis as a contribution to our understanding of the concept. Iyer's discussion of punctuation, for example, sheds new light on language, and Hayakawa helps us to understand the meaning of creativity. Some analyses can even impact the way we live. Bass's essay, for example, might influence someone's approach to college, and Benlow's essay might change how students take on their academic responsibilities.

In Praise of the Humble Comma

Pico Iyer

Our concepts are not concrete or stagnant. They change and are revised. For example, as we grow and have new experiences, we come to think differently about *Santa Claus, education, police officer,* and *smoking.* Whether or not you are moved by Pico Iyer's praise of the comma, his essay illustrates how it is possible to broaden one's understanding of something—not just to know more about it, but to understand it differently.

The gods, they say, give breath, and they take it away. But the same could be said—could it not?—of the humble comma. Add it to the present clause and, of a sudden, the mind is, quite literally, given pause to think; take it out if you wish or forget it and the mind is deprived of a resting place. Yet still the comma gets no respect. It seems just a slip of a thing, a pedant's tick, a blip on the edge of our consciousness, a kind of printer's smudge almost. Small, we claim, is beautiful (especially in the age of the microchip). Yet what is so often used, and so rarely recalled, as the comma—unless it be breath itself?

Punctuation, one is taught, has a point: to keep up law and order. Punctuation marks are the road signs placed along the highway of our communication—to control speeds, provide directions, and prevent head-on collisions. A period has the unblinking finality of a red light; the comma is a flashing yellow light that asks us only to slow down; and the semicolon is a Stop sign that tells us to ease gradually to a halt, before gradually starting up again. By establishing the relations between words, punctuation establishes the relations between the people using words. That may be one reason why schoolteachers exalt it, and lovers defy it ("We love each other and belong to each other let's don't ever hurt each other Nicole let's don't ever hurt each other," wrote Gary Gilmore to his girlfriend.) A comma, he must have known, "separates inseparables," in the clinching words of H. W. Fowler, king of English Usage.

Punctuation, then, is a civic prop, a pillar that holds society upright. (A run-on sentence, its phrases piling up without division, is as unsightly as a sink piled high with dirty dishes.) Small wonder, then, that punctuation was one of the first proprieties of the Victorian Age, the age of the corset, that the modernists threw off: the sexual revolution might be said to have begun when Joyce's Molly Bloom spilled out all her private thoughts in thirty-six pages of panting, unperioded, and officially censored prose; and another rebellion was surely marked when e. e. cummings first committed "god" to the lower case.

Punctuation thus becomes the signature of cultures. The hot-blooded Spaniard seems to be revealed in the passion and urgency of his doubled exclamation points and question marks ("¡Caramba! ¿Quién sabe?"), while the impassive Chinese traditionally added to his so-called inscrutability by omitting all directions from his ideograms. The anarchy and commotion of the sixties were given voice in the exploding exclamation marks, riotous capital letters, and Day-Glo italics of Tom Wolfe's spray-paint prose; and in Communist societies, where the State is absolute, the dignity—and divinity—of capital letters is reserved for Ministries, Subcommittees, and Secretariats.

5   Yet punctuation is something more than a culture's birthmark; it scores the music in our minds, gets our thoughts moving to the rhythm of our hearts. Punctuation is the notation in the sheet music of our words, telling us when to rest, or when to raise our voices; it acknowledges that the meaning of our discourse, as of any symphonic composition, lies not in the units but in the pauses, the pacing, and the phrasing. Punctuation is the way one bats one's eyes, lowers one's voice, or blushes demurely. Punctuation adjusts color and tone and volume till the feeling comes into perfect focus: not disgust exactly, but distaste; not lust, or like, but love.

Punctuation, in short, gives us the human voice, and all the meanings that lie between the words. "You aren't young, are you?" loses its innocence when it loses the question mark. Every child knows the menace of a dropped apostrophe (the parent's "Don't do that" shifting into the more slowly enunciated "Do not do that") and every believer the ignominy of having his faith reduced to "faith." Add an exclamation point to "To be or not to be . . ." and the gloomy Dane has all the resolve he needs; add a comma, and the noble sobriety of "God save the Queen" becomes a cry of desperation bordering on double sacrilege.

Sometimes, of course, our markings may be simply a matter of aesthetics. Popping in a comma can be like slipping on the necklace that gives an outfit quiet elegance, or like catching the sound of running water that complements, as it completes, the silence of a Japanese landscape. When V. S. Naipaul, in his latest novel, writes, "He was a middle-aged man, with glasses," the first comma can seem a little precious. Yet it gives the description a spin, as well as a subtlety, that it otherwise lacks, and it shows that the glasses are not part of the middle-agedness, but something else.

Thus all these tiny scratches give us breadth and heft and depth. A world that has only periods is a world without inflections. It is a world without shade. It has a music without sharps and flats. It is a martial music. It has a jackboot rhythm. Words cannot bend and curve. A comma, by comparison, catches the gentle drift of the mind in thought, turning in on itself and back on itself, reversing, redoubling, and returning along the course of its own sweet river music; while the semicolon brings clauses and thoughts together with all the silent discretion of a hostess arranging guests around her dinner table.

Punctuation, then, is a matter of care. Care for words, yes, but also, and more important, for what the words imply. Only a lover notices the small things: the way the afternoon light catches the nape of a neck, or how a strand of hair slips out from behind an ear, or the way a finger curls around a cup. And no one scans a letter so closely as a lover, searching for the small print, straining to hear its nuances, its gasps, its sighs and hesitations, poring over the secret messages that lie in every cadence. The difference between "Jane (whom I adore)" and "Jane, whom I adore," and the difference between them both and "Jane—whom I adore," marks all the distance between ecstasy and heartache. "No iron can pierce the heart with such force as a period put at just the right place," in Isaac Babel's lovely words; a comma can let us hear a voice break, or a heart. Punctuation, in fact, is a labor of love. Which brings us back, in a way, to gods.

Writing Strategies

1. How does Iyer invite the reader to his text? That is, how does Iyer make his text inviting to the reader?

2. Iyer uses figurative language such as metaphors ("punctuation is a pillar") and similes ("using a comma is like slipping on a necklace"). Find several other uses of figurative language in Iyer's essay. Are they successful? How does his use of figurative language help the reader to understand his point?

3. Iyer says punctuation "gives us the human voice, and all the meanings that lie between the words." (¶ 6) Identify one sentence in any essay besides Iyer's, and punctuate it in three different ways, each way suggesting a different meaning.

4. Study Iyer's organization. How does he introduce new topics in his essay? What strategy does he use to connect one idea to another?

Exploring Ideas

1. What is Iyer trying to accomplish in this essay?

2. How does Iyer encourage the reader to think differently about commas? How might Iyer's essay encourage the reader to think differently about bigger issues than commas?

3. Examine syllabi from several classes that you and/or others are taking. Compare the way different professors use commas and other forms of punctuation. What, if anything, might the writer's punctuation say about the writer?

4. Look further at your study of professors' syllabi begun in #3 above. This time, include word choice, sentence structure, and document design in your analysis. Aside from the content expressed in the syllabus, what message do you get from the way the writer expresses that content? Explain your analysis in several paragraphs.

Ideas for Writing

1. What common object or familiar event can you define in a new and helpful way?

2. What everyday object or event deserves more respect than it gets? Consider objects and events that are so common (such as the comma) that they get overlooked.

If responding to one of these ideas, go to the **Analysis** section of this chapter to begin developing ideas for your essay.

What It Means to Be Creative

S. I. Hayakawa

Analyzing a concept requires some intellectual digging. We have to dig into common terms—ones that we normally take for granted. We also have to imagine a good deal of complexity beneath those common terms. In this essay, S. I. Hayakawa reveals the complexities beneath *creativity*. He goes beyond merely describing creative people to breaking down the concept and showing us what it is and how it works.

What distinguishes the creative person? By creative person I don't mean only the great painter or poet or musician. I also want to include the creative housewife, teacher, warehouseman, sales manager—anyone who is able to break through habitual routines and invent new solutions to old problems, solutions that strike people with their appropriateness as well as originality, so that they say, "Why didn't I think of that?"

A creative person, first, is not limited in his thinking to "what everyone knows." "Everyone knows" that trees are green. The creative artist is able to see that in certain lights some trees look blue or purple or yellow. The creative person looks at the world with his or her own eyes, not with the eyes of others. The creative individual also knows his or her own feelings better than the average person. Most people don't know the answer to the question, "How are you? How do you feel?" The reason they don't know is that they are so busy feeling what they are supposed to feel, thinking what they are supposed to think, that they never get down to examining their own deepest feelings.

"How did you like the play?" "Oh, it was a fine play. It was well reviewed in *The New Yorker.*"

With authority figures like drama critics and book reviewers and teachers and professors telling us what to think and how to feel, many of us are busy playing roles, fulfilling other people's expectations. As Republicans, we think what other Republicans think. As Catholics, we think what other Catholics think. And so on. Not many of us ask ourselves, "How do I feel? What do I think?"—and wait for answers.

5   Another characteristic of the creative person is that he is able to entertain and play with ideas that the average person may regard as silly, mistaken, or downright dangerous. All new ideas sound foolish at first, because they are new. (In the early days of the railroad, it was argued that speeds of twenty-five mph or over were impractical because people's brains would burst.) A person who is afraid of being laughed at or disapproved of for having "foolish" or "unsound" ideas will have the satisfaction of having everyone agree with him, but he will never be creative, because creativity means being willing to take a chance—to go out on a limb.

The person who would be creative must be able to endure loneliness—even ridicule. If he has a great and original idea that others are not yet ready to accept, there will be long periods of loneliness. There will be times when his friends and relatives think he is crazy, and he'll begin to wonder if they are right. A genuinely creative person, believing in his creation, is able to endure this loneliness—for years if necessary.

Another trait of the creative person is idle curiosity. Such a person asks questions, reads books, conducts investigations into matters apparently unrelated to job or profession—just for the fun of knowing. It is from these apparently unrelated sources that brilliant ideas often emerge to enrich one's own field of work.

Finally, the creative person plays hunches. "Pure intellect," says Dr. Hans Selye, the great medical researcher at the University of Montreal, "is largely a quality of the middle-class mind. The lowliest hooligan and the greatest creator in the fields of science are activated mainly by imponderable instincts and emotions, especially faith. Curiously, even scientific research, the most intellectual creative effort of which man is capable, is no exception in this respect."

Alfred Korzybski also understood well the role of undefinable emotions in the creative life. He wrote, "Creative scientists know very well from observation of themselves that all creative work starts as a feeling, inclination, suspicion, intuition, hunch, or some other nonverbal affective state, which only at a later date, after a sort of nursing, takes the shape of verbal expression worked out later in a rationalized, coherent . . . theory."

10   Creativity is the act of bringing something new into the world, whether a symphony, a novel, an improved layout for a supermarket, a new and unex-pected casserole dish. It is based first on communication with oneself, then testing that communication with experience and the realities one has to contend with. The result is the highest, most exciting kind of learning.

Writing Strategies

1. Describe the strategy Hayakawa uses to help the reader to understand the term "creative." That is, how specifically does he make the term clear to the reader?

2. Describe Hayakawa's voice—the way he sounds to the reader.

3. Would you describe Hayakawa's writing as creative? Explain what is or is not creative about his writing.

4. How does Hayakawa lead the reader from one paragraph to another? Select several paragraphs as examples for your explanation.

Exploring Ideas

1. Rate yourself on your own creativity scale. Be ready to support your claim.

2. Hayakawa says that one trait of the creative person is "idle curiosity"—asking questions, reading books, con-ducting investigations into matters "apparently unrelat-ed to job or profession—just for the fun of knowing." Ask others to list several traits of the creative person, and then explain how their ideas about creativity are similar to or different from Hayakawa's.

3. In what ways is writing an essay an act of "creativity"? List Hayakawa's main points (or characteristics) of cre-ativity and apply them to writing an essay. Which ones apply? Which ones don't?

4. Ask several people that you consider to be creative why they do those things that make you consider them to be creative. Explore their creative history and what contin-ues to stimulate their creativity.

Ideas for Writing

1. Based on Hayakawa's definition of "creative," who is not generally considered creative but in fact is?

2. Hayakawa's essay analyzes the concept of "creativity" or "the creative person." What other concepts might you analyze?

good teacher	great band
Thanksgiving dinner	good sermon
best friend	humanitarian
snappy dresser	nice day
bad waitress	good president
rewarding experience	parent

If responding to one of these ideas, go to the **Analysis** sec-tion of this chapter to begin developing ideas for your essay.

"Have It Your Way": Consumerism Invades Education

Simon Benlow

What is a student? This might sound like a silly question, but *student* can be defined in different ways. So can *education*. And the way a person defines or understands these concepts can make a difference in the way that person—and others—acts. In the following essay, Simon Benlow explores what it means to be a student and to participate in an education. Notice how Benlow narrows his focus. He doesn't talk generally about all the characteristics of education, but instead examines the important role consumerism (another concept) plays in education.

Two weeks ago, the faculty and staff received a memo regarding "National Customer Service Week." We were urged to take special efforts in serving our customers—presumably, our students. Certainly, I have no objections to extending extra efforts in helping students feel comfortable and situated in the college environment. However, I am deeply troubled (as are many, or most, instructors and professors) by use of the term "customer" to refer to students. I am concerned, in general, about the slow and subtle infiltration of consumerism into education (by companies buying access to students' brains), and I am downright hostile to the way "customer" has suddenly replaced the word (and maybe idea of) "student" in higher education. And because my concerns may seem ungrounded, I'd like to offer a brief analysis—a quick examination of the basic, and not-so-basic, differences between "customer" and "student."

"The customer is always right." We hear this hollow phrase resound through (almost) every corridor of our consumerist culture. The motive behind the phrase is painfully clear—to keep customers happy, to keep them from complaining, and most importantly, to keep them coming back. (Of course, the meaninglessness of the phrase is well known, too—for those of us who have had the displeasure of talking with Ameritech operators or "customer service" tellers at our banks.) The phrase is meant to maintain a climate in which the substance of anyone's concerns or complaints is obfuscated by friendly and diplomatic clichés—"your business means so much to us"; "we'll do everything we can to address the problem." Ultimately, then, the goal of customer service, in this sense, is to lull customers into a sense of complacency—even though their phones may not be working or their washers are throwing sparks.

"Have it your way!" Of course, we all know the song and the friendly fried food establishment associated with this slogan. It's a harmless phrase, in and of itself, and one that works particularly well for the franchise. It suggests to customers that their particular appetites can be catered to, that their specific tastes, no matter how eccentric (within the continuum of dip n' serve fried food) can be easily satisfied. It promotes the idea that the institution will shift its entire set of processes to meet the desires of the individual.

The meal deal bargain. Recently, in our hyper-drive-thru culture, we've been given a new ticket to ride—a quicker and easier way to get fast food (and a host of other things as well): the combo or meal deal. In the old days, we had to pull up to the drive-thru board, search under "Sandwiches" and THEN go through the labor of exploring "Sides" and "Beverages." It was all too much. Now, we can simply pull up, and say a number. We don't even have to trouble ourselves with uttering all the stuff we want to eat. We just say, "#1 with a diet." The meal deal craze is, of course, not limited to fast food; it is, simply, most explicitly manifested in the fast food industry. That is, in the fast food world, we can clearly see the motives of an increasingly consumerized culture: (1) to limit the interaction between the provider and the customer, (2) to limit the time the customer has to reflect on his/her wants, and 3) to limit the energy the customer has to exert.

5   Passivity. Customers are encouraged to be passive. We are prompted in a variety of ways not to be agents of our own making. Our needs and desires are met by

the work of others. As customers, we pay for someone else's work, for someone else's acts of invention, creation, and production. And we not only hire out our activities (painting our homes, cooking our dinners); we also hire out our imaginations. We don't even have to imagine what is possible. Others have already done the imagining, created a product or service and have told us how we can use it. (They've even taken the extra step of telling us what NOT to do: "Women who are pregnant or who may become pregnant should not take, or even handle, these pills.") In short, *the world of the customer is based on intellectual inactivity;* we merely have to dial the phone, get online, say a number. We don't have to reflect, invent, produce, or research (*Consumer's Reports* has done it already). Nor do we have to shop: they will deliver. Being a customer means being driven by simple and personal desires . . . and ultimately demanding that those desires be met.

Contrary to the passive, personalizing, self-perpetuating, desire-driven customer, students are encouraged to be active. In college, students cannot simply consume knowledge. Even in its most packaged form, the textbook, knowledge must be regenerated, revised, reinterpreted, and remembered in order to be anything beyond an answer on a multiple-choice test. Students who read textbooks, literature, and articles passively will get nothing from them—it is a kind of paralyzing higher education illiteracy. Certainly, they will be able to read something aloud, or even to themselves, and maybe summarize a main point; however, they will not know how to imagine the implications or significance of a textbook chapter. (And this is what academics mean when they say, "Our students don't know how to *make meaning*.")

Students who come to college with a consumerist attitude are lost. Because they are anticipating their most basic desires will be stimulated (because that's how people are massaged into buying stuff they don't need), consumerist students come to college waiting to be tickled, waiting to see the big boom, waiting for the car chase or the sex scene, waiting for the french fry, waiting for the Cherry Coke. What they encounter, however, are rooms filled with ingredients. They see only black and white words—where they anticipate smashy colors and extravagant tools for getting their attention. In the face of pure ingredients (the stuff for making meaning), they will be confused . . . and ultimately, terribly bored.

Consumerist students (or those who have been tricked into thinking like consumers) will also have a difficult time understanding principles. Principles, established doctrines which are to be followed, or evaluated, in the processes of making knowledge, don't really exist in consumer culture (unless you count slogans as doctrines). Because everything is based on the eccentricities of the individual ("hold the pickle, hold the lettuce"), the individual need not ever think outside of his/her own desires and the reality that is created from projecting those desires onto everything and everyone in view. In higher education, principles establish how a discipline works. Physics works on principles of matter and energy. The goal of a physicist is to discover the principles and understand how they can be used. Composition works on principles—conventions of grammar and persuasion. This is not to say that all knowledge is prescribed. On the contrary, students in such classes are encouraged to invent, to break rules, to go beyond. But in order to do so, they need certain ground rules; they need to understand that certain principles exist in the world outside of their own desires. (One cannot do chemistry and simply dismiss algebra because it is distasteful.)

When I think back to the best teachers and professors in my education, I recall those who demanded everything contrary to the consumerist mentality. They insisted on active students; they made us read staggering amounts of material and then actively put that material to use; they prompted us into confusion and disorientation; they made us uncomfortable, and then, sometimes, offered paths to clarity. In short, they made us into critical, reflective agents of our own becoming, rather than passive bags of desire. Everything valuable about my education came from instructors and professors who were free from the ridiculous tyranny of consumerism.

10 There is no way higher education can counter the incredible momentum of consumerist culture. It is far more pervasive than the discourses of physics or composition studies. However, if we continue to allow the term "customer" to replace "student," I fear that students will become increasingly blind to the difference between consumerist culture and college culture. I fear they will become increasingly more confused by the expectations of college, and that in the nightmarish long run, colleges will become simply another extension of the consumerist machine in which everyone is encouraged to pre-package knowledge, to super-size grades, and to "hold" anything even slightly distasteful.

Writing Strategies

1. Evaluate Benlow's title. Is it effective?

2. How is, or isn't, Benlow's voice appropriate to his subject matter?

3. Benlow alludes throughout his essay to pop culture. Find several allusions that you think are successful and explain why. Which, if any, of his allusions do you think fail?

4. If helping Benlow with his essay, what one suggestion would you make?

5. In your view, what makes Benlow's conclusion effective or ineffective?

Exploring Ideas

1. What important distinction does Benlow make between "students" and "consumers"?

2. Interview others to find out if they think students are "customers." Then identify trends in the data you have collected. For example, do certain groups tend to give the same response, or do responses vary?

3. Explain Benlow's reasoning to several people who feel strongly that students are the "customers." Record their responses to Benlow's argument. What aspect of his argument made someone think differently? What were the most convincing, or interesting, responses to what Benlow says?

Ideas for Writing

1. What term is defined, or thought of, incorrectly?

2. Do members of some other group define themselves incorrectly?

If responding to one of these ideas, go to the **Analysis** section of this chapter to begin developing ideas for your essay.

In Search of . . . Something

Skye Bass

Concepts are abstractions—but they operate in the
practice of everyday life. People's concepts prompt
them to make particular decisions and to avoid making
others. And in the rolling unreflective experience of
everyday life, good writers come along and remind us
how our concepts work. In this essay, Skye Bass shakes
loose some common thinking about education, particularly how it gets sold to college students as an illusion.
After she breaks the illusion, she offers a more realistic
understanding of the concept.

College students constantly hear the praises of education as if it were the blueprint to receiving our desires.
There should be a salesman on every major television
network in the country wearing an overpriced suit
screaming: "Education is the answer! Go to school and
everything will come. Just look at what I have." Well,
there are. But they don't come in the form of a salesman. We leave educational promotion to the most
impressive individuals like our fabulously famous
celebrities and our powerfully pleasing politicians. If an
old wrinkly homeless man, with no teeth and no hair,
wearing nothing but rags, did the same commercial,
saying the same things about education, we would turn
the channel. Why? Because we need to see education as
a tool for getting the stuff we want. Put that bum in a
Mercedes-Benz and a double-breasted suit and society
is all ears.

Due to our growing fascination with "pick-me-
ups," we have all become accustomed to believing that
a college education is always a guarantee to an easier
life, a life that includes a well-paying job and a comfortable lifestyle. From birth, our future generations are
force-fed the importance of going to college. Education
is sold like a prescription drug. The symptom is: unhap-
piness in current lifestyle. The cure: high doses of a college education. The concept of obtaining a degree is the
new and improved security blanket.

I was nine years old when my fourth-grade teacher
presented me with an assignment, to write down all of
the things that I wanted in my life. I filled my paper
with things like: own a mansion and have servants to do
my chores; be rich and write books as magnificent as
The Boxcar Children. The next day my teacher handed
back my paper and in red ink she wrote: "GO TO
COLLEGE." For a long time, I was convinced that a
college education was the formula to everything I wanted and therefore once I obtained an education, BAM!
Life would be easier.

Education is not a genie that grants all wishes,
dreams, and desires. Just because we pay for a college
education does not mean that we are paying to receive
our wishes or ensuring a positive future. In "'Have It
Your Way': Consumerism Invades Education," Simon
Benlow argues that society has programmed students to
think like consumers and that in college, they will
expect to be served their education: "Students who
come to college with a consumerist attitude will be lost.
Because they are anticipating their most basic desires
will be stimulated" (152). More and more students are
coming to college to excite their desires and not to truly
learn and evaluate the things they hold true.

5   Society must reject this foolish idea that a college
education's main purpose is to glamorize life, fulfill our
desires, and secure success. Many students believe that
an education will "pick them up" out of their current
minimum-wage-earning, used-vehicle-driving, can't-
get-benefits-without-mom-or-dad situation. They
expect to be propelled into a lifestyle where all of their
dreams come true without effort. But like most challenging things, education is a gamble in which results
depend entirely on the individual's ability to look past
his/her wants to see the realism and reason behind
them. When people "decide" to go to college, they are
opening up the insides of their desires by examining
and dissecting them.

For instance, my first year of college, I took a sociology class. In class, we were taught about Third World
country poverty and income inequalities. We learned

"Education is not a genie that grants all wishes, dreams, and desires."

meant that I had to look past what I had always assumed. Learning is challenging because it doesn't allow the same way of thinking. A student could go into college believing one thing and come out changing his or her beliefs altogether. Being enlightened about the rest of the world required me to examine my own world and desires.

Through the process of education, everything once desired is tested. Wanting something no longer is enough; justification of why we want something becomes imperative to discovering what we really want. When our desires change, we change. Our desires are what drive us to make decisions and value the things we do. When my craving for money changed, everything changed. I stopped longing for money-driven careers and stopped valuing the people who had them. I began to examine the things I purchased and my reason for wanting them. *I wanted an education to get something, not to discover something.*

Education is a tool to be used to develop and advance our desires, so we can discover the things that are truly significant in life. Education is a source to expand our society to see beyond the superficial appeals and the "quick fixes," leaving the notion of an effortless life behind in order to desire a meaningful one.

that our quality of life would be almost impossible for an average person in those countries to achieve. Over the years, consuming ideas of grandeur and money-oriented passions filled my thoughts. The more I read about people suffering from starvation, the more I began to examine my own desire to be insanely rich. To always lust after money felt selfish when knowing others had none at all. Learning about other society's financial situations forced me to look beyond what I wanted. To closely examine another country's financial reality

Work Cited

Benlow, Simon. "'Have It Your Way': Consumerism Invades Education." <u>The Composition of Everyday Life</u>. 2nd ed. Ed. John Mauk and John Metz. Boston: Wadsworth, 2007. 151–53.

Writing Strategies

1. What points does Bass make through personal anecdote? How else might she have made these same points?

2. How does Bass understand the concept of education? How is her essay a response to other understandings of the concept?

3. If workshopping Bass's essay, how would you respond to the following:

   • How does the essay try to help the reader understand the concept differently?

   • What additional information might help the reader?

Exploring Ideas

1. How did Bass's sociology class help her to think differently about the concept of education?

2. How is Bass's sociology class an example of education in action? What did Bass learn? How did she learn it? How did it impact her life outside the classroom?

3. What class or experience helped you to develop your concept of education?

Ideas for Writing

1. Identify times in your life when you had different concepts of education. You might explore how the concepts impacted your life or why they changed.

2. What other concept, besides education, is impacted by materialism or consumerism?

If responding to one of these ideas, go to the **Analysis** section of this chapter to begin developing ideas for your essay.

Why We No Longer Use the "H" Word

Dan Wilkins

In the margins of this essay, a reader's comments point to key ideas and writing strategies. As you read the essay, consider how the comments might influence your own reading and writing.

Words such as "handicapped" are automatic. We don't give them much thought until someone like Dan Wilkins shows us something we didn't know about the concept. As with the other readings in this chapter, this essay not only helps the reader to understand a particular concept differently, but it shows us that our concepts are fluid. Concepts can—and do—change.

Writing Strategies

Title indicates main idea; reader must read on to find out why.

Introduces concept; suggests why analyzing it is important.

Explains origin of the term.

Compares concept/ term to another concept/term.

To develop analysis, discusses an important, relevant, and popular aspect of the concept.

Exploring Ideas

The word "handicap" offends for a couple of reasons.

not the same as "disabled"

"handicap" = pity

Do others agree with Wilkins? Is his opinion popular among disabled people?

Is he being too hard on Jerry? Is Jerry helping or causing damage?

What is it about the word "handicap" that so offends many of us living with disabilities? Within our disability culture, progressive thinking has steered us away from using the word "handicapped" as a label or descriptor for someone living with a disability for a couple of reasons. To begin with, contrary to long-time societal thinking, it is not synonymous with the word "disabled." More on this in a moment.

Most importantly, it is the very origin of the word that leaves such a bad taste in our mouths. It conjures up imagery that perpetuates archaic misperceptions of the value of people living with disabilities and their potential for contribution to their community and to humanity as a whole.

The word comes from old-world England when the only way many with disabilities could survive was to sit on a corner or on the side of the road with a "handy cap" held out for passers-by to fill out of pity. A pretty negative connotation. Not at all an empowering legacy, is it? And, sadly, it is not just a part of our distant past . . . .

I do not wish to break from the "handicap vs. disability" issue, but it is important to point out that this basic premise of projecting pity as a mechanism for exacting funds from the masses is still being used today. If I may rant for a paragraph, children and adults with disabilities continue to be exploited every day, most visibly every Labor Day when Jerry Lewis does his annual Smellathon, er, telethon. Twenty-four hours of patting and hugging "poor, helpless cripples" until FINALLY, in the last five minutes, through red blurry eyes, hair mussed, sleeves uncuffed, bow tie loosened and akimbo, sweat dripping and sleep deprived, he tells us, with all the apparent (or is that transparent) sincerity of a really bad lounge singer, that we "will never walk alone." (Hey, Jerry, I'll never walk

AGAIN! and truth be told, that's OK.) He demands that we, the heart-wrenched public, give, GIVE, until it hurts. GIVE, so that, for another year, we can walk the street unashamed to look someone in the eye; unashamed that we might have fearful, discriminatory thoughts toward "those people," unashamed that our society continues to fight equity and access to all it has to offer. Buy the premise, pay the dues, and it's another year of "no fault insurance."

5   Jerry isn't the only one, just the most notorious. There are others. Be wary. Kahlil Gibran said "the gifts which derive from Justice are greater than those which spring from Charity." There is power in this statement. If you want to make a difference and, at the same time, help put an end to the pattern of pity and paternalization, find an organization that is promoting self-control and independent living; one whose mission is that of building confidence and ability, awareness and community. Try your local Center for Independent Living. It'll be money or time well spent.

Back to disability vs. handicap. Now that we know the origin of the word, we realize that there is little dignity to be found there, except when we look into the souls of those who, over history, wrapped themselves in the label like a banner when there was no other word; who lived, fought, and died defending their right to belong in a world trying so hard to eliminate them or hide them away.

All this is not to say that there is no appropriate context in which to use the word "handicap" or "handicapped." There is. Let me explain.

I have a disability. I broke my neck in an auto accident in 1980. It is an integral part of who I am and, to some degree, it impacts the way I do things in the world. I only become "handicapped" when I cannot reach a goal.

It may be a narrow door, or a set of steps, an inaccessible parking structure, or a restaurant with no accessible bathroom. For some it may be no signage or braille menus, no interpreter or service dogs allowed. It may be someone's attitude out there: "Hey! You can't come in here! We didn't vote for the law and we're not making changes" or my own attitude: "I'm just a quad . . . I'll never amount to anything."

10   Though I'm not big on continuums, let me illustrate it this way. Two lines. One horizontal. One vertical. They form a big plus sign. (See diagram.) The horizontal line represents disability and the (relative, and I stress relative) significance of its involvement and impact on the person,

---

Margin annotations (left):

Concession/Qualifier: Jerry is not the only one.

Suggests what action the reader can take.

Further develops concept: In the past there was no other word.

Further develops the concept by showing what "handicapped" means.

Provides specific examples of challenges he and others face.

Going beyond common thinking about the concept. Introduces and explains visual.

Margin annotations (right):

Wilkins wants readers to think differently, & support organizations that promote independent living, etc.

Does word origin mean there's "little dignity"? Most people don't know the word origin, so does it affect them? How?

"Handicapped" means not being able to reach a goal?

Examples of being "handicapped"? Wilkins wants us to help him and others be self-sufficient.

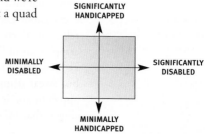

SIGNIFICANTLY HANDICAPPED

MINIMALLY DISABLED — SIGNIFICANTLY DISABLED

MINIMALLY HANDICAPPED

with minimal impact on the left side and significant impact on the right. The vertical line represents the degree to which the external or internal (self-concept, confidence, etc.) handicap limits one from reaching a goal. We'll put minimal impact at the bottom and significant impact at the top.

Now let me tell you the story of two friends. "Friend A" (not his real name) has cerebral palsy as his disability. He uses a word board and head stick to communicate with those who do not understand or speak CP. He uses an electric wheelchair and a chin stick to get around. I stressed parenthetically above the issue of relevance with regard to how we perceive the significance of disability. We, not really knowing Friend A but seeing him on the street, might be quick to place him far along the horizontal continuum of disability, considering him to be pretty significantly disabled. And I would tell you that Friend A's self-perception would put him much farther back toward the minimal end. I would also tell you that Friend A is just finishing up his degree in social work at the local university. Here's a guy who most would consider has a significant disability, yet he's out there making a difference in his life and in the lives of others. He's not allowing his disability or society's low expectations to handicap him. He's going to contribute to his community. I would say he sits pretty low on the handicapped scale. Does this make sense?

"On the other hand," helps reader see relationship between two examples. Illustrates concept with a specific example of two friends.

On the other hand, I have a friend, "Friend B" (not his real name either). He lost a couple of toes in a farm accident. He walks fine. No pain. No limp. Nothing. Pretty minimally disabled, wouldn't you think? But can I get him to go to the beach with me, or swimming? Absolutely not. He'd like to, but he goes nowhere without shoes on. He won't even wear sandals. Pretty minimally disabled but, again, it's relative. He considers himself pretty significantly disabled. So much so that his own attitude, his own self-concept, has him significantly handicapped.

Friend B is minimally disabled but significantly handicapped.

"A final difference" functions as a transition to another idea.

A final difference: if we were to consider these two continuums over a period of time, we would most likely see that the disability continuum, in most people's lives, would remain relatively static when compared to the handicapped continuum, which would fluctuate with every situation and barrier(s) presented.

Disability remains pretty consistent; handicap fluctuates based on situation & barriers.

Conclusion makes general point about understanding the context of words.

It is important to understand the context in which to use the words we use. The best way not to offend someone living with a disability, and I often insert the word "living" because we tend to forget that we are all living, breathing, interacting, supporting, pushing, pulling, etc., basically trying to get from Point A to Point

Makes his main point: that people with disabilities should be viewed as people.

B with as little hassle as possible, the best way not to offend someone living with a disability is to refer to them first as just that: as Someone, as a person, as a teacher, a student, an athlete, whatever they happen to be at that moment. That they have a disability is secondary or even tertiary. People are people. People are not diagnoses, or prognoses. They most certainly are not their disabilities. Their disabilities are a part of who they are, perhaps a tenth or twentieth of who they are completely; affording most of all a unique perspective on the world and one's place in it. It is not something of which to be ashamed but something of which to be proud.

People with disabilities are people. Their disability is secondary or tertiary—only a part of who they are.

Writing Strategies

1. Describe Wilkins's voice—his persona as a writer. Refer to at least three sentences that illustrate your perception.

2. How important is Wilkins's brief etymology (word history) of "handicap"? Does the etymology strengthen his essay? Would the essay do just as well without it? Explain.

3. What tools or strategies does Wilkins use to illustrate his point? What others might he have used?

4. In paragraph 4, Wilkins informs his reader that he is going to "rant." What, if anything, is the effect of this announcement?

5. If workshopping Wilkins's essay, how would you answer the following questions:

   a. The thing I like most about your essay is ____.
   b. I think the main idea of your essay is ____.
   c. The main suggestion I would make about your essay is ____.

Exploring Ideas

1. While Wilkins's essay is focused on the term "handicapped," how does his essay speak to a larger issue—for example, that of language in general?

2. What words, or terms, have been replaced by others, and why? What terms do you think are still in use but shouldn't be?

3. What new term has been most helpful or most harmful? How has the change in terminology affected the concept? How has the change in the term influenced the way people think or act?

Ideas for Writing

1. What two other terms—such as "disability" and "handicap"—require clarification?

2. Have people called you "handicapped," "fat," "skinny," "crazy," "irresponsible," "unapproachable," "beautiful," "lucky"? What word have you had to live with? How has the term been misapplied to you?

3. Ask around until you collect five words that people think should be replaced with another word. Write down (1) the word, (2) the word that the person thinks it should be replaced with, (3) the problem with the original word, and (4) how the new word is an improvement. Which word would make for the most interesting essay? Why?

If responding to one of these ideas, go to the **Analysis** section of this chapter to begin developing ideas for your essay.

"People are not diagnoses, or prognoses."

Outside Reading

Find a written text that analyzes a concept and print it out or make a photocopy. You might focus on a concept related to your major or to a major that you are considering. (To explore a specific field or major, examine a related professional journal such as *Nutrition Health Forum, Law Technology,* or *Education Journal.*) To conduct an electronic search of journals and magazines, go to your library's periodical database or to InfoTrac College Edition (http://infotrac.galegroup.com/itweb/). For your library database, perform a keyword search, or for InfoTrac College Edition, go to the main search box and choose "keywords." Experiment by typing in various concepts, such as *art, society, industry, sportsmanship.* You might limit the search by adding *concept* to the search. (When performing keyword searches, avoid using phrases or articles such as *a, an, the;* instead, use nouns separated by *and.*) The results will yield lists of journal and magazine articles.

You can also search the Internet. Try the search engine Yahoo.com. Like most Internet search engines, Yahoo.com combines words using *and.* In the search box, try various combinations, such as those above.

The purpose of this assignment is to further your understanding of analytical writing. You may discover a text that differs considerably from the essays in this chapter (in tone, rhetorical tools, or organization). As you read through this chapter, keep the text you have discovered close by and notice the elements and strategies the writer uses. Depending on your instructor's suggestions, do one or more of the following:

1. Notice how the writer applies various strategies from this chapter. On the hard copy or photocopy of the text:

   • Highlight the thesis if it is stated. If the thesis is implied, write it in your own words.

   • Identify the major rhetorical strategies (such as narration, description, or figurative language).

   • Identify any passages in which the writer attempts to create public resonance for the topic.

2. Analyze the strategies employed by the writer. The following questions may be helpful:

   • How is the writer's voice different from the essays in this chapter?

   • How does the writer support or illustrate his or her thesis?

   • Who is the audience for this text?

   • How does the audience impact the content of the text?

   • How does the writer go beyond the obvious? (What new idea does the writer offer?)

3. Write at least three "Writing Strategies" questions for the text you found.

4. Write at least three "Exploring Ideas" questions for the text you found.

5. Write two "Ideas for Writing," such as the ones following the essays in this book, for the text you found.

INVENTION

"What does it mean that success is as dangerous as failure? Whether you go up the ladder or down it, your position is shaky."

—Tao Te Ching

Analyzing concepts involves a good deal of reflection. Valuable analysis goes beyond the first impressions a writer may have about a topic. For the writing in this chapter, you must seek out meaning beyond those initial thoughts about a concept. The following sections are designed to help you through this process: specifically, to find a particular concept (in **Point of Contact**), to examine the concept closely (in **Analysis**), to make it relevant to a community of readers (in **Public Resonance**), to develop a focused point (in **Thesis**), and to develop support for that point (in **Rhetorical Tools**). The Invention questions in each section are not meant to be answered directly in your final essay. They are meant to prompt inventive thinking and intensive writing.

POINT OF CONTACT

We carry concepts around with us and, for the most part, do not question them. But writers are willing to get underneath concepts that would otherwise go unquestioned. As you consider a possible topic, imagine the concepts that go unnoticed in your everyday life. To find a concept, investigate the world around you. Take a concept that goes unchallenged, uninspected in your everyday life. The following may prompt a possible topic:

- **Work:** Success, employment, boss, customer, profit, hours, wage, honesty, freedom, career, experience
- **School:** Education, study, discipline, learning, science, humanities, grade, teacher, student, intelligence
- **Home:** Parent, mother, father, pet, living room, divorce, values, God, marriage, privacy, faith
- **Public Life:** Friend, recreation, commitment, travel, woman, man, patriotism, romance, trash, environment
- **Sports:** Team, entertainment, audience, fan, loser, victory, competition
- **Your Major:** Someone majoring in education could analyze a concept such as learning, success, assessment, or high school. Your major itself might be seen as a concept. For example, engineering is a concept, and how one works in that field depends upon one's concept of it.

- **Television:** What does a local news program that devotes 60 seconds to world news and several minutes to sports suggest about news? What does *American Idol* suggest about America or idol? What does *The Real World* suggest about reality? What does *Sex in the City* suggest about sex? What does *The Late Show* suggest about entertainment? What does an automobile commercial suggest about excitement? What does an insurance commercial suggest about neighbors?

As you reflect on the program or commercial, ask yourself if the concept is somehow oversimplified or misrepresented. Or does the program or commercial fairly represent the concept? Remember that you are not evaluating the television program, but using it to prompt an idea, to discover a concept that may need analysis and explanation.

ACTIVITY

Imagine more concepts that define your everyday life. If this can be done in a small group, take turns offering concepts until each participant has chosen a potential topic.

Do not limit yourself to familiar concepts. You might, in fact, choose a concept that is somewhat foreign to your experiences.

What concepts do these images invite you to explore—and to question?

ANALYSIS

Analysis involves investigating particular parts, elements, or ideas within the whole. If we were to analyze an object, we might take it apart and look inside. We might, for instance, analyze a computer by opening the case and looking at the internal wires, the cards, and the connections. But when examining a concept, we cannot take off its cover and simply look inside—at least, not physically. Instead, we have to depend on intellectual inquiry. Rather than physical tools (screwdrivers or wrenches), we have to develop questions that get inside the abstraction. We have to ask questions that point to the particular elements of the concept. For example, consider *college*. To analyze the concept, we must break it down and look at particular issues: What does college suggest for people's lives? Is it a time and place for learning specific skills or for exploring boundless ideas? Is it a place for making choices or for generating options? Such questions are analytical; they help to shed light on specific issues inside the broader, more abstract idea.

As you look closely at the concept you have chosen, use the following Invention questions to break it down:

- Specifically, how does it influence or change people's lives?
- What particular emotions or ideas are associated with it?
- What particular behaviors are associated with it?
- What specific responsibilities come with it?
- What hidden role does it play in everyday life?
- Are there complexities to the concept that people overlook?

Analyzing a concept means breaking it down into smaller elements or qualities.

INVENTION WRITING

In his invention writing, Simon Benlow looks closely at the particular qualities that define student and customer. He attempts to get at root behaviors and attitudes:

How does it influence or change people's lives?

I'm dealing with two concepts: "student" and "customer." "Customer" influences people to buy things and ideas, but the concept also makes people believe certain things about themselves—that they are better off only when they have obtained something or some service. It makes people lazy. When people totally buy into the consumer mentality, they feel as though they should be waited on, catered to, and dealt with, no matter what the circumstances. Being a student is the opposite—or at least, being a good student is the opposite. Students have to discover meaning and to struggle through their own biases, while customers hope to have their biases fed.

What emotions or thoughts are associated with it?

When consumerist students come to college, they get angry and frustrated. Their expectations about institutions have been created, in large part, from their interactions with retail. They've been advertised and sold to for most of their lives. In college when the tables are turned, when they have to do all the discovering, all the inventing, all the developing, they are often freaked out.

Benlow then develops these ideas in his essay. (See the particular development in the first half of his essay on page 151.)

INVENTION WORKSHOP

As you consider the Invention questions, avoid skimming the surface of broad ideas. Enlist the help of at least two other writers. Use one of the Invention questions to launch a focused discussion. As you address the question, try to avoid chatting aimlessly about the topic (which is always tempting!). Instead, follow new ideas that surface. For example, Diana has decided to analyze *conspiracy* after watching an episode of *The X-Files* on television. In a discussion with other students, she discovers more about the concept than she initially expected:

What behaviors are associated with it [*conspiracy*]?

Diana: In the show, the conspiracy is a big network of people from various national governments who are all trying to deal secretly with aliens. It's a giant plot that involves military agencies, doctors, scientists, politicians, FBI agents, and lots of spies. It's great entertainment, but it seems so far-fetched. A conspiracy doesn't have to be so big and involved. If it were, how could it remain secret?

Linda: I know what you mean. I like that show, but I'm always wondering about the big hidden plot with the aliens. Sometimes it seems like only a small handful of people know about it, like when the conspirators, all men by the way, meet in a dark room. There's a lot of cigarette smoke and hard talk about taking control of the world. Then other episodes suggest that all kinds of people, in all parts of the world, are deeply involved.

Marcus: So the show suggests that a conspiracy is a huge underground plot where a bunch of men secretly plan to take over the world. That IS a conspiracy, right?

Diana: Yes, but can't a conspiracy be smaller than that? Does it have to involve several governments and a plan to help aliens take over the Earth?

Linda: What about these corporate executives that construct plans to grab millions of dollars before their companies go belly-up? There's a conspiracy that, maybe, develops pretty quickly—and is shared by only a few people.

The conversation is beginning to open up the concept, to go beyond the idea that Diana first encountered in the television program. This kind of exploration is the key to developing new insights. It takes writers (and their readers) beyond their opinions—and into a realm of possibilities. But Diana, Linda, and Marcus don't stop there:

Marcus: But then the accounting firms get involved, too. Then it gets bigger and bigger.

Diana: But the accountants may not be "in," so to speak; they're simply using the numbers to keep their clients afloat so that they, in turn, have jobs.

Linda: So the people don't always have to be knowledgeable about the beginnings of the conspiracy in order to participate in it.

Marcus: But those accountants are doing something suspicious too, right?

Diana: Right! But they're acting for their own self-interests. They weren't necessarily involved in the plan from the ground up.

Linda: So back to the main point: A *conspiracy* doesn't have to involve governments, dark rooms, and huge cover-ups. It can be a bunch of people doing their own thing (for various different reasons) but working, as best they can, under the covers so they keep jobs and make money.

A review of the discussion turns up the following ideas:

- A conspiracy can be much smaller than many people imagine.
- People don't have to be knowledgeable about the beginnings of the conspiracy in order to participate in it.
- Some (all?) people involved in a conspiracy may simply be acting for their own self-interests—so that they keep their jobs, for example.

These ideas, uncovered through discussion, are beginning to help Diana figure out what a conspiracy is, or can be. As Diana discusses further, even more ideas will emerge—and she must be able to manage all these ideas that are coming at her.

THINKING FURTHER

To explore further, one must:

- Keep an open mind. Great thinkers seek out new, unusual, and challenging ideas.
- Be attentive. Listen and review notes carefully to identify areas worth pursuing further.
- Use particular questions and statements from your previous invention writing as starting points for further exploration.

Imagine that Diana identifies the following statement: *Some people involved in a conspiracy may simply be acting for their own self-interests—so that they keep their jobs, for example.* To explore further, she would ask herself questions to break down the statement.

Some of the Invention questions (page 166) can be used to explore further:

- What particular emotions or ideas are associated with it?
- What hidden role does it play in everyday life?
- Are there complexities to the concept that people overlook?

And newly created questions will also be necessary:

- Do conspiracies require unwitting conspirators?
- How do dictionaries, encyclopedias, and articles define conspiracy?
- Am I involved in a conspiracy? Have I ever been?

As you analyze your own topic even further, return to the questions on page 166 and come up with probing new questions of your own.

To identify areas worth pursuing further, consider:

HELLO
my name is

- **New ideas**
- **Changes in thinking**
- **Differences among people's thinking**
- **What disagreements are based on***

*Is it a basic value or belief, an interpretation of facts, or something else?

EXCERPT OF FURTHER INVENTION WRITING

Am I involved in a conspiracy?

Until now, I had never even imagined that I might be part of a conspiracy. Am I a villain? Or a victim? Am I innocent? What is an unwitting conspirator? A conspiracy is beginning to feel more like a living being to me. It is born. It grows. It takes on certain characteristics. It has various parts. Eventually it dies off. Some parts are like a brain. Others are like feet or hands or the hair on your arms. Is the fist to blame when a punch is thrown? Or is the brain to blame? Or is it something else? Is the brain evil, or just damaged, or just thinking differently?

The invention writing above illustrates a writer letting go and giving herself over to intensive invention. Now she might:

- share ideas with others to discuss them further;
- read essays and articles about the concept to see how others explain it;
- continue exploring on her own.

HOW TO EXPLORE IDEAS EVEN FURTHER

After some initial exploring, keep going. Alone or with others, seek out new and challenging ideas. Question your own thinking! Explore through:

- Discussion
- Invention writing
- Research
- Relaxation

That's right! After you've done some serious thinking, relax. Enjoying a favorite pastime such as running, reading, or watching TV can lead to moments of clarity in one's thinking.

ANALYSIS IN CHAPTER READINGS

In this chapter, S. I. Hayakawa examines *creativity*. He reveals the hidden complexities in the concept and breaks it into several different traits, such as the ability to endure loneliness:

> The person who would be creative must be able to endure loneliness—even ridicule. If he has a great and original idea that others are not yet ready to accept, there will be long periods of loneliness. There will be times when his friends and relatives think he is crazy, and he'll begin to wonder if they are right. A genuinely creative person, believing in his creation, is able to endure this loneliness—for years if necessary. (149)

And it is through an investigation of these particulars that we get a better sense of the concept. Like Hayakawa's essay, good analyses dismantle the whole and show us meaning inside the individual elements. By looking at specifics, they help us to better understand the concept.

ACTIVITY

1. Identify ideas in Diana's invention writing that are worth pursuing further. Why are they worth pursuing?

2. Write down some questions that will help get inside the idea.

3. Spend a few minutes discussing the idea with others, doing more invention writing, or thinking about it during your daily activities.

PUBLIC RESONANCE

It is up to the writer to make a concept relevant to readers. At some level, your concept already resonates with others, because a concept is, by definition, beyond particulars. Whether it is *creativity, college,* or *student,* a concept necessarily involves others. Still, a concept is not always entirely understood—even by those who would, presumably, understand it. Consider *freedom:* As Americans, we often speak of it, sing about it, and even go to war over it, but do most Americans really understand the concept? Even though freedom is part of our collective language, we might not realize its complexities and meaning.

As you consider the social significance of your own topic, use the following questions:

- Is the concept generally agreed upon?
- Does the concept raise controversy? Explain why.
- Why is it important that people have an appropriate understanding of this concept?
- Does the concept need to be rethought? Why?
- What is the possible connection between the topic and public concerns?
- In reconsidering your analysis of the concept, what ideas are most uncommon? What ideas might help people re-see the concept?

If you choose not to directly state the public resonance of your concept, answering these questions serves another goal: To help you envision the relationship between your audience and your topic. In thinking about the public resonance of your chosen concept, you may come across your *purpose*—the reason you are writing. If you believe that the concept is often misunderstood, then the purpose of your analysis might be to educate your audience. Or if your concept is overlooked, the purpose may be to elevate the status of the concept in your reader's mind.

PUBLIC RESONANCE IN CHAPTER READINGS

Because people often miss or ignore a concept's nuances, writers consider it their business to inform, to introduce, or to remind readers of those complexities. For instance, Skye Bass sets out to dispel misconceptions about college. She even directly explains how students' misconceptions work:

> Due to our growing fascination with "pick-me-ups," we have all become accustomed to believing that a college education is always a guarantee to an easier life, a life that includes a well-paying job and a comfortable lifestyle. From birth, our future generations are force-fed the importance of going to college. Education is sold like a prescription drug. The symptom is: unhappiness in current lifestyle. The cure: high doses of a college education. The concept of obtaining a degree is the new and improved security blanket. (154)

At first, a concept may *seem* unrelated to public concerns. However, a writer's job is to create the bridge between a topic (no matter how small or weird) and the surrounding world. Notice Iyer's strategy. His topic, punctuation, may seem totally divorced from the social world. However, he forges a connection. Here, he is making a case for the public resonance of his topic and elevating its significance in readers' minds:

> Punctuation, then, is a civic prop, a pillar that holds society upright. (A run-on sentence, its phrases piling up without division, is as unsightly as a sink piled high with dirty dishes.) Small wonder, then, that punctuation was one of the first proprieties of the Victorian Age, the age of the corset, that the modernists threw off: the sexual revolution might be said to have begun when Joyce's Molly Bloom spilled out all her private thoughts in thirty-six pages of panting, unperioded, and officially censored prose; and another rebellion was surely marked when e. e. cummings first committed "god" to the lower case. (146)

INVENTION WRITING

In the following excerpt, Simon Benlow discovers why *student,* as a concept, is necessary and why people should rethink it. Benlow could have given up early in his exploration. He could have merely stopped with "education will suffer." Instead, he tries to imagine specific effects, and in doing so, he further draws out the difference between customer and student:

Is the concept generally agreed upon?

No! That's the whole problem. Many students don't know what it means to be a student.

Why is it important that people have an appropriate understanding of this concept?

If college students really understand what it means to be a student (and not a consumerist student), their experience at college will be defined by self-discovery and enlightenment rather than petty frustration and grumbling. If colleges across America continue to confuse "student" with "consumer," education will suffer. Much of the time spent in college will be on customer service (keeping students happy) rather than challenging their beliefs, developing their minds, and broadening their horizons. Customers ultimately do not want their ideas about themselves to change; they want products and services to support what they think. If college continues down the present path, it is not hard to imagine colleges being devoid of genuinely new ideas.

Benlow's public resonance shows up directly in the conclusion of his essay, on page 153.

An important part of a writer's job: creating new connections.

RESEARCH

1. Explore what others have said about your topic. Try a periodical database search (such as InfoTrac College Edition or your library's periodical databases). Enter the keywords of the concept you are exploring. To narrow and refine your search, return to your invention writing and seek out words that relate to your most important discoveries so far.

2. Conduct a survey of ten people (classmates and/or people outside of college). Ask them the first thing they think of when they hear _____ (your concept). You might go further and ask them how the topic relates to their lives. Record the answers as they respond (either by an audio recording or by note-taking). You can also conduct this survey via e-mail. Use the responses to further explore your topic. For instance, your respondents might suggest something about your chosen concept that you had not considered.

THESIS

You probably have many different things to say about your topic, but your project will gain focus and intensity with a thesis statement, a single claim that expresses your particular view on the concept. Look over your notes from the Analysis and Public Resonance sections. Find a theme or pattern running through those notes and try to articulate that idea in a sentence. Remember that good writing *reveals* something beyond or beneath common knowledge, and good writers show the extraordinary in the ordinary. Your project might:

- Explain how particular parts or qualities make up a concept.

   Creativity . . . the act of bringing something new into the world . . . is based first on communication with oneself, then testing that communication with experience and the realities one has to contend with. (150)

- Reveal a side or layer of a concept that normally goes unnoticed.

   Education is a collective process in which students join the intellectual traditions of literate culture.

- Show a quality that distinguishes one concept from another.

   Contrary to the passive, personalizing, self-perpetuating, desire-driven customer, students are encouraged to be active. (152)

- Explain the inner workings of a concept.

   Punctuation, in short, gives us the human voice, and all the meanings that lie between the words. (147)

COMMON THESIS PROBLEMS

It is easy to say something broad and general about a concept—especially because concepts are, themselves, generalizations. And while these statements may be true, they do not reveal anything specific about the concept. Writers would do well to re-examine their ideas by asking probing questions that shed light on the concept. Such questions will lead to more focused and revelatory insights.

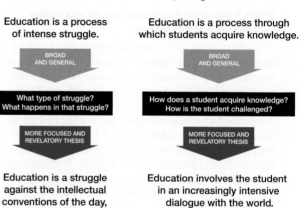

Notice how the two focused and revelatory statements offer a unique point about the way education works. While the statements are broad in scope, they show a particular process (a struggle against conventions and an increasingly intensive dialogue). These statements are rich with possibility and would help a writer to generate an intensive essay.

EVOLUTION OF A THESIS

Remember that a thesis does not materialize out of thin air. It develops over time. It may involve a long process of reflection and discussion. And often, a good thesis emerges only after a writer has thoroughly analyzed the topic. Consider the example from the Analysis section, in which Diana's topic, conspiracy, is developed through a discussion. Her thesis evolves slowly: First, she notices the idea in a television show. Then she analyzes and discovers specific elements. Finally, she refines the point in a focused statement:

- People think that conspiracy means old men meeting in a smoke-filled room and devising an evil plan, but it is far subtler than that.

- In a conspiracy, everyone involved does not have to know each other and purposely act in harmony. In fact, people in a conspiracy can simply be protecting their own interests, and in doing so, carrying out an action under society's radar.

- Although numbers of people sometimes do conspire together, what some call a conspiracy is, in truth, various people with a similar attitude acting independently in their own self-interests.

As you consider your own thesis, remember that narrower points yield more interesting writing. At first, you might think, "I can't possibly write more than a paragraph about something so narrow." However, the process of developing the ideas will generate content for your writing. And the more focused thesis will help you to illustrate particular points rather than listing many marginally related issues.

REVISION

Look back over your invention notes and thesis ideas. Have you discovered a new way of seeing the concept? Have you revealed a specific insight? If not, return to the Analysis section and dig into the Invention questions again. Also, consider the following questions:

- What do people normally say or assume about the concept? How have you complicated or enriched the common way of thinking?

- If you have settled on a thesis, ask yourself: Can I reveal the specifics in any of the terms? Can I more specifically reveal how something works?

Ask yourself: What is the most revealing point I can make about this concept?

RHETORICAL TOOLS

Developing Support

Even though you are dealing with a generalization, an abstract idea that transcends particulars, you can still refer to particular situations or examples to support your take on the concept. In Iyer's essay, for example, he offers the reader numerous examples to illustrate a point. Although he explores punctuation as a concept, he supports his understanding of it with specific examples:

> Punctuation, in short, gives us the human voice, and all the meanings that lie between the words. "You aren't young, are you?" loses its innocence when it loses the question mark. Every child knows the menace of a dropped apostrophe (the parent's "Don't do that" shifting into a more slowly enunciated "Do not do that") and every believer the ignominy of having his faith reduced to "faith." Add an exclamation point to "To be or not to be . . ." and the gloomy Dane has all the resolve he needs; add a comma, and the noble sobriety of "God save the queen" becomes a cry of desperation bordering on double sacrilege. (147)

Benlow uses a detailed scenario to illustrate his concept of *student:*

> In higher education, principles establish how a discipline works. Physics works on principles of matter and energy. The goal of a physicist is to discover the principles and understand how they can be used. Composition works on principles—conventions of grammar and persuasion. This is not to say that all knowledge is prescribed. On the contrary, students in such classes are encouraged to invent, to break rules, to go beyond. But in order to do so, they need certain ground rules; they need to understand that certain principles exist in the world outside of their own desires. (One cannot do chemistry and simply dismiss algebra because it is distasteful.) (152)

In some cases, a writer may use details to illustrate how *not* to conceptualize an idea. Wilkins, for example, alludes to a particular television program to detail a misguided understanding of *handicap*. He uses the "Smellathon" to illustrate the troubling or negative ideas associated with his concept:

> Twenty-four hours of patting and hugging "poor, helpless cripples" until FINALLY, in the last five minutes, through red blurry eyes, hair mussed, sleeves uncuffed, bow tie loosened and akimbo, sweat dripping and sleep deprived, he tells us, with all the apparent (or is that transparent) sincerity of a really bad lounge singer, that we "will never walk alone." (Hey, Jerry, I'll never walk AGAIN! and, truth be told, that's OK.) He demands that we, the heartwrenched public, give, GIVE, until it hurts. GIVE, so that, for another year, we can walk the street unashamed to look someone in the eye; unashamed that we might have fearful, discriminatory thoughts toward "those people," unashamed that our society continues to fight equity and access to all it has to offer. Buy the premise, pay the dues, and it's another year of "no fault insurance." (157–158)

And Benlow goes even further with this strategy by devoting several paragraphs to illustrations of consumerist thinking. (See pages 151–152.)

Each writer in this chapter puts forth a particular way of seeing a concept. And each must support that way of seeing with scenarios (hypothetical accounts), allusions (references to bits of public knowledge), and examples. Because analyzing concepts requires abstract thinking, writers must be extra careful to illustrate points with concrete examples.

To develop support for your topic, ask yourself the following:

- What specific examples in everyday life illustrate my point about the concept?
- Can I construct a hypothetical account that demonstrates the concept?
- What programs, ads, or other examples from everyday life illustrate an inappropriate or oversimplified way of understanding the concept?
- Does anything or anyone from history, current events, popular culture, or literature illustrate my point about the concept?

Even though you are dealing with a generalization, an abstract idea that transcends particulars, you can still refer to particular situations or examples to support your take on the concept.

As you generate a list of possible ideas, allusions, and examples to include in your essay, also imagine how you can explain their significance. Often it is not enough to simply mention an example. A more powerful and convincing strategy is to explain in detail how an example or allusion reveals something relevant. For example, Benlow does not simply mention consumerist slogans; he gives detailed explanations of their significance:

> "The customer is always right." We hear this hollow phrase resound through (almost) every corridor of our consumerist culture. The motive behind the phrase is painfully clear—to keep customers happy, to keep them from complaining, and most importantly, to keep them coming back. (Of course, the meaninglessness of the phrase is well known, too—for those of us who have had the displeasure of talking with Ameritech operators or "customer service" tellers at our banks.) The phrase is meant to maintain a climate in which the substance of anyone's concerns or complaints is obfuscated by friendly and diplomatic clichés—"your business means so much to us"; "we'll do everything we can to address the problem." Ultimately, then, the goal of customer service, in this sense, is to lull customers into a sense of complacency—even though their phones may not be working or their washers are throwing sparks. (151)

Using Definitions

Concepts involve definitions. Sometimes a definition supports a writer's take on a concept; other times a dictionary definition (or *denotation*) is inadequate for exploring a concept's complexities. In all the essays in this chapter, for example, the dictionary definitions associated with the concepts fall short. The writers go far beyond them. Pico Iyer's essay illustrates this point. According to the *American Heritage Dictionary,* punctuation is "[t]he use of standard marks and signs in writing and printing to separate words into sentences, clauses, and phrases in order to clarify meaning." But Iyer's analysis does not involve the formal definition. He is more interested in what punctuation means for people, for cultures, for language—and a dictionary definition will not yield such ideas. Similarly, Benlow does not bother with dictionary definitions. Instead, he is concerned about the realm of *connotations* (meaning created by the social situations), in which society's habits and behaviors shape the meaning of concepts.

Dictionaries can be springboards for ideas.

However, sometimes a dictionary definition comes in handy. Some writers, for instance, begin their essays with a simple definition and then explore the connotation. Most often, the goal is not to prove a definition but to prompt readers to rethink connotations. For example, consider Diana's analysis of *conspiracy* (from the Analysis section). She might begin with the dictionary definition and extend the thinking. Here, the dictionary works only as a springboard. Diana uses the dictionary as a way to begin her analysis:

> Most often, a conspiracy is associated with a direct and charted plan: "We'll collect the money and stash it in the laundry baskets in the basement." In fact, the basic definition of conspiracy suggests a prefigured and collective act. According to the *American Heritage Dictionary,* it is "an agreement to perform together an illegal, treacherous, or evil act." However, more recent events in corporate America invite us to rethink how conspiracies work. Even a quick look at corporate fraud reveals a process in which many people, simply acting in their own self-interests, become part of a bigger covert plan that was begun without them and carries on only because they are unwilling to stand in its way.

For your own topic, ask yourself the following:

- Is a dictionary definition important to my understanding of my chosen concept?
- If so, how do I go beyond it?
- How is the dictionary definition inadequate?
- What does it help me to illustrate about the concept?

Using Outside Sources

Writers often refer to other writers' ideas to substantiate points. For example, in this passage, S. I. Hayakawa first states a point ("the creative person plays hunches") and then uses Selye's words to extend that point:

> Finally, the creative person plays hunches. "Pure intellect," says Dr. Hans Selye, the great medical researcher at the University of Montreal, "is largely a quality of the middle-class mind. The lowliest hooligan and the greatest creator in the fields of science are activated mainly by imponderable instincts and emotions, especially faith. Curiously, even scientific research, the most intellectual creative effort of which man is capable, is no exception in this respect." (149)

This is standard practice when using outside sources. While it may be enticing to begin passages with others' words or even to use long passages from other writers, it is most often best to use sources to help develop or illustrate your points. In other words, be careful not to depend on others' words to make your points for you.

To find outside sources that discuss your concept, go to your library's home page and select a periodical database, such as LexisNexis, InfoTrac College Edition, or EBSCOhost, which contains lists of journal and magazine articles. (Ask a librarian if you are uncertain about the periodical databases your library offers.) Try a keyword search, and type in your concept. The search will yield lists of articles on your topic. You might also try an electronic search engine on the Internet. For instance, using Yahoo.com, type your concept in the search box. (However, on the Internet, be cautious of sites that market materials or services. Because the purpose of such sites is to attract customers, the information they offer may be biased. Marketing sites may contain terms and phrases such as "sale," "low prices," and "large selection." For more guidance in finding and integrating sources, see Chapter 13, Research & Writing.)

INVENTION WORKSHOP

In small groups, collectively develop support for one another's projects. Each writer should announce his or her thesis to the group. Each group member then should offer at least one response to the following:

1. What specific examples in everyday life illustrate the writer's point?

2. Name something from popular culture (such as a television show, movie, advertising campaign) that illustrates the writer's point. Explain how the writer could allude to it.

3. Name something from history (a person, an event, a trend) that shows something about the writer's point.

4. Explain how the writer's point is different than how people normally think about the concept.

As the group members offer ideas, the writer should record the group members' responses so they can be integrated later. Make certain to spend equal time with each person's project.

ORGANIZATIONAL STRATEGIES

How Should I Begin?

Introductions depend on the tone or level of formality of the writing situation. (See more on level of formality on pages 134–135.) An analytical text written for a government agency or a corporate entity would probably begin formally, perhaps with a general discussion about the concept. In less formal situations, introductions vary widely, and the primary goal is to capture the reader's attention, to provoke a sense of curiosity. Among many others, here are three consistent and effective strategies:

- **Give a surprising opening statement.** In Pico Iyer's introduction, he yanks us away from conventional thinking with powerful opening sentence:

  The gods, they say, give breath, and they take it away. But the same could be said—could it not?—of the humble comma. (146)

The statement seems to be hyperbole (an exaggeration). However, as we read on, we realize that his statement fits in with his concept of punctuation. The opening, then, does what good introductions should: Capture the reader's attention and suggest the point of the text.

- **Ask a pointed question.** In Hayakawa's introduction, he asks a question and then qualifies it, directing the reader's attention to a particular line of reasoning. The question thus serves a very particular purpose.

  What distinguishes the creative person? By creative person I don't mean only the great painter or poet or musician. I also want to include the creative housewife, teacher, warehouseman, sales manager . . . (149)

Notice that Hayakawa spends the remainder of his essay answering the question. (This is perhaps the most important issue about raising a question: It ultimately needs to be answered!)

- **Recreate the point of contact.** Explain how you first encountered the idea. This is often more informal, since it requires some personal narration. Notice that Benlow's introduction, for example, begins with the event that provoked his need to write.

  Two weeks ago, the faculty and staff received a memo regarding "National Customer Service Week." We were urged to take special efforts in serving our customers—presumably, our students. (151)

- **Begin with a popular reference.** Writers often invite readers into their ideas by alluding to something in popular culture, such as a television program, an advertisement, a song, a current event. This strategy instantly creates public resonance. It allows readers to enter the world of the essay through a familiar door. In her essay about conspiracy (see the Analysis section on page 166), Diana could begin with an allusion to the *The X-Files:*

  The popular program *The X-Files* stokes our suspicions of and paranoia about the government. It invites us to imagine a vast network of officials, heads of state, military groups, and secret agencies making deals with aliens. Doctors, scientists, politicians, FBI agents, and numbers of spies all share covert plans, meet in smoky, quiet rooms, and plan the future of all humans. It's great entertainment. But conspiracies are often more nuanced, less concocted, less dramatic than what *The X-Files* suggests.

When Should I Change Paragraphs?

Remember that paragraphs are tools for directing a reader's progress. Paragraphs stop the reader and refocus his or her attention on the next point. Hayakawa uses paragraph breaks between each different characteristic of a creative person. Similarly, Iyer begins a new paragraph for each general statement about punctuation: It provides law and order; it is a civic prop; it signifies cultures; it provides movement for our thoughts; it initiates the human voice; it provides aesthetics; it gives depth; and it shows our care for meaning. Each point has its own paragraph, its own space for it to be developed and illustrated.

Paragraphs can also be used to separate specific support strategies. A writer might use paragraphs to separate several examples. Simon Benlow, for instance, dedicates each of his first four paragraphs to a particular element of the consumerist culture. Hayakawa uses paragraphs to separate different elements of creativity. These writers use paragraphs to refocus the reader on a new ingredient or element in the discussion.

How Should I Conclude?

As with introductions, the possibilities for conclusions are limitless. Short explanatory essays (under 1,000 words) usually do not need to summarize main points. Instead, writers often use conclusions to suggest the significance of the ideas expressed in the body of the essay. Consider the strategies used by the authors in this chapter. Iyer concludes by *framing* the essay (returning to the same image or allusion used in the introduction):

Iyer's introduction:
The gods, they say, give breath, and they take it away. But the same could be said—could it not?—of the humble comma. Add it to the present clause and, of a sudden, the mind is, quite literally, given pause to think; take it out if you wish or forget it and the mind is deprived of a resting place. (146)

Iyer's final sentences:
. . . a comma can let us hear a voice break, or a heart. Punctuation, in fact, is a labor of love. Which brings us back, in a way, to gods. (147)

The framing strategy makes an explicit and direct connection between introduction and conclusion. But even if the connection is not as direct as Iyer's, conclusions should not feel divorced from an essay. In fact, the framing strategy makes an important point: A conclusion should feel like an essential part of a formula, necessary for giving meaning and power to all other parts.

Hayakawa concludes by proclaiming the value of the concept:

It is based first on communication with oneself, then testing that communication with experience and the realities one has to contend with. The result is the highest, most exciting kind of learning. (150)

Bass concludes with her main point, describing what education is and how it changes, rather than reinforces, desires:

Education is a tool to be used to develop and advance our desires, so we can discover the things that are truly significant in life. Education is a source to expand our society to see beyond the superficial appeals and the "quick fixes," leaving the notion of an effortless life behind in order to desire a meaningful one. (155)

Each strategy is very different and all are effective, yet none of the writers wastes time summarizing or "wrapping up" points that have already been made. Instead, they use their conclusions to extend their points into the reader's world (by scenarios, direct appeals, or examples).

WRITER'S VOICE

A writer's voice can make the reading experience formal or relaxed, rigorous or casual. Remember that a casual voice does not necessarily mean casual thinking. A very sophisticated analysis can be presented in a casual manner. For example, Wilkins's voice is informal:

> If I may rant for a paragraph, children and adults with disabilities continue to be exploited every day, most visibly every Labor Day when Jerry Lewis does his annual Smellathon, er, telethon. Twenty-four hours of patting and hugging "poor, helpless cripples" until FINALLY, in the last five minutes, through red blurry eyes, hair mussed, sleeves uncuffed, bow tie loosened and akimbo, sweat dripping and sleep deprived, he tells us, with all the apparent (or is that transparent) sincerity of a really bad lounge singer, that we "will never walk alone." (157)

Even though he presents his subject in a casual manner, his analysis is sophisticated. Wilkins makes a complicated point about people's perceptions of disability, but his voice invites the reader to experience the analysis in a comfortable, almost playful, manner.

A writer can also elevate the topic. For example, Pico Iyer's topic, punctuation, is not often described in such grandiose terms, and most people probably conceptualize it as commonplace or boring. But his approach lifts readers' notions about punctuation:

> Thus all these tiny scratches give us breadth and heft and depth. A world that has only periods is a world without inflections. It is a world without shade. It has a music without sharps and flats. It is a martial music. It has a jackboot rhythm. Words cannot bend and curve. A comma, by comparison, catches the gentle drift of the mind in thought, turning in on itself and back on itself, reversing, redoubling, and returning along the course of its own sweet river music; while the semicolon brings clauses and thoughts together with all the silent discretion of a hostess arranging guests around her dinner table. (147)

Using Metaphor

A metaphor is a comparison of two things, in which one thing is made to share the characteristics of another. While metaphors are support strategies, they also help to create a particular voice. A lighthearted or relaxed voice might depend on simple, everyday metaphors. Notice Iyer's use:

> Punctuation marks are the road signs placed along the highway of our communication—to control speeds, provide directions, and prevent head-on collisions. (146)

Using Allusions

Allusions are references to some public bit of knowledge (such as a historical event, a political situation, or a popular culture figure). An allusion can give a personal essay a broader and more public feeling while developing its ideas. But allusions can also help create voice. The allusions one chooses contribute to the voice created in the essay. Alluding to the entertainer Jerry Lewis, for example, is different than alluding to a dark political figure such as Joseph Stalin.

The following allusion helps to characterize Benlow's voice—especially early in the essay when he sounds intolerant of customer life. The nature of the allusion (to a fairly unimportant matter like fast food) helps Benlow to trivialize consumer culture and appear slightly above it.

> "Have it your way!" Of course, we all know the song and the friendly fried food establishment associated with this slogan. It's a harmless phrase, in and of itself, and one that works particularly well for the franchise. It suggests to customers that their particular appetites can be catered to, that their specific tastes, no matter how eccentric (within the continuum of dip n' serve fried food) can be easily satisfied. (151)

Promoting Curiosity

One of the primary jobs of a writer is to pique curiosity in readers. Very rarely does a writer (in any situation) seek only to tell readers what they are already thinking. Instead, writers seek to light a small fire in readers' minds, to make them want to *consider* an issue. One strategy, using metaphor, is illustrated at left. Perhaps the most important strategy for promoting curiosity is to embody it, that is, to be curious as a writer. Curious writers make curious readers. Notice Pico Iyer's own curiosity about the world. Iyer himself seems curious about—even awed by—language. He connects it to both grand performances (symphonies) and minute moments (batting one's eyes). He seems to be totally unafraid of his own imagination:

> Punctuation is the notation in the sheet music of our own words, telling us when to rest, or when to raise our voices; it acknowledges that the meaning of our discourse, as of any symphonic composition, lies not in the units but in the pauses, the pacing, and the phrasing. Punctuation is the way one bats one's eyes, lowers one's voice, or blushes demurely. Punctuation adjusts color and tone and volume till the feeling comes into perfect focus: not disgust exactly, but distaste; not lust, or like, but love. (147)

The person we detect through the language seems full of wonder. And it is not only the content of the passage; notice also the sentence structure. He uses long sentences to keep the reader in his perspective (as though he is holding us underwater without a breath).

As you consider your voice, ask yourself the following:

- What uncommon details reveal my point about the concept?
- Can I avoid telling the reader that something is "interesting," "exciting," and so on, and instead create images or use examples that show it?
- Can I use metaphors to make the reader see the intensity or scope or depth of the concept?
- Can I show the reader a new way to see an everyday phenomenon?

Remember that a casual voice does not necessarily mean casual thinking.

VITALITY

It is easy to fill up pages. But good writers avoid filling. They are careful with their readers' minds. (Sentences, after all, are the only conduit between a writer's thoughts and a reader's life.) Consider the following strategies for making your final text more lively and intense.

Avoid Clichés

Clichés are tired, worn-out phrases. We hear them constantly in everyday life. We use them when there is nothing else left to say—or to make it seem like there is nothing else left to say. We read them on greeting cards, hear them in popular songs or political speeches, and even share them in casual conversations. Think of all the times you have heard phrases such as these:

> You don't know what you've got until it's gone.
> We should expand our horizons.
> Follow your dreams.
> Anything is possible.
> Children are the future.
> I believe in my heart that . . .
> Hang in there.
> Discover who you are as a person.
> People are entitled to their own opinions.

Or even consider smaller phrases that get plugged into sentences but rarely get inspected:

> the real world
> hard work
> the good life
> family values

The list goes on and on. Such common phrases are not tools for thinking—they are substitutes for thinking. Because they have been used repeatedly, and in so many different contexts, their meaning has been emptied.

Clichés blur complex thinking. They actually hide the possibility of further thought. For instance, notice the thinking that might go on behind the cliché: We should expand our horizons.

> What are horizons? How do they form? Are horizons imposed on us, or do we adopt them ourselves? If they are imposed by others, can we simply choose to expand them or do we have to break some rule? How do we know when a horizon expands? What experiences or voices or situations make them expand? Are we just as likely to shrink our horizons? Isn't that human nature? What kind of action broadens our understanding? Is it just a new experience or something else?

All of these questions suggest the complexity behind the idea. But rather than promote hard thinking, clichés invite writers and readers (both!) into quiet, unreflective agreement. In a sense, clichés are strategies for quieting the mind—the opposite goal of academic writing.

ACTIVITY

In a small group, develop a list of clichés. Share this list with the whole class to create a comprehensive list of phrases to avoid.

Clichés stop people from thinking!

Avoid Stilted Language

If clichés are the common, overused phrases of the day, stilted language is the opposite: an overly elaborate jungle of clauses and phrases. Stilted language is unnecessarily elevated—and like a person walking on stilts, it makes the ideas slow and wobbly. For example:

Writer A:
People, in every walk of this big life, should query themselves about the direction of their occupational goals. And they should do this persistently, both before entering into a projected career path and while enduring the veritable ins and outs of said career path. Is it not fitting to examine the very essence of such matters, which would otherwise remain beyond our consciousness in the mundane existence of work? Certainly, we should endeavor to explore the cracks and folds of our lives and thereby free ourselves of any unknown shackles.

Here, the ideas are vague because they are stretched out over unnecessary, but pretty, phrases. The writer injects strings of needless constructions ("in every walk of this big life," "the very essence of such matters") and elaborate language ("their occupational goals," "mundane existence of work") that inflate the importance of the ideas. Writer A also mingles together two competing metaphors at the end of the passage. As readers, we are left exploring the "cracks and folds" while also freeing ourselves from "unknown shackles." Notice a less stilted approach:

Writer B:
Before entering a job, people should ask themselves if it fits their broader career plans. Even after working at a job for months or years, people should return to this question. Otherwise, the workaday lifestyle can prompt us to believe that a present career path is the best—the one that we should continue to walk.

Writer B does use a metaphor at the end, but it works here because it does not compete with other figurative language in the same sentence. Now that the ideas are less ornate, they seem less overwhelming. In fact, when they are stated more plainly, the ideas appear rather ordinary. (And this might even prompt a writer to explore the ideas further.)

These passages reveal two major problems with stilted language: (1) It jumbles ideas so that readers are left guessing or wondering; and (2) it inflates ideas so that they seem beyond exploration. Writers and readers should not be impressed with ornate language, but with intense ideas.

Essays are not performances. They are invitations to think hard.

PEER REVIEW

Exchange drafts with at least one other writer. Before passing your draft to others, underline the thesis, or write it above your essay. This way, reviewers will get traction as they read.

As a reviewer, use the following questions to guide your response.

1. What words or phrases in the thesis could be more focused?

2. Point out passages or sentences that could use more specific illustration. Suggest an example from everyday life that illustrates the writer's point. For example, in an essay about athletics, you might read:

   Athletics are the great motivator of many students. Without sports, many would not feel compelled to attend school at all.

   You might suggest that "the great motivator" could be illustrated more specifically, that the writer show us the particular motivating quality of sports. You might ask: "How do sports work as a motivator? What do they actually do to students?"

3. Suggest an allusion (to popular culture, literature, or history) that illustrates the writer's point. Rather than accept claims as they are, help the writer make a connection to some other time, place, or text so that the concept (whatever it is) connects to a broader set of ideas.

4. If the writer uses a dictionary definition, does he or she take you beyond that definition? The writer might rely on a dictionary to get started, but the ideas should extend beyond that definition. (Hopefully, the essay takes you beyond a definition that you could easily look up yourself.) Where do you feel that "liftoff" away from a standard definition? If there is no liftoff, where might the writer concentrate attention? If you can, offer a path beyond the definition.

5. Consider the paragraphs: Do they focus on one specific point? Point to any paragraphs that seem to stray into several ideas.

6. In which passages does the writer's voice seem most engaging? (Where do you feel yourself, as a reader, most inspired by the ideas?) Why?

7. Point to particular sentences and phrases that could gain vitality and intensity. Use the following:

   • Underline any clichés. On the back of the draft, explain how the cliché conceals or blurs thinking. Suggest an alternative to the cliché.

   • Circle any stilted language. On the back of the draft, suggest an alternative approach to the passage.

   • Consider vitality strategies from other chapters and make editorial changes on the writer's draft:

     —Help the writer experiment with sentence length and brevity. Reconstruct one paragraph, extending some sentences and abbreviating others. Try to create intensity with shorter sentences.
     —Change vague nouns to specific nouns.
     —Change *be* verbs to active verbs.
     —Change clauses to phrases.
     —Change phrases to words.
     —Combine sentences.
     —Repeat structures.
     —Intensify verbs.

8. Help the reader avoid common grammatical errors: comma splices, sentence fragments, or pronoun/antecedent agreement.

Questions for Research

If the writer used outside sources,

• Where must he or she include in-text citations? (See page 650.)

• Are quotations blended smoothly into the argument and punctuated correctly? (See pages 642–648.)

• Where could more direct textual cues or transitions help the reader? (See pages 641–643.)

• Is the Works Cited page formatted properly? (See pages 652–674.)

DELIVERY

College students are always learning new concepts, some clearly related to a chosen career, others more clearly related to everyday life. While professors and textbooks explain "academic" concepts, the rest of us explain "everyday" concepts. Distinguishing between the two is not always possible. Concepts of marketing, engineering, psychology, art, and so on affect our everyday lives, which is one reason for learning about them—even if our major is something else. The concepts learned in college are sometimes more complex or explained in greater depth. But concepts learned outside college—from childhood to old age—are often just as challenging and just as important. What might be the consequences of your essay for this chapter? That is, what effect might your ideas have on your reader's thoughts and actions?

Consider these questions:

- Will the reader better understand the issue about which you wrote?

- Is the reader likely to think or behave differently?

- What might be the benefits to others? How might others be harmed?

- Who besides your instructor might benefit from your ideas?

- How might what you wrote about be affected?

- What might be the effect of these consequences on you, the writer?

Beyond the Essay: Conceptual Mapping

A conceptual map is a graphic presentation of ideas. Using words, shapes, lines, even photographs, the creator of a conceptual map attempts to depict the complexity of ideas—how they relate, what they mean in relation to other ideas. This strategy is well suited for illustrating the various layers of a concept. For instance, on the following two pages, conceptual maps depict cyberspace and Wilkins's essay in this chapter.

Now that you have taken a concept, broken it down, examined its parts and layers, and explored how it works, draw your understanding.

- Try to depict the complexity of your ideas using only key words or phrases from your essay.

- Graphically show how those words and phrases relate.

- Use lines, arrows, and other shapes to depict the relationship between ideas.

- Use colors (if possible) to group ideas or to distinguish between types of ideas.

Present your conceptual map to others. Explain how the map represents the complexity of the ideas in your essay. Also explain how the map reinforces or falls short of the essay.

This conceptual map, designed by Nathan Shedroff for Cyber Geography, represents the relationships in cyberspace: With the placement of each term, line, and graphic, the designer suggests particular connections. Notice, for instance, that one of the outer spheres is "time" and it turns in tandem with "read." This suggests that time, in cyberspace, is dependent on the act of reading. This interesting relationship is part of Shedroff's particular conceptualization.

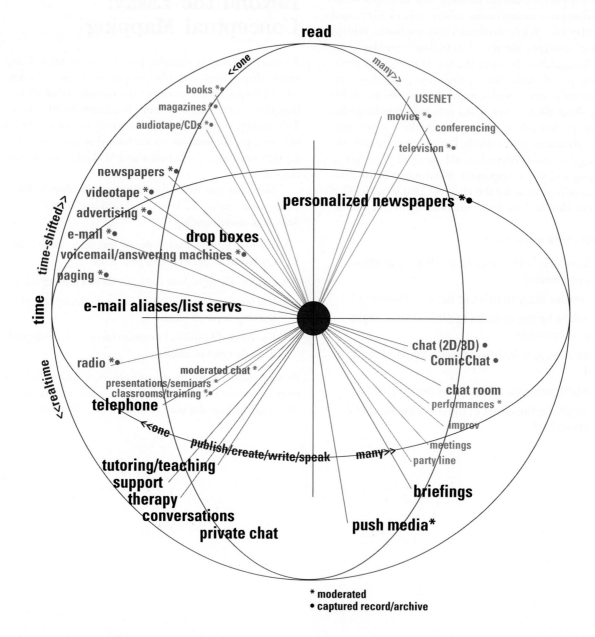

Source: (Nathan Shedroff for Cyber Geography)

Any idea can be mapped graphically. For example, the main idea in Wilkins's essay might be graphically portrayed by the illustration below. Here, the designer places "Handicap" in a contrary position to "Someone." This opposition gets to the tension in Wilkins's essay. In the middle is "Pity."

The map suggests that we must get over pity (and its support tools, such as telethons) to arrive at a conception of "Someone with a disability." In other words, we have to move beyond pity to see the person rather than the handicap. (The map helps us to see new dimensions to Wilkins's idea!)

ANALYZING IMAGES

WHAT'S THE RUSH?

THERE'S A TV SHOW ON SLEDDING I WANT TO WATCH.

IN MY OPINION, TELEVISION VALIDATES EXISTENCE.

TAKE THIS SLED RIDE, FOR INSTANCE. THE EXPERIENCE IS FLEETING AND ELUSIVE. BY TOMORROW, WE'LL HAVE FORGOTTEN IT, AND IT MAY AS WELL HAVE NOT EVEN HAPPENED.

BUT IF WE WERE ON TV NOW COUNTLESS VIEWERS WOULD SHARE IN THE EVENT AND CONFIRM IT! THIS RIDE WOULD BECOME A PART OF MASS CONSCIOUSNESS!

AND ON TV, THE IMPACT OF AN EVENT IS DETER-MINED BY THE IMAGE, NOT ITS SUBSTANCE.

SO WITH SOME STRONG VISUALS, OUR SLED RIDE COULD CONCEIVABLY MAKE US CULTURAL *ICONS*!

INSTEAD OF BEING BORING OL' CALVIN AND HOBBES, WE'D BE "CALVIN AND HOBBES-*AS SEEN ON TV*"! WOULDN'T THAT BE GREAT? DON'T YOU WISH WE WERE ON TV?

AT THIS MOMENT, I LIKE MY ANONYMITY.

I THINK WE SHOULD GO FOR THE HIGH-BROW PUBLIC TV AUDIENCE, DON'T YOU?

Chapter Contents

CHAPTER

"At the speed of light, policies and political parties yield place to the charismatic images."

—Marshall McLuhan

Mainstream life in the United States is deluged with images, not random pictures and photographs, but carefully selected images designed to influence what we think and how we feel. We are surrounded by drawings, computer graphics, digitized photos, and airbrushed faces. The minute details of each appeal to our values, desires, needs, and assumptions. And even after the image itself is gone and its immediate appeal is behind us, it still influences how we see the rest of the world.

There is no doubt about it: The barrage of images in our culture dramatically influences how we think, how we live, what we value, what we believe. But are we victims of everything we see? Is each advertisement, poster, graphic, and illustration another intellectual demand? Can we do more than see and accept? What value is gained from seeing inside the workings of images? Living in an image-soaked culture prompts such questions. Especially since most of the images we encounter were designed to influence our thinking, such questions may be vital.

As images in consumer society become increasingly sophisticated, consumers themselves also need to become more sophisticated seers. As the appeals to our eyes become more nuanced and intense, we have to become equally nuanced in our understanding. Just as we should become sophisticated readers of written language, we should become sophisticated readers of images. We'll then be more able to see what things are about—and what else they are about. When we break down an image, we can better understand how it works, how it conveys meaning, how it conceals values and beliefs. And we can also better understand how that image relates to the world around it. In short, the more analytical we become, the more we see.

Analysis is the act of breaking down something to its basic elements and attempting to understand something of value in the process. Therefore, analyzing images involves breaking down the elements of an image and understanding how those elements convey ideas and feelings, how they work on the consciousness of the viewer, how they speak to a surrounding culture, and how they resonate with surrounding values and beliefs.

At first glance, images might seem simple, coherent, and impenetrable. However, even the most simplistic image has rhetorical tools, strategies for persuading readers of some idea. For example, the following advertisements were posted on the window of a health food store.

The poster on the far left relies on the image of a young woman. She is sassy and vibrant. She asserts herself outward. The image connects the product and health with youth, vitality, and even a fashionable hairstyle and makeup. The poster on the right features a sunflower, a symbol of nature and purity. The sunflower, along with the promotion for a "new look," sits on a green background, which helps convey newness and freshness.

Such details are no accidents. They are closely scrutinized and are meant to impact consciousness in particular ways. But even if they were accidents, the particular elements impact readers. The particulars help convey ideas, assumptions, and values. Any detail, a streak of sunlight through an image or the reflection of a passing car, may also create an effect—whether the artist intended it or not. Regardless of the intent, we should be cognizant of the way details, the minute and the marginal, figure into the meaning of the image.

This chapter will help you analyze a particular image, develop focused explanation, and communicate your ideas in writing. Specifically, the goal is to explain how the elements of an image work to impact the feelings and consciousness of viewers. The following essays will provide valuable insight into various analytical strategies. After reading the essays, you can find an image in one of two ways:

1. Go to the **Point of Contact** section to find a topic from your everyday life.
2. Choose one of the **Ideas for Writing** that follow the essays.

After finding a subject, go to the **Analysis** section to begin developing the evaluation.

The writers in this chapter all attest to the power and pervasiveness of images in mainstream American life. From cartoons to television to print ads, sophisticated and calculated images encircle mainstream public life. For many writers, the sheer volume and intensity of media images prompts concern—and the impetus to think critically about them. The writers in this chapter all focus on a particular set of images (on television or in print ads) and reveal how those images create meaning or impact culture. Each writer attempts to reveal the inner workings or patterns in the images that people might otherwise take for granted.

Addiction as a Relationship

Jean Kilbourne

Advertising populates nearly every facet of everyday life. And that consistent wash of advertising involves a consistent set of themes. For years, Jean Kilbourne has been analyzing those themes and sharing her insights with large audiences. In her analyses, she has discovered the extent to which recurring ideas (such as fragmentation of women's bodies, packaged rebellion, addiction as relationship) haunt the advertising landscape. The following essay shows how many ads attempt to replace interpersonal human relationships with addictive products.

"Do you love beer?" A smooth male voice asks, while the camera lovingly caresses a foaming glass of beer. "If you could have only one thing in your refrigerator, what would it be? . . . How many different languages

can you order beer in? . . . Have you ever spent twenty minutes in the beer aisle? . . . Do you love beer?" This is one in a series of commercials for Sam Adams beer that ask different versions of the same question.

A very powerful 1997 commercial gives the alcoholic's answer to this question. The opening shot is of beer pouring from a tap. A man in his bedroom, looking haggard and anxious, hung over, looks into the mirror and sees an image of Guinness. On the soundtrack we hear the old Platters hit, "My prayer is to linger with you, at the end of the day, in a dream that's divine."

The man hears the ocean roar, looks up at a skylight, and sees the image of Guinness again. He looks at an aquarium and sees the image again. He goes outdoors and sees the image in a puddle. He is in a bar, everything in slow motion, welcomed warmly by friends. A woman looks at him very intensely, but he raises his glass of Guinness, which completely obscures her face. He licks his lips and focuses entirely on the drink. This commercial completely captures the alcoholic's intense focus on his drug—the man sees the bottle everywhere, his drink obliterates the face of the woman looking at him. She is of no importance—only the bottle is real to him.

Advertisers spend an enormous amount of money on psychological research. As the chairman of one advertising agency says, "If you want to get into people's wallets, first you have to get into their lives." As a result, they understand addiction very well. Soon after I began my study of alcohol advertising, I realized with horror that alcohol advertisers understand alcoholism perhaps better than any other group in the country. And they use this knowledge to keep people in denial.

5   The addict's powerful belief that the substance is a friend or lover is constantly reinforced by advertising. In alcohol ads, the bottle itself is sometimes portrayed as the friend or family member. "Bring our family home for the holidays," says a Michelob ad, in which the beer bottles are dressed up as Santa Claus. Another describes a bottle of vodka as "The perfect summer guest." A sign outside a bar at Chicago's O'Hare Airport says, "Why wait at the gate? Your Bud's at the bar." Bud Light takes this theme one step further in an ad featuring two women engrossed in conversation over bottles of beer, with the copy, "Is the best thing about sharing a secret who you share it with or what you share it over?"

Dogs often appear in alcohol ads as a symbol of "man's best friend." A gorgeous Irish setter is pictured in a Johnnie Walker Red ad above the headline, "It's funny how often the comforts of home include Red." A cognac ad, featuring a bloodhound sleeping by the fire, declares "You've been working like one for years, it's time you threw yourself a bone," and a Saint Bernard with a bottle of Chivas Regal around his neck appears above the copy, "It's enough to make you want to get lost." A beer called "Red Dog" uses a picture of a bulldog and the slogan "Be your own dog." More recently, a Miller Lite commercial shows people playing with a puppy and announcing that the beer is "Man's Other Best Friend." The message is clear: Alcohol is loyal and steadfast, just like your dog. Alcohol will never let you down. Alcohol is always there when you need it.

Cigarettes are also often portrayed as friends, companions. Anthropomorphic cigarettes star in a campaign for Benson & Hedges. "Sitting and talking" features two cigarettes on a porch swing. This pitch is especially effective with women because we are socialized to see ourselves in a relational context. Many cigarette ads feature women together, often just talking, with the cigarette as the symbolic bond between them. Sometimes there is deliberate ambiguity about whether the most important relationship is with the friend or the cigarette, as in a Virginia Slims ad featuring two women together with the copy, "The best part about taking a break is who you take it with."

Cigarettes are also used by women, and sometimes by men as well, to facilitate relationships in other ways. They can defuse tense situations or hide anxiety. There is a whole lexicon of smoking as a facilitator for sexual activity, ranging from the man handing a lit cigarette to a woman to her blowing the smoke suggestively in his direction to the two of them sharing a cigarette in the bedroom following their lovemaking.

Even more than a friendship, addiction is a romance—a romance that inevitably goes sour, but that is amazingly intense. As Lou Reed sang in a song called "Heroin," "It's my life and it's my wife." "Your Basic Romance" says a cigarette ad, while another, headlined "Moonlight and Romance," features two cigarettes touching by the light of the moon. And an ad for More features the cigarette leaning against a personal ad that says, "Wanted. Tall dark stranger for long lasting relationship. Good looks, great taste a must. Signed, Eagerly Seeking Smoking Satisfaction." The long brown cigarette is, of course, the "tall dark stranger." And the tobacco industry certainly hopes that the relationship will be long-lasting.

10   A liqueur ad features a loving couple and the headline "The romance never goes out of some marriages." But it turns out the true marriage is of Benedictine and Brandy, the ingredients of the liqueur. "The result is what every marriage should be—unvarying delight. That's why when there is romance in your soul, there should be B and B in your glass." Alcoholics are far more likely than nonalcoholics to be divorced, but maybe that's because they weren't drinking B and B. And smokers are 53 percent more likely to have been divorced than nonsmokers. An important part of the denial so necessary to maintain alcoholism or any other addiction is the belief that one's alcohol use isn't affecting one's relationships. The truth, of course, is that

addictions shatter relationships. Ads like the one for B and B help support the denial and go one step further by telling us that alcohol is, in fact, an enhancement to relationships.

"In life there are many loves. But only one Grande Passion," says an ad featuring a couple in a passionate embrace. Is the passion enhanced by the liqueur or is the passion for the liqueur? For many years I described my drinking as a love affair, joking that Jack Daniels was my most constant lover. When I said this at my lectures or my support group meetings, there were always nods of recognition. Caroline Knapp used this idea as the central metaphor of her memoir about her recovery from alcoholism, *Drinking: A Love Story*, which begins, "It happened this way: I fell in love and then, because the love was ruining everything I cared about, I had to fall out." And Margaret Bullitt-Jonas titled her book about recovering from an eating disorder *Holy Hunger: A Memoir of Desire*.

I can remember loving the names of drinks, from sloe gin fizzes to Manhattans. I loved the look of bottles glowing like jewels in the mirror of a bar—ruby, amber, emerald, topaz. I loved the paraphernalia of drinking—the cherries and olives, the translucent slices of lemon, the salt on the rim of the glass, the frost on the shotglass waiting for the syrupy Stolichnaya straight from the freezer.

Even now, over twenty years since my last drink, if I suddenly catch a glimpse of Jack Daniels on a shelf or in someone's shopping cart, it's a bit like running into an old lover—a lover who was dangerous and destructive, but who completely captured my heart. "You Don't Own Me" was my theme song in high school, a reflection of how frightened I was by intimate relationships, but the truth is that, for many crucial years thereafter, alcohol owned me, heart and soul.

I loved the way alcohol made me feel, the coziness and warmth, the lifting of care. I remember how the first sip of alcohol felt so warm, every time. The glowing feeling in my solar plexus grew more intense as I got high. I felt embraced by alcohol, felt safely enclosed in a little cave of amber light. When I was with another person, I often mistook that little cave for intimacy. The rest of the world went away.

15   I've been struck since by how many ads re-create the glow, the cave of amber light. There is often a golden halo around the bottle or around the drink itself. A cognac ad features two men, perhaps a father and son, embracing. The copy says, "If you've ever come in from the cold, you already know the feeling of Cognac Hennessy." The two men are in black and white, but the label and the glasses of cognac are a rich, deep amber. The alcohol ads not only promise intimacy, they promise spectacular intimacy, a closeness one has never experienced before. The men in the cognac ad were perhaps estranged, they were out in the cold. Now they are inside the circle of warmth, and alcohol has brought them there. For many years I believed, as most alcoholics do, that only alcohol could take me into that circle. Without it, I was outside, alone. It frightens me still to realize how deeply alcohol advertisers understand that precise nature of the addiction and how deliberately and destructively they use their knowledge.

It is one thing when advertisers exploit people's longing for relationship and connection to sell us shoes or shampoo or even cars. It is quite another when they exploit it to sell us an addictive product. . . . [S]ome of the ways that products seem to meet Jean Baker Miller's terms for a growth-enhancing connection—increased sense of zest, empowerment to act, greater clarity and self-knowledge, a greater sense of self-worth, and a desire for more connection—are funny and clever and seemingly harmless. It's a great deal more sinister when the products are potentially addictive. We're not likely really to believe that shampoo is going to improve our sex lives, for example, but we might well believe that champagne will.

It is especially sinister for women because so much of our drinking is connected with our relationships with other people. This begins in childhood when problems in relationships, such as early separation from a parent or sexual abuse, predict a greater likelihood of alcoholism. Later in life a loss or impairment of a close relationship, such as divorce or having a partner with whom we feel unable to talk, often influences women drinkers to drink more heavily. And many women drink in an attempt to facilitate relationships, to reduce sexual inhibition, and to be able to speak more openly, especially when angry or upset. Perhaps we are especially vulnerable to the advertising messages that promise us a relationship with an addictive product.

In the beginning, most addictions seem to fill us with zest and vitality and advertising often plays on this. "Alive with pleasure" and "Fire it up!" say the cigarette ads, while a beer ad proclaims. "Grab for all the gusto you can," as if a product that eventually numbs many of us could help us live more intensely. "Pursue your passion and new possibilities will awaken," claims an ad for Scotch. A gin ad features a man blissfully swimming in a sea of alcohol, with the caption "Innervigoration." Since gin is a clear drink, a huge lemon slice provides the glow, the amber light.

We feel *empowered to act* by our addictions, often foolishly or rebelliously. "Yes, I can!" says a cigarette ad. "Anything can happen," claims a campaign for tequila, featuring young happy people in glamorous outdoor settings. Yet the ads promise us that the only results of such impulsiveness will be adventure and romance. What happens in the ads, of course, is always wonderful—picnics on the beach at sunset, hang-gliding. Even though most of us know, on some level, that the surprises that accompany drinking are not usually so pleasant, the ads are still seductive.

20   In a commercial for Zima, a malt-based alcohol, a young woman sits at an airport bar, her flight to Minneapolis delayed. The bartender pours her a Zima, she takes a sip, she hears the announcement of a flight to Paris, and she spontaneously departs for the City of Light (fortunately, she must have had her passport on hand). The Zima is her magic carpet.

The promise always is that the surprise will be happy—a flight to Paris as opposed to a car crash, falling in love rather than being raped on a date, winning the lottery as opposed to getting AIDS from unprotected drunken sex. Or, less dramatically, picnicking on a beach at sunset rather than throwing up at midnight, being the life of the party as opposed to insulting the host.

"Your night is about to take an unexpected twist," promises an ad for gin. One is supposed to think of adventure, not embarrassment, certainly not catastrophe.

Alcohol gives us the illusion of *clarity*. "In vino veritas," we are told. Alcohol sometimes loosens our tongues so we can speak the truth, but for alcoholics it far more often makes us project our grief and self-hatred onto those closest to us. Through a combination of denial and projection, alcoholism prevents us from seeing the truth about ourselves or our loved ones. And yet sometimes alcohol is very directly advertised as a way to achieve clarity. A scotch ad headlined "Vision" continues, "Seeing clearly is the first step towards acting decisively," as if the drink would contribute to this.

As always, the mythology presented in the alcohol ads is exactly the opposite of the truth about alcohol. Again and again, alcohol is advertised as a way to enhance communication. One ad says, "If the world's biggest problem is a lack of communication, might we suggest a corner table and a fine scotch." Another, featuring a young couple walking together, promises "the art of conversation" along with the cognac.

25   With enough alcohol, the ads tell us, conversation can be dispensed with altogether: "You must be reading my mind" is the caption over a picture of another young couple walking arm in arm on a cobblestone street, beneath golden gaslights.

"Can the generation gap be bridged?" asks another ad, which concludes that perhaps the right kind of scotch can bridge it. Of course, the truth is that alcohol is far more likely to widen gaps between people than to bridge them.

"I love you, man," says a son to his father while the two are fishing in a very successful Bud Light commercial. However, it turns out he just wants his father's beer and his father snaps back, "You're not getting my Bud Light."

"We sat, my father and I, and indulged in fine cigars and the taste of Pinch. Then we did something we rarely do. We talked," says a scotch ad, one of many in which advertisers offer alcohol as a route to intimacy.

The promise of better communication between parents and children is particularly ironic given the devastating effects of parental alcoholism on children and families. Alcohol is involved in over half of all cases of domestic violence and child abuse, and alcoholic families are usually marked by denial and silence (interrupted in many families by emotional and physical explosions, but not by communication). Yet the bottle often represents home itself, as in a Smirnoff vodka campaign with the slogans, "Home is where you find it," and, "Isn't it funny how so many of the places we find Smirnoff feel like home?" "Home improvement," claims an ad for Bacardi rum, while a beer ad tells us that "a man's beer is his castle." Indeed. Almost any child of an alcoholic would find the Absolut ad featuring every window and door of a house in the shape of a bottle an unintentionally ironic picture of the huge and destructive role that alcohol so often plays in families. More accurate, albeit unintentionally, is a rum ad that says, "The dark taste that eclipses everything."

Any kind of addiction gets in the way of communication, mostly because the addict is so focused on the substance. A woman in an ice cream ad says, "I was talking to my boyfriend as I unwrapped my Häagen-Dazs Vanilla Almond Bar. Slowly his voice started to drift away. Completely consumed, I carefully licked the thick Belgian chocolate off. Then I immersed myself in the creamy center. Of all the wonderful things I can say about Häagen-Dazs, I can't say it's great for conversation."

30   Of course, food and drink can be wonderful for conversation. It somehow seems easier to have intimate conversation while sharing something to eat or drink, a glass of wine, a caffe latte, a good meal. I remember the taste of the chicory in the coffee and the powdered sugar on the beignet as I talked with a friend in New Orleans, a few years after I got sober, about my childhood. "You must have thought you were a bad person," she said and, at that moment, I realized that I had thought that for a long, long time but I no longer did. I realized, as I savored the rich taste of the coffee and the southern sun warm on my skin and the compas-

sionate perceptiveness of my friend, that I was happier than I had ever expected to be.

However a glass of wine might enhance a conversation, a bottle of wine will make it at best difficult to recall. When the food or the alcohol or any addictive substance becomes the focal point, relationships inevitably suffer. Countless children grow up with parents whose attention is tragically diverted by an addiction.

Through the miracle of denial, alcohol seems to increase our sense of self-worth, but in fact it mires us more deeply in our self-hatred. "Love thyself," says an ad for scotch, one of many ads offering alcohol as a reward, a gift for oneself. "I.O. ME" declares a billboard ad for whiskey. Ads often offer us alcohol and food as richly deserved rewards, whatever the occasion. It takes an enormous amount of energy to maintain the kind of denial necessary to protect an alcoholic from his or her self-loathing. It is so painful to face the deep belief that one is worthless, unlovable, that many alcoholics, especially male alcoholics, seek refuge in grandiosity—which is, after all, a form of self-hatred. The alcohol advertisers know this—and play on it in ad after ad.

Finally, what is addiction if not a *desire for more connection*? Unfortunately, it is a connection that makes human connection and real intimacy difficult, if not impossible. "More…more…more…gin taste," one ad declares. More gin taste simply means more gin, of course. "More" is even the name of a cigarette brand. "Absolut Attraction," says an ad featuring a cocktail glass leaning toward a bottle of vodka. People are not even present and yet the ad still implies a promise of greater connection.

Most often, the intimate connection that the alcohol ads offer is a sexual experience. Countless ads feature couples passionately embracing with suggestive copy such as, "May all your screwdrivers be Harvey Wallbangers," "Wild things happen in the 'oui' hours," and, "Is it proper to Boodle before the guests arrive?" "If the French can do this with a kiss…," asks an ad featuring a man passionately kissing a woman's neck, "imagine what they can do with a vodka!" Given that the vodka is called Grey Goose, I hate to think.

35   Of course, alcohol has long been advertised to men as a way to seduce women. An ad for Cherry Kijafa from the 1970s features a virginal young woman dressed entirely in white and the headline "Put a little cherry in your life." Such double entendres abound, ranging from a cocktail called "Sex on the Beach" to an ad featuring a young man dressed as a fencer declaring, "I'm as sure of myself on each thrust as I am when choosing my scotch." In a series of suggestive print and television ads in the 1980s, Billy Dee Williams promised that Colt 45 malt liquor "works every time." Years later a radio ad, also for malt liquor and also targeting young African-American men, said, "Grab a six-pack and get your girl in the mood quicker. Get your jimmy thicker with St. Ides malt liquor." Imagine—our kids are growing up in this kind of environment and some people think it's enough to tell them to "just say no" to sex. "Get your jimmy thicker" but keep it in your pants?

An extremely erotic 1999 ad for Kahlua pictures a milkmaid lasciviously pouring milk all over her leg. Her head is tossed back and her eyes closed, as if she were in the throes of orgasm. The goosebumps on her leg are obvious as is the erect state of her exposed nipple. "Anything goes" is the tagline.

Using sex to sell alcohol certainly isn't new. What is new in recent years is the promise in alcohol ads of a sexual relationship with the alcohol itself. No longer a means to an end, the drink has become the end. "You never forget your first girl" is the slogan for St. Pauli Girl's beer. "Just one sip of St. Pauli Girl's rich, imported taste is the start of a beautiful relationship." "Pilsner is a type of beer," says an ad featuring a beautiful young woman, "kind of like Rebecca is a type of woman." The ad concludes that it would be great to meet either one in a bar.

"Six Appeal" is the slogan for an ad that features a six-pack of beer and the copy, "The next time you make eye contact with a six-pack of Cold-Filtered Miller Genuine Draft Longnecks, go ahead and pick one up. You won't be disappointed!" In a 1998 Bud commercial, a group of women are standing in a bar and, nodding toward some leering guys, talk about how men think about "it" every eight seconds. But it turns out that the guys are ogling bottles of Bud. An Absolut ad features the top part of a woman's leg clad in a black silk stocking with a garter in the familiar shape of the Absolut bottle. This focus on one part of the female body, this dismemberment, is common in ads for many products, but especially so for alcohol. The image draws men in, but there is no person, not even a whole body to distract them from the focus of the ad, the bottle.

Women are increasingly encouraged to think of the bottle as a lover too. "If your man won't pour, I will," says an ad for cognac which features the bottle rakishly leaning toward the woman. Another ad pictures a bottle of whisky in a drawstring pouch with the tagline "Smooth operator." In an ad for an Italian wine called Florio, a beautiful and sultry woman says, "For 15 nights I have been with Florio. Never once was it the same." This reminds me of a joke I used to make about my drinking years—that perhaps I had had the same conversation every night over and over again and just didn't know it!

40   In the early 1980s Campari ran a series of ads featuring celebrities such as Geraldine Chaplin and Jill St. John talking lasciviously about their "first time." "There are so many different ways to enjoy it," Chaplin says. "Once I even tried it on the rocks. But I wouldn't recommend that for beginners." The sophomoric campaign used the slogans, "The first time is never the best," and, "You'll never forget your first time." One of the ironies of this campaign is that alcoholics usually do remember their first drink and often romanticize it. For this reason, there's a saying among alcoholics that we should remember our last drunk, not our first drink.

A rawer version of the sexualization of the product was a campaign for the subtly named Two Fingers tequila. Every ad in the campaign featured an older man caressing a beautiful younger woman and saying such things as, "This woman, she is like my tequila. Smooth, but with a lot of spirit," and, "Señor, making good tequila is like looking for a good woman." One of the ads further describes the woman as "the only other love Two Fingers had besides his tequila." Given their age difference, it seems that Two Fingers spent most of his life in love with tequila.

A strange campaign for Hiram Walker liqueurs personifies the product in a series of ads. In one a beautiful young woman says, "Hiram Walker knows the way to Kokomo." She continues, "He took me there late last night. I hadn't packed a bag. But he said all I needed was the right attitude." Another ad in the campaign features a fairly distraught young man saying, "Who is this Hiram Walker guy anyway?" He goes on to say, "My girlfriend couldn't stop talking about him. 'He's spirited . . . and sophisticated . . . and fun. Everything a man should be!' I said, 'Listen, it's him or me. Make up your mind.' She said, 'I want you both.'" The young man ends up having some Hiram Walker, saying, "If you can't beat him, join him." Sadly, this is an attitude many people adopt when dealing with alcoholics.

In this case, the man is introduced to the drink by the woman. Usually, in life and advertising, it is the other way around. Women and girls are usually introduced to alcohol and other drugs by their boyfriends, who generally are older and more experienced. Women often use the drugs to please their men, to have a common activity, or simply to make the relationship bearable.

The advertisers sometimes encourage women to drink in order to keep company with drinking men. "Share the secret of Cristal," says a beautiful woman. The copy continues, "The Columbians kept it to themselves. Men mostly drank it straight. I thought it was pretty tough stuff 'til the night I met him in Miami and he persuaded me to try CRISTAL & O.J. on ice. Very nice!" Often, as in this ad, the man is urged to drink the product straight while the woman is encouraged to cut it with juice, orange juice in this case, or soda (a more "feminine" approach).

45   The increasing sexualization of alcohol in ads parallels the progression of the disease of alcoholism, in which alcohol plays a more and more important role. Alcohol is used initially by many people as an attempt to increase confidence, especially sexual confidence, and for some a drink or two can lead to greater relaxation and less inhibition (although intoxication usually reduces sexual responsiveness). For the alcoholic, however, alcohol eventually becomes the most important thing in life and makes other relationships, including sexual relationships, more difficult, if not impossible. Thus, the ads move from a soft-core promise of sexual adventure and fulfillment with a partner to a more hard-core guarantee of sexual fulfillment without the trouble of a relationship with a human being. Alcohol becomes the beloved. And when alcohol is the beloved, relationships with people—with lovers, children, friends—suffer terribly.

One of the most chilling commercials I've ever seen is a 1999 one for Michelob. It opens with an African-American man and woman in bed, clearly just after making love. A fire is blazing and romantic music is playing. "Baby, do you love me?" the woman asks. "Of course I do," the man replies. "What do you love about me most?" she asks. The man looks thoughtful, "Well, Michelob, I love you more than life itself." "What did you call me?" the woman asks indignantly. "I called you Theresa," he replies. "No, you did not," she says, leaping from the bed. "You just called me Michelob. I'm outta here." "Wait, wait," the man says. "What?" she asks. "While you're up," the man says, "could you get me a Michelob?" On the surface, this commercial is intended to be funny, of course. But on a deeper level, and I believe intentionally on the part of the advertisers, it is meant to normalize and trivialize a symptom of alcoholism. The terrible truth is that alcoholics do love alcohol more than the people in their lives and indeed more than life itself.

The Black Velvet campaign of the late 1970s and early 1980s featured a beautiful blonde wearing a sexy black velvet outfit seductively inviting the viewer to "Feel the Velvet" or "Touch the Velvet" or "Try Black Velvet on this weekend." A few years ago, a product called Nude Beer went further and featured a bikini-topped model on the label. The bikini top could be scratched off, revealing her bare breasts. Even then, however, although the woman was a symbol of the alcohol, the focus was still on her.

In recent years, women's bodies in alcohol ads are often turned into bottles of alcohol, as in the Tanqueray gin ad in which the label is branded on the woman's stomach. A beer ad shows cases of Miller Lite stacked (so to speak) on a beach, with the headline "The perfect 36–24–36." There are women in bikinis in the background but clearly the headline refers to the numbers of cans of beer. "The best little can in Texas" pictures a close-up of a woman's derriere with a beer can held up against it. In these cases, the woman is the intermediary. Sometimes the bottle literally becomes the woman, as in an Original Red ad. At least in these ads, a real woman is present to some degree, although objectified and dismembered. In many alcohol ads these days, the woman is completely dispensed with and the bottle itself is sexualized. A college poster advertising beer features a glass of beer and the caption, "Great head, good body."

"Italy's classics have always had great shapes," declares an ad spotlighting a curvaceous bottle of an Italian liqueur. "Not exactly for the bourbon virgin," says an ad for Knob Creek bourbon featuring an extreme closeup of the bottle with an emphasis on the word "pro" within "proof" (this campaign was so successful, it increased sales by 55 percent). "You'd even know us in the nude," says an ad for scotch, which features a man's hand suggestively peeling back the label from the bottle. Again, the promise is that the alcohol alone will provide a fulfilling relationship, even a sexual relationship—nothing else is necessary.

50   The popular Absolut campaign has several ads in which the bottle is sexualized, including "Absolut Centerfold," which features the bottle without its label, and "Absolut Marilyn," in which the bottle symbolized Marilyn Monroe in her famous dance above the grating.

"A few insights into the dreams of men," says an ad that features four cartoon men dreaming of a bottle of whiskey. "Yes, men dream in color" is the caption above the first man, referring to a drawing of the bottle in a colorful velvet sack. "The average male only remembers 62% of his dreams," is above the second man and the bottle is one-third gone. "5% of all men have a recurring nightmare" is the caption for a picture of an empty bottle. "Every man gets aroused at least once per night,"

depicts a case of whiskey. Women don't exist in this ad, even in the dreams of men. Preoccupation with alcohol is one of the signs of alcoholism. Some alcoholics don't drink all that much, but all alcoholics think about drinking a lot of the time. This ad, in its funny, light-hearted way, normalizes this preoccupation. But the truth is that people who are preoccupied with alcohol create nightmares for themselves and others.

Sometimes it is the drink that is sexualized rather than the bottle. "Peachtree excites soda," proclaims a liqueur ad. A series of ads for Seagram's Extra Dry Gin features extreme close-ups of the gin in a glass with an olive, a piece of lemon, and a cherry with the bold headlines, "Arouse an olive," "Tease a twist," "Unleash a lime," and "It's enough to make a cherry blush."

Even the cork sometimes gets into the act as in a liqueur ad featuring a phallic cork and the words "It's not a stopper. It's a starter." Such suggestiveness might seem silly and trivial or unconscious, as perhaps it sometimes is. However, given the money and energy that advertisers spend on psychological research and the undeniable usefulness of linking sex and power with a product, I contend that most of these visual and verbal puns and symbols are intended by the advertisers as yet another cynical ploy to influence us.

Ad after ad promises us that alcohol will give us great sex. The truth is exactly the opposite. Not only do high-risk quantities of alcohol often lead to sexual dysfunction, for women as well as men, but they are also linked with other unwanted consequences, such as date rape, unwanted pregnancy, fetal alcohol syndrome, and sexually transmitted diseases, including AIDS. Alas, the parody "Absolut Impotence" comes closer to the real relationship between alcohol and sex. Perhaps Shakespeare put it best when he said that drink "provokes the desire, but it takes away the performance."

55   Again and again, advertising tells us that relationships with human beings are fragile and disappointing but that we can count on our products, especially our addictive products. A Winston ad features a greeting card that says, "I never really loved you," with the tagline, "Maybe there shouldn't be a card for every

occasion." Another ad in the same campaign shows a cocktail napkin with a woman's name and phone number written on it. The copy says, "Please check the number and dial again." Oh well, at least we've got our cigarettes.

In truth, addiction increasingly corrupts and co-opts every desirable outcome of real connection. The initial sense of zest and vitality is replaced by depression and despair. Our ability to act productively is severely impaired and our lives stagnate. Blinded by denial, we are unable to see ourselves or others clearly. Corroded with self-hatred, we poison our relationships and end up alienated and alone. Our world narrows as our relationship with alcohol or another drug or substance becomes our central focus. We spiral downward.

Recovery reverses this downward spiral, widening our world and our possibilities. As we break through denial and learn to be honest with ourselves and others, our clarity and our sense of self-worth dramatically increase. All of this leads to a desire for more connection, both with other people and with some kind of life force. We find in recovery everything we had longed to find in addiction—but what addiction had in fact taken from us.

Denial blinds us to the many ironies of addiction, and advertising often supports this denial. In the case of alcohol, we drink to feel glamorous and sophisticated and often end up staggering, vomiting, and screaming. We drink to feel courageous and are overwhelmed by fear and a sense of impending doom. We drink to have better sex, but alcohol eventually makes most of us sexually dysfunctional. We do this to ourselves because of our disease, but we also do it in a cultural climate in which people who understand the nature of our disease deliberately surround us with powerful images associating alcohol with glamour, courage, sexiness, and love, precisely what we need to believe in order to stay in denial.

Above all, we drink to feel connected and, in the process, we destroy all possibility of real intimacy and end up profoundly isolated. Sadly, it is perhaps in recognition of this fact that advertisers so often romanticize and sexualize the bottle. Addicts often end up alone or in very dysfunctional relationships. We turn to alcohol or other drugs or activities for solace, for comfort, for the illusion of intimacy, and even for the illusion of sex appeal or sexual fulfillment. As addiction disrupts our human connections, the substance becomes ever more important, both to numb the pain and to continue the illusion that we are doing all right. What begins as a longing for a relationship, a romance, a grand passion, inexorably ends up as solitary confinement.

Writing Strategies

1. What is Kilbourne's main idea?

2. How does Kilbourne support her main idea?

3. How does Kilbourne support the following statement: "The message is clear: Alcohol is loyal and steadfast, just like your dog. Alcohol will never let you down. Alcohol is always there when you need it." (¶ 6)

4. In paragraphs 12–15, Kilbourne shifts to first person, using the pronoun "I." How does this shift affect Kilbourne's essay? What impact might it have on the reader? Why might she have made the shift?

5. Identify one passage in which Kilbourne addresses an opposing opinion, and explain how it is important to the essay.

6. How does Kilbourne support the following statement: "The terrible truth is that alcoholics do love alcohol more than the people in their lives and indeed more than life itself." (¶ 46)

Exploring Ideas

1. Kilbourne says, "It is one thing when advertisers exploit people's longing for relationship and connection to sell us shoes or shampoo or even cars. It is quite another when they exploit it to sell us an addictive product." (¶ 16) What products or habits, besides alcohol or cigarettes, might be considered addictive? Might shoes, cars, technology, music, shopping, or food be considered addictive?

2. Kilbourne says, "As always, the mythology presented in the alcohol ads is exactly the opposite of the truth about alcohol." (¶ 24) According to Kilbourne, why can this strategy be successful?

3. Write down one statement Kilbourne makes that you disagree with. Then explore the statement further (through research, invention writing, and discussion with others), trying to change your own thinking about it.

4. What picture does Kilbourne paint of advertising?

Ideas for Writing

1. How do images play on other addictions, besides ones to alcohol and cigarettes?

2. Use Kilbourne's strategy to show how advertising works against reality to get people to purchase something (besides alcohol or cigarettes).

If responding to one of these ideas, go to the **Analysis** section of this chapter to begin developing ideas for your essay.

Rise of the Image Culture: Re-Imagining the American Dream

Elizabeth Thoman

Americans are so used to watching TV that they naturally take the commercials for granted, and don't consider the impact these images have on their lives. As Elizabeth Thoman, founder of *Media & Values* magazine, says, "Each commercial plays its part in selling an overall consumer lifestyle." Throughout her essay, Thoman explains how television commercials have become fused with the patterns and habits of everyday life— and how that fusion might be staved off with a new critical awareness.

Like most middle-class children of the '50s, I grew up looking for the American Dream. In those days there were no cartoons in my Saturday viewing, but I distinctly remember watching, with some awe, *Industry on Parade*. I felt both pride and eager anticipation as I watched tail-finned cars rolling off assembly lines, massive dams taming mighty rivers and sleek chrome appliances making life more convenient for all.

When I heard the mellifluous voice of Ronald Reagan announce on *GE Theatre* that "Progress is our most important product," little did I realize that the big box in our living room was not just entertaining me. At a deeper level, it was stimulating an "image" in my head of how the world should work: that anything new was better than something old; that science and technology were the greatest of all human achievements and that in the near future— and certainly by the time I grew up— the power of technology would make it possible for everyone to live and work in a world free of war, poverty, drudgery, and ignorance.

I believed it because I could see it—right there on television.

The American Dream, however, was around long before television. Some believe the idea of "progress" goes back to when humankind first conceived of time as linear rather than cyclical. Certainly the Judeo-Christian heritage of a Messiah leading us to a Promised Land inspired millions to strive for a better world for generations to come.

5   Indeed, it was the search for the "City on the Hill" that brought the Puritans to the American colonies and two centuries later sent covered wagons across the prairies. In 1835, Alexis de Tocqueville observed that Americans "never stop thinking of the good things they have not got," creating a "restlessness in the midst of prosperity" that drives them ever onward.

Even the U.S. Constitution, remember, only promises the pursuit of happiness. It doesn't guarantee that any of us will actually achieve it.

It is this search for "something-more-than-what-we've-got-now" that is at the heart of the consumer culture we struggle with today. But the consumer culture as we know it could never have emerged without the invention of the camera and the eventual mass-production of media images it made possible.

Reproducing Pictures

In 1859 Oliver Wendell Holmes described photography as the most remarkable achievement of his time because it allowed human beings to separate an experience or a texture or an emotion or a likeness from a particular time and place—and still remain real, visible, and permanent. He described it as a "conquest over matter" and predicted it would alter the physics of perception, changing forever the way people would see and understand the world around them. Holmes precisely observed that the emergence of this new technology marked the beginning of a time when the "image would become more important than the object itself and would in fact make the object disposable." Contemporary advertising critic Stuart Ewen describes the photographic process as "skinning" the world of its visible images, then marketing those images inexpensively to the public.

But successive waves of what might be called reality-freezing technology—first the photograph, followed by the phonograph and the motion picture camera—were only some of many 19th-century transformations that paved the way to our present image culture. As the wheels of industrialization began to mass-produce more and more consumer goods, they also increased the leisure time available to use these products and the disposable income required to buy them. Soon the well-being of the economy itself became dependent on an ever-expanding cornucopia of products, goods, and services. The Sears-Roebuck catalogue and the department store emerged to showcase America's new abundance and by the turn of the century, as media critic Todd Gitlin notes, "production, packaging, marketing, advertising, and sales became functionally inseparable." The flood of commercial images also served as a rough-and-ready consumer education course for the waves of immigrants to America's shores and the thousands of rural folk lured to the city by visions of wealth. Advertising was seen as a way of educating the masses "to the cycle of the marketplace and to the imperatives of factory work and mechanized labor"—teaching them "how to behave like human beings in the machine age," according to the Boston department store magnate Edward A. Filene. In a work world where skill meant less and less, obedience and appearance took on greater importance. In a city full of strangers, advertising offered instructions on how to dress, how to behave, how to *appear* to others in order to gain approval and avoid rejection.

10   Granted, the American "standard of living" brought an end to drudgery for some, but it demanded a price for all: consumerism. Divorced from craft standards, work became merely the means to acquire the money to buy the goods and lifestyle that supposedly signified social acceptance, respect, even prestige. "Ads spoke less and less about the quality of the products being sold," notes Stuart Ewen, "and more about the lives of the people being addressed."

In 1934, when the Federal Communications Commission approved advertising as the economic basis of the country's fledgling radio broadcasting system, the die was cast. Even though early broadcasters pledged to provide free time for educational programs, for coverage of religion and for news (creating the famous phrase: the "public interest, convenience, and necessity"), it wasn't long before the industry realized that time was money—and every minute counted. Since free enterprise dictates that it's better to make money than to lose it, the American commercial broadcasting system was born. But it was not until the 1950s that the image culture came into full flower. The reason? Television.

Television was invented in the 1930s, but for many years no one thought it had any practical use. Everyone had a radio, even two or three, which brought news and sports and great entertainment right into your living room And if you tired of the antics of *Fibber McGee and Molly* or the adventures of *Sargent Preston of the Yukon,* you could always go to the movies, which was what most people did at least once a week.

So who needed television? No one, really. What needed television, in 1950, was the economy. The postwar economy needed television to deliver first to America—and then to the rest of the world—the vision, the image, of life in a consumer society. We didn't object because we thought it was, well, just "progress."

What Price Progress?

Kalle Lasn, a co-founder of the Canadian media criticism and environmentalist magazine *Adbusters,* explains how dependence on television first occurred and continues today each time we turn on our sets: "In the privacy of our living rooms we made a devil's bargain with the advertising industry: Give us an endless flow of free programs and we'll let you spend 12 minutes of every hour promoting consumption. For a long time, it seemed to work. The ads grated on our nerves but it was a small price to pay for 'free' television. . . . What we didn't realize when we made our pact with the advertisers was that their agenda would eventually become the heart and soul of television. We have allowed the most powerful communications tool ever invented to become the *command center of a consumer society* defining our lives and culture the way family, community and spiritual values once did."

15 This does not mean that when we see a new toilet paper commercial we're destined to rush down to the store to buy its new or improved brand. Most single commercials do not have such a direct impact. What happens instead is a cumulative effect. Each commercial plays its part in selling an overall *consumer lifestyle.* As advertising executive Stephen Garey noted in a recent issue of *Media&Values,* when an ad for toilet paper reaches us in combination with other TV commercials, magazine ads, radio spots, and billboards for detergents and designer jeans, new cars and cigarettes, and soft drinks and cereals and computers, the collective effect is that they all *teach us to buy.* And to feel somehow dissatisfied and inadequate unless we have the newest, the latest, the best.

Just like our relatives at the turn of the century, we learned quickly to yearn for "what we have not got" and to take our identities from what we own and purchase rather than from who we are or how we interact with others. Through consuming things, through buying more and more, we continue the quest for meaning which earlier generations sought in other ways—conquering the oceans, settling the land, building the modern society, even searching for transcendence through religious belief and action. With few places on earth left to conquer today, the one endless expanse of exploration open to us is the local shopping mall.

Transcending Materialism

Thus the modern dilemma: While few of us would turn in our automatic washing machines for a scrub board or exchange our computers for a slide rule, neither can we expect the images of the past to provide the vision for the future. We must recognize the trade-offs we have made and take responsibility for the society we have created.

For many today, the myth of "progress" is stuttering to a stop. The economic slowdown of the early '90s presents only the most recent example of the human suffering created by the boom and bust cycles of the consumer economy. But even if some magic formula could make steady economic growth attainable, we can no longer afford it. Material limits have been set by the Earth itself. Unlimited exploitation in the name of "progress" is no longer sustainable.

True progress, in fact, would be toward a materially renewable lifestyle that would fulfill the physical, spiritual and emotional needs of all—not just some—of the world's people, while allowing them to live in peace and freedom. Under such a system, communication's most important aim would be to bring people together. Selling things would be a part of its function, but not the whole.

20 Disasters like Chernobyl and the Alaskan oil spill raise hard questions about the long-term social impact of technological innovation. In the U.S., the loss of whole communities to the ravages of drugs, crime, and homelessness threatens the very principles which allow any humane society to flourish.

At the same time, the global events of 1991—the breakup of the Soviet Empire, the struggles for national identity, even the rise of fundamentalist governments in many parts of the Third World—bear witness to a growing desire for meaningful connections as well as material and political progress.

In many ways we are living in a new world, and around that world hungry eyes are turning toward the Western democracies' longstanding promises of freedom and abundance—the promises the media has so tantalizingly presented.

Yet behind the media culture's constantly beckoning shop window lies an ever-widening gap. West or East, North or South, the flickering images of the media remain our window on the world, but they bear less and less relationship to the circumstances of our day-to-day lives. Reality has fallen out of sync with the pictures, but still the image culture continues.

We'll never stop living in a world of images. But we can recognize and deal with the image culture's actual state, which might be characterized as a kind of mid-life crisis—a crisis of identity. As with any such personal event, three responses are typical:

1. *Denial.* Hoping that a problem will go away if we ignore it is a natural response, but business as usual is no solution.

2. *Rejection.* Some critics believe they can use their television dials to make the image culture go away, and urge others to turn it off, too. But it's impossible to turn off an entire culture. Others check out emotionally by using drugs, alcohol, addictions of all kinds to vainly mask the hunger for meaning that comes when reality and images don't converge.

3. *Resistance.* A surprisingly active counterculture exists and is working hard to point out the dangers of over-reliance on the image culture. But such criticism is negative by its very nature, and critics tend to remain voices crying in the wilderness.

25   A positive alternative is needed. What I have called *media awareness*—the recognition of media's role in shaping our lives and molding our deepest thoughts and feelings—is an important step. The three steps I have outlined above provide simple but effective tools for beginning to work through this process. Although they seem basic, they have their roots in the profound state of being that Buddhism calls *mindfulness:* being aware, carefully examining, asking questions, being conscious.

Even a minimal effort to be conscious can make day-to-day media use more meaningful. Being conscious allows us to appreciate the pleasure of a new CD album and then later turn it off to read a bedtime story to a child. Being conscious means enjoying a TV sitcom while challenging the commercials that bait us to buy. Being conscious allows us to turn even weekend sports events into an intergenerational get-together.

But however achieved, media awareness is only a first step. Ultimately, any truly meaningful attempt to move beyond the image culture will recognize the spiritual and emotional emptiness that the material objects it sells cannot fill.

By convincing us that happiness lies at the other end of the cash register, our society has sold us a bill of goods. To move beyond the illusions of the image culture we must begin to grapple with some deeper questions: Where is the fine line between what I want and what all in society should have? What is the common good for all?

Or to rephrase Gandhi: "How do we create a society in which there is enough for everyone's need but not everyone's greed?"

30   Thousands of years ago a philosopher wrote of a cave of illusion in which captive humans were enraptured by a flood of images that appeared before them while they ignored the reality outside the cave. This prophetic metaphor contained its own solutions. Once again we are summoned into the light.

Writing Strategies

1. What connection does Thoman make between images and lifestyle?

2. What is Thoman's main idea, and how does the essay's title help to focus the reader on the main idea?

3. How does Thoman use history (her explanation of history) to develop the main idea? What other strategies does she use?

4. How is Thoman's essay a call to action?

5. What points do you think Thoman could provide better support for? How might you support those points?

Exploring Ideas

1. In paragraph 8, Thoman quotes Oliver Wendell Holmes as saying the "image would become more important than the object itself and would in fact make the object disposable." With others or alone, think of examples to support Holmes's point.

2. Is advertising education? Use your school library's online catalog to find sources that shed light on the relationship between advertising and education.

3. Interview others to find out how they think advertising influences them. Based on the interviews, to what degree would you say others have media awareness? (See paragraph 25.)

4. Read Plato's "Allegory of the Cave" to better help you understand Thoman's conclusion.

Ideas for Writing

1. Explore the relationship between advertising images and the economy.

2. Thoman says, "Most single commercials do not have such a direct impact. What happens instead is a cumulative effect." (¶ 15) Research this idea further, using a certain type of image to support or refute the theory.

If responding to one of these ideas, go to the **Analysis** section of this chapter to begin developing ideas for your essay.

What does this image invite us to value?

Cartoons 'n Comics: Communication to the Quick

Joy Clough

Like any art form or highly publicized text, a comic strip is far more than meets the (untrained) eye. It is a complex form of communication, with a set of conventions and a shared history. The comic strip artists practice a particular set of rhetorical tools—different tools than we might see or use for academic writing. In the following essay, Joy Clough, president of the Chicago Sisters of Mercy, explains how comics appeal to readers by connecting with human psychology and the particular culture of the times.

The comics. They may be worth a glance as you check your horoscope. They may provide a chuckle as you sip your morning coffee. But seriously? You can't take the comics seriously!

Au contraire. The comics are taken quite seriously—by fans whose complaints deluge any newspaper that dares cancel a strip by semi-literate adults who can find in them a sort of pictographic "Ann Landers" and certainly by historians and analysts of popular culture who regard the "funnies" as a revelatory aspect of cultural history.

The comics, say these experts, offer a cross-section of human psychology and capture significant snatches of American life and mores.

The Comics as History

A look at the evolution of the comic strip shows how the "funnies," in their own way, record history. The "Yellow Kid," born in 1895 in the *New York World,* is generally accepted as the first comic character. A violent, gangster-talking figure, the Kid would probably be banned from today's papers. His comments and struggles, however, echoed reality for the city's slum dwellers. Though the Kid died, comics, with their solid psychological appeal, were here to stay.

5   By the Roaring Twenties, such still-familiar strips as "Mutt and Jeff" and "Gasoline Alley" were populating newspaper pages. "Gasoline Alley" made comic strip history by introducing realism and allowing its characters to age. In keeping with the decade, some strips incorporated the emancipated woman. "Nancy," "Winnie Winkle," and "Blondie" (a high-fashion model) were all born in this era.

The Crash and the troubled '30s saw the rise of action comic strips. "Dick Tracy," "Terry and the Pirates," and "Buck Rogers" could take charge and set things right.

With the war in Europe spreading to the U.S., the 1940s became the decade of the comic strip superhero. Welcome "Superman" and "Wonder Woman," both vigorous fighters in the Allied cause. The comics stepped out of newspapers into books of their own with the creation of additional heroes: Batman, Captain Marvel, the Green Lantern.

The 1950s, by and large, grew reflective. Comment could be humorous or biting. "'Lil Abner" grew in popularity. "Pogo" and "Peanuts" offered observations on politics and life. The humorous side of the daily lives of ordinary mortals became the subject of such strips as "Dennis the Menace" and "Beetle Bailey."

If the '60s were an era of protest and questioning, the comics felt the mood. As "Doonesbury" was born, superheroes went into a sharp decline. The self-doubting and reluctant Peter Parker (alias Spiderman) is one of the few superheroes of recent vintage.

The Comic Appeal

10   Old-timer or newcomer, the comic strips apparently owe their ongoing appeal to solid psychology. They mirror human life and respond to the human spirit. When life is bleak, a laugh can help. When life is dull, adventure spells relief. When life seems stupid, humor-become-satire makes its point. When life is lonely, romance provides connections.

These are, in fact, the four major responses the comics offer. Humor strips like "Momma," "Marmaduke," "Hi and Lois," "Hagar," and "For Better or

For Worse" allow us to laugh at life's petty but persistent frustrations.

Adventure series like "Steve Canyon," "The Amazing Spiderman," and the perennial "Dick Tracy" and "Superman" spin stories that keep us wondering (but not worrying) about what will happen next.

Comment comics, including "Doonesbury" and "Peanuts," strike with satire at political, social, or human pretensions.

Romance or soap opera strips like "Mary Worth," "Brenda Starr," and "Dondi" provide a cast of caring characters with which to people our private worlds.

15 This unique media form has marched out of the "funny papers" to an expanded social role: to educate and irritate, tickle and tease, inform and reform.

The comics' universal appeal to the human psyche is strengthened by their universal distribution. Long before television or radio provided cross-country communication links, comic strip characters were known nationally.

They were fantasy figures inciting the imagination. They were mythic heroes proving in varied situations that right overcomes might. They were story-book characters authorized for adults, reflections of daily life, witty crusaders in a variety of causes, 20th-century successors to the likes of King Arthur and Robin Hood.

An American Art Form

Such literary connections come naturally to the comics, which, as an art form indigenous to America, have verbal as well as visual components. No serious discussion of the "funnies" can proceed far without including words like satire, allegory, fable, personification, comedy (in the classical sense), myth, pun, allusion. All these aspects of literary art exist in the comic strip.

However, it is primarily as a visual art form that the comics have made their contribution. They borrowed and refined the tools of the political cartoonist. Before movies were commonplace or television was conceived, comic strips were the storyboards from which later script writers would learn.

20 Panel by panel, they set the scene, introduced the characters, unfolded the action. Comic artists taught movie serial makers how to build to a climax and bring the audience back next week.

The strips developed their own "language" or signals: word balloons indicated dialog; sentences strung across a frame suggested narration; and the very way words were printed "produced" sound effects! Any wonder, then, that comic strips have spawned television series and vice versa?

In the enriching mix of today's media, comic strip characters continue to command considerable attention. They entertain us, exercise our fantasy and reflect wryly on the way life is. They are multiplying. They are leaping off the pages of our papers to live on our movie screens.

In doing so, they continue, like living beings, to adapt to the times. Popeye has proved capable of touching tenderness, Superman and Tarzan have found romance, Zorro has been transformed by satire. The comic strips, in turn, are welcoming into their ranks new figures from other formats—Luke Skywalker, for example, and J. R. Ewing. The comics, quite clearly, remain popular and prosperous. Some are funny. Others, serious. Taken together, however, the comics have much to reveal—about their characters, yes; but more so, about us, their readers!

Writing Strategies

1. According to Clough, why are the comics important? Why should they be taken seriously?

2. What is Clough's purpose in writing? How does she invite the reader to see comic strips differently?

3. How does Clough develop her main idea? What support is most effective?

4. Evaluate Clough's introduction and conclusion. How else might she have begun and ended her essay?

Exploring Ideas

1. In a group, choose a comic or an animated cartoon and explain how it owes its appeal to "solid psychology" and how it mirrors human life.

2. After completing #1 above, consider how your ideas changed because of the group exploration.

3. In a group, create a comic strip that reflects an important aspect of current American culture.

4. Find a comic strip online, study its images and text, and explain what it reveals about its readers.

Ideas for Writing

1. Explain how a particular comic is a "revelatory aspect of cultural history."

2. Explain how a particular ad or ad campaign is a "revelatory aspect of cultural history."

3. Look through one of your college textbooks and explain what the images reveal about the book's readers.

If responding to one of these ideas, go to the **Analysis** section of this chapter to begin developing ideas for your essay.

From your perspective, how have cartoons evolved—in style, intended audiences, and content?

The Mighty Image

Cameron Johnson

In the margins of this essay, a reader's comments point to key ideas and writing strategies. As you read the essay, consider how the comments might influence your own reading and writing.

Although exposed to advertising every day, most Americans are unaware of how advertisements/commercials work in their everyday lives. While ads and commercials seem harmless—or even absurd, as Cameron Johnson explains below—companies spend millions on advertising because it works. Johnson also explains the logic that keeps most people from seeing the effects of advertising in their lives.

Writing Strategies

Begins with public resonance: by addressing a flawed way of thinking among many Americans.

Introduces the issue of images.

Claims that most Americans don't realize the influence images have.

Brief analysis of images and their role in public behavior.

Develops a line of reasoning: millions of products get purchased after a slick marketing campaign; mainstream thinking is that images don't make people buy things; we should explore this logic further.

By the time we Americans are old enough to make hard choices (what to buy, what to wear, what to drive, where to shop, where to buy our degrees, and the like), we imagine ourselves as independent, free, separate, and in control. We like to see ourselves making our own decisions. And because we are attracted to such a self-image, we believe in it. We believe it is *true*. This belief requires us to dismiss the rhetorical power of images in our lives. In fact, most people argue adamantly that they are not influenced by advertising images, that what they purchase is the choice of their own coherent and impenetrable consciousness. Some may concede that images conjure up certain feelings. They may admit, "Those images really moved me" or "That picture brought out lots of feelings in me." But other than the occasional emotional poke, images, say most Americans, have no effect on their reasoning powers—and absolutely no effect on their behaviors.

This is a peculiar stance in a culture that is submerged in advertising images—ones that are highly successful at getting millions of people to wear, drive, buy, and even fight over the same things at the same time. A quick glance at America's spending habits (millions of products suddenly get purchased directly after a slick marketing campaign) reveals the tremendous power of a finely wrought image. Still, the mainstream argument against the power of advertising goes something like this: *Images do not make people buy things. They do not make kids do drugs. They do not make people buy blue jeans or tennis shoes. They do not make adults smoke cigarettes or buy cars or jewelry.* Such statements have an obvious logical ring to them. Of course images do not *make* anyone buy anything. Pictures alone do not *make* people do things. But wait. We should explore this logic a bit further.

Exploring Ideas

To what degree are we independent, free, separate, in control?

How do images influence our thinking?

Spending habits suggest that images influence the way we think.

Pictures alone don't make people buy things. So, how does it work?

In the mainstream perspective, humans are *either* driven by media images or they are entirely independent thinkers. They *either* see something and buy a car or they decide not to buy a car. They *either* want a certain pair of blue jeans or they don't even imagine themselves wanting them. Such a perspective ignores the complexities of desire and the power of images. Of course, people do not simply run to the car lot and buy an SUV after seeing an ad in *Time*. But they consume the image and *the apparent value of the image*. When we see an image (whether it be a hairdo, a body type, or a vehicle), we also get an assumption about its worth in the culture. And this assumption stays with us. It molds into our sense of daily life. (This is, of course, why corporations spend millions of dollars to place images everywhere—so that our ideas about daily life naturally come to include the product or the image.)

Contrary to popular belief, humans are gregarious. We think and act in groups, according to historical trends. About every five years in America, kids laugh at what came five years earlier: "Look at that guy's jeans!" "Hey, check out the hairdo on her!" About every decade or so, certain social behaviors become extinct or come into favor: wearing hats, not wearing hats, getting married at 18, waiting to get married, having multiple sexual partners, being monogamous, and so on. And in the bigger spectrum of history, political consciousness changes: from thinking Indians should die to forgetting they exist, from thinking women should stay home and breed to celebrating female CEOs. How do these trends occur? How can a population make such tremendous shifts in belief in relatively short periods of time? Again, human beings don't think or make decisions in isolation. They decide on their hair, clothing, cars, homes, favorite colors, favorite body types, favorite drinks, and favorite pastimes according to the huge cultural menu of their time. Every important psychologist, anthropologist, and philosopher of the twentieth century taught us this: People do make free choices only insofar as they are free from overt oppression, *but they do not make choices that are free of culture*.

5   Take, for example, the SUV craze in the United States. Certainly, we can point to various causes for the increased sales of SUVs over the past decade: more disposable income, cheap gas prices (relative to other industrialized nations). But given the tremendous escalation of SUV sales, we might assume that significant changes have occurred: dramatic increases in snow throughout the nation, the general depletion of the highway system, rampant mudslides from coast to coast, a sudden migration from cities to

---

Margin notes (left):

Further analyzes the way images work in everyday life—explaining the complexity of how images influence thinking (debunking the oversimplistic view).

Broad cultural allusions help make connections for the reader.

Uses questions *(How do . . . ? How can . . . ?)* to lead the reader to the next point.

Sharp analytical points help make distinctions and reveal the role of images in everyday life.

An extended example about SUVs to illustrate the previous point.

Margin notes (right):

Consuming an image means consuming "the apparent value of the image."

Why do certain behaviors become extinct or come into favor?

People choose from a cultural menu.

Reasons why people shouldn't want to buy an SUV.

mountain hideaways, a dramatic increase in family size, a sudden discovery of free and accessible oil reserves, a sudden realization that SUVs save lives.

None of these occurred. But the opposite in each case has: People are generally moving to warmer climates and to cities; snowfall amounts are diminishing even in "snow belts"; family size is shrinking; oil is increasingly more expensive and coated in political stickiness; SUVs are involved in deadly rollover accidents; the nation is increasingly paved—perhaps the smoothest it's ever been in its paleontological history. And more roads go more places. Generally speaking, people have fewer reasons than ever to drive trucks, fewer reasons than ever to drive big people haulers, fewer reasons than ever to have four-wheel drive, fewer reasons than ever to own humungous, extra-large carrying capacity, super-low-gas-mileage vehicles. But the average suburban family is *more* likely to drive such a vehicle—one originally conceived as a tool for ranches or military operations.

Given the facts, we have to look at the mighty image. Given all the issues at hand (the history, the economics, the politics, the geography, the climate, the demographics), we must analyze what's most prevalent and powerful in our culture: advertising. Take, for example, a typical SUV ad, one for a Toyota 4Runner. The 4Runner descends a rocky cliff—a near-vertical drop—and rocky terrain stretches for miles into the background. The main text proclaims: "No intelligent life out here. Just you." (One wonders if Toyota's marketing executives are terribly ironic or terribly shortsighted.) At the bottom of the ad, a smaller message says, "Daily stops to the middle of nowhere." Certainly, most Americans live nowhere close to the middle of nowhere. Very few people will ever get to a place where they are surrounded by nothing but rocks, and even fewer will ever aim a truck down a cliff.

If we were to examine this ad and then assess the demographics of the buying public, we might guess that it's a joke—or an attempt to ruin Toyota. But the ad obviously works. It conjures up an attractive un-reality for potential consumers. We also might guess that the ad appears in an outdoors magazine—perhaps *Ranchers Quarterly, Mountain Lion News,* or *Rock Slide Specialist.* But the ad appears in *Time*—a decidedly mainstream, middle-class periodical. The vast majority of its readers commute to work on urban streets and suburban highways—and descend the gradual paved slopes of parking garages. Given the distance between read-

---

Margin notes (left):

Develops the extended example about SUVs.

Specific examples help to influence the reader's way of thinking.

With the groundwork laid in the previous two paragraphs, Johnson emphasizes the role of the advertising image.

Specific details from Toyota 4Runner ad help drive home the idea.

Points out the logical absurdity of the Toyota 4Runner ad, while acknowledging that the ad works.

Margin notes (right):

Why SUVs aren't a logical choice.

How prevalent is advertising in our culture? To what extent does it overcome rational thinking?

What other ads work by conjuring up "an attractive un-reality for potential customers"?

Reference to Mars points out logical absurdity.

ers' actual lives and the ad's imagery, Toyota may have just as logically featured the landscape of Mars.

By appealing to underlying values, logically absurd images leave an impression.

But such an image leaves an impression. It resonates with our songs (" . . . purple mountains' majesty . . ."); it appeals to our longing for escape; it captures our desire for solitude and security; it fits into our drive to scoff at nature. And when such imagery pounds the average citizen relentlessly, it begins to reside in the consciousness. It becomes familiar. Even though most Americans will never see the top of a mountain or careen down a cliff (on purpose), they can buy (into) the vehicle attached to the impression.

Advertising images appeal to our values, desires, and underlying beliefs—not our logical reasoning.

Further analysis: The repetition of advertising images has an impact on people's consciousness.

Makes final connection between image and a set of ideas (values, beliefs, assumptions).

10   The image creates an *allure,* that is, an attractive association of the thing (ridiculously large truck) with a set of ideas (escape, individualism, America, majesty, power, etc.). That set of ideas can be entirely divorced from reality, entirely separate from the needs of everyday life. But everyday life doesn't matter, nor does the logic that it might yield. The mighty advertising image makes it all irrelevant.

Writing Strategies

1. Describe Johnson's voice as a writer, and refer to several passages for support. What is, or isn't, inviting about Johnson's voice?

2. How does Johnson's introduction effectively lead into the rest of his essay?

3. Identify one concession Johnson makes, and explain how he uses it to further his own argument.

4. What does Johnson imagine his readers think, and how would he like to change their thinking?

5. Johnson concludes paragraph 8 by saying, "Given the distance between readers' actual lives and the ad's imagery, Toyota may have just as logically featured the landscape of Mars." Based on the preceding paragraphs, how does (or doesn't) Johnson earn the right to make such a claim?

Exploring Ideas

1. Interview people outside of class to find out how they think advertisements influence their thinking. Then use the results of your interviews to support or refute Johnson's claim that advertisements mold our sense of daily life.

2. In his opening sentence, Johnson lists several "hard choices" Americans have to make. Are these really hard choices? What do such choices say about American culture? What do they tell the reader about Johnson?

3. In a group, explore what images Americans consume, settling on several key images. What do those images say about America?

Ideas for Writing

1. What popular image contradicts the facts, and what are the consequences of the contradiction?

2. How are advertising images effective despite their illogical appeals?

If responding to one of these ideas, go to the **Analysis** section of this chapter to begin developing ideas for your essay.

The Power of Images: Creating the Myths of Our Time

J. Francis Davis

How well do you read images? And what impact does your ability to read them have on your life? It might be easy to dismiss such questions. Reading images, after all, may seem fairly brainless, even useless. But the people who craft the millions of images in our popular culture consider the power of every nuance. In the following essay, J. Francis Davis, an adult educator and media education specialist, shows how myths—the ideas and stories that motivate daily behavior—are now emerging from the mass of images that surround us. This article appeared in *Media & Values,* a journal published by the Center for Media Literacy.

We see them everywhere: on billboards, in magazines, on bus placards. They come in the mail and in our Sunday newspapers: glossy pictures of women and men in silk robes, pictures of electric twin-foil shavers and Dirt Devil hand-held vacuums. And we see them on TV: living rooms with two sofas, white-lighted football stadiums, even Wild West gunfights and bloodstained murder scenes.

Images. They are so compelling that we cannot not watch them. They are so seductive that they have revolutionized human social communication. Oral and written communication are in decline because a new form of communication, communication by image, has emerged.

The History of Communication

The history of human social interchange has evolved through three distinct phases: oral, text-based, and now image-centered communication. In oral cultures, learning and tradition were passed on by word of mouth, primarily through storytelling. The invention of writing made it possible to preserve information and literary traditions beyond the capacity of memory, but the circulation of handwritten books was still limited to an elite few.

With the invention of the printing press, written texts were in effect transferred from the exclusive property of those wealthy enough to afford hand-copied manuscripts to a broad reading public. Elizabeth Eisenstien, in *The Printing Press as an Agent of Change,* dramatizes this emergence by considering the case of inhabitants of Constantinople born in 1453, the year that the Byzantine capital fell to the Turks.

5   People born in that pivotal year who lived to be 50 saw more books produced in their lifetimes—some eight million—than had been written in the previous thousand years of Constantinople's existence. The Renaissance, the Protestant Reformation, and the rise of Western science are just a few of the revolutions spurred by the ability to mass-produce books and newspapers and the growing ability of common folk to read them. A similar revolution began about 150 years ago with the invention of photography. For the first time, visual representation of objects in space could be reproduced on a mass scale. Image communication was born.

It only took about 50 years for this new method of representation to become a major player in the communication of social values in American society. The rise of the advertising industry spurred this change, for advertisers quickly learned that the most effective way to sell products was not through stories or plain-text facts, but through the creation of images that appealed to basic human needs and emotions.

Television cemented the era of image communication. In one sense television has turned back the clock to the era of oral storytelling, for television tells stories and we watch and listen just like our ancestors who sat mesmerized around campfires.

But television's most important stories are those not verbalized—the stories and myths hidden in its constant flow of images. These images suggest myths—and thus help construct our world and values—in much the same way that stories did in oral culture.

What Are Images?

Simply put, images are pictures. However, in our culture pictures have become tools used to elicit specific and planned emotional reactions in the people who see them. These pictures—these images—are created to give us pleasure—as when we watch *The Cosby Show*—or to make us anxious when we forget our deodorant or lipstick. Images work best at this task when they are vivid and emotionally saturated. The American flag elicits more powerful emotions than an Idaho potato on a couch, for example. The potato might make us laugh, but the flag is full of multiple and often contradictory meanings and associations—everything from the story of how Francis Scott Key wrote "The Star-Spangled Banner" to flag burning as a protest against the Vietnam War.

10   The flag works as an image because it suggests a long list of stories and myths that are buried inside us. Image makers hope that in the moment it takes to "consume" an ad or commercial frame, their carefully selected graphics—like the image of the flag—will evoke emotions and memories bubbling deep within us. Pictures that evoke these deep memories can be very powerful—and also very spiritual.

In calling up these deep emotions and memories, however, today's images have taken on new meanings and have created new myths that are shrouded—often deliberately—by these deeper memories. These new myths lie at the heart of modern American culture, and illustrate the double-edged power of today's images.

The New Myths

Traditionally, a myth has been defined as a story or idea that explains the culture or customs of a people. Often myths describe heroes or explain why a people revere the sun, or why elders should be respected. Myths are the motivating stories or ideas of common cultural practices.

This understanding of myth leaves little room for the common misperception that myths are simply false or superstitious ideas. Instead, myths are the ideas and stories that motivate daily behavior.

The key to recognizing the new myths of the image culture is to think of them as ideas that emerge from long exposure to patterns of images—not as myths that can be seen readily in one or two images. In fact, these myths are unconvincing unless one thinks of them as emerging from a huge glut of images which come from many sources, including advertising, entertainment, and news.

15   Another way to put this is to say that today's images must be read on two levels. First there is the immediate, emotional level on which we recognize the flag or the sexy body and react in a way that taps our inner stories or emotions.

But second, there is a much broader stage on which we can step back and look at one image in context with hundreds of others. This second level is where we can see the new myths of the image clearly—otherwise these basic ideas are obscured by the powerful stories and emotional connections that are used to sell them. Once identified, however, they are easy to recognize, even among all the media messages that daily bombard us.

MYTH #1. The world is a dangerous place and we need guns, police, and military to protect us.

Media critics often focus on violent entertainment dramas such as cop shows and movies like *Terminator 2*. But graphic reports of crime and terror on the news probably have a greater influence in creating our feeling that the world is unsafe. Newsmakers feature shocking, violent stories because they sell newspapers and raise ratings. And our belief that news stories are "real" and thus could happen to us heightens their impact.

MYTH #2. Leave it to the experts (who are usually white men).

Again, "real life" images—or those we assume to be real—are most important here because they set the pattern for our assumptions about who has power. The authority figures we see presenting the national news are white, middle-aged men. And when an "expert" is interviewed about a crisis or program, as in a study of

Nightline guests by the progressive media criticism organization Fairness and Accuracy in Reporting (F.A.I.R.) the pattern is predictable; nine out of 10 were white males. On *Nightline* and elsewhere, the views of women, persons of color, and representatives of alternate voices of all kinds are customarily absent.

Images found in advertisements and commercials, as well as the national news, reinforce this power structure. Contrast the traditional sex roles of advertisements for Chivas Regal, showing successful professional men in business suits with the stereotypic portraits of women and men in food ads that cast women as kitchen "experts." Many other media images depend on predefined roles based on gender or race.

MYTH #3. The good life consists of buying possessions that cost lots of money.

20   Living well is synonymous with wealth, according to the pictures and advertisements we see of homes and yards and cars. Big houses, yachts, fancy wine, dinner parties with silver and crystal, romantic evenings overlooking the ocean, vacations to Bermuda, sailing, BMWs, fancy two-oven sunlit kitchens: The list goes on and on. All are part of a luxurious lifestyle that is available for our enjoyment—if only we can afford it.

We can even purchase a little of it vicariously, if we can't have it all, by drinking fancy liquors or by driving a car that's out of our price range and financing it over 10 years. Some people call it status—but the myth behind the status myth is that we are getting the "good life."

MYTH#4. Happiness, satisfaction, and sex appeal, just to name a few, are imminent—and available with the next consumer purchase.

Alas, even when we are wealthy, there's always something missing. We don't have the right woman or man, our car stalls at an intersection, we spend too much time doing housework. But a whole group of images imply that we are on the verge of being happy.

These images are largely advertisements. For example, Hope perfume, Joy dishwashing detergent, or "Oh what a feeling—Toyota!" People in these advertisements are gleefully happy, surrounded by lovers, leaping into the air in rapturous joy. Often, the instrument that brings this instant happiness is technology. We can buy the technology to make us happy.

MYTH #5. Your body is not good enough.

Many—if not most—of the women and men we see in the media are slim, muscular, and good-looking. We, on the other hand, are always too fat, out-of-shape, and smelly—though our friends don't always tell us so forthrightly. We are trained to worry, for example, that people will not even tell us if we smell bad because that kind of criticism is embarrassing.

25   Most disturbing, however, is the constant stream of perfect people advertising everything from auto parts to Hanes stockings. We are never told that almost all photoadvertisers make their subjects look better, so that legs are slimmer, eyes are bluer, and faces have no freckles.

MYTH #6. Businesses and corporations are concerned for the public welfare.

Short of an environmental disaster like the Alaskan oil spill we see almost no advertisements and few news stories that shed negative light on corporations or businesses. This is not to suggest that all of these organizations are bad. It is worth noting, however, that most corporate images appear in ads purchased or stories placed by the businesses themselves, so it's hardly surprising that the messages we hear are relentlessly positive.

We see full-page color ads for Chevron talking about its concern for the environment. Or news items reporting that gasoline emissions are down because of a new formula developed by ARCO. Ads from tobacco companies like R.J. Reynolds discourage kids under 18 from smoking. And business-oriented magazines and talk shows like *Wall Street Week* cater to the interests of PBS's upscale audience, reporting business and financial trends, while we see none from a labor perspective.

So Why Does This Matter?

To ask the question another way, how are these myths hurting us? The rest of this issue suggests a variety of answers, but in the *Rise of the Image Culture,* Elizabeth Thoman perhaps put it best when she points out that these myths have become a substitute for the search for meaning which other generations sought in more expansive and significant ways. We no longer face uncharted oceans and unexplored continents, but with a universe of space and time to explore and uncounted problems to solve we need not end all our quests at the shopping mall.

Many of us feel a sense of dissatisfaction, a void that the myths of the image culture and the material goods they sell do little to fill. Besides the money, creativity, and resources that the making and selling of these images waste, they also represent a gigantic "red herring," a signpost to an empty journey, a joust with the windmills of our culture, leaving us like confused Don Quixotes looking for a real opponent.

30   In this sense, the myths of the image culture are "false or superstitious ideas" as well as "motivating stories or ideas behind common cultural practices."

We do have signposts pointing other ways, however, and learning to read images is the first step in the right direction. This issue [of *Media&Values*]and its accompanying Media Literacy Workshop Kit are designed to be a primer on the basic principles of media literacy, using analysis that helps us read images as a beginning point.

Only when we learn to read these myths on a daily basis will we have the power to substitute other motivating ideas and goals of our choosing. Only then can we consciously transcend the Age of Image Communication and stop blindly accepting the myths of the image culture.

Writing Strategies

1. Why is the history of communication important in developing Davis's main idea?

2. How does Davis's definition of "images" go beyond the readers' common understanding of the term?

3. How does Davis define "myths," and how is that definition important to the main idea of the essay?

4. What important relationship does Davis draw between myths and images?

5. How would Davis like people to think? What support strategies help the reader to think differently?

Exploring Ideas

1. With others, make a list of images that are "so compelling that we cannot not watch them." Why are the images so compelling?

2. Explain how a particular advertising image appeals to basic human needs and emotions.

3. Have any myths Davis talks about changed since the original publication of the essay? What myths haven't changed? Are any likely to never change?

4. Why is it difficult for people to question common cultural practices?

Ideas for Writing

1. Davis says that "The flag works as an image because it suggests a long list of stories and myths that are buried inside us." (¶ 10) How does some other image work because it suggests a long list of stories and myths that are buried inside us?

2. How is a particular image (type of image, or group of images) a "signpost" pointing people in the wrong direction?

If responding to one of these ideas, go to the **Analysis** section of this chapter to begin developing ideas for your essay.

Outside Reading

ACTIVITY

Find an Image for the Caption

1. Find an image to go with one of the captions below. Then explain the relationship between the two.
2. Share images with a group of classmates, and explore how the details of each classmate's image gives the caption a different meaning.
3. How do the images classmates found speak to particular values, beliefs, and assumptions?

I'm not a perfect mother.	21st-Century College Student
I don't ride with Bin Laden.	George Bush is bilingual.

INVENTION

Most of the images that constitute everyday life were meant to prompt an idea or emotion—not to be analyzed. (This, say many scholars, is all the more reason to analyze them.) In developing ideas for this project, we have to work against what most images ask of us. We have to see into them, into how they work. We have to break down the parts, and then reassemble them in our own minds to understand how they impact viewers. The following sections are designed to help you through this process: specifically, to find a particular image (in **Point of Contact**), to examine the image closely and understand its relationship to viewers (in **Analysis**), to develop a focused point (in **Thesis**), and to develop support for that point (in **Rhetorical Tools**). The Invention questions in each section are not meant to be answered directly in your final essay, but to prompt inventive thinking and intensive writing.

POINT OF CONTACT

Images are everywhere. And every image contains more meaning than we might initially imagine. Explore the following possibilities to find a specific image for your own analysis:

Consider all the elements of the image: the pictures, text, images, colors, placement, models, clothing, blank space, audience, and even the surrounding materials such as stories and columns.

Image is the root of imagine.

Print Advertisements Print ads range from dense collages of pictures and words to a single image with one slogan. Browse any magazine or newspaper. Also consider print advertisements that lurk in more inconspicuous places, such as your credit card bill, a public bathroom, a phone book, a calendar, and so on.

Internet Images The Internet offers a broad range of images, from shocking photos of war to wondrous shots of space. Do a search by entering a noun, such as "space" or "images."

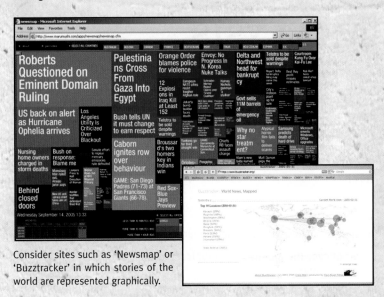

Consider sites such as 'Newsmap' or 'Buzztracker' in which stories of the world are represented graphically.

Posters Most often, posters work like billboards. They are designed to catch a passing eye—to shout loudly enough so that anyone in the vicinity will notice the message.

Billboards Billboards are made to distract people, to yank attention away from the road. Examine one closely to understand how it works toward that goal.

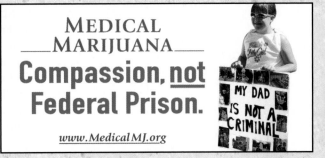

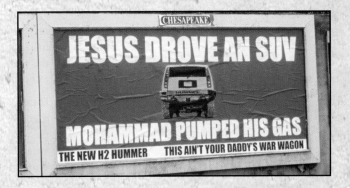

ANALYSIS

Analyzing an image involves looking at the content (the subject matter) of the image, and then considering the particular visual elements, such as shapes, lines, colors, and so on. Since any image consists of various elements, try to focus on one element at a time, and consider how each element creates meaning. Then consider how the various elements work together.

> In this section, we will examine four primary layers:
>
> 1. Image: the pictures or graphics and their specific elements
> 2. Text: any accompanying written language
> 3. Subtext: the unstated meanings and implications beneath the image and text
> 4. Context: the world surrounding the image

"It's not what it's about. It's what else it's about."

—Minor White, Photographer

Image

Even the simplest image contains the following elements:

Content The subject, information, or objects that are pictured. Everything within an image is important—from the largest to the tiniest object or detail. They all figure into the nature of the image; they all impact the consciousness of the viewer.

Framing What has been placed within the boundaries of the image. Whether by choice, by accident, or by necessity, certain objects are included in the image while other objects are left out. Whether a photographer's (or designer's) deliberate move or pure accident, the framing impacts what is seen. It closes in a particular range of objects and closes out the rest of the world.

Composition The way the visual elements of the image are arranged within the frame. Some objects stand in the foreground, others in the background or off to the side. Objects may be crowded, touching, overlapping, far apart. The spatial relationships can be both aesthetic—that is, pleasing to the eye—and meaningful. Composition also includes matters of light and darkness, lines, shapes, focus, and so on.

Focus The degree to which some areas of the image are sharp (or clear) and other areas are blurry. The focus impacts the movement of the eye. Sharper objects automatically attract attention away from blurry or fuzzy objects, thereby prompting the viewer to see, and understand, the image in a particular way.

Lighting The degree to which some areas of the image are brightly lit and other areas are in low light or in shadows. An entire image may be dark or light, or some parts of the image may be in shadows or in bright light. While shadows and light may be a natural consequence of a sunny day or a tall building blocking a photographer's light, the way the elements are lit creates an effect. Like careful planning, accidents can produce strong images.

Texture How the image, or certain objects in the image, looks like it would feel if you could touch it. Images can suggest, or appear to have, texture. Just as tree bark and a marble countertop have different textures, visual images can suggest how they might feel if touched. Even if content, framing, composition, and such are all the same in two images, a smooth or rough texture may suggest a different idea about what is being pictured.

Angle and Vantage Point The angle at which the image is presented, or the vantage point or perspective from which a photograph, for example, is taken. Every image suggests a perspective. A photograph of a politician speaking with a crowd of supporters behind him suggests one meaning, while a shot of the same politician from behind and speaking to a mere handful of people suggests something else. A low-angle shot of the politician might suggest power; a high-angle shot looking down on the politician might suggest weakness.

Significance The collective meaning or impact of all the elements. Our ultimate goal is to figure out how all these elements work together to express ideas, just as the elements of an essay, novel, poem, or movie work together. When analyzing, we focus on one element at a time, but we are always looking at more than one element. For example, when we consider how an image is framed or composed, we are also considering the image's content. When we talk about composition, we are looking at how these various formal elements work together. All elements of an image must be considered, yet some elements will have more impact than others.

Consider the following image: A man, presumably a farmer, plays an acoustic guitar in an open field. The background is nearly empty except for the lower part of a distant building. The distance behind the man matters—perhaps as much as the man himself. Directly beside him sits a small electric amplifier. The man and the amplifier—adjacent, focused, well lit, in the foreground—seem like a mixed pair, like they do not belong together, especially surrounded by an open field of dirt. But all the elements of the image insist that we see them together. Even the angle—seeing both of them from the front—makes us (the viewers) feel like an audience. What do all these elements prompt us to think, to imagine, to assume? What feelings are conjured by the interplay of the elements?

ACTIVITY

In a small group, analyze the following images. Consider content, framing, composition, focus, lighting, texture, angle and vantage point, and the significance of all the elements.

Now examine the image you have chosen for your project. The questions below will help you analyze how the image works—how it affects viewers.

- **Content**

  What content—subject or information—is presented in the image? What are the main objects in the image? Of the main elements, which appear to be most prominent? Which are less prominent?

- **Framing**

  How is the image framed? What has been placed within the boundaries of the image? What has not been included? How do the boundaries influence your focus?

- **Composition**

  How are the elements of the image arranged? Are visual elements symmetrical (distributed evenly) or asymmetrical (not distributed evenly)? Are elements touching, overlapping, close together, or far apart? Are elements above or below each other, or to the left or the right of each other? What is in the background? What might the relationship of elements encourage someone to think?

- **Focus**

  How is the image focused? That is, what objects or areas appear most clear or sharp? What objects or areas are not clear? Is anything unusual or striking about the focus? How does the focus draw your attention? How does it affect the relationship of certain elements?

- **Lighting**

  How is the image lit? That is, what objects or areas are well lit? What areas are dark, or in shadow? Is the light harsh or soft? Is there a contrast of tones from light to dark? What is darkest, and what is lightest? How does the lighting affect what is pictured? How might different lighting change the image?

- **Texture**

  What is the texture of the image? If you could touch what is pictured, how would it feel? How does the photograph's texture relate to its content?

- **Angle and Vantage Point**

  From what angle is the photograph taken? Is it straight-on? Is it exaggerated? How does the angle affect the composition of the image? That is, are some elements more in the foreground or background? Are some more prominent?

You may, in your analysis, consider other elements as well. Colors, for example, may be subdued or bright and splashy. Such details may have significance.

Text

Images—such as photographs, diagrams, and charts—often work in conjunction with written text. In advertising or on posters, meaning is often generated by an interaction of image and text. When text accompanies an image, the two fuse into a single idea. But we can pull them apart and see how they work. For instance, Cameron Johnson examines the way text gives meaning to the image of an SUV:

> The 4Runner descends a rocky cliff—a near-vertical drop—and rocky terrain stretches for miles into the background. The main text proclaims: "No intelligent life out here. Just you." (One wonders if Toyota's marketing executives are terribly ironic or terribly short-sighted.) At the bottom of the ad, a smaller message says, "Daily stops to the middle of nowhere." Certainly, most Americans live nowhere close to the middle of nowhere. Very few people will ever get to a place where they are surrounded by nothing but rocks, and even fewer will ever aim a truck down a cliff. (212)

Many texts speak back to or depend on other texts to make meaning. That is, they exist in dialogue with other texts—a quality called *intertextuality*. Consider the following bumper sticker:

I SEE STUPID PEOPLE

This sticker makes sense alone, but has more impact if the reader knows about *The Sixth Sense,* a movie in which a young boy announces eerily, "I see dead people." If we know the original statement and its context, we are likely to see more significance in the sticker. Or imagine an advertising campaign that includes the statement, "You *Can* Always Get What You Want." While the statement makes sense, it has even more significance if we know the Rolling Stones' song, "You Can't Always Get What You Want." With the Stones' song in the background of our consciousness, the advertising slogan would have even more force. It would speak back to something that we had heard many times before.

The effectiveness of this ad depends upon the viewers' knowledge of the "Got Milk?" ad campaign.

Intertextuality adds layers of meaning to any text. When designers and advertisers make a text speak to other familiar texts, they tap into public domain. They create public resonance.

ACTIVITY

Find an example of an image and/or text that speaks to another familiar text, and explain how the intertextuality adds a layer of meaning

Examine the image you have chosen for your project. If the image has accompanying text, answer the following questions:

- How does the text correlate with the significance of the image?

- How do content, framing, composition, focus, lighting, texture, angle and vantage point help to convey the ideas?

- Does the text echo other texts? (How does the language depend on our familiarity with other texts?)

Subtext

Not all the meaning that comes from a text is stated. Some meaning is *implied*—suggested but not clearly stated. This layer of *implication* is sometimes called *subtext*—meaning that it is under the more visible and obvious layers. Subtext might also be thought of as a collection of assumptions and hidden values, messages that are not obvious but are present nonetheless. For example, when someone asks what you do for a living, the question is about more than your actual job. It implies questions about your status, your identity, your economic situation, your schedule, even your personality. And even if you offer a short answer ("I'm in marketing"), that answer has a subtext.

Images also have subtext. Even if they have no written text, they still imply ideas. In advertising, images and text often work together to suggest a layer of subtext. The following ad relies on a layer of implication (about pregnant women, about relationships, about men, about . . . ice cream).

Examine the image you have chosen for your project, and answer the following questions:

- What seems to be the main idea of the image?
- Besides the obvious statements or ideas, what subtle assumptions or beliefs are suggested by (or lurking in) the image?
- How do content, framing, composition, focus, lighting, texture, angle, and vantage point help to convey the ideas?

INVENTION WRITING

Subtext is invisible, so finding it is hard work. We have to look closely at all the elements (of image and text) and connect them with common values and assumptions. Notice Cameron Johnson's exploration of subtext:

> **Besides the obvious statements or ideas, what subtle assumptions or beliefs are suggested by (or lurking in) the image?**
>
> To accept anything in the ad as attractive, viewers must believe they are independent—that they have lives of rugged off-road exploration. Maybe it isn't so literal. That is, people might not see themselves driving a truck down a cliff, but they have to believe in the value of rugged self-determination—let's add *physical* in there: rugged, physical self-determination. The ad relies on that. It only makes sense (especially within the pages of *Time* magazine!) if readers are caught up in that set of beliefs. The ad implies: "Hey . . . you're the type to bust loose and you need a vehicle to get you where you're going." (Of course, most people don't bust loose—especially the people who can afford such vehicles. Funny.)

Context

Analyzing an image involves examining how the image relates to its context—the things and people surrounding it. We have all seen a copy of the *Mona Lisa*. But how might our response to the painting change if we saw it in the Louvre, as shown on this page.

Specific Context The specific context is the real physical space that surrounds the image—the building, the magazine, the neighborhood, the campus, the wall, and so on. Every image is affected by the specific context in which it appears. In these images, da Vinci's *Mona Lisa* (the world's most reproduced work of art) is surrounded by different contexts. In the first images, the crowded room at the Louvre influences how the *Mona Lisa* is viewed, what it means. In the images on the right, the *Mona Lisa* has been recontextualized (recast in different graphic surroundings, even different clothes!). The contexts drastically change how da Vinci's original image works.

Cultural Context Nothing exists without culture. Beyond the physical space surrounding an image, the broader culture provides meaning. The values and beliefs that shape everyday life also impact the way an image works—why it gets made, how it gets received. In her analysis of cartoons, Joy Clough points to their cultural context:

> Old-timer or newcomer, the comic strips apparently owe their ongoing appeal to solid psychology. They mirror human life and respond to the human spirit. When life is bleak, a laugh can help. When life is dull, adventure spells relief. When life seems stupid, humor-become-satire makes its point. When life is lonely, romance provides connections. (207)

In his analysis of an SUV ad, Cameron Johnson relies on the specific context (the magazine that published the ad) and the cultural context (the lifestyle of *Time* readers):

> If we were to examine this ad and then assess the demographics of the buying public, we might guess that it's a joke—or an attempt to ruin Toyota. But the ad obviously works. It conjures up an attractive un-reality for potential consumers. We also might guess that the ad appears in an outdoors magazine—perhaps *Ranchers*

Quarterly, Mountain Lion News, or *Rock Slide Specialist.* But the ad appears in *Time*—a decidedly mainstream, middle-class periodical. The vast majority of its readers commute to work on urban streets and suburban highways—and descend the gradual paved slopes of parking garages. Given the distance between readers' actual lives and the ad's imagery, Toyota may have just as logically featured the landscape of Mars. (212–213)

Examine the image you have chosen for your project and answer the following questions:

- What beliefs, attitudes, or morals does it support or appeal to?
- What beliefs, attitudes, values or morals does it chafe against?
- What public concern does the image speak to?
- How might people benefit by exploring the possible meanings of the image?

INVENTION WRITING

In his response to the Invention questions on page 227, Cameron Johnson comes to an easy conclusion about his image: a Toyota 4Runner.

> **What beliefs, attitudes, values or morals does it support or appeal to?**
>
> That's easy. The image [for Toyota 4Runner] appeals to the value of independence, individualism. Americans like to think of themselves "out there" alone—doing it on the edge of the frontier. It's in our history. And . . . still . . . we're all caught up in that thinking. Many of our goods are sold to us with this basic belief in mind. We are enamored with the idea of ourselves driving across the open majesty of the country with no rules, no road, no official place to be. In the ad, the truck is aiming down a cliff (a flippin' cliff!) and no sign of civilization ruins the moment. (Apparently, that's a fun thing . . . a sign of one's independence, aiming an expensive truck down a cliff.) The print in the ad says, "No intelligent life out here. Just you." Besides that being pretty funny, it reinforces the appeal to independence. Apparently independence = off the road, off the beaten path.

Johnson is just beginning to get traction with his point. He discovers the main appeal in the ad, and the particular elements that drive the appeal.

THINKING FURTHER

Whenever a question is easy to answer, writers should use that momentum and explore further. They should revel in the ease of the answer and then keep developing nuances, asking more questions. Notice, for instance, what happens when Cameron Johnson continues thinking. He goes beyond the initial answer (that the ad appeals to the idea of independence) and discovers the irony or absurdity of the image:

> What's weird about the appeal is this: Most people aren't at all independent. They follow rules, go to work every day, drive in the correct lanes, park in garages or metered spaces or yellow-lined areas. They trim their lawns to the exact length (about 1/2 inch within the presumed correct length for the neighborhood). They dress according to the rules of their generation. They certainly don't drive their expensive (and very clean) new trucks down cliffs. This ad (and every ad like it) is totally divorced from the real life most people lead. Most Americans are rule followers. We think what the media commentators (or government propaganda) tell us. We do what we can to stay in the lines. But the world of advertising makes it seem like we're all careening down cliffs, splashing through rivers, rockin' it out on the banks of some lake. It ain't true.

This discovery is key to Johnson's essay. That is, only after thinking further does Johnson discover the powerful insights that drive his analysis.

INVENTION WORKSHOP

In a small group, use the Invention questions to explore your image in depth. First, share your image with others in your group. Then apply one of the Invention questions. Once someone in the group offers a possible answer, record the response. Someone else in the group should then continue that thinking (not moving to another topic or question) by asking how the first responder arrived at his or her point.

THESIS

The purpose of this project is to analyze how an image (or set of images) works to impact viewers. The analysis should reveal something that readers would not otherwise see or imagine. It should show the insides, the mechanics, of the image. Consider the following examples:

- Beyond the main image of the Cadillac, the sophisticated background elements make the pitch to potential consumers.

- In trendy music videos, the camera looks up from the ground at the performers, which reinforces the notion that the performers have power over, and speak down to, their audiences.

- Presidential campaign commercials rely on the imagery of middle-class America so that candidates will be seen as normal working Joes.

Notice that each statement focuses on a particular element of an image. Each also explains the significance, the meaning or impact, of that element. Take, for example, the third statement. It focuses on a particular element: *the imagery of middle-class America*. It explains how that particular element works: It casts the candidates as normal working Joes.

We can deduce that a good thesis for this project has two important qualities:

1. Focus on a particular element
2. An explanation of its significance

Look over your invention notes, and focus on a particular element (something in the content, the composition, the framing, etc.). Then try to explain its significance: how that element works to convey meaning or impact the viewer.

COMMON THESIS PROBLEMS

As in most writing projects, the more specific the claims, the more intensive the ideas will be. If you can point to a particular element in an image and explain how that element works, then you are probably on your way to a focused thesis. But notice the problems in the following statement. It lacks significance and focus. It targets "many" ads and offers a sweeping statement about them—they use women. The statement does not explain how something in those ads works, how they influence people, or how the individual elements create messages:

Many *Sports Illustrated* ads use women as the main focus.

The following statement does focus on one text *(Rolling Stone),* but it still lacks focus:

Rolling Stone magazine makes one thing clear: sex sells.

Rolling Stone is a good-sized magazine—with a table of contents, record lists, pictures, ads, articles about politics, CD reviews, movie reviews, and so on. Of course, someone could associate all those elements with sex, but the project would probably lack serious analysis of particular elements. A writer with such a statement needs to look more closely at something specific in *Rolling Stone.*

ACTIVITY

Rewrite the two statements above so they are more focused. Consider the two important qualities: (1) focus on a particular element; and (2) an explanation of its significance.

EVOLUTION OF A THESIS

Thesis statements do not always evolve in a neat fashion. They do not always progress from a broader to a more focused insight. Sometimes (maybe most times), they wander, circle back, and jump around as the writer tries to get traction. Below, we can see Johnson searching out meaning through single sentences. He is trying to connect two things: a particular element of the ad and the meaning of that element for viewers. All of the statements below are attempts, some better than others, at forging that connection.

- SUV ads, like that for the Toyota 4Runner, appeal to Americans through natural imagery.

- Ads like the one for Toyota 4Runner give a vision of life that many Americans strive for.

- Even though most Americans' lives do not resemble the natural imagery of SUV ads, that imagery appeals to what many people imagine about themselves.

- The scenic imagery of SUV ads appeals to a lifestyle that most Americans imagine for themselves but rarely realize.

- The ad for Toyota 4Runner relies on natural imagery that is far outside the experience of most Americans, but the ads still have strong appeal.

- The ad for Toyota 4Runner reveals a trend in SUV advertising: The background imagery connects to an illusive vision of American life—one that is contrary to the situation or needs of most potential consumers.

REVISION

Develop a working thesis statement that includes attention to a specific element of an image and explains its significance. Then, in a small group, discuss each person's statement. Apply the following:

- Does the statement focus on a specific element (something in the content, composition, framing, angle, focus, etc.)? How could the specific element be narrower?

- Beyond the writer's statement, what is the significance (possible meaning or impact) of that specific element? (What else might it suggest about people, lifestyles, nature, America, clothing, social class, race, gender, politics, domestic life, art, music, and so on?) Be creative. Imagine that the significance is not what people initially assume!

- Make a case for the most surprising or hidden significance in the image. Make a connection that seems, at first, outrageous. Try to convince others in the group that your point is valid.

RHETORICAL TOOLS

Developing Support

For analyzing images, support comes in two general categories: (1) details from the image, and (2) evidence outside of the image. The first is essential. Readers will need to see how specific claims correspond to the image itself. The second category includes a wide variety of strategies and will help provide meaningful context to your points.

USING DETAILS FROM THE IMAGE

Any close analysis relies on specific details of the subject. For instance, if you are analyzing an advertisement, readers would expect to see particular features of that ad and an explanation that connects those features to your main point. In her analysis, Jean Kilbourne relies heavily on details from advertisements. Kilbourne's main point is that ads seek to replace interpersonal (human/human) relationships with consumerist (product/human) relationships. In the following passage, she explains how a specific ad works:

> And an ad for More features the cigarette leaning against a personal ad that says, "Wanted: Tall dark stranger for long lasting relationship. Good looks, great taste a must. Signed, Eagerly Seeking Smoking Satisfaction." The long brown cigarette is, of course, the "tall dark stranger." And the tobacco industry certainly hopes that the relationship will be long-lasting. (193)

Likewise, Cameron Johnson uses the details of a specific magazine ad to illustrate his thesis that advertising images are out of sync with the reality of everyday life. Notice that he does not merely mention the details; he also explains how those details illustrate his point:

> Take, for example, a typical SUV ad, one for a Toyota 4Runner. The 4Runner descends a rocky cliff—a near-vertical drop—and rocky terrain stretches for miles into the background. The main text proclaims: "No intelligent life out here. Just you." (One wonders if Toyota's marketing executives are terribly ironic or terribly short-sighted.) At the bottom of the ad, a smaller message says, "Daily stops to the middle of nowhere." Certainly, most Americans live nowhere close to the middle of nowhere. Very few people will ever get to a place where they are surrounded by nothing but rocks, and even fewer will ever aim a truck down a cliff. (212)

Return to any notes you generated from the Analysis section of this chapter. Consider the following questions:

- What details (about the content, focus, composition, framing, lighting, texture, angle, and significance) best illustrate my main point?
- What specific text best illustrates my main point?
- Does subtext help to support my main point?
- Does the context help to support my main point?

USING OTHER EVIDENCE

In some ways, you are attempting to convince readers that your understanding of the image is reasonable. To this end, you can go beyond the image itself and allude to any related events, images, people, or behaviors in the present or past. The readings in this chapter rely heavily on cultural allusions (references to other well-known texts, films, pictures, photos, or events). In the following passage, Elizabeth Thoman alludes to various cultural events to help give meaning to her claims about images in the media:

> Disasters like Chernobyl and the Alaskan oil spill raise hard questions about the long-term social impact of technological innovation. In the U.S., the loss of whole communities to the ravages of drugs, crime, and homelessness threatens the very principles which allow any humane society to flourish.

At the same time, the global events of 1991—the breakup of the Soviet Empire, the struggles for national identity, even the rise of fundamentalist governments in many parts of the Third World—bear witness to a growing desire for meaningful connections as well as material and political progress. (204)

In his analysis of ad images, Cameron Johnson refers to broader cultural trends to support the claim that people are influenced deeply by the messages around them:

Contrary to popular belief, humans are gregarious. We think and act in groups, according to historical trends. About every five years in America, kids laugh at what came five years earlier: "Look at that guy's jeans!" "Hey, check out the hairdo on her!" About every decade or so, certain social behaviors become extinct or come into favor: wearing hats, not wearing hats, getting married at 18, waiting to get married, having multiple sexual partners, being monogamous, and so on. And in the bigger spectrum of history, political consciousness changes: from thinking Indians should die to forgetting they exist, from thinking women should stay home and breed to celebrating female CEOs. How do these trends occur? (211)

Consider the following questions:

- How do cultural trends or events relate to the image I am analyzing?
- Does anything in history show how the image (or type of image) has influenced people?
- Can I create a scenario (a hypothetical situation) to illustrate my point about the image?
- Can I narrate a personal experience to show something important about the image?

RESEARCH

Using a periodical database (such as InfoTrac College Edition) or an Internet search engine (such as Google), explore how others have discussed the image you are analyzing. Most likely, you won't find sources about the specific image (unless you are analyzing an historic piece of art or popular culture). However, you'll likely find sources about the *type* of image—whether an automobile ad, a billboard, a rural photo, and so on. For instance, if Cameron Johnson were exploring for outside sources, he might begin a keyword search with the following combinations:

sport utility vehicle *and* advertisement
sport *and* utility *and* vehicles *and* advertising
automobile *and* advertisements *and* nature

Of course, keyword searches are not an exact science. (They're not a science at all.) They are always attempts—and sometimes require several restarts with substitutions and small changes. For instance, changing *automobile* to *car* or *ad* to *advertisement* may yield significantly different results.

For more assistance with research, see Chapter 13, specifically pages 624–629.

ORGANIZATIONAL STRATEGIES

How Should I Begin?

A common and effective opening strategy is to begin with the personal and then move to the public. For example, notice how Elizabeth Thoman begins her essay with personal reflection but moves steadily toward the public relevance of her topic:

> Like most middle-class children of the '50s, I grew up looking for the American Dream. In those days there were no cartoons in my Saturday viewing, but I distinctly remember watching, with some awe, *Industry on Parade*. I felt both pride and eager anticipation as I watched tail-finned cars rolling off assembly lines, massive dams taming mighty rivers and sleek chrome appliances making life more convenient for all.
>
> When I heard the mellifluous voice of Ronald Reagan announce on *GE Theatre* that "Progress is our most important product," little did I realize that the big box in our living room was not just entertaining me. At a deeper level, it was stimulating an "image" in my head of how the world should work: that anything new was better than something old; that science and technology were the greatest of all human achievements and that in the near future—and certainly by the time I grew up—the power of technology would make it possible for everyone to live and work in a world free of war, poverty, drudgery and ignorance. (202)

While Thoman is relating her own personal memories, those memories are moving the reader into a public discussion—about the rise of the image culture and the American Dream. The personal memories she selects are directly relevant to the public concern she will develop throughout her essay.

Should I Use Headings?

Since many college writing assignments are brief (1,000–2,000 words), headings are not always helpful. But longer essays, such as the ones in this chapter, can be more inviting when the writer breaks the text into sections and uses headings to indicate the general focus of a section of text. This heading strategy is the same as breaking up even longer writings into chapters.

Chapters and headings help the reader to organize major units of thought, and they give the reader a break or a light at the end of the tunnel. For example, Joy Clough provides the reader with three headings:

The Comics as History
The Comic Appeal
An American Art Form

In the same way, J. Francis Davis provides his reader with:

The History of Communication
What Are Images?
The New Myths
So Why Does This Matter?

While headings should not be used indiscriminately, they can be helpful to both writer and reader, especially in organizing longer essays. Of course, headings are like topic sentences, which clearly state the main idea of a paragraph. And in shorter essays, clear topic sentences at the beginning of paragraphs effectively serve the same purpose that headings do in longer essays.

How Should I Integrate Outside Sources?

Writers can integrate outside sources by paraphrasing (expressing the ideas of the source in one's own words), summarizing (compacting the ideas of the source and expressing them in one's own words), or quoting (using the exact wording of the source within quotation marks). In an academic essay, all three strategies require documentation: an in-text citation and a bibliographic citation at the end of the essay. (See more about documentation on pages 649+.)

Any outside research should be carefully woven into the fabric of your own ideas. One of the worst mistakes a writer can make is merely inserting outside sources, dropping a stray passage into a paragraph without a clear sense of its meaning. Often, outside sources are used in a passage only after the idea has been set up. In other words, the writer establishes the momentum of the point and brings in an outside source for reinforcement. Then, after a paraphrase, summary, or quotation, the writer may further explain the significance or meaning.

In the following passage, Elizabeth Thoman first explains how commercials influenced consumerism. Then she reinforces the point with a quotation, and finally further explains the idea in the quotation:

> The flood of commercial images also served as a rough-and-ready consumer education course for the waves of immigrants to America's shores and the thousands of rural folk lured to the city by visions of wealth. Advertising was seen as a way of educating the masses "to the cycle of the marketplace and to the imperatives of factory work and mechanized labor"— teaching them "how to behave like human beings in the machine age," according to the Boston department store magnate Edward A. Filene. In a work world where skill meant less and less, obedience and appearance took on greater importance. In a city full of strangers, advertising offered instructions on how to dress, how to behave, how to *appear* to others in order to gain approval and avoid rejection. (203)

But these three steps are not required with every use of an outside source. Sometimes, the third step is unnecessary—and the writer only sets up the point. In the following passage, Thoman sets up the point about commercials' power. Next, she brings in an outside source (Stephen Garey), to reinforce the point:

> This does not mean that when we see a new toilet paper commercial we're destined to rush down to the store to buy its new or improved brand. Most single commercials do not have such a direct impact. What happens instead is a cumulative effect. Each commercial plays its part in selling an overall *consumer lifestyle*. As advertising executive Stephen Garey noted in a recent issue of *Media&Values,* when an ad for toilet paper reaches us in combination with other TV commercials, magazine ads, radio spots and billboards for detergents and designer jeans, new cars and cigarettes, and soft drinks and cereals and computers, the collective effect is that they all *teach us to buy.* And to feel somehow dissatisfied and inadequate unless we have the newest, the latest, the best. (204)

For more on integrating sources, see Chapter 13, pages 638-648.

WRITER'S VOICE

Creating Intensity

Analysis is an intensive process. It requires intellectual commitment (of both readers and writers). And when writers intensify their voices, they more easily bring readers into that commitment. But what does it mean to intensify a voice? What does it mean to make the voice you've fashioned into something more engaging and insistent? What features create intensity?

The following Cameron Johnson passage seems to insist that the reader pay attention. Johnson creates intensity with repetition, parenthetical phrases, and word choice:

> But such an image leaves an impression. It resonates with our songs (". . . purple mountains' majesty . . ."); it appeals to our longing for escape; it captures our desire for solitude and security; it fits into our drive to scoff at nature. And when such imagery pounds the average citizen relentlessly, it begins to reside in the consciousness. It becomes familiar. Even though most Americans will never see the top of a mountain or careen down a cliff (on purpose), they can buy (into) the vehicle attached to the impression. (213)

What if Johnson's passage were slightly different? Notice the subtle changes in the following passage. How do those changes influence the voice?

> But such an image leaves an impression. Even if you think it does not, it does. The image resonates with common songs (". . . purple mountains' majesty . . ."); it appeals to the longing for escape and captures the desire for solitude and security. Also, such an image supports the idea that we are not slowed down by the perils of nature. When such an image consistently shows up in our magazines and television screens, it begins to take over the consciousness and create familiarity. Even though most Americans will never see the top of a mountain or drive down a cliff in a truck, they can buy the vehicle attached to the impression.

Not all passages in an essay can be intense. Some passages, even in the most ferocious and passionate essays, are more relaxed. They let the reader move along without a fierce intellectual commitment and build a foundation of thought. Such passages are important. In the following passage, Jean Kilbourne analyzes the relationship between alcoholism and alcohol advertising:

> An important part of the denial so necessary to maintain alcoholism or any other addiction is the belief that one's alcohol use isn't affecting one's relationships. The truth, of course, is that addictions shatter relationships. Ads like the one for B and B help support the denial and go one step further by telling us that the alcohol is, in fact, an enhancement to relationships. (193–194)

While this passage is direct, clean, highly analytical, it is not necessarily insistent. But notice the next paragraph in Kilbourne's essay. Something changes slightly:

> "In life there are many loves, but one Grande Passion," says an ad featuring a couple in a passionate embrace. Is the passion enhanced by the liqueur or is the passion for the liqueur? For many years I described my drinking as a love affair, joking that Jack Daniels was my most constant lover. (194)

Kilbourne's voice changes pitch slightly in the second passage. It invites us to ask questions, to enter her life. It becomes slightly more informal and intimate. (But it is no less analytical.) Because reading (like all human activity) depends on a tug and pull, an ebb and flow of consciousness, these subtle changes in pitch help make Kilbourne's writing seem more intense and alive.

ACTIVITY

What else does intensity look like? What does it sound like?

1. In a small group, choose one passage from another chapter reading. As a group, chose specific features of the sentences that help to create an intensive analytical voice. Also, point to features that seem less intense. How do the more intense and less intense passages affect you as readers?

2. Examine any passage you've drafted for this project. How could it be more intense? What statements work against an intensive analytical voice? What words or phrases seem most intense to you? Rewrite the passage while trying to achieve more intensity. Try to abandon the original passage completely. Do something foreign to your habits.

An essay writer tries to create intellectual commitment— for everyone involved.

Using the Personal to Analyze

Analysis does not have to be dry, sterile, or impersonal. It can involve, even rely on, the intimate experiences of the writer. In her essay, Elizabeth Thoman uses the personal to bolster a close examination of images. Notice that she uses her experience as a springboard to take us to a deeper level:

> When I heard the mellifluous voice of Ronald Reagan announce on *GE Theatre* that "Progress is our most important product," little did I realize that the big box in our living room was not just entertaining me. At a deeper level, it was stimulating an "image" in my head of how the world should work: that anything new was better than something old; that science and technology were the greatest of all human achievements and that in the near future—and certainly by the time I grew up—the power of technology would make it possible for everyone to live and work in a world free of war, poverty, drudgery, and ignorance. (202)

Likewise, Jean Kilbourne employs the personal to reveal an important layer of her analysis. In the following passage, Kilbourne shares an intimate vision with us—thereby making the intense examination of advertising more human:

> I can remember loving the names of the drinks, from sloe gin fizzes to Manhattans. I loved the look of the bottles glowing like jewels in the mirror of the bar— ruby, amber, emerald, topaz. I loved the paraphernalia of drinking—the cherries and olives, the translucent slices of lemon, the salt on the rim of the glass, the frost on the shotglass waiting for the syrupy Stolichnaya straight from the freezer. (194)

VITALITY

And now for the hard part: pruning your own language. Once an essay is drafted, it is easy to walk away from it. Returning to your own sentences, with a willingness to trim and vitalize, takes an odd combination of writerly humility and courage. (One has to be humble enough to recognize shortcomings and courageous enough to address them!) Consider the following common issues.

Avoid Blueprinting

Sometimes writers draw attention to their own plans. That is, they tell the reader what they are doing and/or what they are about to do:

> In the following pages, I will explain how the advertising images on MTV influence the present generation.
>
> Next, I will examine the specific framing strategies in the photograph.

This strategy is often called *blueprinting* because it gives the reader a rough plan (like the blueprints for a house). Blueprinting is not inherently wrong, but it does draw attention away from the ideas and toward the writer's processes, which can be distracting. Most readers (and most writing instructors!) would rather stay focused on the ideas themselves. Rather than announcing plans, writers can simply state the points:

> Advertising images on MTV influence the present generation.
>
> Here, removing the blueprinting leaves a relatively vague sentence. So the writer might develop a more focused point: *Advertising images on MTV promote the belief that clothes create identity.*
>
> The specific framing strategies in the photograph . . .
>
> A new verb can be added here to give the sentence more focus: *The specific framing strategies in the photograph help convey the feeling of panic.*

When the blueprinting is removed, the sentences have more potential. More important content can be added. As the previous examples show, blueprinting can fool a writer into thinking that the sentences are saying more than they are.

There are also more subtle forms of blueprinting:

> Next is the composition.
>
> Now, after examining the content, we should explore composition.

These more subtle forms are fairly common. Writers use them as paragraph transitions. While they are generally more accepted, there are still better ways to connect ideas:

> Closely related to content, composition influences how viewers come to an image.

With the blueprinting removed, a sentence can hold more information. Even when the blueprinting is subtle, it diminishes the vitality and intensity of sentences.

Blueprinting diminishes the vitality and intensity of sentences.

Avoid Vague Pronouns

Pronouns help create coherence in and between paragraphs. Pronouns such as *these, this, those,* and *it* are often used to refer back to previous ideas so readers feel a sense of familiarity as they move forward. Notice how *this* works below to keep the reader connected to information in a previous paragraph:

> Even the U.S. Constitution, remember, only promises the pursuit of happiness. It doesn't guarantee that any of us will actually achieve it.
>
> It is <u>this</u> search for "something-more-than-what-we've-got-now" that is at the heart of the consumer culture we struggle with today. (202)

Elizabeth Thoman uses the pronoun to bring the reader from one paragraph to another while maintaining her key point ("this search"). But she also gives us more information, so the transition between paragraphs is smooth: "this search for something-more-than-what-we've-got-now." The additional information keeps the reader in tow. In such a passage, the pronoun offers extra glue between ideas. But imagine if the pronoun had to act alone:

> Even the U.S. Constitution, remember, only promises the pursuit of happiness. It doesn't guarantee that any of us will actually achieve it.
>
> <u>This</u> is at the heart of the consumer culture we struggle with today.

Now the pronoun carries all the burden of the transition between paragraphs. If the reader is not entirely certain what *this* is, the transition is unsuccessful. Consider another example:

> A similar revolution began about 150 years ago with the invention of photography. For the first time, visual representation of objects in space could be reproduced on a mass scale. Image communication was born.
>
> It only took about 50 years for <u>this</u> new method of representation to become a major player in the communication of social values in American society. The rise of the advertising industry spurred <u>this</u> change, for advertisers quickly learned that the most effective way to sell products was not through stories or plain-text facts, but through the creation of images that appealed to basic human needs and emotions. (215)

Here, J. Francis Davis uses *this* to keep readers in tow—to connect information between paragraphs and within the second paragraph. In both instances, *this* does not work alone. It works along with a noun: "this <u>new method of representation</u>" and "this <u>change</u>." Without the nouns, the pronoun would carry the burden of the transition, and the paragraphs would feel less coherent and the ideas less connected.

The most vague pronouns occur when they stand alone and refer to broad ideas:

> While many groups protest the content of advertising images, not enough focus on the presentation of images, particularly the speed and persistence of images. As more and more companies fight over limited air time and limited visual space, the images become increasingly speedy; they zoom past our eyeballs and through our consciousness faster than ever.
>
> <u>This</u> is important. Parent groups, politicians, media analysts basically have it all wrong.

The pronouns in the second paragraph can refer to a broad range of ideas—the speed of images, the fight over air time, the fact that people are not recognizing the speed of images. We just don't know. The pronouns stand alone, and the reader is left to guess at their meaning.

For better vitality and coherence, make certain that pronouns refer directly to, or accompany, specific nouns. (Don't let them go it alone!)

PEER REVIEW

Underline your thesis statement or write your main idea above your draft. Exchange drafts with at least one other writer.

As a reviewer, point to particular sentences and phrases that could gain vitality and intensity. Use the following guidelines:

- Underline any blueprinting passages. Suggest a strategy that keeps the reader focused on the ideas rather than on the structure of the essay.

- Check for vague pronouns. Consider use of *this, these, those, it,* and make certain that they accompany or refer to a specific noun.

- Consider vitality strategies from other chapters and make editorial changes on the writer's draft:
  - Underline any clichés. On the back of the draft, explain how the cliché conceals or blurs thinking. Suggest an alternative to the cliché.
  - Circle any stilted language. On the back of the draft, suggest an alternative approach to the passage.

  - Help the writer experiment with sentence length and brevity. Reconstruct one paragraph, extending some sentences and abbreviating others. Try to create intensity with shorter sentences.
  - Change vague nouns to specific nouns.
  - Change *be* verbs to active verbs.
  - Change clauses to phrases.
  - Change phrases to words.
  - Combine sentences.
  - Repeat structures.
  - Intensify verbs.

- Help the reader avoid common grammatical errors: comma splices, sentence fragments, or pronoun/antecedent agreement.

DELIVERY

We live in a world of images. This chapter has been about how those images communicate and what impact that communication has on individuals and society overall. Now that you have invented and delivered an idea in writing, consider how you might communicate that same idea visually—through an image.

"The statistics—162 million TV sets on seven hours a day, 260,000 billboards, 23,076 newspapers and magazines—are only part of the story."

—Rosalind Silver and Elizabeth Thoman

To communicate your idea visually, first narrow in on your main point. Then consider (but don't limit yourself to) the following options: photograph, sculpture, drawing, painting, diagram, chart, comic, video, map, advertisement, commercial.

After communicating your idea visually, consider the following:

- How did the particular elements of the image communicate the idea to the reader?

- How did the idea change because of the image? That is, how is the visual idea different (in some small or large way) from the idea you communicated in writing?

COLLABORATION

We sometimes rely on others who are more artistic or more technically proficient to help us communicate an idea through images. For example, a writer might work with a graphic artist; a marketing executive might work with an advertising agency. These collaborative efforts, which often produce excellent results, are usually dependent upon the verbal and written communication between the collaborators.

Enlist the help of a friend, classmate, family member, and so on. Ask someone to visually communicate the idea from your essay (or from an essay you've written for one of the other chapters). Then consider the following:

- What difficulties did you have in communicating your vision with the collaborator?

- How was the final creation better, worse, different than you originally imagined?

- How did the visual expression of your idea take on more, or different, meaning?

Collaborate (v) To work together in an intellectual effort.

MAKING ARGUMENTS

Chapter Contents

CHAPTER 6

"Someone who makes an assertion puts forward a claim—a claim on our attention and to our belief."

—Stephen Toulmin

Argument is the art of persuading people how to think. This may sound absurd since most people, we hope, already know how to think, or at least *what* to think about particular issues. But with argument, we can change how people view things, even slightly, and so affect how they approach and process ideas. When was the last time *you* argued with someone—or, at least, tried to change someone's mind about something? Why did you do it? What alternative view were you offering?

Arguments come to us in different forms. We hear them given in speeches, debates, and informal discussions. We hear them every day on talk shows, in break rooms, college hallways, and public meeting places like restaurants and pubs. Arguments get delivered through action. They come explicitly in protests, parades, sit-ins, labor strikes, and elections. They also come in more subtle forms: People donate to charities (thereby expressing their favor of a particular cause); they patronize or boycott a particular store; they choose not to vote (thereby expressing their stance against the entire political process). Arguments get made through art in all media: sculpture, painting, music, and so on. And arguments are major elements of literature. For example, it has been said that Aldous Huxley's book *Brave*

New World argues against the extremes of materialism and industrialization and that Kate Chopin's *The Awakening* argues for a new vision of women's identity. Even poems offer arguments: Walt Whitman's masterpiece *Leaves of Grass* argues for the value of common American workers and their common language.

People in all occupations make or deal with arguments. For example: a human resources manager for a packaging company argues in a report that more supervisors should be hired in the coming fiscal year; several department store sales associates collectively write a letter to store and regional managers in which they claim current scheduling practices minimize sales commissions; the public affairs director of a major automobile company argues that a new advertising campaign should not be offensive to a particular demographic group; the lawyers for a major computer software company argue in a district court that the company's business practices comply with federal anti-trust laws. In academia, argument is everywhere:

- The biology faculty at a state university argue for the need to study cloning and petition the administration for more leeway to do research.

- An historian argues about the number of Native Americans on the continent before European settlers so that people more deeply understand history.
- A psychologist argues that Freudian analysis is overused and that new strategies for exploring patients' psychological makeup should be further developed.
- College administrators argue for more state funds for their schools.
- Students in an architecture class argue that a particular structural design is more sound than competing designs.
- Students in a nursing program must convince others that a new staff management technique is valuable for large hospitals.

In any situation, those who can deliver the most sophisticated and engaging arguments tend to have the most influence. Of course, a sophisticated and engaging argument involves a great deal of strategy. For instance, in academic argument, blatant personal attacks, outright aggression, and sugar-coated language are not valued, nor are empty phrases ("don't question what's in my heart") and mean-spiritedness ("your ideas are simply idiotic"). But while academic writers are not out to squash an opponent or cuddle up to audiences, they do more than simply present their opinions. In providing a new way of thinking about a particular topic, academic writers must also analyze others' ideas and claims and explain how their own claims relate to those of others.

This chapter will help you discover an argumentative topic, explore that topic in depth, develop a sophisticated argument, and communicate your argument in writing. The following essays will provide insight to various argumentative strategies. After reading the essays, you can find a topic in one of two ways:

1. Go to the **Point of Contact** section to find a topic from everyday life.
2. Choose one of the **Ideas for Writing** that follow the essays.

After you find a topic, go to the **Analysis** section to begin developing your argument.

In the following essays, notice how each writer offers a particular stance on an issue and develops that stance throughout the entire essay. But each writer also directly engages other positions on the topic. Whether the essays are long or short, the writers all manage to put forth their own points while also engaging others' opinions, which sometimes compete with their own. In some passages, the writers bring up opposing positions only to refute them; that is, they *counterargue*. In other passages, the writers grant value to opposing positions; that is, they *concede* points.

Crimes Against Humanity

Ward Churchill

In any culture, people learn to accept some language practices and to avoid others. They learn that some words are hurtful and should be avoided while others are perfectly acceptable. Sometimes, minority voices challenge these linguistic habits and the common assumptions they conceal. In "Crimes Against Humanity," Ward Churchill, Keetoowah Band Cherokee and Professor of American Indian Studies at the University of Colorado at Boulder, challenges a seemingly harmless trend in popular entertainment, one that mainstream American culture considers "good clean fun." Because he knows that mainstream thinking is not apt to budge easily, he pushes especially hard in his argument. This argument is challenging—even discomforting. Does he go too far? Does he push us to confront something that we would like to dismiss? What will history say about mainstream American culture? What is the value of all this intellectual discomfort? Such questions lurk beneath Churchill's argument.

During the past couple of seasons, there has been an increasing wave of controversy regarding the names of professional sports teams like the Atlanta "Braves," Cleveland "Indians," Washington "Redskins," and Kansas City "Chiefs." The issue extends to the names of college teams like Florida State University "Seminoles," University of Illinois "Fighting Illini," and so on, right on down to high school outfits like the Lamar (Colorado) "Savages." Also involved have been team adoption of "mascots," replete with feathers, buckskins, beads, spears, and "warpaint" (some fans have opted to adorn themselves in the same fashion), and nifty little "pep" gestures like the "Indian Chant" and "Tomahawk Chop."

A substantial number of American Indians have protested that use of native names, images, and symbols as sports team mascots and the like is, by definition, a virulently racist practice. Given the historical relationship between Indians and non-Indians during what has been called the "Conquest of America," American Indian Movement leader (and American Indian Anti-Defamation Council founder) Russell Means has compared the practice to contemporary Germans naming their soccer teams the "Jews," "Hebrews," and "Yids," while adorning their uniforms with grotesque caricatures of Jewish faces taken from the Nazis' anti-Semitic propaganda of the 1930s. Numerous demonstrations have occurred in conjunction with games—most notably during the November 15, 1992 match-up between the Chiefs and Redskins in Kansas City—by angry Indians and their supporters.

In response, a number of players—especially African Americans and other minority athletes—have been trotted out by professional team owners like Ted Turner, as well as university and public school officials, to announce that they mean not to insult but to honor native people. They have been joined by the television networks and most major newspapers, all of which have editorialized that Indian discomfort with the situation is "no big deal," insisting that the whole thing is just "good, clean fun." The country needs more such fun, they've argued, and a "few disgruntled Native Americans" have no right to undermine the nation's enjoyment of its leisure time by complaining. This is especially the case, some have argued, "in hard times like these." It has even been contended that Indian outrage at being systematically degraded—rather than the degradation itself—creates "a serious barrier to the sort of intergroup communication so necessary in a multicultural society such as ours."

Okay. Let's communicate. We are frankly dubious that those advancing such positions really believe their own rhetoric but, just for the sake of argument, let's accept the premise that they are sincere. If what they say is true, then isn't it time we spread such "inoffensiveness" and "good cheer" around among all the groups so that everybody can participate equally in fostering the national round of laughs they call for? Sure it is—the country can't have too much fun or "intergroup" involvement—so the more, the merrier. Simple consistency demands that anyone who thinks the Tomahawk Chop is a swell pastime must be just as hearty in their endorsement of the following ideas—by the logic used to defend the defamation of American Indians—[to] help us all really start yukking it up.

5   First, as a counterpart to the Redskins, we need an NFL team called "Niggers" to honor Afro-Americans. Half-time festivities for fans might include a simulated stewing of the opposing coach in a large pot while players and cheerleaders dance around it, garbed in leopard skins and wearing fake bones in their noses. This concept obviously goes along with the kind of gaiety attending the Chop, but also with the actions of the Kansas City Chiefs, whose team members—prominently including black members—lately appeared on a

poster, looking "fierce" and "savage" by way of wearing Indian regalia. Just a bit of harmless "morale boosting," says the Chiefs' front office. You bet.

So that the newly-formed Niggers sports club won't end up too out of sync while expressing the "spirit" and "identity" of Afro-Americans in the above fashion, a baseball franchise—let's call this one the "Sambos"— should be formed. How about a basketball team called the "Spearchuckers"? A hockey team called the "Jungle Bunnies"? Maybe the "essence" of these teams could be depicted by images of tiny black faces adorned with huge pairs of lips. The players could appear on TV every week or so gnawing on chicken legs and spitting watermelon seeds at one another. Catchy, eh? Well, there's "nothing to be upset about," according to those who love wearing "war bonnets" to the Super Bowl or having "Chief Illiniwik" dance around the sports arenas of Urbana, Illinois.

And why stop there? There are plenty of other groups to include. Hispanics? They can be "represented" by the Galveston "Greasers" and the San Diego "Spics," at least until the Wisconsin "Wetbacks" and Baltimore "Beaners" get off the ground. Asian Americans? How about the "Slopes," "Dinks," "Gooks," and "Zipperheads"? Owners of the latter teams might get their logo ideas from editorial page cartoons printed in the nation's newspapers during World War II: slanteyes, buck teeth, big glasses, but nothing racially insulting or derogatory, according to the editors and artists involved at the time. Indeed, this Second World War-vintage stuff can be seen as just another barrel of laughs, at least by what current editors say are their "local standards" concerning American Indians.

Let's see. Who's been left out? Teams like the Kansas City "Kikes," Hanover "Honkies," San Leandro "Shylocks," Daytona "Dagos," and Pittsburgh "Polacks" will fill a certain social void among white folk. Have a religious belief? Let's all go for the gusto and gear up the Milwaukee "Mackeral Snappers" and Hollywood "Holy Rollers." The Fighting Irish of Notre Dame can be rechristened the "Drunken Irish" or "Papist Pigs." Issues of gender and sexual preference can be addressed through creation of teams like the St. Louis "Sluts," Boston "Bimbos," Detroit "Dykes," and the Fresno "Fags." How about the Gainsville "Gimps" and the Richmond "Retards," so the physically and mentally impaired won't be excluded from our fun and games?

Now, don't go getting "overly sensitive" out there. None of this is demeaning or insulting, at least not when it's being done to Indians. Just ask the folks who are doing it, or their apologists like Andy Rooney in the national media. They'll tell you—as in fact they have been telling you—that there's been no harm done, regardless of what their victims think, feel, or say. The situation is exactly the same as when those with precisely the same mentality used to insist that Step 'n' Fetchit was okay, or Rochester on the Jack Benny show, or Amos and Andy, Charlie Chan, the Frito Bandito, or any other cutesy symbols making up the lexicon of American racism. Have we communicated yet?

10   Let's get just a little bit real here. The notion of "fun" embodied in rituals like the Tomahawk Chop must be understood for what it is. There's not a single non-Indian example used above which can be considered socially acceptable in even the most marginal sense. The reasons are obvious enough. So why is it different where American Indians are concerned? One can only conclude that, in contrast to the other groups at issue, Indians are (falsely) perceived as being too few, and therefore too weak, to defend themselves effectively against racist and otherwise offensive behavior.

Fortunately, there are some glimmers of hope. A few teams and their fans have gotten the message and have responded appropriately. Stanford University, which opted to drop the name "Indians" from Stanford, has experienced no resulting drop in attendance. Meanwhile, the local newspaper in Portland, Oregon recently decided its long-standing editorial policy prohibiting use of racial epithets should include derogatory team names. The Redskins, for instance, are now referred to as "the Washington team," and will continue to be described in this way until the franchise adopts an inoffensive moniker (newspaper sales in Portland have suf-fered no decline as a result). Such examples are to be applauded and encouraged. They stand as figurative beacons in the night, proving beyond all doubt that it is quite possible to indulge in the pleasure of athletics without accepting blatant racism into the bargain.

Nuremberg Precedents

On October 16, 1946, a man named Julius Streicher mounted the steps of a gallows. Moments later he was dead, the sentence of an international tribunal composed of representatives of the United States, France, Great Britain, and the Soviet Union having been imposed. Streicher's body was then cremated, and—so horrendous were his crimes thought to have been—his ashes dumped into an unspecified German river so that "no one should ever know a particular place to go for reasons of mourning his memory."

Julius Streicher had been convicted at Nuremberg, Germany of what were termed "Crimes Against Humanity." The lead prosecutor in his case—Justice Robert Jackson of the United States Supreme Court—had not argued that the defendant had killed anyone, nor that he had personally committed any especially violent act. Nor was it contended that Streicher had held any particularly important position in the German government during the period in which the so-called Third Reich had exterminated some 6,000,000 Jews, as well as several million Gypsies, Poles, Slavs, homosexuals, and other *untermenschen* (subhumans).

The sole offense for which the accused was ordered put to death was in having served as publisher/editor of a Bavarian tabloid entitled *Der Sturmer* during the early-to-mid 1930s, years before the Nazi genocide actually began. In this capacity, he had penned a long series of virulently anti-Semitic editorials and "news."

15   Stories, usually accompanied by cartoons and other images, graphically depicted Jews in extraordinarily derogatory fashion. This, the prosecution asserted, had done much to "dehumanize" the targets of his distortion in the mind of the German public. In turn, such dehumanization had made it possible—or at least easier—for average Germans to later indulge in the outright liqui-

dation of Jewish "vermin." The tribunal agreed, holding that Streicher was therefore complicit in genocide and deserving of death by hanging.

During his remarks to the Nuremberg tribunal, Justice Jackson observed that, in implementing its sentences, the participating powers were morally and legally binding themselves to adhere forever after to the same standards of conduct that were being applied to Streicher and the other Nazi leaders. In the alternative, he said, the victorious allies would have committed "pure murder" at Nuremberg—no different in substance from that carried out by those they presumed to judge—rather than establishing the "permanent benchmark for justice" which was intended.

Yet in the United States of Robert Jackson, the indigenous American Indian population had already been reduced, in a process which is ongoing to this day, from perhaps 12.5 million in the year 1500 to fewer than 250,000 by the beginning of the 20th century. This was accomplished, according to official sources, "largely through the cruelty of Euro American settlers," and an informal but clear governmental policy which had made it an articulated goal to "exterminate these red vermin" or at least whole segments of them.

Bounties had been placed on the scalps of Indians—any Indians—in places as diverse as Georgia, Kentucky, Texas, the Dakotas, Oregon, and California and had been maintained until resident Indian populations were decimated or disappeared altogether. Entire peoples such as the Cherokee had been reduced to half their size through a policy of forced removal from their homelands east of the Mississippi River to what were then considered less preferable areas in the West.

Others, such as the Navajo, suffered the same fate while under military guard for years on end. The United States Army had also perpetrated a long series of wholesale massacres of Indians at places like Horseshoe Bend, Bear River, Sand Creek, the Washita River, the Marias River, Camp Robinson, and Wounded Knee.

20   Through it all, hundreds of popular novels—each competing with the next to make Indians appear more grotesque, menacing, and inhuman—were sold in the tens of millions of copies in the U.S. Plainly, the Euro American public was being conditioned to see Indians in such a way so as to allow their eradication to continue. And continue it did until the Manifest Destiny of the U.S.—a direct precursor to what Hitler would subsequently call *Lebensraumpolitik* (the politics of living space)—was consummated.

By 1900, the national project of "clearing" Native Americans from their land and replacing them with "superior" Anglo American settlers was complete; the indigenous population had been reduced by as much as 98 percent while approximately 97.5 percent of their original territory had "passed" to the invaders. The survivors had been concentrated, out of sight and mind of the public, on scattered "reservations," all of them under the self-assigned "plenary" (full) power of the federal government. There was, of course, no Nuremberg-style tribunal passing judgment on those who had fostered such circumstances in North America. No U.S. official or private citizen was ever imprisoned—never mind hanged—for implementing or propagandizing what had been done. Nor had the process of genocide afflicting Indians been completed. Instead, it merely changed form.

Between the 1880s and the 1980s, nearly half of all Native American children were coercively transferred from their own families, communities, and cultures to those of the conquering society. This was done through compulsory attendance at remote boarding schools, often hundreds of miles from their homes, where native children were kept for years on end while being systematically "deculturated" (indoctrinated to think and act in the manner of Euro Americans rather than as Indians). It was also accomplished through a pervasive foster home and adoption program—including blind adoptions, where children would be permanently denied information as to who they were/are and where they'd come from—placing native youths in non-Indian homes.

The express purpose of all this was to facilitate a U.S. governmental policy to bring about the "assimilation" (dissolution) of indigenous societies. In other words, Indian cultures as such were to be caused to disappear. Such policy objectives are directly contrary to the United Nations 1948 Convention on Punishment and Prevention of the Crime of Genocide, an element of international law arising from the Nuremberg proceedings. The forced "transfer of the children" of a targeted "racial, ethnical, or religious group" is explicitly prohibited as a genocidal activity under the Convention's second article.

Article II of the Genocide Convention also expressly prohibits involuntary sterilization as a means of "preventing births among" a targeted population. Yet, in 1975, it was conceded by the U.S. government that its Indian Health Service (IHS), then a subpart of the Bureau of Indian Affairs (BIA), was even then conducting a secret program of involuntary sterilization that had affected approximately 40 percent of all Indian women. The program was allegedly discontinued, and the IHS was transferred to the Public Health Service, but no one was punished. In 1990, it came out that the IHS was inoculating Inuit children in Alaska with Hepatitis-B vaccine. The vaccine had already been banned by the World Health Organization as having demonstrated a correlation with the HIV syndrome, which is itself correlated to AIDS. As this is written [March 1993], a "field test" of Hepatitis-A vaccine, also HIV-correlated, is being conducted on Indian reservations in the northern plains region.

25 The Genocide Convention makes it a crime against "humanity" to create conditions leading to the destruction of an identifiable human group, as such. Yet the BIA has utilized the government's plenary prerogatives to negotiate mineral leases "on behalf of" Indian peoples paying a fraction of standard royalty rates. The result has been "super profits" for a number of preferred U.S. corporations. Meanwhile, Indians, whose reservations ironically turned out to be in some of the most mineral-rich areas of North America, which makes us the nominally wealthiest segment of the continent's population, live in dire poverty.

By the government's own data in the mid-1980s, Indians received the lowest annual and lifetime per capita incomes of any aggregate population group in the United States. Concomitantly, we suffer the highest rate of infant mortality, death by exposure and malnutrition, disease, and the like. Under such circumstances, alcoholism and other escapist forms of substance abuse are endemic in the Indian community, a situation which leads both to a general physical debilitation of the population and a catastrophic accident rate. Teen suicide among Indians is several times the national average.

The average life expectancy of a reservation-based Native American man is barely 45 years; women can expect to live less than three years longer.

Such itemizations could be continued at great length, including matters like the radioactive contamination of large portions of contemporary Indian Country, the forced relocation of traditional Navajos, and so on. But the point should be made: Genocide, as defined in international law, is a continuing fact of day-to-day life (and death) for North America's native peoples. Yet there has been—and is—only the barest flicker of public concern about or even consciousness of, this reality. Absent any serious expression of public outrage, no one is punished and the process continues.

A salient reason for public acquiescence before the ongoing holocaust in Native North America has been a continuation of the popular legacy, often through more effective media. Since 1925, Hollywood has released more than 2,000 films, many of them rerun frequently on television, portraying Indians as strange, perverted, ridiculous, and often dangerous things of the past. Moreover, we are habitually presented to mass audiences one-dimensionally, devoid of recognizable human motivations and emotions: Indians thus serve as props, little more. We have thus been thoroughly and systematically dehumanized.

30 Nor is this the extent of it. Everywhere we are used as logos, as mascots, as jokes: "Big Chief " writing tablets, "Red Man" chewing tobacco, "Winnebago"

campers, "Navajo" and "Cherokee" and "Pontiac" and "Cadillac" pickups and automobiles. There are the Cleveland "Indians," the Kansas City "Chiefs," the Atlanta "Braves," and the Washington "Redskins" professional sports teams—not to mention those in thousands of colleges, high schools, and elementary schools across the country, each with their own degrading caricatures and parodies of Indians and/or things Indian. Pop fiction continues in the same vein, including an unending stream of New Age manuals purporting to expose the inner works of indigenous spirituality in everything from pseudo-philosophical to do-it-yourself styles. Blond yuppies from Beverly Hills amble about the country claiming to be reincarnated 17th-century Cheyenne Ushamans ready to perform previously secret ceremonies.

In effect, a concerted, sustained, and in some ways accelerating effort has gone into making Indians unreal. It is thus of obvious importance that the American public begin to think about the implications of such things the next time they witness a gaggle of face-painted and war-bonneted buffoons doing the "Tomahawk Chop" at a baseball or football game. It is necessary that they think about the implications of the grade-school teacher adorning their child in turkey feathers to commemorate Thanksgiving. Think about the significance of John Wayne or Charleton Heston killing a dozen "savages" with a single bullet the next time a western comes on TV. Think about why Land-o-Lakes finds it appropriate to market its butter with the stereotyped image of an "Indian princess" on the wrapper. Think about what it means when non-Indian academics profess—as they often do—to "know more about Indians than Indians do themselves." Think about the significance of charlatans like Carlos Castaneda and Jamake Highwater and Mary Summer Rain and Lynn Andrews churning out "Indian" bestsellers one after the other, while Indians typically can't get into print.

Think about the real situation of American Indians. Think about Julius Streicher. Remember Justice Jackson's admonition. Understand that the treatment of Indians in American popular culture is not "cute" or "amusing," or just "good, clean fun."

Know that it causes real pain and real suffering to real people. Know that it threatens our very survival. And know that this is just as much a crime against humanity as anything the Nazis ever did. It is likely the indigenous people of the United States will never demand that those guilty of such criminal activity be punished for their deeds. But the least we have to expect—indeed to demand—is that such practices finally be brought to a halt.

Writing Strategies

1. Describe Churchill's voice as a writer. Refer specifically to several sentences that support your description. Then explain how Churchill's particular writer's voice might affect his reader. What seems to be Churchill's strategy regarding his writer's voice?

2. Identify places in Churchill's essay where he anticipates his reader's thoughts. How is he able to anticipate them, and how successful is he at responding to them?

3. Describe Churchill's evidence. What type of evidence is it: personal anecdotes, literary allusions, observations, logical reasoning, historical allusions, or something else? What particular evidence did you find most convincing? What evidence did you think fell short?

4. Consider Churchill's opening and closing strategies. How successful are they? How else might he have gotten into and out of his essay?

Exploring Ideas

1. While some people argue that the use of Native American names, images, and symbols is harmless, others argue that it is actually a tribute to Native Americans. Why does Churchill think it isn't a tribute? What values, beliefs, or assumptions create the difference of opinion?

2. Take Churchill's side and respond to the following statement: "I am Irish, and I'm not offended that Notre Dame's mascot is a leprechaun."

3. Why shouldn't a school or team change their name from Redskins to Bears?

4. Search the internet for websites against the use of Native American names for sports teams. How are the arguments put forth on such sites more effective or less effective than Churchill's argument?

Ideas for Writing

1. How can you apply some or all of Churchill's way of thinking to another group or situation?

2. How is Churchill's argument played out in your life? That is, in what ways do you encourage and support or discourage and withdraw your support from the use of Native American images and symbols?

If responding to one of these ideas, go to the **Analysis** section of this chapter to begin developing ideas for your essay.

Why a Great Books Education Is the Most Practical!

David Crabtree, Ph.D.

Academic writers often challenge common assumptions. David Crabtree, president and one of the founders of Gutenberg College in Eugene, Oregon, takes on the common assumption that a specialized education is the best path to a career and financial security. While many college students believe that a narrow focus on a particular set of skills will lead them to successful careers, Crabtree argues that specialization works against students' best interests. Instead, he invites readers to examine the role of "great books" (classical works of literature, philosophy, and religion) in developing a career path and a productive future. Crabtree knows what he's up against: Most people assume that studying great books is contrary to a career path in "the real world." So he begins, in the title of his essay, by taking on that assumption.

Gutenberg College is a great books college. The curriculum is designed to develop good learning skills in students; they read and then discuss in small groups the writings produced by the greatest minds of Western culture as they grappled with the most fundamental questions facing human beings of all ages. When I tell people about Gutenberg College, one of the most common responses is: "It's a good idea, but not practical." The thinking seems to be that if one had unlimited time and money, a great books education would be very good to pursue; but in the real world, food has to be put on the table, and a great books education will not do that. I am convinced, however, that a great books education is not only practical, but, in our day and age, the most practical education available.

Modern society has adopted the historically recent perspective that the purpose of education is training for the workplace. In this view, college should provide students with skills and knowledge that will prepare them to procure reasonably high-paying, satisfying employment for the rest of their lives. The common wisdom says that the best way to achieve this goal is: First, as an undergraduate, select a promising occupation and major in the appropriate field of study; and second, after graduating, enter directly into the work force or attend a graduate or professional school for more specialized training. The logic seems to be that the sooner one concludes one's education and begins work in one's field, the less will be the cost of education and the better the prospects for advancement into secure, high-paying positions. While this was once a reasonable strategy, it is not suited to the economic environment currently developing.

The world is changing at a bewildering pace. Anyone who owns a computer and tries to keep up with the developments in hardware, software, and the accompanying incompatibilities is all too aware of the speed of change. This rapid change, especially technological change, has extremely important implications for the job market. In the past, it was possible to look at the nation's work force, determine which of the existing occupations was most desirable in terms of pay and working conditions, and pick one to prepare for. But the rapid rate of change is clouding the crystal ball. How do we know that a high-paying job today will be high-paying tomorrow?

A photographer told me about a talented and highly skilled artisan who touched up photographs. He was the best in our region of the country, and people knew it; because the demand for his skill was so great, he was unable to keep up with the work. A few years ago, however, this artisan suddenly closed his shop; he did not have enough work to stay in business. Due to developments in computer hardware and software, anyone with just a little training can now achieve results previously attainable by only a few highly skilled artisans. Technology had rendered this artisan's skills obsolete. And this is not an isolated case; technology is antiquating many skills.

5   One could try to avoid this fate by finding an occupation unlikely to be automated, but automation is

not the only cause of job elimination. Historically, mid-management positions in large corporations provided good incomes and considerable job security. However, AT&T's recent layoffs have drawn attention to the growing trend in American companies to eliminate mid-level managers as the companies restructure to compete better in the world market. As a result, a glut of unemployed executives are having great difficulty finding employment in their field of expertise. Most of them never dreamed they would be standing in unemployment lines.

Medicine might be a more promising field. There will always be sick people to treat, and doctors have a reputation for high pay. However, recent news reports have called into question the future of this occupation. There is an excess of doctors in the United States right now, largely due to the number of foreign medical students who decide to remain in this country after they complete their training. And physicians' incomes recently declined for the first time in decades, a change attributed to the proliferation of HMOs and managed health care providers—a trend expected to continue. To further complicate the picture, in the near future a national health care plan may rise from the ashes of President Clinton's ill-fated one. What effect such a program would have on physicians' incomes and working conditions is impossible to predict with certainty, but doctors ought not expect raises under such a plan. In light of such an uncertain future, should a student invest the time and money medical training requires? This is a tough question, but similar uncertainties lie in the future of many professions.

One could forego the traditionally desirable occupations and choose a field certain to grow and develop. Clearly the high demand for programmers, electrical engineers, and computer programmers appears to hold great promise for job security in the foreseeable future, even if one must work for several different employers over the years. However, no one in this field will be able to take his job for granted. Due to the rapid rate of technological change in the computer industry, people in this field need to be constantly learning and updat-

ing their skills to keep up with the new technology. In areas of state-of-the-art development, some companies do not want software writers or engineers over thirty-five years old because their training is out-of-date and they are too set in their ways to approach problems with fresh thinking. These companies prefer to replace older employees with recent graduates. Thus the longevity of one's career in this fast-changing field could be relatively short.

No matter what occupation one chooses, the future is full of question marks. Although this economic dislocation is in its early stages, statistics already indicate a high degree of instability in the job market. According to the United States government, the average American switches careers three times in his or her life, works for ten employers, and stays in each job only 3.6 years.[1]

Such unpredictability calls for a different strategy in preparing for the job market. Rather than spending one's undergraduate years receiving specialized training, one ought to learn more general, transferable skills which will provide the flexibility to adjust to whatever changes may occur. A well-educated worker should be able to communicate clearly with coworkers, both verbally and in writing, read with understanding, perform basic mathematical calculations, conduct himself responsibly and ethically, and work well with others. These skills would make a person well-suited to most work environments and capable of learning quickly and easily the requisite skills for a new career, should the need arise. Thus a hard-headed realism, with long-term economic security as the goal, would seem to dictate an undergraduate educational strategy of focusing on sound general learning skills—just what a great books education provides.

10   Therefore, a great books education makes good sense in terms of dollars spent and dollars gained when calculated over a lifetime, and, therefore, good training for the workplace. This is fortuitous, however, because a great books education is not designed with this as the

---

[1] Sue Brower, "When You Want—or Have—to Make a Career Shift," <u>Cosmopolitan</u> Aug. 1985: 229.

primary goal. It is designed to achieve the even more practical goal historically assigned to education: to teach students how to live wisely. I say this is practical because that which helps one achieve what needs to be done is practical. Living wisely is the most important thing a person can do in his lifetime. Therefore, education with this focus is quintessentially practical.

Wise living means to live as one ought; in other words, to strive to achieve good goals by moral means. This statement immediately evokes an array of fundamental questions: Why are we here? What is valuable or worthwhile? What are the principles of right and wrong? Is there a God? Who is He? What is my relationship to Him? Without having seriously wrestled with these issues, one will be condemned to a life without direction or purpose. Without clearly defined and worthwhile goals, success and fulfillment are impossible. Therefore, one's answers to these questions have very important implications for how one chooses to earn a living.

Is such a goal realistic or attainable by education? It is difficult to teach a person how to live wisely. In a sense, such a skill cannot be taught; it can only be learned. The student must be challenged to think through these fundamental questions for himself; he must be an extremely active participant in his own education. We all derive our wisdom from careful reflection on our experience, and this reflection can be made more profound by considering the reflections of others who have had similar experiences. That is to say, we can benefit from the wisdom others have attained.

A great books education creates an educational environment conducive to the learning of wisdom. Classes are small, personal, and largely discussion-based. The small class size and the discussion format encourage each student to be actively involved in consideration of important issues, and they allow the course of the discussion to be tailored to the concerns of the students. The writings of the most influential thinkers of our cultural tradition are studied, which provides many thought-provoking insights into the fundamental questions. As students work to understand these writings, they develop important learning skills—reading with understanding, thinking clearly, and writing cogently—which equip them to become life-long learners.

A great books education is not for everyone. In order to benefit from such an education, a student has to be highly motivated, mature enough to realize the importance of such a focus, and self-disciplined. Whatever reasons one might have for not pursuing a great books education, it cannot be because it is not practical!

Writing Strategies

1. How does Crabtree make his main idea clear to the reader?

2. Crabtree's introduction puts his essay within a context—that is, he lets the reader know why he is writing about a great books education. Why is he writing? To what argument is his essay responding? To whom is he writing?

3. Does Crabtree clearly define a great books education? If so, how? If not, how might he have defined it more clearly?

4. What kinds of evidence (statistics, examples, allusions, personal testimony, reasoning, and so on) does Crabtree provide as support for his main idea?

5. Does Crabtree make concessions or counterarguments—that is, does he acknowledge weaknesses in his own argument or value in opposing positions (concession), or does he anticipate and respond to likely reactions to his points (counterargument)? If so, how do the concessions and/or counterarguments strengthen his argument? If not, what concessions or counterarguments might he have made that he didn't?

Exploring Ideas

1. What does Crabtree mean by a "great books education"?

2. Crabtree argues that a great books education is the most practical education because the world and workforce are changing at such a rapid rate. Yet many readers disagree with him. Alone or with others, explore what is at the core of these differing opinions.

3. Why else, besides practical training for a job, might a great books education be a good idea?

4. How might a great books education benefit a police officer, a nurse, an accountant?

5. What compromise might college curriculums reach between a purely great books education and purely specialized training?

Ideas for Writing

1. Crabtree argues for the practical value of a great books education, but he does not say that a great books education is for everyone. What else might you argue has practical value, even though you are not arguing that it is for everyone? (Consider a type of education, a way of doing something, a hobby, and so on.)

2. Why are we here? What is valuable or worthwhile? What are the principles of right and wrong? Is there a God? Who is He? What is my relationship with Him? How might you support or refute Crabtree's claim that "one's answers to these questions have very important implications for how one chooses to earn a living" (¶ 11)?

3. Crabtree says that "the writings of the most influential thinkers of our cultural tradition are studied, which provides many thought-provoking insights into the fundamental questions" (¶ 13). Can you think of one such insight that has influenced your thinking?

If responding to one of these ideas, go to the **Analysis** section of this chapter to begin developing ideas for your essay.

Cruelty, Civility, and Other Weighty Matters

Ann Marie Paulin

As with most engaging essays, Paulin's originates in personal circumstance. (See Ann Marie Paulin's invention writing on pages 277–278.) Also, as with most engaging essays, the writer extends her thinking into the public sphere. As you read "Cruelty, Civility, and Other Weighty Matters," notice how Paulin puts forth an argument while keeping herself in the background, only briefly referring to herself in the essay's introduction and conclusion. As you will see, Paulin goes beyond the increasingly common argument against media's portrayal of women; she reveals something about the subtle effects of that portrayal. Paulin, who teaches English and gender studies at Owens Community College in Toledo, Ohio, shows that a writer's voice matters—that savvy use of voice actually creates layers to an argument. That is, her voice re-humanizes the issue and the people involved. If the media have dehumanized "fat people," Paulin does more than argue against the media; she strikes back with an intense, multifaceted presence.

In the margins of this essay, a reader's comments point to key ideas and writing strategies. As you read the essay, consider how the comments might influence your own reading and writing.

Writing Strategies

A strong, emphatic (but informal) voice.

"You" makes the voice more informal.

"Our" is a direct strategy to create public resonance.

This is a qualification of her argument.

Exploring Ideas

Pop culture images are simplistic.

Media images have distorted people's perceptions about life.

I swear, if I have to sit through one more ad proclaiming that life is not worth living if you aren't thin, I'll slug somebody. So much for the theory that fat people are jolly. But, contrary to what magazines, talk shows, movies, and advertisements proclaim, we aren't all a bunch of sorrowful, empty losers with no friends and no self-esteem, either. As with most complex issues—religion, politics, human relationships—most of what we see in mass media is hugely oversimplified and, therefore, wrong. So, if many of us recognize the media are notorious for getting things less than accurate, you might wonder why I let these images bother me so much. Well, if you were one of the millions of fat Americans living in a culture where you are constantly depicted as some sort of weepy loser, ill-dressed buffoon, or neutered sidekick, your good nature might wear a bit thin as well. But far more important than my ill temper is a creepy sense that these inaccurate images have shifted our vision of what is important in life way out of whack, so far out that people are being hurt. What I'm proposing here is that we need to get some perspective on this issue.

First of all, let me make it clear that I'm not advocating that everyone in America go out and get fat. According to the news media, we are doing that very handily on our own, in spite of all the messages to the contrary and the shelves of diet food in every supermarket. (One of my colleagues came by today with a newspaper article on the Krispy Kreme Donut chain; evidently, Americans eat three million Krispy Kreme donuts each day. We may talk tofu, but we gobble glazed.) Americans all need to work on eating healthier and getting some exercise. Of course, the thin fanatics claim to advocate a healthy lifestyle as well, but I question how healthy people are when they are living on low-calorie chocolate milk drinks, or taking herbal supplements containing goodness knows what, or loading up on the latest wonder diet pill. Remember Fen-phen? And most diets don't work. Psychologist Mary Pipher, in her book *Hunger Pains: The Modern Woman's Quest for Thinness,* cites a 1994 study which found that "90 percent of dieters regain all the weight they lost within five years" (32). The evidence is beginning to pile up out there that being fat may not be nearly as bad for a person's health as the crazy things people inflict upon their bodies to lose weight.

But beyond these physical things, we need to get our minds straightened out. We need to get back to recognizing that a human being is a collection of qualities, good and bad, and that appearance is not the ultimate way to judge a person's character or value to society.

Yet there is definitely a prejudice against fat people in this country. Various articles and news magazine programs have reported that Americans of all sizes make far more than simple aesthetic judgments when they look at a fat person. Fat people are assumed to be lazy, stupid, ugly, lacking in self-esteem and pride, devoid of self-control, and stuffed full of a host of other unpleasant qualities that have nothing to do with the size of a person's belly or thighs. But, as anyone who has ever been the victim of such prejudice can tell you, the impact such foolish notions have on people is real and harmful. For example, Marilyn Wann, in her book *Fat! So?,* reports some alarming statistics: "In a 1977 study, half of the landlords refused to rent an apartment to a fat applicant. All of the landlords were willing to rent the same apartment to a thin applicant" (154). What does dress size have to do with whether or not you pay your rent on time? Or do landlords assume that fat people will not keep the apartments clean? Wann also cites an experiment in which "[r]esearchers placed two fake personal ads, one for a woman described as '50 pounds overweight' and the other for a woman described as a drug addict. The drug addict received 79 percent of

Helps with the public resonance. It shows that Paulin is not alone.

Counterargument.

Allusion to a related news event.

Using an authority, Pipher, to support point.

Stating an opposing view—or wrong assumption. Setting up the counterargument.

Counterargument—she's countering the opposing view.

Millions of Americans eat poorly . . . are out of sync with the media images.

Diets don't work . . . and inflict bodily damage.

People's understanding of health has been distorted.

People are more than their body sizes.

The study is almost 30 years old. Has it changed?

Marilyn Wann—fat people are discriminated against.

the responses" (59). I don't even want to know what the thinking was here. And, finally, Wann points out that the average fat woman earns about $7000 less per year than her thinner sisters (80). In my case, I teach English at a community college. Jobs in academia require an advanced degree, so I happen to have a Ph.D., which has nothing to do with my body size, unless you want to count the weight I gained from thousands of hours sitting reading, sitting at a keyboard, sitting grading papers.

Real effects of prejudice. Good support.

Relates the problem to her personal situation. Makes the voice feel personal.

Restatement of the main idea.

5   This weight prejudice hurts real people. When people are denied a place to live or a means of support not because of any bad behavior or lack of character or talent on their part but because of someone else's wrongheaded notions, then we need to start changing things.

The real danger of the media images.

The messages are particularly insidious when they suggest that being thin is more important than a man's or, more often, a woman's relationships with her loved ones or even than her health. The media churn the images out, but the public too often internalizes them. For example, in one commercial for Slim Fast, the woman on the ad is prattling on about how she had gained weight when she was pregnant (seems to me, if you make a person, you ought to be entitled to an extra ten pounds) and how awful she felt. Then there is a shot of this woman months later as a thin person with her toddler in her yard. She joyously proclaims that Slim Fast is "the best thing that ever happened to me!" The best thing that ever happened to her?! I thought I heard wrong. What about that little child romping by her heels? Presumably, there is a daddy somewhere for that little cherub. What about his role in her life? The thought that losing that weight is the most important thing that ever occurred in her life is sad and terrifying. It's even worse for the folks who share that life with her. I kept hoping that was not what she meant. I'm sure her family is really most important. But she didn't say, "Next to my baby, Slim Fast is the best thing that ever happened to me." Advertisers don't spend millions of dollars creating ads that don't say what they intend them to; this message was deliberate. Granted, this is only one ad, but the message is clear: The consumer is the center of the universe, and being thin is the only way to ensure that universe remains a fun place to live. The constant repetition of this message in various forms does the damage to the humans who watch and learn.

Allusion to popular item.

Slim Fast ad that directly values thinness over family, life. Good support.

Thinness ads damage minds/lives.

While we can shrug off advertisements as silly, when we see these attitudes reflected among real people, the hurt is far less easy to brush away. For instance, in her essay, "Bubbie, Mommy, Weight

This addresses an opposing point: That ads are harmless.

Watchers and Me," Barbara Noreen Dinnerstein recalls a time in her childhood when her mother took her to Weight Watchers to slim down and the advice the lecturer gave to the women present: "She told us to put a picture of ourselves on the 'fridgerator of us eating and looking really fat and ugly. She said remember what you look like. Remember how ugly you are" (347).

Analysis of the opposing logic.

I have a problem with this advice. First, of course, it is too darn common. Fat people are constantly being told they should be ashamed of themselves, of their bodies. And here we see another of those misconceptions I mentioned earlier: the assumption that being fat is the same as being ugly. There are plenty of attractive fat people in the world, as well as a few butt-ugly thin ones, I might add. Honestly, though, the real tragedy is that while few people in this world are truly ugly, many agonize over the belief that they are. Dr. Pipher reported: "I see clients who say they would rather kill themselves than be overweight" (91). I never have figured out how trashing a fellow being's self-esteem is going to help that person be healthier.

Ha! The writer is not above judging people . . . this creates an interesting voice.

People would rather die than be fat.

Transition statement creates coherence between points.

Another example of this bullying comes from Pipher's book *Hunger Pains: The Modern Woman's Tragic Quest for Thinness.* Pipher recounts a conversation she overheard one day in a dress shop:

Pipher—women are psychologically damaged by the culture of thinness

> I overheard a mother talking to her daughter, who was trying on party dresses. She put on each dress and then asked her mother how she looked. Time after time, her mother responded by saying, "You look just awful in that, Kathy. You're so fat nothing fits you right." The mother's voice dripped with disgust and soon Kathy was crying. (89)

Follow-up to the quote makes it more engaging and relevant.

Pipher goes on to suggest that Kathy's mother is a victim of the culture, too, because she realizes how hard the world will be on her fat daughter. Unfortunately, what she doesn't realize is how much better her daughter's quality of life would be if she felt loved by her mother. Any person surrounded by loving family members at home is much better equipped to deal with whatever the cruel world outside throws at her or him.

10   Dinnerstein was lucky; she had a grandmother who was very loving and supportive. Her grandmother's advice was, "Be proud, be strong, be who you are" (348). Sound advice for any child, and far more likely to produce an all-around healthy human being than a constant barrage of insults.

But the insensitivity doesn't stop when you grow up. In Camryn Manheim's book *Wake Up! I'm Fat,* the actress discusses her

Keeps returning to the effects on real people—so reader can't dismiss the point.

Another authority used for support . . . a public figure.

But the insensitivity doesn't stop when you grow up. In Camryn Manheim's book *Wake Up! I'm Fat,* the actress discusses her battle with her weight. She expected many of the difficulties she encountered from people in the entertainment industry, which is notorious for its inhuman standards of thinness for women. But when she gained some weight after giving up smoking, she was stunned when her father told her she should start smoking again until she lost the weight (78). In *The Invisible Woman: Confronting Weight Prejudice in America,* W. Charisse Goodman cites a 1987 study that concluded: "When good health practices and appearance norms coincide, women benefit; but if current fashion dictated poor health practices, women might then engage in those practices for the sake of attractiveness" (30). Like taking up smoking to stay slim.

Camryn Manheim—the insensitivity of the industry.

Goodman—women put health below thinness.

Qualifying her main point.

Certainly everyone is entitled to his or her own opinion of what is attractive, but no one has the right to damage another human being for fun or profit. The media and the diet industry often do just that. While no one can change an entire culture overnight, people, especially parents, need to think about what they really value in the humans they share their lives with and what values they want to pass on to their children. We need to wake up and realize that being thin will not fix all our problems, though advertisements for diets and weight loss aids suggest this. Losing weight may, indeed, give a man or woman more confidence, but it will not make a person smarter, more generous, more loving, or more nurturing. It won't automatically attract the dream job or the ideal lover. On the contrary, people who allow the drive to be thin to control them may find that many other areas of their lives suffer: They may avoid some celebrations or get-togethers because of fear they may be tempted to eat too much or the "wrong" foods. They may cut back on intellectual activities like reading or enjoying concerts or art museums because those activities cut into their exercise time too much. The mania for thinness can cause a person to lose all perspective and balance in life. I know. It happened to me. My moment of revelation came about 12 years ago. I was a size ten, dieting constantly and faithfully keeping lists of every bite I ate, trying to lose 15 more pounds. While I was watching the evening news, a story came on about a young woman who was run over by a bus. I vividly recall that as the station played the footage of the paramedics wheeling the woman away on a stretcher, I said to myself, "Yeah, but at least she's thin." I've been lucky enough to

Being thin is not the answer to life.

Back to the personal situation and relaxed voice.

The drive for thinness may shrink other parts of life.

have gained some wisdom (as well as weight) with age: I may be fat, but I'm no longer crazy. There are some things more important than being thin.

Sanity is better than insane thinness.

Conclusion ties back to the intro.

Works Cited

Dinnerstein, Barbara Noreen. "Bubbie, Mommy, Weight Watchers and Me." Worlds in Our Words: Contemporary American Women Writers. Ed. Marilyn Kallet and Patricia Clark. Upper Saddle River: Prentice, 1997. 347–49.

Goodman, W. Charisse. The Invisible Woman: Confronting Weight Prejudice in America. Carlsbad: Gurze, 1995.

Manheim, Camryn. Wake Up! I'm Fat. New York: Broadway, 1999.

Pipher, Mary. Hunger Pains: The Modern Woman's Tragic Quest for Thinness. New York: Ballantine, 1995.

Wann, Marilyn. Fat! So? Because You Don't Have to Apologize for Your Size. Berkeley: Ten Speed, 1998.

Writing Strategies

1. Why do you think Paulin refers to "overweight" people as "fat"? What is the effect of this word on the reader?

2. Paulin helps the reader to understand her main ideas by beginning paragraphs with sentences that state or suggest them. Find three paragraphs in this essay that begin with sentences that state or suggest the main idea. Do those sentences also connect the paragraph to the previous paragraph? If so, describe how.

3. Paulin uses written sources to support her argument. In some places she directly quotes the sources; in others she paraphrases or summarizes (that is, she puts what the source says in her own words). Find an example of each (quote; paraphrase; summary). How do you know the information is from a source? Does Paulin make that clear? Notice how Paulin introduces the information and punctuates it.

4. Paulin's conclusion does not merely summarize points she has already made. Reread the conclusion and describe how it goes beyond mere summary. What does it try to do? Is it successful?

Exploring Ideas

1. How is weight a public issue?

2. In her opening paragraph, Paulin says inaccurate images about weight "have shifted our vision of what is important in life way out of whack, so far out that people are being hurt." Then she calls for perspective. What support can you provide for her claim that our vision of what is important is out of whack? What support can you provide that people are being hurt?

3. Why should or shouldn't comedians refrain from making fat jokes about specific individuals?

4. Paulin says, "[P]eople who allow the drive to be thin to control them may find that many other areas of their lives suffer" (¶ 12). Apply her thinking to some other situation besides body weight, and explain how a particular drive has led to suffering.

Ideas for Writing

1. What point can you help Paulin make by providing different evidence?

2. What idea of Paulin's can you explore further, possibly discovering a different way of seeing it?

If responding to one of these ideas, go to the **Analysis** section of this chapter to begin developing ideas for your essay.

Floppy Disk Fallacies

Elizabeth Bohnhorst

Writing an essay for a class can be difficult. Among the challenges: understanding what you're being asked to do; thinking and writing adventurously without making a mistake that could hurt your grade; not sounding too much like a student writing an essay as a class requirement, even though that's what you are doing. The best student writing, like all good academic writing, puts forth a revelatory claim, has an inviting writer's voice, is to the point and well developed, and ultimately invites readers to think differently about the topic. Elizabeth Bohnhorst's essay, written for a first-semester English course at Northwestern Michigan College, is adventurous. It takes an unusual position and offers a variety of support strategies. If the essay is successful, you may feel slightly different about computer technology in education.

"Another boring PowerPoint," responds Jennifer when I ask about her day at school. I might not find these words so discouraging coming from a company executive after a long meeting or even a college student leaving an informative lecture. But these words of an eleven-year-old elementary school student leave me feeling slightly uneasy. PowerPoint presentations are intended to compel students to become more interested in the subject with the use of neon colors and moving graphic images. But these flashy additions to current educational strategies haven't fooled everyone. The text and material covered is still the same boring grammar and spelling lessons, but the educator has altered: It is a screen.

Computers can undoubtedly contribute wonders to the field of education. In fact, computer education is a must if children intend to thrive in modern society. The possibilities are endless when it comes to surfing the Web or using the thousands of educational programs currently available. These programs are capable of reading text on a computer with icons beside words that take students to a galaxy of options, icons to learn more about the era in which the text was written, fascinating facts about the author, and helpful notes about the morals of the story. But computers are being used more and more frequently as a substitute for books, blackboards, and in some cases, the teachers themselves.

America leads the world in the amount and density of computers in our public schools. In 1992, the typical high school had one computer for every ten students while elementary and middle schools averaged thirteen students per computer ("Computers"). Compared to current numbers, the early 1990s were a time of deprivation. Some schools, such as Kent Central School in rural Connecticut, are considering funding for each student to have his or her own laptop. After visiting the school, Anne Guignon reports that "students use the computers in school, take them home each night, use the computers for homework, and soon will able to tap into the Internet." In such situations, traditional school lingo such as "Take out a piece of paper and a number two pencil" might be replaced with "Take out your floppies and boot up your Toshibas." Unfortunately for some students, dogs cannot digest discs.

And the Texas Board of Education is only steps behind the Kent Central School. "The Texas Board of Education now has state officials seriously examining whether to give all public school students laptops instead of textbooks," states a *New York Times* investigator. The Board "is looking at $1.8 billion in projected costs for textbooks over the next six years, and . . . given technology improvements that have lowered the price of computers, it may be cheaper, to say nothing of innovative, to lease a laptop for each of the state's 3.7 million students" (Guignon).

5   Now, what could possibly be wrong with such a sophisticated device for learning? In reality, "thirty years of research on educational technology has produced almost no evidence of a clear link between using computers in the early grades and improving learning," states Michael Dertouzus, director of MIT Laboratory for Computer Science. In fact, evidence of hazardous effects of frequent use of computers in young children is overwhelming. They do little to promote a healthy

childhood. "Computers are perhaps the most acute symptom of the rush to end childhood. The national drive to computerize schools, from kindergarten on up, emphasizes only one of the many human capacities, one that naturally develops quite late—analytic, abstract thinking—and aims to jump start it prematurely," continues Dertouzus.

Elementary schools are not only responsible for teaching children reading, writing, mathematics, and other basic skills; they also reinforce and indirectly establish guidelines for everyday behavior. Therefore, consistent use of computers in schools ultimately plants the idea in the developing mind that computers are safe, educational, and perhaps one of the most important tools of modern society. Thus, a child returns home from school after hours of staring into an illuminated box, flips through the channels of yet another illuminated box, and then proceeds to play "Final Fantasy Four" on the Macintosh for three more hours. A 1999 study by the Kaiser Family Foundation showed that children ages two to eighteen spent an average of four hours and forty-five minutes per day plugged into electronic media of all kinds. These numbers are excluding the time spent with such machinery during school hours (Dertouzus).

The emotional and social values learned during childhood are also disrupted by computerized education in elementary and middle schools. Students learn more than state capitals and multiplication; they develop a sense of social importance and are taught values or friendship and other relationships. Through interaction with peers, intimacy and companionship are only a few of the many principles computers are unable to relay to children. Dr. Stanley I. Greenspan, former director of the Clinical Infant Development Program, is concerned that the impersonal culture formulated by computerization has serious detrimental effects on children's emotional development: "So-called interactive, computer-based instruction that does not provide true interaction but merely a mechanistic response to the student's efforts," states Greenspan, can be directly linked to "the increasingly impersonal quality that suffuses the experience of

> # "Successful education should not replace children's curiosity to explore the world around them with Internet Explorer."

more and more American children" (qtd. in Dertouzos). He also adds that lack of nurture for children at home and at school can likely result in "increasing levels of violence and extremism and less collaboration and empathy." (qtd. in Dertouzos).

Besides affecting emotional and social development in primary students, computers can also disrupt creative thinking. Like all other electronic viewing systems (television and video games), computers leave little or no room for imagination. Of course, the virtual reality computers create is often full of fantastic images. However, because imagination involves generating one's own images and ideas, consistent exposure to ready-made images only makes it more difficult for children to summon their own creativity. The intensity of the images squashes the need for intensive creativity. Educational psychologist and former school principal Jane Healy has observed that "teachers find that today's video-immersed children can't form original pictures in their mind or develop an imaginative representation. Teachers of young children lament the fact that many now have to be taught to play symbolically or pretend—previously a symptom only of mentally or emotionally disordered youngsters" (qtd. in Dertouzus). Not only do these images affect creativity and imagination; they also have potential to diffuse the sparks of curiosity. For example, if a class is learning about regional watersheds, computerized classrooms will most likely turn to the handy diagrams so conveniently laid out on the screens before the students. In a classroom that values hands-on learning techniques, a school field trip to a local stream or swamp may be an effective strategy. In short, a successful education should not replace children's curiosity to explore the world around them with Internet Explorer.

On the other hand, technology is an effective way to get kids interested in learning, considering "that there is a passionate love affair between children and computers" (Setzer). A colorful computer screen is obviously more attractive to a child than an old novel or a textbook. But this attraction is more likely a fascination with animation and sound effects rather than a genuine exploration of ideas. Dr. Valdemar W. Setzer, a professor of computer science, wonders, "What happens to a student who gets used to learning with computers? Will she be able to tolerate a normal class without all those cosmetic and video game effects?"

10   As technology's role in American society grows, we should observe its influence in public education. It is easy to consider the benefits of computerization: simplicity, standardization, and elimination of other physical controversies. But in the same light we must also consider the hazards and how important traditional education is to children. The obvious concern with traditional education is the students being "left behind" in the rush toward increasing technological advancements.

Educating students in computer skills is and should be a priority in all schools. But when it comes to teaching basic skills and allowing for intellectual development, human interaction and exploration of the real world should never come second to electronic devices. In an effort to preserve the qualities of education, we should not allow ourselves to become mesmerized by teachers that require an electrical outlet and textbooks that require a point-and-click to turn the page.

Works Cited

"Computers in American Schools, 1992: An Overview." IEA Computers in Education. 12 July 1995. 20 July 2005. <http://www.socsci.umn.edu/~iea/>

Dertouzos, Michael. "Developmental Risks: The Hazards of Computers in Childhood." The Alliance for Childhood. 20 July 2005. <http://www.allianceforchildhood.net/projects/computers/computers_reports_fools_gold_2.htm>

Guignon, Anne. "Laptop Computers for Every Student!" Education World. 19 Jan. 1998. 20 July 2005. <http://www.education-world.com/a_curr/ curr048.html>

Setzer, Valdemar W. "A Review of Arguments for the Use of Computers in Elementary Education." Southern Cross Review. 4 (2000) 20 July 2005. <http://www.southerncrossreview.org>

Writing Strategies

1. Why is or isn't Bohnhorst's introduction effective? (What particular sentences or phrases invite you into her thinking? Which do not?)

2. Why does Bohnhorst's reference to PowerPoint strengthen her argument about computers?

3. What additional information could help to bolster Bohnhorst's argument?

4. What does Bohnhorst value and how are those values critical to her argument?

5. How does Bohnhorst deal with specific opposing ideas? Where does she reveal the shortcomings of other positions? Where does she acknowledge the value of other positions?

Exploring Ideas

1. Consider the following claims made by Bohnhorst:

   Computers can undoubtedly contribute wonders to the field of education. (¶ 2)

   In fact, computer education is a must if children intend to thrive in modern society. (¶ 2)

   With others, explore these claims further, trying to discover new ways of thinking about them. Begin by discussing whether or not you think the claims are true, and then pinpoint and explore why people disagree. After several minutes of discussion, how have the claims become more complex?

2. Interview several people who have not read Bohnhorst's argument, and find out specifically what they think computers can contribute to the field of education. Try interviewing people of various backgrounds and age groups. Following your interviews, write down any new ideas you've discovered about computers and education.

3. How might education be better in a school with fewer computers in the classroom? How might computers in the classroom actually interfere with learning? How might education be better in a *nation* with fewer computers in the classroom?

Ideas for Writing

1. What argument might you make by taking a more extreme stance on the role of computers in education?

2. How might you develop an engaging argument on this topic, based on your own experiences with technology and learning?

3. To develop your own argument, research some claim Bohnhorst makes, such as "teachers find that today's video-immersed children can't form original pictures in their mind or develop an imaginative representation" (¶ 8).

If responding to one of these ideas, go to the **Analysis** section of this chapter to begin developing ideas for your essay.

Beware of Drug Sales

Therese Cherry

Extensive use of outside sources can be difficult in a short essay. The writer's voice can easily be drowned out by reliance on statistics and authorities, and the writer's own line of reasoning can be sidetracked by secondary sources. But Therese Cherry manages to use sources in her essay while maintaining a consistent voice and a coherent line of reasoning. Cherry wrote this essay for a first-semester English course at the University of Toledo. The topic emerged from her field of study. At the request of her instructor, she expressed the ideas of the essay in a letter that appears in Chapter 14.

Prescription drug ads are everywhere. You can't turn on the TV or open a magazine these days without finding out if Claritin is "right for you" or being told to ask your doctor about Viagra. Obviously, the makers of prescription drugs want the public to know that there are pills to cure what ails us, and that they don't mind making a little money off our relief. This is how business is run, spending money to make money, marketing the product so that as many consumers as possible are aware of it and will buy it. However, it seems that pharmaceutical companies have taken their role a bit far, marketing their drugs so aggressively that they are actually creating the demand for them. In an industry that sells cars, an ad campaign that sold cars to people who hadn't even realized they wanted to buy one would definitely be a triumph. But to advertise prescription drugs to the extent that people who don't even need them want to buy them is irresponsible and dangerous.

According to the United Nations International Narcotics Control Board (INCB), advanced countries are overdosing on quick-fix pills to ease "non-medical" problems like fat and stress ("Rich States"). INCB also stated that mood-altering drugs are often prescribed for social problems, such as unemployment or relationship problems ("Prescription"). Consumers around the globe are taking medication for this disease called life. The fact that people are spending their hard-earned money on medicine they do not need is bad enough, but the harm these unnecessary drugs can do is a much bigger issue. Yet the drug companies keep on telling us, "It's okay, just ask your doctor." The problem is, the doctors don't have all the answers, either.

Some statistics cited by the FDA reported that toxic reactions to marketed drugs are estimated to cost more than 30 billion dollars per year and to be among the ten leading causes of death in the United States (Pomper 6). So if these drugs are having these kinds of negative effects on people, why are doctors prescribing them? For one, pharmaceutical companies are advertising more aggressively than they have in the past, in part because of loosened restrictions. In 1997 the FDA caved to heavy pressures from the industry, which made it possible for drug companies to advertise on TV without spending huge chunks of time describing side effects (Pomper 6). Now that drug companies can market directly to consumers, suddenly patients are telling their doctors what drugs they want to use. A recent study published by *Health Affairs* reported that three-quarters of the respondents who saw a drug on TV and asked their doctors for it were successful (Pomper 6).

Another reason these drugs are being prescribed is because some doctors are influenced to prescribe drugs which are marketed more aggressively, according to the January 2000 *Journal of the American Medical Association*. And since the most heavily advertised drugs tend to be the newest drugs, the long list of possible side effects cannot be known. In fact, six new drugs approved since mid-1996 have been pulled off the market, and 150 deaths were linked to the drugs before they were pulled (Pomper 8).

5   Perhaps the most unjust and appalling fact about this considerably new trend of pharmaceutical peddling is the industry's knowledge of the damage this marketing technique is causing to the health of the public: "Even people in the industry will concede off the record that groups acting as advertising agents for manufacturers should be subject to FDA regulations" (Pomper 10). The INBC stated in its 2000 report that there was a "continuing existence of aggressive sales methods and

even some cases of financial support to various advocacy groups to foster sales" and appealed to the pharmaceutical industry to demonstrate social responsibility and voluntary cooperation ("Rich States"). We all need to make this same appeal to the drug companies. A business has every right to turn a profit, but should it really be at the risk of good health? Without your health, money means nothing. So, until the pharmaceutical industry can agree with that, buyer beware.

Works Cited

Pomper, Steven. "Drug Rush." The Washington Monthly Online. May 2000: 6–10. 23 Jan. 2002 <http://www.washingtonmonthly.com/features/2000/0005.pomper.html>

"Prescription Drugs 'Over-Used.'" BBC News Online. 21 Feb. 2001. 21 Jan. <2002 http://news.bbc.com.uk/low/english/heath/newsid_1182000/1182115.stm>

"Rich States Overdosing on Feel-Good Pills." Dawn the Internet Edition. 21 Feb. 2001. 21 Jan. 2002 <http://www.dawn.com/2001/02/21/int13.htm>

Writing Strategies

1. What strategy, or strategies, does Cherry use to draw the reader's attention to the point of her essay?

2. What type of evidence does Cherry provide to support her claim? How successful is her evidence? What other evidence might she have provided?

3. Identify any concessions Cherry makes in this essay. That is, where does she acknowledge the validity of a differing viewpoint?

Exploring Ideas

1. In groups, explore Cherry's claim: "A business has every right to turn a profit, but should it really be at the risk of good health?" (¶ 5) Consider each part of her claim:

   - Does a business have every right to turn a profit? What businesses don't?
   - What businesses, besides major pharmaceutical companies, threaten their customers' health?
   - How do pharmaceutical companies actually threaten their customers' health?
   - What businesses should be prohibited from advertising on television and why?
   - What legal businesses should be illegal? What illegal ones should be legal?

   After exploring through discussion, in what ways has the issue become more complex?

2. Is it all right for Americans to take prescription drugs to ease non-medical problems like fat and stress (¶ 2)? What problems should prescription drugs be used for? Consider the following problems: fat, stress, attention, anger, worry, doubt, blood pressure, fear, vision, hearing, sleep, energy, income. Add several more items to the list and explore their relationship to the prescription drug solution.

3. Why do Americans take so many prescription drugs?

Ideas for Writing

1. Like prescription drug ads, what other type of ad is irresponsible and dangerous, and why?

2. What industry commonly perceived as beneficial is endangering the public?

If responding to one of these ideas, go to the **Analysis** section of this chapter to begin developing ideas for your essay.

Outside Reading

Find a written argument and print it out or make a photocopy. You might find an argument about a social or political issue in a general readership publication (such as *Time, Newsweek,* or the *New York Times*). For an argument related to your major, explore an academic journal such as *Journal of the American Medical Association, Texas Nursing,* or *Psychology of Women Quarterly.* To conduct an electronic search of journals and magazines, go to your library's periodical database or to InfoTrac College Edition (http://infotrac.galegroup.com/itweb/). For your library's database, perform a keyword search, or go to the main search box for InfoTrac College Edition and select "keywords." Enter word combinations such as *debate and community, opinion and politics, argument and politics, debate and sports, argument and art.* (When performing keyword searches, avoid using phrases or articles such as *a, an, the;* instead, use nouns separated by *and.*) The search results will yield lists of journal and magazine articles.

You can also search the Internet. Try the search engine Dogpile.com. Like most Internet search engines, Dogpile combines words using *and.* In the search box, try various combinations, such as those above.

The purpose of this assignment is to further your understanding of argument and to introduce a broad range of argumentative strategies. As you are probably discovering, argument appears in many different places and in many different contexts. Even among the essays in this chapter, arguments range in tone, style, length, and strategy. As you read through this chapter, keep the written argument you have discovered close by and notice the elements and strategies the writer uses. Depending on your instructor's suggestions, do one or more of the following:

1. Notice how the writer applies various strategies from this chapter. On the hard copy or photocopy:

   - Highlight the thesis if it is stated in the argument. If the thesis is implied, write it in your own words.

   - Highlight the major support strategies, and write "support" next to each one in the margin.

   - Highlight any passages in which the writer addresses other opinions on the topic, and write "counterargument" or "ca" next to each one in the margin.

   - Highlight any passages in which the writer grants value to another position, and write "concession" or "c" in the margin.

2. Analyze the strategies employed by the writer. The following questions may be helpful:

   - Does this text seem more or less argumentative than the readings in this chapter? Why?

   - How does the writer support his or her argument?

   - Who is the audience for this argument?

   - How does the audience impact the kinds of things said in the argument?

3. Write at least three "Writing Strategies" questions for the argument.

4. Write at least three "Exploring Ideas" questions for the argument.

5. Write two "Ideas for Writing," such as the ones following the essays in this book, for the argument.

INVENTION

Academic audiences demand more than "three reasons why I believe X" arguments. They want to experience more in an argument than a writer's personal beliefs; they want to learn a new way of thinking about a topic. So academic writers often look for a new stance, a way to make people rethink an issue entirely. In general, a successful argument creates a new position on a familiar topic or offers a position on a fresh topic. And good writers do not merely *choose* topics; instead, they *build* topics from the novel and surprising moments of everyday life.

The following sections are designed to help you develop ideas for your argument: specifically, to discover a topic (in **Point of Contact**), develop particular points about the topic (in **Analysis**), make it relevant to a community of readers (in **Public Resonance**), focus your position (in **Thesis**), and create support for that position (in **Rhetorical Tools**). The questions in each section will help you generate intense ideas and start writing. Your responses to the Invention questions may take you in a variety of directions, and some of your responses may get left behind. That is to be expected in academic work—or in any work that seeks to discover something valuable.

POINT OF CONTACT

Some situations in everyday life are obviously significant—what they mean for our lives, or for the lives of others, is apparent. When our country goes to war or when a new president is elected, for example, most Americans understand the significance. Many situations, however, are far more subtle; their potential meaning is hidden by life's hustle and bustle. To understand their meaning, we must stop in our tracks and focus on them.

Use the following suggestions and questions to explore possible topics. If a question seems particularly engaging to you, or if you associate some emotion or idea with the question, start writing.

Work Do my co-workers get along? Do supervisors treat workers fairly? Are the work expectations fair? Are the working hours suitable? Are the hours fair to workers? Do fellow workers do a good job?

School Does my school address all the students' academic needs? Do my instructors address the students' needs? Do my classes fit the goals of my education (my major)? Do my peers interfere with my learning? Was my high school education adequate? What other daily tension lurks at my institution?

Home Is my living situation conducive to my goals as a student? Does living with my family reinforce or oppose my goals as a student? Is the government in touch with my family's needs?

Community Does my town offer adequate social events for youth? Does the water taste funny? Does my town offer ample mass transit? Does my neighborhood feel like a neighborhood? Are strangers as kind as they should be?

Culture Are people's lives too busy? Does my generation have the right priorities? What doesn't the older generation understand about kids today? What doesn't the younger generation understand about older generation(s)?

Your Major Look through a current journal in your field to find controversial issues. Are entry-level personnel in my field treated fairly? Is some research in my field or major controversial? Is my field undervalued by the public? Has my field changed any of its practices, for better or worse, in recent years? Should my field be more diverse (in gender and/or ethnicity)?

Question everything, especially those things that seem unquestionable.

Ask yourself: "Can I change someone's mind about this situation or issue?" If you can, you may have a topic. Once you have decided on a topic, proceed to the Analysis section to develop the argument.

What attitude or basic assumption lies beneath some troubling behavior or policy?

DO NOT AVOID A TOPIC BECAUSE YOU CANNOT, AT THIS EARLY PHASE, IMAGINE WRITING SEVERAL PAGES ON IT. NO WRITER CAN EVER IMAGINE HOW A TOPIC WILL DEVELOP INTO THE FINAL TEXT. WRITING EMERGES OUT OF THE PROCESS OF WRITING.

ACTIVITY

With a small group of peers or alone, make a list of other questions that draw attention to troubling situations in the world around you. Ask yourself: What behavior or situation or policy is wrong? What could be different? What could be better than it is?

ANALYSIS

Analysis cracks open the layers of a topic—and helps a writer to see more than his or her initial thoughts about it. Without analysis, writers may find themselves with little new to say. As you answer the Invention questions, avoid answering too quickly. Instead, use the questions to search for deeper understanding, which will then translate into more intensive writing. Allow time and space for your own thinking to develop:

- What is the particular point of crisis or tension?
- How has the situation (or condition, behavior, policy) come about, and why does it continue?
- What are the effects of the situation (or condition, behavior, policy)?
- What caused me to hold my particular beliefs?
- Why is this belief valuable?

Try to go beyond broad complaints and vague generalities.

INVENTION WORKSHOP

Enlist the help of at least one other writer in answering one of the Invention questions. Use the question to initiate a discussion. Explore further by questioning one another's responses to the questions. For example, Jack is focusing on his high school education. Notice how the discussion with Marcus goes beyond Jack's initial response:

What is the particular point of crisis or tension?

Jack: My high school education was inadequate. I graduated with a B average and I came to college having to take developmental courses before I could even begin taking credit courses.

Marcus: But is that the high school's fault?

Jack: Well, if I couldn't cut the mustard in entry-level college courses, why did I get mostly Bs in high school? It seems like something's out of whack.

Marcus: OK. So the standards are too low in high school?

Jack: Yeah, I think so.

Marcus: Were you ever warned about the standards in college?

Jack: Sure. All the time, teachers would scare us with things like "Wait 'til you get in college; you've got to work constantly to keep your grades up."

Marcus: But did anyone ever share specifics with you? Did you know what kinds of writing, for instance, you would be doing in college?

Jack: Not really. It's all been a big surprise.

Marcus: Maybe that's the issue: High school students (and maybe teachers and administrators) don't really know what kinds of things go on in entry-level college courses.

Jack: Yes—and so there's this huge gap in between, and some students fall right into it.

It would be easy to reinforce Jack's initial idea—the inadequacy of high school—by sharing examples of bad teachers or rotten classes, but Marcus and Jack do better. They develop the initial idea into something more specific and revealing: the gap between high school and college standards.

INVENTION WRITING

In her responses to the Invention questions, Ann Marie Paulin begins to discover something about the rotten behavior of others: it is supported by trends in the media. Like Marcus and Jack, Paulin looks beneath the initial tension or problem and discovers a hidden layer. She goes beyond being "angry" and discovers that media trends indirectly support, even "encourage," mistreatment and incivility:

Why do I have an opinion on this topic?

I have been fat since I was a kid. For about two days in my twenties I starved my way down to a size ten, thereby earning this head-turning compliment from the guy I was then dating: "You'd be a real fox if you'd just lose a few more pounds." I've had complete strangers say the most astonishing things to me on the street. For example, on my way through a parking lot to get to my car, I passed a young man who looked over at me and shouted: "I don't !@#$ fat chicks!" Who was asking? While these behaviors have sometimes hurt me, they mostly make me angry. And when I look around at the society in which I live, I don't see any signs that this kind of behavior is discouraged. Indeed, the media seems to suggest that fat people, by their very existence, seem to deserve contempt and abuse.

How has this situation come about?

Where it gets tricky is that by the media's definition, damn near everyone is fat. How has this situation come about? I'm not sure, but I've watched it develop. When my mother was young, a size ten or twelve was a respectable dress size. When I was in my twenties, a size eight was a respectable size. Now, you must be a size four, two, or even better, a zero to be considered thin. Now, a six-foot-tall model who wears a size twelve dress is considered plus size. She only gets her photo in Lane Bryant ads and such. It's as if society has completely forgotten the concept of "normal size," and so a person is either thin (if you can count all her bones when she appears in a bathing suit) or she's fat. And that leaves the majority of women believing they are fat and hating themselves for it.

Good writing goes further than the writer or reader initially expects.

ANALYSIS IN CHAPTER READINGS

Following the idea from her invention notes, Ann Marie Paulin goes beyond the complaint about the media and body images (which is an increasingly common concern) and reveals the real, harmful effects those images have when they become ingrained in everyday life:

> This weight prejudice hurts real people. When people are denied a place to live or a means of support not because of any bad behavior or lack of character or talent on their part but because of someone else's wrongheaded notions, then we need to start changing things. (261)

Paulin's thinking shows how writers work: They often begin with various points, and in the process of analyzing ideas, create various possible writing directions. However, as they begin to develop their projects, writers also become more focused and revelatory; they go beyond the common complaints and reveal a particular quality, effect, or layer of the issue.

THINKING FURTHER

Analysis is not about answering a question and finding an answer. The real insights lie beneath the answers. Return to your responses to the Invention questions and try to find the most valuable ideas:

- What statements reveal something specific?
- Which statements or phrases seem new to you?
- Which statements or phrases make a new connection, one that you had not considered before?

Now, you can take the statements or phrases forward and use them to develop increasingly intense ideas for your argument. If nothing stands out at this point consider reapproaching the Invention questions, and invite another person to join your exploration. And this time, deliberately take the ideas further:

- What behavior, policy, or quality is at the heart of the topic? (What is beneath the tension you initially discovered?)
- What attitude, value system, or assumption rests beneath the actions of people who are involved?

PUBLIC RESONANCE

Writers transform issues or personal concerns into arguable topics, issues that matter in some way to other people. Making a personal concern resonate with a public issue is simply a process of extension. To this end, the Invention questions below can be used as springboards from personal concerns to public issues. For example, examine the following question: *Is my living situation conducive to my goals as a student?* You may have answered: "Yes. I live at home with my parents and commute to school." Your situation is not unique. Many college students struggle with their living situations—with the decision of living on campus, in a nearby apartment complex, or at home with their parents, away from the campus altogether. This decision involves more than a simple personal choice. It has something to do with college funding, with the success of college students, with the entire college experience. In this sense, your situation resonates with a more public issue. The initial (more personal) question might evolve into a more public question: *Is it beneficial for college students to live at home while going to school?*

You can use the following questions to connect your topic and potential readers:

- Who might care about this issue? Why?
- How are my readers involved in this issue?
- What group of people might understand or sympathize with my situation?
- Is this issue an example of some trend?
- Why is it important that others hear my opinion about this issue?
- What else has been said about this issue, and how are my ideas different?

INVENTION WRITING

Public resonance is key in Ann Marie Paulin's project. Her essay shows that the more a topic affects people, the more attention it may deserve. In her responses to the Invention questions to the left, she explores the hidden messages in ads and the unstated assumptions lurking in the public domain. Paulin's responses show her making connections between her own situation and many others:

Who might care about this issue? Why?

This is certainly a very public issue because it is almost impossible to escape the media: magazines, newspaper ads, billboards, radio, TV, movies, ads plastered in public restrooms and on the walls of buses, ads in your e-mail every day. And every one of those images that deals with weight or beauty makes it clear that to be fat is completely unacceptable and completely fixable if only a person tries hard enough and buys the right products.

Now, if this were just an issue of vanity, it might be something that could be shrugged off. But it goes much deeper than that. If you really pay attention to those ads, their real message is often that if you are fat, no one will love you. Your husband will leave you (if you ever manage to get one to begin with). Your children will be ashamed of you. Your friends will give up on you. You will be alone and unloved because you are fat. That is the message that really hits us where we live. Who wants to be some lonely outcast? We must conform to whatever it takes.

And so, most of us try the diets, the pills, the exercise classes, the wonder machines, and sometimes even more extreme measures like stomach stapling surgery. But in spite of all the time, money, and effort we expend, most of us are still fat. If you look at the studies done, the results are all about the same: Anywhere from 90% to 98% of the people who lose weight gain it all back within five years.

Paulin explains that advertisements hit "us" where "we" live. She also discovers that the messages of ads speak to women, in general, in much the same way: "No one will love you. Your husband will leave you. . . ." By extending her thinking outward, Paulin is developing the public dimensions of her thinking.

Sometimes writers need to go beyond the *actual* effects or consequences of an issue and *imagine* the possible ways others are involved. Consider the following: A writer is arguing about college students living at home. The issue seemingly affects only college students, and maybe their parents. But the writer makes the issue resonate with many other potential readers by transforming a personal issue into a more public one:

> How college students live is not simply a matter of personal choice and comfort. It is a public issue, a public education issue. At the federal, state, and local levels, Americans are increasingly focused on the out-of-school living conditions of elementary and secondary students. Whenever people talk about the quality of education, invariably they end up discussing the living situation of students—the stability of their homes, the qualities of the neighborhoods. Why? Because people are beginning to realize that education does not occur in a vacuum, that how and where students live impact how they learn. But for some reason, we don't seem to be concerned once students are in college. Consequently, millions of college students swarm off to school every fall, often without deeply considering the implications of where they will live. And when millions of dollars of loans and grants go down the drain when students fail out their first year, we don't seem to ask the same questions we ask about elementary and secondary students.

Because a college issue now connects to national concerns about education, a wider audience, not just college students and their parents, can participate in the claims made in the argument.

Use the following questions to further develop the public resonance of your topic:

- Who *should* care about this issue? Why?
- How *could* my reader(s) be involved in this issue?

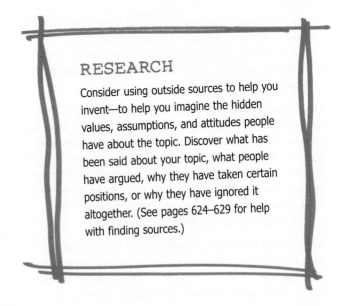

RESEARCH

Consider using outside sources to help you invent—to help you imagine the hidden values, assumptions, and attitudes people have about the topic. Discover what has been said about your topic, what people have argued, why they have taken certain positions, or why they have ignored it altogether. (See pages 624–629 for help with finding sources.)

Going from Private to Public

Private Concern:
Is my living situation conducive to my goals as a student?

Public Concern:
Is it beneficial for college students to live at home while going to school?

THESIS

An argumentative thesis invites debate or suggests that opposing claims exist. For example:

> But far more important than my ill temper is a creepy sense that these inaccurate images [about body type] have shifted our vision of what is important in life way out of whack, so far out that people are being hurt. (259)

Developing a thesis early on in the process will help to develop focus for the writer as well as for the reader. In fact, the process of narrowing down an argument to an intensive single sentence helps writers to understand the heart of their idea. At an early stage in your project, you need not settle into an exact wording, but trying to generate a focused statement can help you focus—and help your ideas gain intensity.

An arguable thesis should have four qualities:

Arguability It should be arguable. That is, an arguable thesis should take a stand on an issue that has two or more possible positions. If you can conceive of other possible positions on the topic, you are probably in arguable territory.

Scope It should be appropriately narrow. Scope can be addressed by asking narrow enough questions. Be careful of broad questions: *Is my town boring?* To answer such a question, one would have to consider all of the town's complexities, all of its goings-on, all of its people, all of its places, and so on. However, the question *Does my town offer sufficient activities for teens?* is more easily answerable—and ultimately arguable.

Public Resonance It should address an issue that resonates with the readers. A good argument addresses a concern that others have *or that a writer thinks they should have*. In other words, a thesis should express something that matters (that has some significance) to readers. It should involve others.

Revelation Academic writers attempt to do more than argue for their own opinions. They try to *reveal* an unfamiliar topic or reveal a new layer to a familiar topic. *Revelatory* thesis statements change readers' (and the writer's) thinking because they show something new. They clear away the mundane thinking and reveal the roots of an issue. Often, revelatory thesis statements:

- Include a reference to the opposition.
- Overturn or contradict popular opinion.
- Show a particular effect or relationship.
- Uncover a hidden layer.

ACTIVITY

Transform the following into revelatory thesis statements:

- The Internet has changed the world.
- Video games are bad for kids.
- Sixteen-year-olds who commit crimes should be punished as adults.

EVOLUTION OF A THESIS

A writer can always increase the focus and revelation of a thesis. The following idea evolves into an increasingly sophisticated point:

- College students benefit from living at home.
- Traditional college students still need the support structure of their home lives to deal with the new challenges of college.
- Because college culture demands intense intellectual and social change from high school culture, traditional college students need the support structure of home.

The first statement announces a simple opinion. The second narrows in on a specific tension: "the new challenges of college." But the statement is still a bit vague, and the idea will intensify with even more focus on that tension. The third statement brings us up close to the primary tension and shows us something that might otherwise escape our awareness: the "intense intellectual and social change" between high school and college culture. The reader of the last two theses, especially the third, has been given a novel insight about schooling. In this way, revelatory thesis statements are more than personal opinion; they are particular and persuasive insights.

COMMON THESIS PROBLEMS

The Question Problem A question is not a thesis, because it offers no stance. People sometimes use questions to imply a stance: *Isn't that the point of college? Why can't you be like your sister?* But this is generally an informal strategy—something people do in everyday talk. A formal argumentative stance should suggest a particular position amidst a realm of many others.

The Obvious Fact Problem An argument that simply announces a commonly known condition is no argument at all. Imagine someone arguing: *Many people go to college for their futures; Americans love cars;* or *Space exploration is expensive.* Such statements do not invite opposition because they are widely held beliefs. They are safe statements about

the condition of our civilization. But the statement *Space exploration is too expensive to continue at its present pace* invites opposition.

The Personal Response Problem Argument depends upon the presence of several other perspectives peering at the same topic. However, when people proclaim a personal response (about their tastes, likes, dislikes, or desires), they merely make public their own state of mind. "I really liked the movie" is not an argumentative stance. It is a statement about a person's tastes. But the statement, "Johnny Depp's portrayal of a wayward pirate illustrates his superior range as an actor" invites opposition. Other positions can engage the point critically.

REVISION

Before moving on, try to express the main point of your argument in a single sentence. Then evaluate the statement, using the following questions:

- How is the statement arguable? (What other positions might be taken?)
- Can the statement be narrower? (What words are too vague or broad?)
- With what public issue or concern does the statement resonate?
- How does the statement reveal a unique insight or hidden layer of the issue?

You might also exchange your working thesis statement with two to three peers and use these questions to generate helpful responses.

RHETORICAL TOOLS

Crafting an essay, or any written text, is a recursive process: Writers move back and forth, drafting, rethinking, redrafting. It is not a simple step-by-step journey through a chapter. But all writers benefit from a large collection of strategies, various tools they can use according to their particular needs, situations, and voices. The strategies in this section will help you build a sophisticated and engaging text—one that emerges from your particular ideas.

Academic argument involves four basic ingredients or elements:

- Main Claim/Thesis
- Support
- Counterargument
- Concession

Support

Support is the material that gives substance and legitimacy to an argumentative claim. Support comes in a variety of forms.

Consider the following as a collection of usable support strategies, a toolbox for persuading readers of your position.

Examples Specific cases or illustrations of a phenomenon. (See Paulin ¶ 6.)

Allusions References to history, science, nature, news events, films, television shows, or literary texts. (See Crabtree ¶ 5, Churchill ¶ 11, Paulin ¶ 2.)

Personal testimonies/anecdotes Individual accounts or experiences. (See Paulin ¶ 1–2.)

Scenarios Hypothetical or fictionalized accounts. (See Crabtree ¶ 6, Churchill ¶ 4–8.)

Statistics Information (often given in numerical value) collected through experimentation, surveys, polls, and research. (See Paulin ¶ 4, Cherry ¶ 3.)

Authorities References to published (most often written) sources. (See Crabtree ¶ 8, Paulin ¶ 2.)

Facts Agreed-upon events or truths, or conclusions drawn from investigation. (See Crabtree ¶ 5, Churchill ¶ 19–25.)

Arguments depend on appeals, which make a connection between the topic and the audience's thought process. In fact, appeals have such rhetorical force that they give meaning to and can even dominate over other forms of evidence.

Appeal to logic Relates the argument to the audience's sense of reason or creates a line of reasoning for the audience to follow. (See Churchill ¶ 4, Paulin's conclusion.)

Appeal to emotion Relates the argument to an emotional state of the audience, or attempts to create a particular emotional state in the audience. (See Churchill ¶ 32.)

Appeal of character Relates the argument to a quality of the author/speaker. (See Paulin ¶ 1.)

Appeal to need Relates the argument to people's needs (spiritual, economic, physical, sexual, familial, political, etc.). (See Cherry ¶ 5.)

Appeal to value Relates the argument to people's values (judgments about right/wrong, success, discipline, selflessness, moderation, honesty, chastity, modesty, self-expression, etc.). (See Crabtree ¶ 9, Churchill ¶ 32.)

The first three appeals (to logic, emotion, and character) are often discussed using three ancient Greek terms: *logos* (for logic), *pathos* (for emotion), and *ethos* (for character). These are sometimes referred to as the Classical appeals. The appeal to logic, or *logos*, is the most valued appeal in formal argument. It requires the arguer to establish premises—claims that must be accepted in order for the main claim (or conclusion) to be acceptable. One example is the *syllogism,* which asserts two premises and a conclusion: A is true and B is true; therefore, C must also be true. The other two Classical appeals, *pathos* and *ethos,* have worked into everyday English usage: e.g., *He has a particularly engaging* ethos. *The newspaper dramatized the* pathos *of the events*.

Developing Support

Too often, writers limit themselves by assuming that facts and statistics are the primary support tools for a good argument, when the truth is that facts and statistics are merely a fragment of what's possible—and what's most valuable. Writers have the whole world of culture and history within reach. Good writers find connections to historical events, literary texts, news, science, nature, and their own personal lives. For example, perhaps you believe that your topic relates to the plot of a book. You can explain the basic plot of the book in a paragraph (or more) and tell why it shows the validity of your ideas. The same thing goes for a movie or a news event.

Use the following questions to develop support for your argument:

- How does my topic appear in history? (How does a historical event or figure illustrate something important about my topic?)

- Does a historical situation or trend (say, the rise of a particular fashion, organization, or individual) illustrate something about my topic?

- How has popular culture treated my topic? Does it show up in television shows, movies, or commercials? If so, how is it characterized, mishandled, or celebrated?

- How has literature (novels, poetry, drama, short stories) dealt with my topic? Have fictional characters illustrated something important about the topic or some behavior related to it?

- How does nature (animals, life cycles, plants, biological processes, and so on) demonstrate something about my topic?

- What has science taught people about my topic?

- Do any news events illustrate my point or stance?

- What have I witnessed or experienced that illustrates my point?

- What hypothetical situation could illustrate my point?

- What do other writers or authorities on the matter say about the topic?

When using authorities, writers must formally document the use of any information, ideas, and expressions taken from sources. For an extended explanation of formal documentation and integration of sources, see Chapter 13, Research & Writing.

Facts and statistics are a small part of what's possible in an argument.

Imagine a writer developing the argument about college residence policies. The argument might develop from the question about popular culture:

How has popular culture treated my topic? Does it show up in television shows, movies, or commercials? If so, how is it characterized, mishandled, or celebrated?

In movies and popular television shows, college is nearly always portrayed as a raucous social engagement. The typical movie college student (like those in *American Pie* or *Animal House*) is a dormitory, apartment, frat or sorority house dweller who thrives or suffers in the family-free environment. The whole point of college in mainstream movies is to create a living situation in which the students just tread the line between responsible participation in society and utter immersion in bohemian life. It's no wonder that going to college seems synonymous with "going away" to college. When students long to avoid living in the chaotic social climate of campus life, they are working against more than some college policies. They are working against popular culture.

The most valuable support may seem, at first, the least obvious. Don't stop thinking.

Using Appeals

While other forms of support involve pointing or referring to something (such as an allusion or authority), an *appeal* involves engaging the audience. In using appeals, writers must frame ideas in ways that directly engage the opinions, beliefs, values, and emotions of their audience. Creating an appeal is often difficult work, but it can make an argument connect deeply with readers. The various appeals can be applied to nearly any topic. Notice how a writer might tie an argument about college students to broader values:

> Going to college should not have to mean going away to college. The intellectual commitment required of a student should not necessarily require a domestic commitment. Coming into an institution should not necessarily mean abandoning the intimacy of family. And entering college should not mean entering a compulsory social climate. But policies that require first-year students to live on campus impose a domestic and social arrangement onto students.
>
> Colleges and universities should be bastions of intellectual and social diversity. They should embody the greatest good of our democracy. And any policies that impose arbitrary domestic habits or social arrangements should be looked upon with great suspicion.

As in this example, writers can look beyond the topic itself and discover what his or her audience values (such as freedom, family intimacy, self-determination) and then connect the position of the argument with those values.

The most valued strategy in formal academic argument is the appeal to logic. When writers create a *line of reasoning*, they create an intellectual path for readers. Consider the topic from the previous section: college students living at home. If we want to convince readers to believe that colleges should not require students to live on campus, we might create the following line of reasoning:

a. The shift from high school to college culture is significant.

b. Many students experience a kind of culture shock in the transition.

c. This culture shock negatively impacts their academic performance.

Each of these statements requires further explanation, examples, illustration, evidence, and appeal. In other words, this line of reasoning might require several lengthy passages of text. But if the readers could accept each claim, then they would be led directly to our main point—that college policies should not require on-campus residence for all first-year students.

Use the following questions to develop appeals for your argument:

- How can I connect the topic to people's values (sense of right and wrong, success, discipline, selflessness, moderation, honesty, chastity, modesty, self-expression, etc.)?

- How can I connect the topic to people's basic needs (spiritual, economic, physical, sexual, familial, political, etc.)?

- How can I connect the topic to people's emotions (fear, hope, sadness, happiness)?

- How can I connect to people's sense of logic? What line of reasoning can I create for the reader to follow?

- Does my life (my role in a relationship, on a job, in school, on a team) lend credibility to my position on this topic?

Create lines of reasoning for your readers to follow.

ACTIVITY

Generate a variety of appeals for each of the following claims:

- Although war illustrates human cruelty and malice, it also illustrates human compassion and sympathy.

- Most proponents of capital punishment fail to consider the impact on the executed person's loved ones.

- Democracy cannot thrive in a two-party system.

- Excessive marketing leads to a lack of civility and respect among the citizens.

Counterargument

Counterarguments anticipate and refute claims or positions that oppose those being forwarded by the writer. Writers must anticipate and account for positions outside of or opposed to their own claims(s) and include reasoning to offset that potential opposition. For example, a savvy teenager who wants to attend a party will imagine his parents' concerns and work them into his argument about why he should be allowed to go to the party. A politician will anticipate her opponent's position on an issue and formulate her speech accordingly.

The most successful arguers are good counterarguers. They address and even dismantle the specifics of opposing claims. In her essay, Ann Marie Paulin counterargues by summing up advice given by Barbara Dinnerstein's mother, then in the following paragraph explaining why she disagrees:

> While we can shrug off advertisements as silly, when we see these attitudes reflected among real people, the hurt is far less easy to brush away. For instance, in her essay, "Bubbie, Mommy, Weight Watchers and Me," Barbara Noreen Dinnerstein recalls a time in her childhood when her mother took her to Weight Watchers to slim down and the advice the lecturer gave to the women present: "She told us to put a picture of ourselves on the 'fridgerator of us eating and looking really fat and ugly. She said remember what you look like. Remember how ugly you are" (347).
>
> I have a problem with this advice. First, of course, it is too darn common. Fat people are constantly being told they should be ashamed of themselves, of their bodies. And here we see another of those misconceptions I mentioned earlier: the assumption that being fat is the same as being ugly. There are plenty of attractive fat people in the world, as well as a few butt-ugly thin ones, I might add. Honestly, though, the real tragedy is that while few people in this world are truly ugly, many agonize over the belief that they are. Dr. Pipher reported: "I see clients who say they would rather kill themselves than be overweight" (91). I never have figured out how trashing a fellow being's self-esteem is going to help that person be healthier. (261–262)

USING COUNTERARGUMENT TO DEVELOP POINTS

In academic argument, opposing claims are vital. Instead of ignoring or fearing them, good writers *use* them to develop points. An argument essay sets out not only to support a main claim, but also to refute the opposing claims—to show why opposing claims are not as valid or valuable. In developing your argument, try to address opposing claims. Doing so will make your argument more complex, more developed, and more persuasive.

Apply the following questions:

- Who might disagree with my position? Why?
- What reasons do people have for disagreeing with me?
- What would support an opposing argument?

ACTIVITY

The Devil's Advocate This activity is designed to generate counterarguments. The process involves an intensive group exchange. Follow these steps:

- Assemble writers into small groups (three or four per group work best).
- Each writer should have his or her thesis statement (main argumentative claim) written down.
- The first writer should read his or her thesis statement aloud to the group.
- Taking turns, each group member then should attempt to refute the position given in the statement. The idea is to play devil's advocate, to complicate the writer's ideas.
- The writer should record each opposing claim that is offered.
- After everyone in the group has given an opposing claim to the first writer, the second writer should recite his or her thesis, and the process begins again.

Sometimes, counterarguing can constitute a significant amount of an essay. For example, in "Crimes Against Humanity," Churchill uses opposing claims (even particular phrases and words) to develop his own reasoning. First he summarizes the claims of others (in first paragraph below) and then he counterargues in response to those claims (subsequent paragraphs):

In response, a number of players—especially African Americans and other minority athletes— have been trotted out by professional team owners like Ted Turner, as well as university and public school officials, to announce that they mean not to insult but to honor native people. They have been joined by the television networks and most major newspapers, all of which have editorialized that Indian discomfort with the situation is "no big deal," insisting that the whole thing is just "good, clean fun." The country needs more such fun, they've argued, and a "few disgruntled Native Americans" have no right to undermine the nation's enjoyment of its leisure time by complaining. This is especially the case, some have argued, "in hard times like these." It has even been contended that Indian outrage at being systematically degraded— rather than the degradation itself—creates "a serious barrier to the sort of intergroup communication so necessary in a multicultural society such as ours."

Okay. Let's communicate. We are frankly dubious that those advancing such positions really believe their own rhetoric but, just for the sake of argument, let's accept the premise that they are sincere. If what they say is true, then isn't it time we spread such "inoffensiveness" and "good cheer" around among all the groups so that everybody can participate equally in fostering the national round of laughs they call for? Sure it is—the country can't have too much fun or "intergroup" involvement—so the more, the merrier. Simple consistency demands that anyone who thinks the Tomahawk Chop is a swell pastime must be just as hearty in their endorsement of the following ideas—by the logic used to defined the defamation of American Indians—[to] help us all really start yukking it up.

First, as a counterpart to the Redskins, we need an NFL team called "Niggers" to honor Afro-Americans. (248–249)

USING COUNTERARGUMENT TO QUALIFY YOUR THESIS

Thesis statements become narrower and more meaningful when they include an understanding of the broader argument (others' positions on the subject). Let's examine the opposition to a working thesis: *College students benefit from living at home while attending school.* Many college students insist that living away from home during college helps to define "the college experience." They might develop an argument using personal or anecdotal evidence. They might illustrate personal (hence, intellectual) growth that comes from living away from home, away from one's family, away from familiar turf. They might point to stories in literature in which a character leaves her or his homeland to seek knowledge or wisdom in the world and gains insight only because of the new surroundings. They might point to movies in popular culture that promote that same idea. We would do well to consider these points, and perhaps work against some of them directly. We might even include part of the logic into our own thesis: *Despite the attraction of living away from home and experiencing life in unfamiliar territory, college students benefit from living at home while attending school.*

A writer should always anticipate objections.

Concession

While counterarguments refute objections, concessions acknowledge the value of others' claims. Put another way, if the writer says that an objection or alternative is wrong, the response is a counterargument; but if the writer says that the objection or alternative is right, that response is a concession.

Concession is a vital aspect of academic argument. Notice how Crabtree concedes a point in the conclusion of his essay. Although he argues for the value of a great books education throughout his essay, he does concede that it demands a particular kind of commitment:

> A great books education is not for everyone. In order to benefit from such an education, a student has to be highly motivated, mature enough to realize the importance of such a focus, and self-disciplined. Whatever reasons one might have for not pursuing a great books education, it cannot be because it is not practical! (257)

Concessions might acknowledge the limitations of, or make clear boundaries for, the writer's own argument. In this case, they are sometimes called *qualifiers*. When giving a speech on the evils of corporate tax evasion, a senator qualifies her statements: "Granted, most companies in America pay taxes responsibly, but we must focus on those few rogue and politically powerful companies." When arguing for a salary increase, a union leader acknowledges a point made by the opposition: "We understand that economic times ahead could be perilous and that a salary increase could make the company more financially vulnerable to outside forces, but the future of the company certainly depends upon the well-being of its loyal employees."

MAKING CONCESSIONS

Conceding in academic argument does not make an argument wishy-washy. In fact, a good concession shows that a writer has a broad sense of his or her claims—that they fit into a larger context. A good writer might discuss the logic of another position and show, *to some degree,* how that position has validity. This does not mean that the writer's own point is weak; on the contrary, it means that his or her point is so strong and valid that it can even acknowledge the soundness of other positions. (See more on this in the Writer's Voice section.)

Consider the following questions for your argument:

- Are there other valid positions that one could take on my topic?
- Are there legitimate reasons for taking another position on this topic?
- Does my argument make any large, but necessary, leaps?

If the answer is "yes" to any of these questions (and it probably is), then you might address those directly in your argument.

The idea in conceding and qualifying is to acknowledge any legitimate concerns that the reader has; otherwise, readers might assume that the writer has not sufficiently thought through the issue. For instance, if a writer were making a generalization about college students, he or she might note an opposing fact but still move on with the argument:

> Younger college students are often overwhelmed by the amount of new experiences in their lives. *Of course, not all younger students are consumed by the novelty of social freedom;* however, many find themselves swimming in a sea of lifestyle options that work against their abilities to focus on schoolwork.

In this example, the writer qualifies the generalized statement about college students, understanding that readers may not accept the idea that *all* college students are affected the same way. This reveals the writer's depth and understanding.

REVISION

Consider the four elements of argument: thesis, support, counterargument, and concession. Look over the material you have generated so far. Is the thesis revelatory? Is the support varied and specific? Could you better plot out your line of reasoning and help your reader follow your logic? Have you anticipated major objections to your position?

Caution: Logical Fallacies Ahead

Logical fallacies are flaws in the structure of an argument that make the claims invalid. A fallacy is a falsehood, so a logical fallacy is a logical falsehood that makes no sense within a given situation. For example, consider this familiar line:

> If you break a mirror, you'll have seven years of bad luck.

We may recognize this as superstition. In academic terms, it is called *faulty cause/effect*. That is, the broken mirror does not actually cause misfortune in one's life. The statement seems categorically faulty. However, the success (or logic) of any argument depends on the particular situation. All argumentative statements exist in situations that give those statements credibility. (If someone's entire fortune were tied to a mirror, then the previous statement would be more logical!) Statements are logical or illogical based on the situation.

In academia, recognizing logical fallacies is part of being a critical thinker in all disciplines (and there is no quicker way to make readers of your own work suspicious than committing logical fallacies). Be careful not to commit any of the following when making an argument.

Logical Fallacies

Ad hominem (Latin for *to the person*) Attacks a person directly rather than examining the logic of the argument.

- We cannot possibly consider Ms. Smith's proposal because she is a Catholic.
- Mr. Mann's argument is suspicious because he is a socialist.

Strawperson Exaggerates a characteristic of a person or group of people and then uses the exaggeration to dismiss an argument.

- Islamic fundamentalists are crazy. They only want to destroy Americans. We cannot accept their claims about imperialism.
- Environmentalists are radical. They want to end everyone's fun by taking cars and boats away.

Faulty cause/effect Confuses a sequential relationship with a causal one. Assumes that event A caused event B because A occurred first.

- Since the construction of the new baseball stadium, homelessness in the downtown area has decreased.
- The tax cut made energy rates drop.

Either/or reasoning Offers only two choices when more exist.

- Either we destroy Russia or it will destroy us.
- The American people will choose to control their own lives or give away their wills to socialist candidates.

Hasty generalization Draws a conclusion about a group of people, events, or things based on insufficient examples (often, the logical flaw behind racist, sexist, or bigoted statements).

- Men are too possessive. My ex-boyfriend would never let me go out alone.
- French people are rude. When I went to France, the civilians grunted French statements when I asked for help.

Non sequitur (Latin for *it does not follow*) Skips several logical steps in drawing a conclusion.

- If we do not trash the entire tax code, the downtown area will slowly deteriorate.
- A new baseball stadium downtown will help with the homelessness problem.

Oversimplification Does not acknowledge the true complexity of a situation or offers easy solutions to complicated problems.

- If we could give kids something to do, they wouldn't get depressed.
- This credit card will end all of my financial problems.

Slippery slope Assumes that a certain way of thinking or acting will necessarily continue or extend in that direction (like a domino effect). Such an argument suggests that once we begin down a path, we will inevitably slip all the way down, and so the effects of a particular action or idea are exaggerated.

- If the college makes students take more mathematics, the next thing we know, advanced calculus and quantum physics will be requirements for all graduates.
- If North Vietnam succeeds in making South Vietnam communist, it will eventually threaten the shores of the United States of America.

False analogy Makes a comparison between two things that are ultimately more unlike than alike. The differences between the things make the comparison ineffective or unfair, or the comparison misrepresents one or both of the things involved.

- Writing is like breathing: You just do what comes naturally.
- Like Galileo, Bill Clinton was breaking new ground, but no one understood him.

Begging the question Attempts to prove a claim by using (an alternative wording of) the claim itself.

- Girls should not be allowed into the Boys' Military Academy because it is for boys only.
- All cigarette smoking should be banned from public places because I believe it in my heart.

ACTIVITY

Explain the problem with the logic in the bumper stickers below, and name the fallacy.

Chocolate fixes everything

**YOU DESERVE
WHAT YOU ACCEPT**

IF ALL ELSE FAILS
STOP USING ALL ELSE

NEVER BELIEVE GENERALIZATIONS

DON'T BLAME ME.
I voted.

CONCEIVE. BELIEVE. ACHIEVE.

POLITICAL CORRECTNESS IS A DISEASE

STRIP MINING
PREVENTS FOREST FIRES

ORGANIZATIONAL STRATEGIES

How Should I Begin?

As with all essays, the sky is the limit. Remember some of the basic introductory tools (anecdote, provocative question, shocking statement). Remember, too, that introductions not only create focus for the topic, but also establish the tone of the essay. They are the invitation to *start* thinking. But if an introduction is flat, typical, or vague, it is an invitation to *stop* thinking. Notice this typical, vague introduction:

> There are many critical issues facing today's public schools. They have to consider violence, financial constraints, teacher training, drugs, and student apathy, just to name a few. But in this difficult era, educators have become enamored with a saving grace: technology. Computers are everywhere in our public schools. But the problem is that the technology isn't the saving grace that it seems. Schools should rethink their allegiance to computers.

This introduction illustrates a few critical mistakes. First, the writer begins with a statement that nearly everyone knows. It is not an invitation to think rigorously or explore an issue. Second, it is far too broad for the reader to get traction. Third, because the introduction begins so broadly, it makes at least two large intellectual leaps in the goal of getting to the writer's thesis at the end. Fourth, the attempt to place the thesis at the end of the paragraph makes all the other information seem contrived and formulaic.

To the contrary, in her essay Elizabeth Bohnhorst takes us directly to the critical issue, showing a specific example. She does not need to rush through several vague statements to suggest her position on the issue. She makes it indirectly from the outset:

> "Another boring PowerPoint," responds Jennifer when I ask about her day at school. I might not find these words so discouraging coming from a company executive after a long meeting or even a college student leaving an informative lecture. But these words of an eleven-year-old elementary school student leave me feeling slightly uneasy. PowerPoint presentations are intended to compel students to become more

interested in the subject with the use of neon colors and moving graphic images. But these flashy additions to current educational strategies haven't fooled everyone. The text and material covered is still the same boring grammar and spelling lessons but the educator has altered: It is a screen. (266)

Bohnhorst does go on in her essay to speak about computer technology in general, but here she focuses on a specific program, PowerPoint, which gives her argument, and her readers, a focal point.

> Check the essays in this chapter. Notice the difference among introduction strategies. Do the introductions help to establish the tone in each essay?

Where Should I Put Counterarguments?

Counterarguments can be tricky, but they need not be. First, they can be placed anywhere in a paper: at the beginning, throughout the body, and even at the conclusion. You might explain an opposing point and then counter, explain another opposing point and then counter. (Depending on the amount of detail given to each counter, each point might be an entire paragraph, or more, with supporting evidence.)

Opposing Point A

Your counterargument

Opposing Point B

Your counterargument

Opposing Point C

Your counterargument

Some writers use a turnabout paragraph for counterarguments. A turnabout paragraph begins with one point and then shifts to an opposing or alternative point while giving the reader a clear sign of the shift. For example, you might begin a paragraph explaining an opposing position, and then counterargue in that same paragraph. In the following example, the opposing claim (that global warming is not a real problem) is addressed within the paragraph. The paragraph also includes the change of direction ("This argument, however . . ."):

> Some people argue that global warming is not a problem at all. They suggest that all the discussion about the ozone layer is merely fear-mongering by left-wing political activists. This argument, however, ignores the volumes of evidence compiled by scientists (many of whom are Nobel Prize winners) from around the world—scientists from different cultures, from different religious contexts, from different political systems, and with different political agendas. The amount of data they have collected and the sheer din of their collective voices ought to be enough to convince people that global warming is much more than the delusions of a few environmental groups.

You might decide that the opposing viewpoint(s) require significant explanation, and that it would be best to keep them grouped together. Therefore, you might devote a chunk of space at the beginning of your paper before countering:

Opposing Point A

Opposing Point B

Opposing Point C

Your counterargument to A

Your counterargument to B

Your counterargument to C

You also might decide that your argument only needs a single main counterargument. That counter might come after you have given your supporting evidence and appeals, or it might even begin the argument. Or several opposing claims might be discussed, and addressed, in one paragraph. (See Paulin ¶ 2.)

> Examine the essays in this chapter for counterarguments. Notice their different organizational strategies.

How Should I Make Transitions?

Regardless of your general organization strategy, make certain to cue the reader when giving a counterargument. It is important that the reader understand when the focus is shifting from counter to main argument. You might begin a paragraph with an opposing viewpoint: "Some opponents might argue that. . . ." If so, you will need to shift the reader back to your logic: "But they do not understand that. . . ." Here is a list of some strategic transitions when doing counterargument:

On the other hand,

Contrary to this idea,

Although many people take this stance,

However, (; however,)

Despite the evidence for this position,

But

WRITER'S VOICE

Argument need not be cast as an act of aggression or belligerence. While arguments are sometimes heated and intense, they need not attempt to belittle their opponents. In fact, the fastest way to alienate, or turn off, a reader is to sound narrow-minded, mean, arrogant, or intimidating. A good argument attracts readers and engages those who might oppose the claims being made; a bad or unsuccessful argument loses readers. Here are some strategies for maintaining a cool tone—one that invites readers rather than alienates them.

Making Concessions

Conceding or qualifying a point can make an argument seem more controlled and more inviting; therefore, even when writers have a very strong conviction, they will often acknowledge the value of some other point or the limits of their own argument. Imagine the following argument:

> First-year college students are not mature enough to live on their own, without the guidance of parents and the familiarity of home turf. Dorm life is a celebration of self-destruction and disorientation. The social distractions draw students away from the real purpose of college and defeat even the most focused and determined students. Colleges should rethink the requirements for first-year students to live on campus.

While these claims unfairly generalize college students (see *logical fallacies*) and threaten the logical soundness of the argument, they also project a hasty or pushy voice. Such unqualified claims create a certain character in readers' minds—someone who is overly anxious and forceful. But the same argument can be cast with a different voice (which uses concession):

> Dorm life does hold some value for young students. It can create a climate of inquiry and academic engagement. However, many young college students are overcome by the utter freedom, lack of genuine guidance, and constant social distractions. And too many students who would otherwise succeed in their first years at college are suffering or failing because they are forced to live on campus. Colleges should, at least, begin to reevaluate requirements for on-campus living.

This paragraph acknowledges some value in dorm life. The voice seems fairer and less alienating.

While conceding can create a more engaging voice, conceding unnecessarily, or too often, can have negative results. Imagine the same argument, but with a distracting degree of concession:

> Living in dorms can be the best thing possible for a college student; however, dorm life can also defeat many students. Sometimes, even the brightest and most determined students can be overcome by the social distractions. Although it all depends on the individual student's personality and upbringing, college dorm life can actually work against the whole purpose of going to college. Certainly, each college should consider the characteristics of its own student body, but policies that require students to live on campus should be reevaluated.

All the concessions undermine the importance of the argument. The voice behind the text seems concerned about offending potential readers. But, ironically, such writing makes readers feel distant or detached from the ideas. Because the writer seems uncommitted, readers have no reason to engage the ideas. (Be cautious not to concede away your argument—and your level of commitment.)

Avoiding Harsh Description

It is often easy to use the most emotionally loaded terms to describe something or someone, to proclaim an opposing view as "dumb" or "evil." Such description, however, is most often exaggerated, and suggests that the writer has not fully investigated the subject. In the following, Paulin does not attack the media and the diet industry with aggressive adjectives, but argues that they damage people's lives. This is a far more sophisticated and useful strategy than merely dismissing them with a simple negative word or phrase:

> Certainly everyone is entitled to his or her own opinions of what is attractive, but no one has the right to damage another human being for fun or profit.
> The media and the diet industry often do just that.
> While no one can change an entire culture overnight, people, especially parents, need to think about what they really value in the humans they share their lives with and what values they want to pass on to their children. (263)

Avoiding Character Slams and Preaching Problems

It is often easy to attack the character of opponents, but it is more engaging, and more persuasive, to direct the argument at behaviors, policies, or attitudes rather than people. In Ward Churchill's essay, he refrains from attacking those who advocate using American Indian symbols in sports media. Rather than attack his opponents, Churchill uses their logic in his own argument:

Okay. Let's communicate. We are frankly dubious that those advancing such positions really believe their own rhetoric but, just for the sake of argument, let's accept the premise that they are sincere. If what they say is true, then isn't it time we spread such "inoffensiveness" and "good cheer" around among all the groups so that everybody can participate equally in fostering the national round of laughs they call for? Sure it is—the country can't have too much fun or "intergroup" involvement—so the more, the merrier. Simple consistency demands that anyone who thinks the Tomahawk Chop is a swell pastime must be just as hearty in their endorsement of the following ideas—by the logic used to defend the defamation of American Indians—[to] help us all really start yukking it up. (249)

His opponents argue that the American Indian images are actually inoffensive, that they are used for a simple game, and that American Indians should be honored by their use. Churchill, then, borrows their logic and applies it to other ethnic and religious groups.

> First, as a counterpart to the Redskins, we need an NFL team called "Niggers" to honor Afro-Americans. Half-time festivities for fans might include a simulated stewing of the opposing coach in a large pot while players and cheerleaders dance around it, garbed in leopard skins and wearing fake bones in their noses. This concept obviously goes along with the kind of gaiety attending the Chop, but also with the actions of the Kansas City Chiefs, whose team members—prominently including black members—lately appeared on a poster, looking "fierce" and "savage" by way of wearing Indian regalia. Just a bit of harmless "morale boosting," says the Chiefs' front office. You bet. (249)

When Churchill applies the logic of his opponents, the result is a surprising list of offensive names and characterizations. His strategy, then, reveals the sloppy argument of his opponents.

But imagine a less sophisticated approach:

> These people need to realize they are wrong. No matter how much fun they might be having with their Tomahawk Chop and other silly pastimes, they are offending thousands of people. They need to realize that defaming any group of people in America is wrong, and that other groups would not tolerate it.

This approach is fundamentally different from Churchill's. While Churchill points to the logic of his opponents, the latter approach preaches about "these people." While Churchill invites the reader into an analysis of ideas, the latter approach calls on the reader to condemn people. It does not invite reflection; it merely states that certain people "are wrong." While Churchill invites the reader to see flawed logic, the latter approach shuts down reflection and makes a simplistic statement. Another, more serious problem with such an approach is that it could be used by any position. For instance, the following preachy passage does not invite reflection or analysis; it merely spouts a flatly worded opinion. And besides the logical problems, it serves to alienate any reader who might have a different opinion:

> These people need to realize that they are wrong. No matter how much they complain about the Tomahawk Chop and other great pastimes, they are keeping thousands of people from having fun. They need to realize that people are not trying to be harmful.

Rather than using such heavy-handed rhetoric, writers such as Churchill avoid preaching or condemning people. They bring readers into an intensive analysis—even if that analysis reveals troubling logic.

Talking with, Not Arguing at, Readers

An academic argument is not an argument with readers. It is a *conversation with readers about an argumentative position.* And if that conversation is compelling, the reader may find that position valuable. In other words, argumentative writing speaks with the reader about a particular position or set of positions and attempts to make one position more logical and/or valuable than others.

To help visualize the role of the writer and reader, imagine the following: The writer sits beside the reader, pointing at and directing attention to a set of claims. The writer does not sit in front of and point his or her finger at the reader. This may seem like a subtle difference, but notice how it may change a passage. In the example below, Crabtree speaks to the reader about the need for workers in America to be intellectually capable of changing work environments. He does not command the reader:

> Such unpredictability calls for a different strategy in preparing for the job market. Rather than spending one's undergraduate years receiving specialized training, one ought to learn more general, transferable skills which will provide the flexibility to adjust to whatever changes may occur. A well-educated worker should be able to communicate clearly with co-workers, both verbally and in writing, read with understanding, perform basic mathematical calculations, conduct himself responsibly and ethically, and work well with others. These skills would make a person well-suited to most work environments and capable of learning quickly and easily the requisite skills for a new career, should the need arise. (256)

But imagine a different approach if Crabtree had talked at us directly:

> Such unpredictability should make you realize the need to be ready for a shifting job market. Rather than spending undergraduate years receiving specialized training, you ought to learn more general, transferable skills which will provide the flexibility to adjust to whatever changes may occur.

Here, the writer tries to convince the reader ("you") to change his or her behavior. Rather than speak with the reader about an issue, this passage targets the reader's own behavior, which is generally avoided in academic writing.

ACTIVITY

What creates a particular writer's voice in each of the sentences to the right?

Arguments aren't all about aggression or belligerence.

Argument need not be cast as an act of aggression or belligerence.

Don't be so belligerent!

VITALITY

While the editing strategies in other chapters can be applied here, argumentative writing has potential difficulties of its own. Because argument is such a common everyday practice, writers have to be especially mindful of some informal habits that can make formal written argument less intense and vital.

Avoid Unnecessary Attention to *I*

In argumentative writing, it is especially tempting to use the first-person pronouns *I, me,* and *my.* As in the following two sentences, personal pronouns can distract the reader from the argument itself and bog down the sentences.

> *I think that* social security ought to be tied to the marketplace.

> *It is my personal belief that* social security should not be a gamble.

In each of these sentences, the main idea is subordinated in a *that* clause. *I* statements such as these are unnecessary in argumentative writing because the claims are already attributed to the writer. By simply attaching his or her name to an essay, the writer has already implied "I believe." Saying it again is redundant.

However, writers do occasionally choose to insert personal pronouns. When dealing with several claims or outside sources, writers may insert the first-person pronoun in order to make a clear distinction between their own thoughts and others', as Ann Marie Paulin does:

> For instance, in her essay, "Bubbie, Mommy, Weight Watchers and Me," Barbara Noreen Dinnerstein recalls a time in her childhood when her mother took her to Weight Watchers to slim down and the advice

the lecturer gave to the women present: "She told us to put a picture of ourselves on the 'fridgerator of us eating and looking really fat and ugly. She said remember what you look like. Remember how ugly you are" (347).

> <u>I have a problem with this advice.</u> First, of course, it is too darn common. (261–262)

Paulin could also have avoided the first-person pronoun:

> But this advice is dangerous to young women.

But Paulin chose the first-person pronoun, perhaps because it is less formal and coincides with the personal voice she has established in her essay. While it is good practice to avoid unnecessary use of first-person pronouns, writers like Paulin can make effective, occasional use of it.

Writers also use *I* for personal narratives—telling a story or anecdote involving their own experiences. Such uses are legitimate and important. Narratives draw attention to the relevant experience of the writer, which requires use of the first-person pronoun.

Unnecessary *I* Statement

I think that history should be taught with more attention to the lives of everyday people.

Appropriate Personal Narrative

When I was in high school, my history courses focused almost exclusively on big battles and big governmental moments.

Avoid Unnecessary Attention to *You*

The second-person pronoun *you* refers directly to the reader—the person holding your text and reading from it. And because academic essays are invitations to a broad audience (to instructors, peers, and even the broader community of thinkers that they represent), *you* is generally avoided. Like the first-person singular pronouns *(I, me, my), you* distracts the reader from the issue at hand. But *you* is especially hazardous in academic writing because it makes writers shift into the imperative mood—the mood of commands. Here, the writer shifts focus and mood:

> Political parties do their best to keep people from closely examining issues. Instead, they wash over complexities and invite voters to stand on one side or another. You should consider your allegiance to any political party.

The first two sentences focus on political parties, people, and voters. But the final sentence shifts and suddenly speaks at the reader. To most academic audiences, this shift is unacceptable. (See more about speaking *with* versus *at* the reader in Writer's Voice.)

Avoiding the first- and second-person pronouns keeps the writer, and therefore the reader, focused on the ideas— on the argument itself, which is generally valuable in academic writing.

Vitalize with Verbs

Verbs are the engine of a sentence. And they are the agent of motion for the reader's mind: They move the reader's thoughts. Weak verbs make for little movement. In the following, the first sentence depends on a weak verb:

> Telemarketers *are* bad for home life.
>
> Telemarketers *have diminished* the sanctity of the home.

The verb of the first sentence, *are,* is often called a *linking verb.* When linking verbs act as the main engine of a sentence, they limit what's possible. Often, they corner the writer into using a vague adjective, in this case *bad.* The second sentence uses an active and more intensive verb: *diminished.* The second sentence creates a more engaging image. Using active verbs rather than linking verbs vitalizes writing. This is not to say that using linking verbs is always a mistake. (Sometimes, they are necessary.) However, changing to more active verbs can dramatically impact your writing, creating more focused statements, more intensive ideas, and more revelatory thinking.

Good writers use intense verbs to move the consciousness of their readers.

PEER REVIEW

Exchange drafts with at least one other writer. Before passing your draft to others, underline the thesis, or write it on the top of your essay. This way, reviewers will get traction as they read.

As a reviewer, use the following questions to guide your response:

1. Could the thesis be more narrow and revelatory? How? (What words or phrases are too broad?)

2. Can you think of another cultural, literary, historical, or political allusion that relates to the writer's position?

3. How well can you follow the writer's line of reasoning? (See appeals to logic, page 283.) Imagine the line of reasoning as though it is a stone path. If the path is well laid out, you should feel a stone at every step. If it is not, you might miss a step; you might feel like some intellectual step is missing.

4. Suggest specific points that the writer should concede or qualify. For instance, the writer's position might seem too extreme; the claims might include too many people or a large, diverse group without making any distinctions. Point out such claims, and help the writer to see the need to acknowledge subtlety, complexity, and exceptions.

5. Can you imagine another opposing point that the writer could address in a counterargument? While the writer may have dealt with several opposing positions, you might think of an additional issue that should be addressed.

6. Consider the writer's voice. Circle passages or sentences that shift mood and speak *at*, rather than *with*, the reader. Suggest an alternative strategy or phrasing.

7. Do paragraphs focus on one main point? Point to sentences in paragraphs that stray from the initial idea put forth in the paragraph.

8. What is the most engaging passage in the draft so far? Why?

9. Check for sentence vitality.

   • Where can the writer change linking verbs to active verbs?

   • Where can the writer avoid drawing attention to *I* and *you*?

   • Consider vitality strategies from other chapters:

     —Help the writer change unnecessary clauses to phrases.

     —Help the writer change unnecessary phrases to words.

     —Point to expletives (such as *there are* and *it is*).

     —Help the writer change passive verbs to active verbs for more vitality.

     —Help the reader avoid common grammatical errors: comma splices, sentence fragments, or pronoun/antecedent agreement.

Questions for Research

If the writer used outside sources,

• Where must he or she include in-text citations? (See page 650.)

• Are quotations blended smoothly into the argument and punctuated correctly? (See pages 642–648.)

• Where could more direct textual cues or transitions help the reader? (See pages 641–643.)

• Is the Works Cited page formatted properly? (See pages 652–674.)

DELIVERY

Academic essays are not merely vehicles for communicating thought. They are intellectual playing fields—places for writers and readers to discover something. Those discoveries do not exist in the vacuum of an essay; they resonate outward through the lives of the writers and readers. An argument essay in particular sets out to assert something about the world, and that assertion is bound to impact reality—because people live according to the arguments they accept.

Now that you have written an argumentative essay, respond to the following:

- How do your claims challenge something in your life? The lives of your friends and family?
- Do your words support mainstream intellectual life? Or does your essay challenge something about the way most people live and think?
- What particular groups, organizations, or people should read your essay? How might it impact their behavior?

Beyond the Essay: The Open Letter

Argumentative essays have changed the world; they've started revolutions, supported religious movements, initiated new scientific organizations, spotlighted atrocities, and prompted a broad range of political events. But sophisticated arguments can impact the world through other genres.

The open letter is closely related to the essay. It is aimed at a particular audience, a particular reader or set of readers, but it also resonates with a broader audience. An open letter draws both writer and reader, and an otherwise private discussion, into a public setting—a powerful move! For example, Martin Luther King's "Letter from Birmingham Jail" (see page 734) was originally aimed at nine fellow clergy members, but the letter also speaks to millions of others. In effect, King performs a response to a particular audience for a broader audience. The conversation occurs between a few particular people, but the issues and claims involve many. Or consider the apostle Paul's letters to the Romans that now constitute part of the New Testament. They have become known to millions of readers, but they were originally aimed at a particular group of people. Or more currently, newspapers and magazines often print open letters to the president, to an editor, or to corporate heads.

Because letters are written with a particular audience in mind, they may draw attention to specifics about the readers' life, such as specific behaviors, policies, attitudes, or events. The writer may then draw out the significance, explaining the impact on or meaning for others. Return to your essay and imagine a particular person or group of people who should read and accept your claims.

Using the points in your essay, develop an open letter addressed to that particular audience. The following questions may help shape your ideas:

- Who has the power or authority over the issue?
- How can you make a specific connection between them and the issue?
- To what specific behavior, attitude, event, or policy can you draw attention?
- What is the public significance of that behavior?

> "People don't operate based on reality. They operate based on their perceptions of reality. And with language, we can change those perceptions."
>
> —David Hawes

RESPONDING TO ARGUMENTS

Chapter Contents

CHAPTER 7

"We hold these truths to be self-evident, that all men are created equal, that they are endowed by their Creator with certain inalienable rights, that among these are life, liberty, and the pursuit of happiness."

—The Declaration of Independence

Arguments are all around us. They lurk in nearly every behavior and event of our lives, and we often respond to arguments that hover but are not stated directly. Imagine an American citizen protesting nuclear energy; she carries a sign that says, "Nuclear energy ≠ clean energy!" Her sign is a response to the argument that nuclear energy is cleaner than energy from oil and coal. The protester is not responding to a particular text or person, but to an argument made by many people (such as politicians) in many different contexts. The sign actually evokes (or brings to mind) this argument and directly refutes it. Someone might also respond to the argument suggested by an advertisement that cigarettes promote social and physical pleasures. Such an ad argues that a certain kind of cigarette provides pleasure beyond inhaling the smoke and feeling the nicotine, and a writer might (quite easily) argue the opposite.

In academia, writers most often respond to arguments that are formally delivered (in an essay or editorial). They respond to a particular text or person and to particular statements or claims:

- A psychologist responds to Freud's theory of ego development, explaining that such a theory is not valuable in treating female patients.
- A political science student supports a revised historical account of U.S. foreign policy that holds Henry Kissinger partly responsible for atrocities in Chile during the 1970s.
- Law students respond to a Supreme Court ruling that upholds the rights of law enforcement officers to detain citizens for traffic violations. They argue that the ruling erodes protections against "unreasonable search and seizure."
- An English professor reviews a controversial new book and defends its claims against rampant consumerism.

As these examples suggest, responding to an argument does not necessarily mean disagreement. The initial argument (whether a court ruling, a book, an essay, or a historical account) provides the position on a topic. A writer has many options beyond agreement or disagreement. For instance, he or she might agree with the initial argument and extend the ideas with additional points, disagree with a particular point, redefine the issue, or point out some logical flaws.

As you can imagine, this is a somewhat more sophisticated task than what we examined in Chapter 6, Making Arguments. However, responding to arguments is an engaging activity, one that is not only vital to and valued in academia, but also necessary for maintaining a democracy.

Although a writer can respond to many different kinds of argument, this chapter primarily focuses on arguments that are formally delivered. The chapter will help you discover and analyze an argument, develop a sophisticated argumentative response, and communicate your position in writing. Read the following essays, which illustrate a variety of arguing strategies. After reading the essays, you can find an argument in one of several ways:

1. Go to the **Point of Contact** section to find an argument from everyday life.
2. Choose one of the **Ideas for Writing** that follow the essays.
3. Respond to any argumentative essay from another chapter in this book.

After you find a topic, go to the **Analysis** section to begin developing your response.

Most of the essays in this chapter respond to written arguments. For instance, Betsy Taylor's response to Juliet Schor's essay (which appears in Chapter 9, Searching for Causes) points to specific claims in the original argument and explains why those claims are either sound or unsound. (You may also notice that Taylor's response points to some of Schor's assumptions.) All of the essays in this chapter develop their own arguments, using their own logic and support. Daniel Bruno, for example, spends the majority of his essay developing an idea beyond the original. Lani Guinier's and Ann Causey's essays respond to arguments that are not written, but that hover around the issues they address, majority rule and hunting.

The Tyranny of the Majority

Lani Guinier

Are Americans by and large ignorant of the existence, let alone the details, of electoral systems other than their own? And if they are, how might they benefit from being more knowledgeable about other systems? What if a fairer system were available, but Americans just didn't know about it? In the following essay (which was originally an introduction to her book *The Tyranny of the Majority: Fundamental Fairness in Representative Democracy*), Harvard Law professor Lani Guinier argues for change in the present voting system. Notice, too, that Guinier refers to the criticism she got for her views after she was nominated to be U.S. Assistant Attorney General for Civil Rights. Her nomination was later withdrawn.

I have always wanted to be a civil rights lawyer. This lifelong ambition is based on a deep-seated commitment to democratic fair play—to playing by the rules as long as the rules are fair. When the rules seem unfair, I have worked to change them, not subvert them. When I was eight years old, I was a Brownie. I was especially proud of my uniform, which represented a commitment to good citizenship and good deeds. But one day, when my Brownie group staged a hatmaking contest, I realized

that uniforms are only as honorable as the people who wear them. The contest was rigged. The winner was assisted by her milliner mother, who actually made the winning entry in full view of all the participants. At the time, I was too young to be able to change the rules, but I was old enough to resign, which I promptly did.

To me, fair play means that the rules encourage everyone to play. They should reward those who win, but they must be acceptable to those who lose. The central theme of my academic writing is that not all rules lead to elemental fair play. Some even commonplace rules work against it.

The professional milliner competing with amateur Brownies stands as an example of rules that are patently rigged or patently subverted. Yet, sometimes, even when rules are perfectly fair in form, they serve in practice to exclude particular groups from meaningful participation. When they do not encourage everyone to play, or when, over the long haul, they do not make the losers feel as good about the outcomes as the winners, they can seem as unfair as the milliner who makes the winning hat for her daughter.

Sometimes, too, we construct rules that force us to be divided into winners and losers when we might have otherwise joined together. This idea was cogently expressed by my son, Nikolas, when he was four years old, far exceeding the thoughtfulness of his mother when she was an eight-year-old Brownie. While I was writing one of my law journal articles, Nikolas and I had a conversation about voting prompted by a *Sesame Street Magazine* exercise. The magazine pictured six children: four children had raised their hands because they wanted to play tag; two had their hands down because they wanted to play hide-and-seek. The magazine asked its readers to count the number of children whose hands were raised and then decide what game the children would play.

5   Nikolas quite realistically replied, "They will play both. First they will play tag. Then they will play hide-and-seek." Despite the magazine's "rules," he was right. To children, it is natural to take turns. The winner may get to play first or more often, but even the "loser" gets something. His was a positive-sum solution that many adult rule-makers ignore.

The traditional answer to the magazine's problem would have been a zero-sum solution: "The children—all the children—will play tag, and only tag." As a zero-sum solution, everything is seen in terms of "I win; you lose." The conventional answer relies on winner-take-all majority rule, in which the tag players, as the majority, win the right to decide for all the children what game to play. The hide-and-seek preference becomes irrelevant. The numerically more powerful majority choice simply subsumes minority preferences.

In the conventional case, the majority that rules gains all the power and the minority that loses gets none. For example, two years ago Brother Rice High School in Chicago held two senior proms. It was not planned that way. The prom committee at Brother Rice, a boys' Catholic high school, expected just one prom when it hired a disc jockey, picked a rock band, and selected music for the prom by consulting student preferences. Each senior was asked to list his three favorite songs, and the band would play the songs that appeared most frequently on the lists.

Seems attractively democratic. But Brother Rice is predominantly white, and the prom committee was all white. That's how they got two proms. The black sen-

iors at Brother Rice felt so shut out by the "democratic process" that they organized their own prom. As one black student put it: "For every vote we had, there were eight votes for what they wanted . . . [W]ith us being in the minority we're always outvoted. It's as if we don't count."

Some embittered white seniors saw things differently. They complained that the black students should have gone along with the majority: "The majority makes a decision. That's the way it works."

10   In a way, both groups were right. From the white students' perspective, this was ordinary decision making. To the black students, majority rule sent the message: "we don't count" is the "way it works" for minorities. In a racially divided society, majority rule may be perceived as majority tyranny.

That is a large claim, and I do not rest my case for it solely on the actions of the prom committee in one Chicago high school. To expand the range of the argument, I first consider the ideal of majority rule itself, particularly as reflected in the writings of James Madison and other founding members of our Republic. These early democrats explored the relationship between majority rule and democracy. James Madison warned, "If a majority be united by a common interest, the rights of the minority will be insecure." The tyranny of the majority, according to Madison, requires safeguards to protect "one part of the society against the injustice of the other part."

For Madison, majority tyranny represented the great danger to our early constitutional democracy. Although the American revolution was fought against the tyranny of the British monarch, it soon became clear that there was another tyranny to be avoided. The accumulations of all powers in the same hands, Madison warned, "whether of one, a few, or many, and whether hereditary, self-appointed, or elective, may justly be pronounced the very definition of tyranny."

As another colonist suggested in papers published in Philadelphia, "We have been so long habituated to a jealousy of tyranny from monarchy and aristocracy, that we have yet to learn the dangers of it from democracy."

Despotism had to be opposed "whether it came from Kings, Lords, or the people."

The debate about majority tyranny reflected Madison's concern that the majority may not represent the whole. In a homogeneous society, the interest of the majority would likely be that of the minority also. But in a heterogeneous community, the majority may not represent all competing interests. The majority is likely to be self-interested and ignorant or indifferent to the concerns of the minority. In such case, Madison observed, the assumption that the majority represents the minority is "altogether fictitious."

15 Yet even a self-interested majority can govern fairly if it cooperates with the minority. One reason for such cooperation is that the self-interested majority values the principle of reciprocity. The self-interested majority worries that the minority may attract defectors from the majority and become the next governing majority. The Golden Rule principle of reciprocity functions to check the tendency of a self-interested majority to act tyrannically.

So the argument for the majority principle connects it with the value of reciprocity: You cooperate when you lose in part because members of the current majority will cooperate when they lose. The conventional case for the fairness of majority rule is that it is not really the rule of a fixed group—The Majority—on all issues; instead it is the rule of shifting majorities, as the losers at one time or on one issue join with others and become part of the governing coalition at another time or on another issue. The result will be a fair system of mutually beneficial cooperation. I call a majority that rules but does not dominate a Madisonian Majority.

The problem of majority tyranny arises, however, when the self-interested majority does not need to worry about defectors. When the majority is fixed and permanent, there are no checks on its ability to be overbearing. A majority that does not worry about defectors is a majority with total power.

In such a case, Madison's concern about majority tyranny arises. In a heterogeneous community, any faction with total power might subject "the minority to the caprice and arbitrary decisions of the majority, who instead of consulting the interest of the whole community collectively, attend sometimes to partial and local advantages."

"What remedy can be found in a republican Government, where the majority must ultimately decide," argued Madison, but to ensure "that no one common interest or passion will be likely to unite a majority of the whole number in an unjust pursuit." The answer was to disaggregate the majority to ensure checks and balances or fluid, rotating interests. The minority needed protection against an overbearing majority, so that "a common sentiment is less likely to be felt, and the requisite concert less likely to be formed, by a majority of the whole."

20 Political struggles would not be simply a contest between rulers and people; the political struggles would be among the people themselves. The work of government was not to transcend different interests but to reconcile them. In an ideal democracy, the people would rule, but the minorities would also be protected against the power of majorities. Again, where the rules of decision making protect the minority, the Madisonian Majority rules without dominating.

But if a group is unfairly treated, for example, when it forms a racial minority, *and* if the problems of unfairness are not cured by conventional assumptions about majority rule, then what is to be done? The answer is that we may need an *alternative* to winner-take-all majoritarianism. In [my] book, a collection of my law review articles, I describe the alternative, which, with Nikolas's help, I now call the "principle of taking turns." In a racially divided society, this principle does better than simple majority rule if it accommodates the values of self-government, fairness, deliberation, compromise, and consensus that lie at the heart of the democratic ideal.

In my legal writing, I follow the caveat of James Madison and other early American democrats. I explore decision making rules that might work in a multi-racial society to ensure that majority rule does not become majority tyranny. I pursue voting systems that might disaggregate The Majority so that it does not exercise power unfairly or tyrannically. I aspire to a more cooperative political style of decision making to enable all of the students at Brother Rice to feel comfortable attending the same prom. In looking to create Madisonian Majorities, I pursue a positive-sum, taking-turns solution.

Structuring decision making to allow the minority "a turn" may be necessary to restore the reciprocity ideal when a fixed majority refuses to cooperate with the minority. If the fixed majority loses its incentive to follow the Golden Rule principle of shifting majorities, the minority never gets to take a turn. Giving the minority a turn does not mean the minority gets to rule; what it does mean is that the minority gets to influence decision making and the majority rules more legitimately.

Instead of automatically rewarding the preferences of the monolithic majority, a taking-turns approach anticipates that the majority rules, but is not overbearing. Because those with 51 percent of the votes are not assured 100 percent of the power, the majority cooperates with, or at least does not tyrannize, the minority.

25 The sports analogy of "I win; you lose" competition within a political hierarchy makes sense when only one team can win; Nikolas's intuition that it is often possible to take turns suggests an alternative approach. Take family decision making, for example. It utilizes a taking-turns approach. When parents sit around the kitchen table deciding on a vacation destination or activities for a rainy day, often they do not simply rely on a show of hands, especially if that means that the older children always prevail or if affinity groups among the children (those who prefer movies to video games, or those who prefer baseball to playing cards) never get to play their activity of choice. Instead of allowing the majority simply to rule, the parents may propose that everyone take turns, going to the movies one night and playing video games the next. Or as Nikolas proposes, they might do both on a given night.

Taking turns attempts to build consensus while recognizing political or social differences, and it encourages everyone to play. The taking-turns approach gives those with the most support more turns, but it also legitimates the outcome from each individual's perspective, including those whose views are shared only by a minority.

In the end, I do not believe that democracy should encourage rule by the powerful—even a powerful majority. Instead, the ideal of democracy promises a fair discussion among self-defined equals about how to achieve our common aspirations. To redeem that promise, we need to put the idea of taking turns and disaggregating the majority at the center of our conception of representation. Particularly as we move into the twenty-first century as a more highly diversified citizenry, it is essential that we consider the ways in which voting and representational systems succeed or fail at encouraging Madisonian Majorities.

To use Nikolas's terminology, "it is no fair" if a fixed, tyrannical majority excludes or alienates the minority. It is no fair if a fixed, tyrannical majority monopolizes all the power all the time. It is no fair if we engage in the periodic ritual of elections, but only the permanent majority gets to choose who is elected. Where we have tyranny by The Majority we do not have genuine democracy.

My life's work, with the essential assistance of people like Nikolas, has been to try to find the rules that can best bring us together as a democratic society. Some of my ideas about democratic fair play were grossly mischaracterized in the controversy over my nomination to be Assistant Attorney General for Civil Rights. Trying to find rules to encourage fundamental fairness inevitably raises the question posed by Harvard professor Randall Kennedy in a summary of this controversy: "What is required to create political institutions that address the needs and aspirations of all Americans, not simply whites, who have long enjoyed racial privilege, but people of color who have long suffered racial exclusion from policymaking forums?" My answer, as Professor Kennedy suggests, varies by situation. But I have a predisposition, reflected in my son's yearning for a positive-sum solution to seek an integrated body politic in which all perspectives are represented and in which all people work together to find common ground. I advocate empowering voters and their representatives in ways that give even minority voters a chance to influence legislative outcomes.

30   But those in the majority do not lose; they simply learn to take turns. This is a positive-sum solution that allows all voters to feel that they participate meaningfully in the decision-making process. This is a positive-sum solution that makes legislative outcomes more legitimate.

My work did not arise in a vacuum. Lost in the controversy over my nomination was the long history of those before me who have sought to change the rules in order to improve the system. There have been three generations of attempts to curb tyrannical majorities. The first generation focused directly on access to the ballot on the assumptions that the right to vote by itself is "preservative of all other rights." During the civil rights movement, aggrieved citizens asserted that "tyrannical majorities" in various locales were ganging up to deny black voters access to the voting booth.

The 1965 Voting Rights Act and its amendments forcefully addressed this problem. The act outlawed literacy tests, brought federal registrars to troubled districts to ensure safe access to polls, and targeted for federal administrative review many local registration procedures. Success under the act was immediate and impressive. The number of blacks registered to vote rose dramatically within five years after passage.

The second generation of voting rights litigation and legislation focused on the Southern response to increased black registration. Southern states and local subdivisions responded to blacks in the electorate by switching the way elections were conducted to ensure that newly voting blacks could not wield any influence. By changing, for example, from neighborhood-based districts to jurisdiction-wide-at-large representatives, those in power ensured that although blacks could vote, and even run for office, they could not win. At-large elections allowed a unified white bloc to control all the elected positions. As little as 51 percent of the population could decide 100 percent of the elections, and the

black minority was permanently excluded from meaningful participation.

In response, the second generation of civil rights activism focused on "qualitative vote dilution." Although everyone had a vote, it was apparent that some people's votes were qualitatively less important than others. The concerns raised by the second generation of civil rights activists led Congress to amend the Voting Rights Act. In 1982, congressional concern openly shifted from simply getting blacks the ability to register and vote to providing blacks a realistic opportunity to elect candidates of their choice. Thus, the new focus was on electing more black officials, primarily though the elimination of at-large districts, and their replacement by majority-black single-member districts. Even if whites continued to refuse to vote for blacks, there would be a few districts in which whites were in the minority and powerless to veto black candidates. The distinctive group interests of the black community, which Congress found had been ignored in the at-large, racially polarized elections, were thus given a voice within decision making councils.

35   The second generation sought to integrate physically the body politic. It was assumed that disaggregating the winner-take-all at-large majority would create political access for black voters, who would use that access to elect black representatives.

In many places, second-generation fights continue today. A number of redistricting schemes have been challenged in court, and not all courts agree on the outcomes, let alone the enterprise itself. Nevertheless, few disagree that blacks continue to be underrepresented in federal, state, and local government.

Even in governments in which minority legislators have increased, the marginalization of minority group interests has often stubbornly remained. Third-generation cases have now begun to respond. Third-generation cases recognize that it is sometimes not enough simply to ensure that minorities have a fair opportunity to elect someone to a legislative body. Under some unusual circumstances, it may be necessary to police the legislative voting rules whereby a majority consistently rigs the process to exclude a minority.

The Supreme Court's recent decision in *Presley v. Etowah County* heralds the arrival of this concern. Although black representatives for the first time since Reconstruction enjoyed a seat on the local county commission in Etowah and Russell counties in Alabama, they did not enjoy much else. Because of second-generation redistricting, black county commissioners were elected to county governing bodies in the two counties. Immediately upon their election, however, the white incumbents changed the rules for allocating decision-making authority. Just like the grandfather clauses, the literacy tests, the white primary, and the other ingenious strategies devised to enforce white supremacy in the past, rules were changed to evade the reach of the earlier federal court decree.

In one county the newly integrated commission's duties were shifted to an appointed administrator. In the other county, its duties were shifted from individual commissioners to the entire commission voting by majority rule. Because voting on the commission, like voting in the county electorate, followed racial lines, "majority rule" meant that whites controlled the outcome of every legislative decision. The incumbents defended this power grab as simply the decision of a bona fide majority.

40 This happened as well in Texas when the first Latina was elected to a local school board. The white majority suddenly decided that two votes were henceforth necessary to get an item on the agenda. In Louisiana, the legislature enacted a districting plan drawn up by a group of whites in a secret meeting in the subbasement of the state capitol, a meeting from which all black legislators were excluded.

Through these three generations of problems and remedies, a long trail of activists has preceded me. In 1964, ballot access was defended eloquently by Dr. Martin Luther King, Jr., and Fannie Lour Hamer. In 1982, redistricting was the consensus solution to electoral exclusion championed by the NAACP, the League of Women Voters, the Mexican American Legal Defense Fund, and many others.

My ideas follow in this tradition. They are not undemocratic or out of the mainstream. Between 1969 and 1993, the Justice Department under both Democratic and Republican presidents disapproved as discriminatory over one hundred sets of voting rules involving changes to majority voting. None of these rules was unfair in the abstract, but all were exclusionary in practice. President Bush's chief civil rights enforcer declared some of them to be "electoral steroids for white candidates" because they manipulated the election system to ensure that only white candidates won.

This history of struggle against tyrannical majorities enlightens us to the dangers of winner-take-all collective decision making. Majority rule, which presents an efficient opportunity for determining the public good, suffers when it is not constrained by the need to bargain with minority interests. When majorities are fixed, the minority lacks any mechanism for holding the majority to account or even to listen. Nor does such majority rule promote deliberation or consensus. The permanent majority simply has its way, without reaching out to convince anyone else.

Any form of less-than-unanimous voting introduces the danger that some group will be in the minority and the larger group will exploit the numerically smaller group. This is especially problematic to defeated groups that do not possess a veto over proposals and acts that directly affect them or implicate concerns they value intensely. Thus, the potential for instability exists when any significant group of people ends up as permanent losers.

45 The fundamentally important question of political stability is how to induce losers to continue to play the game. Political stability depends on the perception that the system is fair to induce losers to continue to work within the system rather than to try to overthrow it. When the minority experiences the alienation of complete and consistent defeat, they lack incentive to respect laws passed by the majority over their opposition.

As Tocqueville recognized, "[T]he power to do everything, which I should refuse to one of my equals,

I will never grant to any number of them." Or as Hamilton put it, when the many are given all the power, "they will oppress the few." The problem is that majoritarian systems do not necessarily create winners who share in power. Politics becomes a battle for total victory rather than a method of governing open to all significant groups.

This is what happened in Phillips County, Arkansas, where a majority vote runoff requirement unfairly rewarded the preferences of a white bloc-voting majority and, for more than half a century, excluded a permanent voting minority. Predominantly rural and poor, Phillips County has a history of extremely polarized voting: Whites vote exclusively for white candidates and blacks vote for black candidates whenever they can. In many elections, no white person ever publicly supports or endorses a black candidate. Although qualified, when highly regarded black candidates compete, local election rules and the manipulation of those rules by a white bloc have meant that no black person in over a century had been elected to any countywide office when I brought a lawsuit in 1987. Yet blacks were just less than half of the voting-age population.

Reverend Julious McGruder, a black political candidate and a former school board member, testified on the basis of fifteen years of working in elections that "no white candidate or white person has come out and supported [a] black." Black attorney Sam Whitfield won a primary and requested support in the runoff from Kenneth Stoner, a white candidate he had defeated in the first round. In a private conversation, Stoner told Whitfield that he personally thought Whitfield was the better remaining candidate but that he could not support him. As Whitfield recounted the conversation at trial, Stoner said "[h]e could not support a black man. He lives in this town. He is a farmer. His wife teaches school here and that there is just no way that he could support a black candidate."

Racially polarized voting is only one of the political disadvantages for blacks in Phillips County. Blacks, whose median income is less than three thousand dollars annually, also suffer disproportionately from poverty,

which works to impede their effective participation in the political process. For some example, 42 percent of blacks have no car or truck, while only 9 percent of the white population are similarly encumbered; and 30 percent of blacks, compared to 11 percent of whites, have no telephone. Thus isolated by poverty, black voters are less able to maneuver around such obstacles as frequent, last-minute changes in polling places. County officials have moved polling places ten times in as many elections, often without prior notice and sometimes to locations up to twelve to fifteen miles driving over dirt and gravel roads. Moreover, because of the relative scarcity of cars, the lack of public transportation in the county, all the expense of taxes, the election campaigns of black candidates must include a get-out-and-vote kind of funding effort that a poor black community simply cannot afford.

50   Black candidates who win the first round come up against one particular local election rule—the majority vote runoff law that doubles the access problem by requiring people to get to the polls two times within a two-week period. Because this rule combines with local racism, almost half the voters for over a century never enjoyed any opportunity to choose who represents them. As a numerical, stigmatized, and racially isolated minority, blacks regarded the majority vote requirement as simply a tool to "steal the elections"—a tool that has the effect of demobilizing black political participation, enhancing polarization rather than fostering debate, and in general excluding black interest from the political process. As Rev. McGruder testified, running twice to win once *just kill[s] all the momentum, all of the hope, all of the faith, the belief in the system.* Many voters "really can't understand the situation where you say 'You know, Brother Whitfield won last night' and then come up to a grandma or my uncle, or auntie and say 'Hey, you know, we're going to have to run again in the next 10 days and—because we've got a runoff.'"

In fact, between the first and second elections, turnout drops precipitously, so that the so-called majority winner in the runoff may receive fewer votes than the plurality winner in the first primary. In fact, in all three black-white runoff contests in 1986, the white runoff victor's majority occurred only because the number of people who came out to vote in the second primary went down.

Indeed, the district court that heard the challenge in 1988 to the Arkansas law did not dispute the facts: that no black candidate had ever been elected to countywide or state legislative office from Phillips County and that "race has frequently dominated over qualifications and issues" in elections. The court, nonetheless, preferred to stick with this obviously unfair electoral scheme, reasoning that The Majority should prevail even when The Majority is the product of a completely artificial and racially exclusionary runoff system. It is decisions like this one that continue to inspire me to work for a better way.

The court failed to see that the unfairness wrought by winner-take-all majority rule was inconsistent with democratic fair play in this county. At first blush, the unfairness of 51 percent of the people winning 100 percent of the power may not seem obvious. It certainly seems to be much less that the unfairness of a professional hatmaker competing against kids. But in some ways it is worse. For example, when voters are drawn into participation by seemingly fair rules, only to discover that the rules systematically work against their interests, they are likely to feel seduced and abandoned. Moreover, those Brownies who made their own hats could at least be assured that others would sympathize with their having been taken advantage of. People who have been systematically victimized by winner-take-all majority rules usually get little sympathy from a society that wrongfully equates majority tyranny with democracy.

As the plaintiffs' evidence demonstrated, this was precisely the situation in Phillips County, where the fairness of the majority requirement was destroyed by extreme racial polarization, the absence of reciprocity, and the artificial majorities created in the runoffs. Judge Richard Arnold put it simply in a related case: Implementation of the majority vote requirement in eastern Arkansas represented a pattern of actions in which "a systematic and deliberate attempt" was made to "close off" avenues of opportunity to blacks in the affected jurisdictions.

55   In other words, my project has been to return the inquiry to its most authoritative source—voters themselves. For example, Milagros Robledo, a Latino voter in Philadelphia, is one of many voters who say they are angry, confused and more cynical than ever about the political process. After a recent scandal involving the solicitation of absentee ballots in a hotly contested local election, Mr. Robledo lamented, "After going through this whole thing, I now really know the value of my vote. It means nothing to me, and it means a lot to the politicians." For Mr. Robledo, his community has continuously been shortchanged by elected officials who are more interested in getting elected than in representing the people.

I take my cue from people like Milagros Robledo. I seek to keep their faith that votes should not count more than voters. I struggle to conceptualize the representatives' relationship with voters to make that relationship more dynamic and interactive.

It is in the course of this struggle that I made my much maligned references to "the authenticity assumption." Authenticity is a concept I describe within my general criticism of conventional empowerment strategies. The Voting Rights Act expressly provides that black and Latino voters must be afforded an equal opportunity "to participate in the political process and to elect representatives of their choice." The question is: Which candidates are the representatives of choice of black or Latino voters?

Authenticity subsumes two related but competing views to answer that question. The first version of authenticity seeks information from election results to learn how the voters perceive elected officials. In this view, voting behavior is key. Authentic representatives are simply those truly chosen by the people. The second authenticity assumption is that voters trust elected officials who "look like" or act like the voters themselves. In this view, authenticity refers to a candidate who shares common physical or cultural traits with constituents. In this aspect of authenticity, the nominally cultural becomes political.

Despite the importance of voter choice in assessing minority-preferred or minority-sponsored candidates, those who support the second authenticity assumption substitute the concept of presumptive or descriptive representativeness in which candidates who look like their constituents are on that basis alone presumed to be representative. In the name of authenticity, these observers have argued that the current voting rights litigation model is effective because it provides blacks or Latinos an opportunity to elect physically black or culturally Latino representatives. This is an understandable position, and I present it as such, but it is not my position. Indeed, I term it "a limited empowerment concept."

60   My preference is for the first view of authenticity, the one that focuses on the voter, not the candidate. In *Thornburg v. Gingles,* a 1986 Supreme Court opinion, Justice William Brennan stressed that it is the "status of the candidate as the chosen representative of a particular racial group, not the race of the candidate, that is important."

This leads to two complementary conclusions that are firmly embedded in the case law and the literature. First, white candidates can legitimately represent non-white voters if those voters elected them. I state this explicitly in my *Michigan Law Review* article . . . . And second, the election of a black or Latino candidate will not defeat a voting rights lawsuit, especially if those black or Latino elected officials did not receive electoral support from their community. Just because a candidate is black does not mean that he or she is the candidate of choice of the black community.

Borrowing from the language of the statute, I say voters, not politicians, should count. And voters count most when voters can exercise a real choice based on what the candidates think and do rather than what the candidates look like.

As I wrote these law review articles, my thinking evolved. New ideas emerged and old ones were rejected as I struggled to understand the tyranny of different majorities. But one idea remained constant: I am a dem-ocratic idealist, committed to making American politics open to genuine participation by all voters. It is as part of this life-long commitment to democratic fair play that I explore the many dimensions of majority tyranny.

Concern over majority tyranny has typically focused on the need to monitor and constrain the substantive policy outputs of the decision-making process. In my articles, however, I look at the *procedural* rules by which preferences are identified and counted. Procedural rules govern the process by which outcomes are decided. They are the rules by which the game is played.

65   I have been roundly, and falsely, criticized for focusing on outcomes. Outcomes are indeed relevant, but *not* because I seek to advance particular ends, such as whether the children play tag or hide-and-seek, or whether the band at Brother Rice plays rock music or rap. Rather, I look to outcomes as *evidence* of whether all the children—or all the high school seniors—feel that their choice is represented and considered. The purpose is not to guarantee "equal legislative outcomes"; equal opportunity to *influence* legislative outcomes regardless of race is more like it.

For these reasons, I sometimes explore alternatives to simple, winner take-all majority rule. I do not advocate any one procedural rule as a universal panacea for unfairness. Nor do I propose these remedies primarily as judicial solutions. They can be adopted only in the context of litigation after the court first finds a legal violation.

Outside of litigation, I propose these approaches as political solutions if, depending on the local context, they better approximate the goals of democratic fair play. One such decision-making alternative is called cumulative voting, which could give all the students at Brother Rice multiple votes and allow them to distribute their votes in any combination of their choice. If each student could vote for ten songs, the students could plump or aggregate their votes to reflect the intensity of their preferences. They could put ten votes on one song; they could put five votes on two songs. If a tenth of the students opted to "cumulate" or plump all their votes for one song, they would be able to select one of every ten or so songs played at the prom. The black seniors could have done this if they chose to, but so could any other cohesive group of sufficient size. In this way, the songs preferred by a majority would be played most often, but the songs the minority enjoyed would also show up on the play list.

Under cumulative voting, voters get the same number of votes as there are seats or options to vote for, and they can then distribute their votes in any combination to reflect their preferences. Like-minded voters can vote as a solid bloc or, instead, form strategic, cross-racial coalitions to gain mutual benefits. This system is emphatically not racially based; it allows voters to organize themselves on whatever basis they wish.

Corporations use this system to ensure representation of minority shareholders on corporate boards of directors. Similarly, some local municipal and county governments have adopted cumulative voting to ensure representation of minority voters. Instead of awarding political power to geographic units called districts, cumulative voting allows voters to cast ballots based on what they think rather than where they live.

70 Cumulative voting is based on the principle of one person-one vote because each voter gets the same total number of votes. Everyone's preferences are counted equally. It is not a particularly radical idea; thirty states either require or permit corporations to use this election system. Cumulative voting is certainly not antidemocratic because it emphasizes the importance of voter choice in selecting public or social policy. And it is neither liberal nor conservative. Both the Reagan and Bush administrations approved cumulative voting schemes pursuant to the Voting Rights Act to protect the rights of racial—and language—minority voters.

But, as in Chilton County, Alabama, which now uses cumulative voting to elect both the school board and the county commission, any politically cohesive group can vote strategically to win representation. Groups of voters win representation depending on the exclusion threshold, meaning the percentage of votes needed to win one seat or have the band play one song. That threshold can be set case by case, jurisdiction by jurisdiction, based on the size of minority groups that make compelling claims for representation.

Normally the exclusion threshold in a head-to-head contest is 50 percent, which means that only groups that can organize a majority can get elected. But if multiple seats (or multiple songs) are considered simultaneously, the exclusion threshold is considerably reduced. For example, in Chilton County, with seven seats elected simultaneously on each governing body, the threshold of exclusion is now one-eighth. Any group with the solid support of one-eighth the voting population cannot be denied representation. This is because any self-identified minority can plump or cumulate all its votes for one candidate. Again, minorities are not defined solely in racial terms.

As it turned out in Chilton County, both blacks and Republicans benefited from this new system. The school board and commission now each have three white Democrats, three white Republicans, and one black Democrat. Previously, when each seat was decided in a head-to-head contest, the majority not only ruled but monopolized. Only white Democrats were elected at every prior election during this century.

Similarly, if the black and white students at Brother Rice have very different musical taste, cumulative voting permits a positive-sum solution to enable both groups to enjoy one prom. The majority's preferences would be respected in that their songs would be played most often, but the black students could express the intensity of their preferences too. If the black students chose to plump all their votes on a few songs, their minority preferences would be recognized and played. Essentially, cumulative voting structures the band's repertoire to enable the students to take turns.

75 As a solution that permits voters to self-select their identities, cumulative voting also encourages cross-racial coalition building. No one is locked into a minority identity. Nor is anyone necessarily isolated by the identity they choose. Voters can strengthen their influence by forming coalitions to elect more than one representative or to select a range of music more compatible with the entire student body's preferences.

Women too can use cumulative voting to gain greater representation. Indeed, in other countries with similar, alternative voting systems, women are more likely to be represented in the national legislature. For example, in some Western European democracies, the national legislatures have as many as 37 percent female members compared to a little more than 5 percent in our Congress.

There is a final benefit from cumulative voting. It eliminates gerrymandering. By denying protected incumbents safe seats in gerrymandered districts, cumulative voting might encourage more voter participation. With greater interest-based electoral competition, cumulative voting could promote the political turnover sought by advocates of term limits. In this way, cumulative voting serves many of the same ends as periodic elections or rotation in office, a solution that Madison and others advocated as a means of protecting against permanent majority factions.

A different remedial voting tool, one that I have explored more cautiously, is supermajority voting. It modifies winner-take-all majority rule to require that something more than a bare majority of voters must approve or concur before action is taken. As a uniform decisional rule, a supermajority empowers any numerically small but collusive group of voters. Like cumulative voting, it is race-neutral. Depending on the issue, different members of the voting body can "veto" impending action.

Supermajority remedies give bargaining power to all numerically inferior or less powerful groups, be they black, female, or Republican. Supermajority rules empowered the minority Republicans in the Senate who used the Senate filibuster procedure in the spring of 1993 to "veto" the President's proposed economic stimulus package. The same concept of a minority veto yielded the Great Compromise in which small-population states are equally represented in the Senate.

80   I have never advocated (or imagined) giving an individual member of a legislative body a personal veto. Moreover, I have discussed these kinds of exceptional remedies as the subject of court-imposed solutions only

when there has been a violation of the statute and only when they make sense in the context of a particular case. I discuss supermajority rules as a judicial remedy only in cases where the court finds proof of consistent and deeply engrained polarization. It was never my intent that supermajority requirements should be the norm for all legislative bodies, or that simple majority voting would ever in itself constitute a statutory or constitutional violation.

Both the Reagan and Bush administrations took a similar remedial approach to enforcement of the Voting Rights Act. In fact, it was the Reagan administration that *approved* the use of supermajority rules as a remedial measure in places like Mobile, Alabama, where the special five-out-of-seven supermajority threshold is still in place today and is credited with increasing racial harmony in that community.

But—and here I come directly to the claims of my critics—some apparently fear that remedies for extreme voting abuses, remedies like cumulative voting or the Mobile supermajority, constitute "quotas"—racial preferences to ensure minority rule. While cumulative voting, or a supermajority, is quite conventional in many cases and race neutral, to order it as a remedy apparently opens up possibilities of nonmajoritarianism that many seem to find quite threatening.

Indeed, while my nomination was pending, I was called "antidemocratic" for suggesting that majority voting rules may not fairly resolve conflict when the majority and minority are permanently divided. But alternatives to majority voting rules in a racially polarized environment are too easily dismissed by this label. As Chief Justice Burger wrote for the Supreme Court, "there is nothing in the language of the Constitution, our history, or our cases that requires that a majority always prevail on every issue." In other words, *there is nothing inherent in democracy that requires majority rule.* It is simply a custom that works efficiently when the majority and minority are fluid, are not monolithic, and are not permanent.

Other democracies frequently employ alternatives to winner-take-all majority voting. Indeed, only five

Western democracies, including Britain and the United States, still use single-member-district, winner-take-all systems of representation. Germany, Spain, the Netherlands, and Sweden, among other countries, elect their legislatures under some alternative to winner-take-all majority voting. As the *New Yorker,* in a comment on my nomination, observed, President Clinton was right in calling some of my ideas "difficult to defend," but only because "Americans, by and large, are ignorant of the existence, let alone the details, of electoral systems other than their own."

85 No one who had done their homework seriously questioned the fundamentally democratic nature of my ideas. Indeed, columnists who attacked my ideas during my nomination ordeal have praised ideas, in a different context, that are remarkably similar to my own. Lally Weymouth wrote, "There can't be democracy in South Africa without a measure of formal protection for minorities." George Will has opined, "the Framers also understood that stable, tyrannical majorities can best be prevented by the multiplication of minority interests, so the majority at any moment will be just a transitory coalition of minorities." In my law journal articles, I expressed exactly the same reservations about unfettered majority rule and about the need sometimes to disaggregate the majority to ensure fair and effective representation for all substantial interests.

The difference is that the minority I used to illustrate my academic point was not, as it was for Lally Weymouth, the white minority in South Africa. Nor, did I write, as George Will did, about the minority of well-to-do landlords in New York City. I wrote instead about the political exclusion of the black minority in many local county and municipal governing bodies in America.

Yet these same two journalists and many others condemned me as antidemocratic. Apparently, it is not controversial to provide special protections for affluent landlords or minorities in South Africa but it is "divisive," "radical," and "out of the mainstream" to provide similar remedies to black Americans who, after centuries of racial oppression, are still excluded.

Talking about racial bias at home has, for many, become synonymous with advocating revolution. Talking about racial divisions, in itself, has become a violation of the rules of polite society.

We seem to have forgotten that dialogue and intergroup communication are critical to forging consensus. In my case, genuine debate was shut down by techniques of stereotyping and silencing. As Professor Randall Kennedy observes, I was "punished" as the messenger reporting the bad news about our racial situation. I dared to speak when I should have been silent.

90 My nomination became an unfortunate metaphor for the state of race relations in America. My nomination suggested that as a country, we are in a state of denial about issues of race and racism. The censorship imposed against me points to a denial of serious public debate or discussion about racial fairness and justice in a true democracy. For many politicians and policymakers, the remedy for racism is simply to stop talking about race.

Sentences, words, even phrases separated by paragraphs in my law review articles were served up to demonstrate that I was violating the rules. Because I talked openly about existing racial divisions, I was branded "race obsessed." Because I explored innovative ways to remedy racism, I was branded "antidemocratic." It did not matter that I had suggested race-neutral election rules, such as cumulative voting, as an alternative to remedy racial discrimination. It did not matter that I never advocated quotas. I became the Quota Queen.

The vision behind my by-now-notorious law review articles and my less-well-known professional commitments has always been that of a fair and just society, a society in which even adversely affected parties believe in the system because they believe the process is fair and the process is inclusive. My vision of fairness and justice imagines a full and effective voice for all citizens. I may have failed to locate some of my ideas in the specific factual contexts from which they are derived. But always I have tried to show that democracy in a heterogeneous society is incompatible with rule by a racial monopoly of any color.

By publishing these law journal articles as a collection, I hope to spark the debate that was denied in the context of my nomination. We will have lost more than any one individual's opportunity for public service if we fail to pursue the public thirst for information about, and positive-sum solutions to, the issues at the heart of this controversy. The twentieth-century problem—the problem of the color line, according to W. E. B. Du Bois—will soon become a twenty-first-century problem if we allow opposing viewpoints to be silenced on issues of race and racism.

I hope that we can learn three positive lessons from my experience. The first lesson is that those who stand for principles may lose in the short run, but they cannot be suppressed in the long run. The second lesson is that public dialogue is critical to represent all perspectives; no one viewpoint should be permitted to monopolize, distort, caricature, or shape public debate. The tyranny of The Majority is just as much a problem of silencing minority viewpoints as it is of excluding minority representatives or preferences. We cannot talk at once, but that does not mean only one group should get to speak. We can take turns. Third, we need consensus and positive-sum solutions. We need a broad public conversation about issues of racial justice in which we seek win-win solutions to real-life problems. If we include blacks and whites, and women and men, and Republicans and Democrats, and even people with new ideas, we will all be better off.

95 New ideas about how to resolve old problems are critical to shaping consensus solutions. To reach consensus we must do more than simply maneuver to avoid controversy. Consensus must be built, not just located. We have become so polarized that we have difficulty speaking to each other, as demonstrated by the controversy over recent judicial opinions condemning race-conscious districting. I believe we may forge a genuine consensus if we consider anew some of the ideas discussed in this collection of essays—the very same ideas previously dismissed as "out of the mainstream."

I am grateful for the opportunity provided by the publication of my law journal articles to participate in a national, public conversation about race, justice, and fundamental fairness. I would like to lower the decibel level but increase the information level on public discussion that surrounds race. I hope that those who actually read what I wrote will challenge decision makers—from politicians to pundits—to represent fairly and more carefully the broad spectrum of public opinion about race.

Most of all, I hope we begin to consider the principle of taking turns as a means to bring us closer to the ideal of democratic fair play. Justice Potter Stewart wrote in 1964 that our form of representative self-government reflects "the strongly felt American tradition that the public interest is composed of many diverse interests, [which] . . . in the long run . . . can better be expressed by a medley of component voices than by the majority's monolithic command." In that "strongly felt American tradition," I hope more of us aspire to govern like Madisonian Majorities through "a medley of component voices." In that "strongly felt American tradition," I hope more of us come to reject the "monolithic command" of The Fixed Majority.

After all, government is a public experiment. Let us not forget Justice Louis Brandeis's advice at the beginning of this century: "If we guide by the light of reason, we must let our minds be bold." At the close of the same century, I hope we rediscover the bold solution to the tyranny of The Majority, which has always been more democracy, not less.

Writing Strategies

1. How effective is Guinier's opening strategy?

2. What example, instead of Brother Rice High School, might better illustrate Guinier's point?

3. What support strategies are most important to Guinier's argument?

4. In paragraph 42, why does Guinier state: "My ideas follow in this tradition. They are not undemocratic or out of the mainstream." How does this strengthen her argument?

5. How persuasive are particular examples, such as paragraphs 48, 49, 50?

Exploring Ideas

1. Beyond the examples Guinier gives, how does the tyranny of the majority work in everyday life?

2. Illustrate "the rule of shifting majorities" (¶ 16) by providing an example.

3. Describe each of the three generations of attempts to curb tyrannical majorities.

4. In paragraph 53, Guinier says, "People who have been systematically victimized by winner-take-all majority rules usually get little sympathy from a society that wrongfully equates majority tyranny with democracy." Do primary research, interviewing several people outside of class to find out if they sympathize with those who have been victimized by winner-take-all majority rules.

5. Why are Americans by and large "ignorant of the existence, let alone the details, of electoral systems other than their own"? Why should they be more aware of alternatives?

Ideas for Writing

1. Choose a particular claim and explore its complexities. Consider the following: "The fundamentally important question of political stability is how to induce losers to continue to play the game" (¶ 45).

2. In paragraph 76 Guinier says, "Women too can use cumulative voting to gain greater representation." Research why women aren't more represented in Congress, and make an argument in response to the current voting system.

If responding to one of these ideas, go to the **Analysis** section of this chapter to begin developing ideas for your essay.

Entitlement Education

Daniel Bruno

We often respond to the people (and arguments) that we agree with the most. As with Betsy Taylor's essay that follows, Daniel Bruno agrees with most of the original argument. His introduction explains: "But he fails, it seems, to emphasize enough a most harmful effect of this sense of entitlement." Bruno's response will not disagree, but will *emphasize* a crucial point in an attempt to make the reader more aware of it.

Writing Strategies

Overall summary of original argument.

Main response to the original argument.

(Attention to "I") Bruno's thesis, and distinction between his argument and the original.

Turnabout paragraph.

Analysis of several possible arguments about the results of student entitlement.

In his book *Generation X Goes to College,* Peter Sacks describes, among other things, the sense of entitlement that some students in today's consumerist culture have toward a college education. One entire chapter explores this issue alone, providing examples of this "sense" and looking into its "humble beginnings." Sacks shows how consumerism has invaded education, leading some students to expect good grades for little effort. But he fails, it seems, to emphasize enough a most harmful effect of this sense of entitlement. The biggest problem, as I see it, is that although students are able to graduate from high school (and even some colleges) with minimal effort, those students may find themselves cheated in the long run.

How might they be cheated? One might argue that students get cheated because entitlement doesn't go on forever. At some point it stops. For example, a college graduate with a marketing degree, but especially weak thinking or writing skills, may find himself disadvantaged on the job. It is not that his boss puts her foot down; instead, the job does. Our student finds himself not well prepared for it. He gets cheated because he is disadvantaged at his job—a job that he paid money to learn how to do. Of course the point isn't about marketing majors. The same is true of students in any field. (Marketing is just what came to mind.)

One might also claim that students will be cheated because their lives will somehow *be less.* This argument claims that a person's intelligence contributes to his quality of life. Here we must remember that "intelligence" is not just "knowledge." Instead, it is being able to use knowledge, to make connections and figure things out, to see causes and solve problems. A person may have much knowledge—that is, he may have accumulated a lot of facts—but not have much intelligence . . . or so the argument goes. As one goes from

Exploring Ideas

Entitlement: Expecting to get good grades for little effort.

Cheated out of adequate job preparation.

Cheated out of quality of life.

first grade to twelfth, from twelfth grade to college, and from freshman to senior, education shifts focus from mere accumulation of information (knowledge) to application of information (intelligence). And while we may accumulate more knowledge as a senior in college than we did as a senior in high school, the focus in college has (or should have) shifted from mere knowledge to intelligence—that is, to the ability to make good use of one's knowledge.

Intelligence = being able to use knowledge.

Other standard arguments claim other ways students might be cheated. For example, we might feel sorry for someone who doesn't get a joke—or a reference. Allusions to literature, history, philosophy, and so on allow us to say much in few words. But does the listener understand? If a person is unaware of common references—the Battle of the Bulge, Normandy, Existentialism, T. S. Eliot, World War I, Rasputin, John the Baptist, Gandhi, apartheid, Jonas Salk, Johnny Appleseed, Lewis and Clark, the Trail of Tears, slavery, the Donner Party, and so on—he misses out on conversations, on meaning, on *connecting with his fellow inmates.* Of course, here one might counter that you don't need to know all of these things. And, I agree, you don't. People tend to hang out with people who have similar interests and tastes.

Cheated out of standard cultural knowledge.

5   One more argument claims that because we live in a democracy, we must be well-educated. Since all the citizens are responsible for the government, our forefathers promoted public education so that all citizens—not just the wealthy and elite—would know how to read and write. Thomas Jefferson wrote,

Cheating the whole democracy.

> I know no safe depository of the ultimate powers of society but the people themselves; and if we think them not enlightened enough to exercise their control with a wholesome discretion, the remedy is not to take it from them, but to inform their discretion by education. This is the true corrective of abuses of constitutional power. (278)

In what ways can educated citizens correct abuses in a democracy? A person's way of life, his purchases and activities—not just a person's vote or protest march—is part of the responsibility. Thus, consumers and neighbors and co-workers and so on should behave responsibly and think intelligently. It is our responsibility as citizens of a democracy.

True enough, these are all ways that students who are allowed to just slide by end up getting cheated. But another way (and one less talked about) strikes me as being far more offensive. This reason hinges on the fact that many students are not just sliding by.

Transition

Uses historical and other allusions to prove his point about allusions.

Concession.

This gives the topic extra public resonance (since the democratic process is at stake).

Transition paragraph that leads us to Bruno's particular stance.

Return to the original argument.

In *Generation X Goes to College,* Peter Sacks illustrates that all of today's college students cannot just be thrown in the same big barrel. In describing the modern/post-modern clash in education, he spends the majority of his time talking about those students who are underprepared, who lack the basic study skills required in academic work, and who demonstrate little real commitment to their own education. Yet, he does not discuss this problem in isolation. He also mentions another type of student. For example, he introduces the reader to Marissa and Carol: "As very good students, [their views] were virtually excluded by The College in order to accommodate the whiners and complainers" (61). And he says they "suffered not only educationally" (63). In addition to discussing specific good students, an entire chapter presents survey results about students' attitudes toward education. While he makes claims such as "nearly a quarter of the students . . . harbored a disproportionate sense of entitlement," this very statement tells the reader that a full three-quarters (that is, three out of four) students *do not* "harbor a disproportionate sense of entitlement" (54–59). He wraps up the book by focusing on another student, Andie, who he describes as "a good student, constantly picking [his] brain for information and feedback on her work" (186–87). His final paragraph, before the Epilogue, says, "Let's create a system that encourages people like Andie at least as much as the ones who don't give a damn" (187). Thus, Sacks shows that today's students are a more diverse group—in skill level, background, and attitude toward education—than has ever before been gathered together in the college classroom.

Quotations illustrate particular points of the original. A properly used colon—to introduce a quote with words that could be punctuated as a sentence—provides coherence. The reader knows immediately the relationship of the words on the left and right of the colon. Quotation marks provide coherence by making clear that the words inside them are from a source.

More summary of the original argument.

Modern = marked by distinctions between lowbrow and highbrow thought. Postmodern = marked by chaos and blurring of boundaries.

1/4 students feel entitled.

3/4 students do not.

Diversity in skill and attitude.

Transition paragraph.

Now when we connect two things—the present grade-inflated, entitlement-driven education system that has got a foothold in most of America's high schools and colleges AND the diversity in skill and attitude toward education of today's college students—two problems appear.

10   One problem is that the motivated students are not being as challenged as they could be. Although their situation is not ideal, it is far from hopeless. They have at least three options: (1) take advantage of the easy system and learn a little along the way; (2) motivate themselves, working harder (and learning more) than the system requires them to; and (3) attend a more academically rigorous school (of course such schools still exist, though they are likely to cost more to attend).

Motivated students are cheated.

While motivated students suffer in our too-lax system, so do the un- (or under-) motivated ones. And these students, who need

Under-motivated students are cheated.

Sacks's quotation supports
Bruno's argument.

our help the most, are the ones most cheated. As Sacks says, "I now
believe the students are the real victims of this systematic failure of
the entitlement mindset" (189). The students who are allowed to
slide by, who are content to slide by, who perhaps don't even realize that they are sliding by because sliding by is all they know—
those students find themselves arriving at college less prepared and
less motivated than the "better students." And what happens next?
Sadly, the gap between these two groups grows even wider.

Gap between students
grows bigger.

Scenarios are the main
support tool.

    The motivated student with good study skills (the one who has
had at least an adequate high school education) attends class, takes
notes, understands reading assignments, follows instructions, develops even better habits of mind, gains even more knowledge, and
learns ways of making that knowledge work for her and her fellow
humans. But in a system where B's are average and C's might indicate that although a student "tried" she did not demonstrate understanding or skill, the poorer students continue to advance through
the system while remaining trapped at the bottom. Their level of
thinking does not change much, while that of their better-prepared
peers does.

Sacks and Bruno argue the
same point.

    The injustice, then, has been done to the students (as Sacks
says, the students are the victims). While the student has happily
skipped (or unhappily slogged) along through sixteen years of formal education, she is allowed, if she wants, to come away with very
little in terms of education. She is allowed, unfortunately, to escape
practically unscathed by learning. The problem, of course, is that
the two students have entered college on different academic levels
and the one on the higher level has graduated on an *even higher* level
while the one on the lower level has remained pretty much the same.

They do not even realize
they are being cheated.

    Students would do well to look around them, at the room full
of fellow classmates. They should imagine that many of those students will be graduating one day. And they should imagine the students in the classroom next door and across the hall and in all the
other buildings on campus. They will be graduating, too. They
should also imagine all those students at the more than 4,000 other
colleges throughout the country: Ohio State, Michigan, Michigan
State, Findlay College, Iowa State, Oklahoma A&M, The University of Utah, California This or That. (*The Chronicle of Higher Education*'s 2000–2001 "Almanac" lists 4,096 colleges in the United
States.) Many of those students are well-prepared, working hard,
and developing even better habits and thinking skills.

The statistic creates some
alarm for student readers.

Qualifier.

15   In our competitive world, the sad truth is that even some of the very good students, though their college dreams were to be doctors and lawyers and pharmacists and engineers, will be waiting tables. Don't get me wrong: There is no shame in that. The point is, that's not why they went to college. The truth is that for some students, college will be a tough uphill climb (a climb that could have been avoided with a more adequate high school education). A sadder truth, I am afraid, is that because of skills and attitudes developed in high school, for some students the reality of genuine learning (as opposed to just getting by) might already be too late.

Competition for jobs and status.

The "I" draws attention to Bruno's personal concern.

It's too late for many!

Works Cited

"Almanac." <u>The Chronicle of Higher Education</u>. 18 Oct. 2000 <http://chronicle.com/free/almanac/2000/almanac.htm>.

Sacks, Peter. <u>Generation X Goes to College</u>. Chicago: Open Court, 1996.

Writing Strategies

1. Are you able to understand Bruno's response to Peter Sacks, even if you have not read *Generation X Goes to College*? What helpful background information does Bruno provide? What other information might have been helpful?

2. Bruno defines "intelligence" in his essay. How is this definition important? Might he have deleted this definition without damaging his essay?

3. What is Bruno's main idea? Does he state it explicitly or imply it? Why is or isn't his strategy successful?

4. Explain how Bruno's essay has public resonance. That is, how is what he says important to others besides himself?

5. What evidence does Bruno provide to support his claim? Does he refer to statistics, outside sources, experience, logical reasoning? What other kind of evidence might he have provided?

Exploring Ideas

1. What do you think is Bruno's purpose in writing?

2. Which of Bruno's points do you think is most important or interesting?

3. How convincing is Bruno's support? What support strategies are used, and how successful is each strategy?

4. How might you respond to Bruno's essay with an essay of your own? Write down your main claim in one clear and concise sentence, and then jot down your ideas for support.

Ideas for Writing

1. What does Bruno get wrong?

2. If you agree with Bruno, what new and important point might you add?

If responding to one of these ideas, go to the **Analysis** section of this chapter to begin developing ideas for your essay.

Response to Juliet Schor

Betsy Taylor

Some responses fall into the "yes, but" or "yes, and" category. These responses acknowledge and even draw out and applaud the value of the original argument. They then go on to contribute something further to the debate or discussion. In essence, the responding essay says, "Yes, good point, BUT here's something further to consider," or "Yes, good point, AND here's an additional point about that." Betsy Taylor's essay is a valuable illustration of how a response can (1) argue for (not against) the validity of another argument, and then (2) contribute something further to the discussion.

This essay is a response to Juliet Schor's essay, "The Politics of Consumption," which appears in Chapter 9, Searching for Causes.

Americans are consuming like there may be no tomorrow. The dominance of consumerism is arguably more pervasive now than at any time in human history. Our most popular national pastime is watching television, followed closely by recreational shopping. The United States has the highest per capita consumption rate in the industrial world. While our material gains have improved the quality of life in some notable ways, there are many hidden costs to our "more is better" definition of the American dream. Juliet Schor is one of the few intellectuals to rigorously examine these costs. Her call for a new politics of consumption warrants serious debate.

Schor does an excellent job of exposing the underbelly of our consumerist culture. Her analytic work, including her recent book *The Overspent American*, focuses primarily on how our work-and-spend lifestyles undermine the quality of our lives. In the chase for more, Americans are working longer hours, racking up more debt, while finding fewer hours to enjoy their material acquisitions. Schor's research also reveals a troubling new trend: our collective tendency to always want much more than we have. In a culture that reveres Bill Gates, the rising stock market, and status goods, people are no longer comparing themselves to the textbook Joneses, but rather to the wealthy celebrities they see on television. For many, this never-ending expansion of wants leads to conspicuous consumption, psychological stress, and a preoccupation with meeting non-material needs materially.

In her essay, Schor points to the other hidden costs of excessive consumerism. Perhaps most troubling, though—and something Schor might have addressed in greater detail—is the environmental damage wreaked by American consumption. With less than 5 percent of the world's population, the United States consumes nearly 30 percent of global resources. Since 1940, Americans alone have used up as large a share of the Earth's mineral resources as all previous humans put together. We use twice as much energy and generate more than twice as much garbage as the average European. The typical American discards nearly a ton of trash per year. We consume 40 percent of the world's gasoline and own 32 percent of the world's cars. The average new house built in the United States has doubled in size since 1970. Two-thirds of those homes have two-car garages. To offer some perspective, scientists recently issued a study for the Earth Council indicating that if everyone on Earth consumed as the average North American does, we would need four extra planets to supply the resources and absorb the waste.

What does this mean for the environment? Every product comes from the earth and returns to it. To produce our cars, houses, hamburgers, televisions, sneakers, newspapers, and thousands upon thousands of other consumer items, we rely on chains of production that stretch around the globe. The unintended consequences of these chains include global warming, rapid deforestation, the depletion of over 25 percent of the world's fish stocks, and the permanent loss of hundreds of plant and animal species—including the very real possibility of losing all large mammals in the wild within the next 50 years.

5   Along with taking a heavy toll on our quality of life and the planet, consumerism is also placing tremendous pressure on low-income families. The American preoc-

cupation with acquisition afflicts the rich and poor alike. But our collective fixation on keeping up with commercial consumerist norms often wreaks havoc for those in low-income communities and exacerbates the growing gap between the rich and poor. Few would dispute that those living on the economic margins need more material goods. But the culture of consumerism weighs heavily on the 35 million Americans living below the poverty line. The relentless marketing of status footwear, high-cost fashion, tobacco, and alcohol to low-income neighborhoods is one of the most pernicious aspects of consumer culture. The politics that Schor describes would challenge a culture that encourages people to define themselves through their stuff and would especially support and empower young Americans who feel enormous pressure to acquire things as the only avenue for gaining love, respect, and a sense of belonging.

Schor describes seven basic elements to a new "politics of consumption." Her elements—or guiding principles for an emerging movement—invite a fusion of those working for justice with those working for environmental sustainability. Her first principle, the right to a decent standard of living, requires affluent environmentalists and progressives to look anew at what structures must be put in place to ensure a level of safety and security for all Americans. If people don't feel safer—about the future and about their kids—they can't entertain the deeper moral and environmental question "How much is enough?" Schor does not specify the components necessary to give people greater security, but the litany of real needs is well known: affordable housing, quality healthcare, living wage jobs, medical care in old age, funds for retirement, and affordable college education for children. People feel alone. It's hard to stop the chase for money, if not stuff, when you feel no support structures. Unless progressives re-embrace these concerns, those in poor and middle class families will have difficulty connecting with Schor's politics. Too many progressives have become seduced by the culture of desire: We, too, look up instead of down. We spend too much time in isolation from those living in poverty. With some exceptions, we have lost our edge. Perhaps we are just too comfortable. Perhaps this is unavoidable in a noisy culture that bombards us with 3,000 commercial messages a day.

Schor's other principles ring true. Millions of Americans obviously share her call for more fun, less stuff. Millions are opting to downshift, choosing to make less money in search of more time. A growing number of people also affirm her call for responsible consumption—a call for a much higher consciousness about the environmental and human costs of each consumer decision we make. Her call to democratize consumer markets seems a bit naïve, since humans have probably always sought to define themselves in part through their stuff. But in an age of excessive materialism, the times may be ripe to challenge the dominant ethos. Perhaps we can make it cool to shun fashion and footgear with corporate logos and redefine hip as simple, real, and non-commercial.

Her fifth principle taps into growing opposition to globalization and a dismaying recognition that Bangkok and New York look the same. After two decades of mega-mergers and five years of intense globalization, the homogenization of retail environments is destroying local businesses and cultures. A recommitment to local economies, independent small businesses, and consumer products that are locally designed and produced could be good for jobs, the environment, and cultural diversity.

The only principle that seems missing to me is one that goes to the heart of our values. Progressives tend to squirm when encouraged to examine values at a personal level. We want to change the system yet we remain uncomfortable with "soft" discussions of individual transformation. But there is a huge churning underway about values, purpose, and spirit. Progressives can dogmatically dismiss these forces as elements of religious dogmatism or New Age narcissism, or they can connect with this churning. I would argue that a politics of consumption—and we need a better name for this—should include guiding principles of humility and compassion. Humility and awe in surrendering to the "not knowing" about the cosmology of things, coupled with an affirmation of all those who hunger to experience the Light, however one defines that. We need a politics that embraces compassion for the Earth, for each other as individuals of equal human value, and especially for children who will inherit the future. Can we not come together with new energy, passion, and vision—combining forces for justice and sustainability with the hunger for rekindled spirits? Does a critique of consumer culture open up this discussion in new and encouraging ways? Schor argues that it does. I am persuaded that she is on to something.

Writing Strategies

1. Describe the nature of Taylor's response. Would you say she disagrees completely, agrees completely, disagrees on a few minor points, or something else? What is her primary reason for responding to Schor?

2. Describe the tone of Taylor's essay. Is it hostile, friendly, patient, praising, distant, cold? Provide examples to support your claim.

3. What kind of evidence does Taylor provide to support her argument? Does she use statistics, personal experience, written sources, hypotheticals, or other kinds?

4. In Schor's response to Taylor, she says,

   I appreciate Taylor's pointing out that I gave short shrift to the environmental effects of consumption, and that those must play a central role in any political discourse of consumption. Coming to terms with our current destruction of the planetary ecology will be an important part of coming to a new set of values.

   Has Taylor, in your opinion, communicated her main idea successfully, and has Schor understood it? In two sentences, summarize Taylor's conclusion, and compare your summary to that of several classmates.

Exploring Ideas

1. Taylor says that "while our material gains have improved the quality of life in some notable ways, there are many hidden costs to our 'more is better' definition of the American dream" (¶ 1). Generate a list of as many "hidden costs" as you can, and then explain what you think is the most dangerous one.

2. According to Taylor, "Few would dispute that those living on the economic margins need more material goods" (¶ 5). Interview others and observe your community to define what you and others mean by "economic margins." How is your understanding of "economic margins" similar to or different from others' understanding of the term?

3. Explore the "chase for money" that Taylor refers to. Is it, as Taylor says, "hard to stop the chase for money, if not stuff, when you feel no support structures"(¶ 6)? What makes it so hard? In what ways is this chase harmful? How is it beneficial?

4. Taylor says that we need a better name than the "politics of consumption." In groups or alone, come up with a better name. Then present to the class your new name and your reasons for why it is a better one.

Ideas for Writing

1. Contribute some important point to an argument you agree with. (Make a "Yes, and" or "Yes, but" argument.)

2. Respond by elaborating on an argument's strengths.

If responding to one of these ideas, go to the **Analysis** section of this chapter to begin developing ideas for your essay.

Is Hunting Ethical?

Ann F. Causey

We can become entrenched in our own way of thinking, and argument can be antagonistic: two sides battling to the death. Or an argument can be an open exploration, as we challenge our own way of thinking and try to accept an idea before rejecting it. "Is Hunting Ethical?" illustrates how a writer can step back and analyze an argument or debate, acknowledge the value of more than one way of thinking, and create a path for better understanding.

The struggling fawn suddenly went limp in my arms. Panicked, I told my husband to pull the feeding tube out of her stomach. Though Sandy had quit breathing and her death was clearly imminent, I held her head down and slapped her back in an attempt to clear her trachea. Warm, soured milk ran from her mouth and nose, soaking my clothes and gagging us with its vile smell. I turned Sandy over in my arms, and my husband placed his mouth over her muzzle. While he blew air into her lungs, I squeezed her chest as a CPR course had taught me to do for human infants in cardiac arrest.

After a minute or so I felt her chest for a pulse. Nothing at first, then four weak beats in rapid succession. "She's alive! Keep breathing for her."

My husband gagged, then spit to avoid swallowing more of the soured milk, and continued his efforts to revive Sandy. I kept working her chest, hoping that through some miracle of will she would recover. Come on, Sandy, wake up. Please wake up!

Sandy never woke up. My husband, a wildlife biologist, and I had nursed over two dozen white-tailed deer fawns that summer for use in a deer nutrition and growth study he was conducting. Most of the animals were in poor shape when we got them. People around the state found them—some actually orphaned, others mistakenly thought to be abandoned. After a few days of round-the-clock feedings, the fun gave way to drudgery and frustration. That's when they would call their county conservation officer, who in turn called us.

5   All the animals we raised required and got from us loving care, attention, and patience, no matter how sick or recalcitrant they may have been. All were named, and we came to know each one as an individual with unique personality traits and behavior patterns. Though most lived to become healthy adults, each fatality was a tragic loss for us, and we mourned each and every death.

The afternoon Sandy died, however, was not convenient for mourning. We were going to a group dinner that evening and had to prepare a dish. Through tears I made a marinade for the roast. While the meat smoked over charcoal and hickory, we brooded over Sandy's death.

When the roast was done, we wiped away our tears, cleaned up, and went to the dinner. Our moods brightened as our roast was quickly gobbled up, and the evening's high point came when several guests declared that our roast was the best venison they'd ever eaten. The best deer meat. Part of an animal my husband, an avid hunter, had willfully killed and I had gratefully butchered, wrapped, and frozen—a deer that once was a cute and innocent little fawn . . . just like Sandy.

If any one word characterizes most people's feelings when they reflect on the morality of killing an animal for sport, it is "ambivalence." With antihunters insisting that hunting is a demonstration of extreme irreverence for nonhuman life, thoughtful hunters must concede, albeit uncomfortably, the apparent contradiction of killing for sport while maintaining a reverence for life. Yet I know of few hunters who do not claim to have a deep reverence for nature and life, including especially the lives of the animals they seek to kill. It seems that this contradiction, inherent in hunting and increasingly the focus of debate, lies at the core of the moral conundrum of hunting. How can anyone both revere life and seek to extinguish it in pursuit of recreation? The opponents of hunting believe they have backed its proponents into a logical corner on this point, yet the proponents have far from given up the battle for logical supremacy. Is either side a clear winner?

None who know me or my lifestyle would label me "antihunting." Most of the meat in my diet is game. And many is the time I've defended hunting from the attacks of those who see all hunters as bloodthirsty, knuckle-dragging rednecks.

10   Yet I have on occasion found myself allied with antihunters. But it's an uneasy and selective alliance, my antihunting sentiments limited to diatribes against such blatantly unethical behavior as Big Buck contests, canned Coon Hunt for Christ rallies, and bumper stickers proclaiming "Happiness Is a Warm Gutpile."

There is also a subtler reason for my concerns about hunting, stemming, I believe, from my disappointment with the responses of many hunters and wildlife managers to questions concerning the morality of hunting. In the interest of enlivening and, I hope, elevating the growing debate, it is these moral questions, and their answers, I wish to address here.

To begin, I should point out some errors, common to ethical reasoning and to the current debate, that we should do our best to avoid. The first is confusing prudence with morality. Prudence is acting with one's overall best interests in mind, while morality sometimes requires that one sacrifice self-interest in the service of a greater good.

While thorough knowledge is all that's required to make prudent decisions, the making of a moral decision involves something more: conscience. Obligations have no moral meaning without conscience. Ethical hunters do not mindlessly follow rules and lobby for regulations that serve their interests; rather, they follow their consciences, sometimes setting their own interests aside. In short, ethics are guided by conscience.

Another important distinction is between legality and morality. While many immoral activities are prohibited by law, not all behavior that is within the law can be considered ethical. The politician caught in a conflict of interest who claims moral innocence because he has broken no laws rarely convinces us. Nor should hunters assume that whatever the game laws allow or

tradition supports is morally acceptable. The ethical hunter is obligated to evaluate laws and traditions in light of his or her own moral sense. Conscience is not created by decree or consensus, nor is morality determined by legality or tradition.

15   Finally, it's all too tempting to dismiss the concerns of our opponents by questioning their motives and credentials instead of giving serious consideration to the questions they raise. Hunters do hunting no favors by hurling taunts and slander at their opponents. The questions raised about hunting deserve a fair hearing on their own merits. Consideration of antihunting messages must not be biased by personal opinions of the messengers, nor should hunters' efforts remain focused on discrediting their accusers. Rather, ethical hunters must undertake the uncomfortable and sometimes painful processes of moral deliberation and personal and collective soul-searching that these questions call for.

The first difficulty we encounter in addressing the morality of hunting is identifying and understanding the relevant questions and answers. To me, the most striking feature of the current debate is the two sides' vastly different understanding of the meaning of the question, Is hunting a morally acceptable activity?

Those who support hunting usually respond by citing data. They enumerate the acres of habitat protected by hunting-generated funds; how many game species have experienced population increases due to modern game management; how much the economy is stimulated by hunting-related expenditures; how effectively modern game laws satisfy the consumptive and recreational interests of the hunting community today while assuring continued surpluses of game for future hunters; and how hunters, more than most citizens, care deeply about ecosystem integrity and balance and the global environment.

While these statements may be perfectly true, they're almost totally irrelevant to the question. Antihunters are not asking whether hunting is an effective management tool, whether it's economically advisable, or whether hunters love and appreciate nature. Rather, they're asking, Is it ethical to kill animals for sport? Are any forms of hunting morally right?

The hunter says yes; the antihunter says no, yet they are answering entirely different questions. The hunter answers, with data, what he or she perceives as a question about utility and prudence; the antihunter, though, has intended to ask a question about morality, about human responsibilities and values. It's as if one asked what day it is and the other responded by giving the time. While the answer may be correct, it's meaningless in the context of the question asked.

20 The point is that moral debates, including this one, are not about facts but about values. Moral controversy cannot be resolved by examination of data or by appeal to scientific studies.

An obsession with "sound, objective science" in addressing their opponents has led many hunters not only to avoid the crucial issues but to actually fuel the fires of the antihunting movement. Animal welfare proponents and the general public are primarily concerned about the pain, suffering, and loss of life inflicted on hunted animals, and the motives and attitudes of those who hunt. They're offended by references to wild animals as "resources." They're angered by the sterile language and, by implication, the emotionally sterile attitudes of those who speak of "culling," "controlling," "harvesting," and "managing" animals for "maximum sustained yield." And they're outraged by those who cite habitat protection and human satisfaction data while totally disregarding the interests of the sentient beings who occupy that habitat and who, primarily through their deaths, serve to satisfy human interests.

Antihunters insist that nontrivial reasons be given for intentional human-inflicted injuries and deaths—or that these injuries and deaths be stopped. An eminently reasonable request.

Even when hunters acknowledge the significance of the pain and suffering inflicted through hunting, they too often offer in defense that they feel an obligation to give back more than they take, and that hunters and wildlife professionals successfully have met this obligation. Granted, it may be that the overall benefits

to humans and other species that accrue from hunting outweigh the costs to the hunted. Nevertheless, this utilitarian calculation fails to provide moral justification for hunting. Is it just, hunting's detractors ask, that wild animals should die to feed us? To clothe us? To decorate our bodies and den walls? To provide us with entertainment and sport?

These are the questions hunters are being asked. *These* are the questions they must carefully consider and thoughtfully address. It will not suffice to charge their opponents with biological naïveté, as theirs are not questions of science. Nor will charges of emotionalism quiet their accusers, since emotion plays an integral and valid part in value judgments and moral development. Both sides have members who are guided by their hearts, their minds, or both. Neither side has a monopoly on hypocrisy, zealotry, narrow-mindedness, or irrationalism. Opposition to hunting is based in largest part on legitimate philosophical differences.

25 It has been said that hunting is the most uncivilized and primitive activity in which a modern person can legally engage. Therein lies ammunition for the biggest guns in the antihunters' arsenal; paradoxically, therein also lies its appeal to hunters and the source of its approval by many sympathetic nonhunters.

Hunting is one of few activities that allows an individual to participate directly in the life and death cycles on which all natural systems depend. The skilled hunter's ecological knowledge is holistic and realistic; his or her awareness involves all the senses. Whereas ecologists study systems from without, examining and analyzing from a perspective necessarily distanced from their subjects, dedicated hunters live and learn from within, knowing parts of nature as only a parent or child can know his or her own family. One thing necessary for a truly ethical relationship with wildlife is an appreciation of ecosystems, of natural processes. Such an appreciation may best be gained through familiarity, through investment of time and effort, through curiosity, and through an attitude of humility and respect. These are the lessons that hunting teaches its best students.

Not only have ethical hunters resisted the creeping alienation between humans and the natural out-of-doors, they have fought to resist the growing alienation between humans and the "nature" each person carries within. Hunters celebrate their evolutionary heritage and stubbornly refuse to be stripped of their atavistic urges—they refuse to be sterilized by modern culture and thus finally separated from nature. The ethical hunter transcends the mundane, the ordinary, the predictable, the structured, the artificial. As Aldo Leopold argues in his seminal work *A Sand County Almanac,* hunting in most forms maintains a valuable element in the cultural heritage of all peoples.

Notice, though, that Leopold does not give a blanket stamp of moral approval to hunting; nor should we. In fact, Leopold recognized that some forms of hunting may be morally depleting. If we offer an ecological and evolutionary defense for hunting, as Leopold did and as many of hunting's supporters do today, we must still ask ourselves, For which forms of hunting is our defense valid?

The open-minded hunter should carefully consider the following questions: To what extent is shooting an animal over bait or out of a tree at close range after it was chased up there by a dog a morally enriching act? Can shooting an actually or functionally captive animal enhance one's understanding of natural processes? Does a safari to foreign lands to step out of a Land Rover and shoot exotic animals located for you by a guide honor your cultural heritage? Does killing an animal you profess to honor and respect, primarily in order to obtain a trophy, demonstrate reverence for the animal as a sentient creature? Is it morally enriching to use animals as mere objects, as game pieces in macho contests where the only goal is to out-compete other hunters? Is an animal properly honored in death by being reduced to points, inches, and pounds, or to a decoration on a wall? Which forms of hunting can consistently and coherently be defended as nontrivial, meaningful, ecologically sound, and morally enriching?

30 Likewise, we who hunt or support hunting must ask ourselves: Does ignoring, downplaying, and in some cases denying the wounding rate in hunting, rather than taking all available effective measures to lower it, demonstrate reverence for life? Does lobbying for continued hunting of species whose populations are threatened or of uncertain status exemplify ecological awareness and concern? Is the continued hunting of some declining waterfowl populations, the aerial killing of wolves in Alaska, or the setting of hunting seasons that in some areas may sentence to slow death the orphaned offspring of their legally killed lactating mothers, consistent with management by hunters—or do these things verify the antihunters' charges of management primarily *for* hunters?

These questions and others have aroused hunters' fears, indignation, defensive responses, and collective denial. Yet no proponent of ethical hunting has anything to fear from such questions. These are questions we should have been asking ourselves, and defensibly answering, all along. The real threat comes not from outside criticism but from our own complacency and uncritical acceptance of hunting's status quo, and from our mistaken belief that to protect *any* form of hunting, we must defend and protect *all* forms. In fact, to protect the privilege of morally responsible hunting, we must attack and abolish the unacceptable acts, policies, and attitudes within our ranks that threaten all hunting, as a gangrenous limb threatens the entire body.

The battle cry "Reverence for Life" has been used by both sides, at times with disturbing irony. Cleveland Amory, founder of the Fund for Animals, described in the June 1992 issue of *Sierra* magazine the perfect world he would create if he were appointed its ruler: "All animals will not only be not shot, they will be protected—not only from people but as much as possible from each other. Prey will be separated from predator, and there will be no overpopulation or starvation because all will be controlled by sterilization or implant."

A reverence for life? Only if you accept the atomistic and utterly unecological concept of life as a characteristic of individuals rather than systems.

But neither can all who hunt legitimately claim to hold a reverence for life. In a hunting video titled "Down to Earth," a contemporary rock star and self-proclaimed "whack master" and "gutpile addict" exhorts his protégés to "whack 'em, stack 'em, and pack 'em." After showing a rapid sequence of various animals being hit by his arrows, the "master whacker" kneels and sarcastically asks for "a moment of silence" while the viewer is treated to close-up, slow-motion replays of the hits, including sickening footage of some animals that clearly are gut shot or otherwise sloppily wounded. A reverence for life? Such behavior would seem to demonstrate shocking *irreverence,* arrogance, and hubris. As hunters, we toe a fine line between profundity and profanity and must accept the responsibility of condemning those practices and attitudes that trivialize, shame, and desecrate all hunting. To inflict death without meaningful and significant purpose, to kill carelessly or casually, or to take a life without solemn gratitude is inconsistent with genuine reverence for life.

35   To be ethical, we must do two things: We must *act* ethically, and we must *think* ethically. The hunting community has responded to its critics by trying to clean up its visible act: We don't hear many public proclamations of gutpile addictions anymore; we less frequently see dead animals used as hood ornaments while the meat, not to be utilized anyway, rapidly spoils; those who wound more animals than they kill are less likely nowadays to brag about it; and, since studies show that the public opposes sport hunting as trivial, hunters are coached to avoid the term "sport" when they address the public or their critics.

What's needed, though, for truly ethical hunting to flourish is not just a change of appearance or vocabulary but a change of mindset, a deepening of values. Hunters may be able to "beat" antihunters through a change of tactics, but to win the wrong war is no victory at all. Some morally repugnant forms of hunting are *rightfully* under attack, and we can defend them only by sacrificing our intellectual and moral integrity. We should do all we can to avoid such "victories." Hunters must reexamine and, when appropriate, give up some of what they now hold dear—not just because doing so is expedient but because it's *right.* As T. S. Eliot, quoted by Martin Luther King, Jr., in his "Letter from Birmingham Jail," reminds us, "The last temptation is the greatest treason: To do the right deed for the wrong reason."

Can anyone give us a final answer to the question, Is hunting ethical?

No.

For one thing, the question and its answer depend heavily on how one defines "hunting." There are innumerable activities that go by this term, yet many are so different from one another that they scarcely qualify for the same appellation. Moreover, there is no one factor that motivates one hunter on each hunt; nor is there such a thing as the hunter's mind-set.

40   Second, and even more important, is the recognition that in most cases one cannot answer moral questions for others. Two morally mature people may ponder the same ethical dilemma and come to opposite, and equally valid, conclusions. The concept of ethical hunting is pluralistic, as hard to pin down as the definition of a virtuous person. Unlike our opponents, we who are hunting proponents do not seek to impose a particular lifestyle, morality, or spirituality on all citizens; we merely wish to preserve a variety of options and individualities in all our choices concerning responsible human recreation, engagement with nature, and our place in the food web. It's doubtful that any one system, whether it be "boutique" hunting, vegetarianism, or modern factory farming, is an adequate way to meet the ethical challenges of food procurement and human/nonhuman relationships in our diverse culture and burgeoning population.

Like education of any sort, moral learning cannot be passively acquired. In fact, the importance of answering the question of whether hunting is ethical is often exaggerated, for the value of ethics lies not so much in the product, the answers, as in the process of deep and serious deliberation of moral issues. To ponder the value of an animal's life versus a hunter's material and spiritual needs and to consider an animal's pain, suffering, and dignity in death is to acknowledge deeper values and to demonstrate more moral maturity than one who casually, defensively dismisses such ideas.

No matter the result, the process of moral deliberation is necessarily enriching. Neither side can offer one answer for all; we can only answer this question each for ourself, and even then we must be prepared to offer valid, consistent moral arguments in support of our conclusions. This calls for a level of soul-searching and critical thinking largely lacking on both sides of the current debate.

Today's ethical hunter must abandon the concept of hunting as fact and replace it with the more appropriate concept of hunting as challenge—the challenge of identifying and promoting those attitudes toward wildlife that exemplify the values on which morally responsible hunting behavior is based. Heel-digging and saber-rattling must give way to cooperation, to increased awareness and sensitivity, to reason and critical analysis, and to honest self-evaluation and assessment.

The Chinese have a wonderful term, *wei chi,* that combines two concepts: crisis . . . and opportunity. The term conveys the belief that every crisis presents an opportunity. I submit that the hunting community today faces its greatest crisis ever and, therein, its greatest opportunity—the opportunity for change, for moral growth, for progress.

Writing Strategies

1. Do you consider Causey's opening narrative (¶ 1–7) to be effective? Explain how her opening is or is not a strength of her essay.

2. How does Causey make the purpose of her essay clear to the reader?

3. Examine Causey's essay for coherence. Provide several examples of how she connects ideas for the reader. What different strategies does she employ?

4. What writing decisions does Causey make to avoid alienating hunters? What decisions does she make to avoid alienating nonhunters?

5. What, if anything, about Causey's essay alienated you as a reader? Why?

Exploring Ideas

1. What is Causey trying to accomplish with this essay?

2. What points do you find most interesting, and why? Which of Causey's ideas make you think differently?

3. Interview various people to find out their views on hunting. Record their responses, and then write several paragraphs explaining how others' views are similar to or different from Causey's.

4. What issues, in addition to hunting, can Causey's ethical approach be applied to? That is, what issue do others discuss in terms of data or legality when you feel the issue should be ethics?

Ideas for Writing

1. What point that Causey makes can you respond to? What point might you expand on or refute?

2. How can hunting be made more ethical?

If responding to one of these ideas, go to the **Analysis** section of this chapter to begin developing ideas for your essay.

Outside Reading

Every academic discipline (such as sociology, chemistry, history, and so on) rests on, and puts forth, arguments. Even disciplines that seem objective (beyond opinion) are highly argumentative. Claims that seem uncontested are often debated, so that disciplines are always changing and evolving. Notice the following statements taken from various books used in college classes. What arguable claims are offered?

> Indeed, it is an important fact that we can think about combinations of pictures and words, abstract ideas and concrete ones, and so forth. Therefore, there must be somewhere in the mind that all these contents can be brought together "under one roof"; how else could we think about these combinations?
>
> *Cognition: Exploring the Science of the Mind*

> Constituted as they are of people with their inbuilt frailties, institutions are built of vices as well as virtues. When the vices—in-group versus out-group loyalties, for example—get compounded by numbers, the results can be horrifying to the point of suggesting (as some wag has) that the biggest mistake religion ever made was to get mixed up with people.
>
> *The World's Religions*

> Only one fear was greater than the fear of black rebellion in the new American colonies. That was the fear that discontented whites would join black slaves to overthrow the existing order. In the early years of slavery, especially, before racism as a way of thinking was firmly ingrained, while white indentured servants were often treated as badly as black slaves, there was a possibility of cooperation.
>
> *A People's History of the United States*

> An anxiety disorder, as the term suggests, has an unrealistic, irrational fear or anxiety of disabling intensity at its core and also as its principal and most obvious manifestation.
>
> *Abnormal Psychology and Modern Life*

Find an argument in another textbook, and use the following questions to analyze the claims:

1. How is the passage you found an argument?

2. What evidence or reasoning does the passage offer?

3. Does the passage make any attempt to convince the reader that the argument is sound (or is it assumed that the reader will accept the claims)?

4. What view of people or behavior or physical reality does it take?

5. Who might challenge the view put forward by the book? Why?

6. Does the passage use a metaphor to illustrate a concept? (How is the metaphor an argument?)

INVENTION

Responding to an argument involves some sophisticated thinking and planning. In a sense, this project is an argument^2, an argument to the second power. You are not only taking on another argument (with its own layers and nuances) but you are also developing a layered argument of your own. The following sections are designed to help you through the invention process: specifically, to find an argument (in **Point of Contact**), to discover the mechanics of that argument (in **Analysis**), to understand how the points relate to a community of readers (in **Public Resonance**), to invent a focused stance of your own (in **Thesis**), and to develop your own support (in **Rhetorical Tools**).

POINT OF CONTACT

In this chapter, the point of contact is an actual argument. You will be responding to an explicit argument that someone else has formulated or to an argument that is expressed by many people. Remember that an argument need not be an essay; arguments are also made by advertisements, posters, and billboards. To find an argument that may relate directly to the goings-on of your life and community, examine the following options:

- **Local/City/Campus Newspapers:** Search the editorial pages and letters to the editor for arguments.

- **National Newspapers:** Publications such as the *New York Times, USA Today,* and *The Wall Street Journal* have editorial pages and columnists who offer arguments on various political and social issues.

- **Magazines:** Popular weeklies (such as *Newsweek, The Nation, Time, US News and World Report*) and monthly or quarterly magazines (such as *Utne Reader* or *The New Republic*) are filled with argumentative articles and personal columns on social and political issues.

- **A Publication from Your Major** (such as *Education Journal, Nursing, Applied Science and Engineering*): Examine not only main articles, but also reviews and personal columns.

- **Disciplinary Databases** (databases that focus on specific disciplines): Go to your library and check the electronic databases for your major or a closely related one.

- **Websites:** Go to your favorite search engine (such as Yahoo.com, Dogpile.com, or Google.com) and enter topical keywords (*dogs, skateboards, economy,* etc.). You might find argumentative sites or pages more quickly if you combine potential topics with words such as *law, policy, argument, crisis,* or *debate.*

Search the Web:	dogs and law and debate	Search

You can also explore websites devoted to college, community, cultural, or political issues. For links, go to this textbook's website: http://english.wadsworth.com/maukmetz_2.

Choose an argument that interests you and that you can address with some authority. Once you have found a potentially interesting argument, answer the following question:

- Why does the argument interest me?
  —Because something or someone has been omitted?
  —Because something or someone has been misrepresented?
  —Because I disagree or agree with it?
  —Because it raises an important issue that should be further discussed?
  —Because it changed my mind on a topic?
  —Because it is potentially important (helpful or dangerous)?

Remember that you need not strongly disagree or agree with a particular argument. A powerful response often comes from a slight agreement or disagreement.

For a detailed explanation of support strategies, see page 283 in Chapter 6.

ANALYSIS

When responding to an argument, you are not simply agreeing or disagreeing. You are evaluating claims and analyzing an issue—one that has already been defined by someone else. It is not enough to simply say, "I don't agree with this argument." Instead, you must discover *why* you agree or disagree with *particular points* in an argument. But even beyond your personal agreement or disagreement, you will also need to analyze the argument in front of you—and to do this, you will need some particular analytical tools.

The First Layer: The Four Elements of Argument

Thesis Before we can respond to an argument, we must know *exactly* what is being argued. That is, we must figure out the thesis, the particular stance the writer takes on the topic. Finding the thesis for a written argument can be trickier than it seems. While some essays have explicit theses (stated directly), others are implied (not stated, but suggested by the supporting points). Most often, in sophisticated academic essays, the thesis does not come at the end of the first paragraph. Instead, it comes along later, after the debate has been explained—and even after other perspectives have been addressed. (Notice, for instance, Juliet Schor's essay on page 410. The thesis comes along eighteen paragraphs into the argument.) Once we locate the thesis (or understand it based on the details of the argument), we can then see how it is supported.

Explicit: stated directly in the text

Implied: not stated, but suggested by supporting points

Support Initially, the thesis might seem outlandish, but good support strategies will invite readers to accept even the most extreme thesis statements. Remember that support comes in a variety of forms:

Statistics	Scenarios
Authorities	Appeal to Logic
Facts	Appeal to Emotion
Examples	Appeal of Character
Allusions	Appeal to Need
Personal Testimonies/Anecdotes	Appeal to Value

Depending on the medium of the argument (essay, poster, etc.), the support may be varied. Or the writer may depend on a single key support strategy. Remember that all these support strategies can help create a powerful argument. (Don't be fooled into believing that statistics are the only certain support strategy.) The key question, however, lies in their connection to the thesis. We might ask: *How well does the support strategy connect to the thesis?* Or, *Given this argument, how appropriate is the support strategy?*

Counterargument Sophisticated arguments counterargue. That is, they anticipate and refute opposing claims. In fact, the success of an argument may depend on its counterarguments—on the ability of the writer to fend off opposing claims. Remember a key counterargument strategy, the turnabout paragraph, in which a writer explains an opposing perspective and then responds directly.

Concession Concessions acknowledge the value of opposing claims. Writers who concede acknowledge that others' positions may offer some insight outside of the writers' own claims. When writers concede points, their arguments do not lose force; instead, they appear more fair-minded. A writer who concedes shows that he or she has considered a range of other ideas.

Now, examine the argument to which you are responding. To fully understand the first layer of the argument,
answer the following questions:

- What is the main claim/thesis?
- What are the means of support for the main claim?
- Do the support strategies sufficiently prove the
  thesis?
- How does argument address opposing claims? Are
  those claims sufficiently refuted?
- Does the argument concede to outside positions?
  What is the effect of those concessions?
- Does the writer define the issue correctly?

INVENTION WRITING

Here, Daniel Bruno responds to one of these Invention
questions. He uses the question as a springboard to discover
a specific shortcoming in Sacks's book:

Does the writer define the issue correctly?

Sacks defines the issue correctly as far as he defines it.
Entitlement education has the negative effect that he says
it does, but he fails, it seems, to discuss or focus on an
important aspect of the issue, which is that some students,
who don't have an entitlement mentality, learn a great deal
in school while others, who do, don't learn a great deal, or
very much at all. The students who have the entitlement
mentality slide by while their classmates are learning more
and more. The gap between the two groups widens. So,
what does this mean to those students who feel entitled to
good grades because they showed up (high school) or paid
the tuition (college)? They get grades, but did they learn
anything? Did they get an education?

The Second Layer:
Warranting Assumptions

Beneath the first, most visible, layer of an argument lurk
warranting assumptions: the beliefs that connect points in
an argument. Warranting assumptions are the root system of
an argument; although they most often go unstated, they are
as important as the most directly worded points. And when
we dig up warranting assumptions and investigate them
closely, we can decide for ourselves if they are reasonable.

We need intellectual tools for digging up assumptions.
Philosopher Stephen Toulmin has developed a powerful analytical system for this job. In his perspective, every argument
has a structure with interrelated parts. Using this, we can see
how those parts relate, and how well they function. Here are
the three basic elements:

Claim: The main argumentative position (or thesis)
being put forward.

Grounds: The support for the position (evidence,
examples, illustrations, etc.).

Warranting Assumption: The idea, often unstated,
that connects the claim and the grounds—or that justifies the use of the grounds for the claim.

**Three Basic Elements
of Argumentative Statements**

Claim

↑

Warranting Assumption

↓

Grounds

IDENTIFYING WARRANTING ASSUMPTIONS

The warranting assumption lies (often hidden) between the claim and the grounds. See how the elements work in the following example:

Claim:	Sport utility vehicles (SUVs) are dangerous.
Grounds:	Many different models roll over easily.
Warranting Assumption:	Vehicles that roll over easily are dangerous.

The assumption lies between the claim and the grounds, connecting them logically.

In this example, the rollover frequency of SUVs supports the claim that they are dangerous. The warranting assumption (vehicles that roll over easily are dangerous) lies between the claim and the grounds. The assumption is entirely acceptable; few people would challenge it. But consider a different argument:

Claim:	Sport utility vehicles are valuable to the average American driver.
Grounds:	The extra-large carrying capacity and four-wheel drive capability meet traveling needs.
Warranting Assumption:	Extra-large carrying capacity and four-wheel drive are valuable for the average American driver's traveling needs.

The assumption here is less acceptable. Someone might argue against this warranting assumption on the grounds that the average American driver does not need extra-large carrying capacity and four-wheel drive, and that these aspects are actually unnecessary for most drivers. Stating the assumption thus reveals a particular weakness in the argument and provides an opportunity to respond.

RESPONDING TO GROUNDS AND/OR ASSUMPTIONS

Dissecting arguments in this fashion allows for various critical opportunities. Writers can focus attention on (take exception or agree with) two different layers of an argument: grounds and/or assumptions. Consider, for example, the first claim: *Sport utility vehicles are dangerous.* Although the assumption *vehicles that roll over easily are dangerous* is acceptable, the grounds for the claim *many models roll over easily* can be challenged. Someone might agree with the assumption but cite statistics showing that only a few models are prone to rollover accidents.

Claim:	Sport utility vehicles are dangerous.	
Grounds:	Many different models roll over easily.	(Questionable)
Warranting Assumption:	Vehicles that roll over easily are dangerous.	(Acceptable)

Responding with such statistics could help a writer challenge the original argument. In this case, the responding writer would be challenging the grounds. For other arguments, both the grounds and assumption might be arguable:

Claim:	The environment is not in danger from human influence.	
Grounds:	The environment is supporting the Earth's population today.	(Questionable)
Warranting Assumption:	The present human population directly illustrates the health of the environment.	(Questionable)

Here, both the grounds and the warranting assumption are questionable. While the grounds could be refuted on their own terms (by illustrating the vast numbers of people starving throughout the world), the more interesting response might point to the warranting assumption. The mere presence of people, of course, does not indicate the health of the environment. Someone, for instance, might point to dramatic increases in skin and other cancers to illustrate the effects of greenhouse gases and environmental contamination. In this case, discovering the warranting assumption would allow a responding writer to point out a flaw in the logic.

ACTIVITY

In groups, decide on the warranting assumption for the following claims and explain why each assumption is acceptable or questionable.

Claim: Consumerism is out of control in American life.

Grounds: Many people are going into debt to pay for luxury items.

Claim: America is losing a sense of community and social connectedness.

Grounds: The number of bowling teams has steadily decreased in the past 20 years.

Claim: People rely too much on technology that puts us out of touch with our neighbors and our own bodies.

Grounds: Leaf blowers are increasingly popular.

Now go to the argument you have chosen to examine, and answer the following questions. They will help you to develop a response.

- What is the warranting assumption?
- Is the assumption acceptable or arguable?
- Can I prove that the assumption is incorrect?
- What else does the author of the argument assume (about life, identity, society, people's behavior, time, politics, human nature, etc.)?

Writers can focus on (take exception or agree with) two different layers of an argument: grounds and/or assumptions.

PUBLIC RESONANCE

Public resonance refers to the way in which a topic (or argument) relates to a community. In most cases, any published argument that you find will already have public resonance, especially if it comes from a newspaper, magazine, or journal. Your job, however, is not complete. As a responding writer, you can draw attention to the effects of the original argument on its readers and on the community at large.

To develop public resonance, examine the argument to which you will respond, and answer the following questions:

- Has the argument had an impact on readers? Any specific person or people?
- How *could* the argument affect people (negatively or positively)?
- What other issues or situations does the argument relate to or address?
- How can I relate the argument to the needs/wants of my audience (or anyone who is involved in the topic)?

INVENTION WORKSHOP

In a small group of writers, use one of the Invention questions to start a discussion about your topic. First, briefly explain the original argument (the argument to which you are responding) to your group members. Then pose the question. (It may be helpful to write the question on a board or have all group members focus on this page so the question does not get lost in the discussion.)

Diana is responding to Ward Churchill's essay (in Chapter 6, Making Arguments). In a discussion with peers, her argument takes on several layers. Notice how Diana's thinking begins to extend beyond her initial reaction. At first, she is simply offended by Churchill's argument—a gut reaction. But then she starts to consider the public effects of that reaction. This is an important intellectual turn. It is easy to have a gut reaction, but good writers ask questions about the feelings they have. Like Diana, they seek out intellectual turns.

How could the argument affect people (negatively or positively)?

Diana: Churchill's argument made me mad, and I think it may do the same to a lot of people. It basically suggests that everyone who supports certain professional sports teams is somehow tied to genocide.

Jack: I think that's his point, isn't it?

Diana: Yes, and I don't buy it, and I don't think most people would.

Jack: Does that mean that most people are right, or that most people don't see their own racism? Like Churchill says, during World War II most Americans were okay with the racist stereotypes of Japanese people. So, does that make such stereotyping okay?

Diana: Of course not. But making such an extreme point as Churchill seems counterproductive. When he comes out and says that wearing a Cleveland Indians baseball hat is like committing genocide, I think he's setting himself up for a certain amount of disagreement.

Marcus: But is he really making the connection that clearly?

Diana: Well, maybe not, but I think most people would see it that way . . . and they wouldn't like it.

Jack: Maybe that's an important point. Churchill's argument is probably more involved than what people want to hear.

Diana: And that's usually the case with arguments about race. But, still, calling mainstream America racist and making a connection between a national pastime and the Holocaust is going too far.

Jack: Why? Are you afraid of offending mainstream Americans who like sports?

Diana: No. I just wonder how valuable it is.

Jack: But isn't that what mainstream America said to the civil rights activists of the '60s? They didn't want activists to be offensive or confrontational, but most people are not going to change their thinking unless they are moved deeply—and sometimes that means they have to be offended.

Diana: So you're saying that mainstream America needs to be pushed before it will accept new ideas? Maybe.

Jack: Yeah, I think that's been shown throughout history. People don't just change their minds and suddenly become more enlightened.

INVENTION WRITING

In this excerpt, Daniel Bruno explores *what* and *how* people might think about the topic of student entitlement. Here, Bruno has narrowed in on a particular issue from the original argument (Peter Sacks's book about college students). It's not merely that students shouldn't feel entitled to high grades. Bruno goes further and discovers the double jeopardy of entitlement: Those who feel entitled are "missing out" on their own educations:

How can I relate the argument to the needs/wants of my audience (or anyone who is involved in the topic)?

Some students feel entitled, which means expecting a good grade automatically, without working or learning anything. Some don't. The wants of the entitlement students are different than their needs. They want a grade or degree but need to learn and work. Interestingly, the students who feel entitled are the ones missing out, while the ones who don't feel entitled benefit. Maybe the students who believe they are entitled would benefit from thinking about the students who think differently, the ones who they will be competing against in the future, the ones who perhaps will be better prepared and have a better work ethic. The entitlement-minded students may find out too late that others are working hard and developing good skills and attitudes.

RESEARCH

What have others said about your topic? If you are responding to a specific text (like an article or a book), go beyond that author's views and seek out other perspectives. Examine your invention writing and seek out keywords. Enter them into a periodical database search. (Remember that periodical databases, such as InfoTrac College Edition, rely on keywords rather than phrases.) Enter main nouns linked together with *and*. If you have no luck, keep changing the nouns; try replacing them with synonyms. For instance, Bruno might enter: *students and college and entitlement*. Then, he might try: *students and college and attitude*. He might replace *attitude* with *achievement, success, study skills, apathy,* or a combination of these.

THESIS

Responding to arguments is complicated because another set of claims must be engaged. But do not let those other claims confuse you. Resist chasing ideas throughout the original argument, and instead focus on a particular issue and then springboard into your own reasoning. Your argument might do one or more of the following:

- Redefine the issue according to your understanding.

    Sacks shows how consumerism has invaded education, leading some students to expect good grades for little effort. But he fails, it seems, to emphasize enough a most harmful effect of this sense of entitlement. (318)

- Argue for the value of a particular point or assumption in the original text.

    In "Technology, Movement, and Sound," Ed Bell argues against our culture's increasing love affair with technology. The real value of his argument is its focus on the relationship between personal technology and public effects.

See Bell's essay on page 470.

- Argue against a particular point or assumption in the original text.

    Simon Benlow insists that students are increasingly more consumerist in their approach to education, but consumption is not inherently passive or anti-educational.

See Benlow's essay on page 151.

- Extend the original argument to include a broader set of ideas.

    A great books education is practical, as David Crabtree argues; however, it is not practical because it makes one "wise," as he suggests. Instead, a great books education develops key intellectual skills that, in turn, help students succeed in various academic and professional pursuits.

See Crabtree's essay on page 255.

- Narrow the argument and suggest an important emphasis.

    As Jayme Stayer argues in "Whales R Us," theme parks such as Sea World are a "reflection of American culture . . . not a promoter of political change." His argument shows us that mainstream American culture may entirely lack a language for political change.

See Stayer's essay on page 366.

As you can see in these statements, it is not enough to say "I disagree" or "I agree." Instead, a project such as this benefits from a more focused point—one that shows something (important, harmful, inaccurate, valuable, etc.) in the original argument.

Use the following questions to help generate the thesis of your argumentative response:

- With what *particular* point do I agree or disagree?
- How are my assumptions different from or similar to those of the writer?
- How is the original argument too narrow or too exclusive?
- What particular point in the original argument might readers fail to see? Why is it so important?
- How can I extend or broaden the original argument?

EVOLUTION OF A THESIS

Diana's thesis (first developed in the Public Resonance section) focuses on how people might respond to Churchill's argument. In the following, notice how her idea evolves from summary, to gut reaction, to analytical insight:

- In "Crimes Against Humanity," Ward Churchill argues that the use of Native American symbols for sports teams is racist.   **Summary**

- Churchill's argument made me mad, and I think it may do the same to a lot of people. It basically suggests that everyone who supports certain professional sports teams is somehow tied to genocide.   **Gut reaction**

- Mainstream America might need to be pushed before it will accept new ideas.   **Analytical insight**

- Churchill's "Crimes Against Humanity" reminds us that mainstream opinions often do not change unless they encounter shocking, even offensive, claims.   **Focused statement**

Diana goes from summary statement to a gut reaction to an analytical statement about that reaction to an insight about mainstream opinions. Throughout this intellectual journey, she discovers something specific about Churchill's argument and its potential effect on readers. Diana also moves from dismissing the argument to revealing a quality in it.

THINKING FURTHER

Writers may decide that their gut reaction to an argument will suffice as a thesis statement. However, while gut reactions get a writer started, they are often too vague. The following statements show what someone might feel directly after reading Paulin's, Crabtree's, or Churchill's arguments (which all appear in Chapter 6). While these initial feelings are valuable, they are only the beginning:

- Ann Marie Paulin's argument is right on target.
- David Crabtree's argument is important for college students to hear.

- In "Crimes Against Humanity," Ward Churchill is just making a mountain out of a molehill.

See Paulin on page 259, Crabtree on 255, and Churchill on page 248.

Now, those initial reactions must be explored. The writers might ask:

- What particular idea or assumption of Paulin's argument is insightful or valuable? Why is it insightful or valuable?
- Why is Crabtree's argument important? What particular aspect is valuable to college students?
- Why might the issue really be a mountain?

In asking such questions, the writers can take their gut reaction to the next level—to more focused ideas:

- Ann Marie Paulin reveals the quiet everyday prejudices against overweight people.
- David Crabtree's argument correctly challenges the common misconception that college courses translate directly into real-world experience.
- Churchill describes a view of American history and sports that most people do not consider.

REVISION

With a group of peers, explore your thesis statements. Each group member should share his or her thesis in turn. Then the group should collectively attempt to narrow it by asking questions like those above. Go after broad adjectives (*valuable, wrong, irresponsible, good, intense,* etc.). Try to prompt the writer to give specific descriptors or explanations.

Also, check out the Common Thesis Problems in Chapter 6 on page 281. The same problems may lurk in this project as well. Make certain to avoid them!

RHETORICAL TOOLS

Even though you are responding to someone else's argument, you still creating your own argument. Consider all the argumentative strategies introduced in Chapter 6.

Using Support

Remember that you have the whole world beyond the original argument to support your points. You can use various forms of evidence (such as personal testimony, examples, and facts, as well as allusions to history, popular culture, and news events) and appeals.

- What particular examples from everyday life show my point?

- Does a historical situation or trend (say, the rise of a particular fashion, organization, or individual) illustrate something about my topic?

- How has popular culture treated my topic? Does it show up in television shows, movies, or commercials? If so, how is it characterized, mishandled, or celebrated?

- How has literature (novels, poetry, drama, short stories) dealt with my topic? Have fictional characters illustrated something important about the topic or some behavior related to it?

- How does nature (animals, life cycles, plants, biological processes, and so on) demonstrate something about my topic?

- How can this topic relate to people's sense of logic? What line of reasoning can I create for the reader to follow?

(See pages 283–285 in Chapter 6, Making Arguments, for more help in developing evidence and appeals for your argument.)

Counterarguing

Good writers try to address specific opposing claims. Notice, for example, that Ann Causey takes on claims individually as she develops her argument:

> Those who support hunting usually respond by citing data. They enumerate the acres of habitat protected by hunting-generated funds; how many game species have experienced population increases due to modern game management; how much the economy is stimulated by hunting-related expenditures; how effectively modern game laws satisfy the consumptive and recreational interests of the hunting community today while assuring continued surpluses of game for future hunters; and how hunters, more than most citizens, care deeply about ecosystem integrity and balance and the global environment.
>
> While these statements may be perfectly true, they're almost totally irrelevant to the question. . . . (330)

As you develop your own argument, examine the particular points of the original argument with which you disagree or find fault.

Consider the following questions for your own argument:

- Apart from the author of the original argument, who might disagree with my position? Why?

- What reasons do people have for disagreeing with me?

- What evidence would support an opposing argument?

See a list and examples of logical fallacies in Chapter 6, page 290.

Conceding and Qualifying Points

When responding to argument, a writer should be especially mindful of giving credit to others' points. For example, in Bruno's response to Peter Sacks's book, he acknowledges several important elements of Sacks's argument:

> His final paragraph, before the Epilogue, says, "Let's create a system that encourages people like Andie at least as much as the ones who don't give a damn" (187). Thus, Sacks shows that today's students are a more diverse group—in skill level, background, and attitude toward education—than has ever before been gathered together in the college classroom. (322)

Answering the following questions will help you to see possible concessions for your own argument:

- Does the original argument make any valid points?
- Does my argument make any large, but necessary, leaps? (Should I acknowledge them?)
- Do I ask my audience to imagine a situation that is fictional? (Should I acknowledge the potential shortcomings of a fictional or hypothetical situation?)
- Do I ask my audience to accept generalizations? (Should I acknowledge those generalizations?)

Remembering Logical Fallacies

Logical fallacies are logical stumbles—gaps or shortcomings in reasoning. Examine the original argument closely to determine if it is free of fallacies. Finding logical fallacies in an argument can help you to generate a response. For example, in the following passage, the writer points to a logical shortcoming in the original argument:

Smith argues that incoming college students cannot handle the intellectual rigors of academia. He characterizes an entire generation as "undisciplined and whimsical." But like all arguments about entire generations, Smith's depends upon a hasty generalization. The truth about today's college students is far more complex than Smith's assertions, and any statement that seeks to characterize them as a whole should be looked upon with suspicion.

INVENTION WORKSHOP

Need some help? Borrow the brains of your peers. In a small group, share thesis statements, and then use the following questions to generate ideas for one another's arguments.

Support

- Can you offer the writer a scenario to support his or her stance?
- What popular cultural, historical, or literary references come to mind as you consider this topic—and the writer's stance?

Counterargument/Concession

- What valid points or perspectives does the original argument offer? (If the writer takes an opposing position, should he or she concede?)
- Why might the writer be wrong (oversimplifying, mischaracterizing, misjudging)?

ORGANIZATIONAL STRATEGIES

Should I Quote the Original Argument?

Quoting is like putting a spotlight on a key passage. Responding writers sometimes want to draw attention not only to a point, but also to the particular way the author delivered it. A quote can flag the shortcoming in the original text:

> In her argument, Ross claims banks "only share customers' personal information with affiliated companies" (43). However, an "affiliated company" in the present economic environment can be any company with which a bank does business. Because most financial institutions are parts of huge conglomerates, they can be justified in "sharing" information with a practically unlimited number of companies seeking to exploit people and invade their personal lives. In other words, Ross's argument only further conceals the exploitive policies of many financial institutions.

Sometimes writers quote the original argument to illustrate the importance or value of a particular point, or to extend an idea. Notice Bruno's quotation of Peter Sacks:

> While motivated students suffer in our too-lax system, so do the un- (or under-) motivated ones. And these students, who need our help the most, are the ones most cheated. As Sacks says, "I now believe the students are the real victims of this systematic failure of the entitlement mindset" (189). The students who are allowed to slide by, who are content to slide by, who perhaps don't even realize that they are sliding by because sliding by is all they know—those students find themselves arriving at college less prepared and less motivated than the "better students." And what happens next? Sadly, the gap between these two groups grows even wider. (322–323)

Here, Bruno builds his argument from Sacks's point. That is, he begins with Sacks's idea, and then goes further to show the greater extent of the problem.

Using quotation can be a powerful strategy in drawing attention to key passages. However, be careful not to quote too often. (Notice how seldom the writers in this chapter use direct quotation.) Rather than quote the original argument (or any outside source), you have two other tools available: summary and paraphrase.

INTEGRATING SUMMARY

A summary is a restated and abbreviated version of the original passage. Writers can abbreviate (shorten) a passage of any length (from a paragraph to an entire chapter). For instance, in the introduction to his essay, Daniel Bruno summarizes Peter Sacks's book in a few sentences. Also notice how Betsy Taylor briefly summarizes Schor's essay (see ¶ 2).

INTEGRATING PARAPHRASE

A paraphrase is a restatement in your own words of an original passage. Occasionally (but not in this chapter), writers restate ideas in their own words without abbreviating, or shrinking, the original passage. This is done when writers want to discuss particular points in great detail.

> For more information on quoting, summary, and paraphrase, see Chapter 13, Research & Writing.

How Should I Structure My Response?

The structure of your essay largely depends on what you intend to address from the original argument. You can use some standard organization strategies for argument essays, such as:

> Point A (from original argument)
> Your evaluation and response
>
> Point B (from original argument)
> Your evaluation and response
>
> Point C (from the original argument)
> Your evaluation and response

Of course, you also might have points D, E, F, and so on. And each of your evaluations and responses can vary in length, from a sentence to several paragraphs, depending on the main point of your essay.

You might decide that the opposing viewpoint requires significant explanation, and that it would be best to keep all your points grouped together rather than separating them with passages from the original:

> Point A (from original argument)
> Point B (from original argument)
> Point C (from original argument)
> Your evaluation and response to A
> Your evaluation and response to B
> Your evaluation and response to C

Remember that the turn-about paragraph (see page 293) is a good strategy for counterargument. A turn-about paragraph begins with one point, and then changes directions at some point—always giving the reader a clear indication of that change.

How Can I Integrate Toulminian Analysis, Argument, and Counterargument?

Responding to arguments might involve various elements and rhetorical tools. But it need not be confusing. You might consider all the elements as ingredients of the bigger argumentative project. Notice how Ann Causey analyzes (or inspects particular points within) the hunting debate and then evaluates those points.

> Antihunters insist that nontrivial reasons be given for intentional human-inflicted injuries and deaths—or that these injuries and deaths be stopped. An eminently reasonable request.
>
> Even when hunters acknowledge the significance of the pain and suffering inflicted through hunting, they too often offer in defense that they feel an obligation to give back more than they take, and that hunters and wildlife professionals successfully have met this obligation. Granted, it may be that the overall benefits to humans and other species that accrue from hunting outweigh the costs to the hunted. Nevertheless, this utilitarian calculation fails to provide moral justification for hunting. (331)

This passage works to support a broader point about the hunting debate. Causey is analyzing others' claims about hunting, and at the same time building her own argument about the debate. In short, the analysis helps to support her argument.

WRITER'S VOICE

Rogerian Argument

Because argument can potentially create hostility and turn people away from each other, Carl Rogers developed an argumentative perspective that emphasizes building connections between different positions. People who use Rogerian argument look for similarities, rather than differences, between arguments. Such a strategy creates an engaging voice—one that invites exploration of ideas rather than harsh dismissals. Notice, for example, Betsy Taylor's Rogerian strategy:

> Schor's other principles ring true. Millions of Americans obviously share her call for more fun, less stuff. Millions are opting to downshift, choosing to make less money in search of more time. A growing number of people also affirm her call for responsible consumption—a call for a much higher consciousness about the environmental and human costs of each consumer decision we make. Her call to democratize consumer markets seems a bit naïve, since humans have probably always sought to define themselves in part through their stuff. But in an age of excessive materialism, the times may be ripe to challenge the dominant ethos. Perhaps we can make it cool to shun fashion and foot-gear with corporate logos and redefine hip as simple, real, and non-commercial. (327)

Although she finds one of Schor's ideas "a bit naïve," Taylor focuses much of her essay on the value of Schor's argument. Similarly, as you examine arguments, see if you can find claims and/or assumptions that resonate with your own. (But be cautious to avoid excessive enthusiasm, simply celebrating the argument without offering an analysis of the ideas.)

The Invisible/Present "I"

Writers often wonder if they should include the first-person pronoun *I* in their writing. It may be especially tempting to include *I* in argumentative writing. However, many academic disciplines favor writing that does not draw attention to the writer (to the *I*). And writing for English courses, which often focuses on personal insights and reflection, avoids unnecessary attention to *I* as well. This is because argumentative writing implies or assumes the presence of the writer. In other words, every claim or position in a paper that is not attributed to some other source belongs to the writer; therefore, phrases such as "I think that," "In my opinion," or "I believe" are often unnecessary.

However, the first-person pronoun occasionally can be used to make a distinction between an outside argument and the writer's own opinion. If the writer is dealing with several ideas or outside opinions, he or she might decide that using the first-person pronoun refocuses attention on the main argument. In the following passage, Taylor uses the phrase "I would argue" to draw attention to "the only principle" she wants to raise, the only idea that is excluded from Schor's argument:

> Progressives can dogmatically dismiss these forces as elements of religious dogmatism or New Age narcissism, or they can connect with this churning. I would argue that a politics of consumption—and we need a better name for this—should include guiding principles of humility and compassion. (327)

Although this strategy is helpful, it is still unnecessary; that is, Taylor could still make the distinction without attention to *I*. And so this often becomes a choice about formality and style: Inserting *I* can help create a less formal or more intimate style.

ACTIVITY

If you are enrolled in multiple courses, ask each instructor about his or her stance on first-person pronouns in writing. You might also ask about the standard practice of your major, or examine a professional journal in your field of study to see how (and how often) first-person pronouns are used.

As you examine your chosen argument (the one to which you are responding) and your own position, consider tone. Ask yourself the following:

- Has the tone been established by someone else's argument?
- Do I want to change the tone slightly, or dramatically?
- What effect would a change in tone have on the argument?

Consider Tone

If you are responding to a specific argument, you are encountering a tone (the color or mood of a writer's voice). Sometimes writers who are responding to an argument choose to mimic the tone of the original argument. In other words, if you are responding to a very sober and formal argument, you might do well to respond in kind. On the other hand, changing the tone of a discussion can be a powerful rhetorical tool. When writers want to challenge an argument, they may not only argue against the ideas but also shift the tone to their own particular liking. For example, imagine a politician arguing against the comedic rants of Howard Stern. The politician might put forth a very sober argument against Stern—thereby arguing on her own ground rather than on Stern's comedic turf. The opposite is often done: Many writers (and public figures) argue informally to challenge a seemingly formal argument. Consider programs such as *The Daily Show with Jon Stewart* and *Saturday Night Live* or Michael Moore's film *Roger & Me.* They respond to "serious" political arguments by spoofing them—by revealing their flaws and deliberately changing their tone.

Changing the tone of a discussion can be a powerful rhetorical tool.

VITALITY

For any essay project, boiling down text is a key strategy. When writers approach a final draft, they benefit from taking time away and then returning to the draft with one goal in mind: to make it more concise and intensive. This requires the willingness to boil away unnecessary phrases, clauses, and sentences. To help you make decisions at the sentence level, consider the following.

Avoid Over-Embedding

Sometimes sentences can become over-embedded, or jumbled by too many overlapping clauses. In the following sentences, notice how dependent clauses (those beginning with *that, because, if, how, which, what,* etc.) keep you from linking the main ideas in the sentence.

1. The problem <u>that Thoreau has with the government that</u> depends upon the majority is that the majority often fails to think of what is right and what is wrong.

2. King wonders <u>if because the white moderate assumes the wrong thing about time,</u> they will not want to change society for the better for all people.

3. The moderate does not <u>consider about the way</u> time really works to the goals of evil.

Good writers delete unnecessary words and sentences.

In each case, the sentence offers a long clause where a specific noun would help the reader connect ideas. For example, in the first sentence, we have to traverse two *that* clauses before we know what "the problem" is. The clauses overlap, piling up on us as we try to connect the subject ("the problem") and its verb ("is"). The sentence might be re-written:

> According to Thoreau, a government of the majority has a key problem: Majorities often fail to distinguish between right and wrong.

Notice that the revised sentence contains fewer clauses and phrases. Instead, it relies on more direct connections between nouns and verbs.

ACTIVITY

Rewrite the second and third sentences to the left. Try to avoid overlapping clauses.

Clean Up Attributive Phrases

Attributive phrases connect an author and his or her ideas: *According to Biff Harrison; in Jergerson's argument; as Jacobs points out,* and so on. Because you are dealing with another text, you may need to draw consistent attention to the author's words and use attributive phrases. But be cautious of clumsy phrasing such as the following:

1. In "Letter from Birmingham Jail," by Martin Luther King, Jr., King writes about how society can be unjust.

2. In Jayme Stayer's perspective, Sea World reveals the shallowest qualities of American culture. He believes that "[t]he American traits that Sea World reflects most clearly are its gullibility and irrationality."

3. Ann Marie Paulin wrote an essay about incivility and obesity. It is called "Cruelty, Civility, and Other Weighty Matters."

Each of these sentences makes a similar error: Each draws an unnecessary degree of attention to the act of writing or to the author's thoughts. Each could be boiled down. For the first sentence, Martin Luther King, Jr., only needs mentioning once:

1. In "Letter from Birmingham Jail," Martin Luther King, Jr. writes about injustice.

For the second sentence, a colon can replace "he believes that." (Generally, a colon says to readers, "Here's the quotation that proves my point," so it can replace any statement that suggests this idea.)

2. In Jayme Stayer's perspective, Sea World reveals the shallowest qualities of American culture: "The American traits that Sea World reflects most clearly are its gullibility and irrationality."

For the third, the fact that Paulin wrote the essay does not need to be stated. It is better to imply the point:

3. Ann Marie Paulin's essay "Cruelty, Civility, and Other Weighty Matters" shows the deeply personal impact of media images.

Generally speaking, writers do not need an entire sentence or clause to name a title or make a connection between a writer and her words. It is sufficient to use possessive phrases, such as "Paulin's essay."

Try Absolutes!

Absolute phrases consist of a noun, modifiers, and a participle. Absolutes can help intensify ideas—weaving them together to create a more sophisticated, yet concise, sentence. Consider the following two sentences:

> The beauty pageant had finally concluded and the whole ordeal had finally come to an end. Cindy Bosley could now escape the desperate feelings around her.

Although these sentences are correct and functional, they can be combined with an absolute phrase. The verbs of the first sentence will be omitted, the ideas slightly compressed into an absolute phrase and attached to the clause:

> The beauty pageant concluded and the whole ordeal finally over, Cindy Bosley could escape the desperate feelings around her.

If they are used intermittently, and sparingly, absolute phrases can add subtle variety to an essay. They help writers (and their readers) escape the march of subject/verb, subject/verb sentence patterns.

PEER REVIEW

Exchange drafts with at least one other writer. Before exchanging, underline your thesis (or write it on the top of the first page) so that others will more quickly get a sense of your main idea.

Use the following questions to respond to specific issues in the drafts:

1. Can any phrases or terms in the thesis be narrowed? If so, circle them and make some suggestions for more focus.

2. Is the main idea of the original argument sufficiently summarized? (Could the summary be shorter? How?)

3. Where could the writer support broad statements with specific evidence (allusions, examples, facts, personal testimony, scenario)? Writers often fall into the habit of making broad claims that should be illustrated. For instance, someone might argue, "All students learn differently." But such a statement needs to be supported with specifics. Otherwise, a reader has no reason to accept it, no reason to see it as true.

4. Where might the writer oversimplify the original argument/issue or mischaracterize the original author's position? (Look especially for ad hominem or strawperson logical fallacies. See page 290.)

5. What paragraphs shift focus? Where do you sense gaps in the lines of reasoning? How could the writer fill those gaps?

6. Circle any clichés or overly broad statements that could be transformed into specific and revelatory insights.

7. Consider sentence vitality:

   • What sentences are over-embedded? (Point to any clauses that overlap with other clauses, causing a disconnect between ideas.)

   • Examine attributive phrases. Point out unnecessary phrases or sentences that could be boiled down.

   • Consider vitality strategies from other chapters:

   —Where can the writer change linking verbs to active verbs?

   —Where can the writer avoid drawing attention to *I* and *you*?

   —Help the writer change unnecessary clauses to phrases.

   —Help the writer change unnecessary phrases to words.

   —Point to expletives (such as *there are* and *it is*).

   —Help the writer change passive verbs to active verbs for more vitality.

   —Help the reader avoid common grammatical errors: comma splices, sentence fragments, or pronoun/ antecedent agreement.

Questions for Research

If the writer used outside sources:

• Where must he or she include in-text citations? (See page 650.)

• Are quotations blended smoothly into the argument and punctuated correctly? (See pages 642–648.)

• Where could more direct textual cues or transitions help the reader? (See pages 641–643.)

• Is the Works Cited page formatted properly? (See pages 652–674.)

DELIVERY

Just as we discuss (or explore ideas) with others, we play out discussions internally, in our own minds. And the ideas, the thoughts and opinions, that we express outwardly to others often originate in our own internal dialogues.

Have you ever considered how you explore ideas internally through imaginary dialogue with others?

- For several days keep a journal, jotting down imaginary (internal) discussions you have. (To do this, you will have to catch yourself having one of these internal discussions. Remember, you have them often throughout the day, so often that you may have trouble stepping back and noticing one. Instead of simply thinking, you will have to step back and *think about your thinking*.)

Then examine the content of your internal dialogues:

- What is the purpose of each discussion? (Does it have a thesis?)
- How, in the discussion, are you responding to an argument?
- How do your ideas develop?
- Is the imaginary discussion helpful or counterproductive?
- How does your thinking (from the imaginary discussion) play out externally?

Consider the invention writing you did for the essay in this chapter. You may have relied on written responses to Invention questions, public dialogue, internal dialogue, or previous internal dialogues (before you began the assignment).

- Which did you rely on most? And which might you have utilized more?
- Identify several key points in your essay and explain how they developed. What role did writing in response to chapter questions, public dialogue, internal dialogue, or previous dialogue (prior to the assignment) play in the development of those points?
- If you can recall internal dialogues, describe how they worked:

  —Who were your imaginary discussion partners?

  —What was the nature of the discussion? Cooperative? Combative? Something else?

  —What new thinking emerged from the imaginary discussions?

Beyond the Essay

1. Find or create an image that responds to an argument.

   - What response does the image make to the argument?
   - How do particular visual elements help to make the response?

2. Find or create an image that corresponds to the argument you made in your essay for this chapter.

EVALUATING

Chapter Contents

CHAPTER

"The trouble with normal is it always gets worse."

—Bruce Cockburn

Evaluating is the act of judging the value or worth of a given subject. We make informal judgments constantly throughout our daily lives: We decide that we like a particular car more than another, or that one song on the radio is better than another. Such evaluations are informal because they involve little analysis; that is, we do not usually take the time to thoroughly analyze each song we hear on the radio as we are sweeping through stations. We also take part in formal evaluation, a process that goes beyond an expression of likes and dislikes: Teachers must evaluate student performance; jury members must evaluate events, people, and testimony; voters must evaluate political candidates; members of unions must evaluate contracts; managers must evaluate employees; executives must evaluate business proposals; citizens must evaluate laws and lawmakers. In such situations, mere personal tastes cannot dictate evaluative decisions. Instead, a formal process—sometimes entirely intellectual, sometimes organized in visible steps—is necessary for sound evaluation.

The ability to make formal evaluations is essential to academic thinking and writing:

- Biologists at a national conference evaluate the success of a particular molecular research process.
- Law enforcement students are assigned to evaluate a new highway safety program.
- Crime lab scientists evaluate a particular procedure for gathering evidence.
- University civil engineers evaluate a downtown rezoning plan.
- English professors evaluate a new textbook for the department literature courses.
- Education faculty members and graduate students evaluate the state's controversial new standardized tests.
- Art students evaluate a set of paintings from the early Modernist era.

Much literary work is also evaluative. William Copeland's book *Generation X,* for example, may be viewed as an evaluation of the culture created by the baby boomer generation. Toni Morrison's *Jazz* may be seen as an evaluation of 1920s culture. And Jonathan Swift's *Gulliver's Travels,* perhaps one of the most famous examples of evaluative literature, critiques (or satirizes) political and economic institutions of eighteenth-century England.

Whether one is an author, jury member, civil engineer, or voting citizen, the person who can evaluate well and make judgments outside of his or her personal tastes is able to make valuable decisions, to help distinguish the best course of action, to clarify options when many seem available. And in a culture that is increasingly filled with choices (among political candidates, retirement plans, religious paths, and lifestyles, to name just a few), it is increasingly important for the literate citizen to evaluate well.

This chapter will help you develop a formal evaluation of a particular subject and communicate your evaluation in writing. The following essays will provide valuable insight to various evaluation strategies. After reading the essays, you can find a subject in one of two ways:

1. Go to the **Point of Contact** section to find a topic from your everyday life.
2. Choose one of the **Ideas for Writing** that follow the essays.

After finding a subject, go to the **Analysis** section to begin developing the evaluation.

The essays in this chapter all make judgments and, in doing so, present the subjects to the reader in a particular light. In other words, each writer gives an opinion about a subject (be it a theme park, a television show, etc.) and then supports that opinion by showing selected details of the subject. While the writers give some form of overview (some general summary about the subject), they also focus the reader's attention on the details that support their judgments. This is fair play. In drawing attention to certain details (and ignoring others), they are simply creating argumentative positions—the positions they want the reader to accept. Notice, also, that the writers tend to draw on support outside their subjects; that is, they refer to other like subjects to show particular points, which gives credibility to their judgments. Ebert, for instance, points to other movies, Stayer refers to another theme park, and Bell and Benlow refer to other television shows. This strategy helps the reader to share in the writer's perspective.

Star Wars

Roger Ebert

A good evaluation prompts readers to see the subject in a particular light—not to simply see its worth or shortcomings, but to see how it relates to their lives. In this review, Roger Ebert, one of America's best-known film critics, goes beyond saying what is good about *Star Wars*. He explains why and how the movie resonates with people, and he argues why it deserves its standing among the great artifacts of popular culture.

To see *Star Wars* again after 20 years is to revisit a place in the mind. George Lucas's space epic has colonized our imaginations, and it is hard to stand back and see it simply as a motion picture because it has so completely become part of our memories. It's as goofy as a children's tale, as shallow as an old Saturday afternoon serial, as corny as Kansas in August—and a masterpiece. Those who analyze its philosophy do so, I imagine, with a smile in their minds. May the Force be with them.

Like *Birth of a Nation* and *Citizen Kane, Star Wars* was a technical watershed that influenced many movies that came after. These films have little in common, except that they came along at crucial moments in cinema history, when new methods were ripe for synthesis. *Birth of a Nation* brought together the developing language of shots and editing. *Citizen Kane* married special effects, advanced sound, a new photographic style, and a freedom from linear storytelling. *Star Wars* melded a new generation of special effects with the high-energy action picture; it linked space opera and soap opera, fairy tales and legend, and packaged them as a wild visual ride.

Star Wars effectively brought to an end the golden era of early-1970s personal filmmaking and focused the industry on big-budget special-effects blockbusters, blasting off a trend we are still living through. But you can't blame it for what it did; you can only observe how well it did it. In one way or another all the big studios have been trying to make another *Star Wars* ever since (pictures like *Raiders of the Lost Ark, Jurassic Park,* and *Independence Day* are its heirs). It located Hollywood's center of gravity at the intellectual and emotional level of a bright teenager.

It's possible, however, that as we grow older, we retain the tastes of our earlier selves. How else to explain how much fun *Star Wars* is, even for those who think they don't care for science fiction? It's a good-hearted film in every frame, and shining through is the gift of a man who knew how to link state-of-the-art technology with a deceptively simple, very powerful story. It was not by accident that George Lucas worked with Joseph Campbell, an expert on the world's basic myths, in fashioning a screenplay that owes much to man's oldest stories.

5   By now the ritual of classic film revival is well established: An older classic is brought out from the studio vaults, restored frame by frame, re-released in the best theaters, and relaunched on home video. With this "special edition" of the *Star Wars* trilogy (which includes new versions of *Return of the Jedi* and *The Empire Strikes Back*), Lucas has gone one step beyond. His special effects were so advanced in 1977 that they spun off an industry, including his own Industrial Light & Magic Co., the computer wizards who do many of today's best special effects.

Now Lucas has put ILM to work touching up the effects, including some that his limited 1977 budget left him unsatisfied with. Most of the changes are subtle; you'd need a side-by-side comparison to see that a new shot is a little better. There are about five minutes of new material, including a meeting between Han Solo and Jabba the Hutt that was shot for the first version but not used. (We learn that Jabba is not immobile, but sloshes along in a spongy undulation.) There's also an improved look to the city of Mos Eisley ("a wretched hive of scum and villainy," says Obi-Wan Kenobi). And the climactic battle scene against the Death Star has been rehabbed.

The improvements are well done, but they point up how well the effects were done to begin with: If the changes are not obvious, that's because *Star Wars* got the look so right in the first place. The obvious comparison is with Stanley Kubrick's *2001: A Space Odyssey*, made in

1968, which also holds up perfectly well today. (One difference is that Kubrick went for realism, trying to imagine how his future world would really look, while Lucas cheerfully plundered the past; Han Solo's Millennium Falcon has a gun turret with a hand-operated weapon that would be at home on a World War II bomber, but too slow to hit anything at space velocities.)

Two Lucas inspirations started the story with a tease: He set the action not in the future but "long ago," and jumped into the middle of it with "Chapter 4: A New Hope." These seemingly innocent touches were actually rather powerful; they gave the saga the aura of an ancient tale, and an ongoing one.

As if those two shocks were not enough for the movie's first moments, I learn from a review by Mark R. Leeper that this was the first film to pan the camera across a star field: "Space scenes had always been done with a fixed camera, and for a very good reason. It was more economical not to create a background of stars large enough to pan through." As the camera tilts up, a vast spaceship appears from the top of the screen and moves overhead, an effect reinforced by the surround sound. It is such a dramatic opening that Lucas paid a fine and resigned from the Directors Guild rather than obey its demand that he begin with conventional opening credits.

10　The film has simple, well-defined characters, beginning with the robots C-3PO (fastidious, a little effete) and R2-D2 (childlike, easily hurt). The evil Empire has all but triumphed in the galaxy, but rebel forces are preparing an assault on the Death Star. Princess Leia (pert, sassy Carrie Fisher) has information pinpointing the Death Star's vulnerable point and feeds it into R2-D2's computer; when her ship is captured, the robots escape from the Death Star and find themselves on Luke Skywalker's planet, where soon Luke (Mark Hamill as an idealistic youngster) meets the wise, old, mysterious Kenobi (Alec Guinness) and they hire the freelance space jockey Han Solo (Harrison Ford, already laconic) to carry them to Leia's rescue.

The story is advanced with spectacularly effective art design, set decoration, and effects. Although the scene in the intergalactic bar is famous for its menagerie of alien drunks, there is another scene—when the two robots are thrown into a hold with other used droids—that equally fills the screen with fascinating details. And a scene in the Death Star's garbage bin (inhabited by a snake with a head shaped like E.T.'s) also is well done.

Many of the planetscapes are startlingly beautiful, and owe something to fantasy artist Chesley Bonestell's imaginary drawings of other worlds. The final assault on the Death Star, when the fighter rockets speed between parallel walls, is a nod in the direction of *2001*, with its light trip into another dimension: Kubrick showed, and Lucas learned, how to make the audience feel it is hurtling headlong through space.

Lucas fills his screen with loving touches. There are little alien rats hopping around the desert and a chess game played with living creatures. Luke's weather-worn "Speeder" vehicle, which hovers over the sand, reminds me of a 1965 Mustang. And consider the details creating the presence, look and sound of Darth Vader, whose fanged face mask, black cape, and hollow breathing are the setting for James Earl Jones's cold voice of doom.

Seeing the film the first time, I was swept away, and have remained swept ever since. Seeing this restored version, I tried to be more objective and noted that the gun battles on board the spaceships go on a bit too long; it is remarkable that the Empire marksmen never hit anyone important; and the fighter raid on the enemy ship now plays like the computer games it predicted. I wonder, too, if Lucas could have come up with a more challenging philosophy behind the Force. As Kenobi explains it, it's basically just going with the flow. What if Lucas had pushed a little further, to include elements of non-violence or ideas about intergalactic conservation? (It's a waste of resources to blow up star systems.)

15　The film's philosophies that will live forever are the simplest-seeming ones. They may have profound depths, but their surfaces are as clear to an audience as a beloved old story. I know this because the stories that seem immortal— *The Odyssey, Don Quixote, David Copperfield, Huckleberry Finn*—are all the same: a brave but flawed hero, a quest, colorful people and places, sidekicks, the discovery of life's underlying truths. If I were asked to say with certainty which movies will still be widely known a century or two from now, I would list *2001, The Wizard of Oz*, Keaton and Chaplin, Astaire and Rogers, and probably *Casablanca . . .* and *Star Wars,* for sure.

Writing Strategies

1. What criteria—or standards of judgment—does Ebert rely on when evaluating *Star Wars*? What other standards might he have used?

2. Ebert uses support outside the subject, such as other movies, to develop his evaluation. How does this outside support help to develop his evaluation?

3. Does Ebert seem credible? Does his information seem reliable? Upon what would you base your decision about his credibility?

4. What is Ebert's main point about *Star Wars*?

Exploring Ideas

1. What standards of judgment besides "entertaining" might be used to evaluate a film? That is, what might be the purpose or value of a film beyond or in addition to mere entertainment?

2. With a small group, come up with at least three films that have value beyond mere entertainment. What is their value?

3. Select a film that you think is especially good, and then do research to help you explain how earlier films influenced it.

Ideas for Writing

1. What film set a trend that other films have followed? What film do you believe is likely to set a trend that other films will follow?

2. What CD, music video, television show, or work from some other form of media has been influential?

If responding to one of these ideas, go to the **Analysis** section of this chapter to begin developing ideas for your essay.

Whales R Us

Jayme Stayer

Evaluations are sometimes heated arguments: They insist that we see shortcomings or values that we'd otherwise ignore—or would like to ignore. In fact, good writers often either invite or force us to confront ideas we would rather not examine. In his evaluation of Sea World, Jayme Stayer, a professor of literature, sheds new light on the park. His evaluative points might seem unreasonable at first. After all, why should someone target a theme park? But Stayer's essay illustrates an important move in academic writing: uncovering the layers of meaning behind the propaganda of everyday life.

Mickey Mouse scares the bejesus out of me. Shamu, on the other hand, simply makes me queasy. I'm not the first to express loathing for Mickey & Co.: a giggling rodent as mascot for a nasty, litigious, multimedia *Über*-corporation. But you don't hear too many people railing against Sea World, though Shamu has a dark side too.

One of the first things to irk me at a Sea World park happened during a bird show. A perky blonde was displaying a few parrots, and she kept up a stream of banter about their feeding habits and origins. "When our ancestors came to this continent," she breezily explained to an audience chock full of non-Europeans, "they brought with them this breed of parrot from Africa." Since I'm almost certain that slaves brutally shipped to the Americas were not allowed bird cages as carry-on luggage, what she should have said was that European—not "our"—ancestors stopped off in Africa and loaded up with parrots and slaves. One needn't be a fanatical multiculturalist to be ruffled by inaccurate history and specious assumptions about an audience's makeup.

In America, unexamined notions of history and the coercive politics of majority identity go hand in hand with boorish nationalism. (See, for example, the debate over the Confederate flag and its supposed sta-

tus as symbol of a unitary "Southern" culture.) Oddly, the bird show at Sea World confirmed this. Her parrots now retired, the perky woman waltzed around the stage with a bald eagle while the audience was subjected to a chummy patriotic tune. So the eagle was presented not as the largest or most impressive of birds, or as indigenous to Canada, or even as another instance of the marvels of creation, but as the Bird of American Democracy—this, in spite of the fact that eagles' politics tend to the monarchist side and that their feeding habits indicate a predisposition for brutal dictatorship. The bird becomes valued, in other words, for the cultural associations "we" Americans slapped onto it, not for any of its intrinsic properties. The eagle, in Sea World's monistic version of the world, becomes just another happy commodity—like parrots, slaves, designer clothes sweatshops—that makes America the Great Nation It Has Always Been.

But not all employees were as chipper as the bird show people. There are two types of teenagers who work at Sea World: the aggressively happy and the sullenly aggrieved. These two opposed mentalities are as old as the summer job itself: namely, the optimism of youths who want to change the world vs. the cynicism of kids who despise their jobs, resent their pay, and wouldn't give a hooey if they were fired because some enraged Yuppie did not get good service with a grovelling smile when he bought his Sno-Cone. I personally sided with the disaffected and wished I had brought copies of *The Communist Manifesto* to slip into their pockets.

5   The most important job at Sea World—and teenagers are particularly good at it—is making lots of noise. Since most Americans are terrified of being alone in a store without Muzak, Sea World willingly obliges its customers with rock-concert levels of decibels. All of the shows keep up a noxious patter complete with ear-splitting sound effects; the walkways have abrasively loud music piped over them; and even the exhibits have teenagers chained there with microphones in hand, droning their mantra of dull facts.

It is ironic that a park putatively designed to extol the wonders of nature is obsessed with high-tech wizardry and mega-voltage noise, noise, noise—even when it is extolling the wonders of nature's silence. Another talking point of the bird show featured how silently an owl could fly. The bird's flight began in blissful silence, but halfway through its flight the soundtrack faded back in with a shimmer of violins, followed by a cymbal crash when the owl landed. Even the absence of noise is packaged with noise: The owl's silence is first framed with amplified yakking (noise), then underlined as it happens (quiet noise), then punctuated (big noise) so the audience knows when to clap (make more noise).

One of the most ludicrous moments of the Shamu show was an assertion by another relentlessly cheerful teenager: "We here at Sea World believe we have the greatest jobs in the world." With its overtones of Orwellian party-speak, it was only slightly risible until she added: "We get to work with nature's most wonderful animals and contribute to the world's knowledge about them." Her jejune assumption that "world knowledge" exists as some kind of huge, accumulative spittoon—rather than a set of competing claims and shifting paradigms—was hilarious enough, particularly coming from a kid who is probably still struggling with basic algebra and who wouldn't recognize "world knowledge" if it landed on her in a heap. I imagined her logging on to a marine biology chat group and making an announcement—in all caps, no doubt—followed by an emoticon: "SHAMU DID A BACK FLIP TODAY!!! :)" Thus does the world's cup of knowledge runneth over.

And that insistent refrain of "We here at Sea World believe" was another thing that rankled me, because it was usually followed by patronizing flimflam. Some prime examples: "We here at Sea World believe that animals should not be taken from their natural habitat." Or: "We here at Sea World believe only in the use of positive reinforcement in the training of animals." The audience is supposed to believe that these are lovely sentiments. How noble that they try to find injured or orphaned animals to "befriend." How comforting to know Shamu isn't being shocked with electricity or poked in the eye when he's tired or just damned fed up with giving piggyback rides. Most disturbing was that these credos came mostly out of the mouths of the teenage staff, whose inexperience made their We-Believe proclamations ring even more hollowly.

Taken individually, some of these moments were only mildly unnerving, but there was one occurrence that stood out as gratuitous. Situated on a lake, the Sea World I visited featured a water show with ski jumps and corny skits. The theme of that year's show was *Baywatch*, which involved—predictably enough—nubile bodies in poorly choreographed dance routines, the bold rescue of someone in the water, and the odd appearances of two buffoons (fat old man with hysterical wife), all of which was irritatingly narrated by an emcee's we-havin'-fun-yet? voice-over. At one point, the old man and his wife were "accidentally" pulled into view: the man (vertical) on skis, the woman (horizontal) with her legs wrapped around his torso. They were in the unmistakable position of sex, the two actors in a flurry of feigned embarrassment at having been "caught." (Whut in tarnation cud be more funny than ol' fat folks havin' sex? Har dee har har.) The emcee and other characters on stage slyly absolved themselves of complicity in this vulgarity by shrugging their shoulders, as if to say: "Golly, what was that all about?" Sea World, by the way, bills itself as a place for the whole family.

10   You might think that a park that sponsors PG-13 shows would divest itself of prudishness. Alas, there was more self-righteousness there than at a revival. Case in point: the shark exhibit. Before we could enter, we were forced to watch a short film about sharks; the doors to the exhibit were pointedly barred until after the film was over. The film gave us a hellfire-and-damnation scolding: you thought that sharks were human predators? WRONG. You thought sharks were abundant in the ocean? WRONG AGAIN. After airing its grievances with us—the ill-informed public—it asserted that much damage had been inflicted on these misunderstood fishies. Because we've all been shark-haters at

heart, fishermen have felt free to kill them. Quivering with virtue, the film called "intolerable" the fishermen who "senselessly" destroyed the sharks, either because the sharks got caught in the nets or because the sharks fed on prized fish. With vast self-contentment Sea World then relayed how they had successfully worked to stop this great evil.

While I'm pleased to have my horror-film notions of sharks corrected, the film's smugness was unbearable. And in spite of Sea World's professed vigilance, I'm not convinced that sharks aren't still being arbitrarily killed somewhere in the world. Even so, I wonder if sharks, given the choice, would prefer to stay in a Sea World bathtub for the rest of their lives or take a chance with those fishnets.

Of the many inanities hurled at me, my favorite was an emcee's sign-off: "And remember," she intoned from a precipitously high moral ground, "before we can have peace *on* the Earth, we have to make peace *with* the Earth." Indeed. As if, in the interest of world peace, the United Nations agenda should be scuttled in favor of dotting the globe with Sea Worlds to promote feel-good vibes between humans and dolphins. Here's more glib reasoning: to make peace *with* the Earth implies the Earth was a peaceful place before we humans mucked things up. Yet the last time I looked, the Earth was full of viruses, earthquakes, predatory animals, and a survival-of-the-fittest mentality that Sea World has apparently never heard of.

And maybe it was petty of me to be irked when the woman narrating Shamu's activities insisted that whales scratch their backs on the pebbled shores when they're contented. There was captive Shamu scratching his back on the simulated shore. The audience oohed and aahed. Nevermind that Shamu had been explicitly directed to scratch his back, and that to have disobeyed would have resulted not in a whack on the head (lucky for him) but in the withholding of food (not so lucky). Is that contentment then? With the help of an extraordinarily costly visual aid, the audience was expected to "learn" a fact of whale behavior that could be shown only at the cost of candor.

"Sea World . . . was desperately trying to present itself as a place where education occurs."

Sea World, I realized after an afternoon of learning very little, was a place that was desperately trying to present itself as a place where education occurs. And for twenty-some bucks, your educational experience goes roughly like this: You can give up an afternoon of watching vapid TV shows and take your whole family to watch a skit based on a vapid TV show. You get to ogle busty women and hirsute men. You get to have constant noise crowd out any independent thoughts that might be percolating to the surface of your brain. You get to harbor the illusion that America is a happy, white, European family, as well as a leading maker of world knowledge, and that Sea World is largely responsible for such happiness and abundance. You get to imagine you hold the key to world peace (remember to give the dog a kiss when you get home). You get to indulge in patriotic goosebumps ("the *American* eagle!"), have your heart-strings jolted ("Ah—Shamu's happy to be here!"), get your sluggish sense of morality jump-started ("*baaaad* fishermen, *gooood* sharkie"). And if you're willing to invest another three bucks, you can fling a sardine at dolphins that have been petted to within an inch of their lives. Best of all, at the end of the day you get to go home with the vaguely self-congratulatory feeling that you've *learned* something, by God.

15   I'm an educator, and I pay close attention when someone is trying to teach me something. So on my way out of Sea World, I asked myself what I had learned. Like a student who has crammed for an exam, I was able to recall lots of idiocies, but could only say I had truly learned two things. (1) Thanks to the film, I

learned that sharks attack humans only when provoked, and, (2) thanks to their anthropomorphizing skits, I learned that sea otters are cute little buggers. Even if these elements were judicious pedagogical objectives (which they are not), they still don't add up to anything resembling education. In fact, the entire experience of Sea World is suspiciously similar to the exact opposite of education: mind control.

It was only in retrospect that I realized that these annoyances were related: the high-pitched entertainment and trivial sexual jokes, the shut-up-and-listen attitude, the constant noise and verbal presence, the Big Brotherly refrains of exactly what "We here at Sea World believe." These are all rhetorical strategies of a government diverting its citizens, masking something it doesn't want the public to know. And what is it that Sea World doesn't want its customers to think about?

In a review lambasting Disney World, an author hilariously describes the ideology of the place as "benign fascism": The streets are immaculately clean; the worker-bees wear impossibly happy smiles; the rides and trains run on time; and every day, the gloved hero appears on parade, where the hordes worship him and his lickspittles with songs and fireworks. The author's comparison of Mickey to Mussolini is more than just amusing: He ties it into his critique of how history is portrayed at the Epcott center. Because Disney does not want to offend any of its ethnically and racially diverse customers (Sea World: take note), their film on American history carefully controls the emotional barometer of its vacationers. The Disney film of American history is whitewashed to the point of banality, and such central topics as the atomic bomb, racial conflict, and imperialist genocide are entirely avoided. The point is that fascists, benign or not, always have political and economic reasons for telling history the way they do. And like Disney World and other fascist operations, Sea World likes to keep a tight grip on what and how its visitors think.

Take, for example, the "we-believe-animals-should-be-treated-in-this-way" gestures that continually crop up. These assertions pose as facts the audience ought to memorize in preparation for an exit quiz. Yet the nervous tic of emphasizing the politically correct means of treating animals in captivity belies Sea World's uneasiness with the larger, unasked question: Should we even have animals in captivity for our bourgeois amusement? Nowhere in their literature, exhibit signs, or rehearsed prattle of their miked minions is this basic question broached or answered.

Part of the way Sea World can get away with ignoring the obvious fact that these animals are there for our entertainment is that it nervously insists that it is a place of science and research, and disingenuously implies that entertainment easily meshes with education and research. While I scoff at the idea that important research gets done at Sea World, the problem isn't really with what kinds of knowledge Sea World makes, or how much, or how important it is. Rather, the problem is Sea World's communication of that knowledge, or to be more explicit, their refusal to level with its visitors about its real cultural role and worth. If they would fess up to the fact that Sea World is essentially a playground and not a classroom, that might be a start towards a real educational experience.

20 Sea World keeps up its image of itself as a classroom by propagating signs with facts and statistics on them. These factoids—and their Post-it Note ubiquity—are a peculiar manifestation of "textbook knowledge": boring chunks of data unconnected to any larger, compelling theme. There were a plethora of facts swimming around at Sea World and a dearth of ideas, which is why I couldn't remember anything at the end of my day. Like the eager student who has a bad teacher, I was given no complex or interesting framework inside of which ideas jostled about; so I was reduced to cramming lists of unconnected information in preparation for a never-to-be-taken exam.

I'm not suggesting that Sea World become a place that sponsors round-table discussions of animal rights and lets biology students present their theses during Shamu intermissions. But I do think that instead of slavishly subscribing to popular notions of science, Sea World might call them into question. This is what real education does.

As it stands, none of our deeply rooted cultural beliefs are explored or challenged at Sea World. After a trip there the visitor is likely to keep thinking that facts are equivalent to knowledge; that America is synonymous with Europe; that science and technology are the greatest goods imaginable; that education means being fed a list of facts in a condescending manner; and that sated, docile fish—who decorously eat buckets of non-cute sardines—are practically vegetarians.

A skit in which a lovably frisky sea otter has its head chomped off by a hungry predator is not the kind of bloody epiphany Sea World is likely to promote. Imagine the screams of the unsuspecting children. Imagine the lawsuits of offended suburbanites who like their nature sanitized and safe. But imagine, too, how such a moment would educate an audience about the dangers of humanizing certain animals at the expense of others. Such a skit might end with a question to the audience about why its government enacts laws to protect the habitat of owls but not of insects or low-income humans.

The only cultural assumption that was seriously challenged at Sea World was the premise of *Jaws*—and that was much too heavy-handed, not to mention incorrect, as events in Florida have shown. It turns out that sharks *will* attack idle swimmers. It should come as no surprise that a capitalist venture like Sea World can't even get its basic facts straight. Neither can the tobacco industry seem to grasp what everyone else knows about nicotine addiction. Nor is Disney equipped to navigate the treacherous waters of American history.

25   Surely the most real moments at Sea World occurred when the fascists lost control, for example, when the staff had trouble getting the animals to obey their directions. Such glitches in the program put their slapstick routines and canned jokes on hold, and forced them to talk to the audience about fixing this problem. It also gave the teenage apparatchiks an opportunity for some inspired ad-libbing, disburdening them from their less endearing lecture notes.

If the ideology of Disney is benign fascism, then the ideology of Sea World is exploitative spectacle masquerading as education. Too occupied with obscuring the real moral, environmental, and scientific issues at stake, Sea World is constitutionally incapable of teaching respect for nature. Love of nature is spiritually informed and politically assertive. It is not the kind of passive, sentimental quackery Sea World prefers, and it cannot be taught with the crude tools in Sea World's lesson plans: glib moralizing, base pandering, and clichés masquerading as insights.

But in the last analysis, Sea World—to paraphrase Auden—makes nothing happen. Sea World is a reflection of American culture: a consequence, not a cause; a mirror of consumerist desires, not a promoter of political change via education. The American traits Sea World reflects most clearly are its gullibility and irrationality. It's a consolation, albeit a small one, to consider that Americans are likewise gullible to the very real beauty of nature. It's that kind of openness—and not Sea World's preaching—that makes the connection between humans and dolphins seem worth investigating. It's less of a comfort to consider another analogy between Americans and marine life that Sea World leaves unexplored: America's exorbitant arms race, its rape of the environment, its valorization of guns and violence, its giddy, media-fueled acclamation of the death sentence that disproportionately murders minorities: Are these not strikingly similar to the fierce logic of the food chain? Screw the little guy; I'm hungry and more powerful.

So my advice is to go to Sea World anyway. Even inside the ideological frame where they are forced, the creatures there—including the teenagers—are amazing, hilarious, and terrifying. Who can remain unimpressed when a mammal the size of a Mack truck lifts itself out of the water? As for Sea World itself: If aided by earplugs and skepticism you can ignore what they're trying to teach you, you just might learn something.

Work Cited

Alexander, Maxwell. "Promise Redeemed: At Long Last Mickey." <u>Johns Hopkins Magazine</u> Apr. 1995: 5.

Writing Strategies

1. What word would you use to describe the tone of this essay—humorous, serious, urgent, angry, light, or something else? Identify several passages to support your description.

2. In evaluation, understanding the purpose of the subject—Sea World, in this case—is essential. According to Stayer, what is, or should be, the purpose of Sea World? Point to a specific passage to support your answer.

3. If workshopping Stayer's essay, what suggestion would you make, and why?

4. How does Stayer use Sea World to make broader points about American culture?

Exploring Ideas

1. Based on this essay, how is the way that Stayer sees entertainment parks similar to or different from the way you see them?

2. Based on this essay, how are Stayer's thoughts, values, beliefs, or feelings similar to or different from yours?

3. How does Stayer's thinking go beyond one's initial ideas about entertainment parks?

4. How might you evaluate some entertainment activity (theme park, concert, movie, race track, etc.), going beyond one's initial thinking about that activity?

Ideas for Writing

1. What public place—such as Sea World—does not achieve the purpose that it should or that it claims to?

2. What public place does achieve its purpose?

If responding to one of these ideas, go to the **Analysis** section of this chapter to begin developing ideas for your essay.

The Andy Griffith Show: Return to Normal

Ed Bell

In the margins of this essay, a reader's comments point to key ideas and writing strategies. As you read the essay, consider how the comments might influence your own reading and writing.

Evaluations invite readers to see why something is valuable or deficient. To do this, a writer may propose a new standard of judgment (a criterion) upon which the evaluation is based. For example, a writer might suggest that a television show should not only entertain but also *comfort* its audience. In this essay, Ed Bell does just that, first establishing comfort as a potential criterion for a prime-time television sitcom, then arguing how well *The Andy Griffith Show* meets that criterion. (Ed Bell's writing also appears in Chapter 10.)

Writing Strategies

Introduction discusses what sitcoms do (their purpose): instruct, entertain, comfort. Evaluation of show can be based on how well the shows do this.

Main claim: "More than any other sitcom . . ."

Criteria for evaluation. How *Andy Griffith* differs from other shows—it's more comforting because things return to normal.

Develops argument by discussing what happens in other shows: Things work out okay, but we can tell a new crisis will loom.

From those early days of Lucy and Ricky to our own Dharma and Greg, situation comedies have been part of American culture. And for all the advancements, it still seems like the plots of most of them are something cooked up by Lucy who dragged along Ethel and got caught (and ultimately forgiven) by Fred and Barney . . . uh . . . Fred and Ricky, I mean. Whether or not these shows instruct is, I suppose, debatable. But what is not debatable is that over the past 50 years they have entertained millions. And, I would suggest, through that very act of entertaining us, they have comforted us—the most comforting of them all being *The Andy Griffith Show.*

More than any other sitcom, *The Andy Griffith Show* leaves its viewers with a sense that everything is all right. While *Three's Company* or *Dharma and Greg* or *MASH* may also wind things up happily after 30 minutes, there is—even though the complication of that particular week's crisis has been worked out—always a sense on those shows that things are not quite right. Yet *The Andy Griffith Show* leaves us with the feeling that, even though our friends sometimes get big-headed ideas or strangers from Raleigh come driving or dancing or swindling their mixed-up way into our peacefulness, life will eventually return to normal, all warm and wonderful.

On *Three's Company* or *Seinfeld* or *Friends,* things work out in the end. The friends are getting along just fine, but we can see that they are bound for another conflict in a week or so. Though this week's crisis has worked itself out, the pace of their lives or their natural temperaments or their complicated living conditions are still spinning wildly and we know next week they're in for trouble again. On *Dharma and Greg* or *Green Acres* or *I Love Lucy* (even on

Exploring Ideas

Connects to life of viewer: Do sitcoms instruct? How?

They entertain. Do they comfort? Probably.

Okay, but there must be "other" shows like *Andy*—such as *Leave It to Beaver.*

The Dick Van Dyke Show), the family has once again survived, but as with the shows about friends, on the shows about families there seems to be only temporary comfort in the happy ending. Dharma and Greg are still bound for a divorce. Lisa, on *Green Acres,* is only putting up with the farm life a little while longer and Oliver loves it so much that he is never going back to the city. Though she is ironically more suited to the place than he is, she longs always to live elsewhere. No one could possibly put up with all Lucy's scheming. And as for Richard and Laura Petrie, the most stable of our sample couples, to the average American they seem only a step away from falling into the New York swinger crowd. On *MASH* or *Hogan's Heroes* or *Gomer Pyle,* they are either at war or could be. There's little real and lasting comfort in these folks who are gathered together out of necessity so far from home. Yes, they're buddies and that's nice, but it's all so temporary.

This seems to go beyond initial thinking. (I've never thought about it.)

Author concedes that there are other sitcoms and other types of sitcoms.

This doesn't exhaust all the sitcoms or all the types, but it does set up the reasons that *The Andy Griffith Show* comforts us more than the others. The show's main character, Andy, is full of southern wisdom. He is quiet and listens and makes better decisions in the midst of all the madness than we could have. That is comfort number one: Someone—the general, the man in charge, *the sheriff*—has things under control. All the madness results from one of three things: either intruders, but Andy gets rid of them after they have caused only a little trouble; or just boys (Opie and sometimes his friends) going through what is natural to go through growing up, but Andy deals with this expertly, too; or ego, ambition, and pride—usually Barney is having the trouble here, though it could be Aunt Bea or one of the others. Andy understands all of this, though not so well or right away that the show isn't a little bit interesting. The plot is better than most sitcoms: There is always a solution that takes a little while to get to, and we believe it when we finally do.

Goes beyond initial thinking here. Gets specific. Show provides comfort because someone's wise. Madness because of:
1) intruders,
2) natural growing up,
3) ego, ambition, pride.

Develops argument through specific analysis of *The Andy Griffith Show.* Shows specifically why/how AG comforts us.

5   What's most comforting about this show, however, is that things return to normal. That is, *The Andy Griffith Show* offers us a normal that can be returned to. With *Andy Griffith* we get a sense that the complication has blown through like a summer thunderstorm, instead of us getting the sense that a little blue sky has blown through a place where it is otherwise always thunderstorming. The characters are at home. They're not strangers thrown together, and they haven't been transplanted in some strange land (such as Hooterville, New York City, or Postmodern America). They are familiar with their surroundings and like (both "similar to" and

Main idea: Says what is most comforting about the show (relates to title of essay).

"fond of") each other. The zaniness on *Andy Griffith* could just as well not ensue . . . but it does. On all those other shows, it must ensue. How couldn't it?

> This seems to go beyond initial thinking: Things are normal and get wacky, instead of things generally just being wacky.

The situation itself—small-town people in a small town—is comforting. The show develops this sense with Andy's quiet wisdom, but also with the integrity of the wacky supporting characters. All of them to some degree are like Barney—a liability and an asset all at once. They are, like us, good people flawed. We are all familiar with the show's gentle theme song, whistled as Andy and Opie walk along with fishing poles. And the black and white camera shots are always perfectly composed, like a photo we'd see in *Life* magazine. The dialog is quiet, engaging, funny, real. For 30 minutes we are practically back in the womb of Mayberry—a place that doesn't exist, but does. It is a place that, whether we ever felt it as a child or not, as adults we feel that we once knew. We can feel it now, and *The Andy Griffith Show* captures what we all now think that we once felt back then.

> Connects to reader (public resonance): They are, like *us*, good people flawed. The use of "we" (though not required) helps make this connection.

> Is this true? Doesn't it have to ensue because of Barney, etc.?

> The situation itself (small-town life) contributes to comforting.

Not all sitcoms set out to comfort, though all do set out to entertain. Some, such as *All in the Family* or *Soap* or *Will and Grace*, might even set out to challenge us, to make us think. But *The Andy Griffith Show*, I believe, sets out to entertain and comfort and it succeeds as no other show ever has . . . or ever will. *The Cosby Show* could only circle in *Andy's* orbit. The reason is, I suppose, because the times have changed. Today an attempt to create the comfort of Mayberry (an attempt to say your small-town life is idyllic) would somehow fail. It would seem a lie without any of the twenty-first-century issues (drugs, pregnancy, homosexual kissing), without any of the edgy technology, the music, the rapid-fire slick wit, the self-aware writing and directing. Mayberry exists, cliché as it sounds, in our hearts. The show, like no other, captured what we want to remember, whether it happened or not. It tells us that blue skies are normal.

> Concession/Qualifier: Not all sitcoms set out to comfort. Some may even do the opposite.

> The show captures something. What is it?

> Concludes by providing a possible reason why *The Andy Griffith Show* is more comforting than today's shows.

> Connects to viewers because it is comforting. Assures viewer that blue skies, not storms, are normal. (Even if this is not true? Is it?)

Writing Strategies

1. What criteria (standards of judgment) does Bell use to evaluate *The Andy Griffith Show*? List several other criteria he might have used but didn't.

2. Highlight any background or summary information necessary to understand the evaluation. Where does such information appear? Why is it helpful? Where might more or less background information have been presented?

3. If workshopping Bell's essay, what suggestion would you make, and why?

4. Would you say that Bell's essay is an argument? Why or why not?

Exploring Ideas

1. How does Bell's essay encourage the reader to think differently about TV sitcoms?

2. How does Bell's essay encourage the reader to think differently about entertainment?

3. Interview others until you discover three television shows that people think impact the quality of the viewer's life. Explain how each show might influence the way that people think or act.

Ideas for Writing

1. What television show is overestimated or underestimated? Why do audiences have the wrong take on it?

2. What person, place, or thing can you evaluate, focusing your evaluation on a less usual (less obvious) purpose of that thing?

If responding to one of these ideas, go to the **Analysis** section of this chapter to begin developing ideas for your essay.

"The situation itself—small town people in a small town—is comforting."

Revealing the Ugly Cartoonish Truth: *The Simpsons*

Simon Benlow

Evaluating entertainment can be dangerous, because writers might be tempted to give a list of likes and dislikes. Based on this essay, we can assume that Simon Benlow "likes" *The Simpsons,* but the essay does more than share Benlow's approval of the show. It argues about the purpose of mainstream entertainment—what it should or could do for American audiences. While celebrating *The Simpsons* and analyzing its specific qualities, Benlow reveals the shortcomings of mainstream American entertainment, and even pokes fun at the institutions of everyday life.

It's not often that a television sitcom does more than tickle our most simplistic pleasures. The vast majority of sitcoms, past and present, fill twenty-two minutes (or is it nineteen?) with cliché moralism, empty characters, and adolescent dialog. Every fall we can look forward to a new parade of bad jokes and simpleton plots—created primarily to allow American viewers to gawk at the latest celebrity hairstyles and tight shirts.

However, amidst an exhausting list of here-and-then-gone "real-life" sitcoms, *The Simpsons* has managed to create a new class of television. It has stretched what can (and should) be expected in prime-time entertainment. It goes where most sitcoms, most American entertainment, will not. It satirizes everything (and nearly anything) mainstream America cherishes. From SUVs to friendly fast-food chains, the familiar elements of everyday life are revealed as ridiculous creations of a culture blind to its own vices. Certainly, it takes shots at big targets: nuclear power, organized labor, corporate fraud, slick politicians, organized religion, hyper-consumerism, hyper-consumption, and even television programming (often slamming its own network, FOX). But these are more than easy targets; these are the entities that seem to run amuck consistently, the institutions that maintain their status despite repeated failings,

the bullies of our culture that always seem in need of a punch to their maniacal eye sockets.

In "Homer's Odyssey," an episode from the first season, the show does its usual deconstruction of everyday life. The episode reveals some ugly truth: Beneath the daily façade, there lurks an entire set of systems barely working, hardly accomplishing anything beyond their own survival. In the first scene, in front of Springfield Elementary, the children wait for the tardy, pot-smoking bus driver, Otto (who loves to "get blotto"). Once they get settled, they drive in circles through town. They pass by the toxic waste dump where happy workers casually pour mysterious fluid into the river; they pass the prison where they are greeted by hosts of prisoners (who were set free during the children's last field trip). They pass the Springfield tire yard (which becomes the Springfield tire fire in later episodes), and finally arrive at the nuclear power plant. At the gate, several signs announce "employees only," but the guard is sucking on a beverage and watching Krusty the Clown on television, so the children pass on through unnoticed.

In the power plant, we see the gross fumblings and even grosser cover-ups of an unchecked system. While Joe Fission, a cartoon icon, feeds the children pronuclear propaganda, Homer flummoxes his job and wreaks havoc in the plant. Homer is the poster boy of incompetence—yet he's granted a typical place in the ill-defined bureaucracy of power: Is he the "supervising technician" or the "technical supervisor"? No one knows. Through the episode, Homer is fired and then, for no good reason, hired back. The status quo prevails; three-eyed fish swim happily in the lake and the town continues to live on the brink of nuclear disaster.

5 In the animated town of Springfield, nothing is worthy of the praise it wants. Schools are not great institutions of learning; they are poorly funded bureaucracies run by flawed and desperate individuals. Government is not "of the people"; it is a mob of self-perpetuating boozers and womanizers. Business is not ethical or productive; it is a race to monopolize and swindle everyone in sight. These are the hard truths that *The Simpsons* offers us. Of course, we get these truths

Some may argue that *The Simpsons* is just a show; it can't possibly have that much meaning. However, one thing we've learned in America is that our entertainment has more significance than history, literature, philosophy, and politics. Mainstream society gets its values, its slogans, its hairstyles, even its dialects from entertainment. We are, as the world knows, an over-entertained nation. The average American citizen reads very little (maybe a few books per year), but fills thousands of hours being massaged by the television. As the last thirty years proves undoubtedly, Americans can change their minds at the drop of a hat (about almost anything) if the television set prompts us to do so. When television maintains such influence, it is significant and meaningful when the television itself plays with, pokes at, and parodies that influence.

In a swirling array of giddy and capricious entertainment, *The Simpsons* is far more real than any "real-life" sitcom hopes to be (or wants to be). In its relentless pursuit to overturn our romantic notions of ourselves and our lovely creations, it is probably more real than the audience it attracts (and certainly more real than those whom it doesn't). In fact, if we take the show as seriously as it deserves, we might even see the broad strokes of its irony: that *we* are the cartoons, drawn and colored by the ridiculous institutions that constitute our society. However, as soon as we go that far, Homer belches, Bart moons a head of state, and Grandpa soils himself; *The Simpsons* won't allow anything, including itself, to be taken seriously.

thrown at us in sanctimonious movies and bad morning talk shows, but *The Simpsons* manages to reveal these ideas without romanticizing its own characters or actors.

The Simpsons throws at us what we all might be thinking had we not been programmed to dismiss it. We all might briefly consider the lies the nuclear power industry feeds us, the laziness and self-righteousness of city governments, or the emptiness and humiliation of most jobs, but we've been trained out of being appalled. We've become distracted by our own lives, and the constant barrage of material goodness, so we allow our own institutions to bully us, to humiliate us, to dismiss our general welfare entirely. But *The Simpsons* reminds us of the slip-shod work and flagrant thievery going on just outside our own television sets.

Writing Strategies

1. What purpose or goal of *The Simpsons* does Benlow focus on?

2. In your own words, what is Benlow's main idea?

3. What details from Benlow's essay are most helpful in developing his main idea?

4. Identify one counterargument Benlow makes, and explain how it is important to his essay.

Exploring Ideas

1. Why does Benlow think *The Simpsons* is important?

2. Watch several episodes of *The Simpsons,* finding support for Benlow's argument.

3. After exploring the following statement with others, explain what Benlow means when he says we are "drawn and colored by the ridiculous institutions that constitute our society":

In fact, if we take the show as seriously as it deserves, we might even see the broad strokes of its irony: that *we* are the cartoons, drawn and colored by the ridiculous institutions that constitute our society. (¶ 8)

Ideas for Writing

1. Evaluate some other sitcom, focusing on how it does more than "tickle our most simplistic pleasures."

2. Evaluate some form of entertainment, focusing on why it deserves to be taken more seriously.

If responding to one of these ideas, go to the **Analysis** section of this chapter to begin developing ideas for your essay.

Rethinking Divorce

Barbara Dafoe Whitehead

Although we live in a world of complex issues, we often reach for simple solutions: *Guns don't kill; people do. If you think video games are violent, don't play 'em.* And so on. Unfortunately, the mainstream American media encourage us to see complex issues in oversimplistic—and unrealistic—ways. In college courses, thinkers such as Barbara Dafoe Whitehead invite us to consider complex issues without grasping for the easy answers. Her essay is not simply an argument against divorce. Instead, it analyzes how divorce impacts people (especially children) and evaluates the *rationale* for it. She is not merely criticizing parents who divorce; she is critiquing the reasoning for many divorces.

During the past 30 years, divorce has moved from the margin of society into the mainstream. It is now an American way of life and a commonplace childhood event. Close to half of all children in the United States will experience divorce before they reach age 18. Half of those are also likely to go through a second divorce. This alone is cause for concern, since a mounting body of evidence shows that divorce creates hardship, loss, and disadvantage for many of the roughly 1 million children each year who experience it firsthand.

But the harmful impact of divorce goes far beyond just those lives. Widespread divorce has also given rise to a set of ideas and values that are antithetical to the interests of all the nation's children and destructive of the social commitments that promote their well-being. It is no coincidence that the cruel loss of the welfare entitlement for children has come on the heels of the divorce revolution. For the current rationale for divorce also undermines the case for public support for the next generation as a whole.

This rationale has emerged as the result of a historic change in the way Americans think about divorce and its consequences.

Divorce has been a feature of Western social life for 300 years, and, until recently, most Americans believed that divorce caused such severe and sometimes lasting damage to children that it should be avoided, except in cases where marriages were torn apart by violence or other severe abuse. Consequently, parents were enjoined to work out their marital problems (or at least conceal them), so that they could preserve the marriage, as the popular saying had it, "for the sake of the children."

5 This social injunction was not designed to ruin the lives of parents. Rather, its main purpose was to acknowledge that children are stakeholders in the parents' marriage, and so deserve to have their interests represented. According to this way of thinking, marriage was children's most basic form of social insurance. It tied both parents to the child's household and also brought together two families whose help and support might be turned to the child's advantage. Marriage also attached fathers to their biological children and promoted steady, ongoing parental support and sponsorship. The legal dissolution of a marriage weakened the child's claim on these resources and thus was not to be entered into lightly.

Underlying this injunction against parental divorce was a child-centered ethic. It assumed that parents, as independent adults, had an obligation to represent and serve the interests of their dependent children. It viewed parents as emotionally resilient and able to withstand adversity, whereas children were emotionally vulnerable and should be protected from it.

After the mid-1960s, this injunction lost support and credibility, both as a statement about the sources of security for children and as a statement about the obligations of parents to their children. In 1972, advice columnist Ann Landers announced that she also no longer believed in staying together for the children. Academics, therapists, even clergy counseled against it. Women increasingly rejected the idea that parents should remain in unhappy marriages. In 1962, women were evenly divided over this question. Fifteen years later, 80 percent of women said parents should not stay together.

A new rationale emerged that justified divorce. It argued that a child's happiness depended on the happiness of the individual parent, especially the mother, rather than on the marriage itself. Thus, parents should look out for their own well-being first, and the children would benefit as well—a view one scholar has called "psychological trickledown."

This reversed the ethic. It was no longer child-centered. Now it was adults who were the emotionally fragile ones and thus had to be protected against adversity while children were the resilient ones and could take it. Not surprisingly, as this new ethic gained broad acceptance in the culture, the percentage of divorces involving children increased. Today 6 out of every 10 divorces occur in families with children.

10   As a consequence of this cultural shift, middle-class Americans today see divorce as an individual entitlement that must be protected against challenge, criticism, or infringement. They reject the idea that children have an independent stake in the marriage partnership, and thus reject any social norm that affirms the child's stake. Indeed, so thoroughly does this sense of individual entitlement shape public thinking that any expression of concern for the children of divorce is interpreted as an unfeeling attack on the divorced themselves.

For this reason, politicians of every stripe duck the issue of middle-class divorce. Democrats avoid it, too, because they do not want to anger their large constituency of women who see divorce as a hard-won freedom and prerogative, nor do they want to seem unsympathetic to divorced mothers. Republicans do not want to antagonize their wealthy constituents or the party's libertarian wing, both of whom favor easy divorce. Nor does either party wish to call attention to divorce among its own leadership.

This bipartisan consensus has been politically expedient, but it has taken an enormous toll on our public commitment to children.

For one thing, it allows the middle class to define family breakup as a "them" problem—concentrated among the poor and underclass—rather than a problem that also implicates "us": the divorcing middle class. Mainstream America clings to the comfortable illusion that the declining well-being of children has to do almost solely with the behavior of unwed teenage mothers or poor women on welfare rather than with the instability of marriage and the fragility of parental commitment within its own ranks.

This isolates poor children and weakens our sense of shared obligation to improve their lot. It leads to the scapegoating of the nation's most vulnerable families. Policy makers focus on the eclipse of marriage among the most economically stressed members of the society as the root cause of family decline in the nation today. Welfare legislation urges poor parents to get married and stay married. But no one is selling this marriage to the country club crowd.

15   Moreover, and even more troublingly, today's divorce ethic undermines the social foundation for our public commitment to children. A society cannot sustain a public ethic of obligation to children if it also embraces a private ethic that devalues and disenfranchises children. If parents are entitled to put their needs and interests before those of their own children, why should they or any other adults feel an obligation to help somebody else's children?

Despite marches on Washington, D.C. and media campaigns, children's advocates are having trouble gaining support for their cause. Their struggles remind us that altruism cannot be generated by exhortation alone. For the foundation of altruism lies chiefly in family life, where it must be cultivated and practiced. A sense of obligation to others grows out of a sense of binding obligation to kith and kin. Durable social bonds depend heavily on the existence of lasting and dependable family bonds.

Yet today's children are coming of age at a time when bonds are increasingly fragile and commitments notably weak. According to survey research, high school students say that they aspire to long-lasting, mutually satisfying relationships, but despair that they will be able to achieve them. Theirs is not the angst of adolescence but realistic expectation based on life experience. Children whose parents are divorced are two to three times more likely to get divorced themselves. So the breaking of the bonds is gaining cultural and generational momentum.

Unfortunately, the weakening of commitment to children could not have come at a worse time. Today's children need higher levels of both public and parental investment if they are to succeed in a demanding global economy. The characteristics that are most essential to making one's way in a dynamic world—initiative, resourcefulness, independence, risk taking—are the very characteristics that children are less likely to acquire if they lose permanence and security in their primary family bonds. At the very time the world is asking more of today's children, we are giving them less and less.

Consequently, there is an urgent need to begin a conversation about divorce. Its purpose should not be to second-guess or criticize divorced adults. Divorce is a necessary institution. Instead, the conversation should help us reconsider our current philosophy of divorce. What's at stake is the ability of children and young adults to fulfill their desires for durable bonds and lasting commitments.

Writing Strategies

1. What is Whitehead claiming about divorce? That is, what is her overall judgment? And what criteria—or standards of judgment—does Whitehead use to evaluate divorce?

2. What type of evidence does Whitehead use to support her claims (anecdotes, allusions, statistics, etc.)? What evidence do you think is most convincing?

3. How does Whitehead help the reader go from one idea to another? Provide several examples of strategies she uses to make her writing flow.

4. How does Whitehead use her writer's voice to keep from offending or alienating the reader?

Exploring Ideas

1. How is the way that you see divorce similar to or different from the way Whitehead sees it? What accounts for the difference in thinking?

2. Ask various people about the effects of divorce in their own lives. Be sure to accurately record their responses. Then compare what they say to Whitehead's ideas. Which responses support what Whitehead says? Which refute what she says?

3. How might you participate in this discussion about divorce? Consider expanding on a point, clarifying a point, redirecting the discussion, and so on.

Ideas for Writing

1. Whitehead says, "[T]here is an urgent need to begin a conversation about divorce" (¶ 19). What other issue needs to be discussed? How might you begin that conversation?

2. What during the past 30 years has moved from the margin of society into the mainstream, and what has been its effect?

If responding to one of these ideas, go to the **Analysis** section of this chapter to begin developing ideas for your essay.

Outside Reading

Find a written evaluation, and make a photocopy or print it out. You might find an evaluation of a government policy or politician in a news magazine (such as the *National Review, Slate,* or *Pundit*). General readership magazines such as *Spin* and *Rolling Stone* regularly feature reviews of movies, music CDs, and performances. Your local city or campus newspaper may feature reviews of movies, music, and restaurants.

To conduct an electronic search of journals and magazines, go to your library's periodical database or to Info-Trac College Edition (http://infotrac.galegroup.com/itweb/). For your library database, perform a keyword search, or for InfoTrac College Edition, go to the main search box and click on "keywords." Type in subjects that interest you (such as *books, political policy, music, restaurant*) and combine that keyword with an evaluative term (*critique, review, evaluation*), such as *book and review, political and policy and critique, restaurants and reviews, punk and music and review.* (When performing keyword searches, avoid using phrases or articles such as *a, an, the;* instead, use nouns separated by *and.*) The search results will yield lists of journal and magazine articles. This same strategy can be used with a newspaper database.

You can also search the Internet. Try the search engine Altavista.com. Like most Internet search engines, Altavista.com combines words using *and.* In the search box, try various combinations, such as those above.

The purpose of this assignment is to further your understanding of evaluation and to introduce a broad range of evaluation strategies. As you are probably discovering, evaluation appears in many different places and in many different contexts. But despite the subject or the audience, some elements of evaluation are consistent. As you read through this chapter, keep the written evaluation you have discovered close by and notice the elements and strategies the writer uses. Depending on your instructor's suggestions, do one or more of the following:

1. Notice how the writer applies various strategies from this chapter. On the hard copy or photocopy:
   - Highlight the thesis if it is stated. If the thesis is implied, write it in your own words.
   - Identify (or write in the margins) the criteria, or standards of judgment, the writer uses to judge the subject.
   - Identify any counterarguments or concessions (elements of argument from Chapter 6).

2. Analyze the strategies employed by the writer. The following questions may be helpful:
   - Do you believe the writer uses appropriate criteria? Why?
   - How does the writer support his or her judgment about the subject?
   - Who is the audience for this evaluation?
   - How does the audience impact the kinds of things said in the evaluation?

3. Write at least three "Writing Strategies" questions for the evaluation.

4. Write at least three "Exploring Ideas" questions for the evaluation.

5. Write two "Ideas for Writing," such as the ones following the essays in this book.

INVENTION

"I criticize by creation . . . not by finding fault."

—Marcus Tullius Cicero

Invention is the primary strategy for producing writing that goes beyond common assumptions. As you work through the following sections, imagine possibilities beyond your initial thoughts. The **Point of Contact** section will help you to find a subject for the evaluation; **Analysis** will help you to develop particular points about the subject; and **Public Resonance** will help you to make it relevant to a community of readers. The **Thesis** and **Rhetorical Tools** sections will help you develop a specific claim and support it appropriately. As in the other chapters, the Invention questions in each section are not meant to be answered directly in your final written assignment. They are meant to prompt reflection and discovery; however, your answers may translate directly into your drafts.

POINT OF CONTACT

An evaluator needs to have particular insight into his or her subject, so choose something that you can examine carefully. Your instructor may provide subjects, or you can use the suggestions and questions below to seek out and focus on a particular subject. Once you've focused on a subject, gather information on it by taking notes:

- **Place** (such as a restaurant, movie theater, night club, amusement park, college classroom or campus, shopping mall, grocery store, etc.): Gather information about the place. How do people behave? What behavior is tolerated, supported, ignored? What is on the walls? How does this influence the mood of the place? How much open space is available? Is the place empty, crowded, stuffy, clean, lonely, isolated, intense?

- **Event** (such as a carnival, circus, beauty pageant, dance, tractor pull, art show, concert, poetry reading, company meeting, college class, etc.): What happens before the event? What is the mood? How are the participants treated during the event? What kinds of interaction occur during the event? Where does the event take place? What impact does the location have on the event?

- **Person** (such as a government official, doctor, religious leader, talk show host, roommate, professional athlete, work supervisor or manager, work associate, etc.): Evaluating a person can be tricky because it is easy to fall into an explanation of one's likes and dislikes. Instead, focus on the qualities or actions of the person in terms of his or her particular position or title. Is he or she willing to listen to people? For how long? What does he or she do while listening to someone? How do people respond or react to this person? Are people comfortable around this person? Is this person entertaining, enlightening, engaging, comforting, informative, energizing (or the opposite of any of these)?

- **Movie or Show** (such as a motion picture, sitcom, documentary, television drama, music video): Gather information and details, going beyond simple likes and dislikes. Does the dialogue reveal something about the characters that their actions do not? What kinds of graphic or sexually explicit images appear? Is the movie/show humorous or frightening in some way? How? What message(s) does the movie/show offer? Does the movie/show have stereotypes (of rich people, poor people, women, men, racial groups, children, elderly)?

- **Text** (such as a book, article, poster, letter, website, etc.): Consider texts from your major. In this case, go to one of the journals for your major, or to a database in your library. In some ways, evaluating a text is easy because it can be examined closely without having to rewind or travel somewhere. However, a written text can be a complicated mass of elements. What is the main idea or main argument of the text? What kind of evidence or support is used? How formal is the language? What is the tone of the text? If the text is an argument, does it address counterarguments? Does it use concession? What strategies are used to draw the reader into the ideas of the text?

Like a detective, gather all the information you can. Ask hard questions. Ask weird questions.

INVENTION WORKSHOP

These prompts are only a starting point; many other categories are possible. Consider, for example, evaluating a law, policy, philosophy, or even an attitude.

Once you have settled on a subject, try to generate more questions for recording details. Think of the questions as tools of exploration, as strategies for revealing everything that's occurring, as flashlights for lighting up different aspects of your subject. If groups are available, each person within a small group (three to four people) should take turns informing the group of his or her chosen subject. Then the other members should take turns offering a question about the subject while the writer records each question.

ANALYSIS

Imagine taking your car to a mechanic because you heard a strange knocking sound when you accelerate. As you pull into the garage, the mechanic smiles and exclaims, "Hey, nice car! I love Ford Mustangs! There's nothing wrong with *that* car." Obviously, you'd be a bit disoriented, and maybe a little grumpy. You would also probably complain: "Hey, I want you to tell me what's wrong with the car—tell me why it's making that sound!" The problem with this scenario is that the mechanic does no analysis and uses no *criteria* (the standards on which judgments are based). The evaluation of the car is based on the mechanic's own likes and dislikes.

Or imagine reading a review of a fine Italian restaurant. While ignoring the wine list, entrees, and presentation of the food, the reviewer gives the restaurant a very low rating because of a limited number of ice cream flavors. In this scenario, the reviewer uses the *wrong* criteria. The reviewer evaluates a fine dining establishment with criteria for judging an ice cream shop. This would be similar to judging a historical drama negatively because it is not funny: Historical dramas are not necessarily supposed to be funny, nor are fine Italian restaurants supposed to have wide varieties of ice cream.

Two challenges for evaluating:
1. Creating criteria.
2. Creating appropriate criteria.

DISCOVERING THE PURPOSE OF THE SUBJECT

The first analytical step is to discover the subject's purpose or goal—to understand, in other words, what the subject is attempting to achieve. We can only develop criteria and then evaluate a subject if we know the subject's purpose and audience. For example, we can evaluate a movie only if we understand what the movie is attempting to do: to succeed as a comedy for teens, to maintain high action for adults, or to retell a classic fairy tale for children. Evaluating something means understanding what that subject is attempting to do. For example, Sea World attempts to entertain and educate visitors. But Jayme Stayer argues that it falls short as an educational park—and even that its purpose is confused. His essay gives specific illustrations of the park's educational shortcomings.

While the specifics you recorded from the Point of Contact section tell you what your subject *does*, the following Invention questions will help you discover the *purpose* of your subject and criteria for the evaluation:

- What does this subject try to achieve? (Be specific. For example, an Italian restaurant may be attempting to provide an elegant dining experience with a particular ethnic cuisine. This is different from the goal of a general chain restaurant such as Denny's, which attempts to provide economically priced food from a general menu.)

- What do other like subjects try to achieve? (Think about subjects similar to yours—other teachers, other comedic movies, other restaurants, and so on.)

- What is the subject's audience? (Whom does your subject attempt to engage or attract?) If you have not already considered the audience, imagine who might use, benefit from, and interact with the subject.
- What goals *should* this subject, or all subjects like it, have? (It might be argued, for instance, that a restaurant should attempt to elevate the dining experience, to transform the mundane act of eating into a cultural and social event. Once this criterion is established, someone might then use it to judge a particular restaurant.)

The answer to these questions can be used directly in an evaluation. In other words, an evaluation might include a discussion about the particular criteria, or argue for the application of some criteria. For example:

> Some people have argued that teachers need not worry about their ability to entertain. Teachers, it is often said, need not consider how boring their presentations are. Such a claim, however, ignores the needs of the student. No matter how old or literate, students benefit from engaging presentations, intensive interaction, and good old-fashioned excitement. Teachers should, in fact, be judged on their skill at arousing attention in their students.

APPLYING CRITERIA TO THE SUBJECT

Now that you have criteria, you can begin making specific evaluative points about your subject. Answering the following questions will provide you with the raw material for your evaluation.

Refer to your notes from the Point of Contact section and answer the following:

- In what particular ways does the subject achieve its goal? What specific parts, tools, or strategies help the subject to achieve its goal? (For example, a restaurant depends upon such things as servers, atmosphere, and interior design, in addition to the actual food.)
- In what particular ways does the subject fall short of achieving its goal?
- What goals does the subject ignore?
- How does the subject compare to and contrast with other similar subjects?
- What is unique about your subject's approach or strategy to achieving its goal?

INVENTION WRITING

In his exploration of *The Simpsons,* Simon Benlow discovers something critical about his subject. He goes beyond a simple answer ("the show tries to make people laugh") and finds a deeper layer of that humor ("Really, every episode shows us the crummy work of our institutions day in and day out—the stuff that we've been trained to ignore.").

What does this subject try to achieve?

On the surface, *The Simpsons* tries to make people laugh. But laugh at what? We laugh at Homer falling down, Bart screwing up, Milhouse wetting the bed, etc. (In these moments, we are the bully, Nelson, when he does his famous derisive "Ha Ha!" at the other characters.) But the real target of *The Simpsons,* the real object of the laughter, must be the politicians, nuclear power plants, schools, churches, bus drivers, pot smokers, dads, moms, bullies, nerds—everyone, really. And maybe it wants us to laugh hardest at the people and institutions that seem beyond evaluation—the people and organizations that get away with crappy behavior constantly. The show wants us to laugh at ourselves and the world we've created. The show wants us to say, "We keep getting it wrong!"

In what particular ways does the subject achieve its goal?

Any given episode shows us the ugly side of things—the behavior that goes on behind the scenes when no one is looking. We get to see what teachers really think of their students. We hear them laughing in the teacher's lounge; we see principal Skinner jockeying numbers and reports to make the school look good; we see him throw together a shoddy field trip just to get the students out for the day. And we see other glimpses into ugly truth: Homer screwing up at the power plant (pushing whatever button he chooses on a control panel), persistent prison escapes, a persistent tire fire on the edge of town, etc. Really, every episode shows us the crummy work of our institutions day in and day out—the stuff that we've been trained to ignore. (When I watch, I often find myself smirking quietly in realization of the creeps running our society.)

THINKING FURTHER

Through his initial invention writing, Benlow discovers an important point: "Really, every episode shows us the crummy work of our institutions day in and day out—the stuff that we've been trained to ignore." In more invention writing, he takes this point and runs with it:

> In a way, we're living in a fantasy land ourselves when we gladly look away from the villains, rogues, thieves, charlatans running our towns, cities, and country. We put up with so much lying, cheating, and good old-fashioned sloth that the people running things are responsible to no one. We're asleep in the back seat of the car. People drunk on power are driving. Who's really living in the cartoon?

And the idea shows up in the conclusion of his final essay:

> In a swirling array of giddy and capricious entertainment, *The Simpsons* is far more real than any "real-life" sitcom hopes to be (or wants to be). In its relentless pursuit to overturn our romantic notions of ourselves and our lovely creations, it is probably more real than the audience it attracts (and certainly more real than those whom it doesn't). In fact, if we take the show as seriously as it deserves, we might even see the broad strokes of its irony: that *we* are the cartoons, drawn and colored by the ridiculous institutions that constitute our society. However, as soon as we go that far, Homer belches, Bart moons a head of state, and Grandpa soils himself; *The Simpsons* won't allow anything, including itself, to be taken seriously. (377)

Benlow has gone far beyond an initial opinion of the television show. He has *revealed* how *The Simpsons* works—how its comedy involves the audience and society at large. Like Benlow, academic writers seek to reveal something about their subjects.

As you consider your own writing project, try to see the subtle, almost hidden, mechanics of the subject. Ask yourself: *What's going on beneath the surface? (And what's going on beneath that?)*

What's going on beneath the surface? And what's going on beneath that?

PUBLIC RESONANCE

A meaningful evaluation considers how the subject affects or influences people—how it resonates with people's lives and concerns. For example, a movie critic might argue that children's movies carry the responsibility of developing notions of right and wrong. Or someone might suggest that a restaurant affects the health and well-being of a community and influences the image of a neighborhood. Ultimately, it is up to the writer to reveal the influence of a subject.

Use the following questions to develop a sense of public resonance for your evaluation:

- How does the subject influence people's lives (their health, attitudes, living conditions, etc.)?
- Why is this subject important in people's lives?
- What do people expect from the subject?
- Why is it important that the subject meets people's expectations?

INVENTION WORKSHOP

With at least one other writer, use one of the Invention questions to launch an intensive and focused discussion about your subject. Try to go beyond your first thoughts on the subject. For example, Linda, who is evaluating a new restaurant in her town, transcends her initial thoughts. Linda's initial, quick response is to see restaurants as having only one (obvious) purpose. But her discussion leads to a more complicated understanding of the subject and its relationship to people's lives:

Why is this subject important in people's lives?

Linda: That's easy . . . a restaurant serves people food. And people need food.

Marcus: But do restaurants just provide food?

Jack: No, they also provide service—someone bringing you the food. And they also make eating a social event.

Linda: But that isn't the important part.

Marcus: Well, it isn't the main part, but I'd say people need that social aspect in their lives, and eating is natu-rally a social activity. That's what's so enjoyable about eating out—you get to feel social.

Linda: But eating is also a personal thing, right? It's about the home and family, too.

Jack: I would say that restaurants are important because they provide a place where people can feel slightly special—like they're somewhere besides their living room with a bowl of cereal. They make eating feel elevated.

Linda: If that's the case, what's the deal with all these restaurants saying they're "just like home"?

Marcus: Well, that's the goal of those chain restaurants, which really aren't like home at all. They're trying to make people feel close to home.

Linda: So these restaurants provide something psychologically to people. I guess that's why restaurants spend so much on atmosphere and advertising.

Marcus: So what about the particular restaurant Chunky's? Does it make people feel "at home"?

Linda: Not really. It feels like a chain restaurant that's attempting to not feel like a chain restaurant.

Marcus: That's interesting. What things make it feel that way?

Linda has discovered something beyond the obvious about the subject's purpose: Restaurants aren't simply about food; they are also about familiarity. (There's an important psychology to food service!) This discovery could impact how she evaluates the particular restaurant.

Linda is discovering a foundation upon which her essay can rest—not just piling more evidence on top of a shaky thesis.

PUBLIC RESONANCE IN CHAPTER READINGS

Some topics, such as divorce, automatically seem to include public concern. In Whitehead's essay, for example, she does not have to convince the reader that her topic involves a broader public. However, she goes beyond saying that divorce affects people. In fact, she spends much of her essay showing the extent to which divorce influences public life, and public policy and attitude influence divorce:

> Moreover, and even more troublingly, today's divorce ethic undermines the social foundation for our public commitment to children. A society cannot sustain a public ethic of obligation to children if it also embraces a private ethic that devalues and disenfranchises children. If parents are entitled to put their needs and interests before those of their own children, why should they or any other adults feel an obligation to help somebody else's children? (380)

As Whitehead's essay suggests, an evaluation often depends on making the reader see how much the subject relates to the deep layers of public life. Likewise, Stayer makes a deep connection between the values of a theme park and American culture, and Ebert shows the relationship between *Star Wars* and contemporary American life.

INVENTION WRITING

In the following invention notes, Benlow goes deep into his subject, *The Simpsons*. In exploring people's expectations, he discovers some important comparisons between his subject and other subjects.

What do people expect from the subject?

Maybe the show is so successful because it's one of the very few that genuinely and consistently works hard at its goal—at taking the audience beyond dopey slapstick humor. The characters, even though they are hand-drawn and computer animated, are more real than the typical sitcom characters. (Honestly, I think *The Simpsons* characters have a wider range of emotions than the standard crappy sitcom.) So the show goes beyond people's expectations—it sticks out above the flat, faddish, beautiful-but-cliché non-persons that populate other sitcoms. Ironically, the standard new crap-com on NBC, CBS, and ABC this fall (or any fall) will treat its viewers as uninformed, unreflective children—and it will be more adolescent, simplistic, and un-real than *The Simpsons*.

RESEARCH

Consider using outside sources to help you invent, to help you imagine what others have said about the subject. Do not expect to find writers who share your perspective. Instead, explore for various perspectives. Have people generally found the subject valuable, worthy, deficient, dangerous, helpful? If your subject is very specific (such as a local diner) you might search for evaluations in that general category (local diners). (See pages 624–629 for help with finding sources.)

THESIS

An evaluation makes a judgment about a subject. An evaluative thesis statement gives focus to that judgment: The thesis sheds light on a particular element of the subject. For instance, a movie has many elements, such as characters, plot, cinematography, themes, special effects, and dialogue. A thesis can help create focus, telling the reader that the evaluation will deal primarily with plot, not character development and costumes:

> The movie's plot is unnecessarily confusing.

An evaluative thesis need not be completely positive or completely negative. It need not, for example, claim that a particular movie is absolutely great or downright rotten. Many evaluative thesis statements are a mixture of judgments. A statement might concede some value but focus primarily on a shortcoming as in the following:

> While the movie's cinematography is engaging, the plot is unnecessarily confusing.

To focus your evaluation and generate a thesis, answer the following:

- On what particular value or shortcoming do I want to focus?

An evaluative thesis should focus on a particular concern about the subject.

EVOLUTION OF A THESIS

A good thesis gives focus to an entire project. Linda's evaluation of a restaurant (in the Public Resonance section) gains focus as she works to craft a thesis:

The writer discovers the subject's purpose: What does this subject try to achieve?

- Chunky's attempts to give people a variety of good food and friendly service.

In exploring the public resonance, the writer discovers another, less obvious, layer: Why is this subject important in people's lives?

- People like to feel attached to their surroundings, to the places they shop and eat. Therefore, restaurants such as Chunky's try to create the illusion that diners are patronizing a friendly neighborhood grill.

The writer refines the idea into an evaluative claim:

- Although Chunky's attempts to make people feel comfortable in a small neighborhood grill, it doesn't work very well.
- Although Chunky's attempts to make people feel comfortable in a small neighborhood grill, the atmosphere and food still seem prepared by a distant corporate chef.

COMMON THESIS PROBLEMS

The blurry focus problem A sufficiently narrow focus can mean all the difference between intensive and bland writing. First, a writer needs to hone in on a particular subject, such as a particular band, a particular college campus or program. But that is often not enough. As in the following examples, the specific subjects still do not provide intensive points:

- Green Day is a great punk band.
- Big River Community College is a good school.

These statements need more focus. The writers could examine more particular elements (such as the themes of Green Day's songs or the accessible class times at Big River). Or the writers could develop more vital statements by avoiding the broad predicates "is a great . . ." and "is a good. . . ."

The obvious fact problem The goal of evaluative writing is to help readers see the subject in a new light—to help them see some particular value or shortcoming. But writers sometimes fall into the trap of stating the obvious:

- Howard Stern offends people.
- Although some purists did not like it, the *Lord of the Rings* trilogy made a lot of money at the box office.

Both of these statements announce common knowledge, facts about the radio shock jock and the Peter Jackson movies. But neither statement offers an evaluation. The stated facts say nothing about the value or shortcoming of the subjects. Offending people, for instance, may be a good thing. And making lots of money may not mean much about the movies' artistic success.

The noncommittal problem An evaluation is an argument; therefore, the writer should put forth a position. But it may be tempting to back away from the evaluation and to let the reader make up his or her own mind about the subject. The following examples back away; they lack a committed stance:

- The new building will please some and offend others.
- It's up to all readers to decide whether they appreciate Kingsolver's *The Bean Trees* or not.

ACTIVITY

In small groups, revise the problematic thesis statements on this page. Concentrate on making them more focused, more intensive, more committed.

REVISION

Share the thesis statement for your essay with two other writers. As you look over their statements, look for all three common problems: blurry focus, obvious fact, and noncommittal. Suggest strategies for narrowing and intensifying the statements.

RHETORICAL TOOLS

An evaluation puts forth a particular, and potentially debatable, opinion about a subject. And when any debatable opinion is put forth, it should be supported.

Support about the Subject

Most of the claims made in evaluations are supported with specific information about the subject itself. The writer points out particular details that illustrate the main idea and show the value or shortcoming of the subject. Notice Roger Ebert's use of particulars:

> Lucas fills his screen with loving touches. There are little alien rats hopping around the desert and a chess game played with living creatures. Luke's weather-worn "Speeder" vehicle, which hovers over the sand, reminds me of a 1965 Mustang. And consider the details creating the presence, look and sound of Darth Vader, whose fanged face mask, black cape, and hollow breathing are the setting for James Earl Jones's cold voice of doom. (364)

And Simon Benlow points out specifics within a particular episode of *The Simpsons:*

> In the power plant, we see the gross fumblings and even grosser cover-ups of an unchecked system. While Joe Fission, a cartoon icon, feeds the children pro-nuclear propaganda, Homer flummoxes his job and wreaks havoc in the plant. Homer is the poster boy of incompetence—yet he's granted a typical place in the ill-defined bureaucracy of power: Is he the "supervising technician" or the "technical supervisor"? No one knows. Through the episode, Homer is fired and then, for no good reason, hired back. The status quo prevails; three-eyed fish swim happily in the lake and the town continues to live on the brink of nuclear disaster. (376)

Jayme Stayer brings together a list of details about Sea World that a reader might not otherwise connect:

> It was only in retrospect that I realized that these annoyances were related: the high-pitched entertainment and trivial sexual jokes, the shut-up-and-listen attitude, the constant noise and verbal presence, the Big Brotherly refrains of exactly what "We here at Sea World believe." These are all rhetorical strategies of a government diverting its citizens, masking something it doesn't want the public to know. And what is it that Sea World doesn't want its customers to think about? (369)

Stayer's details are critical to his main point. He does not merely explain all the goings-on of the theme park; instead, he focuses on minute elements and connects them to his point. He helps us to see those minute elements in a new light (if we are willing).

For your evaluative claims, be sure to use details about your subject. As you develop support, ask the following:

- Which details best show my point about the subject's worth or shortcomings?

Caution: Beware of Too Much Summary

A writer should present some basic facts about, or summarize, the subject as part of the evaluation. The presentation or summary of the subject should *not* constitute the majority of an evaluation but should offer only the relevant details about the subject. For example, an evaluation using the thesis *While the movie's cinematography is engaging, the plot is unnecessarily confusing* would not devote long passages to the dress or appearance of the characters. Such information would be unnecessary and irrelevant to the evaluation.

Support Outside the Subject

As explained in Chapter 6, writers have the world of history and culture at their disposal. This applies to evaluation as well. Although evaluative writing depends primarily on details about the subject at hand, writers may also refer to outside issues/ideas/subjects to substantiate their claims. To prove a point about the subject, the writer can borrow from other moments in history, from science, nature, popular culture, or merely point out other like subjects. For example, Roger Ebert depends on other like subjects for his evaluation of *Star Wars:*

> Like *Birth of a Nation* and *Citizen Kane, Star Wars* was a technical watershed that influenced many movies that came after. These films have little in common, except that they came along at crucial moments in cinema history, when new methods were ripe for synthesis. *Birth of a Nation* brought together the developing language of shots and editing. *Citizen Kane* married special effects, advanced sound, a new photographic style, and a freedom from linear storytelling. *Star Wars* melded a new generation of special effects with the high-energy action picture; it linked space opera and soap opera, fairy tales and legend, and packaged them as a wild visual ride. (362)

Benlow indirectly refers to other prime-time television shows:

> It's not often that a television sitcom does more than tickle our most simplistic pleasures. The vast majority of sitcoms, past and present, fill twenty-two minutes (or is it nineteen?) with cliché moralism, empty characters, and adolescent dialog. Every fall we can look forward to a new parade of bad jokes and simpleton plots—created, primarily, to allow American viewers to gawk at the latest celebrity hairstyles and tight shirts. (376)

And although Stayer evaluates Sea World, he begins with an allusion to Disney:

> Mickey Mouse scares the bejesus out of me. Shamu, on the other hand, simply makes me queasy. I'm not the first to express loathing for Mickey & Co.: a giggling rodent as mascot for a nasty, litigious, multimedia *Über*-corporation. But you don't hear too many people railing against Sea World, though Shamu has a dark side too. (366)

To develop claims using outside support, consider the following questions:

- Does a historical situation or trend (such as the rise of a particular fashion, organization, or individual) illustrate something about my topic?
- Does my topic or situation appear in any movies or television shows? If so, how is it handled?
- Does my topic appear in any works of literature? If so, how is it handled?
- Does my topic relate to anything in nature?
- Has science taught us anything about my topic?
- Do any news events illustrate my point or stance?
- Have I witnessed or experienced someone or something that illustrates my point?
- Can I construct a hypothetical situation that illustrates my point?

Counterarguments and Concessions

Evaluations can also involve counterarguments and concessions (see Chapter 6, pages 286–288). Because evaluations are argumentative, they must acknowledge that other opinions (other judgments about the subject) are possible. In his evaluation of *The Simpsons,* Simon Benlow addresses, and then counters, a standard argumentative position:

> Some may argue that *The Simpsons* is just a show; it can't possibly have that much meaning. However, one thing we've learned in America is that our entertainment has more significance than history, literature, philosophy, and politics. Mainstream society gets its values, its slogans, its hairstyles, even its dialects from entertainment. We are, as the world knows, an over-entertained nation. The American average citizen reads very little (maybe a few books per year), but fills thousands of hours being massaged by the television. As the last thirty years proves undoubtedly, Americans can change their minds at the drop of a hat (about almost anything) if the television set prompts us to do so.

When television maintains such influence, it is significant and meaningful when the television itself plays with, pokes at, and parodies that influence. (377)

An evaluative argument might also concede some ground, acknowledging some value to another position. In the following passage, Linda admits some value about Chunky's restaurant:

Chunky's does work hard to establish a comfortable environment. And in some ways, it succeeds. The lighting is appropriately low; the tables are spread apart so diners don't feel squashed into a corporate experience.

Even though her main point reveals Chunky's shortcomings, she does give the restaurant some credit. In this way, her evaluation appears more open-minded.

INVENTION WORKSHOP

The Devil's Advocate

This activity is designed to generate counterarguments. The process involves an intensive group exchange. Follow these steps:

- Assemble writers into small groups (three or four per group work best).
- Each writer should have his or her thesis statement (main evaluative claim about the subject) written down.
- The first writer should read his or her thesis statement aloud to the group.
- Taking turns, each group member then should attempt to refute the position given in the statement. The idea is to play devil's advocate, to complicate the writer's ideas.
- The writer should record each opposing claim that is offered.
- After everyone in the group has given an opposing claim to the first writer, the second writer should recite his or her thesis, and the process begins again.

ACTIVITY

In the following everyday evaluations, look for support about the subject, support outside the subject, counterarguments and concessions. Then consider what other support (including counterarguments and concessions) could strengthen the evaluations.

A. Although the employees at the Exxon on Route 191 are friendly, the store has a very limited supply of items: mostly beer, snacks, and so on. Because it serves people who live so far from town, the Exxon would do a better job if it sold more grocery items. Admittedly, the Exxon has limited space, but other small gas station stores, such as the Sinclair on Route 89, utilize their small space better, thus better serving their communities.

B. Dr. Robertson's literature class is interesting, but instead of helping students understand the reading material better, the small-group discussions often turn into small-group gripe sessions, in which students simply tell each other why they didn't like the poem or story: "too long," "boring," "too many details," and so on. Although Dr. Robertson is an excellent professor, she encourages such discussions because students are "expressing themselves." In another literature class, Dr. Kellogg discourages students from explaining why they don't like the reading material, and instead provides specific questions that require students to explain how the poems or stories inspired them to "think differently." Dr. Kellogg's approach encourages students to explore and discover value in the readings.

C. Eric Clapton masterfully plays Robert Johnson songs on *Me and Mr. Johnson,* but subtleties of the songs are lost in the full-band arrangements. It would have been nice had Clapton included some acoustic versions, without bass, drums, and additional instrumentation.

ORGANIZATIONAL STRATEGIES

How Should I Include Support Outside of the Subject?

Like any support tool, the possibilities are limitless. You might reference another similar subject briefly to help describe something, as Ebert does:

> And a scene in the Death Star's garbage bin (inhabited by a snake with a head shaped like E.T.'s) also is well done. (364)

The reference to E.T. is quick. It serves only to describe the scene, and so the attention on the original subject, *Star Wars,* is only briefly interrupted or broken. However, sometimes writers, such as Ed Bell, want to put more attention on something other than the original subject, and so develop a new paragraph entirely:

> From those early days of Lucy and Ricky to our own Dharma and Greg, situation comedies have been part of American culture. And for all the advancements, it still seems like the plots of most of them are something cooked up by Lucy who dragged along Ethel and got caught (and ultimately forgiven) by Fred and Barney . . . uh . . . Fred and Ricky, I mean. Whether or not these shows instruct is, I suppose, debatable. But what is not debatable is that over the past 50 years they have entertained millions. And, I would suggest, through that very act of entertaining us, they have comforted us—the most comforting of them all being *The Andy Griffith Show.* (372)

When Should I Change Paragraphs?

When considering paragraphs, it may be helpful to think of a television documentary of the Civil War. The camera pans across an old battlefield while the host's voice narrates events. Then the scene breaks, and the camera focuses on a city that housed the soldiers; then the scene breaks again to focus on plantations that encircled a key battlefield. And when an in-depth analysis is in order, the camera shifts to a studio where the host sits talking with us about the deeper significance of the scenes; that is, the camera focuses on the speaker, so that she or he can expound on one issue.

Paragraphs in an evaluation can work similarly. They can break when the writer wants the reader to focus on a new aspect of the subject, and they can even shift whenever the writer wants to give an extended analysis of a particular point. For example, notice the beginning sentences of several of Stayer's paragraphs (see the full essay on page 366). He not only uses paragraphs to examine a new part of the subject, Sea World, but he also begins a new paragraph whenever he explores the deeper significance of one point.

How Should I Deal with Counterargument?

As in any argument, counterargument can be addressed in an unlimited number of ways. It may depend on the nature of your subject and on your position. If you are taking a relatively controversial stance or one that is not often taken, you should be prepared to counterargue. For example, imagine a writer giving a negative evaluation of *Good Morning, America,* a popular and seemingly harmless television program. In this turnabout paragraph, the writer briefly addresses an opposing view ("Certainly, many would argue that . . . ") and then immediately counters ("But the problem is not . . . "):

> *Good Morning, America* confuses news with feel-good entertainment. Like an evening sitcom, its primary goal seems to be making the viewer feel that all is right with the world—or, specifically, all is right with the shiny happy middle-class world in America. Certainly, many would argue that feel-good shows are a plus and that a morning show devoted to gloom and doom would be a great disservice. But the problem is not with the feel-good mood. It is that *Good Morning, America* postures itself as a quasi-news program, so any "news" that is given is ultimately framed by dimwitted celebrities making gratuitous appearances and exercise tips for the on-the-go lifestyle. The show smears news of the world across the same screen as the movie of the week. It's newstainment.

But you might decide to develop an opposing view for an entire paragraph and then counter in a new paragraph:

> opposing position ¶
> your counterargument ¶

And if the topic required attention to more opposing points, the pattern can be repeated:

> opposing position ¶
> your counterargument ¶
>
> opposing position ¶
> your counterargument ¶

ACTIVITY

Make a Plan

Now that you have the basic elements of your evaluation, plan how you might organize the parts. Will you state your main judgment in the introduction? Where and how will you address counterarguments? Do you have to include much support outside the subject? After you organize your ideas, present them to a small group of classmates.

WRITER'S VOICE

A good evaluation can be strongly worded without being stilted. A productive evaluation, like a good argument, attracts readers and engages those who might oppose the claims being made; a bad or unsuccessful evaluation loses readers. Here are some strategies for maintaining a cool but engaging tone.

Avoiding Harsh Description

It is often easy to use the most emotionally loaded terms to describe something or someone, to proclaim a subject "ridiculous" or "dumb." Such description, however, is usually exaggerated, and suggests that the writer has not fully investigated the subject. Be cautious of dismissing a subject by using especially harsh words. Imagine the following passage in which a writer evaluates a government official:

> Mayor G. is out of his mind. He has no understanding of the political spectrum and no concept of city governance. He is just some crazy, power-hungry man looking for a soapbox to stand on. If the city really understood the depth of his insanity, it would kick him out of office immediately.

Such language is not only full of logical fallacies, but it also reveals the writer's unfocused aggression more than revealing an interesting and important point about the mayor. Such language distracts readers from the subject, but a successful writerly voice should prompt the reader to investigate the subject closely.

Avoiding the Enthusiasm Crisis

On the other hand, be careful not to overwhelm your reader with enthusiasm. If a writer comes off too amused or too enthralled with a subject, readers may react with suspicion. Imagine a glowing evaluation of a political candidate:

> Zelda Brown is the best politician the country has seen. She has a perfect record as a community leader. Her insights into state politics are responsible for the American dream we are all living.

Certainly, any conscious and critical reader would recognize such claims as overblown and ungrounded. Too much enthusiasm alienates a reader in the same way as excessive negativity does.

Exploring the Boundaries

Some writers perform. Their language suggests, "Look at what I'm saying, and how I'm saying it!" Some writers lay low. Their language says, "I'm here, but only to give you some information." Some writers hide. Their language says, "I hope no one sees me in this essay." Every writer has a comfort zone, the place where he or she feels most at ease. The problem is that our most comfortable voices are not always the most appropriate for the situation, and they do not allow us to explore language. In some situations, the intensely performative writer may need to be invisible and understated. The writer hiding behind sentences may occasionally need to step forward and be noticed.

The best writers in all disciplines, occupations, and walks of life are not locked into a voice. They can work with various voices, depending on the writing situation. As you consider your own voice and your own habits, imagine breaking from your comfort zone. Explore the following:

ASIDES

Writers often use parentheses or dashes to make an aside comment or ask a rhetorical question. The material separated by parentheses or dashes is often a more intimate or personal note (something one might share only with the person sitting closest at the table). These often help create a particular voice because they reveal insights that are less public than other information:

> The theme of that year's show was Baywatch, which involved—predictably enough—nubile bodies in poorly choreographed dance routines, the bold rescue of someone in the water, and the odd appearances of two buffoons (fat old man with hysterical wife) . . . (367)

In both asides Stayer seems to be less public. He is sharing his personal reactions and assumptions. Although the first aside, "predictably enough," seems insignificant, it reveals Stayer's predisposition; that is, we see that he cynically expects Sea World to mimic the television show *Baywatch*. And when we read the aside, we get a little nudge from the writer, as though he is saying in our ear: "We both knew that would happen, eh?"

INTENSIVE DESCRIPTION

When writers stay abstract and general, when they do not commit to particulars, their voices remain less visible. Voices often hide behind abstraction. But when writers characterize their subjects by using particular and focused words, their voices become recognizable. For instance, notice the evaluative passage about Sea World:

> Sea World does not deal with real moral, environmental, and scientific issues, and is unable to teach a true respect for nature. True respect for nature involves the spiritual and political, two directions that Sea World avoids in favor of less important and more shallow entertainment.

And notice Stayer's more descriptive passage:

> Too occupied with obscuring the real moral, environmental, and scientific issues at stake, Sea World is constitutionally incapable of teaching respect for nature. Love of nature is spiritually informed and politically assertive. It is not the kind of passive, sentimental quackery Sea World prefers, and it cannot be taught with the crude tools in Sea World's lesson plans: glib moralizing, base pandering, and clichés masquerading as insights. (370)

Stayer commits to specific characterizations, such as "sentimental quackery," that actually do more than describe. They also create a presence in the writing. A voice that calls something "sentimental quackery" is radically different from one that calls the same thing "shallow entertainment."

As you consider your own writing, revise abstract passages and describe your subject with intense details.

VITALITY

Readers experience the writer's world and vision only through sentences. Sentences are the readers' lenses for seeing the subject. If the lenses are filmy, the reader's vision is blurry and vague. Sharp, intense sentences create a clear vision. Consider the following strategies:

Avoid Unnecessary Interruption

Sometimes writers will inject a phrase or clause between a subject and its verb or between verbs and direct objects—the main parts of a sentence. A modifying clause or phrase, like this one, comes between main parts of a sentence. Interrupting elements can be appropriate when the subject needs explaining. In the following, the interrupting element, *Bart's distempered father,* helps explain the subject. It does not slow down the reading significantly:

> Homer Simpson, <u>Bart's distempered
> father</u>, consistently leads his family
> through a campaign of treacherous
> buffoonery.

**Appropriate
interruption**

But writers sometimes interrupt the sentence flow unnecessarily:

> Nothing, <u>in the animated town of
> Springfield</u>, is worthy of the praise
> it wants.
>
> So I asked myself, <u>on my way out of
> Sea World</u>, what I had learned.

**Unnecessary
interruption**

In many cases, the interrupting element can simply move to the front of the sentence, which keeps the main parts of the sentence together. This helps the reader's consciousness move along more quickly and easily:

> <u>In the animated town of Springfield</u>, nothing is worthy of
> the praise it wants.
>
> <u>So on my way out of Sea World</u>, I asked myself what I had
> learned.

Repeat Clause or Phrase Patterns

Repetition in writing is not always bad. In fact, skillful repetition can add vitality and intensity to sentences. When writers re-create a sentence pattern, they create familiar linguistic territory for readers and drive points home. For example, Simon Benlow repeats a pattern that helps reinforce the ideas:

> Schools <u>are not</u> great institutions of learning; <u>they are</u> poorly funded bureaucracies run by flawed and desperate individuals. Government <u>is not</u> "of the people"; <u>it is</u> a mob of self-perpetuating boozers and womanizers. Business <u>is not</u> ethical or productive; <u>it is</u> a race to monopolize and swindle everyone in sight. (376)

Jayme Stayer repeats not only the sentence pattern but also actual phrases:

> Like a student who has crammed for an exam, I was able to recall lots of idiocies, but could only say I had truly learned two things. (1) <u>Thanks to</u> the film, <u>I learned that</u> sharks attack humans only when provoked, and, (2) <u>thanks to</u> their anthropomorphizing skits, <u>I learned that</u> sea otters are cute little buggers. (368–369)

As in these examples, repetition can make sentences feel more deliberate and intense, more dramatic and lively. Readers can actually feel the word patterns insisting on attention.

In a small group, rewrite the following passage. Try to repeat clause or phrase patterns so that ideas become even more intense:

Star Wars effectively brought to an end the golden era of early-1970s personal filmmaking and focused the industry on big-budget special-effects blockbusters, blasting off a trend we are still living through. But you can't blame it for what it did; you can only observe how well it did it. In one way or another all the big studios have been trying to make another *Star Wars* ever since (pictures like *Raiders of the Lost Ark, Jurassic Park,* and *Independence Day* are its heirs). It located Hollywood's center of gravity at the intellectual and emotional level of a bright teenager. (362–363)

Condense Wordy Phrases

In everyday life, we use lots of common wordy phrases—phrases that contain unnecessary words. But in writing, we have an opportunity to clean out the filler:

black in color	condense to	black
square in shape	condense to	square
try and explain	condense to	explain
due to the fact that	condense to	because
in this day and age	condense to	today (or now)
back in the day	condense to	then
at the present time	condense to	now
for the most part	condense to	mostly or most
in the final analysis	condense to	finally
in the event that	condense to	if
frank and honest	condense to	honest
revert back to	condense to	revert

Notice the wordy and condensed phrases in action:

Wordy

In the event that your sentences are more vital, your grades will likely improve due to the fact that instructors, for the most part, want intense ideas rather than bloated sentences.

Condensed

If your sentences are more vital, your grades will likely improve because most instructors want intense ideas rather than bloated sentences.

Academic writing aims to clear out useless language and make room for intense ideas.

PEER REVIEW

Exchange drafts with at least one other writer. Use the following questions to respond to specific issues in the drafts:

1. Can any phrases or terms in the thesis be narrowed? If so, circle them and make some suggestions for more focus. Does the thesis avoid the common problems? (See page 393.)

2. Does the evaluation summarize or describe the subject thoroughly? (Where might the summary or description be unnecessary or unrelated to the main idea?)

3. Where could the writer support broad evaluative claims with specific details about the subject? For instance, someone might argue "the plot is unnecessarily complicated" but avoid pointing to specific points in the plot. (This is a critical omission for an evaluative argument, so examine the claims closely.)

4. Where might the writer go beyond the specific subject (the place, text, person, etc.) and allude to some other like subject? How could other like subjects help the reader to see the main idea?

5. What other evaluative claims could be made about the subject? How could the writer address other, perhaps opposing, opinions?

6. Do any paragraphs shift focus from one point about the subject to another? Write "shifts focus" in the margins.

7. Identify any passages of harsh description or the enthusiasm crisis (page 400).

8. As a reviewer, point to particular sentences and phrases that could gain vitality and intensity. Use the following:

   a. Look for unnecessary interrupting clauses and phrases. Underline them and/or draw an arrow to show where the phrase or clause can be moved.

   b. Rewrite a sentence to create more intensity with a repeating pattern.

   c. Cross out wordy phrases, and write in more concise options.

   d. Consider vitality strategies from other chapters:

      • What sentences are over-embedded? (Point to any clauses that overlap with other clauses, causing a disconnect between ideas.)

      • Examine attributive phrases. Point out unnecessary phrases or sentences that could be boiled down.

      • Where can the writer change linking verbs to active verbs?

      • Where can the writer avoid drawing attention to *I* and *you*?

      • Help the writer change unnecessary clauses to phrases.

      • Help the writer change unnecessary phrases to words.

      • Point to expletives (such as *there are* and *it is*).

      • Help the writer change passive verbs to active verbs for more vitality.

      • Help the reader avoid common grammatical errors: comma splices, sentence fragments, or pronoun/antecedent agreement.

DELIVERY

Evaluations are serious business. Like other types of writing, they can have important consequences.

- An employee who has been evaluated negatively may not receive a raise or a promotion. Worse yet, she may lose her job.

- If a flawed policy receives a positive evaluation, it will probably not be revised as it should be. This may lead to disastrous results later on.

- A coach who evaluates talent poorly is likely to have a losing team, and talented players will not be given a fair chance to contribute.

- A jury who evaluates evidence poorly (swayed by emotional appeals, for example) may convict an innocent person (or let a guilty one go free).

Make a list of recent evaluations you have made. For example, you have probably evaluated your clothes, your meals, your classes, your friends, your own skills and behaviors, and so on.

Consider the following questions:

- Did you evaluate effectively? If not, where did you go wrong, and why? What circumstances made evaluating difficult?

- What can you learn from your evaluation about yourself, about evaluating, about your world?

- Who besides you was affected? How did your ability to evaluate help or harm others?

Beyond the Essay: Classroom Evaluations

College administrators and faculty consistently examine student classroom evaluations, those forms that you fill out at the end of every semester. Administrators and professors alike argue about their effectiveness at measuring the success of courses. Some argue that evaluations are too prone to bias, that students who do well give good evaluations and

students who do poorly give poor evaluations. Others argue that student evaluations are "popularity contests" that encourage professors to inflate grades. All these arguments are evaluating evaluations!

Part of the debate about student evaluations involves the criteria—the standards that should be used. Some of the criteria in this debate are:

- Rigor of the material
- Convenience for students
- Entertainment quality of the material being presented
- Students' interests
- Instructor's appearance
- Instructor's personality
- Grading policies or standards
- Syllabus/calendar clarity
- Adherence to course objectives
- Adherence to departmental objectives
- Individual student needs
- Acknowledgement of students' personal lives

As a college student, you may have significant insight to this issue. Focus on one of the following activities to explore this issue further:

1. As a class, debate one or more of the following:

   a. Individual student needs should (or should not) be a primary concern of a college course.

   b. The rigor of the material should (or should not) be adjusted to meet students' abilities.

   c. A college class should, above all else, be convenient for the college customer.

2. In small groups, develop a set of questions that could be used to evaluate a college writing course. Ask yourselves: What criteria should be used in a college classroom evaluation? What specific components should be examined for a writing course?

SEARCHING FOR CAUSES

Chapter Contents

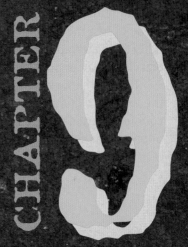

CHAPTER 9

"All human beings should try to learn before they die what they are running from, and to, and why."

—James Thurber

When something happens in a community, everyone wants to know why. Why did the apartment building catch on fire? Why did the incumbent mayor's campaign lose momentum? Why are so many kids absent from school? What causes the traffic jam on I-95 every day? Why did the stock market suddenly drop? Why did the terrorists attack? Of course, everybody has guesses, but it takes a close analysis to discover the possible causes of such phenomena. Fire officials inspect the ashes of a burned apartment building; political scientists examine candidates' speeches and poll results; civil engineers look closely at travel patterns and highway capacity; economists deliberate over consumption trends and overseas markets. In all these cases, the people searching for causes are detectives attempting to find answers amidst a dizzying array of possibilities.

The search for causes constitutes much of the workload in many occupations. Doctors, of course, diagnose patients (looking for the cause of particular symptoms). Psychologists try to understand the causes of personality disorders or behavioral problems. Business executives hold weekly meetings and discuss the causes of production failures. Education specialists work with children to find the cause of scholastic problems. And, as you can imagine (or as you may have witnessed), the search for such causes is not easy. Any number of factors can contribute to an effect. Take, for example, low proficiency test scores in public schools: School administrators might argue that poor teaching is the cause; teachers may point to poor parenting and discipline problems in the classroom; parents may point to bullying on school grounds or drug abuse; others might point to the tests themselves as the cause. The search for this cause, as it turns out, is a heated debate.

In academia, students spend much of their time studying causes:

- In an engineering class, students try to discover what causes one generator to produce more energy than another.

- Educational psychology students discuss why a particular student has lost all motivation.
- In history and economics seminars, students study economic conditions of the 19th century and debate the causes of the American Civil War.
- A class of physics students tries to determine the cause of black holes.

It might even be said that academia prepares people to understand causes in different fields — that is, that the study of a particular discipline gives students the critical perspectives necessary for asking the right questions (to find the right answers) within their fields. But despite the particular field or discipline, the process of discovery (of focusing and analyzing) is much the same, and the act of communicating one's discoveries is key in every situation.

This chapter will help you focus on a particular topic (a behavior, event, trend), discover a possible cause, and then develop an argument in favor of that particular cause. The following essays will provide valuable insight to necessary writing strategies. After reading the essays, you can find a topic in one of two ways:

1. Go to the **Point of Contact** section to find a problem from your everyday life.
2. Read the following essays and choose one of the **Ideas for Writing** that follow.

After finding a subject, go to the **Analysis** section to begin developing the evaluation.

In the following essays, notice how each writer offers a particular stance on an issue and develops that stance throughout the entire essay. The texts in this chapter are arguments in many ways: They put forward a particular belief (about the cause of a phenomenon) and attempt to prove its validity. Some of the essays also make explicit use of counterargument, refuting opposing claims or, more specifically, refuting other interpretations of cause. For example, Schor refutes others' interpretation of the cause of overconsumption. Some of the writers argue about the cause of a phenomenon because they hope for a change in behavior or policy. Jacoby, for instance, explains the cultural causes for girls' deficiency in science and math so that it may be avoided. And Schor hopes to point out the cause of the "consumption problem" in order to redirect Americans' economic habits. As you read, consider how these essays embody the writing strategies discussed in other chapters: observation, concept analysis, the elements of argument, and the elements of evaluation.

The New Politics of Consumption: Why Americans Want So Much More Than They Need

Juliet Schor

A search for causes can be concrete (Why does the sewer system keeping flooding?) or abstract (Why do people want so much stuff?). In this essay, Juliet Schor, an economist and the Director of Women's Studies at Harvard University, explores a number of trends that seem directly related to overconsumption, or what she deems a *new consumerism*. Schor also explains the conclusions of other economists and how they miss the mark.

In contemporary American culture, consuming is as authentic as it gets. Advertisements, getting a bargain, garage sales, and credit cards are firmly entrenched pillars of our way of life. We shop on our lunch hours, patronize outlet malls on vacation, and satisfy our latest desires with a late-night click of the mouse.[1]

Yet for all its popularity, the shopping mania provokes considerable dis-ease: Many Americans worry about our preoccupation with getting and spending. They fear we are losing touch with more worthwhile values and ways of living. But the discomfort rarely goes much further than that; it never coheres into a persuasive, well-articulated critique of consumerism. By contrast, in the 1960s and early '70s, a far-reaching critique of consumer culture was a part of our political discourse. Elements of the New Left, influenced by the Frankfurt School, as well as by John Kenneth Galbraith and others, put forward a scathing indictment. They argued that Americans had been manipulated into participating in a dumbed-down, artificial consumer culture, which yielded few true human satisfactions.

For reasons that are not hard to imagine, this particular approach was short-lived, even among critics of American society and culture. It seemed too patronizing to talk about manipulation or the "true needs" of

---

[1] Sources for much of the data cited in this article can be found in the notes to *The Overspent American: Why We Want What We Don't Need* (New York: Harper, 1999) or by contacting the author.

average Americans. In its stead, critics adopted a more liberal point of view, and deferred to individuals on consumer issues. Social critics again emphasized the distribution of resources, with the more economistic goal of maximizing the incomes of working people. The good life, they suggested, could be achieved by attaining a comfortable, middle-class standard of living. This outlook was particularly prevalent in economics, where even radical economists have long believed that income is the key to well-being. While radical political economy, as it came to be called, retained a powerful critique of alienation in production and the distribution of property, it abandoned the nascent intellectual project of analyzing the consumer sphere. Few economists now think about how we consume, and whether it reproduces class inequality, alienation, or power. "Stuff" is the part of the equation that the system is thought to have gotten nearly right.

Of course, many Americans retained a critical stance toward our consumer culture. They embody that stance in their daily lives—in the ways they live and raise their kids. But the rejection of consumerism, if you will, has taken place principally at an individual level. It is not associated with a widely accepted intellectual analysis, and an associated *critical politics of consumption.*

5   But such a politics has become an urgent need. The average American now finds it harder to achieve a satisfying standard of living than 25 years ago. Work requires longer hours, jobs are less secure, and pressures to spend more intense. Consumption-induced environmental damage remains pervasive, and we are in the midst of widespread failures of public provision. While the current economic boom has allayed consumers' fears for the moment, many Americans have long-term worries about their ability to meet basic needs, ensure a decent standard of living for their children, and keep up with an ever-escalating consumption norm.

In response to these developments, social critics continue to focus on income. In his impressive analysis of the problems of contemporary American capitalism, *Fat and Mean,* economist David Gordon emphasized

income *adequacy.* The "vast majority of US households," he argues, "can barely make ends meet. . . . Meager livelihoods are a *typical* condition, an *average* circumstance." Meanwhile, the Economic Policy Institute focuses on the distribution of income and wealth, arguing that the gains of the top 20 percent have jeopardized the well-being of the bottom 80 percent. Incomes have stagnated and the robust 3 percent growth rates of the 1950s and '60s are long gone. If we have a consumption problem, this view implicitly states, we can solve it by getting more income into more people's hands. The goals are redistribution and growth.

It is difficult to take exception to this view. It combines a deep respect for individual choice (the liberal part) with a commitment to justice and equality (the egalitarian part). I held it myself for many years. But I now believe that by failing to look deeper—to examine the very nature of consumption—it has become too limiting. In short, I do not think that the "income solution" addresses some of the most profound failures of the current consumption regime.

Why not? First, consuming is part of the problem. Income (the solution) leads to consumption practices that exacerbate and reproduce class and social inequalities, resulting in—and perhaps even worsening—an unequal distribution of income. Second, the system is structured such that an *adequate* income is an elusive goal. That is because adequacy is relative—defined by reference to the incomes of others. Without an analysis of consumer desire and need, and a different framework for understanding what is adequate, we are likely to find ourselves, twenty years from now, arguing that a median income of $100,000—rather than half that—is adequate. These arguments underscore the social context of consumption: the ways in which our sense of social standing and belonging comes from what we consume. If true, they suggest that attempts to achieve equality or adequacy of individual incomes without changing consumption patterns will be self-defeating.

Finally, it is difficult to make an ethical argument that people in the world's richest country need more when the global income gap is so wide, the disparity in world resource use so enormous, and the possibility that we are already consuming beyond the Earth's ecological carrying capacity so likely. This third critique will get less attention in this essay—because it is more familiar, not because it is less important—but I will return to it in the conclusion.

10   I agree that justice requires a vastly more equal society, in terms of income and wealth. The question is whether we should also aim for a society in which our relationship to consuming changes, a society in which we consume *differently.* I argue here for such a perspective: for a critique of consumer culture and practices. Somebody needs to be for quality of life, not just quantity of stuff. And to do so requires an approach that does not trivialize consumption, but accords it the respect and centrality it deserves.

The New Consumerism

A new politics of consumption should begin with daily life, and recent developments in the sphere of consumption. I describe these developments as "the new consumerism," by which I mean an upscaling of lifestyle norms; the pervasiveness of conspicuous, status goods and of competition for acquiring them; and the growing disconnect between consumer desires and incomes.

Social comparison and its dynamic manifestation—the need to "keep up"—have long been part of American culture. My term is "competitive consumption," the idea that spending is in large part driven by a comparative or competitive process in which individuals try to keep up with the norms of the social group with which they identify—a "reference group." Although the term is new, the idea is not. Thorstein Veblen, James Duesenberry, Fred Hirsch, and Robert Frank have all written about the importance of relative position as a dominant spending motive. What's new is the redefinition of reference groups: Today's comparisons are less likely to take place between or among households of similar means. Instead, the lifestyles of the upper middle class and the rich have become a more salient point of reference for people throughout the income distribution. Luxury, rather than mere comfort, is a widespread aspiration.

One reason for this shift to "upscale emulation" is the decline of the neighborhood as a focus of comparison. Economically speaking, neighborhoods are relatively homogeneous groupings. In the 1950s and '60s, when Americans were keeping up with the Joneses down the street, they typically compared themselves to other households of similar incomes. Because of this focus on neighbors, the gap between aspirations and means tended to be moderate.

But as married women entered the workforce in larger numbers—particularly in white-collar jobs—they were exposed to a more economically diverse group of people, and became more likely to gaze upward. Neighborhood contacts correspondingly declined, and the workplace became a more prominent point of reference. Moreover, as people spent less time with neighbors and friends and more time on the family-room couch, television became more important as a source of consumer cues and information. Because television shows are so heavily skewed to the "lifestyles of the rich and upper middle class," they inflate the viewer's perceptions of what others have, and by extension what is worth acquiring—what one must have in order to avoid being "out of it."

15   Trends in inequality also helped to create the new consumerism. Since the 1970s, the distribution of income and wealth have shifted decisively in the direction of the top 20 percent. The share of after-tax family income going to the top 20 percent rose from 41.4 percent in 1979 to 46.8 percent in 1996. The share of wealth controlled by the top 20 percent rose from 81.3 percent in 1983 to 84.3 percent in 1997. This windfall resulted in a surge in conspicuous spending at the top. Remember the 1980s—the decade of greed and excess? Beginning with the super-rich, whose gains have been disproportionately higher, and trickling down to the merely affluent, visible status spending was the order of the day. Slowed down temporarily by the recession during the early 1990s, conspicuous luxury consumption has intensified during the current boom. Trophy

homes, diamonds of a carat or more, granite counter-tops, and sport utility vehicles are the primary consumer symbols of the late 1990s. Television, as well as films, magazines, and newspapers ensure that the remaining 80 percent of the nation is aware of the status purchasing that has swept the upper echelons.

In the meantime, upscale emulation had become well-established. Researchers Susan Fournier and Michael Guiry found that 35 percent of their sample aspired to reach the top 6 percent of the income distribution, and another 49 percent aspired to the next 12 percent. Only 15 percent reported that they would be satisfied with "living a comfortable life"—that is, being middle class. But 85 percent of the population cannot earn the six-figure incomes necessary to support upper-middle-class lifestyles. The result is a growing aspirational gap: With desires persistently outrunning incomes, many consumers find themselves frustrated. One survey of US households found that the level of income needed to fulfill one's dreams doubled between 1986 and 1994, and is currently more than twice the median household income.

The rapid escalation of desire and need, relative to income, also may help to explain the precipitous decline in the savings rate—from roughly 8 percent in 1980, to 4 percent in the early 1990s, to the current level of zero. (The stock market boom may also be inducing households not to save; but financial assets are still highly concentrated, with half of all households at net worths of $10,000 or less, including the value of their homes.) About two-thirds of American households do not save in a typical year. Credit card debt has skyrocketed, with unpaid balances now averaging about $7,000 and the typical household paying $1,000 each year in interest and penalties. These are not just low-income households. Bankruptcy rates continue to set new records, rising from 200,000 a year in 1980 to 1.4 million in 1998.

The new consumerism, with its growing aspirational gap, has begun to jeopardize the quality of American life. Within the middle class—and even the upper middle class—many families experience an almost threatening pressure to keep up, both for themselves and their children. They are deeply concerned about the rigors of the global economy, and the need to have their children attend "good" schools. This means living in a community with relatively high housing costs. For some households this also means providing their children with advantages purchased on the private market (computers, lessons, extra-curriculars, private schooling). Keeping two adults in the labor market—as so many families do, to earn the incomes to stay middle class—is expensive, not only because of the second car, child-care costs, and career wardrobe. It also creates the need for time-saving, but costly, commodities and services, such as take-out food and dry cleaning, as well as stress-relieving experiences. Finally, the financial tightrope that so many households walk—high expenses, low savings—is a constant source of stress and worry. While precise estimates are difficult to come by, one can argue that somewhere between a quarter and half of all households live paycheck to paycheck.

These problems are magnified for low-income households. Their sources of income have become increasingly erratic and inadequate, on account of employment instability, the proliferation of part-time jobs, and restrictions on welfare payments. Yet most low-income households remain firmly integrated within consumerism. They are targets for credit card companies, who find them an easy mark. They watch more television, and are more exposed to its desire-creating properties. Low-income children are more likely to be exposed to commercials at school, as well as home. The growing prominence of the values of the market, materialism, and economic success make financial failure more consequential and painful.

20 These are the effects at the household level. The new consumerism has also set in motion another dynamic: It siphons off resources that could be used for alternatives to private consumption. We use our income in four basic ways: private consumption, public consumption, private savings, and leisure. When consumption standards can be met easily out of current income, there is greater willingness to support public goods, save

privately, and cut back on time spent at work (in other words, to "buy leisure"). Conversely, when lifestyle norms are upscaled more rapidly than income, private consumption "crowds out" alternative uses of income. That is arguably what happened in the 1980s and 1990s: resources shifting into private consumption, and away from free time, the public sector, and saving. Hours of work have risen dramatically, saving rates have plummeted, public funds for education, recreation, and the arts have fallen in the wake of a grass-roots tax revolt. The timing suggests a strong coincidence between these developments and the intensification of competitive consumption—though I would have to do more systematic research before arguing causality. Indeed, this scenario makes good sense of an otherwise surprising finding: that indicators of "social health" or "genuine progress" (i.e., basic quality-of-life measures) began to diverge from GDP in the mid-1970s, after moving in tandem for decades. Can it be that consuming and prospering are no longer compatible states?

To be sure, other social critics have noted some of these trends. But they often draw radically different conclusions. For example, there is now a conservative jeremiad that points to the recent tremendous increases in consumption and concludes that Americans just don't realize how good they have it, that they have become overly entitled and spoiled. Reduced expectations, they say, will cure our discontents. A second, related perspective suggests that the solution lies in an act of psychological independence—individuals can just ignore the upward shift in consumption norms, remaining perfectly content to descend in the social hierarchy.

These perspectives miss the essence of consumption dynamics. Americans did not suddenly become greedy. The aspirational gap has been created by structural changes—such as the decline of community and social connection, the intensification of inequality, the growing role of mass media, and heightened penalties for failing in the labor market. Upscaling is mainly defensive, and has both psychological and practical dimensions.

Similarly, the profoundly social nature of consumption ensures that these issues cannot be resolved by pure acts of will. Our notions of what is adequate, necessary, or luxurious are shaped by the larger social context. Most of us are deeply tied into our particular class and other group identities, and our spending patterns help reproduce them.

Thus, a collective, not just an individual, response is necessary. Someone needs to address the larger question of the consumer culture itself. But doing so risks complaints about being intrusive, patronizing, or elitist. We need to understand better the ideas that fuel those complaints.

Writing Strategies

1. Schor's essay is longer than the type of essay often written in college writing classes. What strategies does she employ that help the reader to follow her lengthy discussion/argument?

2. Find one paragraph in Schor's essay that you think is especially well-written. What is the main idea of that paragraph? And how does she support that main idea (example, allusion, statistics, and so on)?

3. How does Schor let the reader know the main idea of her essay? Does she state it or imply it? If implied, is it clear?

4. Schor introduces the reader to new terms and concepts, such as "the new consumerism." What strategy does she use to make this term clear to the reader? What other new terms (or concepts) does she use? How does she make them clear to the reader?

5. Describe Schor's overall organizational strategy. How are her ideas arranged and connected for the benefit of the reader?

Exploring Ideas

1. In a paragraph or so, explain what you think Schor is trying to accomplish in this essay.

2. How does Schor encourage the reader to think about consumerism?

3. How is the way that Schor sees consumerism, or consumption, similar to or different from the way you see it? Write down your major areas of agreement and disagreement. Then explain the reasons you agree or disagree.

4. Keeping in mind Schor's ideas, explore your own spending habits and the habits of those around you. What evidence can you find for Schor's argument? What evidence can you find to refute what Schor says?

5. Discuss Schor's main ideas and how they are or are not played out in your life and the lives of your classmates and others. Then, through discussion, writing, and further research, attempt to discover the causes of the way you consume, and the consequences.

Ideas for Writing

1. What is the cause of some negative trend in behavior?

2. What is the cause of some problem on your campus or in the field you are studying?

If responding to one of these ideas, go to the **Analysis** section of this chapter to begin developing ideas for your essay.

Throwing Up Childhood

Leonard Kress

The most personal or intimate exploration can have significance for others. Even the contents of one's stomach can have public resonance. Good writers can make a personal search for causes resonate with the lives of others. In this essay, Leonard Kress tries to pinpoint his bulimic childhood behavior. In that search, he realizes that his own understanding runs contrary to expert opinion and the official positions of published research. But he focuses on, even seeks out, the tension between his own understanding and the answers he finds. In this sense, Kress's essay illustrates thinking further—exploring the cracks and crevices of what he knows and what others know.

I remember standing breathless and exhilarated in the hotel lobby, the rest of my family still in the dining room finishing their evening meal. I'm not sure whether or not they can see what I see—the thin gray broken line on the carpet, leading all the way to the back entrance. This time I don't make it out to the patio, the swimming pool, down to the beach, inundated this summer with jellyfish and jelly lichen, Portuguese Man O'War. If only they would leave their table, they could easily find me by following the half-digested dinner rolls and the masticated but intact sirloin morsels, the bitter tomato-broth they soak in. Hansel, whom I imagine to be about my age (seven and a half), couldn't have left a better trail for him and his sister to follow back to their woodland cottage. Even if the birds had pecked it clean, that bile-stain would still remain, like a stripe dividing a country highway. We are here in Miami Beach to visit my grandparents, Ada and Max, and since they live in a tiny apartment, we are staying in this beachfront hotel, more luxurious than we are used to. It occurs to me that only the desk clerk has been following my whole grand performance with any interest. Whatever others there might be carefully and kindly turn away their gaze. But the desk clerk glances over to me and across the lobby, as if surveying both the damage and the cause of it. I recognize that smirk and wonder, was he a vomiter too? I don't have a clue and don't really care; he assiduously computes the cleaning bill.

This isn't the first time. As far back as I can remember, meals out with my parents were capped with similar grand gestures. It didn't matter whether it was a Howard Johnson's, a deli, a steakhouse—sometimes I'd conveniently make it to the bathroom sink or toilet; other times I'd leave a pile on the floor, splatter the door, the parking lot, the car. I don't know how it happened; I can't make sense of the progression that leads up to it. I ordered from the menu like my brother and sister—appetizer, entrée, dessert. I didn't steal from anyone's plate, stabbing a slab of beef or spearing a soggy fry while they tied a shoe or fidgeted over a response to some parental inquiry. I didn't pick their dregs, dumping half-gnawed bones onto my own fully gnawed pile, I didn't reach across plates and setting to grab a soppy crust of bread or buttered roll. We were all healthy eaters in my family, and we were all well within the recommended weight guidelines. Granted, I was a fast eater; my father and brother were also fast eaters—we lacked the patience to chew, always anxious to move on to something new. I certainly didn't deliberate over the plate like my younger sister did, who always ate like a bird. She'd barely be attending to her main course while the rest of us scraped up the last of our desserts. Compared to her, I wolfed my food, scarfed it, inhaled it, terms I heard over and over again much later. I was a healthy, active second-grader; dinner meant disjuncture, interruption, tactic of delay constructed by mothers to keep their sons from the real work of childhood—hide and seek, wiffle ball, bikes, backyard Olympiad.

I often wonder now what led me to such disgusting behavior—what might lead any child to such disgusting behavior. Like any good 21st-century questioner/researcher, I go to the Internet, hopeful that a search of current medical literature will provide answers and understanding. So I begin my search, seated in front of my computer. I find a gopher (its name is OVID—aptly named for the ancient Roman writer of *Metamorphoses* or *Transformations*), and it's as versatile as a left-handed shortstop, a triple-threat, able to simultaneously search pediatric, psychology, anthropology, and other allied health databases. I'm confident that with the right *keyword search,* the exact *cross-referencing* or *Boolean limitation,* I will be able to call up some insight. This should be a breeze, I think, *childhood bulimia,* thousands of hits, hundreds of studies from millions of research dollars. After all, anorexia/bulimia was, arguably, *the disease* of the 1990s. I do find something. In *The International Journal of Eating Disorder*s (1995) there's an article titled, "Premorbid Onset of Psychopathology in Long-term Recovered Anorexia Patients." And the abstract tells me that 58% of anorexics reported "childhood anxiety disorders at age ten (plus or minus five years)."

Intensive details.

Paragraph shift indicates the new focus: from describing the behavior to searching for causes.

An allusion to the writer. Are the titles significant?

Narrating the actual searching process.

No obvious reason for his vomiting.

He was not an overeater. He was not obese or unhealthy.

Active & energetic—otherwise "normal"?

Anorexia and bulimia are the same type of disease? ("the disease of the '90s")

Eating disorders associated with psychological problems.

The most common is childhood depression beginning well before the eating disorder. I also locate "Determinants of Adolescent Obesity: A Comparison with Anorexia Nervosa," in *Adolescence* (1988), which claims that "both anorexics and the obese are characterized by overprotectedness and enmeshment, resulting from a poor sense of identity and effectiveness." After a whole week of research, this seems to be the extent of my findings. I can find nothing to urge me to go beyond the abstracts, nothing at all, though I type in "eating disorder," "vomiting," "obesity," "abnormal psychology," "gluttony," "disgusting and destructive behavior"—always cross-referenced with "childhood."

I was a happy child. I really was. And not only in my parents' estimation. I see it now in old snapshots and projected slides. When I was two, the neighbors nicknamed me "Smiley." It stuck. Nothing fazed me—not even the most traumatic incident of my early life, driving my trike over the sides of that same neighbor's screened-in porch, the screens removed for spring cleaning. The tumble left a pus-filled bruise, two weeks in draining. My parents said that I never flinched or lost that smile, even as that neighbor dug and poked and pressed and guiltily reapplied her expert pity dressings, the whole time boasting incessantly about her favorite nephew, a fighter pilot almost blasted out of the Korean sky a few years back. "Praise God," I remember her saying, "that he wasn't tortured or starved." Thank God he returned, intact, and (my parents informed me years later) in time to be chosen as one of the original Mercury 7 astronauts. Somehow it seems that this might have been right about the time that I began my career as a public barfer.

5   Only once do I remember doing it in secret. It was at my grandparents' golden wedding anniversary celebration, a feast my grandmother herself with the help of her Kovno and Litwak sisters, Bronx nieces, and Jersey City daughters prepared. I am not one, however, to gorge on a sumptuous catalogued recitation of the feast (more scrumptious than the feast itself?). For the food itself never seemed to matter. For the most part, I ate whatever was cast in front of me. The party took place at my aunt's apartment in Stuyvesant Town on the East Side, where the shouts of roller skaters and stick-ball players rose up from the playground, mixing with the shrill stab of ambulance, police car, fire truck, and the play-by-play of the Yankees . . . and it is this final detail that I most vividly recall—not the carp swimming all night in the bathtub, walloped against the

Outside source.

The literature does not describe his case.

Paragraph shifts from the search back to describing the past.

Details to show he was healthy and energetic.

Could this be a connection?

Why is this the most vivid detail for him? Is there a connection?

porcelain rim in the morning, then beheaded and sopped in a bucket of brine. Not the pickled tongue or brisket or pot roast, and kasha, knishes, blintzes served up beneath gobs of sour cream, like Chekhov's "crisp bleenies, lacy and plump as the shoulder of a merchant's daughter." There was a full week of food preparation that I gobbled down and then disposed of with great ease and easing. I didn't even have to stick my finger down my throat; I could simply will the partially chewed hearty chunks of meat and potato up from their sour churning stock. It felt so good! *The Encyclopedia of Pediatric Psychology* (1979) reports that children who vomit, farfetched as it sounds, even "those who have learned society's aversions . . . can overcome such scruples and experience vomiting as cathartic, even orgasmic."

I still find it odd that my parents never questioned why I did it. They never seemed to mind, though I'm sure they did, privately. They must have been embarrassed, if not mortified by my behavior. In spite of that, we went out to dinner often, several times a month. Not once did they ask me to modify my order, limit my portion. They never motioned the waitress aside, and with the promise of a bigger tip, asked her to go easy on the fries. My brother and sister were silent, too, as though my barfing were a perfectly acceptable alternative to an after-dinner mint, a toothpick, a wet-wipe wrapped like a condom. Perhaps they were too busy stashing away the details of the affront, safekeeping for a time of need—like Aesop's despicable, self-righteous ant. I can only imagine the hay they might have later made by simple melodramatic evocations of the sounds of my gagging, as it echoed in tiny bathrooms. The deep, throaty sound of plosively expelling vomit. "Well, whatever I did can't be as gross and disgusting as THAT," I can hear them repeating over and over till they got what they wanted. Or did they have their own equally disgusting but self-customized techniques of catharsis and orgasm back then—I wondered. Does everyone, I still wonder? And how could a "D" in French or a detention or a missed meal or a dent in the car compare with what I did, over and over and over?

It couldn't, of course, it would pale in comparison to that cathartic act of throwing up (knowing that others could hear my retching) that left my face bloodless and pale, my extremities tingling, my chest heaving with giddiness. Perhaps earlier generations of parents and child psychologists had a better understanding of its power and attraction. And that's why older writings on the subject,

---

Margin notes:

The details show the culinary tradition of his family.

The outside source integrated (colliding with?) his experiences.

Counterargument?

New paragraph: focus on others around him

Allusion to the ant and grasshopper story.

Public resonance: Does everyone have a technique for releasing tension?

Here's the first connection between the search and his experience: It's pleasurable.

Catharsis = relief/release of tension.

The main cause is need for catharsis?

rare but not unheard of, prescribe such drastic, almost Draconian treatment to stop the behavior. *The Encyclopedia of Pediatric Psychology* (1970) lacks entries for either anorexia or bulimia and refers to it as "psychogenic vomiting." It predates the public and medical concern over the condition, and takes a stern, almost Victorian approach to treatment:

Draconian = code of extreme severity or rigor.

> Karo syrup, Phenobarbital, anticonvulsants, chlorpromazine, antihistamines, chin straps, esophageal blocks, thickened feedings, removal of normal appendix, electric shock therapy, and even intensive prayer are all reported to have been used successfully to resolve the problem.

His situation, again, seems slightly different than the literature suggests.

In some cases, and in my case, I suppose, the patient simply outgrows it.

Writing Strategies

1. Evaluate Kress's introduction. Does it grab the reader's interest? Does it lead purposefully into the body of the essay? Does it establish a tone? What else does it do? What does it fail to do?

2. Identify several sentences that bring Kress's essay to life. Explain why you identified those particular sentences.

3. How does Kress use secondary (written) sources in his essay? Are they helpful? In what way or ways do they help him to make his point?

4. Identify at least two allusions in Kress's essay, and use them to explain not merely what an allusion is, but how an allusion conveys meaning.

Exploring Ideas

1. What is Kress trying to accomplish in his essay?

2. Who might benefit from reading Kress's essay? What might be the benefit?

3. Explore a past behavior of your own, searching for its cause. Research the behavior by reading about it and/or talking to others. Your goal is to arrive not at *the* cause, but at several possible causes. List the possible causes.

4. Evaluate each of the possible causes you discovered for #3 above. Which ones seem most likely to be the cause of your behavior? Provide convincing evidence to support your conclusion.

Ideas for Writing

1. Reflect as an adult on a puzzling childhood experience. What might be the cause of a certain behavior that you have not yet understood?

2. Kress considers his family's reaction to his vomiting. What is the cause of someone else's puzzling reaction to you?

If responding to one of these ideas, go to the **Analysis** section of this chapter to begin developing ideas for your essay.

"[D]id they have their own equally disgusting but self-customized techniques of catharsis and orgasm . . . ? Does everyone?"

Sex, Lies, and Conversation: Why Is It So Hard for Men and Women to Talk to Each Other?

Deborah Tannen

The essays in this chapter are argumentative in nature; that is, they argue that a particular cause is responsible for a behavior. As with any argument, the writers must rely on ample and reasonable evidence, which can take many forms: examples, testimony, anecdotes, statistics, allusions, all the appeals, and so on. In her argument, Deborah Tannen, a linguist and author of many books, relies on testimony and anecdotes to build a case for gender-specific behaviors—a slippery and complex phenomenon. She also points to her own research to support the claims.

I was addressing a small gathering in a suburban Virginia living room—a women's group that had invited men to join them. Throughout the evening, one man had been particularly talkative, frequently offering ideas and anecdotes, while his wife sat silently beside him on the couch. Toward the end of the evening, I commented that women frequently complain that their husbands don't talk to them. This man quickly concurred. He gestured toward his wife and said, "She's the talker in our family." The room burst into laughter; the man looked puzzled and hurt. "It's true," he explained. "When I come home from work I have nothing to say. If she didn't keep the conversation going, we'd spend the whole evening in silence."

The episode crystallizes the irony that although American men tend to talk more than women in public situations, they often talk less at home. And this pattern is wreaking havoc with marriage.

The pattern was observed by political scientist Andrew Hacker in the late '70s. Sociologist Catherine Kohler Riessman reports in her new book *Divorce Talk* that most of the women she interviewed—but only a few of the men—gave lack of communication as the reason for their divorces. Given the current divorce rate of nearly 50 percent, that amounts to millions of cases in the United States every year—a virtual epidemic of failed conversation.

In my own research, complaints from women about their husbands most often focused not on tangible inequities such as having given up the chance for a career to accompany a husband to his, or doing far more than their share of daily life-support work like cleaning, cooking, social arrangements, and errands. Instead, they focused on communication: "He doesn't listen to me," "He doesn't talk to me." I found, as Hacker observed years before, that most wives want their husbands to be, first and foremost, conversational partners, but few husbands share this expectation of their wives.

5   In short, the image that best represents the current crisis is the stereotypical cartoon scene of a man sitting at the breakfast table with a newspaper held up in front of his face, while a woman glares at the back of it, wanting to talk.

Linguistic Battle of the Sexes

How can women and men have such different impressions of communication in marriage? Why the widespread imbalance in their interests and expectations?

In the April [1990] issue of *American Psychologist*, Stanford University's Eleanor Maccoby reports the results of her own and others' research showing that children's development is most influenced by the social structure of peer interactions. Boys and girls tend to play with children of their own gender, and their sex-separate groups have different organizational structures and interactive norms.

I believe these systematic differences in childhood socialization make talk between women and men like cross-cultural communication, heir to all the attraction and pitfalls of that enticing but difficult enterprise. My research on men's and women's conversations uncovered patterns similar to those described for children's groups.

For women, as for girls, intimacy is the fabric of relationships, and talk is the thread from which it is woven. Little girls create and maintain friendships by exchanging secrets; similarly, women regard conversation as the cornerstone of friendship. So a woman expects her husband to be a new and improved version of a best friend. What is important is not the individual subjects that are discussed but the sense of closeness, of a life shared, that emerges when people tell their thoughts, feelings, and impressions.

10 Bonds between boys can be as intense as girls', but they are based less on talking, more on doing things together. Since they don't assume talk is the cement that binds a relationship, men don't know what kind of talk women want, and they don't miss it when it isn't there.

Boys' groups are larger, more inclusive, and more hierarchical, so boys must struggle to avoid the subordinate position in the group. This may play a role in women's complaints that men don't listen to them. Some men really don't like to listen, because being a listener makes them feel one-down, like a child listening to adults or an employee to a boss.

But often when women tell men, "You aren't listening," and the men protest, "I am," the men are right. The impression of not listening results from misalignments in the mechanics of conversation. The misalignment begins as soon as a man and a woman take physical positions. This became clear when I studied videotapes made by psychologist Bruce Dorval of children and adults talking to their same-sex best friends. I found that at every age, the girls and women faced each other directly, their eyes anchored on each other's faces. At every age, the boys and men sat at angles to each other and looked elsewhere in the room, periodically glancing at each other. They were obviously attuned to each other, often mirroring each other's movements. But the tendency of men to face away can give women the impression they aren't listening even when they are. A young woman in college was frustrated: Whenever she told her boyfriend she wanted to talk to him, he would lie down on the floor, close his eyes, and put his arm over his face. This signaled to her, "He's taking a nap." But he insisted he was listening extra hard. Normally, he looks around the room, so he is easily distract-

ed. Lying down and covering his eyes helped him concentrate on what she was saying.

Analogous to the physical alignment that women and men take in conversation is their topical alignment. The girls in my study tended to talk at length about one topic, but the boys tended to jump from topic to topic. The second-grade girls exchanged stories about people they knew. The second-grade boys teased, told jokes, noticed things in the room, and talked about finding games to play. The sixth-grade girls talked about problems with a mutual friend. The sixth-grade boys talked about 55 different topics, none of which extended over more than a few turns.

Listening to Body Language

Switching topics is another habit that gives women the impression men aren't listening, especially if they switch to a topic about themselves. But the evidence of the 10th-grade boys in my study indicates otherwise. The 10th-grade boys sprawled across their chairs with bodies parallel and eyes straight ahead, rarely looking at each other. They looked as if they were riding in a car, staring out the windshield. But they were talking about their feelings. One boy was upset because a girl had told him he had a drinking problem, and the other was feeling alienated from all his friends.

15 Now, when a girl told a friend about a problem, the friend responded by asking probing questions and expressing agreement and understanding. But the boys dismissed each other's problems. Todd assured Richard that his drinking was "no big problem" because "sometimes you're funny when you're off your butt." And when Todd said he felt left out, Richard responded, "Why should you? You know more people than me."

Women perceived such responses as belittling and unsupportive. But the boys seemed satisfied with them. Whereas women reassure each other by implying, "You shouldn't feel bad because I've had similar experiences," men do so by implying, "You shouldn't feel bad because your problems aren't so bad."

There are even simpler reasons for women's impression that men don't listen. Linguist Lynette Hirschman found that women make more listener-noise, such as "mhm," "uhuh," and "yeah," to show "I'm with you." Men, she found, more often give silent attention. Women who expect a stream of listener-noise interpret silent attention as no attention at all.

Women's conversational habits are as frustrating to men as men's are to women. Men who expect silent attention interpret a stream of listener-noise as over-reaction or impatience. Also, when women talk to each other in a close, comfortable setting, they often overlap, finish each other's sentences and anticipate what the other is about to say. This practice, which I call "participatory listenership," is often perceived by men as interruption, intrusion, and lack of attention.

A parallel difference caused a man to complain about his wife, "She just wants to talk about her own point of view. If I show her another view, she gets mad at me." When most women talk to each other, they assume a conversationalist's job is to express agreement and support. But many men see their conversational duty as pointing out the other side of the argument. This is heard as disloyalty by women, and refusal to offer the requisite support. It is not that women don't want to see other points of view, but that they prefer them phrased as suggestions and inquiries rather than as direct challenges.

20 In his book *Fighting for Life,* Walter Ong points out that men use "agonistic" or warlike, oppositional formats to do almost anything; thus discussion becomes debate, and conversation a competitive sport. In contrast, women see conversation as a ritual means of establishing rapport. If Jane tells a problem and June says she has a similar one, they walk away feeling closer to each other. But this attempt at establishing rapport can backfire when used with men. Men take too literally women's ritual "troubles talk," just as women mistake men's ritual challenges for real attack.

The Sounds of Silence

These differences begin to clarify why women and men have such different expectations about communication in marriage. For women, talk creates intimacy. Marriage is an orgy of closeness: You can tell your feelings and thoughts, and still be loved. Their greatest fear is being pushed away. But men live in a hierarchical world, where talk maintains independence and status. They are on guard to protect themselves from being put down and pushed around.

This explains the paradox of the talkative man who said of his silent wife, "She's the talker." In the public setting of a guest lecture, he felt challenged to show his intelligence and display his understanding of the lecture. But at home, where he has nothing to prove and no one to defend against, he is free to remain silent. For his wife, being home means she is free from the worry that something she says might offend someone, or spark disagreement, or appear to be showing off; at home she is free to talk.

The communication problems that endanger marriage can't be fixed by mechanical engineering. They require a new conceptual framework about the role of talk in human relationships. Many of the psychological explanations that have become second nature may not be helpful, because they tend to blame either women (for not being assertive enough) or men (for not being in touch with their feelings). A sociolinguistic approach by which male-female conversation is seen as cross-cultural communication allows us to understand the problem and forge solutions without blaming either party.

Once the problem is understood, improvement comes naturally, as it did to the young woman and her boyfriend who seemed to go to sleep when she wanted to talk. Previously, she had accused him of not listening, and he had refused to change his behavior, since that would be admitting fault. But then she learned about and explained to him the differences in women's and men's habitual ways of aligning themselves in conversation. The next time she told him she wanted to talk, he began, as usual, by lying down and covering his eyes. When the familiar negative reaction bubbled up, she reassured herself that he really was listening. But then he sat up and looked at her. Thrilled, she asked why. He said, "You like me to look at you when we talk, so I'll try to do it." Once he saw their differences as cross-cultural rather than right and wrong, he independently altered his behavior.

25   Women who feel abandoned and deprived when their husbands won't listen to or report daily news may be happy to discover their husbands trying to adapt once they understand the place of small talk in women's relationships. But if their husbands don't adapt, the women may still be comforted that for men, this is not a failure of intimacy. Accepting the difference, the wives may look to their friends or family for that kind of talk.

And husbands who can't provide it shouldn't feel their wives have made unreasonable demands. Some couples will still decide to divorce, but at least their decisions will be based on realistic expectations.

In these times of resurgent ethnic conflicts, the world desperately needs cross-cultural understanding. Like charity, successful cross-cultural communication should begin at home.

Writing Strategies

1. Describe Tannen's voice as a writer, and refer to several passages to support your description.

2. Read several paragraphs from Susan Jacoby's "When Bright Girls Decide That Math Is a 'Waste of Time,'" which follows this essay, and compare Tannen's voice to Jacoby's. How would you say they are similar or different?

3. In your own words, write down Tannen's main idea.

4. Discuss with several peers what you wrote down for #3 above. How is your understanding of Tannen's idea similar to or different from your peers' understanding? After discussing, write one statement of Tannen's main idea that you and your group members agree on.

5. What support, or evidence, does Tannen provide to explain a cause? That is, does she tell stories, provide statistics, or something else?

Exploring Ideas

1. How does Tannen's essay invite others to think about communication?

2. Reflect on your communication habits. You might first jot down any initial ideas you have, and then recall comments others have made about the way you communicate. In several paragraphs, describe your own conversational behavior.

3. Over the course of several days, make your own observations about the way men and women communicate. How are your observations similar to or different from Tannen's?

4. Is it acceptable to generalize, as Tannen does, about men and women? What makes her generalizations valid? Or, why aren't they valid?

Ideas for Writing

1. What is the cause of some other difference in the way men and women think or act?

2. What is the cause of some difference in the way two groups of people think or act?

If responding to one of these ideas, go to the **Analysis** section of this chapter to begin developing ideas for your essay.

When Bright Girls Decide That Math Is a "Waste of Time"

Susan Jacoby

Whenever we wonder about group behavior (why girls do this, why students do that, why boys like this, why Americans hate that), we enter into perilous territory. We have to account for entire trends but at the same time point to particular causes. In this essay, Susan Jacoby takes on a large trend—one surrounded by the nature versus nurture debate: While some argue that nature causes gender-specific behavior, others argue that culture and social conditioning play a primary role. Jacoby, a journalist and book author, enters this debate—and relies heavily on appeals to logic for support.

Susannah, a 16-year-old who has always been an A student in every subject from algebra to English, recently informed her parents that she intended to drop physics and calculus in her senior year of high school and replace them with a drama seminar and a work-study program. She expects a major in art or history in college, she explained, and "any more science or math will just be a waste of my time."

Her parents were neither concerned by nor opposed to her decision. "Fine, dear," they said. Their daughter is, after all, an outstanding student. What does it matter if, at age 16, she has taken a step that may limit her understanding of both machines and the natural world for the rest of her life?

This kind of decision, in which girls turn away from studies that would give them a sure footing in the world of science and technology, is a self-inflicted female disability that is, regrettably, almost as common today as it was when I was in high school. If Susannah had announced that she had decided to stop taking English in her senior year, her mother and father would have been horrified. I also think they would have been a good deal less sanguine about her decision if she were a boy.

In saying that scientific and mathematical ignorance is a self-inflicted female wound, I do not, obviously, mean that cultural expectations play no role in the process. But the world does not conspire to deprive modern women of access to science as it did in the 1930s, when Rosalyn S. Yalow, the Nobel Prize-winning physicist, graduated from Hunter College and was advised to go to work as a secretary because no graduate school would admit her to its physics department. The current generation of adolescent girls—and their parents, bred on old expectations about women's interests—are active conspirators in limiting their own intellectual development.

5   It is true that the proportion of young women in science-related graduate and professional schools, most notably medical schools, has increased significantly in the past decade. It is also true that so few women were studying advanced science and mathematics before the early 1970s that the percentage increase in female enrollment does not yet translate into large numbers of women actually working in science.

The real problem is that so many girls eliminate themselves from any serious possibility of studying science as a result of decisions made during the vulnerable period of mid-adolescence, when they are most likely to be influenced—on both conscious and subconscious levels—by the traditional belief that math and science are "masculine" subjects.

During the teenage years the well-documented phenomenon of "math anxiety" strikes girls who never had any problem handling numbers during earlier schooling. Some men, too, experience this syndrome—a form of panic, akin to a phobia, at any task involving numbers—but women constitute the overwhelming majority of sufferers. The onset of acute math anxiety during the teenage years is, as Stalin was fond of saying, "not by accident."

In adolescence girls begin to fear that they will be unattractive to boys if they are typed as "brains." Science and math epitomize unfeminine braininess in a way that, say, foreign languages do not. High-school girls who pursue an advanced interest in science and math (unless they are students at special institutions like the Bronx High School of Science, where everyone is a brain) usually find that they are greatly outnumbered by boys in their classes. They are, therefore, intruding on male turf at a time when their sexual confidence, as well as that of the boys, is most fragile.

A 1981 assessment of female achievement in mathematics, based on research conducted under a National Institute for Education grant, found significant differences in the mathematical achievements of 9th- and 12th-graders. At age 13 girls were equal to or slightly better than boys in tests involving algebra, problem solving and spatial ability; four years later the boys had outstripped the girls.

10   It is not mysterious that some very bright high-school girls suddenly decide that math is "too hard" and "a waste of time." In my experience, self-sabotage of mathematical and scientific ability is often a conscious process. I remember deliberately pretending to be puzzled by geometry problems in my sophomore year in high school. A male teacher called me in after class and said, in a baffled tone, "I don't see how you can be having so much trouble when you got straight A's last year in my algebra class."

The decision to avoid advanced biology, chemistry, physics, and calculus in high school automatically restricts academic and professional choices that ought to be wide open to anyone beginning college. At all coeducational universities women are overwhelmingly concentrated in the fine arts, social sciences, and traditionally female departments like education. Courses leading to degrees in science and technology-related fields are filled mainly by men.

In my generation, the practical consequences of mathematical and scientific illiteracy are visible in the large number of special programs to help professional women overcome the anxiety they feel when they are promoted into jobs that require them to handle statistics.

The consequences of this syndrome should not, however, be viewed in narrowly professional terms. Competence in science and math does not mean one is going to become a scientist or mathematician any more than competence in writing English means one is going to become a professional writer. Scientific and mathematical illiteracy—which has been cited in several recent critiques by panels studying American education from kindergarten through college—produces an incalculably impoverished vision of human experience.

Scientific illiteracy is not, of course, the exclusive province of women. In certain intellectual circles it has become fashionable to proclaim a willed, aggressive ignorance about science and technology. Some female writers specialize in ominous, uninformed diatribes against genetic research as a plot to remove control of childbearing from women, while some well-known men of letters proudly announce that they understand absolutely nothing about computers, or, for that matter, about electricity. This lack of understanding is nothing in which women or men ought to take pride.

15   Failure to comprehend either computers or chromosomes leads to a terrible sense of helplessness, because the profound impact of science on everyday life is evident even to those who insist they don't, won't, can't understand why the changes are taking place. At this stage of history women are more prone to such feelings of helplessness than men because the culture judges their ignorance less harshly and because women themselves acquiesce in that indulgence.

Since there is ample evidence of such feelings in adolescence, it is up to parents to see that their daughters do not accede to the old stereotypes about "masculine" and "feminine" knowledge. Unless we want our daughters to share our intellectual handicaps, we had better tell them no, they can't stop taking mathematics and science at the ripe old age of 16.

Eight percent of math professors are women.

Writing Strategies

1. Describe Jacoby's voice as a writer, and point to several passages to support your description.

2. What type of evidence does Jacoby provide in explaining a cause? What evidence is most convincing? What other type of support might she have provided?

3. In your own words, write down Jacoby's reasoning for bright girls deciding that math is a waste of time.

4. Discuss what you wrote down for #3 above with a group of classmates. How are their ideas similar to or different from your own?

5. How does Jacoby conclude her essay? Is her strategy effective or ineffective? Why?

Exploring Ideas

1. What decisions have you made that already have limited your academic or professional choices, or might limit them in the future? Why did you make those choices? Were they influenced by any stereotypes, social pressures, or perceived social pressures?

2. How might you respond to Jacoby? Consider expanding, narrowing, or refocusing her discussion.

3. Reconsider your understanding of math or English—whichever is the least attractive to you. What could change your perspective on the field and your abilities to succeed in it?

4. Interview others to find out what they take pride in not knowing. What is their reason for not knowing it? Why do they take pride in not knowing it? How are their reasons similar to or different from the ones Jacoby describes?

Ideas for Writing

1. What thing do some people take pride in not knowing, and why? That is, what is the cause of their (a) not knowing and (b) taking pride in not knowing?

2. What causes many students to think school is a "waste of time"?

If responding to one of these ideas, go to the **Analysis** section of this chapter to begin developing ideas for your essay.

Outside Reading

Find an essay or report that explores causes, and print it out or make a photocopy. To explore a specific field or major, search a related professional journal, such as *Nutrition Health Forum, Law Technology,* or *Education Journal.* Keep an eye out for titles of articles that begin with *why.* You might also find articles about causes in local and national newspapers. For journal or newspaper articles, go to your library's home page, and then choose a magazine or periodical database. (Choose one that says "full text" in the title.) Using a keyword search, enter *cause and* plus any noun that interests you, such as *cause and flu, cause and recession, cause and global warming, cause and traffic jams.*

You can also search the Internet. Try a Google search, but go to Google's special search for government studies and reports: www.Google.com/unclesam. At the site, you will notice that "Google" is red, white, and blue. At the search box, type any topic of interest, and *cause.* (In Google, Boolean operators such as *and* are unnecessary.) The search results will yield only government-sponsored studies and reports.

The purpose of this assignment is to explore the range of possibilities for writing. You may discover a text that differs considerably from the essays in this chapter (in tone, rhetorical strategies, or organization). As you read through this chapter, keep the text you have discovered close by, and notice the elements and strategies the writer uses. Depending on your instructor's suggestions, do one or more of the following:

1. Notice how the writer applies various strategies from this chapter. On the hard copy or photocopy:
   - Highlight the thesis if it is stated. If the thesis is implied, write it in your own words.
   - Identify the major rhetorical strategies (appeals, evidence, counterargument, concession, etc.).
   - Identify any passages in which the writer attempts to create public resonance for the topic.

2. Analyze the strategies employed by the writer. The following questions may be helpful:
   - How is the writer's voice different from the essays in this chapter?
   - How does the writer support or illustrate his or her thesis?
   - Who is the audience for this text?
   - How does the audience impact the kinds of things said in the text?
   - How does the writer go beyond the obvious? (What new idea does the writer offer?)

3. Write at least three "Writing Strategies" questions for the text you found.

4. Write at least three "Exploring Ideas" questions for the text you found.

5. Write two "Ideas for Writing," such as the ones following the essays in this book, for the text you found.

INVENTION

"One great cause of failure is lack of concentration."

—Bruce Lee

Invention is an act of discovery. It involves opening all the intellectual cases we have closed in everyday life. It involves asking questions where we had assumed we knew the answers. For this chapter, invention involves asking why something occurs (or has occurred) and going beyond the first (and second) guess. In **Point of Contact,** ask adventurous questions to find a topic. In **Analysis,** imagine unseen causes. In **Public Resonance,** consider the ways your topic extends outward and affects the public. In **Thesis,** focus your ideas to a particular insight, and in **Rhetorical Tools,** explore a range of possible support strategies. The Invention questions in each section are not meant to be answered directly in your final written assignment. In fact, as you work through the sections, avoid simply answering them and then moving on. Instead, use them to explore and to develop revelatory ideas.

POINT OF CONTACT

The authors of the essays in this chapter have a deep under-standing of their topics. Certainly, Schor, as a professor of economics, has an expert perspective. While you need not have years of training and study about your topic, you will benefit from some degree of personal experience.

The search for a cause begins with a question: Why did something happen? Why does something continue? What causes some phenomenon? The following questions can help you to explore possible topics. After you have decided on a particular topic, go to the Analysis section to continue your search for causes.

Work

- Why are some sections/groups/teams more successful than others?
- Why is workplace efficiency up or down?
- Why are profits for the company or organization up or down?
- Why are some workers more content or fulfilled than others?

Local Events

- Why is urban sprawl taking place in your community?
- Why is a local sports team winning or losing?
- What makes one school perform better than others?
- Why are some areas of town more policed than others?
- Why do so many yards look the same?

Social Trends

- What causes road rage? Teenage rebellion? Conformity to fashion trends?
- Why are the elderly isolated?
- Why is depression on the rise in the United States?
- Why do Americans love sport utility vehicles?
- Why does the condition of streets change throughout a city?
- Why doesn't anyone care about the future?

Campus Issues

- Why do college students binge drink?
- Why do some students cheat? Procrastinate?
- What causes boredom?
- Why are some classes more difficult for large numbers of students?

Politics

- Why have the Democrats consistently lost in recent elections?
- Why do younger generations tend not to vote?
- Why does a certain community consistently vote Democratic or Republican?
- Why do minority voters tend toward Democratic candidates?

Your Major

- What has caused the field to thrive (or deteriorate) in recent years?
- What has fueled a recent debate in the field? Why has the debate continued?
- Find the cause of a phenomenon in your field, for example:
  —*History:* a revolution, a military victory or loss
  —*Art:* a style (such as impressionism), an artistic revolution
  —*Geology:* mudslides, a volcanic eruption
  —*Biology:* an organism's short life span
  —*Criminal Justice:* a jury decision, a Supreme Court decision to hear a case
  —*Business Marketing:* the success or failure of a marketing campaign
  —*Architecture:* the appeal of a recent building design, the change in mid-20th-century buildings

ACTIVITY

Although the chapter readings tend to focus on problems (such as bulimia or overconsumption), you might focus on any phenomenon, good or bad. In a group (in class, on a listserv, or in a chatroom), generate more options for seeking out a topic. Share your ideas with the class.

ANALYSIS

Now that you have a topic (any phenomenon from the above or from your own set of questions), the next step is to begin searching for possible causes. (We use the term *phenomenon* here to refer to anything you are exploring—any behavior, event, situation, attitude, issue, idea, and so on.) You may already have some guesses about the cause. But keep an open mind. Any single phenomenon can be a consequence of many factors, both physical and abstract.

Respond to the following questions and refer back to your notes as you continue the process.

- What events or behaviors led to the phenomenon?
- What social conditions or prevailing attitudes led (or could lead) to the phenomenon?
- What economic conditions led to the phenomenon?
- What state of mind or psychological need may have led to the phenomenon?
- What are all the possible reasons someone would carry out this behavior?

INVENTION WORKSHOP

With several other writers, use one or two of the Invention questions to initiate a discussion about your topics. Even though some questions might seem irrelevant, do not dismiss them quickly. Explore the impact of each question on your topic. For example, in the following workshop, Jack develops his initial thoughts about this topic: why people join cults.

What state of mind or psychological need may have led to the phenomenon?

Jack: These people are obviously sick—mentally ill.

Diana: What kind of mental illness?

Jack: I don't know . . . probably some kind of schizophrenia or something.

Diana: But a lot of the people who join cults are otherwise productive members of society—with jobs, families, homes, social responsibilities. I've even heard that some cults attract people who are smarter than average. It doesn't seem like these people are downright mentally ill—at least in the way most people talk about mental illness.

Jack: So if they aren't sick in some way, why would they possibly leave behind their families and friends, give all their money to a group of strangers, and lose their identities?

Marcus: Well, I've heard that a lot of those people don't have friends—they're lonely.

Jack: How can people be lonely if they have families and jobs?

Marcus: Working a job and supporting a family doesn't necessarily make someone truly connected to others. Think about mid-life crises—where people run out and have wild flings or buy ridiculously expensive sports cars. They're obviously unfulfilled.

Jack: But wouldn't you say that joining a cult is a little more extreme than buying a car or having an affair?

Diana: Sure, but remember that a lot of people long for something more than sex and fast cars. They wonder what's out there, what their purpose is, what's beyond this life.

Jack: And religious cults have all those answers—well, at least that's the argument.

Diana: Yeah, so the whole issue may be related to loneliness and longing rather than sickness.

THINKING FURTHER

Now for the fun part: taking your new ideas and exploring them further. For example, in his dialogue with Diana and Marcus, Jack's thinking evolves:

Beginning of the dialogue:	Sick people join cults.
End of the dialogue:	Loneliness and longing, which run rampant in mainstream culture, drive people to wonder what they're missing. This is where cults come in.

With this new understanding, Jack might come to more insightful conclusions about the perspective of people who join cults:

> I guess in the eyes of a potential cult member, a cult doesn't look like a cult. I mean, a group doesn't hang a "Cult" sign on the door. They don't say, "Hey!! Join our cult!! We'll all kill ourselves next year! It'll be great!!" No. A cult is merely a group of people who offer a web of relationships and a clear purpose in life. Isn't that why people go to college even though they hate it?! Isn't that why people join the Army?? A clear sense of purpose?!! Is college a kind of cult? Is the Army?!! Here's the message of both institutions: "Leave behind everything—your family, etc. Come here. Stay with us. And . . . you have to follow our strict schedule of events. But in the end, you'll be way better off." Holy crap! We're a culture of . . . cults.

Jack's continued exploration of why people join cults has taken him into new intellectual territory. He is exploring the relationship between something he thinks is dangerous (cults) and something he thinks is normal (college, the army).

Use the following questions to think further:

- How has your understanding of the cause developed? What new idea has entered your thinking?
- Why didn't you think about this before?

INVENTION WRITING

In Leonard Kress's invention notes, he explores some personal behaviors from the past—in his attempt to determine what caused his bulimic behavior. Here, Kress begins to note the gap between common assumptions about bulimia and his own experience. And that gap is important, even vital, for Kress's analysis:

What caused your behavior as a child?

I have seen some discussion about high school wrestlers— I even recall a friend who subsisted on popsicles for two days to "make weight" and who occasionally vomited in the boys' room, both with the coach's approval. But children? Young boys? This didn't seem to fit the mold. I have these vivid images of places where I vomited, of scenes I caused, of my parents' quiet exasperation.

RESEARCH

Find an outside source (a website, article, or book) about your concept. (Consult Chapter 13, Research & Writing, to help you explore.) The author(s) of the source may have a different understanding of the causes. Summarize the main points of the source, then answer the following questions:

- Does the source suggest a cause for the phenomenon?
- If not, does the source imply or assume a cause?
- Does the source account for the most direct cause?
- Does the source account for indirect or multiple causes? Hidden causes?

PUBLIC RESONANCE

Some topics automatically resonate with public concerns or interests. Juliet Schor's topic, for instance, involves public interest and even includes the reader, as a consumer, in its analysis. But other topics may seem more difficult to connect with. Local or intensely personal topics, for instance, may seem less linked to broader concerns. Who would think that childhood vomiting could be an interesting topic or make for a valuable essay? But Leonard Kress makes his own vomiting experience resonate (in more than one way) with readers:

> My brother and sister were silent, too, as though my barfing were a perfectly acceptable alternative to an after-dinner mint, a toothpick, a wet-wipe wrapped like a condom. Perhaps they were too busy stashing away the details of the affront, safekeeping for a time of need—like Aesop's despicable, self-righteous ant. I can only imagine the hay they might have later made by simple melodramatic evocations of the sounds of my gagging, as it echoed in tiny bathrooms. The deep, throaty sound of plosively expelling vomit. "Well, whatever I did can't be as gross and disgusting as THAT," I can hear them repeating over and over till they got what they wanted. Or did they have their own equally disgusting but self-customized techniques of catharsis and orgasm back then—I wondered. Does everyone, I still wonder? And how could a "D" in French or a detention or a missed meal or a dent in the car compare with what I did, over and over and over? (419)

In this paragraph, Kress broadens the scope, including his siblings and "everyone." He makes the connection for us: Not everyone throws up for catharsis, but, he supposes, everyone may have some technique for experiencing relief, release, or comfort. This broader scope does not mean that Kress is losing focus—he is bringing others into the issue. As a writer, he knows that his job is to invite others into his exploration, into his search for causes.

Imagine how your topic involves others who are not directly associated with it. Use the following questions to help generate a sense of public resonance for your topic:

- What are the effects of this phenomenon?
- Whom does it affect? How does it affect them?
- How does it affect people indirectly?
- How does my position or understanding relate to popular perspectives on the topic?

INVENTION WRITING

In his exploration, Leonard Kress looks outward and compares his personal search with "pop psychology." He decides that his personal experience (and intellectual response) is different than what he sees in the media. But he doesn't therefore decide that his topic has no public resonance. Instead, he decides to explore the contrast between his experience and common characterizations.

How does your position or understanding relate to popular perspectives on the topic?

In writing this, I guess I am caught in the popular mania of confession. I consider myself to be a fairly private person, but all around I see people (in books, articles, on TV, etc.) revealing the most personal and embarrassing details about their lives. And doing so with relish. The fact that this piece deals with childhood makes it somewhat easier, of course. This is as close as I came to a taboo subject—and it intrigues me that my experience was so different from the media and pop psychology take on eating disorders and adolescent girls.

Kress's move here is vital to academic writing: When a writer discovers contrast or tension between his own experience and that of others, he has discovered something worth exploring more—something worth writing about.

Like Kress's topic, Jack's topic of cult membership might seem to only affect specific people—cult members, their families, maybe the communities surrounding the cult. But Jack goes further than that and imagines the broader and subtler factors:

How does it affect people indirectly?

If people are drawn to cults through deep loneliness, then cults potentially relate to everyone—that is, anyone who cares about family, friends, the quiet neighbor, etc. Our days are filled with constant inattention to others. Most people choose their narrow paths (their jobs and their small circle of friends) and leave everyone else. Many of us will go weeks without truly acknowledging anyone outside of our little circles. Rarely do we invite the quiet guy from work out with us; rarely do we call our cousin to see how she's doing. We leave lonely people behind us every day.

Jack could even explore further, examining the messages that popular culture sends to people: that we must have intense social engagement to achieve happiness and fulfillment, that solitude should be avoided, that excitement and purpose should define every minute of our lives. Jack would then be exploring the culture surrounding cults. He would be thinking like a sociologist, and assuming that any one behavior is linked to a broad system of attitudes, messages, and group behaviors.

ACTIVITIES

1. Make a conceptual map of your ideas thus far. Graphically display the elements: the event, behavior, trend, the most direct cause, other possible causes, and even the public resonance. (See pages 186–187 for examples of conceptual maps.)

2. Present your ideas to a small group of peers. Explain specifically how the phenomenon is caused. Also, explain the public resonance: how this phenomenon relates to the concerns and lives of others. Start a follow-up discussion about the phenomenon by asking the group members to consider how it affects their lives.

Is your thinking out of sync with conventional wisdom? If so, you may have discovered something important!

THESIS

The kind of writing done in this chapter is both analytical and argumentative. Each author of the chapter readings offers an analysis of the topic and an argument for his or her understanding of the cause. Each author has a thesis that focuses on the causes or set of causes most responsible for the phenomenon. As you consider your main point, examine all possible avenues. (You may even begin writing and drafting before your ideas take shape.) Your thesis might:

- Argue for a particular cause.

    Professional sports have gotten more violent because of the intensity of sports coverage in the media.

- Argue that several factors equally cause the phenomenon.

    Writing proficiency among American high school students continues to diminish because of a broader cultural disinterest in reading and a fundamental misunderstanding of language.

- Argue against an apparent cause or widely held belief and for a less obvious or more complicated cause.

    People drive gas guzzlers not because they are selfish and insensitive, but because they are uneducated about their real choices.

    The music industry is losing profits not because college kids are insatiable thieves, but because the industry has not evolved with the listening habits of the new generation.

As you consider your topic, decide on your emphasis:

- Will it be important to thoroughly describe several causes or to focus on one?

EVOLUTION OF A THESIS

Your main idea may not come into focus immediately. Notice how Jack's thesis evolves from his initial thoughts into a sophisticated point.

Jack focuses on a particular phenomenon:

- What makes people leave everything and everyone behind and join cults?

He uses the Invention questions on page 434 to probe for causes:

- What state of mind or psychological need may have led to the phenomenon? Some form of mental disease makes people join cults.

He works through his initial thoughts and discovers a less obvious cause:

- Deep loneliness and lack of purpose in life cause people to leave their families and join cults.

Jack struggles to integrate public resonance into his understanding of the cause:

- The deep loneliness and loss created in our society cause people to crave belonging and purpose in their lives, and cults can meet those needs.

- The deep loneliness and loss fostered by our hurried society create desperate searches for belonging and purpose, and cults sometimes fulfill those needs.

For more related common thesis problems, see Chapter 6, page 281.

COMMON THESIS PROBLEMS

Perhaps the two most common thesis problems are psychological, striking before the writer ever touches a key or marks a paper.

1. **Fear of Ongoing Invention:** Some writers assume that thesis statements are fixed, unchangeable structures that must be strictly adhered to throughout a writing project. As they draft ideas and generate support for their initial point, they avoid asking hard questions and making new connections; that is, they fear continued invention once they've started drafting. But thesis statements are not traps. They are merely statements that help writers focus and intensify their thinking *as they are writing.* The human brain functions in new ways once serious writing and shaping begin; therefore, writers should allow their own writing to help them with new ideas.

2. **Fear of Commitment:** In contrast to the above fear, some writers avoid committing to a focused statement. They wander around without attempting to establish a particular idea, without digging in to a specific intellectual place. Such wandering, if it goes on for too long, often leads to shallow ideas (saying lots of different things about lots of different things). Although invention is key throughout the process, invention is not general wandering. Better ideas come when writers dig in their intellectual heels.

> ### REVISION
>
> Ask yourself: Am I afraid of ongoing invention or commitment? Have I committed to a rigid thesis too early, or have I not even tried to commit? Whatever your tendency, try now to do the opposite: For a rigid thesis, try to imagine a less obvious, subtler or more surprising cause. For non-commitment, follow the path of the sample Evolution of a Thesis. Try to hone in on your thesis using those steps.

Thesis statements are tools for narrowing and intensifying our ideas.

RHETORICAL TOOLS

Remember that you are not simply explaining a cause. You are arguing that a particular cause (or set of causes) could be responsible for a phenomenon, and you also are arguing that your understanding of the cause/effect relationship is worth considering. Therefore, consider the support strategies of argument (from Chapter 6, Making Arguments):

- **Examples:** Specific cases or illustrations of a phenomenon.
- **Allusions:** References to history, science, nature, news events, films, television shows, or literary texts.
- **Personal Testimonies/Anecdotes:** Individual accounts or experiences.
- **Scenarios:** Hypothetical or fictionalized accounts.
- **Statistics:** Information (often given by numerical value) collected through experimentation, surveys, polls, and research.
- **Authorities:** References to published (usually written) sources.
- **Facts:** Agreed-upon events or truths.
- **Appeal to Logic:** Relates the argument to the audience's sense of reason, or creates a line of reasoning for the audience to follow.
- **Appeal to Emotion:** Relates the argument to an emotional state of the audience, or attempts to create a particular emotional state in the audience.
- **Appeal of Character:** Relates the argument to a quality of the author/speaker.
- **Appeal to Need:** Relates the argument to people's needs (spiritual, economic, physical, sexual, familial, political, etc.).
- **Appeal to Value:** Relates the argument to people's values (judgments about right/wrong, success, discipline, selflessness, moderation, honesty, chastity, modesty, self-expression, etc.).

In the essays for this chapter, the writers use a broad range of support strategies. Kress, for instance, depends on information collected in his own everyday life (personal testimony and anecdotes) to support his argument. Personal experience (in the form of narration) is his primary support. He also uses authorities (outside sources). Juliet Schor uses examples, statistics, scenarios, facts, and anecdotes. Tannen uses authorities, testimony, allusions, and examples. And all the writers rely heavily on appeals to logic in order to show the cause/effect relationships between the possible cause and the phenomenon itself (overconsumption, childhood bulimia, gender strife, educational trends).

Use the following questions to develop support for your thesis:

- How can I illustrate the relationship between the cause and the effect? (What line of reasoning can I use?)
- Does a historical event or figure help to show the cause?
- Can I allude to a similar phenomenon (with a similar cause) to support my point?
- Does a literary work (novel, poem, drama) or popular culture text (movie, television program, song) support my point?
- How do other writers discuss this cause?
- Does something in nature (in animal or plant life) support my point?
- Has anyone done scientific study on this phenomenon? Does it support my point?
- Have I witnessed or experienced someone or something that illustrates my point?
- Can I construct a hypothetical situation that illustrates my point?

Integrating Authorities (Outside Sources)

Outside sources must be carefully integrated into your own argument; that is, they must genuinely interact with your own claims. For instance, notice how Deborah Tannen uses the claims of other researchers. Since her own observations resonate with others' conclusions, her claims do not rest exclusively on outside sources. Like all good writers, she does not depend on the sources, but uses them to show how her own ideas fit into a broader discussion on the topic:

> The pattern was observed by political scientist Andrew Hacker in the late '70s. Sociologist Catherine Kohler Riessman reports in her new book *Divorce Talk* that most of the women she interviewed—but only a few of the men—gave lack of communication as the reason for their divorces. (422)

Immediately after referring to other sources, she mentions her own research:

> In my own research, complaints from women about their husbands most often focused not on tangible inequities such as having given up the chance for a career to accompany a husband to his, or doing far more than their share of daily life-support work like cleaning, cooking, social arrangements and errands. Instead, they focused on communication . . . (422)

Research should also relate directly to the writer's claims. Tannen, or any of the writers in this chapter, could appear unbelievable if her claims were disconnected from her research. Imagine if Tannen had gone on in her essay to claim that "women are better talkers than men." Nothing in her research, at least as it is reported to us, would suggest such a conclusion. So, despite years of research, Tannen would lose credibility. However, Tannen's claims are appropriately focused and illustrated by the observations she shares with her readers. In other words, readers accept ideas when the support seems proportional and related to the claims.

See Chapter 13, Research & Writing, for further guidance in integrating and documenting sources.

ACTIVITY

Examine the essays in this chapter. First decide on the thesis of each essay, and then decide on the supporting strategies each uses.

Counterarguing

Counterarguments defend against opposing claims. Writers must anticipate and account for positions outside of or opposed to their own claims(s) and include reasoning to offset that potential opposition. In many cases, writers must contend directly with arguments that forward another cause. Leonard Kress, for example, argues against common views and explains the way his position differs from others'. Here, Kress points to authorities who seem to miss the mark:

> I also locate "Determinants of Adolescent Obesity: A Comparison with Anorexia Nervosa," in *Adolescence* (1988), which claims that "both anorexics and the obese are characterized by overprotectedness and enmeshment, resulting from a poor sense of identity and effectiveness." After a whole week of research, this seems to be the extent of my findings. I can find nothing to urge me to go beyond the abstracts, nothing at all, though I type in "eating disorder," "vomiting," "obesity," "abnormal psychology," "gluttony," "disgusting and destructive behavior"—always cross-referenced with "childhood." (418)

Because Kress mentions these other causes (or other takes on the phenomenon), we get the sense that he has a broad understanding of the topic—he is not simply guessing at a cause, but has explored other possibilities. Juliet Schor also addresses positions outside of her own, and even explains her previous acceptance of another view of the phenomenon of consumption:

> In response to these developments, social critics continue to focus on income. In his impressive analysis of the problems of contemporary American capitalism, *Fat and Mean,* economist David Gordon emphasized income *adequacy.* . . . Meanwhile, the Economic Policy Institute focuses on the distribution of income and wealth, arguing that the gains of the top 20 percent have jeopardized the well-being of the bottom 80 percent. Incomes have stagnated and the robust 3 percent growth rates of the 1950s and '60s are long gone. . . .

It is difficult to take exception to this view. It combines a deep respect for individual choice (the liberal part) with a commitment to justice and equality (the egalitarian part). I held it myself for many years. But I now believe that by failing to look deeper—to examine the very nature of consumption—it has become too limiting. In short, I do not think that the "income solution" addresses some of the most profound failures of the current consumption regime. (411)

Use the following questions to develop counterarguments:

- What other causes could be attributed to this phenomenon? (Why are these other causes less acceptable or less valid?)
- What other reasons do people have for disagreeing with me?
- What would support an opposing argument?

Every phenomenon has many possible causes—and each cause comes with its own argument.

Conceding

Concessions acknowledge the value of positions or claims other than those being forwarded by the writer. Remember that a good writer (with a broad understanding of the topic) is able to concede the value of some points or qualify his or her own points well. For example, Juliet Schor does not mention other points simply to knock them down, but genuinely acknowledges the value of another position:

> In response to these developments, social critics continue to focus on income. In his impressive analysis of the problems of contemporary American capitalism, *Fat and Mean,* economist David Gordon emphasized income adequacy. (411)

Although she ultimately disagrees with David Gordon, Schor acknowledges his "impressive analysis" and clearly understands the value of other arguments.

Susan Jacoby makes a slightly different move. Rather than acknowledge the value of someone else's claims, she *qualifies* her own; that is, she explains that men also have low estimations of their own mathematical abilities. Although Jacoby's essay focuses on women's and girls' self-limiting perspectives, she qualifies or opens up her point. This move puts her argument in a bigger context and shows that she understands that other arguments exist parallel to her own:

> Scientific illiteracy is not, of course, the exclusive province of women. In certain intellectual circles it has become fashionable to proclaim a willed, aggressive ignorance about science and technology. Some female writers specialize in ominous, uninformed diatribes against genetic research as a plot to remove control of childbearing from women, while some well-known men of letters proudly announce that they understand absolutely nothing about computers, or, for that matter, about electricity. (427)

As you consider your own argument, your own position about a cause, use the following questions to develop concessions and qualifiers:

- Are there legitimate reasons for taking another position on this topic?
- Does my argument make any large, but necessary, leaps?
- Do I ask my audience to accept generalizations?

INVENTION WORKSHOP

With a small group of peers, answer the first two Invention questions in this section for each group member's topic. Each writer should announce his or her thesis. Then the other group members should take turns offering responses to the questions. The goal here is to play devil's advocate—to give each writer opposing positions to consider and possibly counterargue.

The writer should not argue back, but instead should take notes, writing down the opposing positions that other group members offer.

ORGANIZATIONAL STRATEGIES

Where Should I Explain the Phenomenon?

As with any argument, the elements of your essay can be arranged in many ways. One tendency among writers, whether using narrative, examples, or illustrations, is to detail the phenomenon (the behavior, event, trend) before getting into a discussion of causes. In Jacoby's introduction, she gives a brief illustration of the phenomenon (girls dropping math and science from their priorities):

> Susannah, a 16-year-old who has always been an A student in every subject from algebra to English, recently informed her parents that she intended to drop physics and calculus in her senior year of high school and replace them with a drama seminar and a work-study program. She expects a major in art or history in college, she explained, and "any more science or math will just be a waste of my time." (426)

Now that Jacoby has given a snapshot of the phenomenon, she can go on to discuss its significance and public resonance and to explore possible causes. However, like the other authors in this chapter, Jacoby continues to describe the phenomenon throughout her essay, developing its complexity and showing how certain causes are linked to it.

How Should I Deal with Other Causes?

Other causes, those that are different than yours, can help develop counterarguments; you can argue against other causes in favor of the cause you put forth. For example, Jack may point to a possible cause of cult membership (mental illness), but refute that idea in favor of another (loneliness). In this case, the argument that mental illness causes people to join cults is an opposing position—one that the writer counters:

> Some may argue that people join cults because they are mentally ill, nuts, freaked out. It is easy to write off cult members as lunatics. They willingly cast away their families and friends, give all of their life belongings to a bunch of strangers, wear uniform-like apparel, and sometimes even cut their hair to match the group. In short, they throw away their identities, something next to insanity in a culture that honors individualism as the greatest good. However, insanity may not be the main reason people join cults. In fact, many cult members are highly intelligent, entirely reasonable, and healthy individuals. But they long for something, something that everyone longs for—belonging and purpose.

If you have potential counterarguments, remember some standard strategies from Chapter 6, Making Arguments. Counterarguments might come directly after opposing points in counterpoint, point, counterpoint, point manner. Depending on the amount of detail given to each counter, each point might be an entire paragraph, or more, with supporting evidence:

> Opposing Point A
> Your counterargument
> Opposing Point B
> Your counterargument

How Should I Include Outside Sources?

If you have already gathered some information and know how you want to use it, keep in mind that any information from your research should only be included as part of your purpose for the paper. In other words, *be careful not to include information just for the sake of including it.* You might include information from outside sources to explain other perspectives on the cause, support your argument about the cause, or help to explain the phenomenon.

Schor and Kress both use outside sources to illustrate what others think about the cause; Schor also uses sources to support her argument for the causes of consumption. Her use of outside research is always part of her purpose. We always know where she stands and how the information she presents relates to her stance. Here, Schor uses statistics and others' research to explain the behavior of increased consumption:

> In the meantime, upscale emulation had become well-established. Researchers Susan Fournier and Michael Guiry found that 35 percent of their sample aspired to reach the top 6 percent of the income distribution, and another 49 percent aspired to the next 12 percent. Only 15 percent reported that they would be satisfied with "living a comfortable life"—that is, being middle class. But 85 percent of the population cannot earn the six-figure incomes necessary to support upper-middle-class lifestyles. (413)

If you have used outside sources, see Chapter 13, Research & Writing, for guidance on integrating and documenting them.

How Should I Use Paragraphs?

As in all academic prose (the language that scholars use to communicate ideas), paragraphs are used to cluster information. But we should also think of paragraphs as rhetorical tools—strategies for focusing and refocusing readers' attention. In this sense, paragraphs focus readers on a single idea, point, or example. For an argument about causes, a single paragraph might focus readers on a single illustration of a cause, an outside source that argues for a particular cause, a personal narrative that coincides or counters the outside source, or a concession to an outside perspective.

Remember that the turnabout paragraph is a good tool for addressing opposing views. It often begins by expressing an opposing position (one different than the writer's) and then turns to counter that position. For example, see Jack's paragraph on the previous page.

Rather than turnabout in the same paragraph, you can also begin a new paragraph when counterarguing. In the following passage, Schor explains a perspective, or "view," outside of her own. She then begins a new paragraph that initially grants value to the perspective but then turns to show its failing.

> If we have a consumption problem, this view implicitly states, we can solve it by getting more income into more people's hands. The goals are redistribution and growth.
>
> It is difficult to take exception to this view. It combines a deep respect for individual choice (the liberal part) with a commitment to justice and equality (the egalitarian part). I held it myself for many years. But I now believe that by failing to look deeper—to examine the very nature of consumption—it has become too limiting. In short, I do not think that the "income solution" addresses some of the most profound failures of the current consumption regime. (411)

WRITER'S VOICE

Creating Credibility

You are now familiar with many different tools for creating an engaging voice. As earlier chapters discuss, good writers are inviting and curious; they avoid preachiness and hostility. Writers also need to create a sense of credibility, the quality that makes points believable. In argumentative writing, and especially in more complicated types such as in this chapter, credibility is very important so readers consider your claims.

A credible voice is not necessarily commanding or domineering. It might simply be very logical or insightful. Juliet Schor seems credible by virtue of her intensive analysis and extensive research. Deborah Tannen offers a slice of her own research to ground her claims and create credibility. Some writers, such as Leonard Kress, use personal experience to build credibility. In his essay, we get the sense that he may know more about the behavior than many of the supposed experts because of his experience. It is not his reference to *The Encyclopedia of Pediatric Psychology* that gives credibility to Kress's voice; rather, it is the manner in which he uses that information to highlight his own understanding. By the time Kress discovers the important passage in the encyclopedia, he has established his own credibility:

> . . . I could simply will the partially chewed hearty chunks of meat and potato up from their sour churning stock. It felt so good! *The Encyclopedia of Pediatric Psychology* (1979) reports that children who vomit, farfetched as it sounds, even "those who have learned society's aversions . . . can overcome such scruples and experience vomiting as cathartic, even orgasmic." (419)

Remember that you can be credible by your examination of personal experiences as well as of others' research. In considering your own writing, ask yourself the following:

- How will my own experiences or insights create credibility?
- How might outside sources add to my credibility?

Projecting Wonder

Some people assume that a sense of credibility means that the writer is unquestionable and unquestioning. However, credibility should not diminish a sense of curiosity. Even though the writers in this chapter have justification for speaking authoritatively about their topics (from research and observation), they also create a sense of curiosity, even wonder. Sometimes, the most authoritative voice is also the most curious. For example, Leonard Kress is curious even though he has reason to be certain about his claims:

> I often wonder now what led me to such disgusting behavior—what might lead any child to such disgusting behavior. Like any good 21st-century questioner/researcher, I go to the Internet, hopeful that a search of current medical literature will provide answers and understanding. So I begin my search, seated in front of my computer. (417)

Now think of your own topic and your stance on it. Ask yourself the following:

- What about my topic is mysterious or unknown?
- How does my topic extend beyond usual perceptions or conventional thinking?
- What details or ideas associated with my topic might make the reader curious?

Avoiding Preachiness

Because this essay is argumentative in nature, it could potentially invite accusatory language. However, remember that most readers do not accept language that demeans people or tells people what they need. Imagine if Jacoby became accusatory toward adolescent girls and their parents:

> Girls should know better than to dump math and science classes. They need to realize that math and science are important for their intellectual development, and that dropping these courses means they will remain behind their male counterparts in many occupations. Their decision to replace math and science courses with drama and art shows their lack of responsibility.

Such language does nothing to help a reader understand the phenomenon or accept a particular cause; it merely spouts opinions about behavior. This passage also moves away from an argument about *why* something occurs to an argument *against* certain people. Most often, academic writing avoids telling readers what people should do and instead shows readers the value or liability of certain behavior. In Jacoby's essay, she does not attack adolescent girls and their parents. Instead, she explains the complicated cultural process by which they accept their own low expectations in scientific and mathematical proficiency. Jacoby's analysis is not a blame game, but an examination of cause and effect:

In saying that scientific and mathematical ignorance is a self-inflicted female wound, I do not, obviously, mean that cultural expectations play no role in the process. But the world does not conspire to deprive modern women of access to science as it did in the 1930s. . . . The current generation of adolescent girls—and their parents, bred on old expectations about women's interests—are active conspirators in limiting their own intellectual development. (426)

As you consider your own voice, avoid condemning people or behaviors. Instead, try to explain *why* situations occur or *why* people act in a particular way. This strategy will help create a voice that is reflective and analytical, rather than condemning.

ACTIVITY

1. In small groups, discuss how you might create credibility or project wonder for your essay.

2. Support your thesis by writing a paragraph that creates credibility or projects wonder.

3. Consider why you should or should not include the paragraph you wrote for #2 in your final essay.

Most academic readers do not accept language that demeans people or tells people what they need.

VITALITY

Academic writing should be clean and intense. Sentences should be sophisticated enough to prompt intensive thinking but concise enough to keep the reader moving briskly. Lively sentences can be any length—but they should not bog down the reader. It's a fine line: A long engaging sentence can help the reader experience an intense idea, but a long rambling phrase can confuse a reader thoroughly. This section focuses on that fine line. On one hand, we should avoid unnecessarily difficult phrases; on the other, we can intensify sentences by deliberately adding a series of clauses.

Avoid Strings of Phrases

Writers sometimes string together several prepositional phrases. (A prepositional phrase begins with a preposition, such as *in, of, between, on, beside, behind, for*, and so on.) Too many prepositional phrases (even two in a row) can slow down the reader. You might think of it as a matter of momentum: Verbs propel readers through sentences. So when too many phrases pile up, the sentence slows down. Without verbs, the meaning thickens up, the sentence gets muddy, and the reader gets bogged down. That's why good writers avoid clustering together too many phrases.

The following sentence begins with three prepositional phrases:

> The celebration of the holiday at the end of the month will attract many tourists to the town.

If the sentence is revised to have fewer prepositional phrases, the verb *(will attract)* will be closer to the beginning, and the sentence becomes less muddy:

> At the end of the month, the holiday celebration will attract many tourists to the town.

ACTIVITY

Rewrite the five following examples. Try to avoid using strings of prepositional phrases, but also try to keep all the information in the sentences.

1. The solving of this problem of racial segregation involves several steps that the people of the United States ought to understand.

2. Because of the nonviolent actions of the protestors in the courtyard, the city council arranged an emergency meeting.

3. The environmental group argued against the increased use of toxic chemicals for the development of the area golf courses.

4. Our present strategy creates the transition from imagining the world as a place full of attainable riches to thinking of the world as a place full of human resources.

5. The end of the first chapter of the book on migrating birds lists several different species and their geographical patterns.

A string of phrases or clauses is not always bad. In fact, good writers intentionally line up several phrases or clauses. What's the difference between a confusing string of phrases and a powerful series of phrases? The answer lies in *repetition:* Good writers use repeating patterns to reinforce ideas.

Intensify with a Series

A series of words creates a pattern for readers. When a chain of words is lined up, readers make an automatic intellectual connection among those words. We most often see single words in a series:

> The land flattens itself out and creates a sense of <u>openness</u>, <u>emptiness</u>, and <u>space</u>.

But phrases can also be put in a series:

> The land flattens itself out and creates <u>a feeling of openness</u>, <u>a sense of emptiness</u>, and <u>an eyeful of space</u>.

Skillful writers can even put entire clauses in a series. Here, the repeating clauses create an intellectual pattern for the reader. They set up a way of thinking—and pull the reader briskly through the images:

> They live in a place <u>where the fields lie uninterrupted</u>, <u>where the houses take the full brunt of the wind</u>, <u>where the horizon simply evaporates</u>.

The same strategy can be applied to any topic:

> The feelings of paranoia increase because the victims are often socially isolated, because they often live far from family, and because they seldom understand the nature of their condition.

> In spring, when the temperatures stay consistently above freezing, when the rain becomes nearly constant, and when the daylight overtakes the darkness, mammalian activity increases sharply.

The previous examples rely on three clauses in each series. Of course, a series can extend far beyond three clauses, but the same effect can be created with only two clauses. To reinforce a way of thinking, writers often use two of the same type of clause. Here, Leonard Kress and Juliet Schor use a double clause pattern to emphasize and develop thinking:

> I often wonder now <u>what led me to such disgusting behavior</u>—<u>what might lead any child to such disgusting behavior</u>. (417)

> For example, there is now a conservative jeremiad that points to the recent tremendous increases in consumption and concludes <u>that Americans just don't realize how good they have it</u>, <u>that they have become overly entitled and spoiled</u>. (414)

What's the difference between a confusing string of phrases and a powerful series of phrases?

PEER REVIEW

Now get help from other writers. Before exchanging drafts with at least one other writer, underline your main idea (your thesis) or write it on the top of your draft.

As a peer reviewer, use the following questions to respond to specific issues in the draft.

1. Can any phrases or terms in the thesis be narrowed? If so, circle them and make some suggestions for more focus. Does the thesis avoid the common problems? (See page 439.)

2. Can you follow the writer's line of reasoning? Do you accept the cause the writer asserts? Why or why not?

3. What other support strategies could the writer employ? (Consider examples, allusions, scenarios, and so on. See page 440.)

4. Do any paragraphs shift focus from one point about the subject to another? Write "shifts focus" in the margins.

5. If the writer uses outside sources, are they integrated smoothly into the argument? (See pages 642–643, in Chapter 13, Research & Writing, for specific strategies.)

6. Consider the writer's voice.
   a. Identify any passages that seem preachy. (See page 447.)
   b. Does the writer seem credible? What passages support your decision? (See page 446.)
   c. Identify a passage that seems flat, without intensity. Suggest a strategy for the writer to create a sense of wonder. (See page 446.)

7. As a reviewer, point to particular sentences and phrases that could gain vitality and intensity. Use the following:
   a. Look for confusing strings of phrases. Suggest a revision.
   b. Rewrite a passage of the draft, and use a series of phrases or clauses to intensify an idea.
   c. Consider vitality strategies from other chapters:
   - Look for unnecessary, interrupting clauses and phrases. Underline them and/or draw an arrow to show where the phrase or clause can be moved.
   - Rewrite a sentence and create more intensity with a repeating pattern.
   - Cross out wordy phrases and write in more concise options.
   - What sentences are overembedded? (Point to any clauses that overlap with other clauses, causing a disconnect between ideas.)
   - Examine attributive phrases. Point out unnecessary phrases or sentences that could be boiled down.
   - Where can the writer change linking verbs to action verbs?
   - Where can the writer avoid drawing attention to *I* and *you*?
   - Help the writer change unnecessary clauses to phrases and phrases to words.
   - Point to expletives (such as *there are* and *it is*).
   - Help the writer change passive verbs to active verbs for more vitality.

DELIVERY

In academia, at work, and at home, understanding causes can have serious consequences. Exploring and writing about issues is likely to have consequences for the reader, the writer, and their community as a whole. What are the possible consequences of the essay you wrote for this chapter?

Consider these questions:

- Will the reader better understand the issue about which you wrote? Is the reader likely to think or behave differently as a result?

- What might be the benefits to others? How might others be harmed? Who besides your instructor might benefit from your ideas?

- What are the possible effects on you, the writer?

Beyond the Essay

Explore a photo (or image) essay How does the photo essay "Road Salt" encourage people to think about a cause? How do the four images work together to make some point? What other images might the writer have used, and why? What other order might the images have been placed in?

Create a photo (or image) essay Use at least four images to encourage people to think about a cause. Select and arrange the images carefully, and then in writing explain how the images work together to make your point.

PROPOSING SOLUTIONS

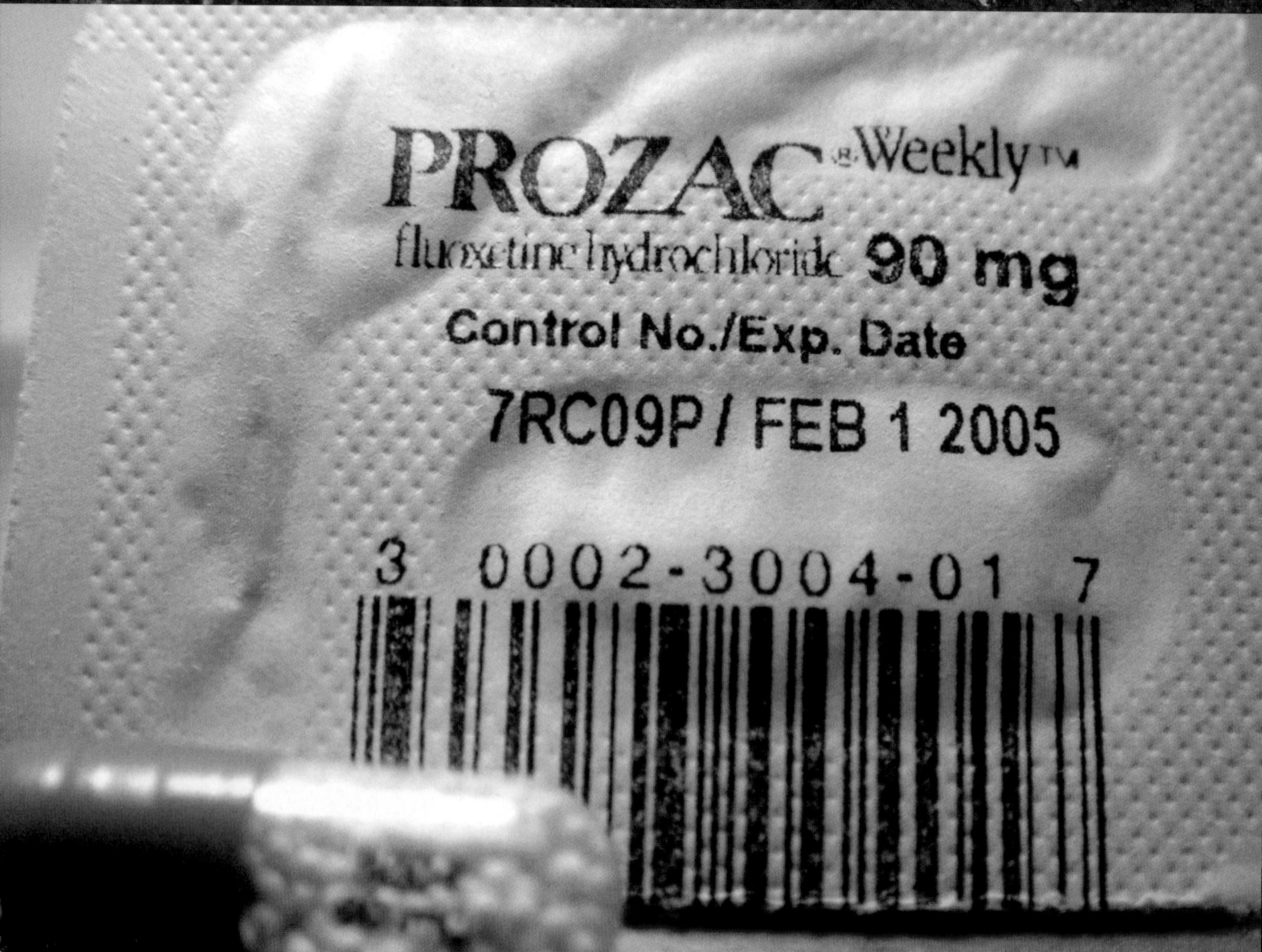

PROZAC ®Weekly™
fluoxetine hydrochloride **90 mg**

Control No./Exp. Date

7RC09P / FEB 1 2005

3   0002-3004-01 7

Chapter Contents

CHAPTER 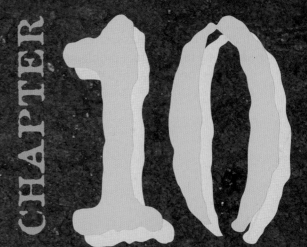 10

"All subjects, except sex, are dull until
somebody makes them interesting."

—Paul Roberts

In everyday life, crisis is a constant. Problems emerge in every facet of our existence: In the work world, problems arise in working conditions, policy implementation, coworker relations, labor/management relations, and government standards; our communities face problems such as homelessness, pollution, school violence, terrorism, and urban sprawl; at home, the list of possible problems can seem endless. While many of us have the privilege of ignoring such problems, someone in some capacity has to address them. Whether elected official, shift supervisor, environmental scientist, department chair, or scout leader, someone ultimately has to engage daily crises and propose solutions.

In academia, people in all disciplines have to propose solutions:

- In an engineering class, students propose solutions to structural problems in a building designed before earthquake construction codes.

- In a business class, students must convince their peers that a particular strategy for solving a company's financial problems is the most efficient.

- In a calculus class, students explore several different ways to solve a problem and then convince their peers and instructor that one particular way is the best.

- For a national conference on employment trends, graduate students and faculty members propose strategies to counter the increasing demand for low-salary instructors.

When writers propose solutions to problems, they are involved in many layers of analysis. They must analyze the problem to discover its causes—some of which may lie hidden in abstraction. They must also consider all the possible ways for addressing the problem and then come to some conclusion about the most appropriate. Proposing solutions also involves argument: Writers have to convince readers that the problem must be addressed, that action is necessary. They also must argue for the value of their particular solution. This is what politicians do for a living; members of Congress, after all, spend much of their time arguing, first, that particular problems deserve allocated funds and, second, that those funds should be used in particular ways.

You might think of proposing a solution as a double-layered argument: First, you must argue that a problem worthy of attention or action exists and, second, that a particular solution will best solve it. Proposing a solution involves all the elements of an argument (thesis, support, counterargument, and concession).

This chapter will help you discover a problem, develop a solution, and develop a written argument for the solution. The following essays will provide valuable insight to necessary strategies for proposing solutions. After reading the essays, you can uncover a problem in one of two ways:

1. Go to the **Point of Contact** section to find a problem from your everyday life.
2. Choose one of the **Ideas for Writing** that follow each essay.

After finding a subject, go to the **Analysis** section to begin developing ideas for your essay.

In the following essays, each writer addresses a specific problem and gives many illustrations or examples for that problem. Some writers go to great lengths to express the degree of the problem being discussed. As you may notice, the more abstract or hidden the problem, the more the writer has to work to illustrate it. (The effect of pesticides on human life, for instance, is a fairly difficult problem to illustrate, so Carson goes to considerable lengths to make it apparent.) For some problems, the solution is equally complex. Writers who acknowledge the true complexities of their problems and solutions will better engage their readers and will meet with less opposition. Some solutions, as Didion's essay illustrates, are not necessarily complicated physical solutions, but simple reconsiderations—that is, new ways of thinking about an inescapable problem.

The Obligation to Endure

Rachel Carson

The following essay is as much an historical document as is the *Declaration of Independence* or *The Emancipation Proclamation*. In "The Obligation to Endure," an excerpt from *Silent Spring,* published in 1962, Rachel Carson puts forth ideas that were revolutionary at the time—and that are as relevant today as they were then, if not more relevant. As you read, consider how Carson's argument reminds us that writing from over 40 years ago (or from 100 or 1,000 years ago) can be as relevant now as it was then.

The history of life on earth has been a history of interaction between living things and their surroundings. To a large extent, the physical form and the habits of the earth's vegetation and its animal life have been molded by the environment. Considering the whole span of earthly time, the opposite effect, in which life actually modifies its surroundings, has been relatively slight. Only within the moment of time represented by the present century has one species—man—acquired significant power to alter the nature of his world.

During the past quarter century this power has not only increased to one of disturbing magnitude but it has changed in character. The most alarming of all man's assaults upon the environment is the contamination of air, earth, rivers, and sea with dangerous and even lethal materials. This pollution is for the most part irrecoverable; the chain of evil it initiates not only in the world that must support life but in living tissues is for the most part irreversible. In this now universal contamination of the environment, chemicals are the sinister and little-recognized partners of radiation in changing the very nature of the world—the very nature of its life. Strontium 90, released through nuclear explosions into the air, comes to earth in rain or drifts down as fallout, lodges in soil, enters into the grass or corn or wheat grown there, and in time takes up its abode in the bones of a human being, there to remain until his death. Similarly, chemicals sprayed on croplands or forests or gardens lie long in soil, entering into living organisms, passing from one to another in a chain of poisoning and death. Or they pass mysteriously by underground streams until they emerge and, through the alchemy of air and sunlight, combine into new forms that kill vegetation, sicken cattle, and work unknown harm on those who drink from once pure wells. As Albert Schweitzer has said, "Man can hardly even recognize the devils of his own creation."

It took hundreds of millions of years to produce the life that now inhabits the earth—eons of time in which that developing and evolving and diversifying life reached a state of adjustment and balance with its surroundings. The environment, rigorously shaping and directing the life it supported, contained elements that were hostile as well as supporting. Certain rocks gave out dangerous radiation; even within the light of the sun, from which all life draws its energy, there were short-wave radiations with power to injure. Given time—time not in years but in millennia—life adjusts, and a balance has been reached. For time is the essential ingredient; but in the modern world there is no time.

The rapidity of change and the speed with which new situations are created follow the impetuous and heedless pace of man rather than the deliberate pace of nature. Radiation is no longer merely the background radiation of rocks, the bombardment of cosmic rays, the ultraviolet of the sun that have existed before there was any life on earth; radiation is now the unnatural creation of man's tampering with the atom. The chemicals to which life is asked to make its adjustment are no longer merely the calcium and silica and copper and all the rest of the minerals washed out of the rocks and carried in rivers to the sea; they are the synthetic creations of man's inventive mind, brewed in his laboratories, and having no counterparts in nature.

5   To adjust to these chemicals would require time on the scale that is nature's; it would require not merely the years of a man's life but the life of generations. And even this, were it by some miracle possible, would be futile, for the new chemicals come from our laboratories in an endless stream; almost five hundred annually find their way into actual use in the United States alone. The figure is staggering and its implications are not easily grasped—500 new chemicals to which the bodies of men and animals are required somehow to adapt each year, chemicals totally outside the limits of biologic experience.

Among them are many that are used in man's war against nature. Since the mid-1940s over 200 basic chemicals have been created for use in killing insects, weeds, rodents, and other organisms described in the modern vernacular as "pests"; and they are sold under several thousand different brand names.

These sprays, dusts, and aerosols are now applied almost universally to farms, gardens, forests, and homes—nonselective chemicals that have the power to kill every insect, the "good" and the "bad," to still the song of birds and the leaping of fish in the streams, to coat the leaves with a deadly film, and to linger on in soil—all this though the intended target may be only a few weeds or insects. Can anyone believe it is possible to lay down such a barrage of poisons on the surface of the earth without making it unfit for all life? They should not be called "insecticides," but "biocides."

The whole process of spraying seems caught up in an endless spiral. Since DDT was released for civilian use, a process of escalation has been going on in which ever more toxic materials must be found. This has happened because insects, in a triumphant vindication of Darwin's principle of the survival of the fittest, have evolved super races immune to the particular insecticide used, hence a deadlier one has always to be developed—and then a deadlier one than that. It has happened also because, for reasons to be described later, destructive insects often undergo a "flareback," or resurgence, after spraying, in numbers greater than before. Thus the chemical war is never won, and all life is caught in its violent crossfire.

Along with the possibility of the extinction of mankind by nuclear war, the central problem of our age has therefore become the contamination of man's total environment with such substances of incredible potential for harm—substances that accumulate in the tissues of plants and animals and even penetrate the germ cells to shatter or alter the very material of heredity upon which the shape of the future depends.

10   Some would-be architects of our future look toward a time when it will be possible to alter the human germ plasm by design. But we may easily be doing so now by

inadvertence, for many chemicals, like radiation, bring about gene mutations. It is ironic to think that man might determine his own future by something so seemingly trivial as the choice of an insect spray.

All this has been risked—for what? Future historians may well be amazed by our distorted sense of proportion. How could intelligent beings seek to control a few unwanted species by a method that contaminated the entire environment and brought the threat of disease and death even to their own kind? Yet this is precisely what we have done. We have done it, moreover, for reasons that collapse the moment we examine them. We are told that the enormous and expanding use of pesticides is necessary to maintain farm production. Yet is our real problem not one of *overproduction*? Our farms, despite measures to remove acreages from production and to pay farmers *not* to produce, have yielded such a staggering excess of crops that the American taxpayer in 1962 is paying out more than one billion dollars a year as the total carrying cost of the surplus-food storage program. And is the situation helped when one branch of the Agriculture Department tries to reduce production while another states, as it did in 1958, "It is believed generally that reduction of crop acreages under provisions of the Soil Bank will stimulate interest in use of chemicals to obtain maximum production on the land retained in crops."

All this is not to say there is no insect problem and no need of control. I am saying, rather, that control must be geared to realities, not to mythical situations, and that the methods employed must be such that they do not destroy us along with the insects.

The problem whose attempted solution has brought such a train of disaster in its wake is an accompaniment of our modern way of life. Long before the age of man, insects inhabited the earth—a group of extraordinarily varied and adaptable beings. Over the course of time since man's advent, a small percentage of the more than half a million species of insects have come into conflict with human welfare in two principal ways: as competitors for the food supply and as carriers of human disease.

Disease-carrying insects become important where human beings are crowded together, especially under conditions where sanitation is poor, as in time of natural disaster or war or in situations of extreme poverty and deprivation. Then control of some sort becomes necessary. It is a sobering fact, however, as we shall presently see, that the method of massive chemical control has had only limited success, and also threatens to worsen the very conditions it is intended to curb.

15   Under primitive agricultural conditions the farmer had few insect problems. These arose with the intensification of agriculture—the devotion of immense acreages to a single crop. Such a system set the stage for explosive increases in specific insect populations. Single-crop farming does not take advantage of the principles by which nature works; it is agriculture as an engineer might conceive it to be. Nature has introduced great variety into the landscape, but man has displayed a passion for simplifying it. Thus he undoes the built-in checks and balances by which nature holds the species within bounds. One important natural check is a limit on the amount of suitable habitat for each species. Obviously then, an insect that lives on wheat can build up its population to much higher levels on a farm devoted to wheat than on one in which wheat is intermingled with other crops to which the insect is not adapted.

The same thing happens in other situations. A generation or more ago, the towns of large areas of the United States lined their streets with the noble elm tree. Now the beauty they hopefully created is threatened with complete destruction as disease sweeps through the elms, carried by a beetle that would have only limited chance to build up large populations and to spread from tree to tree if the elms were only occasional trees in a richly diversified planting.

Another factor in the modern insect problem is one that must be viewed against a background of geologic and human history: the spreading of thousands of different kinds of organisms from their native homes to invade new territories. This worldwide migration has been studied and graphically described by the British ecologist Charles Elton in his recent book *The Ecology of Invasions.* During the Cretaceous Period, some hundred million years ago, flooding seas cut many land bridges between continents and living things found themselves confined in what Elton calls "colossal separate nature reserves." There, isolated from others of their kind, they developed many new species. When some of the land masses were joined again, about 15 million years ago, these species began to move out into new territories—a movement that is not only still in progress but is now receiving considerable assistance from man.

The importation of plants is the primary agent in the modern spread of species, for animals have almost invariably gone along with the plants, quarantine being a comparatively recent and not completely effective innovation. The United States Office of Plant Introduction alone has introduced almost 200,000 species and varieties of plants from all over the world. Nearly half of the 180 or so major insect enemies of plants in the United States are accidental imports from abroad, and most of them have come as hitchhikers on plants.

In new territory, out of reach of the restraining hand of the natural enemies that kept down its numbers in its native land, an invading plant or animal is able to become enormously abundant. Thus it is no accident that our most troublesome insects are introduced species.

20 These invasions, both the naturally occurring and those dependent on human assistance, are likely to continue indefinitely. Quarantine and massive chemical campaigns are only extremely expensive ways of buying time. We are faced, according to Dr. Elton, "with a life-and-death need not just to find new technological means of suppressing this plant or that animal"; instead we need the basic knowledge of animal populations and their relations to their surroundings that will "promote an even balance and damp down the explosive power of outbreaks and new invasions."

Much of the necessary knowledge is now available but we do not use it. We train ecologists in our universities and even employ them in our governmental agencies but we seldom take their advice. We allow the chemical death rain to fall as though there were no alternative, whereas in fact there are many, and our ingenuity could soon discover many more if given opportunity.

Have we fallen into a mesmerized state that makes us accept as inevitable that which is inferior or detrimental, as though having lost the will or the vision to demand that which is good? Such thinking, in the words of the ecologist Paul Shepard, "idealizes life with only its head out of water, inches above the limits of toleration of the corruption of its own environment. . . . Why should we tolerate a diet of weak poisons, a home in insipid surroundings, a circle of acquaintances who are not quite our enemies, the noise of motors with just enough relief to prevent insanity? Who would want to live in a world which is just not quite fatal?"

Yet such a world is pressed upon us. The crusade to create a chemically sterile, insect-free world seems to have engendered a fanatic zeal on the part of many specialists and most of the so-called control agencies. On every hand there is evidence that those engaged in spraying operations exercise a ruthless power. "The regulatory entomologists . . . function as prosecutor, judge and jury, tax assessor and collector and sheriff to enforce their own orders," said Connecticut entomologist Neely Turner. The most flagrant abuses go unchecked in both state and federal agencies.

It is not my contention that chemical insecticides must never be used. I do contend that we have put poisonous and biologically potent chemicals indiscriminately into the hands of persons largely or wholly ignorant of their potentials for harm. We have subjected enormous numbers of people to contact with these poisons, without their consent and often without their knowledge. If the Bill of Rights contains no guarantee that a citizen shall be secure against lethal poisons distributed either by private individuals or by public officials, it is surely only because our forefathers, despite their considerable wisdom and foresight, could conceive of no such problem.

25 I contend, furthermore, that we have allowed these chemicals to be used with little or no advance investigation of their effect on soil, water, wildlife, and man

himself. Future generations are unlikely to condone our lack of prudent concern for the integrity of the natural world that supports all life.

There is still very limited awareness of the nature of the threat. This is an era of specialists, each of whom sees his own problem and is unaware of or intolerant of the larger frame into which it fits. It is also an era dominated by industry, in which the right to make a dollar at whatever cost is seldom challenged. When the public protests, confronted with some obvious evidence of damaging results of pesticide applications, it is fed little tranquilizing pills of half truth. We urgently need an end to these false assurances, to the sugar coating of unpalatable facts. It is the public that is being asked to assume the risks that the insect controllers calculate. The public must decide whether it wishes to continue on the present road, and it can do so only when in full possession of the facts. In the words of Jean Rostand, "The obligation to endure gives us the right to know."

Writing Strategies

1. Evaluate Carson's introduction and conclusion. Why is, or isn't, each effective? How else might she have begun and concluded her essay?

2. Write a new introduction and conclusion for Carson's essay. Then discuss with classmates the advantages and disadvantages of the introduction and conclusion you wrote.

3. What strategies (allusion, hypothetical situation, personal experience, observation of a trend, statistics/data, and so on) does Carson use to support her main idea? (Refer to the **Delivery** section of this chapter for more help.)

4. A convincing argument is likely to include both concessions and counterarguments. Identify one of each in Carson's essay, and then explain how each strengthens her argument.

5. Identify at least three transitional words or expressions used to help the reader more easily go from one idea to another.

Exploring Ideas

1. What is Carson trying to accomplish with this essay?

2. What change does Carson want the reader to consider?

3. What ideas of Carson's are still relevant today? What ideas are no longer relevant?

4. Spend several days observing your environment, looking for evidence from your everyday life to support or refute any of Carson's ideas. Write down each piece of evidence you discover and the way it relates to what Carson says.

5. How might you participate in this discussion about the environment? Consider various ways of expanding, narrowing, redirecting, or updating the discussion.

Ideas for Writing

1. Carson questions commonly accepted practices, such as a farmer devoting "immense acreages to a single crop." What problem (environmental or other) can you think of that is the result of a commonly accepted practice? What is the problem, what caused it, and how might it be solved?

2. For what problem on campus can you propose a solution?

If responding to one of these ideas, go to the **Analysis** section of this chapter to begin developing ideas for your essay.

In Bed

Joan Didion

It is easy to be fooled into thinking that every problem can be solved (with a number, a pill, a bullet, a check, a degree, a credit card). But most human problems are complicated, and many simply *cannot be fixed*. Instead, we have to learn new approaches to old problems. In this essay, Joan Didion explains a personal problem that resonates with many people; she also asserts her solution, which is, in some ways, no solution, and in other ways, the only possible solution. The essay, then, is not simply about migraines; it is about the process of re-seeing problems.

Three, four, sometimes five times a month, I spend the day in bed with a migraine headache, insensible to the world around me. Almost every day of every month, between these attacks, I feel the sudden irrational irritation and the flush of blood into the cerebral arteries which tell me that migraine is on its way, and I take certain drugs to avert its arrival. If I did not take the drugs, I would be able to function perhaps one day in four. The physiological error called migraine is, in brief, central to the given of my life. When I was 15, 16, even 25, I used to think that I could rid myself of this error by simply denying it, character over chemistry. "Do you have headaches *sometimes? frequently? never?*" the application forms would demand. "Check one." Wary of the trap, wanting whatever it was that the successful circumnavigation of that particular form could bring (a job, a scholarship, the respect of mankind and the grace of God), I would check one. *"Sometimes,"* I would lie. That in fact I spent one or two days a week almost unconscious with pain seemed a shameful secret, evidence not merely of some chemical inferiority but of all my bad attitudes, unpleasant tempers, wrongthink.

For I had no brain tumor, no eyestrain, no high blood pressure, nothing wrong with me at all: I simply had migraine headaches, and migraine headaches were, as everyone who did not have them knew, imaginary. I

fought migraine then, ignored the warnings it sent, went to school and later to work in spite of it, sat through lectures in Middle English and presentations to advertisers with involuntary tears running down the right side of my face, threw up in washrooms, stumbled home by instinct, emptied ice trays onto my bed and tried to freeze the pain in my right temple, wished only for a neurosurgeon who would do a lobotomy on house call, and cursed my imagination.

It was a long time before I began thinking mechanistically enough to accept migraine for what it was: something with which I would be living, the way some people live with diabetes. Migraine is something more than the fancy of a neurotic imagination. It is an essentially hereditary complex of symptoms, the most frequently noted but by no means the most unpleasant of which is a vascular headache of blinding severity, suffered by a surprising number of women, a fair number of men (Thomas Jefferson had migraine, and so did Ulysses S. Grant, the day he accepted Lee's surrender), and by some unfortunate children as young as two years old. (I had my first when I was eight. It came on during a fire drill at the Columbia School in Colorado Springs, Colorado. I was taken first home and then to the infirmary at Peterson Field, where my father was stationed. The Air Corps doctor prescribed an enema.) Almost anything can trigger a specific attack of migraine: stress, allergy, fatigue, an abrupt change in barometric pressure, a contretemps over a parking ticket. A flashing light. A fire drill. One inherits, of course, only the predisposition. In other words I spent yesterday in bed with a headache not merely because of my bad attitudes, unpleasant tempers and wrongthink, but because both my grandmothers had migraine, my father has migraine and my mother has migraine.

No one knows precisely what it is that is inherited. The chemistry of migraine, however, seems to have some connection with the nerve hormone named serotonin, which is naturally present in the brain. The amount of serotonin in the blood falls sharply at the onset of migraine, and one migraine drug, methysergide, or

Sansert, seems to have some effect on serotonin. Methysergide is a derivative of lysergic acid (in fact Sandoz Pharmaceuticals first synthesized LSD-25 while looking for a migraine cure), and its use is hemmed about with so many contraindications and side effects that most doctors prescribe it only in the most incapacitating cases. Methysergide, when it is prescribed, is taken daily, as a preventive; another preventive which works for some people is old-fashioned ergotamine tartrate, which helps to constrict the swelling blood vessels during the "aura," the period which in most cases precedes the actual headache.

5   Once an attack is under way, however, no drug touches it. Migraine gives some people mild hallucinations, temporarily blinds others, shows up not only as a headache but as a gastrointestinal disturbance, a painful sensitivity to all sensory stimuli, an abrupt overpowering fatigue, a strokelike aphasia, and a crippling inability to make even the most routine connections. When I am in a migraine aura (for some people the aura lasts fifteen minutes, for others several hours), I will drive through red lights, lose the house keys, spill whatever I am holding, lose the ability to focus my eyes or frame coherent sentences, and generally give the appearance of being on drugs, or drunk. The actual headache, when it comes, brings with it chills, sweating, nausea, a debility that seems to stretch the very limits of endurance. That no one dies of migraine seems, to someone deep into an attack, an ambiguous blessing.

My husband also has migraine, which is unfortunate for him but fortunate for me: perhaps nothing so tends to prolong an attack as the accusing eye of someone who has never had a headache. "Why not take a couple of aspirin," the unafflicted will say from the doorway, or "I'd have a headache, too, spending a beautiful day like this inside with all the shades drawn." All of us who have migraine suffer not only from the attacks themselves but from this common conviction that we are perversely refusing to cure ourselves by taking a couple of aspirin, that we are making ourselves sick, that we "bring it on ourselves." And in the most

immediate sense, the sense of why we have a headache this Tuesday and not last Thursday, of course we often do. There certainly is what doctors call a "migraine personality," and that personality tends to be ambitious, inward, intolerant of error, rather rigidly organized, perfectionist. "You don't look like a migraine personality," a doctor once said to me. "Your hair's messy. But I suppose you're a compulsive housekeeper." Actually my house is kept even more negligently than my hair, but the doctor was right nonetheless: perfectionism can also take the form of spending most of a week writing and rewriting and not writing a single paragraph.

But not all perfectionists have migraine, and not all migrainous people have migraine personalities. We do not escape heredity. I have tried in most of the available ways to escape my own migrainous heredity (at one point I learned to give myself two daily injections of histamine with a hypodermic needle, even though the needle so frightened me that I had to close my eyes when I did it), but I still have migraine. And I have learned now to live with it, learned when to expect it, how to outwit it, even how to regard it, when it does come, as more friend than lodger. We have reached a certain understanding, my migraine and I. It never comes when I am in real trouble. Tell me that my house is burned down, my husband has left me, that there is gunfighting in the streets and panic in the banks, and I will not respond by getting a headache. It comes instead when I am fighting not an open but a guerrilla war with my own life, during weeks of small household confusions, lost laundry, unhappy help, canceled appointments, on days when the telephone rings too much and I get no work done and the wind is coming up. On days like that my friend comes uninvited.

And once it comes, now that I am wise in its ways, I no longer fight it. I lie down and let it happen. At first every small apprehension is magnified, every anxiety a pounding terror. Then the pain comes, and I concentrate only on that. Right there is the usefulness of migraine, there in that imposed yoga, the concentration on the pain. For when the pain recedes, ten or twelve hours later, everything goes with it, all the hidden resentments, all the vain anxieties. The migraine has acted as a circuit breaker, and the fuses have emerged intact. There is a pleasant convalescent euphoria. I open the windows and feel the air, eat gratefully, sleep well. I notice the particular nature of a flower in a glass on the stair landing. I count my blessings.

Writing Strategies

1. Study several of Didion's paragraphs. How are they organized? Does she state or imply main ideas? How does her organization help or hinder the reader?

2. Does Didion's essay resonate with the public—that is, do her points relate to others beyond herself? How does her essay convey this public resonance?

3. Compare Didion's conclusion to one you might have written. How does she begin her conclusion? How does she end it? Why is, or isn't, her conclusion effective?

4. How does Didion help the reader understand the problem? What did you learn about migraine from this essay?

Exploring Ideas

1. How does Didion see migraine?

2. What is Didion's solution?

3. How might others benefit by reading Didion's essay?

4. Summarize Didion's essay, and ask several migraine sufferers for their response. How is the way others see migraine similar to or different from the way Didion sees it?

5. How might you participate in Didion's discussion? What interesting point might you add to her discussion of migraine, or how might you apply her way of thinking to some other problem? Might you apply a completely different way of thinking to some problem?

Ideas for Writing

1. What problem is central to the "given" of your life, and how might one deal with such a problem?

2. What physical condition have you come to terms with?

If responding to one of these ideas, go to the **Analysis** section of this chapter to begin developing ideas for your essay.

How to Say Nothing in 500 Words

Paul Roberts

College has a particular set of problems and a corresponding set of familiar solutions. For the college writing student, the recurring problem is fulfilling an assignment on time. And many (most?) students have accumulated strategies for "knocking out" or "getting" through" the chore. But, as Paul Roberts argues, those familiar strategies work against students. That is, the common solutions for getting through a writing assignment actually create another problem—bad grades. Roberts first names and illustrates the common solutions (or writing strategies) and then offers an alternative path for better dealing with college writing assignments.

It's Friday afternoon and you have almost survived another week of classes. You are just looking forward dreamily to the weekend when the English instructor says: "For Monday you will turn in a five-hundred-word composition on college football."

Well, that puts a good hole in the weekend. You don't have any strong views on college football one way or the other. You get rather excited during the season and go to all the home games and find it rather more fun than not. On the other hand, the class has been reading Robert Hutchins in the anthology and perhaps Shaw's "Eighty-Yard Run," and from the class discussion you have got the idea that the instructor thinks college football is for the birds. You are no fool. You can figure out what side to take.

After dinner you get out the portable typewriter that you got for high school graduation. You might as well get it over with and enjoy Saturday and Sunday. Five hundred words is about two double-spaced pages with normal margins. You put in a sheet of paper, think up a title, and you're off:

Why College Football Should Be Abolished

College football should be abolished because it's bad for the school and also for the players. The players are so busy practicing that they don't have any time for their studies.

This, you feel, is a mighty good start. The only trouble is that it's only thirty-two words. You still have four hundred and sixty-eight to go, and you've pretty well exhausted the subject. It comes to you that you do your best thinking in the morning, so you put away the typewriter and go to the movies. But the next morning you have to do your washing and some math problems, and in the afternoon you go to the game. The English instructor turns up too, and you wonder if you've taken the right side after all. Saturday night you have a date, and Sunday morning you have to go to church. (You can't let English assignments interfere with your religion.) What with one thing and another, it's ten o'clock Sunday night before you get out the typewriter again. You make a pot of coffee and start to fill out your views on college football. Put a little meat on the bones.

Why College Football Should Be Abolished

In my opinion, it seems to me that college football should be abolished. The reason why I think this to be true is because I feel that football is bad for the colleges in nearly every respect. As Robert Hutchins says in his article in our anthology in which he discusses college football, it would be better if the colleges had race horses and had races with one another, because then the horses would not have to attend classes. I firmly agree with Mr. Hutchins on this point, and I am sure that many other students would agree too.

One reason why it seems to me that college football is bad is that it has become too commercial. In the olden times when people played football just for the fun of it, maybe college football was all right, but they do not play college football just for the fun of it now as they used to in the old days. Nowadays college football is what you might call a big business. Maybe this is not true at all schools, and I don't think it is especially true here at State, but certainly this is the case at most colleges and universities in America nowadays, as Mr. Hutchins points out in his very interesting article. Actually the coaches and alumni go around to the high schools and offer the high school stars large salaries to come to their colleges and play football for them. There was one case where a high school star was offered a convertible if he would play football for a certain college.

Another reason for abolishing college football is that it is bad for the players. They do not have time to get a college education, because they are so busy playing football. A football player has to practice every afternoon from three to six and then he is so tired that he can't concentrate on his studies. He just feels like dropping off to sleep after dinner, and then the next day he goes to his classes without having studied and maybe he fails the test.

(Good ripe stuff so far, but you're still a hundred and fifty-one words from home. One more push.)

Also I think college football is bad for the colleges and the universities because not very many students get to participate in it. Out of a college of ten thousand students only seventy-five or a hundred play football, if that many. Football is what you might call a spectator sport. That means that most people go to watch it but do not play it themselves.

(Four hundred and fifteen. Well, you still have the conclusion, and when you retype it, you can make the margins a little wider.)

These are the reasons why I agree with Mr. Hutchins that college football should be abolished in American colleges and universities.

5   On Monday you turn it in, moderately hopeful, and on Friday it comes back marked "weak in content" and sporting a big "D."

This essay is exaggerated a little, not much. The English instructor will recognize it as reasonably typical of what an assignment on college football will bring in. He knows that nearly half of the class will contrive in five hundred words to say that college football is too commercial and bad for the players. Most of the other half will inform him that college football builds character and prepares one for life and brings prestige to the school. As he reads paper after paper all saying the same thing in almost the same words, all bloodless, five hundred words dripping out of nothing, he wonders how he allowed himself to get trapped into teaching English when he might have had a happy and interesting life as an electrician or a confidence man.

Well, you may ask, what can you do about it? The subject is one on which you have few convictions and little information. Can you be expected to make a dull subject interesting? As a matter of fact, this is precisely what you are expected to do. This is the writer's essential task. All subjects, except sex, are dull until somebody makes them interesting. The writer's job is to find the argument, the approach, the angle, the wording that will take the reader with him. This is seldom easy, and it is particularly hard in subjects that have been much discussed: College Football, Fraternities, Popular Music, Is Chivalry Dead?, and the like. You will feel that there is nothing you can do with such subjects except repeat the old bromides. But there are some things you can do which will make your papers, if not throbbingly alive, at least less insufferably tedious than they might otherwise be.

Avoid the Obvious Content

Say the assignment is college football. Say that you've decided to be against it. Begin by putting down the arguments that come to your mind: it is too commercial, it takes the students' minds off their studies, it is hard on the players, it makes the university a kind of circus instead of an intellectual center, for most schools it is financially ruinous. Can you think of any more arguments, just off hand? All right. Now when you write your paper, make sure that you don't use any of the material on this list. If these are the points that leap to your mind, they will leap to everyone else's too, and whether you get a "C" or a "D" may depend on whether the instructor reads your paper early when he is fresh and tolerant or late, when the sentence "In my opinion, college football has become too commercial," inexorably repeated, has brought him to the brink of lunacy.

Be against college football for some reason or reasons of your own. If they are keen and perceptive ones, that's splendid. But even if they are trivial or foolish or indefensible, you are still ahead so long as they are not everybody else's reasons too. Be against it because the colleges don't spend enough money on it to make it worthwhile, because it is bad for the characters of the spectators, because the players are forced to attend classes, because the football stars hog all the beautiful women, because it competes with baseball and is therefore un-American and possibly Communist-inspired. There are lots of more or less unused reasons for being against college football.

10 Sometimes it is a good idea to sum up and dispose of the trite and conventional points before going on to your own. This has the advantage of indicating to the reader that you are going to be neither trite nor conventional. Something like this:

> We are often told that college football should be abolished because it has become too commercial or because it is bad for the players. These arguments are no doubt very cogent, but they don't really go to the heart of the matter.

Then you go to the heart of the matter.

Take the Less Usual Side

One rather simple way of getting into your paper is to take the side of the argument that most of the citizens will want to avoid. If the assignment is an essay on dogs, you can, if you choose, explain that dogs are faithful and lovable companions, intelligent, useful as guardians of the house and protectors of children, indispensable in police work—in short, when all is said

and done, man's best friends. Or you can suggest that those big brown eyes conceal, more often than not, a vacuity of mind and an inconstancy of purpose; that the dogs you have known most intimately have been mangy, ill-tempered brutes, incapable of instruction; and that only your nobility of mind and fear of arrest prevent you from kicking the flea-ridden animals when you pass them on the street.

Naturally personal convictions will sometimes dictate your approach. If the assigned subject is "Is Methodism Rewarding to the Individual?" and you are a pious Methodist, you have really no choice. But few assigned subjects, if any, will fall in this category. Most of them will lie in broad areas of discussion with much to be said on both sides. They are intellectual exercises, and it is legitimate to argue now one way and now another, as debaters do in similar circumstances. Always take the side that looks to you hardest, least defensible. It will almost always turn out to be easier to write interestingly on that side. This general advice applies where you have a choice of subjects. If you are to choose among "The Value of Fraternities" and "My Favorite High School Teacher" and "What I Think About Beetles," by all means plump for the beetles. By the time the instructor gets to your paper, he will be up to his ears in tedious tales about a French teacher at Bloombury High and assertions about how fraternities build character and prepare one for life. Your views on beetles, whatever they are, are bound to be a refreshing change.

Don't worry too much about figuring out what the instructor thinks about the subject so that you can cuddle up with him. Chances are his views are no stronger than yours. If he does have convictions and you oppose him, his problem is to keep from grading you higher than you deserve in order to show he is not biased. This doesn't mean that you should always cantankerously dissent from what the instructor says; that gets tiresome too. And if the subject assigned is "My Pet Peeve," do not begin, "My pet peeve is the English instructor who assigns papers on 'my pet peeve.'" This was still funny during the War of 1812, but it has sort of lost its edge since then. It is in general good manners to avoid personalities.

Slip out of Abstraction

If you will study the essay on college football [near the beginning of this essay], you will perceive that one reason for its appalling dullness is that it never gets down to particulars. It is just a series of not very glittering generalities: "football is bad for the colleges," "it has become too commercial," "football is big business," "it is bad for the players," and so on. Such round phrases thudding against the reader's brain are unlikely to convince him, though they may well render him unconscious.

15   If you want the reader to believe that college football is bad for the players, you have to do more than say so. You have to display the evil. Take your roommate, Alfred Simkins, the second-string center. Picture poor old Alfy coming home from football practice every evening, bruised and aching, agonizingly tired, scarcely able to shovel the mashed potatoes into his mouth. Let us see him staggering up to the room, getting out his econ textbook, peering desperately at it with his good eye, falling asleep and failing the test in the morning. Let us share his unbearable tension as Saturday draws near. Will he fail, be demoted, lose his monthly allowance, be forced to return to the coal mines? And if he succeeds, what will be his reward? Perhaps a slight ripple of applause when the third-string center replaces him, a moment of elation in the locker room if the team wins, of despair if it loses. What will he look back on when he graduates from college? Toil and torn ligaments. And what will be his future? He is not good enough for pro football, and he is too obscure and weak in econ to succeed in stocks and bonds. College football is tearing the heart from Alfy Simkins and, when it finishes with him, will callously toss aside the shattered hulk.

This is no doubt a weak enough argument for the abolition of college football, but it is a sight better than saying, in three or four variations, that college football (in your opinion) is bad for the players.

Look at the work of any professional writer and notice how constantly he is moving from the generality, the abstract statement, to the concrete example, the facts and figures, the illustrations. If he is writing on juvenile delinquency, he does not just tell you that juve-

niles are (it seems to him) delinquent and that (in his opinion) something should be done about it. He shows you juveniles being delinquent, tearing up movie theatres in Buffalo, stabbing high school principals in Dallas, smoking marijuana in Palo Alto. And more than likely he is moving toward some specific remedy, not just a general wringing of the hands.

It is no doubt possible to be too concrete, too illustrative or anecdotal, but few inexperienced writers err this way. For most the soundest advice is to be seeking always for the picture, to be always turning general remarks into seeable examples. Don't say, "Sororities teach girls the social graces." Say, "Sorority life teaches a girl how to carry on a conversation while pouring tea, without sloshing the tea into the saucer." Don't say, "I like certain kinds of popular music very much." Say, "Whenever I hear Gerber Sprinklittle play 'Mississippi Man' on the trombone, my socks creep up my ankles."

Get Rid of Obvious Padding

The student toiling away at his weekly English theme is too often tormented by a figure: five hundred words. How, he asks himself, is he to achieve this staggering total? Obviously by never using one word when he can somehow work in ten.

20   He is therefore seldom content with a plain statement like "Fast driving is dangerous." This has only four words in it. He takes thought, and the sentence becomes:

In my opinion, fast driving is dangerous.

Better, but he can do better still:

In my opinion, fast driving would seem to be rather dangerous.

If he is really adept, it may come out:

In my humble opinion though I do not claim to be an expert on this complicated subject, fast driving, in most circumstances, would seem to be rather dangerous in many respects, or at least so it would seem to me.

Thus four words have been turned into forty, and not an iota of content has been added.

Now this is a way to go about reaching five hundred words, and if you are content with a "D" grade, it is as good a way as any. But if you aim higher, you must work differently. Instead of stuffing your sentences with straw, you must try steadily to get rid of the padding, to make your sentences lean and tough. If you are really working at it, your first draft will greatly exceed the required total, and then you will work it down, thus:

> It is thought in some quarters that fraternities do not contribute as much as might be expected to campus life.
> Some people think that fraternities contribute little to campus life.

> The average doctor who practices in small towns or in the country must toil night and day to heal the sick.
> Most country doctors work long hours.

> When I was a little girl, I suffered from shyness and embarrassment in the presence of others.
> I was a shy little girl.

> It is absolutely necessary for the person employed as a marine fireman to give the matter of steam pressure his undivided attention at all times.
> The fireman has to keep his eye on the steam gauge.

You may ask how you can arrive at five hundred words at this rate. Simple. You dig up more real content. Instead of taking a couple of obvious points off the surface of the topic and then circling warily around them for six paragraphs, you work in and explore, figure out the details. You illustrate. You say that fast driving is dangerous, and then you prove it. How long does it take to stop a car at forty and at eighty? How far can you see at night? What happens when a tire blows? What happens in a head-on collision at fifty miles an hour? Pretty soon your paper will be full of broken glass and blood and headless torsos, and reaching five hundred words will not really be a problem.

Call a Fool a Fool

Some of the padding in freshman themes is to be blamed not on anxiety about the word minimum but on excessive timidity. The student writes, "In my opinion, the principal of my high school acted in ways that I believe every unbiased person would have to call foolish." This isn't exactly what he means. What he means is, "My high school principal was a fool." If he was a fool, call him a fool. Hedging the thing about with "in-my-opinion's" and "it-seems-to-me's" and "as-I-see-it's" and "at-least-from-my-point-of-view's" gains you nothing. Delete these phrases whenever they creep into your paper.

The student's tendency to hedge stems from a modesty that in other circumstances would be commendable. He is, he realizes, young and inexperienced, and he half suspects that he is dopey and fuzzyminded beyond the average. Probably only too true. But it doesn't help to announce your incompetence six times in every paragraph. Decide what you want to say and say it as vigorously as possible, without apology and in plain words.

25 Linguistic diffidence can take various forms. One is what we call euphemism. This is the tendency to call a spade "a certain garden implement" or women's underwear "unmentionables." It is stronger in some eras than others and in some people than others but it always operates more or less in subjects that are touchy or taboo: death, sex, madness, and so on. Thus we shrink from saying "He died last night" but say instead "passed away," "left us," "joined his Maker," "went to his reward." Or we try to take off the tension with a lighter cliché: "kicked the bucket," "cashed in his chips," "handed in his dinner pail." We have found all sorts of ways to avoid saying "mad": "mentally ill," "touched," "not quite right upstairs," "feebleminded," "innocent," "simple," "off his trolley," "not in his right mind." Even such a now plain word as "insane" began as a euphemism with the meaning "not healthy."

Modern science, particularly psychology, contributes many polysyllables in which we can wrap our thoughts and blunt their force. To many writers there is no such thing as a bad schoolboy. Schoolboys are maladjusted or unoriented or misunderstood or in the need of guidance or lacking in continued success toward satisfactory integration of the personality as a social unit, but they are never bad. Psychology no doubt makes us better men and women, more sympathetic and tolerant, but it doesn't make writing any easier. Had Shakespeare been confronted with psychology, "To be or not to be" might have come out, "To continue as a social unit or not to do so. That is the personality problem. Whether

'tis a better sign of integration at the conscious level to display a psychic tolerance toward the maladjustments and repressions induced by one's lack of orientation in one's environment or—" But Hamlet would never have finished the soliloquy.

Writing in the modern world, you cannot altogether avoid modern jargon. Nor, in an effort to get away from euphemism, should you salt your paper with four-letter words. But you can do much if you will mount guard against those roundabout phrases, those echoing polysyllables that tend to slip into your writing to rob it of its crispness and force.

Writing Strategies

1. Is Roberts's essay engaging (or inviting)? That is, does it make you want to read on? Why or why not?

2. What strategy does Roberts use to make the problem clear to the reader? Must he convince his reader of a problem before offering a solution? Explain.

3. Roberts supports his points by giving specific examples. Did any stand out to you? Without rereading, recall several examples, and then connect them to the main points they illustrate. Why might those examples have stood out to you?

4. Are Roberts's headings helpful? Should, or might, he have used more? When might *you* use headings (love letters, business reports, college essays, shopping lists)? What drawbacks do headings have?

5. Roberts uses lively language. Identify at least five lively words or expressions that struck you as you read. What makes these expressions lively? What is the value of such lively language?

Exploring Ideas

1. What is the purpose of Roberts's essay?

2. Have you experienced the problem that Roberts describes? Discuss with several classmates or others outside of class any difficulties you have had coming up

with ideas for an essay. Take notes on what people say as you explore this problem. Then draw conclusions: Why do some people have a hard time coming up with good ideas for their essays?

3. How does writing an essay help students to develop worthwhile thinking skills?

4. How might Roberts's ideas be important beyond merely writing an essay? That is, how might they be of value in schoolwork that does not involve essay writing; how might they be of value in the workplace; and how might they be of value in everyday life?

5. Why is Roberts's essay, first published in 1958, still relevant today?

Ideas for Writing

1. What can you tell someone how to do? Avoid a simple step-by-step instructional approach, and instead make worthwhile points that could benefit your reader.

2. How can a student succeed either (a) at college, (b) at his or her freshman year of college, or (c) at the first two weeks of college? Narrow your focus to suit your comfort level. For example, if you have been in college only a few months, you may not feel comfortable telling others how to succeed for all four years.

If responding to one of these ideas, go to the **Analysis** section of this chapter to begin developing ideas for your essay.

Technology, Movement, and Sound

Ed Bell

Good solutions can be involved and complex. Or they can be simple. In this essay, Ed Bell takes a "back to the basics" approach. Such approaches are dangerous—they often rely on oversimplistic thinking or the assumption that *things were a whole lot better back in the good old days*. A successful "back to basics" argument, however, gets at the root of a problem. As in this essay, it questions our unquestioning faith in technological "advancements." As you read Bell's essay, consider the value, and dangers, of such "back to basics" thinking.

In the margins of this essay, a reader's comments point to key ideas and writing strategies. As you read the essay, consider how the comments might influence your own reading and writing.

Writing Strategies

Begins with concession and main point. Narrows focus to leaf blowers—a specific example of the larger issue (technology).

Makes a concession. Shows public resonance—how ideas matter to others.

Lists and numbers main supporting ideas for the reader's benefit.

Develops points 1 and 2.

Provides common sense/observational support for first point.

Provides reasoning to support the second point.

Exploring Ideas

Technology used "indiscriminately."

Leaf blowers, for example

Leaf blowers can be okay (when?).

Benefits of Raking:
1. Does as good a job
2. Time well spent
3. Provides needed exercise
4. Sounds nice? Must mean more—is natural, pleasant, maybe, good for the soul?

True
Good point

Like rowing machine, stair climber, spinning, etc., machines at student rec center are based on natural activities people avoid.

Although technology has improved society in many ways, we use it indiscriminately, not distinguishing the good uses from the bad. We could talk about cell phones, oversized SUVs, fast food, or a variety of other advancements. But the cool air and falling leaves of autumn bring to mind the leaf blower—a monster whose decibel level far exceeds her practical value.

While I'm willing to admit that under certain circumstances the leaf blower can be useful, I think most people are missing out on the natural benefits of using a rake:

1. Raking does just as good a job as blowing.
2. If it actually does take longer to rake (a fact of which I'm not certain), the time "saved" and used otherwise would in many ways have been better spent raking.
3. Raking provides more exercise—the necessary physical movement our twenty-first-century bodies are lacking.
4. Raking makes <u>only</u> the most wonderful sound as it scratches across the leafy ground.

As for point one, beautifully raked yards existed long before noisy leaf blowers—there's no denying that it is, at the very least, possible to rake leaves and not have to blow them. As for point two, how many Americans who argue they don't have time to rake all those leaves will stand there blowing them, then rush off to the health club to use a rowing machine or a stair-climber? How long will it be until the most popular workout machine is the one that simulates leaf raking? But if you don't rush off to a health club (no doubt because you don't have the time), you're probably too busy working. After all, you have bills to pay: the new leaf blower, the new cell phone, the new computer, the new car, and that badly needed vacation to get away from it all.

But even if it does take longer to rake than to blow, the extra time spent raking provides the exercise that we need. One look at the human body will tell you it is built for raking—it *wants* to rake! According to Pete Egoscue, renowned anatomical functionalist and author of *The Egoscue Method of Health Through Motion,* "movement is as much a biological imperative as food and water." Many people today, he says, don't "move enough to beat the overwhelming odds that one day this motionless lifestyle will catch up with them." Do we sit at computers and cash registers doing repetitive movements, then relax with a little TV? Should we add standing and holding a noisy leaf blower to our routine? Just think about all the various body movements required by leaf raking.

5   The human body is built to move, yet we treat our physical human movement as an inconvenience. Egoscue says that "what all of us must do is deliberately and systematically get our bodies back in motion despite a modern lifestyle that discourages movement, and even encourages us to believe that we can survive and prosper as sedentary beings who treat motion as an inconvenience that can be minimized with the help of technology." A few sore muscles (and blisters) from a little leaf raking is, I would say, just what we need.

The man who blows the leaves on my campus wears special equipment—big spaceman goggles for his eyes and headphone-like muffs to protect his ears. His get-up alone indicates a problem to me: If you can't gather up leaves without protecting your own eyes and ears, perhaps there's a better way of doing it. Stop and compare the man with the rake to the one with the leaf blower. Which one is better off? The rake is simple; it stores easily; it doesn't cost much; it is quiet and doesn't bother the neighbors; it encourages necessary body movement; it's not very dangerous; and so on. But the leaf blower is bound to break down; it takes up more space and, combined with its cousins (the weed-whacker, the electric hedge trimmers, and so on), it will eventually convince you to build a bigger garage; it (and machines like it) costs more money, which is why you are working too much to rake leaves; it is loud, which is unpleasant, if not for you, for the neighbors; it is apparently dangerous—I'm assuming this because of the equipment the man on campus wears.

Marginal annotations (left):

Develops third point by providing evidence from an outside source.

Introduces source and quotes sparingly (only the information that is most helpful in making the point).

Makes point through asking the reader questions and to think about leaf raking.

Continues to develop third point.

Provides support from a source.

Concludes paragraph by commenting.

Through description and reasoning argues that rakes are better than leaf blowers.

Provides specific evidence to compare rakes and leaf blowers.

Marginal annotations (right):

Point: no time to rake; must pay for leaf blower + stuff like it.

Bell cares about exercise, movement, health. He's arguing that people aren't exercising in natural ways. He's saying they work to pay for things so they don't have to move their bodies, then claim they don't have time to move their bodies.

Interesting point: Why is so much protection required? Maybe not because leaf blowers are dangerous, but because of lawsuits. Still, leaf blowers probably are more dangerous than rakes.

Rakes are simple, convenient. Leaf blowers, etc., break down.

Main point: Leaf blowers bug the neighbors. Bell cares about this, too. And this deals with community.

Technology is likely to come along and solve all of these problems. It's not hard to imagine a quieter leaf blower someday. Of course, the old-fashioned leaf-blowing folk will long for the good old days when a leaf blower could be heard for blocks away. But soon enough they'll all have the newer, lighter, more ergonomically correct models too. And then, of course, we'll have another problem to deal with—a problem that we can't even imagine until it occurs. Through all of that, however, two things will remain true: (1) We should not make too much noise around other people and (2) we should get our bodies moving. We should, I suggest, use our technology more discriminately—instead of using it just because we can.

Tech will solve problems + create new ones.

Makes closing point— general, main idea.

Main point: Use technology more discriminately. Why not (1) exercise, (2) be considerate of others?

Work Cited

Egoscue, Pete. <u>The Egoscue Method of Health Through Motion: Revolutionary Program That Lets You Rediscover the Body's Power to Rejuvenate It</u>. New York: Harper, 1992.

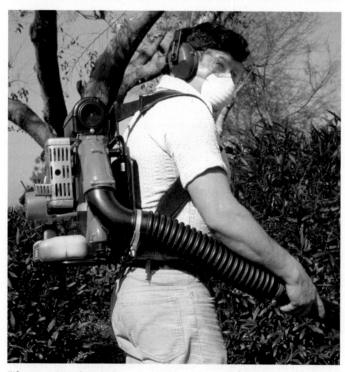

"If you can't gather up leaves without protecting your own eyes and ears, perhaps there's a better way of doing it."

Writing Strategies

1. What types of evidence (statistics, facts, allusions, anecdotes, scenarios, analogies) does Bell use to support his claims (opinions)?

2. Does Bell make any concessions (acknowledging possible weaknesses in his argument or value in opposing positions) or counterarguments (anticipating and responding to his reader's possible questions and concerns)? Write down at least one concession and one counterargument that he might have made, but didn't.

3. Bell uses one secondary source, Pete Egoscue. How does he let the reader know when he is referring to Egoscue and when he is not? After reviewing the entire essay, can you distinguish between when Bell is expressing Egoscue's ideas and when Bell is expressing his own?

4. Bell uses concrete words such as "cell phones," "stair climber," "goggles," and "blisters." These words create images (you see them in your mind when you hear the word). Refer to previous essays you have written or one you are writing now to see what concrete words you have used. Are there places where you have been abstract ("communication device") and could have been concrete ("cell phone")?

5. Bell uses nearly every form of punctuation. Did you notice his punctuation throughout the essay? Or was it "invisible" to you? Where might he have punctuated differently in order to help you more readily understand his points?

Exploring Ideas

1. Explain the relationship Bell sees between three things: technology, movement, and sound.

2. Explain how Bell moves from an individual concern (point of contact) to a community concern (public resonance).

3. In your own words, describe the problem Bell writes about and the solution he proposes.

4. Share your description (from #3) with several classmates, and discuss the similarities and differences in the way you and they understood Bell's essay.

5. Share Bell's ideas with several people outside of class and get their responses. (You may have them read the essay, or you may summarize it for them.) How is the way others think about technology and movement different from the way Bell thinks about it? What difference might be worth further exploration?

6. With others, generate a list of concepts such as "technology," "movement," "noise," "cars," "school," "work," "family," "food," "fast food," "homelessness," "money," and so on. As you generate your list, think in categories (food, shelter, clothing; local, national, international; work, play; etc.) and make connections (for example, "food" might lead you to think of "fast food," which might lead you to think of "hamburgers," which might lead you to think of "feed lots"). Then discover a relationship among three of the ideas, as Bell does among "technology," "movement," and "sound." (Admittedly, this exercise is artificial, but it can be fun and helps to develop thinking skills.)

Ideas for Writing

1. What common practice, some generally accepted way of doing something, can you point out a problem with?

2. What technology (cell phone, portable music player, air conditioning, lawn sprinkler, recliner chair, etc.) possesses some lesser-known danger?

If responding to one of these ideas, go to the **Analysis** section of this chapter to begin developing ideas for your essay.

A Uterus Is No Substitute for a Conscience

Barbara Ehrenreich

The chapters of this book might suggest that personal essays fall easily into certain categories: analyzing images, responding to arguments, proposing solutions, and so on. While essays do have emphases, they often overlap categories. Writers might observe, remember, argue, and solve a problem in one project. In this essay, Barbara Ehrenreich, a widely acclaimed author, analyzes an image, responds to an argument, and finally proposes a solution. In some ways, the essay does the intellectual work of three chapters in this book: Chapter 5, Chapter 7, and Chapter 10. Although the essay is intellectually complex and layered, Ehrenreich's logic is easy to follow.

Even those people we might have thought were impervious to shame, like the Secretary of Defense, admit that the photos of abuse in Iraq's Abu Ghraib prison turned their stomachs.

The photos did something else to me, as a feminist: They broke my heart. I had no illusions about the U.S. mission in Iraq—whatever exactly it is—but it turns out that I did have some illusions about women.

Of the seven U.S. soldiers now charged with sickening forms of abuse in Abu Ghraib, three are women: Spc. Megan Ambuhl, Pfc. Lynndie England, and Spc. Sabrina Harman. It was Harman we saw smiling an impish little smile and giving the thumbs-up sign from behind a pile of hooded, naked Iraqi men—as if to say, "Hi Mom, here I am in Abu Ghraib!" It was England we saw with a naked Iraqi man on a leash. If you were doing PR for Al Qaeda, you couldn't have staged a better picture to galvanize misogynist Islamic fundamentalists around the world.

Here, in these photos from Abu Ghraib, you have everything that the Islamic fundamentalists believe characterizes Western culture, all nicely arranged in one hideous image—imperial arrogance, sexual depravity, . . . and gender equality.

5   Maybe I shouldn't have been so shocked. We know that good people can do terrible things under the right circumstances. This is what psychologist Stanley Milgram found in his famous experiments in the 1960s. In all likelihood, Ambuhl, England, and Harman are not congenitally evil people. They are working-class women who wanted an education and knew that the military could be a stepping-stone in that direction. Once they had joined, they wanted to fit in.

And I also shouldn't be surprised because I never believed that women were innately gentler and less aggressive than men. Like most feminists, I have supported full opportunity for women within the military—1) because I knew women could fight, and 2) because the military is one of the few options around for low-income young people.

Although I opposed the 1991 Persian Gulf War, I was proud of our servicewomen and delighted that their presence irked their Saudi hosts. Secretly, I hoped that the presence of women would over time change the military, making it more respectful of other people and cultures, more capable of genuine peacekeeping. That's what I thought, but I don't think that anymore.

A certain kind of feminism, or perhaps I should say a certain kind of feminist naïveté, died in Abu Ghraib. It was a feminism that saw men as the perpetual perpetrators, women as the perpetual victims, and male sexual violence against women as the root of all injustice. Rape has repeatedly been an instrument of war and, to some feminists, it was beginning to look as if war was an extension of rape. There seemed to be at least some evidence that male sexual sadism was connected to our species' tragic propensity for violence. That was before we had seen female sexual sadism in action.

But it's not just the theory of this naïve feminism that was wrong. So was its strategy and vision for change. That strategy and vision rested on the assumption, implicit or stated outright, that women were morally superior to men. We had a lot of debates over whether it was biology or conditioning that gave women the moral edge—or simply the experience of being a woman in a sexist culture. But the assumption of superiority, or at least a lesser inclination toward cruelty and violence, was more or less beyond debate. After all, women do most of the caring work in our culture, and in polls are consistently less inclined toward war than men.

10 I'm not the only one wrestling with that assumption today. Mary Jo Melone, a columnist for the St. Petersburg (Fla.) Times, wrote on May 7: "I can't get that picture of England [pointing at a hooded Iraqi man's genitals] out of my head because this is not how women are expected to behave. Feminism taught me 30 years ago that not only had women gotten a raw deal from men, we were morally superior to them."

If that assumption had been accurate, then all we would have had to do to make the world a better place—kinder, less violent, more just—would have been to assimilate into what had been, for so many centuries, the world of men. We would fight so that women could become the generals, CEOs, senators, professors, and opinion makers—and that was really the only fight we had to undertake. Because once they gained power and authority, once they had achieved a critical mass within the institutions of society, women would naturally work for change. That's what we thought, even if we thought it unconsciously—and it's just not true. Women can do the unthinkable.

You can't even argue, in the case of Abu Ghraib, that the problem was that there just weren't enough women in the military hierarchy to stop the abuses. The prison was directed by a woman, Gen. Janis Karpinski. The top U.S. intelligence officer in Iraq, who also was responsible for reviewing the status of detainees before their release, was Major Gen. Barbara Fast. And the U.S. official ultimately responsible for managing the occupation of Iraq since October was Condoleezza Rice. Like Donald H. Rumsfeld, she ignored repeated reports of abuse and torture until the undeniable photographic evidence emerged.

What we have learned from Abu Ghraib, once and for all, is that a uterus is not a substitute for a conscience. This doesn't mean gender equality isn't worth fighting for for its own sake. It is. If we believe in democracy, then we believe in a woman's right to do and achieve whatever men can do and achieve, even the bad things. It's just that gender equality cannot, all alone, bring about a just and peaceful world.

In fact, we have to realize, in all humility, that the kind of feminism based on an assumption of female moral superiority is not only naïve; it also is a lazy and self-indulgent form of feminism. Self-indulgent because it assumes that a victory for a woman—a promotion, a college degree, the right to serve alongside men in the military—is by its very nature a victory for all of humanity. And lazy because it assumes that we have only one struggle—the struggle for gender equality—when in fact we have many more.

15 The struggles for peace and social justice and against imperialist and racist arrogance, cannot, I am truly sorry to say, be folded into the struggle for gender equality.

What we need is a tough new kind of feminism with no illusions. Women do not change institutions simply by assimilating into them, only by consciously deciding to fight for change. We need a feminism that teaches a woman to say no—not just to the date rapist or overly insistent boyfriend but, when necessary, to the military or corporate hierarchy within which she finds herself.

In short, we need a kind of feminism that aims not just to assimilate into the institutions that men have created over the centuries, but to infiltrate and subvert them.

To cite an old, and far from naïve, feminist saying: "If you think equality is the goal, your standards are too low." It is not enough to be equal to men, when the men are acting like beasts. It is not enough to assimilate. We need to create a world worth assimilating into.

Writing Strategies

1. What does Ehrenreich convey about herself in her opening sentence? How might that influence her reader?

2. What problem does Ehrenreich write about, and what solution does she propose?

3. How is Ehrenreich's approach to the problem broader, more complex, than other approaches?

4. Why does Ehrenreich use ellipsis in the following sentence:

   Here, in these photos from Abu Ghraib, you have everything that the Islamic fundamentalists believe characterizes Western culture, all nicely arranged in one hideous image—imperial arrogance, sexual depravity, . . . and gender equality. (¶ 4)

5. In paragraph 5, Ehrenreich makes reference to the famous experiments of Stanley Milgram. What does Ehrenreich's reference to Milgram suggest about her audience?

6. How does Ehrenreich support her argument? (What specific rhetorical tools does she use?)

Exploring Ideas

1. How did the images from Abu Ghraib change Ehrenreich's thinking?

2. How did the images from Abu Ghraib change your thinking? If you aren't familiar with the images or don't recall them, do research to find the Abu Ghraib images she is referring to, then respond.

3. According to Ehrenreich, how should women infiltrate and subvert institutions, and why?

4. In her concluding paragraph, Ehrenreich says, "To cite an old, and far from naïve, feminist saying: 'If you think equality is the goal, your standards are too low.'" In groups, explore what the old saying means, and provide examples to illustrate it.

Ideas for Writing

1. Ehrenreich says, "But the assumption of superiority, or at least a lesser inclination toward cruelty and violence, was more or less beyond debate" (¶ 9). What else seems more or less *beyond debate,* but isn't—or shouldn't be? What problem is caused by such thinking, and what's the solution?

2. What can bring about a just and peaceful world?

If responding to one of these ideas, go to the **Analysis** section of this chapter to begin developing ideas for your essay.

Television: Destroying Childhood

Rose Bachtel

Even though people commonly say television is bad (especially for children), mainstream America remains enamored with, and locked into, television life. In this essay, Rose Bachtel argues that television destroys something in children. As you read, imagine how you might expand on what Bachtel says or how you might offer an alternate way of seeing the problem.

When my grandparents were little, they spent their free time riding bicycles outside, playing dolls or dress-up, or curling up with a good book. Nowadays, my younger siblings consume every free moment they have in front of a television. "Times have changed. It is just another form of entertainment," some say. Should this obsession be handled so lightly? Is there nothing wrong with sitting in front of a television set all day? Of course this poses a problem, especially where children are concerned! They are at a vital growing period in their lives, and how they are raised will play a strong role in who they will become. Watching television will not work any muscle groups, so a child will not get the proper amount of exercise he or she needs. This will lead to future health problems, whether it be in the near future or years down the road. Also, because TV does not demand effort or interaction of the person watching it, children who watch television often become lazy and expect that everything should come to them instantaneously and without work. This lowers a child's patience because he or she wants instant gratification and will not engage in activities or events that require time or complicated components. These same children will also experience a decline in creativity because the television is creative for them. This is not healthy because childhood is the most vital time for stimulating a young person's mind and forcing him or her to develop it.

How can parents stop their children's bodies and minds from eroding? My solution is quite simple. Parents should not keep a television in the home. It may sound a bit drastic at first, but when analyzed, it makes sense. Without the convenience of a television, children are forced to think of other forms of keeping themselves entertained. This would lead them to exercise more, since most activities involve using more muscle groups than are involved in stagnantly watching television. Also, since children would be forced to seek out other forms of entertainment, they would be, in turn, forced to use their brains more and think creatively in order to come up with something to do. They would have to use their minds to search for information about their world instead of having it handed to them by TV. Also, since a child is no longer confined to inside the house, he or she can venture outside and explore nature while getting fresh air and vitamin D from the sun's rays. Another problem with TV is that many television show producers feel that sex and violence sell, so consequently many of today's programs contain these elements. Since people at a young age are very impressionable, they pick up on these messages and are influenced by them. Without a television set in the home, children will be less exposed to sex and violence. Another benefit of my proposal is the fact that parents do not have to worry about monitoring the content of the television shows their children watch if there is no TV set in the home to begin with. Their kids will not be able to watch unapproved shows when the parents are not home to supervise.

Still, many people may feel apprehensive towards this proposal because they have lived with televisions for so long that they cannot imagine functioning without them. "How will we know what's going on in the world or what the weather is going to be like?" they might ask. Sure, television stations provide very useful information, but so do other forms of communication, such as newspapers and magazines. These sources of information can be just as convenient as television. Of course, a news program can give more up-to-date information, but written periodicals are not far behind.

There is also the Internet, which is perhaps more current than television. "What about all of the shows on TV that the adults want to watch?" Television does offer a great deal of American entertainment, but it is not the only way to be entertained. People could try reading a good book, going out on the town, or enjoying the outdoors. Adults will find that if there is not TV in the house to distract them, they will have a lot more free time on their hands to really enjoy life. A good argument brought up by television supporters is the point that there are a lot of educational programs that teach children. These programs keep the attention of children and help them grow mentally. Yes, these stations are helpful, but what would be better and more effective to children is if someone taught them about the world in a "hands on" fashion instead of through a television set. Another protest against my proposal is that TV acts as a sort of babysitter for children. It keeps them quiet and entertained so that the parents can get all of their tasks accomplished. My response to that argument is that raising the children should be a parent's number one priority. The best way to raise a child is to constantly interact with him or her, spending many hours of quality time, because it shows the child that he or she is important and loved. This aspect of raising a young one will be lost if he or she is constantly sat in front of the TV.

Granted, many television shows are not moral and should be kept away from children. That is not the problem. The real problem with TV is the fact that it consumes so much of an American's time that could be invested into a more productive activity. Sure, television use could just be minimized, but I think that it would be better to get rid of televisions in the home altogether. The problem with owning one but not watching it as often is that it is easier said than done. When the temptation is there, it is hard to resist. Paul Klein, who worked for NBC in the 1950s, believed that people would watch TV just to watch TV, meaning that even if nothing interesting is on, people will still sit in front of a television set. For example, when I first moved into my apartment, I did not have a TV for a few days. During those few days, I was very efficient, using every minute of my time to study, clean, or perform any other needed task. I accomplished a lot of things in those first few days. However, when my television finally arrived, I found myself turning on the set and watching shows that I did not necessarily have any interest in. I was also not keeping up on my studies as well as I had before or cleaning as much. This scenario is true for many Americans. The television does not have one single essential use. People functioned perfectly fine before this invention. Sure, it is entertaining, informative, and convenient, but it also has many hidden side effects that are hurting the younger generations. By getting rid of televisions in the home, children will spend their childhood as they should, not watching television, but playing, creating, and learning about their world through their own eyes.

Writing Strategies

1. What evidence does Bachtel provide to explain the problem? What evidence does she provide to support her solution?

2. Describe Bachtel's voice as a writer, referring to several passages as evidence.

3. Write a new introduction and conclusion for Bachtel's essay, taking a very different approach for each.

4. In small groups, discuss the introductions and conclusions (from #3 above) that you and your classmates wrote. What are the advantages and disadvantages of each introduction and conclusion? Which introduction and conclusion do you prefer?

5. Provide several examples of how Bachtel helps the reader go from one idea to another.

Exploring Ideas

1. Based on this essay, describe how Bachtel is concerned about community and others.

2. How is the way that you see television similar to or different from the way Bachtel sees it?

3. Briefly summarize Bachtel's main idea, and then ask others to respond to it. Write down the three responses that interest you the most and explore what you find to be interesting about them. How are each of the responses similar to or different from what Bachtel says?

4. How might you respond to Bachtel's ideas? Write down at least three ways you might contribute something worthwhile to this discussion.

5. One way you might respond to #4 above is to expand on Bachtel's solution by suggesting various benefits of giving up television. Some will be obvious, but think of some less obvious ones, too. Then explore these benefits further through discussion. Finally, write down the benefits you discovered through your exploration—ones that you did not think of right away.

Ideas for Writing

1. What else is destroying childhood?

2. How might television be used better, instead of not at all?

If responding to one of these ideas, go to the **Analysis** section of this chapter to begin developing ideas for your essay.

Outside Reading

Find a text that proposes a solution, and make a photo-copy or print it out. Solutions for social problems are often published in general readership publications (*Time* or *Newsweek),* and in national or local newspapers (on opinion pages). More in-depth solutions might appear in monthly or quarterly journals (*Utne Reader* or the *New Republic*). You also might find an interesting solution related to your major. For that, explore academic journals such as *Criminal Law, Engineering,* or *Elementary Education.* To conduct an electronic search of journals and magazines, go to your library's periodical database or to InfoTrac College Edition (http://infotrac.galegroup.com/itweb/). For your library database, perform a keyword search, or go to the main search box for InfoTrac College Edition and choose "keywords." Enter word combinations such as *problems and schools, problems and flying, problems and food, solutions and sewage, solutions and farms,* and so on. (When performing keyword searches, avoid using phrases or articles such as *a, an, the.*) The search results will yield lists of journal and magazine articles.

You can also search the Internet. Try the search engine Yahoo.com. Like most Internet search engines, Yahoo! combines words using *and.* In the search box, try various combinations, such as those above; however, if using *solutions* in your search, be cautious of the many business and corporate sites in the search results.

The purpose of this assignment is to further your understanding of writing that proposes solutions. As you are probably discovering, such writing is sometimes very argumentative, and other times appears to be neutral; however, even the most neutral-sounding text offers a position—a stance that requires support. As you read through this chapter, keep the text you have discovered close by and notice the elements and strategies the writer uses. Depending on your instructor's suggestions, do one or more of the following:

1. Notice how the writer applies various strategies from this chapter. On the photocopy or hard copy:
   - Identify the passage that most clearly states the problem and write "problem" in the margin.
   - Identify the passage that most clearly states the solution and write "solution" in the margin.
   - Identify the passages in which the author offers support for the solution and write "support" next to each one in the margin.
   - Find any passages in which the writer addresses other opinions on the topic and write "counter-argument" or "ca" next to each one in the margin.
   - Find any passages in which the writer grants value to another position (or alternative solution) and write "concession" or "c" in the margin.

2. Analyze the strategies employed by the writer. The following questions may be helpful.
   - Does this writer seem more or less argumentative than the readings in this chapter? Why?
   - How does the writer support his or her proposed solution?
   - Who is the audience for this argument?
   - How does the audience affect the kinds of things said in the argument?

3. Write at least three "Writing Strategies" questions for the text you found.

4. Write at least three "Exploring Ideas" questions for the text you found.

5. Write two "Ideas for Writing," such as the ones following the essays in this chapter.

INVENTION

"No problem can withstand the assault of sustained thinking."

—Voltaire

For this chapter, your topic will be a particular problem — some situation that needs to be changed or an idea that needs to be rethought. Be wary of global problems like hunger, poverty, or racism. They are not unapproachable or unsolvable, but such big problems usually have local or particular expressions, and it is the local or particular that is often the most appropriate place to start. Focusing on a particular problem also sets the ground for a manageable solution. For example, solving financial difficulty for single-parent students is more manageable than solving poverty in general.

The following sections are designed to help you through the invention process: specifically, to discover a problem (in **Point of Contact**), to develop an understanding of its causes and develop a possible solution (in **Analysis**), to make it relevant to a community of readers (in **Public Resonance**), to develop a focused statement about the problem and solution (in **Thesis**), and to develop support for your argument (in **Rhetorical Tools**). The Invention questions in each section are not meant to be answered directly in your final written assignment. They will, however, help you to think further into your topic, to develop intense claims and insightful points.

POINT OF CONTACT

Social problems are not necessarily physical or material; they can be intellectual, spiritual, or psychological. Consider problems related to bad policies (all first-year students must live on campus), narrow thinking (a government administration that assumes energy must come from fossil fuels), or troubled systems (a bureaucracy in which all decisions must be made at the executive level before action can be taken).

Writers often do best with topics with which they are familiar, or with which they can become familiar. To discover particular problems, consider the different circles of your life. Use the following suggestions and questions to help dig up a problem that you, as a writer, witness or experience; and attempt to see problems that others might disregard. See the problems that lurk behind the obvious. If one of the suggestions prompts you to see a problem, begin by recording details—that is, try to explain the particulars of the problem.

School

- Are students missing too many classes?
- Do my instructors communicate poorly with students?
- Are my peers lazy?
- Are enough courses offered to students?
- Do instructors give enough or too many exams?
- Did my high school education adequately prepare me for college?
- Is the curricular gap between high school and college too wide?

Community

- Are the elderly people in my family or community isolated?
- Do people in my neighborhood ignore one another?

- Are there too few animals in people's lives? (Too many?)
- Does traffic in my community interfere with daily life?
- Are billboards tasteless or boring?
- Are there too many chain stores or strip malls in my community?

Government

- Does the city government do enough for children? For senior citizens?
- Does state government overlook the particular needs of my community?
- Are citizens sufficiently involved in local government?
- Do average citizens know how tax dollars are spent?
- Are there enough minorities in public office?

Television

- Is prime-time television too adolescent?
- Are sports televised too often?
- Is there something wrong with the way sports are televised?
- Are talk shows tasteless, moronic, or disrespectful?
- Has art been abandoned by popular culture?

Your Major

- What are the problems related to employment in my field?
- What about job security? Safety for the workers? Safety for the public?
- Are there problems with government regulations?

RESEARCH

In addition to the questions above, outside sources such as websites, articles, or books can be great points of contact.

ACTIVITY

Now go beyond these suggestions. In groups or alone, develop more strategies for encountering and exploring social problems. Imagine what might be wrong, or what can be better than it is.

ANALYSIS

Problems

Any solution must address the causes of a problem. Therefore, analyzing a problem to discover all possible causes is essential to developing a good solution. Often the causes of a problem are not clear, however. A problem may originate from an abstract source, such as a long tradition, a widely held attitude, or a flawed assumption. And writers must search through such abstractions to find the possible causes.

To understand the full complexities of your problem, respond to the following questions:

- What are the causes of the problem?
- What are the most troubling or alarming images associated with the problem?
- What are its short-term effects? Long-term effects?
- How might this problem snowball?
- What other situation (event, attitude) does this problem resemble?

Your goal in answering these questions is to see different layers of the problem and all its possible effects. The questions, then, are opportunities for probing meaning. Avoid moving too quickly as you imagine answers. Consider the hidden effects, the invisible consequences.

RESEARCH

You may respond to the questions to the left on different levels, first providing your own initial responses, and then gathering information from outside sources. Such sources may include friends, coworkers, family members, websites, articles, and books. (Consult Chapter 13, Research & Writing, to help you explore.) As you research, look not just for ideas that support your initial responses but, more importantly, for ideas that might change the way you think.

- What ideas support my initial thinking?
- How might ideas that question my thinking be valid and worth considering?

INVENTION WRITING

Ed Bell's early analysis relies upon his personal—perhaps selfish—reaction: Leaf blowers are noisy and therefore annoying to him.

What are its short-term effects? Long-term effects?

The short-term effects: hmmm. People get woken up. People might get angry and get in fights. I don't see that happening, to be honest. But maybe people are just grouchy. Maybe one inconsideration leads to another, which may be more of a long-term effect. It's just noisy, which may create tension in individual lives and in interaction among people. Another effect is that standing there holding a leaf blower for an hour might be easy, but it's loud and annoying and the person doing it isn't getting much exercise. Raking would be better for the person. It'd take more time, maybe, but in the "long term," it would be more peaceful, because it'd be quieter and the person would get their body moving, get some exercise, work up a sweat, and not impose on everyone else in the neighborhood. I guess I'm saying "Hey! Your standing outside my bedroom window with that leaf blower isn't good for YOUR health!"

If Bell were to stop at his initial reaction, his essay might sound like more of a gripe—a personal and self-indulgent complaint. He might come off just sounding grumpy. But Bell's analysis develops beyond the personal complaint.

THINKING FURTHER

Notice how Ed Bell's invention writing extends outward, beyond himself. He's imagining possibilities: fights, grouchiness, further inconsiderations, and ultimately, physical inactivity—and its effects on one's physical and mental well-being. Bell forces himself to think beyond the personal inconvenience the noise creates for him, and thus he finds the public resonance of the issue: *everyone's* physical and mental health. And the ideas become more developed in his essay, in which he traces the source of the problem to the cultural trend of an unhealthy lifestyle brought on by indiscriminate use of technology.

INVENTION WORKSHOP

After you have answered the questions on your own, convene with a small group of other writers. The goal is to help one another explore the hidden causes of the problems. You can use any of the questions from this section, or you can develop more general questions; for example: *Do you believe _____ is a problem? Why? What causes it? Have you had experience with _____?* Record each person's answers in writing. You might include the answers and opinions in your explanation of the problem. If one of the group members has had a unique or significant experience, you might include it to illustrate the nature of the problem.

PROBLEMS IN CHAPTER READINGS

Joan Didion's problem, migraine headaches, is commonly misunderstood, and many people assume the wrong thing about their cause. Didion, therefore, spends a good deal of her essay dismissing some causes while explaining the true complexities of the problem:

No one knows precisely what it is that is inherited. The chemistry of migraine, however, seems to have some connection with the nerve hormone named serotonin, which is naturally present in the brain. The amount of serotonin in the blood falls sharply at the onset of migraine, and one migraine drug, methysergide, or Sansert, seems to have some effect on serotonin. (461–462)

Writers sometimes must include a discussion of the effects (long- and short-term) in order for readers to understand the full extent of the issue. For example, Rachel Carson discusses long-term consequences of pesticides:

To adjust to these chemicals would require time on the scale that is nature's; it would require not merely the years of a man's life but the life of generations. And even this, were it by some miracle possible, would be futile, for the new chemicals come from our laboratories in an endless stream; almost five hundred annually find their way into actual use in the United States alone. The figure is staggering and its implications are not easily grasped—500 new chemicals to which the bodies of men and animals are required somehow to adapt each year, chemicals totally outside the limits of biologic experience. (457)

Solutions

Before settling on a solution, consider how the solution will work, how it will address the causes of the problem, and how it might fail. Answers to the following questions will be vital to developing your solution and to making it persuasive to readers. While you will benefit from understanding all of the following issues, your readers may need some points emphasized over others. Ask yourself what points seem least obvious, or most debatable, to your audience.

Respond to the following questions to develop your solution:

- What action will best address the causes of the problem?
- What might stand in the way of this action?
- How will the action change the situation?
- Has this kind of solution been tried before (in other situations)? How did it go?
- Does this solution have potential shortcomings or limitations?

INVENTION WRITING

In this excerpt from his notes, Ed Bell asks some far-reaching questions. He's no longer just focused on the leaf blower and the rake; he's wondering about his neighbors' everyday behaviors and priorities. He's wondering why everything couldn't be different:

What action will best address the causes of the problem?
Raking instead of leaf blowing. Why? Because the raker gets exercise, burns calories, feels better, and doesn't make so much noise. This improves the quality of everyone's life. People will say they're too busy to rake, but busy doing what? What are they busy doing? It seems important, running around, but what if they didn't do it? What if they raked leaves instead? What would happen?

Bell's intellectual move is vital. He's not limited by what he's supposed to think. We're supposed to think: "Of course, raking leaves is not as important as all our errands!" But . . . Bell wonders: *Maybe it is!*

Notice how Bell discovers some public resonance during his analysis (484–485). Then he fleshes it out even further (left and below). It is important to realize that insights about public resonance may come at any time during the invention process. Since the process of exploration and discovery cannot be divided simply into separate steps or stages (analysis, public resonance), one must always be on the lookout for insights.

SOLUTIONS IN CHAPTER READINGS

For Joan Didion, the solution is somewhat complicated. It is not a particular drug, behavior, or policy change. It is merely an intellectual shift—from resistance to acceptance. Because the cause of migraine is so evasive, she (like many others) cannot discover a perfect solution. Instead, she develops a new awareness about the problem:

> I have tried in most of the available ways to escape my own migrainous heredity . . . but I still have migraine. And I have learned now to live with it, learned when to expect it, how to outwit it, even how to regard it, when it does come, as more friend than lodger. (462)

Didion shows us the broad range of possible maneuvers a writer can make in addressing a problem. She does not oversimplify the problem, or conjure a fake solution, or dodge the issue altogether. Instead, she offers a subtle solution to migraines, and then goes on to explain how that solution works:

> And once [the migraine] comes, now that I am wise in its ways, I no longer fight it. I lie down and let it happen. At first every small apprehension is magnified, every anxiety a pounding terror. Then the pain comes,

and I concentrate only on that. Right there is the usefulness of migraine, there in that imposed yoga, the
concentration on the pain. For when the pain recedes,
ten or twelve hours later, everything goes with it, all
the hidden resentments, all the vain anxieties. The
migraine has acted as a circuit breaker, and the fuses
have emerged intact. (462–463)

Rachel Carson's proposal may seem modest given the nature
of the problem. After all, she describes the constant introduction of toxic chemicals into the environment, and her
solution simply involves making the public aware:

We urgently need an end to these false assurances, to
the sugar coating of unpalatable facts. It is the public
that is being asked to assume the risks that the insect
controllers calculate. The public must decide whether
it wishes to continue on the present road, and it can
do so only when in full possession of the facts. In the
words of Jean Rostand, "The obligation to endure
gives us the right to know." (460)

As Carson's argument shows, a solution need not wipe the
problem clean away. Solutions to complicated problems, in
fact, might simply *begin* the process of change. A solution
might change the intellectual environment so that physical
changes can take place later; a solution might alter conditions so that significant changes can *begin* to occur; a solution might merely propose a way of talking about a
complicated problem. Of course, many solutions involve
physical steps and implementation, but as Didion and Carson show, genuine solutions do not require physical or structural changes.

A solution might change the *intellectual* environment so that *physical* changes can take place later.

ACTIVITY

Challenge your solution before proposing it to others.
Just as pesticides solved one problem but created others, how might your solution create another problem?

PUBLIC RESONANCE

Some topics may seem difficult to connect to a broad public concern, but good writers bring *seemingly* marginal topics into the center of public consciousness. The problem you have chosen may obviously affect (or potentially affect) a community or society at large. However, no matter how much your problem involves or affects people, you still must make it known.

As you consider your own topic, respond to the following questions to help develop public resonance:

- Who should care about this issue? Why?
- What particular community, place, or thing does this issue affect?
- How might my reader(s) be involved in this issue?
- Is this issue an example of some broader trend?
- Why is it important that others hear my opinion about this issue?

INVENTION WORKSHOP

Avoid moving too quickly through the Invention questions. The public resonance may not be clear at first, but working through all the possibilities can help your topic to expand in interesting ways. Enlist the help of other writers, and in a small group, answer one of the questions above for your topic. As a group, work at collectively building a sophisticated answer to the question.

In the following, Marcus has discovered a problem in his community: Elderly people in nursing homes and senior living centers are isolated from others. In a discussion with peers, Marcus develops his initial thinking:

What group of people might understand or sympathize with this situation?

Marcus: Primarily the elderly. Senior citizens are primarily concerned about this issue, and as medical advances allow people to live longer, it seems like we all should be worried—because we'll all be old someday.

Linda: But shouldn't the younger generations be concerned about the isolation of the elderly, too—I mean beyond just caring about themselves as they age?

Diana: Yeah . . . even if they don't care, it seems like stuffing the elderly away from mainstream society can't be a good thing, for anybody.

Marcus: It's like we are ignoring a huge group of people—the group that probably has the most insight and experience about big social problems.

Linda: And I would even say personal and family problems. I know in my family, it was always my grandmother who understood everyone's problems and could talk through them without getting angry or mean. She was the one that gave everyone a sense of direction.

Marcus: So when society shuts away its elderly, maybe the biggest victims are the younger generations. Of course, it's bad for the elderly, but in a more indirect and long-term way, maybe their absence from mainstream society is an even bigger wrong. Maybe the younger generations feel the effects in the long term without their patience, insights, and experience.

Marcus could then develop this thinking further, and perhaps explain how younger generations suffer from the absence of older generations.

INVENTION WRITING

In this excerpt from his notes, Bell makes an important connection between a simple act, leaf blowing, and people's bodies. Bell's project evolves here. It is not simply about leaf blowing; it is an argument about the relationship between the human body and the tendencies of mainstream culture.

To what trends (in living/working/socializing) does my topic point?

This has to do with the trend of people using technology because they can. Talking about nothing on cell phones while not paying attention to their driving. That sounds pretty cranky, but I think it's true. It's about people going to a gym to work out and not wanting to walk a few hundred yards in their daily lives. Raking leaves would be good for people in lots of ways, but they'd rather stand there blowing them with a noisy machine. So, machines, not all of them but a lot of them, are noisy and annoying and make people "lazy" or make them not move their bodies as much as people used to. They don't get exercise. People should get more exercise and wonder if the noise they are making might be bothering OTHERS.

PUBLIC RESONANCE IN CHAPTER READINGS

The thinking in Ed Bell's invention notes evolves into his essay:

> But even if it does take longer to rake than to blow, the extra time spent raking provides the exercise that we need. One look at the human body will tell you it is built for raking—it *wants* to rake! According to Pete Egoscue, renowned anatomical functionalist and author of *The Egoscue Method of Health Through Motion,* "movement is as much a biological imperative as food and water." Many people today, he says, don't "move enough to beat the overwhelming odds that one day this motionless lifestyle will catch up with them." Do we sit at computers and cash registers doing repetitive movements, then relax with a little TV? Should we add standing and holding a noisy leaf blower to our routine? Just think about all the various body movements required by leaf raking. (471)

In her essay, Rachel Carson makes pesticide use relevant to American citizens and suggests the impact of the problem on future generations. Although the topic itself naturally involves public well-being, Carson pushes the reader to see how it relates to public doctrines, even the Bill of Rights:

> We have subjected enormous numbers of people to contact with these poisons, without their consent and often without their knowledge. If the Bill of Rights contains no guarantee that a citizen shall be secure against lethal poisons distributed either by private individuals or by public officials, it is surely only because our forefathers, despite their considerable wisdom and foresight, could conceive of no such problem. (459)

Any writer can use public resonance by pointing out the effects of a problem on a community or on a society at large.

THESIS

Your thesis for this project should offer a specific strategy for addressing a specific problem. The following examples show a range of possible strategies:

- If the sales associates at Dalworth's had more discretion over break time, the management/employee tension would decrease significantly.

- The budget crisis at Midland State College can only be addressed with a tuition increase.

- Small group work can help writers get beyond their frustration with invention.

- The degradation of rural areas cannot be stopped with peaceful public rhetoric. Significantly higher gasoline taxes would, however, keep people from building homes farther away from their jobs.

- If the country could begin to take back the airwaves from corporate interests, democracy might then begin to flourish.

- When America's hunters and fishermen see their shared interests with strong environmental groups, their combined political force will help counter the unchecked movement into wildlife areas.

Thesis statements tend to go off track for a few consistent reasons. Before committing to a statement (to something that may impact everything hereafter!), see the Common Thesis Problems in Chapter 6 (page 281), which overlap with this chapter.

EVOLUTION OF A THESIS

Notice how a thesis might evolve out of the invention process. Marcus's topic (isolation of the elderly) can be developed into a focused and sophisticated point. He begins by articulating the problem. Then he tries to make the problem more specific. Finally, he works to integrate the solution:

- In the long run, younger generations may feel the effects of the elderly's isolation.

- Older generations are isolated—their experiences, insights, and wisdom cut off from the people who need it most: everyone else.

- We have to make our grandparents the center of our families, not the marginal human satellites they are presently.

- Because older generations are isolated, their experiences, insights, and wisdom cut off from those who need them most, families should rethink how grandparents figure into everyday life.

- The lost experiences, insight, and wisdom of the older generations can only be reintegrated into culture through families; therefore, each family should work to place its grandparents at the center of everyday life.

Try to express your own problem and your solution in a sentence or two before moving on.

REVISION

Could your thesis be narrower? Writers sometimes seek out problems that are simply too big: hunger, racism, sexism, political deceit, and so on. But such giant problems have too many causes and too many forms. Writers are more apt to create a focused argument and offer an important insight if they take on a specific problem—one that can be located in a particular place and time. Before moving on, make certain that your problem is narrow—as narrow as possible.

RHETORICAL TOOLS

Remember that proposing a solution is a form of arguing. In fact, the process may involve two layers of argument: (1) persuading the reader about the nature or degree of the problem and (2) showing the value of a particular solution. The goal is not necessarily to convince readers that only one solution is possible, but that a particular solution to an important problem has merit.

Although the act of proposing solutions can vary greatly, good proposal essays have certain key elements (which you have already begun to develop):

> • **Problem:** Includes illustrations or examples, an explanation of causes, and a picture of short- and long-term effects.
>
> • **Solution:** Includes an explanation of how that solution will address, confront, or stop the causes of the problem.
>
> • **Counterargument:** Addresses concerns about or opposing claims to the solution or the articulation of the problem.
>
> • **Alternative Solutions:** Include any other potential strategies for addressing the problem. Articulating alternative solutions requires an explanation of why these are less desirable than the main solution being offered.
>
> • **Concession/Qualifier:** Acknowledges any possible shortcomings of the solution, or concedes value to some opposing claim or alternative solution.

Proposing Solutions: The Double-Layer Argument

1. Argue about the nature of the problem.
2. Argue for the value of your solution.

The development of these elements depends upon your particular problem and solution. Some problems, for instance, require significant explanation; that is, you might need to work hard just to make the reader aware of the complexities of the problem (as do Carson and Didion). Or perhaps you have a problem that is rather apparent (such as abandoned buildings plaguing an entire section of town). Consider how your audience may view the problem, and make certain to convince your readers to see the problem as you do.

Also, remember the strategies from Chapter 6, Making Arguments. Writers have the whole world of culture, history, and science within reach. By alluding to key historical moments, relevant literary texts, news events, or popular culture figures, a writer can make claims more persuasive to readers or show that his or her position is shared by others.

Use the following questions to help construct supporting points for your argument (and see the examples in the chapter readings):

• Does a historical event or figure illustrate something about my topic? (See Didion ¶ 3.)

• Does a historical situation or trend (the rise of a particular fashion, organization, or individual) illustrate something about my topic? (See Carson ¶ 8, 17–18, and Bell.)

• Does my topic relate to anything in nature? (See Carson.)

• Has science taught us anything about my topic? (See Carson and Bell.)

• Do any news events illustrate my point or stance? (See Ehrenreich.)

• Have I witnessed or experienced someone or something that illustrates my point? (See Bell ¶ 6 and Didion.)

• Can I construct a hypothetical situation that illustrates my point? (See Roberts ¶ 1–9.)

Discovering Counterarguments

In proposing a solution, you are arguing that a problem exists and that a particular solution will address it. But someone might argue with you about several different points: that the problem is no problem at all, that your solution will not work, that your solution is inappropriate—too costly, inhumane, unmanageable, and so on. A good arguer addresses those possible objections. And an especially sophisticated writer can dig into opponents' assumptions. For example, in the following passage, Barbara Ehrenreich briefly points to a flawed assumption: that women are naturally more humane, more caring, than men. At the end of the paragraph, Ehrenreich counters that assumption:

> If that assumption [that women are more caring than men] had been accurate, then all we would have had to do to make the world a better place—kinder, less violent, more just—would have been to assimilate into what had been, for so many centuries, the world of men. We would fight so that women could become the generals, CEOs, senators, professors, and opinion makers—and that was really the only fight we had to undertake. Because once they gained power and authority, once they had achieved a critical mass within the institutions of society, women would naturally work for change. That's what we thought, even if we thought it unconsciously—and it's just not true. Women can do the unthinkable. (475)

Ehrenreich continues pointing to and refuting opposing positions. In the following, she imagines how certain readers might characterize the causes of the problems at Abu Ghraib and then counters:

> You can't even argue, in the case of Abu Ghraib, that the problem was that there just weren't enough women in the military hierarchy to stop the abuses. The prison was directed by a woman, Gen. Janis Karpinski. The top U.S. intelligence officer in Iraq,

who also was responsible for reviewing the status of detainees before their release, was Major Gen. Barbara Fast. And the U.S. official ultimately responsible for managing the occupation of Iraq since October was Condoleezza Rice. Like Donald H. Rumsfeld, she ignored repeated reports of abuse and torture until the undeniable photographic evidence emerged. (475)

Use the following questions to help anticipate opposition to your argument:

- Who might not see this as a problem? Why?
- Why might the solution not work?
- Who might be offended by or resistant to my solution? Why?

Considering Alternative Solutions

Every problem has many possible solutions, and a good writer acknowledges other possibilities. But acknowledging solutions other than your own involves explaining their shortcomings. That is, as you mention other solutions, you must also make it clear that they are not as valuable as yours for some reason. Other solutions, for instance, might be less efficient, more dangerous, less ethical, less manageable, or simply inadequate.

Apply the following questions to your own proposal:

- What other solutions could be (or have been) attempted?
- Why did (or how could) these solutions fail or fall short?
- Why is the solution I am proposing better?

Considering other solutions can also help you understand the strengths and shortcomings of the solution you are promoting. For instance, imagine Marcus's problem (from the Public Resonance section): isolation of the elderly. His solution might involve refiguring the concept of the nuclear family to include grandparents, uncles, aunts, and cousins. Only in reconceptualizing the basic family unit, he might argue, will elderly members of society find more genuine social engagement. But he might also address other solutions, such as programs that bring together schoolchildren and nursing home residents. According to his argument, such solutions might fall short of creating deep and lasting relationships for the elderly.

Avoiding Logical Fallacies

Logical fallacies are flaws in the structure of an argument that can make readers call the claims into question. (See further explanation of logical fallacies in Chapter 6, pages 289–290.) In proposing solutions, be especially cautious of the following fallacies: faulty cause/effect, non sequitur, and slippery slope. When considering the possible long-term effects of a solution, writers may make any of several logical errors:

- Creating an effect unrelated to the factors of the present (**faulty cause/effect**).
- Skipping several logical steps between a cause and a possible effect (**non sequitur**).
- Extending present circumstances to their most dramatic or disastrous conclusion without sufficient logical clause (**slippery slope**).

Consider Marcus's topic: *Mainstream society isolates the elderly.* It might be valuable for Marcus to project the long-term effects of this problem. However, he should be cautious; it may be tempting to overstate the effects.

Logically sound

- Without the insight of older generations, mainstream society may continuously forget the social crises of the past and have to re-live many burdens.

- As older generations are further isolated, the difficulties they have lived through are isolated with them. And without constant real-life reminders in our midst, younger generations are likely to ignore a past that is not written by official voices of history.

Logically unsound

- America will have to go through another two world wars because it has completely forgotten the past.

- Everyone will eventually think like children without the elderly in everyday life.

- Society will eventually keep everyone over 50 years old locked away.

ACTIVITY

With a small group, describe logical problems in the unsound statements above.

ORGANIZATIONAL STRATEGIES

How Should I Separate Problem and Solution?

Many components go into a proposing solutions text: the problem, illustrations or support for the problem, the solution, support for the solution, the alternative solutions, shortcomings of those solutions, counterarguments, and concessions. These can be arranged in any imaginable order. Here are two standard strategies:

- Problem
  Examples/Illustrations

- Solution
  Examples/Illustrations

- Alternative Solution
  Explanation
  Shortcoming

- Alternative Solution
  Explanation
  Shortcoming

OR

- Problem

- Alternative Solution A/Shortcoming

- My Solution

- Alternative Solution B/Shortcoming

- My Solution

- Alternative Solution C/Shortcoming

- My Solution

Of course, these strategies depend upon the amount of detail and illustration the writer develops. A problem can be developed in great detail, and in cases such as Carson's essay, the problem actually requires significant explanation and illustration. Generally, the more a writer vividly portrays the problem, the more the reader will see a need for solving it.

If the causes of the problem are explained well enough, a brief articulation of the solution may suffice. In Didion's essay, for example, her solution comes at the very end of her essay, in one paragraph:

> And once it comes, now that I am wise in its ways, I no longer fight it. I lie down and let it happen. At first every small apprehension is magnified, every anxiety a pounding terror. Then the pain comes, and I concentrate only on that. Right there is the usefulness of migraine, there in that imposed yoga, the concentration on the pain. For when the pain recedes, ten or twelve hours later, everything goes with it, all the hidden resentments, all the vain anxieties. The migraine has acted as a circuit breaker, and the fuses have emerged intact. There is a pleasant convalescent euphoria. (462–463)

When the solution involves many meticulous steps, it needs significant explanation. In the Roberts essay, for example, the problem, the task of writing a 500-word essay, is presented quickly. The solution is developed with specific details, specific how-to strategies.

How Should I Include Counterarguments?

Counterarguments (responses to those opposing your claims) often are arranged in separate paragraphs. You might develop a counter in an entire paragraph—explaining why, for example, some people are opposed to your understanding of the problem. Then, in a new paragraph, you might explain why your understanding is most appropriate or correct or valuable. Some writers use the turnabout paragraph for counterarguments. A turnabout paragraph begins with one point and then changes directions at some point, always giving the reader a clear indication of that change. For example, you might begin a paragraph with an opposing claim, and then counterargue in that same paragraph as in the following passage from Bachtel's essay. Notice Bachtel's turnabout phrase, "but so do other forms . . .":

> Still, many people may feel apprehensive towards this proposal because they have lived with televisions for so long that they cannot imagine functioning without them. "How will we know what's going on in the world or what the weather is going to be like?" they might ask. Sure, television stations provide very useful information, but so do other forms of communication, such as newspapers and magazines. These sources of information can be just as convenient as television. (477)

Counterarguments can also be addressed in a subtler manner. Joan Didion, for example, first refers to the notion that migraines are merely imaginary and then lists real physical consequences of migraines. She acknowledges an opposing point and makes it irrelevant by showing the opposite to be true:

> For I had no brain tumor, no eyestrain, no high blood pressure, nothing wrong with me at all: I simply had migraine headaches, and migraine headaches were, as everyone who did not have them knew, imaginary. I fought migraine then, ignored the warnings it sent,

went to school and later to work in spite of it, sat through lectures in Middle English and presentations to advertisers with involuntary tears running down the right side of my face, threw up in washrooms, stumbled home by instinct, emptied ice trays onto my bed and tried to freeze the pain in my right temple, wished only for a neurosurgeon who would do a lobotomy on house call, and cursed my imagination. (461)

Where Should I Put Alternative Solutions?

Alternative solutions, those strategies other than the one forwarded by the writer, can come early or late in an essay. Some writers acknowledge other possibilities soon after their introductions. Notice Roberts's strategy: In his scenario, a student hands in an essay using typical get-it-done strategies and receives a "D." The hypothetical writing process of the student is the alternative solution, which, Roberts argues, is not a very good one. He explains this after showing us the hypothetical paper on college football:

> On Monday you turn it in, moderately hopeful, and on Friday it comes back marked "weak in content" and sporting a big "D." (465)

Once Roberts shows the negative side of such a strategy, he goes on to give a detailed solution to the problem of writing assignments.

Didion's strategy is much the same: She offers some alternative, and rather ineffective, methods for dealing with migraine (such as "taking a couple of aspirin") before giving her new way of coping in the conclusion. Other writers wait to mention alternative methods until they have fully explained what they deem the best.

WRITER'S VOICE

Because proposing a solution is an argumentative process, the Writer's Voice strategies from Chapter 6, Making Arguments, apply here as well (see pages 294–297). But proposing solutions brings with it some particular concerns and strategies. The following strategies will help you develop and maintain an engaging writer's voice.

Creating Reasonable Tone

It might be said that *tone* is the way a writer treats readers. In argumentative writing, tone is vital to maintaining readers' interest. One that is too emotional can overwhelm; one that is condescending is apt to alienate. When proposing solutions, writers must be careful not to force problems *at* readers. Instead, it is the writer's job to present a problem and illustrate its significance *for* readers. For example, notice Carson's strategy for making the reader understand the significance of a problem:

> In this now universal contamination of the environment, chemicals are the sinister and little-recognized partners of radiation in changing the very nature of the world—the very nature of its life. Strontium 90, released through nuclear explosions into the air, comes to earth in rain or drifts down as fallout, lodges in soil, enters into the grass or corn or wheat grown there, and in time takes up its abode in the bones of a human being, there to remain until his death. (456)

Be careful not to force problems at readers.

It would be easy, or at least tempting, for Carson to scream and shout at her readers about the state of the environment. Imagine the following:

> With evil chemicals, humankind has completely and utterly ruined the environment and is in the process of transforming nature, indeed, the world itself. Through nuclear explosions, we release terrible chemicals such as Strontium 90 into the air, which then fall to the ground and contaminate the plants that human beings eventually eat. And then, in an insanely nightmarish process, the unsuspecting humans ingest this horrific chemical until it eventually kills them.

This passage is over the top. It forces the problem at its readers and demands that they feel a particular emotion. Carson's passage is less confrontational, while still intense. She does not make emotional demands on the reader; instead, she presents the rather gristly details of environmental contamination and leaves the reader to reflect on them.

Inviting the Reader

Writerly invitations are phrases that promote curiosity in readers, phrases that entice them to examine a particular topic.

Question Asking the right question can make a reader concerned about the subject: *Why are the computer labs at University Hall a problem? How safe is the drinking water in our community?* In her essay, Rachel Carson invites the reader to consider hard questions that bring the reader into the center of the problem:

> All this [life] has been risked—for what? Future historians may well be amazed by our distorted sense of proportion. How could intelligent beings seek to control a few unwanted species by a method that contaminated the entire environment and brought the threat of disease and death even to their own kind? (458)

Group inclusion A writer can include potential readers in a relevant group (small or large) that is affected by the subject. Didion creates an "us" for those who have migraine:

> All of us who have migraine suffer not only from the attacks themselves but from this common conviction that we are perversely refusing to cure ourselves by taking a couple of aspirin . . . . (462)

Statement A simple claim that calls the reader's attention to the matter is often the most effective. Notice Carson's strong statement at the beginning of her essay:

> The most alarming of all man's assaults upon the environment is the contamination of air, earth, rivers, and sea with dangerous and even lethal materials. (456)

Considering Verb Mood

There are three moods in English: *indicative* (used for stating facts or statements about the world), *subjunctive* (used to express conditions that are not facts, such as a recommendation, a wish, a requirement, or a statement contrary to fact), and *imperative* (used for issuing commands or suggestions). Many passages in this text are in the imperative mood. (Find one right now.) Rather than informing the reader about possible ways to act (as in the subjunctive), imperative mood orders the reader to act.

Imperative mood is not often used in academic essays or formal proposals because it puts the reader in the position of action. Of course, there are exceptions. Roberts's essay is written, almost entirely, in the imperative mood. Because his strategy is to give his audience the particular steps to solving a problem, the imperative mood is appropriate. It is also appropriate because his audience is very specific—college writers. He assumes that the audience has (or will have) a personal encounter with the problem.

ACTIVITY

Draft a paragraph that makes your topic inviting to the reader. Apply one of the three strategies:

1. Ask an important question.
2. Include the reader in an effected group.
3. Call attention to the matter with a strong statement.

VITALITY

In his essay "How To Say Nothing in 500 Words," Paul Roberts offers college students sound advice. The problem students face: a standard college assignment that requires a certain page length. The solution Roberts proposes: less obvious approaches and less usual positions.

Avoid the Obvious Content

In his essay, Roberts argues that writers should avoid saying what everyone knows. He urges writers to make a list of the first ideas that come to mind on any topic, and then to avoid those initial ideas: "If these are the points that leap to your mind, they will leap to everyone else's too. . . ." Even at the sentence level, writers can avoid the obvious. They can trim out the statements that readers will simply infer on their own. Notice the following obvious content:

> It is wrong when people cheat others. And when the Enron executives cheated thousands of employees out of their pensions, they ruined retirement years for many families.

The entire first sentence is unnecessary, and it detracts from the intensity of the ideas. When writers force such obvious statements onto readers, they make readers less involved. Obvious statements actually tell readers to turn off!

Get Rid of Obvious Padding

Padding occurs when writers stuff their sentences with unnecessary material. The sentences become longer but contain no added meaning. In his essay, Roberts begins with a brief sentence and a simple idea: "Fast driving is dangerous."

The brief idea then gains words but no meaning:

> In my humble opinion though I do not claim to be an expert on this complicated subject, fast driving, in most circumstances, would seem to be rather dangerous in many respects, or at least so it would seem to me. (467)

The padded sentence is full of unnecessary qualifiers and attention to the writer. While qualifiers can be valuable and first-person pronouns can be important, they can be overused. They can slow down sentences and inflate simple ideas so they sound important.

But when writers begin pruning and trimming their essays, when they really get good at vitalizing their sentences, their drafts are apt to shrink. This may seem like bad news if the goal is, in fact, to reach a certain length requirement. But Roberts again gives good advice:

> Instead of taking a couple of obvious points off the surface of the topic and then circling warily around them for six paragraphs, you work in and explore, figure out the details. You illustrate. You say that fast driving is dangerous, and then you prove it. How long does it take to stop a car at forty and at eighty? How far can you see at night? What happens when a tire blows? What happens in a head-on collision at fifty miles an hour? Pretty soon your paper will be full of broken glass and blood and headless torsos, and reaching five hundred words will not really be a problem. (468)

So it all comes back to invention. Developing more intensive ideas from the beginning means writers can avoid padding.

Call a Fool a Fool

Academic audiences value intensity and directness. But some writers may avoid directly stating points. Roberts gives the following scenario:

> The student writes, "In my opinion, the principal of my high school acted in ways that I believe every unbiased person would have to call foolish." This isn't exactly what he means. What he means is, "My high school principal was a fool." If he was a fool, call him a fool. Hedging the thing about with "in-my-opinion's" and "it-seems-to-me's" and "as-I-see-it's" and "at-least-from-my-point-of-view's" gains you nothing. Delete these phrases whenever they creep into your paper. (468)

PEER REVIEW

Exchange drafts with at least one other writer. Before passing your draft to others, underline the thesis, or write it above your essay. This way, reviewers will get traction as they read.

As a reviewer, use the following questions to guide your response:

1. After reading the draft, do you believe that the problem the writer describes is worthy of attention? Do you think it's a problem worth solving? If not, what might the writer do to make the problem more significant? (Consider the Public Resonance section of the chapter.)

2. Do you think the writer's solution is appropriate for the problem? Will it address specific causes? Is it manageable? Realistic? Humane?

3. Try to imagine a reason why the writer's solution will not work. What unforeseen forces or variables should the writer consider?

4. What other solutions might be as or more productive in solving the problem?

5. Consider the organization of the essay. Do any paragraphs shift focus without sufficient cues? Do you feel like any paragraphs move away from their initial points without taking you along? Point to specific places in the essay that move too abruptly from one idea to another.

6. How would you describe the writer's tone? (See pages 496–497.) Do you feel invited into the topic, or do you have to work at keeping your attention focused? (Is the writer's voice too flat, too uninteresting, too typical?) Rewrite a short passage of the draft using a different voice. Help the writer to imagine how a different voice might sound.

7. Consider sentence vitality:
   a. Help the writer to avoid obvious content. Circle any sentences or passages that seem obvious to you. (Write "obvious?" next to the passage.)
   b. Help the writer to avoid padding. Underline phrases that inflate simple ideas and draw out sentences unnecessarily.
   c. Help the writer to "call a fool a fool." Rewrite any phrases or sentences that seem to hedge, that circle around a more direct and intense wording.
   d. Consider vitality strategies from other chapters.

Academic audiences value intensity and directness.

DELIVERY

The real value of everything in this book lies in how you apply it to real-life situations. To do this, imagine the essay as a sort of practice field, and see all the lessons you learn from writing an essay as important knowledge you can now apply in your everyday life—at work, at home, at school, and everywhere else. What problems do you and others face in real life? And what are the possible solutions?

- Do you drive too far to work?
- Are you strapped financially?
- Why, surrounded by modern conveniences, don't you have enough free time?

Consider the essay you wrote for this chapter:

- Will the reader better understand that a problem exists?
- How might others act differently from reading your essay?
- How did writing the essay help you, the writer, with the problem?

Beyond the Essay

The comic on the following page encourages you to express the idea from your essay in some other form: a letter, speech, and so on.

Why?

Students sometimes see education—or certain college courses such as this one—as separate from their actual lives. However, the course is not only related to your major; it is, more importantly, related to your *life*. Writing courses such as this one go out into the real world and bring that real world back into the classroom.

Such courses look at what really goes on in everyday life, and they present what goes on (invention strategies, rhetorical strategies, and so on) in an organized way. College courses gather and organize the untidy ideas of disorganized real life, and they present those ideas in an orderly, more graspable way. Admittedly, the college writing course can be a confusing and seemingly irrelevant place. But if you can remember that the invention and delivery strategies in this book are a description (not a prescription) of how everyday people think and communicate effectively, you can more successfully fuse schoolwork and real life. This fusion is the intended purpose of all education.

A student's job is to connect classroom work to everyday life.

A student's job is to connect everyday life to classroom work.

EXPLORING THE ARTS

Chapter Contents

CHAPTER **11**

"One of the most compelling aspects of literature is its relationship to human experience. Reading is an act of engagement and participation. It is also, simultaneously, an act of clarification and discovery."

—Jeffrey D. Hoeper

I f reading literature is an act of discovery, then the same thing might be said about listening to music and taking in the visual arts. Art is more than entertainment. It calls on readers, listeners, or viewers to participate in the creation of ideas. Whether they are involved in novels, Shakespeare's plays, folk songs, or Picasso's paintings, people engaging art are inventing as they take it in: They are developing thoughts, envisioning situations, seeing connections, and imagining worlds that they had not previously encountered. While the arts help us imagine other worlds, they also help us to make sense of our own. Art, in whatever form, offers something to everyday experience—maybe answers to the gnawing uncertainties of daily existence; maybe mystery and intensity in a world that seems too plain; maybe a framework for exploring human behavior; or maybe a deeper understanding of our place in society. Exploring and responding to the arts, then, is the process of developing and communicating ideas, not simply about a story, poem, song, or painting, but about life.

Of course, not all works that could be considered art promote valuable insight. More sophisticated pieces of art tend to promote more sophisticated ideas, which, perhaps, is why college courses focus on art that is more complex than popular romance novels or teen dance music. Although art varies in complexity and form, we will assume art is *any creative work that intends to provoke new ideas or insights in its audience.*

Key Terms and Concepts

The following terms are helpful in reading and writing about art:

Arrangement: The structure of a song

Ensemble: The collection and placement of instruments or voices in a performance

Genre: A category of artistic work based on form, style, and subject matter

Narrator: The voice speaking to the audience, which may also be a character

Plot: The arrangement or course of events

Setting: The place and time in which events occur

Stanza: A unit of verse in poetry

Style: An artist's particular characteristics that distinguish his or her work from others

Theme: The controlling idea or primary message

Such a definition does create some boundaries, excluding, for example, a piece of work produced to make preadolescents thoughtlessly excited— but any definition creates boundaries.

The formal study of the arts can become a highly specialized practice, dependent on particular theories and terms. Such advanced study is often relegated to particular disciplines: English departments study literature, drama, and poetry; art schools study painting and sculpture; music majors examine the formalities of composition. However, the arts transcend any one discipline or academic field:

- In addition to reading government publications, military records, and personal memoirs, historians study the literature and art of a given era to understand its culture.
- Sociologists, anthropologists, and political scientists study the literature and art of a culture to understand its perspectives, moral crises, and attitudes.
- Psychologists study the arts to further their understanding of the human experience.
- Lawyers and law officials study the arts to explore the relationship between individual action and civic duty, or to understand the workings of the criminal mind.

All of these disciplinary approaches emphasize an important point: The arts are deeply connected to how and what people think. Exploring art is not simply an examination of one person's expression; it is an investigation into human thought and imagination, as well as culture and society.

The definition of art has been contested for thousands of years, and it continues to be today. If our definition does not suit you, create another one. Ask five people for their definitions of art (either in class or by surveying non-classmate peers). Considering those ideas, write out a definition that you can use in your exploration for this chapter.

This chapter will help you examine and analyze a subject (one or more works of art) and develop a specific point about it in a formal essay. The chapter readings include works of art and analytical essays. You can find a topic in one of two ways:

1. Go to the **Point of Contact** section for help finding an artistic work outside of this chapter.
2. Choose one of the **Ideas for Writing** that follow each work of art or essay.

After finding a subject, go to the **Analysis** section to begin developing your ideas.

The readings for this chapter include both artistic works and analytical essays about artistic works. Even though the artistic works are of different genres (or categories), they have some similarities: They create a vivid reality for the reader; they promote a sense of wonder; and they bring a particular idea or situation into sharp focus so the reader can experience it in a new way. Like all artistic works, the ones in this chapter intend to show the reader a new or particularly intensive way of imagining something, and thereby change the reader's perspective.

Encountering an artistic work calls for a certain degree of intellectual adventure. We must be willing to follow the artist into a way of thinking and seeing. And while it is impossible to leave behind all of our biases and opinions, we benefit by being willing to explore the subtleties of language, image, and thought.

The essays in the chapter attempt to show what effect various artistic works have on people—how they promote ideas and influence thinking. Of course, to discuss what art does, writers must understand how it works; that is, they must *analyze* the artistic work. Notice how the writers use analysis and how they draw attention to particular lines, images, or characters. Notice also that each writer offers a focused point about an artistic work, group of works, or genre.

Two essays (Whitehead's and Bennett's) focus on works by several artists. Although the subjects may be broad, their main points are very specific. McCovey's essay, however, focuses on only one work. Although the subjects are different (an art form, a specific genre, or one particular work), the authors use many similar strategies for supporting their claims.

ARTISTIC WORKS

A Very Old Man with Enormous Wings

Gabriel García Márquez

Gabriel García Márquez, born in 1928 in Colombia, has published many novels and short story collections. His novel *One Hundred Years of Solitude* (1967) has been hailed as one of the greatest novels ever written. He was awarded the Nobel Prize for literature in 1982.

On the third day of rain they had killed so many crabs inside the house that Pelayo had to cross his drenched courtyard and throw them into the sea, because the newborn child had a temperature all night and they thought it was due to the stench. The world had been sad since Tuesday. Sea and sky were a single ash-gray thing and the sands of the beach, which on March nights glimmered like powdered light, had become a stew of mud and rotten shellfish. The light was so weak at noon that when Pelayo was coming back to the house after throwing away the crabs, it was hard for him to see what it was that was moving and groaning in the rear of the courtyard. He had to go very close to see that it was an old man, a very old man, lying face down in the mud, who, in spite of his tremendous efforts, couldn't get up, impeded by his enormous wings.

Frightened by that nightmare, Pelayo ran to get Elisenda, his wife, who was putting compresses on the sick child, and he took her to the rear of the courtyard. They both looked at the fallen body with mute stupor. He was dressed like a ragpicker. There were only a few faded hairs left on his bald skull and very few teeth in his mouth, and his pitiful condition of a drenched great-grandfather had taken away any sense of grandeur he might have had. His huge buzzard wings, dirty and half-plucked, were forever entangled in the mud. They looked at him so long and so closely that Pelayo and Elisenda very soon overcame their surprise and in the end found him familiar. Then they dared speak to him, and he answered in an incomprehensible dialect with a strong sailor's voice. That was how they skipped over the inconvenience of the wings and quite intelligently concluded that he was a lonely castaway from some foreign ship wrecked by the storm. And yet, they called in a neighbor woman who knew everything about life and death to see him, and all she needed was one look to show them their mistake.

"He's an angel," she told them. "He must have been coming for the child, but the poor fellow is so old that the rain knocked him down."

On the following day everyone knew that a flesh-and-blood angel was held captive in Pelayo's house. Against the judgment of the wise neighbor woman, for whom angels in those times were the fugitive survivors of a celestial conspiracy, they did not have the heart to club him to death. Pelayo watched over him all afternoon from the kitchen, armed with his bailiff's club, and before going to bed he dragged him out of the mud and locked him up with the hens in the wire chicken coop. In the middle of the night, when the rain stopped, Pelayo and Elisenda were still killing crabs. A short time afterward the child woke up without a fever and with a desire to eat. Then they felt magnanimous and decided to put the angel on a raft with fresh water and provisions for three days and leave him to his fate on the high seas. But when they went out into the courtyard with the first light of dawn, they found the whole neighborhood in front of the chicken coop having fun with the angel, without the slightest reverence, tossing him things to eat through the openings in the wire as if he weren't a supernatural creature but a circus animal.

5 Father Gonzaga arrived before seven o'clock, alarmed at the strange news. By that time onlookers less frivolous than those at dawn had already arrived and

they were making all kinds of conjectures concerning the captive's future. The simplest among them thought that he should be named mayor of the world. Others of sterner mind felt that he should be promoted to the rank of five-star general in order to win all wars. Some visionaries hoped that he could be put to stud in order to implant on earth a race of winged wise men who could take charge of the universe. But Father Gonzaga, before becoming a priest, had been a robust woodcutter. Standing by the wire, he reviewed his catechism in an instant and asked them to open the door so that he could take a close look at that pitiful man who looked more like a huge decrepit hen among the fascinated chickens. He was lying in a corner drying his open wings in the sunlight among the fruit peels and breakfast leftovers that the early risers had thrown him. Alien to the impertinences of the world, he only lifted his antiquarian eyes and murmured something in his dialect when Father Gonzaga went into the chicken coop and said good morning to him in Latin. The parish priest had his first suspicion of an imposter when he saw that he did not understand the language of God or know how to greet His ministers. Then he noticed that seen close up he was much too human: he had an unbearable smell of the outdoors, the back side of his wings was strewn with parasites and his main feathers had been mistreated by terrestrial winds, and nothing about him measured up to the proud dignity of angels. Then he came out of the chicken coop and in a brief sermon warned the curious against the risks of being ingenuous. He reminded them that the devil had the bad habit of making use of carnival tricks in order to confuse the unwary. He argued that if wings were not the essential element in determining the difference between a hawk and an airplane, they were even less so in the recognition of angels. Nevertheless, he promised to write a letter to his bishop so that the latter would write to his primate so that the latter would write to the Supreme Pontiff in order to get the final verdict from the highest courts.

His prudence fell on sterile hearts. The news of the captive angel spread with such rapidity that after a few

hours the courtyard had the bustle of a marketplace and they had to call in troops with fixed bayonets to disperse the mob that was about to knock the house down. Elisenda, her spine all twisted from sweeping up so much marketplace trash, then got the idea of fencing in the yard and charging five cents admission to see the angel.

The curious came from far away. A traveling carnival arrived with a flying acrobat who buzzed over the crowd several times, but no one paid any attention to him because his wings were not those of an angel but, rather, those of a sidereal bat. The most unfortunate invalids on earth came in search of health: a poor woman who since childhood had been counting her heartbeats and had run out of numbers; a Portuguese man who couldn't sleep because the noise of the stars disturbed him; a sleepwalker who got up at night to undo the things he had done while awake; and many others with less serious ailments. In the midst of that shipwreck disorder that made the earth tremble, Pelayo and Elisenda were happy with fatigue, for in less than a week they had crammed their rooms with money and the line of pilgrims waiting their turn to enter still reached beyond the horizon.

The angel was the only one who took no part in his own act. He spent his time trying to get comfortable in his borrowed nest, befuddled by the hellish heat of the oil lamps and sacramental candles that had been placed along the wire. At first they tried to make him eat some mothballs, which, according to the wisdom of the wise neighbor woman, were the food prescribed for angels. But he turned them down, just as he turned down the papal lunches that the penitents brought him, and they never found out whether it was because he was an angel or because he was an old man that in the end he ate nothing but eggplant mush. His only supernatural virtue seemed to be patience. Especially during the first days, when the hens pecked at him, searching for the stellar parasites that proliferated in his wings, and the cripples pulled out feathers to touch their defective parts with, and even the most merciful threw stones at him, trying to get him to rise so they could see him standing. The only time they succeeded in arousing him was when they burned his side with an iron for branding steers, for he had been motionless for so many hours that they thought he was dead. He awoke with a start, ranting in his hermetic language and with tears in his eyes, and he flapped his wings a couple of times, which brought on a whirlwind of chicken dung and lunar dust and a gale of panic that did not seem to be of this world. Although many thought that his reaction had been one not of rage but of pain, from then on they were careful not to annoy him, because the majority understood that his passivity was not that of a hero taking his ease but that of a cataclysm in repose.

Father Gonzaga held back the crowd's frivolity with formulas of maidservant inspiration while awaiting the arrival of a final judgment on the nature of the captive. But the mail from Rome showed no sense of urgency. They spent their time finding out if the prisoner had a navel, if his dialect had any connection with Aramaic, how many times he could fit on the head of a pin, or whether he wasn't just a Norwegian with wings. Those meager letters might have come and gone until the end of time if a providential event had not put an end to the priest's tribulations.

10 It so happened that during those days, among so many other carnival attractions, there arrived in town the traveling show of the woman who had been changed into a spider for having disobeyed her parents. The admission to see her was not only less than the admission to see the angel, but people were permitted to ask her all manner of questions about her absurd state and to examine her up and down so that no one would ever doubt the truth of her horror. She was a frightful tarantula the size of a ram and with the head of a sad maiden. What was most heartrending, however, was not her outlandish shape but the sincere affliction with which she recounted the details of her misfortune. While still practically a child she had sneaked out of her parents' house to go to a dance, and while she was coming back through the woods after having danced all night without permission, a fearful thunderclap rent the sky in two and through the crack came the lightning bolt of brimstone that changed her into a spider. Her only nourishment came from the meatballs that charitable souls chose to toss into her mouth. A spectacle like that, full of so much human truth and with such a fearful lesson, was bound to defeat without even trying that of a haughty angel who scarcely deigned to look at mortals. Besides, the few miracles attributed to the angel showed a certain mental disorder, like the blind man who didn't recover his sight but grew three new teeth, or the paralytic who didn't get to walk but almost won the lottery, and the leper whose sores sprouted sunflowers. Those consolation miracles, which were more like mocking fun, had already ruined the angel's reputation when the woman who had been changed into a spider finally crushed him completely. That was how Father Gonzaga was cured forever of his insomnia and Pelayo's courtyard went back to being as empty as during the time it had rained for three days and crabs walked through the bedrooms.

The owners of the house had no reason to lament. With the money they saved they built a two-story mansion with balconies and gardens and high netting so that crabs wouldn't get in during the winter, and with iron bars on the windows so that angels couldn't get in. Pelayo also set up a rabbit warren close to town and gave up his job as bailiff for good, and Elisenda bought some satin pumps with high heels and many dresses of iridescent silk, the kind worn on Sunday by the most desirable women in those times. The chicken coop was the only thing that didn't receive any attention. If they washed it down with creolin and burned tears of myrrh inside it every so often, it was not in homage to the angel but to drive away the dungheap stench that still hung everywhere like a ghost and was turning the new house into an old one. At first, when the child learned to walk, they were careful that he not get too close to the chicken coop. But then they began to lose their fears and got used to the smell, and before the child got his second teeth he'd gone inside the chicken coop to play, where the wires were falling apart. The angel was no less standoffish with him than with other mortals, but he tolerated the most ingenious infamies with the patience of a dog who had no illusions. They both came down with chicken pox at the same time. The doctor who took care of the child couldn't resist the temptation to listen to the angel's heart, and he found so much whistling in the heart and so many sounds in his kidneys that it seemed impossible for him to be alive. What surprised him most, however, was the logic of his wings. They seemed so natural on that completely human organism that he couldn't understand why other men didn't have them too.

When the child began school it had been some time since the sun and rain had caused the collapse of the chicken coop. The angel went dragging himself about here and there like a stray dying man. They would drive him out of the bedroom with a broom and a moment later find him in the kitchen. He seemed to be in so many places at the same time that they grew to think that he'd been duplicated, that he was reproducing himself all through the house, and the exasperated and unhinged Elisenda shouted that it was awful living in that hell full of angels. He could scarcely eat and his antiquarian eyes had also become so foggy that he went about bumping into posts. All he had left were the bare cannulae of his last feathers. Pelayo threw a blanket over him and extended him the charity of letting him sleep in the shed, and only then did they notice that he had a temperature at night, and was delirious with the tongue twisters of an old Norwegian. That was one of the few times they became alarmed, for they thought he was going to die and not even the wise neighbor woman had been able to tell them what to do with dead angels.

And yet he not only survived his worst winter, but seemed improved with the first sunny days. He remained motionless for several days in the farthest corner of the courtyard, where no one would see him, and at the beginning of December some large, stiff feathers began to grow on his wings, the feathers of a scarecrow, which looked more like another misfortune of decrepitude. But he must have known the reason for those changes, for he was quite careful that no one should notice them, that no one should hear the sea chanteys that he sometimes sang under the stars. One morning Elisenda was cutting some bunches of onions for lunch when a wind that seemed to come from the high seas blew into the kitchen. Then she went to the window and caught the angel in his first attempts at flight. They were so clumsy that his fingernails opened a furrow in the vegetable patch and he was on the point of knocking the shed down with the ungainly flapping that slipped on the light and couldn't get a grip on the air. But he did manage to gain altitude. Elisenda let out a sigh of relief, for herself and for him, when she saw him pass over the last houses, holding himself up in some way with the risky flapping of a senile vulture. She kept watching him even when she was through cutting the onions and she kept on watching until it was no longer possible for her to see him, because then he was no longer an annoyance in her life but an imaginary dot on the horizon of the sea.

Exploring Ideas

1. According to the events and descriptions of this story, do angels exist? If so, what are they? What is their relationship to humanity? (Or, what is humanity's relationship to angels?)

2. The people's reaction in the story is perhaps as important as the winged old man's presence. What does their reaction say about people? Their fears? Their treatment of strangers?

3. With the events in this story as your basis, explain our fear of the unknown and how it influences behavior.

Fire

Joy Harjo

Joy Harjo, born in 1951 in Tulsa, Oklahoma, has pub-
lished several books of award-winning poetry. "Fire"
appears in *How We Became Human, New and Selected
Poems* (2003), and first appeared in *What Moon Drove
Me to This?* (1979). Her poetry often focuses on Native
American life and identity.

a woman can't survive
by her own breath
alone
she must know
the voices of mountains
she must recognize
the foreverness of blue sky
she must flow
with the elusive
bodies
of night winds
who will take her
into herself

look at me
i am not a separate woman
i am the continuance
of blue sky
i am the throat
of the mountains
a night wind
who burns
with every breath
she takes

Exploring Ideas

1. How is the message of this poem important for women
   living at the dawn of the 21st century?

2. Does this poem speak only to women? Does it offer anything to men? Explain what this poem may or may not
   offer to men.

Dover Beach

Matthew Arnold

Matthew Arnold (1822–1888) was an English poet and essayist. While he produced poetry in his early years, he devoted much of his later life to essays on literature and culture. His most famous essay, *Culture and Anarchy,* is often quoted in discussions about the role of morality in societies. "Dover Beach," which is set on the coast of England, was published in 1867 in his second book of poetry.

The sea is calm to-night.
The tide is full, the moon lies fair
Upon the straits;—on the French coast the light
Gleams and is gone; the cliffs of England stand,
Glimmering and vast, out in the tranquil bay.
Come to the window, sweet is the night-air!

Only, from the long line of spray
Where the sea meets the moon-blanch'd land,
Listen! you hear the grating roar
Of pebbles which the waves draw back, and fling,
At their return, up the high strand,
Begin, and cease, and then again begin,
With tremulous cadence slow, and bring
The eternal note of sadness in.

Sophocles long ago
Heard it on the Aegean, and it brought
Into his mind the turbid ebb and flow
Of human misery; we
Find also in the sound a thought,
Hearing it by this distant northern sea.

The Sea of Faith
Was once, too, at the full, and round the earth's shore
Lay like the folds of a bright girdle furl'd.
But now I only hear
Its melancholy, long, withdrawing roar,
Retreating, to the breath
Of the night-wind, down the vast edges of drear
And naked shingles of the world.

Ah, love, let us be true
To one another! for the world, which seems
To lie before us like a land of dreams,
So various, so beautiful, so new,
Hath really neither joy, nor love, nor light,
Nor certitude, nor peace, nor help for pain;
And we are here as on a darkling plain
Swept with confused alarms of struggle and flight,
Where ignorant armies clash by night.

Exploring Ideas

1. What is the "Sea of Faith" (stanza 4)? How is the idea similar to or different from other religious or philosophical metaphors that you have used or heard?

2. Sophocles was a playwright in ancient Greece who wrote the tragic story of Oedipus. How does the allusion to Sophocles support the main idea of the poem?

3. How does Arnold make you rethink your connection to other people and societies, both in the present and in the distant past?

Running to Stand Still

U2

From Dublin, Ireland, U2 has been on popular music charts around the world since 1980. Emerging from the punk scene, U2 developed worldwide attention as a band with highly charged political and social messages. The band's lead singer, Bono, has rallied political and religious leaders to help poor and oppressed people throughout the world. "Running to Stand Still" appears on *The Joshua Tree* (1987).

And so she woke up
Woke up from where she was
Lying still
Said I gotta do something
About where we're going
Step on a steam train
Step out of the driving rain, maybe
Run from the darkness in the night
Singing ha, ah la la la de day
Ah da da da de day Ah la la de day
Sweet the sin
Bitter taste in my mouth
I see seven towers
But I only see one way out
You got to cry without weeping
Talk without speaking
Scream without raising your voice
You know I took the poison
From the poison stream
Then I floated out of here
Singing . . . ha la la la de day
Ha la la la de day
Ha la la de day

She runs through the streets
With her eyes painted red
Under a black belly of cloud in the rain
In through a doorway she brings me
White gold and pearls stolen from the sea
She is raging
She is raging
And the storm blows up in her eyes
She will . . .
Suffer the needle chill
She's running to stand . . .
Still.

Exploring Ideas

1. Explain how the images in this song help us to see a life of addiction.

2. What does "Running to Stand Still" suggest about art's relationship to life?

3. Listen to "Heroin" by the Velvet Underground (off the album *Velvet Underground & Nico*). What qualities do "Heroin" and "Running to Stand Still" share? Explain how U2's song plays off "Heroin" and what this might suggest about influence and art.

Knuckle Down

Ani DiFranco

Ani DiFranco has been described as a "folk punk" singer/songwriter. Her eclectic style has gained her significant notoriety and acclaim in the music industry. DiFranco's songs, like the following (on her 2005 release, *Knuckle Down*) often rely on personal narrative to reveal political and social issues.

that's just my cowgirl alter-ego
riding on her bar room bull
dripping with the sweat of irony
as the cowboys whoop and drool
shooting glances at the mirror
to see if her scar is showing
she is truly going nowhere tonight

lecherous old lady wanna-be
much too young and shy
flailing her whole life
just thinking she can teach herself to fly
vehement romantic
frantic for forever right now
but forever's going nowhere tonight

sick of goading her self-loathing
she thinks, i think i'd better leave
'course whiskey makes me smarter
and i'm happy as can be
but please excuse me darlin
it's not you
it's me

and there's a dusty old dust storm on mars, they say
so tonight you can't see it too clear
still i stood in line to look through their telescope
looked like a distant ship light
as seen from a foggy pier
and i know that i was warned
still it was not what i hoped
yes i know that i was warned
still it was not what i hoped

i think i'm done gunnin to get closer
to some imagined bliss
i gotta knuckle down
and just be ok with this
i'm gonna knuckle down
just be ok with this
'course that star struck girl is already someone i miss

i swear some stuff you just see better from further
  away
and i think i communicate best now, the less i say
and i can't dance if the band can't play
and the vibe is going nowhere tonight

'cuz somewhere between Hollywood and its pretty
  happiness
and an anguish so infinite it's anybody's guess
is a place where people are all teachers
and this just one long class
and that ass will get you nowhere tonight

there's a dusty old dust storm on mars they say
so tonight you can't see it too clear
still i stood in line to look through their telescope
looked like a distant ship light
as seen from a foggy pier
and i know that i was warned
still it was not what i hoped
yeah i know that i was warned
still it was not what i hoped

i think i'm done gunnin to get closer
to some imagined bliss
i gotta knuckle down
just be ok with this
gotta knuckle down
just be ok with this

'course that star struck girl
is already someone i miss

Exploring Ideas

1. How would you describe the speaker in the song (the "I")?

2. What new perspective or idea is that speaker trying to offer you? Cite specific lines or words to support your answer.

3. Visit DiFranco's record company site, Righteous Babe Records. Read the lyrics of another song from *Knuckle Down*. How do they overlap with the lyrics of the song above?

Train at Night in the Desert

Georgia O'Keeffe

Georgia O'Keeffe (1887–1986) helped to define American art in the 20th century. Much of her work explores life in the American Southwest, where she spent the last half of her life. This painting illustrates O'Keeffe's dramatization of everyday life. Like many of her paintings, it reveals the intensity of a single moment or experience.

Exploring Ideas

1. If art attempts to prompt a new way of seeing or thinking about a subject, how does this painting invite you to think about the desert? About trains? About distance?

2. What other ideas does the painting prompt? What specific elements of the painting stir up those ideas?

3. Research O'Keeffe online. Examine other O'Keeffe works, and read what some scholars have said about her contribution to art.

ESSAYS RESPONDING TO THE ARTS

The Plight of High-Status Women

Barbara Dafoe Whitehead

Many people assume that literature is separate from real life—that the reality of books is entirely divorced from the reality of everyday life. However, even a brief study of literature reveals how closely fiction mirrors, records, and chronicles the lives of real humans in real conditions. Literature often focuses on themes that define and give meaning to people's lives. In this essay, Barbara Dafoe Whitehead, a sociologist and widely published author, explains how one type of popular fiction corresponds to the tensions and questions in the lives of professional women. Notice how Whitehead refers to specific books and characters to support her main idea. (Whitehead also appears in Chapter 8.)

Women's tastes in popular reading have long favored two kinds of romances. One is the romance of falling in love and making a brilliant marriage. This centuries-old staple traces the progress of true love from wooing to wedding, through all the confusions and complications along the way. The other is more contemporary and appears prominently in women's magazines, especially those aimed at educated women in the Baby Boom generation. It is the romance of finding a job and making a brilliant career. Here the progress is from first job to first six-figure salary. Complications arise in this narrative as well, but it ends happily with the acquisition of an executive title, a great wardrobe, and a bicoastal social life. What the two romances have in common is the optimistic and essentially liberal faith that a young woman can get what she wants through the shrewd

exercise of her own intelligence, talents, and discerning judgment.

Now, however, a vastly different kind of popular literature is emerging. It is written for and about the privileged members of a new generation. These young women, the highly educated daughters of educated Baby Boomers, are in their twenties and thirties, living and working on their own. Compared with earlier generations, they spend a long time in the mating market, and thus face prolonged exposure to the vicissitudes of love, including multiple breakups, fears of sexually transmitted disease, and infertility anxieties. They must also go through a prolonged period of higher education and career apprenticeship in order to establish themselves in a demanding job market. During these years they may be laid off, downsized, or fired at least once or twice. Neither their love life nor their work life is settled or secure.

The new literature reflects these dual realities. Like traditional women's stories, it deals with themes of love and work, often interweaving the two, but it breaks sharply with the romantic view of both. The defining theme in this literature isn't finding the dream guy or landing the great job but precisely the opposite. It's getting dumped—by a boyfriend or a boss or both. What's more, these books challenge the idea that a young woman blessed with talent and education, and filled with desire and ambition, can get what she wants.

The purest statement of the signature theme in this literature can be found in a batch of self-help books published over the past few years, with titles such as *Dumped!; He Loved Me, He Loves Me Not; The Heartbreak Handbook; Getting Over Him; Exorcising Your Ex; How to Heal the Hurt by Hating;* and *The Woman's Book of Revenge.* There is also a *Complete Idiot's Guide to*

Handling a Breakup. But this theme is not limited to self-help literature. It crosses over into other genres. Suzanne Yalof's *Getting Over John Doe* is a mini-memoir. Candace Bushnell's *Sex and the City* is a collection of her columns in the *New York Observer*. Perhaps the most thorough treatment of the theme is found in recent coming-of-age fiction such as Melissa Bank's critically acclaimed *The Girls' Guide to Hunting and Fishing*, Amy Sohn's *Run Catch Kiss*, Kate Christensen's *In the Drink,* and Laura Zigman's *Animal Husbandry.*

5   Like Jane Austen's *Emma*, the young women in these four books are handsome, clever, and rich in educational advantage (a good education is the contemporary equivalent of propertied wealth). After graduating from elite colleges they move to Manhattan, find minuscule apartments, and seek their fortunes. Eventually they land jobs in the glamorous media or entertainment industry. But their jobs are low-level and short-term; they are temps, part-timers, and freelancers. What's more, their employment prospects don't improve as time goes on: Instead of moving up the career ladder, they get stuck at the level of the temp job. Far from making brilliant careers, they forever remain Girl Fridays.

Their love lives aren't much more successful. They go out with attractive, high-profile men, but these men are not looking for a lifelong mate—they're already encumbered by a wife or a live-in girlfriend, or they have weird habits (wearing mouse slippers to bed) or "multiple substance issues." Far from making brilliant marriages, these smart, funny, talented women forever remain girlfriends or ex-girlfriends.

Consider Claudia Steiner, the twenty-nine-year-old protagonist of *In the Drink*. A Swarthmore graduate, she has spent nine post-college years in New York City in low-level jobs (receptionist, dog walker, phone-sex scriptwriter, temp, waitress, housecleaner, and temp again) when she lands an $18-an-hour position as a personal assistant to and ghostwriter for a celebrity author of mystery romances. Her boss, Jackie del Castellano, turns out to be egotistical and tyrannical; she insists on pretending that Claudia, who is turning

Jackie's literary straw into best-selling gold, is merely providing a fresh insight or two. What's more, Jackie routinely yells at, humiliates, and mistreats Claudia, and finally dumps her.

Claudia's home life isn't much better. She lives alone in a "rathole on an airshaft," eats takeout, and drinks too much. She says, "I was like a tiny version of the city itself: all my systems were a welter of corruption and neglect." And her love life is a mess. Although she is desperately in love with William, her childhood friend, she can't find the "bridge between friendship and romance." Instead she falls into and out of relationships that follow a predictable course: "bantering dive-bar pickup, drunken sex, a rushed exchange of phone numbers afterwards on a subway platform, then other nights with more dive-bar bantering and drunken sex."

Bosses and boyfriends behave a lot alike in the novels. They make nice to you (ever so briefly). Then they dump you. The bosses are invariably vain, capricious, self-centered, and hard-shelled women, not mentors but tormentors. In *The Girls' Guide to Hunting and Fishing*, Jane Rosenal is a rising star in her publishing company until Mimi Howlett, her new boss, arrives. Mimi demotes Jane from the promising position of associate book editor to de facto personal assistant. She also relentlessly criticizes Jane's professional work while generously offering her tips on how to improve her appearance.

10   Jobs go from bad to worse following a firing. After Ariel Steiner, the protagonist in *Run Catch Kiss,* is dumped from her freelance job as a sex columnist and from her temp job in a Manhattan publishing company, she slides from a temp job in a bank in Queens to a part-time job in Brooklyn before hitting bottom with a waitressing job at a twelve-table restaurant in the Village. (Her salary plummets from a high of $18 an hour to a low of $5.50 an hour plus tips.) Jane Rosenal languishes as a temp worker in a bank.

Boyfriends look good on paper—they're a mostly upscale crowd of writers, publishers, artists, fund managers, and investment bankers—but they turn out to be cruel, careless, self-absorbed, socially clueless, and sexually inept. What's more, as prospective mates they're virtually indistinguishable.

In the traditional romance there was one special guy for every special girl. The special girl found her special guy by administering a set of means and morals tests and then using her powers of discernment to pick him out of the pack. Dump literature rejects this premise. It takes the opposing view—that men are all the same. "I've gone out with the short, fat, and ugly," says a woman journalist in *Sex and the City*, "and it doesn't make any difference. They're just as unappreciative and self-centered as the good-looking ones." In short, the existence of many men doesn't guarantee the existence of many choices. There's just One Guy. Take him or leave him. More precisely, take him and he'll leave you.

Part II

When it comes to ending a relationship, male behavior is entirely predictable. According to dump literature, it's over when he says (pick one): (a) "I think maybe we should cool things for a while," (b) "I've been doing a lot of thinking," (c) "God, this week is going to be terrible . . . I'm completely swamped," or (d) "It's not you, it's me."

Once dumped, however, the ex-girlfriends and ex-Girl Fridays don't get downhearted. They get even. In these books the functional equivalent of romantic passion is revenge, served up fast and hot. The self-help books reject the therapeutic approach of grieving over a loss, which was popular in an earlier generation of books aimed mainly at divorcing couples. The best therapy, many of them advise, is to work through your grief on his property. Since many contemporary breakups involve a household as well as a relationship, the revenge schemes focus on destroying or defacing his stuff, including his car and clothing. Some of this is intended as mere fantasy, or played for laughs. But some scenarios recur so frequently—obsessively calling his answering machine and driving past his place, shredding his pictures or clothes, getting mutual friends to spy on him—that it is hard not to assume that they have been battle-tested.

15   For the characters in the novels, writing is the best revenge. As one observes, "It's the ultimate revenge fantasy. You get rich and famous writing about something you're already obsessed with." In *Run Catch Kiss*, Ariel Steiner takes revenge on the disgusting men she goes out with by lampooning them in her popular sex column. After her boyfriend dumps her, Jane Goodall, the protagonist in *Animal Husbandry*, turns to animal research for evidence on why men flee. She invents a theory based on the observation that a bull will ditch an old cow as soon as a new cow appears, and then gets a job writing about her "Old-Cow-New-Cow" theory as a pseudonymous science columnist for a men's magazine. Bosses are likewise targets for revenge. In a twist on the writing-as-revenge tactic, Claudia Steiner strikes back by unwriting: she erases the disk containing the text of her boss's nearly completed book.

Revenge is psychologically expedient, but it does not accomplish lasting personal transformation, much less social change. What is striking is how little this literature protests the cycle of temping and dumping and how little hope it holds out for an end to it. This is all the more surprising because these books are about young women blessed by all the advantages that education, fond parents, and a good therapist can provide. Nevertheless, the challenge for these women is not to avoid, let alone alter, the bleak disjunctions of life but merely to survive them—to get over them and move on.

In a world so blindly indifferent to individual merit and mettle a woman's chief psychological resource is humor, and her only form of activism is to laugh it off and get back in the game. Despite its resignation, this literature is hardly weary or despondent. It is full of riffs, spoofs, quips, and mordant observations about men, women, and their mating and relating problems. The most appealing element of this humor is not its acidulous portrait of men and bosses but its unsparing view of women's weaknesses and self-deceptions. "I couldn't get enough of the most unsuitable men," one character says. Another explains why she and her female boss were attracted to each other: "She was desperate, and I was available."

However, an undercurrent of anxiety runs through the hilarity. After all, what is funny at twenty-five might be less so at thirty-five. Some of the characters are haunted by a vision of themselves in the future, living alone in a dark studio apartment, eating out of an open refrigerator, and earning a meager wage stuffing envelopes at home. And although the fiction resorts to the expedient of the happy ending, the girl-gets-guy resolutions that some employ are thoroughly unconvincing and entirely at odds with everything that has come before.

Of course, no one believes that dump literature offers a documentary portrait of today's educated young women. In its depiction of work it draws heavily on the experience of the authors (themselves young), who, like aspiring actors, may have taken part-time or temp jobs in order to devote themselves more fully to their craft. Theirs is a very narrow slice of work life, hardly representative of the experience of the many post-college single women who enjoy far greater success in their careers than these fictional characters. Nor can the sex lives of these women be taken as typical. Few young women spend every night at clubs or have sex, drunken or otherwise, with a string of partners. What does ring true, however, is the depiction of what might be called the plight of the high-status woman.

20 Given the high divorce rate, today's young women cannot rely on marriage for economic security. Even if they aspire to marriage (and according to survey research, most do), they have to be ready and able to support themselves with their own earnings. This has meant ever-increasing education beyond high school. For women pursuing high-status professions the schooling can extend several years beyond college, well into their twenties. Then, for as much as another decade, such women must invest heavily in developing their careers. Indeed, women on the make adopt the same priorities as men on the make. Work is in the foreground, love in the middle distance or the background. Neither men nor women have the time or a pressing desire for marriage, especially when they can get some marriagelike benefits without

it. So they put it off and enter into relationships that offer some combination of sex, companionship, convenience, and economies of scale.

By the time high-status single men and women reach their early thirties, however, their marriage prospects begin to diverge. Men's educational and career achievements enhance their marriageability and increase the pool of prospective mates, because men tend to marry women of similar or lesser education, and the supply at or below their achievement level is large. For women of the same age and education the opposite is the case: high-status women tend to seek husbands of higher levels of education and achievement, and their lofty status decreases the pool of eligible mates. For men, age is no barrier to attracting women. A few gray hairs can be sexy. For women, age is no asset. A few gray hairs can send a woman racing to the colorist.

Moreover, intragender competition can be fierce. High-status women find themselves in competition not only with other high-status women but also with younger women of lesser education, in lower occupations. The classic example is thirtyish female physicians who, having finished their rigorous training, are ready for marriage. They find themselves up against slightly younger residents and interns along with a large pool of twentysomething nurses and other health professionals. Since the nurses and the physical therapists are in careers that can be disrupted and then picked up again, they may be more willing than the female physicians to stay home and raise children while their husbands pursue careers. This, too, can be a source of competitive disadvantage for the female physicians.

By this stage in life single women of talent and accomplishment begin to grasp the principle that life is unfair in at least one key domain. Men may be able to pursue their careers singlemindedly during their twenties and postpone marriage until their thirties without compromising their fertility or opportunities to find a suitable mate, but women cannot. Just at the moment when they are ready to slow down and share the pleasures of life with similarly successful mates, they look around and find that many of the most desirable men are already taken. What is left is an odd assortment: married men who want a girlfriend on the side; divorced men with serious financial, child-custody, or ex-wife problems; and single men who invite suspicion simply because they're still single. These mating patterns lead to a plaint familiar among upscale single women in their thirties: "There are no good men left."

Thus the career strategy now favored by well-educated young women, in part to establish their own economic viability as a cushion against the likelihood of an eventual divorce, exacts a maddening cost of its own: It makes it less likely that they will marry in the first place. This is a classic case of what is known as goods in conflict.

25   Taken separately, most of the dump books can be read as entertainments; taken together, however, they suggest that an important and recent change is occurring in the lives of educated young women. The romance of love and marriage took its inspiration from a long-standing mating system, but the defining institutions of the old system are breaking down. Courtship is dead. Marriage is in decline. A new mating system is emerging, with its own complications and confusions, including the conflict that faces high-status women. These books are field reports on the new rules of engagement—and disengagement.

Writing Strategies

1. In your own words, write down Whitehead's main idea.

2. Identify one concession Whitehead makes, and explain why it is worth making.

3. Describe Whitehead's introduction and conclusion. How does each function—that is, what does Whitehead seem to be trying to achieve with her introduction and conclusion?

4. Find one colon and semicolon in Whitehead's essay and explain how they function.

Exploring Ideas

1. How does Whitehead view "dump literature"? What point does she think it is making, and how does it make it?

2. How is your view of the plight of high-status women similar to or different from Whitehead's view?

3. Interview a variety of people to discover their views on the present courtship, marriage, and mating system. Attempt to interview people of different backgrounds, ages, and gender. How are their views similar to or different from Whitehead's?

4. You may not read "dump literature," but instead might watch a certain type of movie or television show or read a certain type of magazine. Taken together, what do these movies, shows, or magazines suggest about the status of a certain group?

Ideas for Writing

1. What type of literature, film, music, and so on suggests something interesting about a certain group?

2. What form of art suggests a new trend?

If responding to one of these ideas, go to **Recording the Basics** (page 538) to begin developing ideas for your essay.

The Parting Breath of the Now-Perfect Woman

Chester McCovey

In the margins of this essay, a reader's comments point to key ideas and writing strategies. As you read the essay, consider how the comments might influence your own reading and writing.

Literature often comments on human foibles and social ills. Authors allow fictional characters to live out the worst and best human traits and reveal their psychological and social effects. But the commentary, the meaning behind characters' actions, often lurks quietly in the events of a story; the points are not blatant. Writers like Chester McCovey bring that meaning to the surface. In this essay, McCovey sheds light on the meaning lurking In Nathaniel Hawthorne's short story "The Birthmark." Notice that McCovey works to make this 19th-century story relevant to the lives of his readers.

Writing Strategies

Introduces main idea: "The Birthmark is relevant today." It has public resonance.

Uses direct quote to convey story's theme. Indents long quote and does not use quotation marks.

States a main idea and supports it with a quote from the story.

Quotation marks are used because a character from the story is speaking, not because the source is quoted.

A masterpiece of literature offers its readers unlimited opportunities for thought, analysis, discovery, insight, interpretation. Though an old story's language may be difficult for some, if that old story is a masterpiece, its characters and plot develop a timeless theme as relevant today as it was yesterday. Nathaniel Hawthorne's "The Birthmark" is such a story.

Hawthorne's theme is clear. In the story's opening paragraph we read:

> The higher intellect, the imagination, the spirit, and even the heart might all find their congenial ailment in pursuits which, as some of their ardent votaries believed, would ascend from one step of powerful intelligence to another, until the philosopher should lay his hand on the secret of creative force and perhaps make new worlds for himself. We know not whether Aylmer possessed this degree of faith in man's ultimate control over Nature.

See what I mean about the language? But the point here is that even though we now speak—and write—differently, Aylmer *did* apparently possess this degree of faith in man's ultimate control over nature. And in attempting to remove his young wife's only blemish—a small, hand-shaped birthmark on her left cheek—he "removes" her very life. The story's climax comes when after much science, Aylmer is successful—the birthmark is gone:

> "By Heaven! It is well-nigh gone!" said Aylmer to himself, in almost irrepressible ecstasy. "I can scarcely trace it now.

Exploring Ideas

Claim: old story still relevant—timeless theme.

Man believes he can control nature.

Don't mess with nature?

Success! success! And now it is like the faintest rose color. The lightest flush of the blood across her cheek would overcome it. But she is so pale!"

And while Georgiana is now "perfect" and Aylmer's science has been "successful," Georgiana is, of course, not just "pale." She is dying . . . then dead. And the young beauty—who because she had been told so often that her birthmark was a charm was, in her own words, "simple enough to imagine that it might be so"—now speaks her dying words:

> "My poor Aylmer," she repeated, with a more than human tenderness, "you have aimed loftily; you have done nobly. Do not repent that with so high and pure a feeling, you have rejected the best the earth could offer. Aylmer, dearest Aylmer, I am dying."

Reading "The Birthmark" for a second time, one plainly sees that the author laid everything out in the first paragraph. It could, of course, turn out no other way. And today's reader, raised on "Frankenstein" and stories like it, is probably not surprised by the ending. After the bombing of Hiroshima and Nagasaki, Americans spent their 1950s watching ("Birthmark"-like) movies in which havoc-wreaking mutants warned us about the dangers of man's faith in his ultimate control over Nature. Yet Hawthorne's masterpiece is so perfectly crafted, one eagerly reads on to find out what is about to happen.

As a masterpiece of literature, "The Birthmark" deserves much attention: attention to Hawthorne's plot, which contains perfect foreshadowing throughout; attention to his characters—poor Aylmer, and simple Georgiana who one cannot help but fall in love with; attention to word choice and sentence structure, though these are not so easy to be attracted to because of our modern tastes in writing. And also deserving attention, the theme of the story—a story written in the early nineteenth century—is not only *worth* pondering today— at the dawn of a twenty-first century—but it would be, in fact, difficult to imagine how someone could *not* ponder it.

5   The attentive reader is already a step ahead of me: cloning, stem cell research, genetic engineering. The incidents of humans "perfecting" nature—or fiddling with nature in attempts to perfect it—are forever in today's headlines. But cloned sheep and the possibility of cloned people is not the only science "The Birthmark" asks today's reader to think about.

Side annotations:

The quotation shows the tension between the natural world and human arrogance.

Develops idea with historical and literary references.

Discusses literary elements of the story: plot, style, theme.

Thinks he had success, but she is dying.

He rejects "the best the earth" could offer.

We are used to such stories now: since A-bomb, technological advances.

Why it's a masterpiece of literature: plot, style (word choice, sentence structure), theme (timeless, still relevant).

How it's relevant (public resonance): cloning, stem cell research, genetic engineering.

Relates "The Birthmark" to today's world. Shows how it's relevant.

Concession

Discusses further public resonance: We attempt to perfect nature today as Aylmer did in the story.

Summary of the story with a few small quotes.

Quotes are used sparingly—worked into a summary of the story.

McCovey restating his main idea.

While Georgiana's birthmark represents abstract imperfection, and Aylmer's faith in man represents humankind's efforts to perfect nature in general, the birthmark obviously reminds us of today's little "imperfections": (too small) breasts, a (too large) nose, (no) chin, (fat) thighs, and so on. The reader should not miss the point. No one is saying that cleft palates or clubbed feet should not be corrected—at least no one is saying that in this essay. But Georgiana's birthmark was "of the smallest pygmy size" and her lovers were "wont to say that some fairy at her birth hour had laid her tiny hand upon the infant's cheek, and left this impress there in token of the magic endowments that were to give her such sway over all hearts. Many a desperate swain would have risked life for the privilege of pressing his lips to the mysterious hand." The "mad scientist" is us—eager to erase these "imperfections" of Nature.

Perhaps the story's most important warning—indeed! It *is* the story's most important warning—comes so subtly that one might overlook it. When Georgiana, for the first time, goes into her husband's off-limits laboratory where he is working on one last concoction, she is scolded for her lack of faith in him. But she *has* faith and tells him so, and then she fails to tell him her reason for coming. She has felt a "sensation in the fatal birthmark, not painful, but which induced a restlessness throughout her system." One can hardly imagine the sensation was nothing at all, that it was just an excuse for a master storyteller to prolong his story. It is also unlikely that this sensation was a *negative* reaction to Aylmer's first treatment—after all, it was a "sensation" and it was not "painful." We thus imagine that Aylmer's first treatment was on its way to working, then he went too far.

Earlier in the story Aylmer shows Georgiana a powerful drug, and says, "With a few drops of [it] in a vase of water, freckles may be washed away as easily as the hands are cleansed." When asked, "Is it with this lotion that you intend to bathe my cheek?" Aylmer replies, "Oh, no . . . this is merely superficial. Your case demands a remedy that shall go deeper." And so, Aylmer's remedy ends up going too far. To him, the birthmark is not "superficial," but something that "has clutched its grasp into [her] being." His cure *does* work. The birthmark is removed. And his young wife is perfect, just as he planned . . . but only for a moment.

Great literature survives—it survives time, and multiple readings, and critical analysis, and skeptical hearts and minds. And it not only survives, but it thrives. Read "The Birthmark" twice and you will know what I mean. Hawthorne's theme is just as relevant

What is beauty? What is perfection? How does "society" determine this?

Aylmer went too far. We, today, are going too far (McC claims). Are we?

Can we improve on nature? Have we gone too far in trying? Are we out of control?

today. And Georgiana's dying words express the real complexity of the issue.

Pointing out the complexity of this issue.

10   As for physical imperfection in the twenty-first century, it seems odd that on one level we promote respect for all sorts of human "imperfections," yet on another level, we strive as we do to eliminate them whenever we can. It seems odd because so many times they are not imperfections at all.

Have we gone too far in trying to improve what is natural? And what is the cost?

Concludes with relevant quote from the story.

Alas! It was too true! The fatal hand had grappled with the mystery of life, and was the bond by which an angelic spirit kept itself in union with a mortal frame. As the last crimson tint of the birthmark—that sole token of human imperfection—faded from her cheek, the parting breath of the now-perfect woman passed into the atmosphere, and her soul, lingering a moment near her husband, took its heavenward flight.

Writing Strategies

1. Describe McCovey's voice, and identify several specific passages to support your description.

2. Identify at least one counterargument McCovey makes. What other counterargument might he have made to strengthen his argument?

3. Study the ways in which McCovey refers to the story "The Birthmark" in his essay. Look for quotes and paraphrases. When he quotes, look for (a) long passages set off by themselves, (b) shorter passages quoted within McCovey's sentences, and (c) individual words from the story worked into McCovey's sentences. Based on McCovey's essay (and at least two others in this text) write a one- or two-page essay explaining various ways in which writers can refer to sources (in this case a story) in their text.

4. How does McCovey convey the point of "The Birthmark" to the reader? How does he convey the point of his own essay to the reader?

Exploring Ideas

1. In a paragraph, explain how McCovey connects Hawthorne's story to 21st-century America.

2. State McCovey's main idea in no more than a few sentences, and then compare your statement with those of several classmates. Discuss the similarities and differences in the way you and your classmates understand McCovey's essay. Then revise your statement of his main idea, and explain how your understanding changed, if it did, through discussion.

3. Explain McCovey's main idea to several friends, coworkers, and family members, asking for their input. Do others agree or disagree with McCovey's ideas? Why?

Ideas for Writing

1. How is the theme of a short story written before 1850 still relevant—even more relevant—today?

2. What work of art relates to a contemporary issue that concerns you?

If responding to one of these ideas, go to **Recording the Basics** (page 538) to begin developing ideas for your essay.

Hip-Hop: A Roadblock or Pathway to Black Empowerment?

Geoffrey Bennett

Throughout American history, popular art forms and entertainment have pushed against mainstream tastes and mores: slam poetry, jazz, vaudeville, swing, rock and roll, punk, heavy metal, rap, hip-hop. Each of these shocked the sensibilities of the mainstream culture. And when they gained popularity, writers, politicians, church groups, sociologists, and thinkers of all stripes asked questions about the state of the civilization. In the past twenty years, hip-hop music has been the source (and target) of such commentary. In this essay, Geoffrey Bennett (former editor-in-chief of the *Maroon Tiger* college newspaper at Morehouse College) explores the relationship between hip-hop and the black community. The essay originally appeared in the *Black Collegian Online* (2001).

In the early 1980s, a highly percussive, cadenced, and repetitious musical form seeped from the inner city streets of the South Bronx to a virtually exclusive African-American audience. Harbingered by originators such as Run DMC, the Sugar Hill Gang, Public Enemy, Afrika Bambaata, and others, the medium was a simple reflection of the daily lives of its creators with topics ranging from the trivial, such as the style of one's new Adidas sneakers, to the significant, like the infuriation spurred by police harassment.

Rap music, as it came to be known, lacked major commercial support in its early stages, and, as a result, it was authentic and unaffected; it was truly "CNN for the streets," as Chuck D once commented. Twenty years later, however, hip-hop culture has since flooded mainstream culture, and rap music is as prevalent in suburban homes as it once was in its native environment, moving from American subculture to the forefront of American attention. "Hip-hop is more powerful than any American cultural movement we've ever had," said rap music impresario Russell Simmons.

Hip-hop is one of the fastest-growing music genres in the United States, accounting for $1.84 billion in sales last year out of a $14.3 billion total for the U.S. recording industry, according to industry statistics. Interestingly, nearly 70 percent of those sales are to white suburban youth, a striking transformation considering rap music's beginnings. Most importantly, perhaps, rap music and its associated hip-hop culture have become a new component of the Black cultural aesthetic. With its rhythmical roots firmly planted in African tradition, hip-hop music is more than just musical expression. For some, it is a way of life, affecting their speech, style of dress, hairstyle, and overall disposition.

Like any other expressive art form, rappers have tested the boundaries of social responsibility, legality, free speech, and old-fashioned "good taste." Labeled as misogynistic, reckless, and even criminal, rappers endured years of public scrutiny with African Americans among some of their most relentless critics. After years of incessant scrutiny, hip-hop mogul Russell Simmons organized a three-day hip-hop music summit for 200 rappers, industry executives, and African-American politicians, the first event of its kind. Sean Combs, LL Cool J, Queen Latifah, Wyclef Jean, Wu-Tang Clan, Chuck D, Jermaine Dupri, KRS-1, Luther Campbell, Ja Rule, and Talib Kweli were just a few of the influential hip-hop artists in attendance at the conference held last June in New York City.

5   Stars joined forces with some of Black America's intellectual and political elite, including NAACP president Kweisi Mfume; Urban League president Hugh Price; Nation of Islam minister Louis Farrakhan; Martin Luther King, III, leader of the Southern Christian Leadership Council; Georgia Democratic congressional representative Cynthia McKinney; and authors Cornel West and Michael Eric Dyson. The summit ended with musicians and industry executives agreeing to follow voluntary guidelines to advise parents of music's lyrical content while vowing to protect rap artists' freedom of speech by fighting Congressional efforts to censor the music. Minister Louis Farrakhan of the Nation of Islam, one of the political activists who attended the summit,

told rappers, "You've now got to accept the responsibility you've never accepted. You are the leaders of the youth of the world."

Today's African-American college students, many of whom as youth were the original fans during rap music's formative years, still remain avid rap music connoisseurs. Rap music, however, has taken a decidedly different direction in recent years. Since rap music is clearly a profitable commercial commodity, rappers consequently perpetuate images and stereotypes that will sell their products, ranging from the excessively violent to the extravagantly wealthy. "Many rappers do not live the type of lives they claim. Those that claim to be affluent often are not, and those that claim to be poor gang-bangers are often millionaires. Fortunately, most college students have the ability to decipher between rap's glamorous image and the realities of life.

A problem arises for the younger, impressionable audience, many of whom buy into rap's surface image," said Morehouse College Student Government Association president Christopher J. Graves.

As role models, accepting of the designation or not, rappers have a unique responsibility to be cognizant of their message and their intended audience. Since American pop culture reveres stardom, rappers often garner more attention and respect than they deserve. Consequently, rap music and hip-hop culture have the power to either adversely or positively affect African Americans in specific, and the larger culture in general. While a summit on rap music cannot adequately address all of its dilemmas, a dialogue between interested parties must continue in order to preserve the distinctive art form, while protecting the rich heritage of the African-American cultural aesthetic.

Writing Strategies

1. Describe how Bennett's introduction functions. What is he attempting to do? How does it assist the reader in understanding the rest of the essay? What, if anything, else do you think it does?

2. Describe Bennett's voice and evaluate its appropriateness for this subject matter. Provide several passages to support your evaluation.

3. How does Bennett get his main idea across to the reader? Does he state his main idea or imply it? What type of background information and evidence does he provide?

4. Evaluate the effectiveness of Bennett's sources. How do they help the reader to understand his argument or to accept his claims?

Exploring Ideas

1. How does Bennett encourage the reader to look at hip-hop?

2. How does Bennett's idea fit into a larger discussion? That is, how can what he says be applied not just to hip-hop but to other art forms?

3. Observe the relationship between different art forms (hip-hop, country music, film, painting, etc.) and people in your community. How does art seem to influence their thoughts and behavior? How do they seem to influence the art form?

4. In addition to art, what influences people? Go out and observe how people in your community choose to live—how they move around, shop, eat, work, play. What are the major influences on what they wear, what they eat, how they get around, what they do for a living, what they do in their spare time?

Ideas for Writing

1. What responsibility do you think rappers have? What responsibility do artists in some other art form have?

2. What problems arise when people buy into the surface images of some particular art form?

If responding to one of these ideas, go to **Recording the Basics** (page 538) to begin developing ideas for your essay.

The Faces of the *Mona Lisa*

Vincent Pomarède

It is hard to imagine anyone who is not familiar in some way with Leonardo DaVinci's *Mona Lisa*. As Vincent Pomarède, curator in the Paintings Department of the Louvre Museum in Paris, says, "the *Mona Lisa* is beyond doubt the best known painting in the world. . . ." But our knowledge of such famous works (the *Mona Lisa,* Beethoven's Fifth Symphony, Shakespeare's *Macbeth*) is often limited. Pomarède's essay provides necessary background information about the painting. Based on Pomarède's background information and the painting itself, you might begin to consider why the *Mona Lisa* is the best-known painting in the world.

What is the mysterious connection that is established over time between a work of art and its public? What are the factors, profound motivations and secret techniques which can explain that the Winged Victory of Samothrace, the Venus de Milo, or the *Angelus* of Jean-François Millet have become universal objects of admiration and contemplation, of adoration almost, to the extent that all modern mediums, from end-of-the-year calendars to advertising, have used them and even sometimes excessively so? The study of the unequalled success over three centuries of Leonardo da Vinci's *Mona Lisa* will perhaps enable a better understanding of the numerous and complex motivations which make visitors of a museum only remember a single work from amongst thousands of others. Indeed, the *Mona Lisa* is beyond doubt the best-known painting in the world, today completely identified with the Louvre Museum and even with the general notion of art. If we were able to penetrate the origins of its creation, its aesthetic qualities, and its history following the death of its creator, we would perhaps be able to identify some rules explaining a work of art's success.

It is possible to identify four areas of research which are closely connected to the *Mona Lisa*'s unequalled success with its public: the marginal, whimsical, and brilliant personality of its creator, Leonardo da Vinci (1452–1519); the perfection of his pictorial technique; the mysteries, which are moreover still unresolved, surrounding the identity of the model who posed for the work; the developments in its history, which are as surprising and numerous as a detective story.

Was Leonardo da Vinci a painter, engineer, inventor, or philosopher?

Born in 1452 in a small Toscan village called Vinci, which gave him its name, Leonardo da Vinci was the illegitimate son of the village's lawyer and one of his servants, Catarina Vacca. Statements concerning his appearance and personality differ, particularly as legend grew up very early on in his biographical accounts. He is sometimes described as a prodigiously strong colossus, capable of bending a horseshoe in his hands, and often as a young adolescent, effeminate and dreamy. He is sometimes presented to us as a man who loved physical exercise and violent sports, sometimes as an adolescent playing the lyre and singing with perfection. His artistic gifts must however have already appeared during his childhood, because in 1469, at the age of 17, he had already spent three years in the studio of the Florentine painter and sculptor Andrea Verrochio (1435–1488). In this famous artist's studio, in the company of other important painters such as Sandro Botticelli or Perugino, he spent thirteen years learning the technique of painting and the secrets of the execution of a picture. He also began to study the subjects which were then considered indispensable for an artist: mathematics, perspective, geometry, and all the sciences of observation and study of the natural environment. He also began to study architecture and sculpture.

After completing his training, he began his career as a painter with portraits and religious paintings, receiving commissions from the leading citizens or monasteries of Florence. But, from this period onwards, it is very difficult (and this continues throughout his career) to know with certitude whether he considered himself as a painter, multidisciplinary artist, or engineer. The limits between the professions had not then been fixed as they are today and a man of talent could move with ease from one function to another. Leonardo then came under the protection of the most influential person in Florence, Lorenzo di Medici, named the Magnificent, a politician and exceptionally rich patron of the arts, who brought him many clients and whom, in 1482, sent him to Milan to serve the Duke Sforza. He wrote at the time an astonishing letter to the Duke of Milan, reading like a curriculum vitae, in which he revealed his ambitions as engineer, inventor, and also soldier: "I can build very light bridges, solid, robust, easily transportable, to pursue and sometimes flee from the enemy [. . .] I also have the means to make bombardments, very practical and easy to transport, which throw stones almost like a storm, terrorizing the enemy with their smoke [. . .] In peace time, I believe that I am also able to give complete satisfaction to anyone, whether in architecture, the building of public and private buildings, or in conveying water from one place to another."

5   Later, he placed his engineering talents at the service of the cities of Pisa and Venice, the sovereigns of Mantua, the Este family, and, of course, the King of France, François I, who invited him to come and work in the Loire valley, where the monarch then resided. This unusual quality of being able to tackle any subject with talent (during his lifetime he was to be better known as a hydraulic engineer than as a painter!) astonished all his contemporaries, as did also the insatiable curiosity with which he ceaselessly studied natural phenomena: "Where does urine come from? Where does milk come from? How does food spread through the veins? Where does drunkenness come from? And vomiting? And gravel and stone? [. . .] Where do tears come from?", he confided to the pages of his notebooks in a continual quest for answers to every imaginable kind of question. His perfect knowledge of anatomy, the effects of light, and the most complex chemical combinations obviously guided his career as painter and, from his first masterpieces the *Virgin on the Rocks* (Paris, Louvre Museum), begun in 1483, the *Last Supper* (Milan, Convent of Santa Maria del Gracia), which he painted in 1493, or the *Battle of Anghiari* (missing), for which he

obtained a commission in 1503 after a hard struggle with Michelangelo, he showed to what an extent his scientific and technological knowledge enriched the creation of his paintings.

Even though his technical experimentations in painting were not always successful—the *Last Supper* and the *Battle of Anghiari* were ruined by badly mastered pictorial innovations, which attracted him the contempt and jeering of certain professionals—Leonardo da Vinci was famous for the unequalled level of perfection of his portraits and some of his religious paintings, such as *Saint Anne, the Virgin and the Infant Jesus* (Paris, Louvre Museum).

The perfect technique of the *Mona Lisa*

Indeed, the search for perfection was a true obsession with Leonardo da Vinci: "Tell me, tell me, has one ever finished anything?", he groaned in his notebooks, in which he frequently insisted upon his desire to equal the perfection of divine creation in his own artistic creations.

Painted on a thin backing of poplar wood, which is now extremely fragile (this is why it is today preserved behind a glass case) the *Mona Lisa* is an exemplary creation, thanks to the subtle effects of light on flesh and the panache of the landscape in the painting's background. The modeling of the face is astonishingly realistic. Leonardo executed the painting with patience and virtuosity: After preparing the wooden panel with several layers of coating, he first of all drew his motif directly onto the picture, before painting it in oil, adding very weak turpentine, which enabled him to paint on innumerable layers of transparent color, known as glaze, and to endlessly remodel the face. The glaze, skillfully worked, heightens the effects of light and shade on the face, constituting what Leonardo himself called "sfumato." This technique enables the perfect imitation of flesh, due to refined treatment of the human figure plunged into half-obscurity or chiaroscuro, and enabled Leonardo to satisfy his preoccupation with realism.

During his lifetime, Leonardo was indeed above all famous for his evident talent for imitating nature to perfection and when his first biographer, the painter Vasari, described the *Mona Lisa,* he above all insisted on the work's realism: "Its limpid eyes had the sparkle of life: ringed by reddish and livid hues, they were bordered by lashes whose execution required the greatest delicacy. The eyelashes, in places thicker or more sparse according to the arrangement of the pores, could not be truer. The nose, with its ravishing delicate, pink nostrils, was life itself. [. . .] In the hollow of the throat, the attentive spectator can catch the beating of the veins." Through "sfumato" Leonardo could attain one of his primary artistic objectives, that of interesting himself mainly in his model's personality: "The good painter has essentially two things to represent: the individual and the state of his mind," said Leonardo. To paint the soul rather than the body was in fact the ultimate aim of his work and the "sfumato," lighting the portrait through "chiaroscuro," accentuated the work's mysteries: "to plunge things into light is to plunge them into the infinite."

10   It is here important to recall to what extent the question of the model's realism is connected to its identity. To this day, we still do not know whether Leonardo da Vinci faithfully represented an existing model, whether he idealized a portrait of a woman of his circle, or if he entirely imagined a type of universal woman.

The mystery of the model's identity

Every kind of possibility, including the most far-fetched, has been envisaged concerning the model's identity: Isabelle of Este, who reigned at Mantua during Leonardo da Vinci's stay there (we know a drawing by him showing her); a mistress of Giuliano di Medici's or of Leonardo himself; perhaps an ideal woman; and even an adolescent boy dressed as a woman, or possibly a self-portrait.

The first statement concerning the model for the *Mona Lisa* dates from the last years of Leonardo's life, and talks of a portrait "of a certain Florentine lady done from life at the request of the magnificent Giuliano di Medici." We know that Leonardo da Vinci took the portrait to France during his stay at the court of François I (and no doubt he was still working on it), but he had begun it during his stay in Florence between 1503 and 1506. It therefore appears likely that the model, whoever it was, could have been Florentine. A later second statement by Vasari described the portrait of Mona Lisa, the wife of a Florentine gentleman, Francesco del Giocondo. This latter, a rich bourgeois holding a position of political authority in his city, really existed, but we know little about the life of his wife, Lisa Gherardini, born in 1479. We do know that she had married del Giocondo in 1495 but we in fact have no proof that she could have been the mistress of a Medici. A later anonymous statement creates a certain confusion, linking the *Mona Lisa* to a portrait of Francesco del Giocondo—the origin of the risky idea that it is the portrait of a man. Lastly, a later text, dated 1625, refers to a "half-figure portrait of a certain Gioconda," which permanently gave the painting its French title.

Even today, we possess no final proof of the identity of the woman shown by Leonardo. Indeed, it is astonishing to consider that we now remember more the universal aspects of the picture (the evident idealization of the portrait, the painter's imaginative rendering of the landscape, the balance of the model's posture), more than the reference to a personality who really existed. Even if he painted a woman's face with realism, it is clear that Leonardo lastingly freed himself from any obligations to accuracy to search for an abstract description of the human figure.

The detective story of the history of the *Mona Lisa*

These intrinsic qualities in Leonardo's work, which had already impressed art lovers and professionals, would not have sufficed to give the *Mona Lisa* its worldwide success if its history had not also been exceptional.

15   Acquired by François I, either directly from Leonardo da Vinci during his stay in France or upon his death from his heirs, the painting remained in the royal collections from the beginning of the sixteenth century

to the creation of the Central Arts Museum at the Louvre in 1793. We know that it was kept at Versailles under the reign of Louis XIV and that it was in the Tuileries during the First Empire. Since the Restoration, the *Mona Lisa* has always remained in the Louvre Museum, a key piece of the national collections. Studied by historians and painters, who copied it frequently, the *Mona Lisa* became world famous after its theft in 1911. On August 21, 1911, a slightly mad Italian painter, Vincenzo Peruggia, stole it to return it to its country of origin. After a long police enquiry, during which everyone was suspected, including the Cubist painters and the poet Guillaume Apollinaire, who had one day shouted that "the Louvre should be burnt," the *Mona Lisa* was rediscovered in Italy almost two years later and rehung in the Louvre, treated with the honors accorded to a head of state, after having occupied, throughout this period, the front pages of the world's newspapers.

Since then, the painting has truly become a cult object, considered as sacred to an excessive degree.

The two journeys which she made during the twentieth century, in 1963 to the United States and in 1974 to Japan, were unprecedented successes, the work being welcomed by the crowds like a film star. These two journeys moreover played a major role in building its notoriety, as did the theft of 1911, and the Japanese and American publics have ever since worshipped the work which spent a few weeks in their countries and in front of which hundreds of thousands of visitors filed.

An exceptional artist and faultless technique, combined with the mysteries of its model and its history, were therefore at the origin of the extraordinary craze for the *Mona Lisa* which no other work of art has up until now known. Perhaps too the fact that the painting shows a human figure, that is to say neither a religious or profane scene, subjects that always date and are forgotten as soon as their fashions fade, nor a landscape or still life, subjects sometimes too intellectual, surely explains the crowds' passion. Indeed, the portrait genre, which is accessible for the public, has always been popular, and did not Leonardo himself already seem to predict the portrait's success when he wrote: "Can you not see that amongst human beauties, it is a beautiful face that stops passers by, and not the rich ornaments . . . ", thereby insisting on the mysteries of the look that is exchanged between the visitor and the strange, smiling face.

Writing Strategies

1. Based on his introduction, how does Pomarède intend to discuss the painting? Why does he think it is worth discussing?

2. What is Pomarède's main point about the *Mona Lisa*?

3. How does Pomarède support his main idea?

4. Describe Pomarède's voice as a writer. Why is or isn't it inviting to the reader?

5. Pomarède's essay was published on the Louvre Museum's website; he is curator in the Paintings Department at the Louvre. How does Pomarède's position and the place of publication (the Louvre website) influence the content and style of his writing?

Exploring Ideas

1. How important is Leonardo da Vinci's biography to the popularity of the *Mona Lisa*?

2. Interview others regarding their impression of the *Mona Lisa*. What do they know about the painting, and how do they know it? Then in groups, discuss what people know and don't know about the painting. Why do you think they should know more about it?

3. What other works of art are most people familiar with? How might knowing more about those works benefit them?

4. What work of art is more important or more popular because of its history, and why?

Ideas for Writing

1. What work of art expresses "the soul rather than the body"?

2. Why is a particular work of art as popular as it is?

If responding to one of these ideas, go to **Recording the Basics** (page 538) to begin developing ideas for your essay.

Outside Reading

Find an article that discusses a particular piece or type of art (novel, painting, poem, short story, and so on), and print it out or make a photocopy. It might examine the art's significance, worth, or general relationship to society. To conduct an electronic search of journals and magazines, go to your library's periodical database or to InfoTrac College Edition (http://infotrac.galegroup.com/ itweb/). For your library database, perform a keyword search, or go to the main search box and click on "keywords" for InfoTrac College Edition. In the search box, you might enter a genre or form of art (such as *modern painting, poetry, contemporary fiction*), or a particular artist or work of art (such as *Hillman* or *The Sound and the Fury*). Focus your search by entering other keywords, such as art, society, culture, value. You might even explore specific topics; for example: *women and Hispanic and poetry* or *rap and art and society.* (When performing keyword searches, avoid using phrases or articles such as *a, an, the;* instead, use nouns separated by *and.*) The search results will yield lists of journal and magazine articles. This same strategy can be used with a newspaper database.

You can also search the Internet. Try the search engine Google.com. Like most Internet search engines, Google combines keywords (nouns and proper nouns), but Google does not require joining words (Boolean operators) such as *and.* In the search box, try various word combinations, such as those above.

The purpose of this assignment is to explore the range of options in writing about art. As you read through this chapter, keep the text you have discovered close by and notice the elements and strategies the writer uses. Depending on your instructor's suggestions, do one or more of the following:

1. Notice how the writer applies various strategies from this chapter. On the hard copy or photocopy:
   - Highlight the thesis if it is stated. If the thesis is implied, write it in your own words.
   - Identify (or write in the margins) passages that are argumentative, evaluative, descriptive, narrative.
   - Identify any counterarguments or concessions (elements of argument from Chapter 6).

2. Analyze the strategies employed by the writer. The following questions may be helpful.
   - Do you believe the writer shows the public resonance of the art? How?
   - How does the writer support his or her point about the art?
   - Who is the audience for this text?
   - How does the audience influence the rhetorical tools?

3. Write at least three "Writing Strategies" questions for the article.

4. Write at least three "Exploring Ideas" questions for the article you found.

5. Write two "Ideas for Writing" questions, such as the ones following the essays in this book.

INVENTION

"Only through art can we emerge from ourselves and know what another person sees."

—Marcel Proust

For this chapter, the writing project focuses on discovering something specific about a work of art. Use the following sections to develop ideas for your essay. The **Point of Contact** questions will help you choose a subject (an artistic work or form of art) and collect some basic information about it. The **Analysis** section will help you closely examine different elements of the work. The **Public Resonance** section will help you consider the relevance of the work to your readers. In the **Thesis** section, you will come to terms with a specific point and in **Rhetorical Tools** develop supporting ideas. The Invention questions in each section are not meant to be answered directly in your final written assignment; they will help you explore the subject and develop ideas.

Choosing a subject for your writing might be a simple process of choosing your favorite literary text, musical piece, or visual work. However, your favorite work of art may not be the best subject to examine. Remember that you are not simply explaining how much you like a particular work; rather, you are exploring what the work, or a particular form of art, means for people, what it offers an audience. To that end, look for a work or set of works that might have some value beyond your likes and dislikes.

POINT OF CONTACT

As in all the previous chapters of this book, the Point of Contact section here is designed not only to help you find a subject, but also to create focus: to draw your attention to details about the subject that might otherwise go unnoticed. First, choose a literary text, a musical work, or a visual piece.

- Browse through a literary anthology or go to a library and search for a collection of short stories or poems by a writer you have never read.

- Visit a museum or browse through an art book (such as Gardner's *Art Through the Ages*).

- Search a library database or the Internet for an artist or writer of particular ethnicity or from a particular time period. For example, you might try a search using words such as: *African-American writers, Hispanic writers, women writers, contemporary painters, Renaissance painters, Impressionists.*

- Watch an artistic film. For ideas, check out the following websites: The Berkeley Art Museum and Pacific Film Archive (http://www.bampfa.berkeley.edu), The British Academy of Film and Television Arts (http://www.bafta.org), The Independent Movie Database (http://indie.imdb.com).

Recording the Basics

After you have found your subject (work of art), address the questions below that correspond to your chosen work.

Literary works Literature comes in many categories or genres: drama, poetry, novels, short stories, and an unlimited combination of all these. Within each genre, individual pieces can vary widely; in fact, many of the most successful and widely read authors consistently transcend the rules or conventions of a genre.

- What is the *plot* (the arrangement or course of events)?
- What is the *setting* (the time and place in which events occur)?
- Who is the *narrator* (the main voice speaking to the audience)?
- Who are the characters?

Musical works Musical works include everything from Mozart to hip-hop. Like other works of art, musical pieces may transcend conventions and go beyond the audience's expectations. While the lyrics of a song may point to themes, create characters, or even develop a story, the music itself influences the listener's understanding of the lyrics.

- If the piece contains lyrics, what events, ideas, or feelings do they communicate?
- If the piece does not have lyrics, what moods does it take the listener through?
- What is the *ensemble* (the collection and placement of instruments or voices in the performance)?
- What is the *arrangement* (the structure of the song)?

Visual arts Painting, sculpture, architecture, and a vast array of other mediums, such as weaving and embroidery, are all types of visual arts. All of these can communicate complex ideas to an audience; of course, the communicative tools are vastly different than in literary and musical arts. Visual artists must rely on images, color, and placement to convey meaning, although titles can help establish a concept.

- What is the title?
- What is the *medium* (the materials used in creation of the work)?
- What is the *form* (the shape and structure)?
- What is the *composition* (the placement or arrangement of images and color)?

Film Because movies often depend on celebrity actors to live out oversimplified, predictable, and formulaic plots, many people do not consider movies to be art. However, many movies, or films, attempt to do more. Like a good painting, short story, or ballad, they attempt to provoke new ideas and insights, and some even attempt to redefine audiences' expectations.

- What is the title?
- What is the plot?
- Who are the main characters?
- What is the setting?

ANALYSIS

While knowing the basic features of a work is important, we have to go further: We have to learn how those basic features function in the work. Either with a small group of peers or alone, ask questions to examine each feature of your subject and discover how it functions. For instance, when considering the title, you might ask:

- Why is the title important?
- What does the title make people think?
- Should a work of art have a title?

As you explore the features of your subject, use the categories and questions that follow. Ask what each feature means, what it does for the work, and how it might affect its audience.

In analysis, it is easy to trick oneself into seeing an answer where another question is waiting. And often the easy answer is the least valuable.

Themes

In the same way that essays have thesis statements, artistic works have themes, which are controlling ideas. The following themes appear in countless films, songs, and literary works, and in visual art: Governments produce and conceal corruption; love overcomes selfishness; nature provides freedom; racism destroys lives; technology can control humans; the grace of god redeems human life; war is not a romantic adventure. Themes may be made obvious (as they tend to be in songs) or they can lurk with more subtlety.

- What themes emerge in the images or plot?
- What point, idea, or issue does the artist explicitly bring out?
- What hidden idea or issue lurks in the piece?

Conflict

When you think of conflict, struggle, or crisis, you may imagine overt struggle, such as hostility between people, wars between countries, people against time. (These are the kinds of conflicts that typically propel Hollywood movies.) However, artistic works often deal with more abstract conflicts, such as moral, psychological, or spiritual dilemmas. The conflict may not be obvious; it can be subtle or implied by the placement of details.

- How are conflicts dealt with or resolved?
- How does conflict or tension help to develop the theme?
- How does the conflict prompt the audience to think differently?

Characters

Art, especially fiction and drama, often shows the development or evolution of characters. How a character appears or changes throughout a story can illustrate key points to the audience. Sometimes the changes are subtle—or even different than what the character believes about him- or herself. It is up to the audience to understand those changes and how they impact the whole work of art.

- How do the characters evolve or transform throughout the text?
- Who or what might the characters represent?
- What human quality (weakness or strength) do the characters illustrate?
- What do the characters show the audience about human life—or life in general?

Conventions

All art forms have conventions, or commonly accepted strategies, for conveying ideas. Some conventions are so common that we do not even think about them: Novels depend on a series of chapters that help create the story; contemporary pop songs have repeating choruses. Sometimes artists work to transcend the conventions, or break the rules, of a given genre, which may result in a piece that seems bizarre at first glance or listen. However, breaking the rules is often the most vital aspect of art. When artists make audiences stand back and wonder, "What's really going on here?" they are actively promoting a new way of thinking.

- How is the piece a typical example of its genre? (For example, how is it a typical pop song or short story?)
- How does the piece challenge or transcend the conventions of the genre?
- What value does the piece have? What does it offer to people?
- Why is this work especially valuable?

Style

Artists have particular characteristics, or styles, that distinguish their work from others'. Style may be associated with a consistent artistic device or way of representing ideas. The novelist William Faulkner, for instance, is known for lengthy and complex sentences, and Emily Dickinson is known for short lines of poetry separated with dashes. Style affects how ideas are communicated and impressions are made. Style also factors into mediums such film. Certain directors such as Jim Jarmusch, Spike Lee, or Tim Burton have established distinct and recognizable styles.

- What is the artist's style?
- How does it affect the ideas being communicated?
- How does the style influence the audience's possible response or impression?

ACTIVITY

Select a particular artist (painter, poet, musician, etc.) or a particular work of art (film, CD, poster) and describe its style.

Context

Every piece of art emerges out of a context (a specific, historical time and place), and understanding that context can deepen the analytical process. For instance, knowing that the Beatles' "Revolution" was written during a time of significant social and political unrest helps give it meaning. Some artistic works explicitly function to recall or memorialize a past era. In these cases, the context is important, because it may reveal the values of the age in which the art was produced.

- What is the context of the work? (When and where was the work created?)
- What was the social and political climate? (Was it a time of war, oppression, class tension, national expansion, technological advancement, economic boom, or industrial revolution?)
- Does the context show up or manifest itself in the work?
- How does understanding the context help the audience understand the work or an important idea related to the work?

All art emerges from a particular social situation— a context.

ACTIVITY

Consider the following works of art. In groups, discuss how each work may have been influenced by its context. You may have to research the work by doing a quick Internet search. Try Google.com.

- —The Empire State Building
- —the movie *Titanic*
- —"Respect" by Otis Redding
- —*Guernica* by Picasso
- —"This Land Is Your Land" by Woodie Guthrie
- —the Taj Mahal

INVENTION WRITING

In his invention writing, Chester McCovey discovers a theme in "The Birthmark" by Nathanial Hawthorne. McCovey connects this theme to another popular text, Mary Shelley's *Frankenstein*:

What themes emerge in the images or plot?
The old sci-fi theme: Some guy starts messing with chemicals trying to improve on nature and it backfires. Frankenstein, etc. Once again, man tries to control nature, instead of accepting nature. Man tries imposing his will. So, Hawthorne says man can improve on life (or perfect it) only by destroying it? When the blemish goes, Georgiana dies. But Hawthorne pre-dates Frankenstein, etc. He seems ahead of his time in that sense. The theme is still relevant today, though the story was written in the 1800s.

THINKING FURTHER

Making an important connection between two works of art—"The Birthmark" and *Frankenstein*—shows that McCovey is analyzing. But McCovey's thinking doesn't stop there. Through further exploration of "The Birthmark," he discovers an insight about life in the 21st century. McCovey zeros in on the very title of Hawthorne's short story, exploring the significance of the birthmark: It is something very small ("of the smallest pygmy size") and harmless (Georgiana's admirers were "wont to say that some fairy at her birth hour had laid her tiny hand upon the infant's cheek, and left this impress there in token of the magic endowments that were to give her such sway over all hearts"). McCovey says:

> The attentive reader is already a step ahead of me: cloning, stem cell research, genetic engineering. . . . But cloned sheep and the possibility of cloned people is not the only science "The Birthmark" asks today's reader to think about.
>
> While Georgiana's birthmark represents abstract imperfection, and Aylmer's faith in man represents humankind's efforts to perfect nature in general, the birthmark obviously reminds us of today's "little imperfections": (too small) breasts, a (too large) nose, (no) chin, (fat) thighs, and so on. (524–525)

McCovey finds meaning in the smallness of the imperfections and prompts the reader to consider our desire to "perfect" the tiniest of "imperfections." What, he asks, does this say about us?

PUBLIC RESONANCE

All art has a certain degree of public resonance because it attempts to address people. Art deals with issues that go beyond the artist and the single reader, viewer, or listener. For example, the poem "Fire" by Joy Harjo is not necessarily about one woman (the speaker of the poem). It resonates, or seeks to resonate, with all women. García Márquez's story "A Very Old Man with Enormous Wings" tells about a particular village, but the ideas about supernatural beings and people's treatment of others echo in many (maybe all) societies.

When writing about the arts, writers should attempt to emphasize or highlight issues of public value, pointing to the important or significant issues in the work, thereby making it resonate even more with readers. You might say that the goal of the writing in this chapter is to connect readers and art—to emphasize important issues that lurk within an artistic work.

As you consider your chosen subject, use the following questions to develop public resonance for your own writing:

- What value does the work have?
- Does the particular conflict, characters, or theme have any bearing on people's lives today?
- How does the work help us to understand society? Individual life?
- How does the work challenge our assumptions about beauty or art?

INVENTION WRITING

McCovey's response illustrates a reflective thought process: He does not simply answer the question, but explores intellectual directions. He makes a connection between particular issues in the work and the world around him (or "the 21st-century reader"), going far beyond the original question.

What value does the work have?

It is a well-written story in various ways. It is beautifully pieced together. Reading it a second time, you see that Hawthorne lays it all out in the opening paragraph. Also, we do more of Aylmer's sort of thing now than ever before. Our society wants to fix life (animal and plant). We want to genetically engineer rhubarb. We want to get rid of our hideous birthmarks. So, what's wrong with that? Is anything wrong with that? Can that be taken too far? It's not that all these attempts at improvement lead to death. What do they lead to? More and more attempts at improving more and more things, perhaps. Just like Aylmer who may have been onto something, but came up with something stronger. Perhaps engineering bigger tomatoes or insect-resistant apples is not a problem. (Or is it?) But where does it stop? (Be careful of a lame slippery slope argument here.) Are we fixing things that are fine? Are we fixing things that are beautiful, and calling them hideous? By fixing these things that can be seen as either beautiful or hideous are we heading down a path where we can't see natural beauty . . . or beauty? The 19th-century work says to the 21st-century reader: Be careful about trying to perfect nature; instead of improving it (or as you improve it), you may be destroying it.

PUBLIC RESONANCE IN CHAPTER ESSAYS

If the goal is to connect readers and art, the essays in this chapter work explicitly toward that goal. For example, notice Bennett's rather direct explanation of hip-hop's public resonance. His main idea is tied to hip-hop's role in popular culture, so the public resonance is an especially important part of his essay:

> Since American pop culture reveres stardom, rappers often garner more attention and respect than they deserve. Consequently, rap music and hip-hop culture have the power to either adversely or positively affect African Americans in specific, and the larger culture in general. (529)

Whitehead's essay focuses on the relationship between a genre of art and popular culture. She makes the connection in her conclusion:

> Taken separately, most of the dump books can be read as entertainments; taken together, however, they suggest that an important and recent change is occurring in the lives of educated young women. The romance of love and marriage took its inspiration from a long-standing mating system, but the defining institutions of the old system are breaking down. Courtship is dead. Marriage is in decline. A new mating system is emerging, with its own complications and confusions, including the conflict that faces high-status women. These books are field reports on the new rules of engagement—and disengagement. (521)

In his introduction, McCovey explains the public resonance of "The Birthmark":

> A masterpiece of literature offers its readers unlimited opportunities for thought, analysis, discovery, insight, interpretation. Though an old story's language may be difficult for some, if that old story is a masterpiece, its characters and plot develop a timeless theme as relevant today as it was yesterday. Nathaniel Hawthorne's "The Birthmark" is such a story. (523)

Art deals with issues that go beyond the artist and the single reader, viewer, or listener.

THESIS

While a thesis statement is apt to evolve during the writing process and may not even be stated directly in an essay, writers benefit from having a sense of their main ideas. Your thesis depends primarily on the goal of your project, which might do any of the following:

- Argue for or against the value of a given work of art or a particular art form.

    Political satire, such as *The Daily Show,* is vital to a democracy because it seeks to reveal the real governmental machinery behind the spin.

- Argue that a specific element (characters, theme, conflict, setting, etc.) in a work of art influences people in a particular way.

    The conflict in Shakespeare's *Hamlet* reminds us that revenge is not a simple, automatic human reaction but a complex response with tragic layers and consequences.

- Explain how the conflict in a work of art or art form relates to people in a given time and place.

    Aldous Huxley's *Brave New World* points directly at mainstream America, our blind overconsumption and self-stimulating giddiness, and shows the real danger to political freedom: the relentless pursuit of happiness.

- Explain how any feature of a given work or art form might influence the audience's perspective or challenge conventional thinking.

    Punk rock music challenges, and even accosts, the mainstream attraction to artificial beauty.

EVOLUTION OF A THESIS

Thesis statements do not come out of thin air. They evolve through inventive thinking and rethinking. Notice how the following ideas develop and twist their way to a thesis:

The writer discovers something valuable about her subject.

- "Running to Stand Still" is more than a pop song—it raises a social issue.

The writer discovers a particular issue in the work.

- U2's "Running to Stand Still" reveals the contradictory world of a drug addict.

The writer considers how public resonance develops the idea.

- In mainstream accounts of drug use, addicts are hopeless, one-track waste cases, but U2's "Running to Stand Still" reveals a different identity.

The writer struggles to narrow the point but maintain the complexity of the idea.

- To a society that treats addiction as criminal behavior, U2's "Running to Stand Still" offers a much-needed glimpse into the complexities of drug addiction.

- Mainstream rhetoric about drug use characterizes addicts as criminals and hopeless fiends, but U2's "Running to Stand Still" reveals a person who is full of hope and confusion.

As your ideas develop, return consistently to your main point. Let it evolve into an increasingly focused yet powerful point.

COMMON THESIS PROBLEMS

As with any project, writing about the arts comes with some potential perils. The following represent possible missteps:

The obvious fact problem Academic writing seeks to reveal something about a subject. The obvious fact statement does just the opposite: It merely states what many people already know:

> Leonardo da Vinci's *Mona Lisa* is adored by people everywhere, in various cultures, and throughout centuries.

The personal opinion problem Writing about art can be dangerous—especially if the writer feels deeply about the subject. But announcing a deeply felt opinion does not necessarily help readers. The most obvious form of the opinion statement includes phrases such as "I think," "I love," or "I believe." But personal opinions can be worded in a variety of ways. The following statement offers very little to readers beyond a writer's personal liking for a song:

> DiFranco's "Knuckle Down" is the most powerful song on her most recent CD.

The overstated claim problem It's easy to imagine a favorite artist being critically acclaimed throughout society, the world, even history. But writers must be cautious about projecting their inclinations too far and ultimately saying something that cannot be proven. Overstated claims such as the following can make readers doubtful:

> *Train at Night in the Desert* shows why O'Keeffe is the best American artist of the twentieth century.

The summary problem Part of this project involves summarizing the work of art—explaining to readers what exactly occurs in the work. However, summary should only be a part of the project, and it should work only to support a more analytical point. The following statement might work as part of a summary or as an introductory idea, but it would not work well as a main point in an essay:

> "A Very Old Man with Enormous Wings" shows how a small village responds to an injured angel.

A writer's deeply held opinion is not an automatic invitation to readers.

RHETORICAL TOOLS

Writing for this chapter might involve any number of rhetorical tools, such as the elements of argument and evaluation or the focus on detail from observation. In many ways, the writing for this chapter is argumentative, putting forth a potentially arguable claim about a subject. But the exploration of the artistic work also involves analyzing concepts and conventions of art.

Remember that writing about art is like building a bridge between your readers and the work of art. For this reason, it is important to have a copy of the work close by so that you can return to it often and discover (or rediscover) details. Also, it is important to consider your readers, who are not experiencing the art along with you. Remember to keep your readers involved in the art and bring them along as you develop ideas. During the drafting process, you may discover new ideas or details about the work. In that case, do not hesitate to rethink your main ideas.

INVENTION WORKSHOP

A Little Help from Your Friends

After exploring ideas further by considering your rhetorical tools, prepare a briefing for a small group of writers. (See pages 728–729.) In the briefing, summarize the artistic work you plan to write about, and write down your thesis about it. Then ask others to help you answer some of the Invention questions in this section (on pages 548–550). If your class is set up to communicate electronically, send the briefing (no longer than a paragraph) along with your questions, and elicit electronic responses.

Using Support about the Subject

Regardless of any particular stance or thesis, claims about the work of art should be supported with specific details. For example, a writer making a claim about the relevance of a particular theme would have to support that idea in at least two different ways. First, the writer would have to show the theme being played out in the work. This would involve highlighting elements of the work (part of the plot, some of the lyrics, part of an image) featuring that theme. For example, in Whitehead's essay, she refers to the characters in several different novels to illustrate her points. Notice that she refers only to specific scenes and situations that prove her thesis:

> Bosses and boyfriends behave a lot alike in the novels. They make nice to you (ever so briefly). Then they dump you. The bosses are invariably vain, capricious, self-centered, and hard-shelled women, not mentors but tormentors. In *The Girl's Guide to Hunting and Fishing*, Jane Rosenal is a rising star in her publishing company until Mimi Howlett, her new boss, arrives. Mimi demotes Jane from the promising position of associate book editor to de facto personal assistant. She also relentlessly criticizes Jane's professional work while generously offering her tips on how to improve her appearance. (518)

As you consider your ideas, ask the following question:

- What particular features or details of the work illustrate my point?

Using Support Outside the Subject

Pointing to details within the work is not enough if the writer is claiming something about its relevance, importance, or value in the world. The writer also has to use support outside the subject. Beyond the particular work of art, writers have the world of everyday life, history, popular culture, and other art to support their claims. For example, Whitehead uses trends in everyday life to support her claims about a literary genre:

> Given the high divorce rate, today's young women cannot rely on marriage for economic security. Even if they aspire to marriage (and according to survey research, most do), they have to be ready and able to support themselves with their own earnings. This has meant ever-increasing education beyond high school. For women pursuing high-status professions the schooling can extend several years beyond college, well into their twenties. Then, for as much as another decade, such women must invest heavily in developing their careers. Indeed, women on the make adopt the same priorities as men on the make. (520)

Or imagine a writer is arguing that García Márquez's story challenges readers to rethink popular notions of angels. She would not only discuss particular passages from the story; she would also point to the treatment of angels in popular culture. Only then could she support her claim. In other words, the writer would use details from the specific work of art and from everyday life to make her claims.

Use the following questions to find support outside the subject:

- Does anything in everyday life help illustrate my point about the work of art?
- Does anything in nature or science help illustrate my point about the work of art?
- Do any other works of art exemplify my point?

Counterarguing

In asserting any debatable point, writers may need to counterargue and defend their claims against opposition. This is especially true in writing about art, which can be interpreted so many different ways.

Imagine a writer arguing for the value of punk rock music. The writer takes on a position that counters her own and defends punk music from critics:

> Critics of punk rock argue that it merely panders to the most basic and simplistic desires of its listeners. But in societies that tend toward artificiality and hyper-materialism, punk rock is a necessary art form. Its simplicity reminds people that absurd amounts of luxury and thoughtless reverence of money can be overcome—or drowned out with primal noise.

She might then go on to cite particular examples of punk music that support her point.

As you consider your own point and your own argument about the worth of the art, consider how other perspectives might help to clarify your points. Ask yourself the following questions:

- Who might disagree with my claims about the artistic work, and what would they say?
- What claims about the artistic work might oppose my own?

Conceding

Argumentative writing benefits from concessions, passages that grant value to opposing claims. In his essay, Chester McCovey argues that the scientist in "The Birthmark" can symbolize contemporary desires to erase human imperfection. McCovey suggests that this desire is perilous and uncontrolled, but he also acknowledges the good that can come from medical reconstruction. That is, he does not argue that all science is bad; such a claim could be dismissed too easily.

> No one is saying that cleft palates or clubbed feet should not be corrected—at least no one is saying that in this essay. But Georgiana's birthmark was "of the smallest pygmy size" and her lovers were "wont to say that some fairy at her birth hour had laid her tiny hand upon the infant's cheek, and left this impress there in token of the magic endowments that were to give her such sway over all hearts. Many a desperate swain would have risked life for the privilege of pressing his lips to the mysterious hand." The "mad scientist" is us—eager to erase these "imperfections" of Nature. (525)

As you consider your own points, consider the following questions:

- Are there other valid claims one could make about the artistic work?
- Do my claims make any large, but necessary, leaps?
- Do I ask my audience to accept generalizations?

Using the Elements of Evaluation

Your project may involve evaluation. That is, you may need to convince your readers that your chosen subject (work of art) is good, bad, superior, and so on. If assessing the value of the work is important to your overall project, use the elements of evaluation. The first step in evaluation is to develop criteria, which involves finding the subject's purpose and audience.

- What does this subject try to achieve?
- What do other similar subjects try to achieve?
- Who is the audience for the subject?
- What goals *should* this subject, or all subjects like it, have?

After you have established criteria (the standards by which that particular kind of art can be judged) apply them to your subject.

- Through what particular ways does the subject achieve its goal? What specific parts, tools, or strategies help the subject to achieve its goal? (For example, a song might rely solely on lyrics, ensemble, . . . or marketing!)
- In what particular ways does the subject fall short of achieving its goal?
- What is unique about your subject's approach or strategy?

Evaluation need not constitute a major part of your essay; in fact, it might simply help show the value of your chosen work of art. Notice below how evaluation might serve as a particular part of an essay. Imagine a writer arguing about the qualities of U2's "Running to Stand Still."

> A good pop song should do more than titillate its listeners. In fact, as we learned with the protest songs of the late 1960s and early 1970s, popular music can be an agent of political and social change. Artists such as Bob Dylan and Neil Young helped create political awareness, which led to significant social action and civic dialogue. Although politically aware artists went out of style in the disco era and stayed on the fringes of the '80s metal scene, some artists continued to use popular music as a medium for exploring social issues. Perhaps the most successful, and most committed to this goal, was U2.
>
> On U2's acclaimed album *The Joshua Tree*, "Running to Stand Still" depicts the life of addiction, particularly its inherent contradiction and tension. The voice in the song seems to speak back to a culture that too easily dismisses addiction as a simple problem of will.

Here, the writer uses the elements of evaluation in the introduction to establish the idea of a "good pop song," and then alludes to other artists (Dylan and Young) to illustrate the point. Once the idea is established, the writer introduces the particular song and begins the analysis.

Criteria are standards of judgment that make an evaluation acceptable to others.

ORGANIZATIONAL STRATEGIES

Where Should I Summarize or Detail the Work?

Imagine you are about to go on a bus tour of New York City. After you take your seat on the bus, the tour guide, standing in the front talking over the intercom, begins to explain the tour itinerary. She explains the details of every single block you will see on the tour. After twenty minutes of hearing the minute details, you think: "OK, already! Let's go!" The problem is that the tour guide is giving too much introductory summary. She could more easily, and more appropriately, give a more general description: "The bus will take us through midtown Manhattan where we will see Times Square, and then we will head toward the Village."

Similarly, writers can create a problem by spending too much time introducing their subject. A brief introductory summary, however, may be an appropriate strategy for settling the reader into the work of art. You may decide to give a brief general summary of the subject (especially for longer literary works) at the beginning of your own text, and then mention only pertinent specifics as they relate to each point. A general summary need not take several paragraphs; in fact, a lengthy retelling of events or details, with no guiding point, should be avoided in shorter papers (fewer than 1,000 words). An introductory summary can even be a few sentences:

> In Gabriel García Márquez's story "An Old Man with Enormous Wings," an angelic figure falls to earth in a storm. The figure, an old man, is taken into town and kept in a barn where people come to stare, taunt, gawk, and wonder at him. Eventually, the old man's wings recover from his stormy fall, and he flies off into the sky again.

From here, the writer could go on to develop a particular point, and then refer to more particular events or details from the story as they are needed to support claims. Such a general summary gives readers the gist of the work without putting off analysis.

How Should I Begin?

One strategy is to begin with a brief overall summary of the work. For instance, McCovey explains the timelessness of his subject, "The Birthmark," and Bennett gives a historical account of his subject, hip-hop music.

However, the main idea need not be completely introduced in the first paragraph. For instance, Whitehead's essay takes three paragraphs to set up the main idea. Her opening paragraph simply begins an explanation of romance novel themes. It is not until the third paragraph that Whitehead focuses the reader on her specific point, which she then illustrates throughout the rest of her essay:

> The new literature reflects these dual realities. Like traditional women's stories, it deals with themes of love and work, often interweaving the two, but it breaks sharply with the romantic view of both. The defining theme in this literature isn't finding the dream guy or landing the great job but precisely the opposite. It's getting dumped—by a boyfriend or a boss or both. What's more, these books challenge the idea that a young woman blessed with talent and education, and filled with desire and ambition, can get what she wants. (517)

As in all essays, you have many options available for introducing your ideas. Focusing on a work of art does not erase the possible introductory strategies from other chapters, such as personal anecdote, scenario, question, statement, and so on.

How Should I Integrate Lines of Songs, Poems, or Stories?

Integrating others' words into your own writing can be tricky business. While there are many strategies for doing so, the rule of thumb is to avoid free-standing quotations (quotations that are not introduced by your own words). In other words, a reader should not encounter an artist's words without first understanding why they are referenced. The words of an artistic piece should be included only to illustrate a point that is already expressed, so the reader understands how to process the words.

When essay writers integrate the language of other writers into their own texts, they can often work the lines in directly:

> As the philosopher Diana Raffman has pointed out, "our ability to discriminate or compare values considerably exceeds our ability to identify or recognize them."

They can do this because the language is from the same genre (an essay). However, integrating poetry or song lyrics into an essay is different, and most often the artist's lines need to be clearly separated. A colon is a standard strategy for introducing a longer literary passage or poetic line:

> The story's climax comes when after much science, Aylmer is successful—the birthmark is gone:
>
> > "By Heaven! It is well-nigh gone!" said Aylmer to himself, in almost irrepressible ecstasy. "I can scarcely trace it now. Success! success! And now it is like the faintest rose color. The lightest flush of the blood across her cheek would overcome it. But she is so pale!" (523–524)

Quoting poetry involves yet another step. A slanted line (/) represents a line break in the poem:

> Joy Harjo's poem "Fire" announces a universal feminine identity: "look at me / i am not a separate woman / i am the continuance / of blue sky."

Quote only to shine a spotlight on a key passage.

WRITER'S VOICE

Avoiding the Enthusiasm Crisis

Imagine going to a movie, and in the theater lobby an usher begins jumping up and down and screaming, "That is the best movie ever! I love it! I love it!" Besides drawing attention away from the movie and onto his own giddiness, the usher may even make you apprehensive and think, "How could a movie be *that* good?" This is the enthusiasm crisis. It is easy to appear overenthusiastic about an artistic work or an artist. Imagine the following passage about a popular song, the Indigo Girls' "Galileo":

> The Indigo Girls are a great folk duo who write songs about all kinds of issues. Their outstanding vocal harmonies and angelic voices create an amazing listening experience, but more interestingly, their lyrics create a powerful intellectual experience. The lyrics to "Galileo" are a perfect example of their stellar abilities to consume a listener's thoughts.

Ironically, such glowing praise does not invite a reader into reflection about the art. In fact, such dramatic and puffy language excludes and overwhelms the reader. To avoid raw enthusiasm, be cautious of the following:

1. Overly positive adjectives. Vague descriptive words such as *great, outstanding, superior, excellent, perfect* leave little room for reflection.

2. Unsupported judgments. Readers would prefer not to have judgments forced upon them; instead, they want to experience a new idea about the subject.

3. Overly broad claims about the art or artists. Often baldly enthusiastic claims have little focus. They generalize about the art or artist's worth, so perhaps the best defense against alienating your reader with enthusiasm is to develop a focused thesis.

Avoiding Harsh Description

Like the enthusiasm crisis, excessively harsh description draws attention to the emotions of the speaker rather than inviting reflection. For example, imagine a writer arguing about the value of a museum exhibit:

> "Art of the World" offers nothing artistic to viewers. It is entirely devoid of worth, and it should be avoided at all costs.

Like most harsh description, such language overshadows any particular elements of the subject and draws attention to itself. A better strategy is to steer toward subtlety:

> "Art of the World" does not invite the reader into various cultures of the world. Instead, it displays paintings that represent only dominant countries: China, France, Russia, United States, Brazil, India. Moreover, the paintings themselves offer stereotypical representations of their homelands, for example, a Chinese painting of rice fields.

This passage, while still negative, gives a more specific examination of the subject, so the reader can share in the point being made.

Promoting Wonder

While writers do not want to alienate readers with their enthusiasm, they also do not want to dull the reader's senses. Writing about art should create a certain degree of intensity. It should make both writer and reader feel a sense of wonder. Wonder is probably best achieved by showing the reader powerful aspects of the artistic work. But beyond that, writers can embody the kind of wonder they want to bestow in readers. They can use language and sentence structure that dramatizes the thoughts and feelings associated with the artistic work. In his essay about the *Mona Lisa,* Vincent Pomarède encourages readers to wonder at the work's power:

> The study of the unequalled success over three centuries of Leonardo da Vinci's *Mona Lisa* will perhaps enable a better understanding of the numerous and complex motivations which make visitors of a museum only remember a single work from amongst thousands of others. Indeed, the *Mona Lisa* is beyond doubt the best-known painting in the world, today completely identified with the Louvre Museum and even with the general notion of art. If we were able to penetrate the origins of its creation, its aesthetic qualities, and its history following the death of its creator, we would perhaps be able to identify some rules explaining a work of art's success. (531)

ACTIVITY

Write a paragraph that promotes wonder about your topic. Encourage your readers to re-see specific qualities of the artwork, to look at the work with new curiosity and awe.

Considering the Tone of the Art

A writer's voice certainly depends on the subject. Even the most strategic writer would have some difficulty maintaining a comedic voice when discussing a very sober tale such as Joseph Conrad's "Heart of Darkness." However, writers need not fall entirely in line with their subjects. Notice, for example, that Geoffrey Bennett maintains a formal voice even though he is discussing hip-hop, an art form characterized by slang or "street" language. And Chester McCovey does not echo the highly formal language in "The Birthmark":

> Hawthorne's theme is clear. In the story's opening paragraph we read:
>
> > The higher intellect, the imagination, the spirit, and even the heart might all find their congenial ailment in pursuits which, as some of their ardent votaries believed, would ascend from one step of powerful intelligence to another, until the philosopher should lay his hand on the secret of creative force and perhaps make new worlds for himself. We know not whether Aylmer possessed this degree of faith in man's ultimate control over Nature.
>
> See what I mean about the language? But the point here is that even though we now speak—and write— differently, Aylmer *did* apparently possess this degree of faith in man's ultimate control over nature. (523)

Although he draws attention to the formality of the story's language, McCovey's voice is informal. McCovey, like Bennett and Whitehead, has a voice that is distinct from the art he discusses.

VITALITY

All writers can make their sentences more vitalized—more full of life and intensity. As many of the earlier chapters suggest, vitalizing often means trimming down unnecessary words and phrases. It means making things more concise. But it can also mean rearranging sentence parts.

Break Apart Noun Clusters

Noun clusters occur when several nouns are used consecutively to describe something or someone:

- The mid-twentieth-century underground comic book hero represented American values.
- The local high school English class students are reading *Romeo and Juliet.*

Noun clusters can seem like a wall of words to readers. They can slow or stop forward movement, often making readers return to the beginning of the sentence to build up momentum and get through them. Notice how the above clusters can be broken apart. In both cases, a prepositional phrase can break apart the cluster of nouns:

- In the mid-twentieth century, the underground comic book hero represented American values.
- At the local high school, the English classes are reading *Romeo and Juliet.*

Change Nouns to Verbs

Vitalizing often revolves around verbs. Whenever writers can make the main verb of a sentence more important and central to the sentence, they increase vitality. This may involve replacing nouns with verbs as in the following two sentences:

- Antonia makes the decision to stay on the Plains and create the family her father had imagined.
- This culture has a love for everything big.

The nouns in these constructions can be replaced with verbs. *Decision* can become *decides* and *love* can become *loves:*

- Antonia decides to stay on the Plains and create the family her father had imagined.
- This culture loves everything big.

Avoid Unnecessary Modifiers

It is tempting to rely on modifiers such as *very, certainly, really, clearly, extremely, undoubtedly,* and so on. Such words seem like they intensify statements. But they don't. As in the following sentences, such modifying words can slow down statements and artificially puff up the importance of an idea:

- The characters are very realistic.
- He has really powerful voice control.
- Certainly, we should hope for something more intense out of a film.

Without the qualifiers, the sentences seem weaker, which might encourage a writer to revise. For example, the second sentence could be more focused:

- His voice controls the entire listening experience.

ACTIVITY

Rewrite the following passage to create more vitality:

It is seldom that American movie theater audiences encounter such subtlety in a single event. But with *Napoleon Dynamite,* we were thankfully spared the smashy ending, overblown slapstick, and throwaway stereotypes. The script is highly sensitive to the interesting politics of outsider high school life.

PEER REVIEW

Exchange drafts with at least one other writer. Before passing your draft to others, underline the thesis, or write it above your essay. This way, reviewers will get traction as they read.

As a reviewer, use the following questions to guide your response.

1. Could the thesis be more narrow and revelatory? How? (What words or phrases are too broad?)

2. In what passages could the writer use more details about the work of art?

3. Where might the writer use other means of support (allusions to history, popular culture, other art, examples from everyday life, etc.)?

4. Suggest specific points that the writer should concede or qualify. For instance, the writer's position might seem too extreme; the claims might include too many people or include a large, diverse group without making any distinctions. Point out such claims and help the writer to see the need to acknowledge subtlety, complexity, and exceptions.

5. Imagine another perspective that the writer has ignored. Try to propose an alternative way of seeing and valuing the work of art so that the writer can counterargue or concede to this new perspective.

6. Consider the writer's voice. Does the writer create wonder or intensity? How? What particular passages achieve that? If not, what particular passages seem flatly informational? Suggest an alternative strategy or phrasing.

7. Has the writer focused too much on summarizing the work of art? (In other words, does a majority of the essay merely explain the work without developing a specific point about it?) Write "summary" in the margins next to all passages that only inform you about the work.

8. What is the most engaging passage in the draft so far? Why?

9. Check for sentence vitality.

   a. Check for any noun clusters. If you encounter any noun clusters, suggest a revision of the sentence.

   b. When possible, replace nouns (such as in *make a decision*) with verbs (*decide*).

   c. Circle any unnecessary modifiers (*very, really, certainly,* and so on).

   d. Consider vitality strategies from other chapters:

   - Where can the writer avoid drawing attention to *I* and *you*?
   - Where can the writer change linking verbs to active verbs?
   - Help the writer change unnecessary clauses to phrases.
   - Help the writer change unnecessary phrases to words.
   - Point to expletives (such as *there are* and *it is*).
   - Help the writer change passive verbs to active verbs for more vitality.
   - Point to padding or obvious content.
   - Identify any stilted language.
   - Help the reader avoid common grammatical errors: comma splices, sentence fragments, or pronoun/antecedent agreement.

Questions for Research

If the writer used outside sources,

- Where must he or she include in-text citations? (See page 650.)
- Are quotations blended smoothly into the argument and punctuated correctly? (See pages 642–648.)
- Where could more direct textual cues or transitions help the reader? (See pages 641–643.)
- Is the Works Cited page formatted properly? (See pages 652–674.)

DELIVERY

What you say about an individual work of art or a body of work can change how people think and how they live. Helping people to better understand a particular work of art, a body of work, or art in general can provide them with a valuable new way of thinking. Written works about art can also influence the field of art itself. Consider these questions:

- How have you added to people's understanding of art?
- How has your thinking developed, changed, shifted, even slightly?
- Why is your take on the work of art important in a society that focuses so much attention on profit and economic growth?

Transform the Essay: Create a Found Poem

Poets often use the language around them, building poems by selecting key words and phrases from texts in everyday life. The passage on page 559 is from the introduction to this chapter. Below the original paragraph is a poem, created from key words were that were selected and rearranged.

1. How does the poem change the reading experience for you? What does it invite you to do differently as a reader?
2. How does the poem's visual component (its layout) impact the ideas?
3. Is the poem more or less effective than the original passage? Why?

"A mind that is lively and inquiring, compassionate, curious, angry, full of music, full of feeling, is a mind full of possible poetry."

—Mary Oliver

[Passage from chapter introduction (page 504):]

If reading literature is an act of discovery, then the same thing might be said about listening to music and taking in the visual arts. Art is more than entertainment. It calls on readers, listeners, or viewers to participate in the creation of ideas. Whether they are involved in novels, Shakespeare's plays, folk songs, or Picasso's paintings, people engaging art are inventing as they take it in: They are developing thoughts, envisioning situations, seeing connections, and imagining worlds that they had not previously encountered. While the arts help us imagine other worlds, they also help us to make sense of our own. Art, in whatever form, offers something to everyday experience: maybe answers to the gnawing uncertainties of daily existence; maybe mystery and intensity in a world that seems too plain; maybe a framework for exploring human behavior; or maybe a deeper understanding of our place in society. Exploring and responding to the arts, then, is the process of developing and communicating ideas, not simply about a story, poem, song, or painting, but about life.

a poem about art

an act of discovery
listening to music
taking in the visual arts

Shakespeare, Picasso
folk songs, paintings

imagining other worlds
to make sense of our own

gnawing uncertainties, daily existence
mystery and intensity in a world that seems plain
—too plain

Art is more than entertainment.
It calls on us to participate
in the creation
of ideas.

Return to the essay you wrote for this chapter. Select key words and arrange them into a poem that communicates your essay's main idea.

THINKING RADICALLY:
RE-SEEING THE WORLD

Chapter Contents

CHAPTER 12

"We must therefore look in the most obscurest corners and summon up courage to shock the prejudices of our age if we want to broaden the basis of our understanding of nature."

—Carl Jung

Living in a society demands a certain degree of conformity. As individuals in a society, we conform to laws, clothing styles, hairstyles, and even culinary tastes (most Americans like french fries but not raw oysters). We also conform to ways of thinking; we learn to follow intellectual conventions. This is not to say that we all think alike, not by a long shot, but we do buy into conventional modes or patterns of thought that, on the one hand, allow us to participate in shared knowledge but, on the other hand, limit intellectual possibilities.

Mainstream thought invites us to accept a particular view of reality, and with it, certain assumptions. Consider the following:

- Progress involves technological advancement.
- The past is behind us.
- People who make lots of money are successful.
- Poor people are worse off than rich people.
- We make individual choices.
- Time is constant.

Such ideas are what we might call *common sense,* in that they represent widely held, and largely unexamined, beliefs. But some people have examined and even challenged such common ideas. For example, thinkers such as

Wendell Berry challenge the idea that human progress necessarily involves increased dependence on technology; several important religious figures (Jesus, Buddha, Mohammed) overturned the inherent value of monetary riches; and Albert Einstein showed the world that time is not constant but relative. We might say that such figures transcend and challenge commonsense thinking. They call into question those beliefs that rest beneath layers of intellectual practice and everyday life. They show us questions where we may have assumed solid answers.

People who transcend conventional thinking are not *radical* in the sense that they want to destroy mainstream life. (We are not talking here about anarchists, religious zealots, or specific political positions.) Rather, they are radical *thinkers:* They escape conventional thought patterns. While convention calls on us to think within the lines, radical thinkers work to see beyond those lines, and then communicate what ideas are possible. Their writing seeks to reform conventional thinking.

Radical thinking is not necessarily a matter of topic choice; in fact, topics are not, in themselves, radical. Radical thinking involves an adventurous *approach* to a topic and offers a new way to think. For example, in 1784, Benjamin

Franklin first put forth the idea of daylight savings time. After waking at an unusually early hour in the morning and finding that the sun had risen, he imagined that people could change their clocks to coincide with sunrise throughout the seasons.

In 1543, Nicolaus Copernicus challenged the conventional theory that the Earth is the center of the universe. He defied church law and common sense of the day and claimed that the Earth rotates around the sun. History is filled with such intellectual adventurers, those who transcended norms to see relationships beyond the obvious, to find meaning outside of cultural norms, and to imagine perspectives beyond the present:

- W. E. B. Dubois argued against mainstream thinking about African Americans' place in society. While most politicians, educators, and civic leaders walked a moderate line, assuming that black people in America could thrive in subservient positions, Dubois imagined that African Americans should act as leaders for national and global change.

- Psychologist Carl Jung broke away from his colleague Sigmund Freud (and the conventional wisdom of the psychological community) to argue that human unconscious is, in part, a collective rather than an individual phenomenon.

- Georgia O'Keeffe transcended artistic conventions by focusing on the organic. While art and popular culture were increasingly transfixed on the abstract, O'Keeffe sought out the most pure and basic forms of identity in images such as flowers and landscapes.

Radical thinkers have changed how laws, government, and institutional policy work. People such as Thomas Jefferson, Mahatma Gandhi, Eleanor Roosevelt, Martin Luther King, Jr., and Martin Luther articulated ideas and policies that were beyond conventional thinking of their times.

In academic study and everyday life, methods often evolve because real people transcend the common sense of their fields; that is, they imagine the possibilities beyond what is assumed. The people who are able to think beyond *what is* and to conjure images of *what could be* are those who most often provide direction for improvement in the quality of daily work and daily life. As you explore this chapter, remember that all those people who have helped bring about change are those who first had to imagine a reality beyond the status quo.

This chapter will help you transcend conventional thought, focus on a particular topic, develop a focused thesis, and communicate your ideas in writing. The following essays will provide valuable insight to various strategies. After reading the essays, you can find a topic in one of two ways:

1. Go to the **Point of Contact** section to find a topic from everyday life.
2. Choose one of the **Ideas for Writing** following the essays.

After finding a subject, go to the **Analysis** section to begin developing your thoughts.

The writing in this chapter exemplifies thinking that transcends convention. The authors go beyond standard, comfortable notions about farming, corporations, the female body, and everyday life. The authors understand, and even point to, conventional thought and attempt to take the reader to a new intellectual place. At first their claims may seem shocking or offensive. A writer such as Michael Moore, for example, may be attempting to ask questions that initially seem absurd. However, being shocked or offended can be a valuable intellectual experience—if the reader is ready. It is easy to dismiss claims when they collide with our prejudices, but it is often more enriching (and valuable) to transform shock into curiosity. As you read, be prepared to accept, or at least consider, a new way of thinking.

Farming and the Global Economy

Wendell Berry

The first entry under "radical" in *The American Heritage College Dictionary* says: "1. Arising from or going to a root or source; basic." In this essay (as in other essays in this chapter and throughout the book), the writer thinks radically because he is getting at a root, or a source. This may sound like an easy thing to do, but because we are immersed in the ideology that surrounds us, we are often unable to see or imagine the root. In this essay, Wendell Berry, a novelist, farmer, and essayist, points out some root principles of food, energy, and consumption and argues that abandoning those principles comes with significant consequences.

We have been repeatedly warned that we cannot know where we wish to go if we do not know where we have been. And so let us start by remembering a little history.

As late as World War II, our farms were predominantly solar powered. That is, the work was accomplished principally by human beings and horses and mules. These creatures were empowered by solar energy, which was collected, for the most part, on the farms where they worked and so was pretty cheaply available to the farmer.

However, American farms had not become as self-sufficient in fertility as they should have been—or many of them had not. They were still drawing, without sufficient repayment, against an account of natural fertility accumulated over thousands of years beneath the native forest trees and prairie grasses.

The agriculture we had at the time of World War II was nevertheless often pretty good, and it was promising. In many parts of our country we had begun to have established agricultural communities, each with its own local knowledge, memory, and tradition. Some of our farming practices had become well adapted to local conditions. The best traditional practices of the Midwest, for example, are still used by the Amish with considerable success in terms of both economy and ecology.

5   Now that the issue of sustainability has arisen so urgently, and in fact so transformingly, we can see that the correct agricultural agenda following World War II would have been to continue and refine the already established connection between our farms and the sun and to correct, where necessary, the fertility deficit. There can be no question, now, that that is what we should have done.

It was, notoriously, not what we did. Instead, the adopted agenda called for a shift from the cheap, clean, and, for all practical purposes, limitless energy of the sun to the expensive, filthy, and limited energy of the fossil fuels. It called for the massive use of chemical fertilizers to offset the destruction of topsoil and the depletion of natural fertility. It called also for the displacement of nearly the entire farming population and the replacement of their labor and good farming practices by machines and toxic chemicals. This agenda has succeeded in its aims, but to the benefit of no one and nothing except the corporations that have supplied the necessary machines, fuels, and chemicals—and the corporations that have bought cheap and sold high the products that, as a result of this agenda, have been increasingly expensive for farmers to produce.

The farmers have not benefited—not, at least, as a class—for as a result of this agenda they have become one of the smallest and most threatened of all our minorities. Many farmers, sad to say, have subscribed to this agenda and its economic assumptions, believing that they would not be its victims. But millions, in fact, have been its victims—not farmers alone but also their supporters and dependents in our rural communities.

The people who benefit from this state of affairs have been at pains to convince us that the agricultural practices and policies that have almost annihilated the farming population have greatly benefited the population of food consumers. But more and more consumers are now becoming aware that our supposed abundance of cheap and healthful food is to a considerable extent illusory. They are beginning to see that the social, ecological, and even the economic costs of such "cheap food" are, in fact, great. They are beginning to see that a system of food production that is dependent on massive applications of drugs and chemicals cannot, by definition, produce "pure food." And they are beginning to see that a kind of agriculture that involves unprecedented erosion and depletion of soil, unprecedented waste of water, and unprecedented destruction of the farm population cannot by any accommodation of sense or fantasy be called "sustainable."

From the point of view, then, of the farmer, the ecologist, and the consumer, the need to reform our ways of farming is now both obvious and imperative. We need to adapt our farming much more sensitively to the nature of the places where the farming is done. We need to make our farming practices and our food economy subject to standards set not by the industrial system but by the health of ecosystems and of human communities.

10 The immediate difficulty in even thinking about agricultural reform is that we are rapidly running out of farmers. The tragedy of this decline is not just in its numbers; it is also in the fact that these farming people, assuming we will ever recognize our need to replace them, cannot be replaced anything like as quickly or easily as they have been dispensed with. Contrary to popular assumption, good farmers are not in any simple way part of the "labor force." Good farmers, like good musicians, must be raised to the trade.

The severe reduction of our farming population may signify nothing to our national government, but the members of country communities feel the significance of it—and the threat of it—every day. Eventually urban consumers will feel these things, too. Every day farmers feel the oppression of their long-standing problems: overproduction, low prices, and high costs. Farmers sell on a market that because of overproduction is characteristically depressed, and they buy their supplies on a market that is characteristically inflated—which is necessarily a recipe for failure, because farmers do not control either market. If they will not control production and if they will not reduce their dependence on purchased supplies, then they will keep on failing.

The survival of farmers, then, requires two complementary efforts. The first is entirely up to the farmers, who must learn—or learn again—to farm in ways that minimize their dependence on industrial supplies. They must diversify, using both plants and animals. They must produce, on their farms, as much of the required fertility and energy as they can. So far as they can, they must replace purchased goods and services with natural health and diversity and with their own intelligence. To increase production by increasing costs, as farmers have been doing for the last half century, is not only unintelligent; it is crazy. If farmers do not wish to cooperate any longer in their own destruction, then they will have to reduce their dependence on those global economic forces that intend and approve and profit from the destruction of farmers, and they will have to increase their dependence on local nature and local intelligence.

The second effort involves cooperation between local farmers and local consumers. If farmers hope to exercise any control over their markets, in a time when a global economy and global transportation make it possible for the products of any region to be undersold by the products of any other region, then they will have to look to local markets. The long-broken connections between towns and cities and their surrounding landscapes will have to be restored. There is much promise and much hope in such a restoration. But farmers must understand that this requires an economics of cooperation rather than competition. They must understand also that such an economy sooner or later will require some rational means of production control.

If communities of farmers and consumers wish to promote a sustainable, safe, reasonably inexpensive supply of good food, then they must see that the best, the safest, and most dependable source of food for a city is not the global economy, with its extreme vulnerabilities and extravagant transportation costs, but its own surrounding countryside. It is, in every way, in the best interest of urban consumers to be surrounded by productive land, well farmed and well maintained by thriving farm families in thriving farm communities.

15 If a safe, sustainable local food economy appeals to some of us as a goal that we would like to work for, then we must be careful to recognize not only the great power of the interests arrayed against us but also our own weakness. The hope for such a food economy as we desire is represented by no political party and is spoken for by no national public officials of any consequence. Our national political leaders do not know what we are

talking about, and they are without the local affections and allegiances that would permit them to learn what we are talking about.

But we should also understand that our predicament is not without precedent; it is approximately the same as that of the proponents of American independence at the time of the Stamp Act—and with one difference in our favor: In order to do the work that we must do, we do not need a national organization. What we must do is simple: We must shorten the distance that our food is transported so that we are eating more and more from local supplies, more and more to the benefit of local farmers, and more and more to the satisfaction of local consumers. This can be done by cooperation among small organizations: conservation groups, churches, neighborhood associations, consumer co-ops, local merchants, local independent banks, and organizations of small farmers. It also can be done by cooperation between individual producers and consumers. We should not be discouraged to find that local food economies can grow only gradually; it is better that they should grow gradually. But as they grow they will bring about a significant return of power, wealth, and health to the people.

One last thing at least should be obvious to us all: The whole human population of the world cannot live on imported food. Some people somewhere are going to have to grow the food. And wherever food is grown the growing of it will raise the same two questions: How do you preserve the land in use? And how do you preserve the people who use the land?

The farther the food is transported, the harder it will be to answer those questions correctly. The correct answers will not come as the inevitable by-products of the aims, policies, and procedures of international trade, free or unfree. They cannot be legislated or imposed by international or national or state agencies. They can only be supplied locally, by skilled and highly motivated local farmers meeting as directly as possible the needs of informed local consumers.

Writing Strategies

1. Describe Berry's opening strategy. How does his introduction lead the reader into the body of his essay?

2. Make an outline of Berry's essay, dividing it into several major sections. Describe Berry's organizational strategy.

3. Describe Berry's voice as a writer and identify several passages to support your description.

4. How does Berry express the public resonance of his ideas? That is, how does he relate his ideas to the reader?

5. How is Berry's essay an example of radical thinking?

Exploring Ideas

1. Based on this essay, what is Berry concerned about?

2. How is the way that you see farming different from the way that Berry sees it?

3. What does your response to the reading tell you about the way that you view the world?

4. How might you benefit by reconsidering your views of farming?

5. Based on interviews and observations, how do you think others view farming? What do they think is important, and how are their views similar to or different from Berry's and your own?

Ideas for Writing

1. What other idea is "represented by no political party and is spoken for by no national public officials of any consequence" (¶ 15)?

2. What major problem has a simple solution?

If responding to one of these ideas, go to the **Analysis** section of this chapter to begin developing ideas for your essay.

Why Doesn't GM Sell Crack?

Michael Moore

A common assumption in mainstream America is that society should work for the advancement of business. People don't often assume (or say!) that a democratic society should come first and that business should advance society. In fact, whenever such a notion comes up, it is often cast away with scorn. In this essay, Michael Moore applies a line of reasoning (appeal to logic) to pull readers away from the most common assumptions about business.

People in the business world like to say, "Profit is supreme." They like chanting that. "Profit is king." That's another one they like to repeat. They don't like to say, "I'll pick up the check." That means less profit. Profit is what it's all about. When they say "the bottom line," they mean their *profit*. They like that bottom line to contain a number followed by a lot of zeroes.

If I had a nickel for every time I heard some guy in a suit tell me that "a company must do whatever is necessary to create the biggest profit possible," I would have a very big bottom line right now. Here's another popular mantra: "The responsibility of the CEO is to make his shareholders as much money as he can."

Are you enjoying this lesson in capitalism? I get it every time I fly on a plane. The bottom-line feeders have all seen *Roger & Me,* yet they often mistake the fuselage of a DC-9 for the Oxford Debating Society. So I have to sit through lectures ad nauseam about the beauties of our free market system. Today the guy in the seat next to me is the owner of an American company that makes office supplies—in Taiwan. I ask the executive, "How much is 'enough'?"

"Enough what?" he replies.

5   "How much is 'enough' profit?"

He laughs and says, "There's no such thing as 'enough'!"

So, General Motors made nearly $7 billion in profit last year—but they could make $7.1 billion by clos-ing a factory in Parma, Ohio, and moving it to Mexi-co—that would be okay?"

"Not only okay," he responds, "it is their duty to close that plant and make the extra $.1 billion."

"Even if it destroys Parma, Ohio? Why can't $7 billion be enough and spare the community? Why ruin thousands of families for the sake of *$.1* billion? Do you think this is *moral*?"

10   "Moral?" he asks, as if this is the first time he's heard that word since First Communion class. "This is not an issue of morality. It is purely a matter of economics. A company must be able to do whatever it wants to make a profit." Then he leans over as if to make a revelation I've never heard before.

"Profit, you know, is supreme."

So here's what I don't understand: if profit is supreme, why doesn't a company like General Motors sell crack? Crack is a *very* profitable commodity. For every pound of cocaine that is transformed into crack, a dealer stands to make a profit of $45,000. The dealer profit on a two-thousand-pound car is less than $2,000. Crack is also safer to use than automobiles. Each year, 40,000 people die in car accidents. Crack, on the other hand, kills only a few hundred people a year. And it doesn't pollute.

So why doesn't GM sell crack? If profit is supreme, why not sell crack?

GM doesn't sell crack because it is illegal. Why is it illegal? Because we, as a society, have determined that crack destroys people's lives. It ruins entire communities. It tears apart the very backbone of our country. That's why we wouldn't let a company like GM sell it, no matter what kind of profit they could make.

15   If we wouldn't let GM sell crack because it destroys our communities, then why do we let them close facto-ries? *That, too,* destroys our communities.

As my frequent-flier friend would say, "We can't prevent them from closing factories because they have a right to do whatever they want to in order to make a profit."

No, they don't. They don't have a "right" to do a lot of things: sell child pornography, manufacture chemical weapons, or create hazardous products that could conceivably make them a profit. We can enact laws to prevent companies from doing anything to hurt us.

And downsizing is one of those things that is hurting us. I'm not talking about legitimate layoffs, when a company is losing money and simply doesn't have the cash reserves to pay its workers. I'm talking about companies like GM, AT&T, and GE, which fire people at a time when the company is making record profits in the billions of dollars. Executives who do this are not scorned, picketed, or arrested—they are hailed as heroes! They make the covers of *Fortune* and *Forbes*. They lecture at the Harvard Business School about their success. They throw big campaign fund-raisers and sit next to the President of the United States. They are the Masters of the Universe simply because they make huge profits regardless of the consequences to our society.

Are we insane or what? Why do we allow this to happen? It is *wrong* to make money off people's labor and then fire them after you've made it. It is *immoral* for a CEO to make millions of dollars when he has just destroyed the livelihood of 40,000 families. And it's just plain *nuts* to allow American companies to move factories overseas at the expense of our own people.

20 When a company fires thousands of people, what happens to the community? Crime goes up, suicide goes up, drug abuse, alcoholism, spousal abuse, divorce—everything bad spirals dangerously upward. The same thing happens with crack. Only crack is illegal, and downsizing is not. If there was a crack house in your neighborhood, what would you do? You would try to get rid of it!

I think it's time we applied the same attitudes we have about crack to corporate downsizing. It's simple: If it hurts our citizens, it should be illegal. We live in a democracy. We enact laws based on what we believe is right and wrong. Murder? Wrong, so we pass a law making it illegal. Burglary? Wrong, and we attempt to prosecute those who commit it. Two really big hairy guys from Gingrich's office pummel me after they read this book? Five to ten in Sing Sing.

As a society, we have a right to protect ourselves from harm. As a democracy, we have a responsibility to legislate measures to protect us from harm.

Here's what I think we should do to protect ourselves:

1. Prohibit corporations from closing a profitable factory or business and moving it overseas. If they close a business and move it within the U.S., they must pay reparations to the community they are leaving behind. We've passed divorce laws that say that if a woman works hard to put her husband through school, and he later decides to leave her after he has become successful, he has a responsibility to compensate her for her sacrifices that allowed him to go on to acquire his wealth. The "marriage" between a company and a community should be no different. If a corporation packs up and leaves, it should have some serious alimony to pay.

2. Prohibit companies from pitting one state or city against another. We are all Americans. It is no victory for our society when one town wins at another's expense. Texas should not be able to raid Massachusetts for jobs. It is debilitating and, frankly, legal extortion.

3. Institute a 100 percent tax on any profits gained by shareholders when the company's stock goes up due to an announcement of firings. No one should be allowed to profit from such bad news.

4. Prohibit executives' salaries from being more than thirty times greater than an average employee's pay. When workers have to take a wage cut because of hard times, so, too, should the CEO. If a CEO fires a large number of employees, it should be illegal for him to collect a bonus that year.

5. Require boards of directors of publicly owned corporations to have representation from both workers and consumers. A company will run better if it has to listen to the people who have to build and/or use the products the company makes.

For those of you free-marketers who disagree with these modest suggestions and may end up on a plane sitting next to me, screaming, "You can't tell a business how it can operate!"—I have this to say: Oh, yes, we can! We legally require companies to build safe products, to ensure safe workplaces, to pay employees a minimum wage, to contribute to their Social Security, and to follow a host of other rules that we, as a society, have deemed necessary for our well-being. And we can legally require each of the steps I've outlined above.

25   GM can't sell crack. Soon, I predict, they and other companies will not be able to sell us out. Just keep firing more workers, my friends, and see what happens.

Writing Strategies

1. Describe Moore's voice and how it is or is not effective in this essay.

2. Summarize Moore's argument. Show how he gets from closing factories to selling crack, and how he makes his point in doing so.

3. Whether you agree or disagree with Moore, look for gaps in his argument. That is, how would someone who disagrees with him argue against his reasoning? Where might his argument be most vulnerable?

4. Identify what you consider to be several of Moore's most interesting points. How does he support them? Why do you think these points are interesting?

5. Evaluate Moore's introduction and conclusion. Are they effective? Why or why not?

Exploring Ideas

1. What change does Moore call for?

2. How does Moore encourage the reader to think about capitalism?

3. Summarize Moore's essay in a paragraph or two, and then discuss your understanding of his essay with several classmates. How is your understanding of his essay similar to or different from your classmates'?

4. Interview a variety of people of different ages and professions to find out what they think about Moore's ideas. How are their views similar to or different from Moore's? Write down the differing viewpoints that you think are most interesting or most convincing.

5. With classmates, discuss the differing viewpoints you discovered for #4 above. Select two or three of the strongest arguments against what Moore says and develop a counterargument for them. What evidence can you provide to help support Moore's argument?

Ideas for Writing

1. Write an editorial for your college paper titled "Why Doesn't [Your College's Name Here] Sell Crack?" Use Moore's reasoning, or reasoning similar to Moore's, to make your point. (Change the title of your editorial as you see fit.)

2. What generally accepted practice is clearly inappropriate?

If responding to one of these ideas, go to the **Analysis** section of this chapter to begin developing ideas for your essay.

The Menstrual Cycle

Christiane Northrup, M.D.

Certain topics are off-limits, or taboo. They are not to be talked about in public or in mixed company (among people of different genders, social standing, religions, races, and so on). But what determines this is social custom and emotional aversion to the topic. While some topics are certainly inappropriate for some audiences, we might also examine how opening up a public discussion can be enlightening and a benefit to all. In "The Menstrual Cycle," a chapter from Christiane Northrup's book *Women's Bodies, Women's Wisdom,* considers the impact social custom and emotional aversion has on this topic and on your reaction to it. Also, notice how Northrup escapes a fundamental assumption in our culture: that the individual human body is a closed system, separate from the world and separate from others.

> How might it have been different for you if, on
> your first menstrual day, your mother had given
> you a bouquet of flowers and taken you to lunch,
> and then the two of you had gone to meet your
> father at the jeweler, where your ears were
> pierced, and your father bought you your first
> pair of earrings, and then you went with a few of
> your friends and your mother's friends to get your
> first lip coloring; and then you went,
>> for the very first time,
>>> to the Women's lodge,
>>>> to learn
>>>>> the wisdom of women?
> How might your life be different?
>
> <div align="right">Judith Duerk, <i>Circle of Stones</i></div>

We can reclaim the wisdom of the menstrual cycle by tuning in to our cyclic nature and celebrating it as a source of our female power. The ebb and flow of dreams, creativity, and hormones associated with different parts of the cycle offer us a profound opportunity to deepen our connection with our inner knowing. This is a gradual process for most women, one that involves unearthing our personal history and then, day by day, thinking differently about our cycles and living with them in a new way.

Our Cyclical Nature

The menstrual cycle is the most basic, earthy cycle we have. Our blood is our connection to the archetypal feminine. The macrocosmic cycles of nature, such as the ebb and flow of the tides and the changes of the seasons, are reflected on a smaller scale in the menstrual cycle of the individual female body. The monthly ripening of an egg and subsequent pregnancy or release of menstrual blood mirrors the process of creation as it occurs not only in nature, unconsciously, but in human endeavor. In many cultures, the menstrual cycle has been viewed as sacred.

Even in modern society, where we are cut off from the rhythms of nature, the cycle of ovulation is influenced by the moon. Studies have shown that peak rates of conception and probably ovulation appear to occur at the full moon or the day before. During the new moon, ovulation and conception rates are decreased overall, and an increased number of women start their menstrual bleeding. Scientific research has documented that the moon rules the flow of fluids (ocean tides as well as individual body fluids) and affects the unconscious mind and dreams.[1] The timing of the menstrual cycle, the fertility cycle, and labor also follows the moon-dominated tides of the ocean. Environmental cues such as light, the moon, and the tides play a documented role in regulating women's menstrual cycles and fertility. In one study of nearly two thousand women with irregular menstrual cycles, more than half of the subjects achieved regular menstrual cycles of twenty-nine days' length by sleeping with a light on near their beds during the three days around ovulation.[2]

The menstrual cycle governs the flow not only of fluids but of information and creativity. We receive and process information differently at different times in our cycles. I like to describe menstrual cycle wisdom this way: From the onset of menstruation until ovulation, we're ripening an egg and—symbolically, at least—

preparing to give birth to someone else, a role that society honors. Many women find that they are at their peak of expression in the outer world from the onset of their menstrual cycle until ovulation. Their energy is outgoing and upbeat. They are filled with enthusiasm and new ideas. At midcycle, we are naturally more receptive to others and to new ideas—more "fertile." Sexual desire also peaks for many women at midcycle, and our bodies secrete into the air hormones that have been associated with sexual attractiveness to others.[3] (Our male-dominated society values this very highly, and we internalize it as a "good" stage of our cycle.) One patient, a waitress who works in a diner where many truckers stop to eat, has reported to me that her tips are highest at midcycle, around ovulation. Another man described his wife as "very vital and electric" during this time of her cycle.

The Follicular and Luteal Phases

5   The menstrual cycle itself mirrors how consciousness becomes matter and how thought creates reality. On the strictly physical level, during the time between menses and ovulation (known as the follicular phase) an egg grows and develops, while deep within the wall of the uterus circular collections of immune system cells, known as lymphoid aggregates, also begin to develop.[4] On the expanded level of ideas and creativity, this first half of the cycle is a very good time to initiate new projects. A researcher friend of mine tells me that she has the most energy to act on ideas for new experiments during this part of her cycle. Ovulation, which occurs at midcycle, is accompanied by an abrupt rise in the neuropeptides FSH (follicle-stimulating hormone) and LH (luteinizing hormone). The rise in estrogen levels that accompanies this has been associated with a rise in left-hemisphere activity (verbal fluency) and a decline in right-hemisphere activity (visual-spatial ability, such as the ability to draw a cube or read a map).[5] Ovulation represents mental and emotional creativity at its peak; the FSH-LH surge that accompanies ovulation may be the biological basis for this. The weeks following ovulation lead up to the menses; this is evaluative and reflec-

tive time, looking back upon what is created and on the negative or difficult aspects of our lives that need to be changed or adjusted. My researcher friend notes that during this part of her cycle, she prefers to do routine tasks that do not require much input from others or expansive thought on her part.

Our creative biological and psychological cycle parallels the phases of the moon; recent research has found that the immune system of the reproductive tract is cyclic as well, reaching its peak at ovulation, and then beginning to wane. From ancient times, some cultures have referred to women having their menstrual periods as being "on their moon." When women live together in natural settings, their ovulations tend to occur at the time of the full moon, with menses and self-reflection at the dark of the moon. Scientific evidence suggests that biological cycles as well as dreams and emotional rhythms are keyed into the moon and tides as well as the planets. Specifically, the moon and tides interact with the electro-magnetic fields of our bodies, subsequently affecting our internal physiological processes. The moon itself has a period when it is covered with darkness, and then slowly, beginning at the time of the new moon, it becomes visible to us again, gradually waxing to fullness. Women, too, go through a period of darkness each month, when the life-force may seem to disappear for a while (premenstrual and menstrual phases).[6] We need not be afraid or think we are sick if our energies and moods naturally ebb for a few days each month. In many parts of India, it's perfectly acceptable for women to slow down during their periods and rest more. I have come to see that all kinds of stress-related disease, ranging from PMS to osteoporosis, could be lessened a great deal if we simply followed our body's wisdom once per month. Demetra George writes that it is here, at the dark of the moon, that "life cleanses, revitalizes, and transforms itself in its evolutionary development, spiraling toward attunement with its essential nature."[7] Studies have shown that most women begin their menstrual periods during the dark of the moon (new moon) and begin bleeding between four and six A.M.—the darkest part of the day.[8] Many women, including me, have noticed that on the first day or two of our periods, we feel an urge to organize our homes or work spaces, cleaning out our closets—and our lives. Our natural biological cleansing is accompanied by a psychological cleansing as well.

If we do not become biologically pregnant at ovulation, we move into the second half of the cycle, the luteal phase—ovulation through the onset of menstruation. During this phase, we quite naturally retreat from outward activity to a more reflective mode. During the luteal phase we turn more inward, preparing *to develop or give birth to something that comes from deep within ourselves.* Society is not nearly as keen on this as it is on the follicular phase. Thus we judge our premenstrual energy, emotions, and inward mood as "bad" and "unproductive." (See Figures 1 and 2.)

Since our culture generally appreciates only what we can understand rationally, many women tend to block at every opportunity the flow of unconscious "lunar" information that comes to them premenstrually or during their menstrual cycle. Lunar information is reflective and intuitive. It comes to us in our dreams, our emotions, and our hungers. It comes under cover of darkness. When we routinely block the information that is coming to us in the second half of our menstrual cycles, it has no choice but to come back as PMS or menopausal madness, in the same way that our other

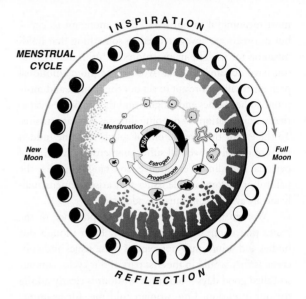

Figure 2

feelings and bodily symptoms, if ignored, often result in illness.[9]

The luteal phase, from ovulation until the onset of menstruation, is when women are *most in tune with their inner knowing and with what isn't working in their lives.* Studies have shown that women's dreams are more frequent and often more vivid during the premenstrual and menstrual phases of their cycles.[10] Premenstrually, the "veil" between the worlds of the seen and unseen, the conscious and the unconscious, is much thinner. We have access to parts of our often unconscious selves that are less available to us at all other times of the month. In fact, it has been shown experimentally that the right hemisphere of the brain—the part associated with intuitive knowing—becomes more active premenstrually, while the left hemisphere becomes less active. Interestingly enough, communication between the two hemispheres may be increased as well.[11] The premenstrual phase is therefore a time when we have greater access to our magic—our ability to recognize and transform the more difficult and painful areas of our lives. Premenstrually, we are quite naturally more in tune with what is

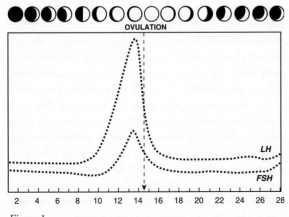

Figure 1

most meaningful in our lives. We're more apt to cry—but our tears are always related to something that holds meaning for us. The many studies of Dr. Katerina Dalton have documented that women are more emotional premenstrually, more apt to act out their anger, and more prone to headaches and fatigue, and they may even experience exacerbations of ongoing illnesses such as arthritis. To the extent that we are out of touch with the hidden parts of ourselves, we will suffer premenstrually. Years of personal and clinical experience have taught me that the painful or uncomfortable issues that arise premenstrually are always real and must be addressed.

10   Women need to believe in the importance of the issues that come up premenstrually. Even though our bodies and minds may not express these issues and concerns as they would in the first part of our cycle—on our so-called good days—our inner wisdom is clearly asking for our attention. One woman told me, for example, that whenever she becomes premenstrual, she worries that the house, car, and investments are in her husband's name only. When she mentions this to her husband, he replies, "What's wrong? Don't you trust me?" I'd call that a premenstrual reality check that needs attention! One husband reported that in the follicular phase of his wife's cycle, she was great, was always cheery, kept the house in order, and did the cooking. But after ovulation she "let herself go" and talked about wanting to go back to college and get out of the house more. I told him that these issues that arise premenstrually should be treated seriously, and I asked him to consider what his wife's needs were for her full personal development. I pointed out that her difficult behavior premenstrually was her way of expressing those needs.

There is an intimate relationship between a woman's psyche and her ovarian function throughout the menstrual cycle. Before we ovulate we are outgoing and upbeat, while ovulating we are very receptive to others, and after ovulation (premenstrually) we are more inward and reflective. An astounding study done in the 1930s supports my observations. The psychoanalyst Dr. Therese Benedek studied the psychotherapy records of a group of patients, while her colleague Dr. Boris Ruben-

stein studied the ovarian hormonal cycles of the same women. By looking at a woman's emotional content, Dr. Benedek was able to predict where she was in her menstrual cycle with incredible accuracy. The authors wrote, "We were pleased and surprised to find an exact correspondence of the ovulative dates as independently determined by the two methods"—that is, psychoanalytic material compared with physiological findings. They found that before ovulation, when estrogen levels were at their highest, women's emotions and behavior were directed toward the outer world. During ovulation, however, women were more relaxed and content and quite receptive to being cared for and loved by others. During the post-ovulatory and premenstrual phase, when progesterone is at its highest, women were more likely to be focused on themselves and more involved in inward-directed activity. Interestingly, in women who had periods but did not ovulate, the authors saw similar cycles of emotions and behavior, except that around the time when ovulation should have occurred, these women missed not only ovulation but the accompanying emotions; that is, they were not relaxed, content, or receptive to being cared for by others.[12]

Given our cultural heritage and beliefs about illness in general and the menstrual cycle in particular, it is not difficult to understand how women have come to see their premenstrual phase not as a time for reflection and renewal but as a disease or a curse. In fact, the language that our culture uses regarding the uterus and ovaries has been experimentally shown to affect women's menstrual cycles. Under hypnosis, a woman who is given positive suggestions about her menstrual cycle will be much less apt to suffer from menstruation-related symptoms.[13] On the other hand, one study found that women who were led to believe that they were premenstrual when they weren't reported more adverse physical symptoms, such as water retention, cramps, and irritability, than another group who were led to believe they were not premenstrual.[14] These studies are excellent examples of how our thoughts and beliefs have the power to affect our hormones, our biochemistry, and our subsequent experience.

Healing through Our Cycles

Once we begin to appreciate our menstrual cycle as part of our inner guidance system, we begin to heal both hormonally and emotionally. There is no doubt that premenstrually, many women feel more inward-directed and more connected to their personal pain and the pain of the world. Many such women are also more in touch with their own creativity and get their best ideas premenstrually, though they may not act on them until later. During the premenstrual phase, we need time to be alone, time to rest, and time away from our daily duties, but taking this time is a new idea and practice for many women. Premenstrual syndrome results when we don't honor our need to ebb and flow like the tides. This society likes action, so we often don't appreciate our need for rest and replenishment. The menstrual cycle is set up to teach us about the need for both the in-breath and the out-breath of life's processes. When we are premenstrual and feeling fragile, we need to rest and take care of ourselves for a day or two. In the Native American moon lodge, bleeding women came together for renewal and visioning and emerged afterward inspired and also inspiring to others. I think that the majority of PMS cases would disappear if every modern woman retreated from her duties for three or four days each month and had her meals brought to her by someone else.

I've personally found that simply and *unapologetically* stating my needs for a monthly slowdown to my husband is all that is needed. When I show respect for myself and the processes of my body, he shows respect as well, and my body responds with comfort and gratitude. Indeed, my experience of my own menstrual cycle began to change after I noticed that my most meaningful insights about myself, my life, and my writing came on the day or two just before my period. In my mid-thirties, I began to look forward to my periods, understanding them to be a sacred time that our culture didn't honor. When I am premenstrual, the things that make me feel teary are the things that are most important to me, things that I know tune me in to my power and my deepest truths. My increased sensitivity feels like a gift of insight. I don't become angry, though if I did, I would pay attention and not chalk it up to "my stupid hormones." I like to keep track of the phases of the moon in my daily calendar to see if I'm ovulating at the full moon, the dark of the moon, or in between. When I ovulate at the full moon and menstruate at the dark of the moon, my inner reflective time is synchronized with the moon's darkness. Getting my period at the time of the full moon results in a more intense period: I am more emotionally charged than usual, and my bleeding is often heavier than normal. I've found that sometimes simply intending to bleed at the dark of the moon tends to move my cycles in this direction, though not always. (I don't "try" to control this.) Noting my individual cycle in relationship to the moon's cycle consciously connects me with the earth and helps me to feel connected with women past and present.

Notes

[1] E. Hartman, "Dreaming Sleep (The D State) and the Menstrual Cycle," *Journal of Nervous and Mental Disease* 143 (1966): 406–16; E. M. Swanson and D. Foulkes, "Dream Content and the Menstrual Cycle," *Journal of Nervous and Mental Disease* 145.5 (1968): 358–63.

[2] F. A. Brown, "The Clocks: Timing Biological Rhythms," *American Scientist* 60 (1972): 756–66; M. Gauguelin, "Wrangle Continues over Pseudo-scientific Nature of Astrology," *New Scientist* 25 Feb. 1978; W. Menaker, "Lunar Periodicity in Human Reproduction: A Likely Unit of Biological Time," *American Journal of Obstetrics and Gynecology* 77.4 (1959): 905–14; E. M. Dewan, "On the Possibility of the Perfect Rhythm Method of Birth Control by Periodic Light Stimulation," *American Journal of Obstetrics and Gynecology* 99.7 (1967): 1016–19.

[3] R. P. Michael, R. W. Bonsall, and P. Warner, "Human Vaginal Secretion and Volatile Fatty Acid Content," *Science* 186 (1974): 1217–19.

[4] Charles Wira, "Mucosal Immunity: The Primary Interface Between the Patient and the Outside World." Course syllabus. Dartmouth Hitchcock Medical Center, 20–21 Sept., 1996.

[5] E. Hampson and D. Kimura, "Reciprocal Effects of Hormonal Fluctuations on Human Motor and Perceptual Skills," *Behavioral Neuroscience* 102 (1988): 456–59.

[6] Wira.

7 Demetra George, *Mysteries of the Dark Moon: The Healing Power of the Dark Goddess* (San Francisco: Harper, 1992) 70–71.

8 Menaker.

9 Lunar data adapted from Caroline Myss.

10 Hartman; Swanson and Foulkes.

11 M. Altemus, B. E. Wexler, and N. Boulis, "Neuropsychological Correlates of Menstrual Mood Changes," *Psychosomatic Medicine* 51 (1989): 329–36.

12 Therese Benedek and Boris Rubenstein, "Correlations Between Ovarian Activity and Psychodynamic Processes: The Ovalutory Phase," *Psychosomatic Medicine* 1.2 (1939): 247–70.

13 Bernard C. Gindes, "Cultural Hypnosis of the Menstrual Cycle," *New Concepts of Hypnosis* (London: George Allen, 1953).

14 Diane Ruble, "Premenstrual Symptoms: A Reinterpretation," *Science* 15 July, 1977: 291–92.

Writing Strategies

1. Who is Northrup's intended reader? That is, to whom do you think she is writing? Explain. (Consider, for example, her opening sentence.)

2. What is the public resonance of Northrup's essay? That is, how might her essay matter to others? Who might benefit from reading it—and how? How does she convey the public resonance?

3. Describe Northrup's voice and how it is or isn't appropriate to her subject matter. Provide examples to support your opinion.

4. Identify three of Northrup's strongest points. What type of evidence does she use to support them? Would the points be as strong without the evidence? Explain.

5. Northrup chooses to begin with an excerpt from Judith Duerk's *Circle of Stones*. Why? What effect does this excerpt have as an opening?

Exploring Ideas

1. In your own words, write down how Northrup views the menstrual cycle. How does she encourage others to view it differently?

2. How do you view the menstrual cycle, or menstruation? How is your view different from Northrup's?

3. Interview others regarding their views on the menstrual cycle. How are their views similar to or different from Northrup's and your own?

4. How might the reader benefit by reading Northrup's essay? Who is her intended audience, and what is she trying to achieve?

5. In a paragraph or two, explain why the menstrual cycle is or is not appropriate reading material and an appropriate topic of discussion in this class.

6. Discuss your responses to #5 above with classmates and others. How are their views on this subject similar to or different from your own? What is the strongest evidence others offer to support their views? What is the strongest evidence you offer to support your own?

Ideas for Writing

1. Northrup says, "In my mid-thirties, I began to look forward to my periods, understanding them to be a sacred time that our culture didn't honor" (¶ 14). What time, place, or thing do you think is sacred but not honored by our culture?

2. Northrup believes that "replacing the harmful myths about our menstrual cycles with accurate information is part of women's healing." How might accurate information—education—help to heal another situation?

If responding to one of these ideas, go to the **Analysis** section of this chapter to begin developing ideas for your essay.

An Apology to Future Generations

Simon Benlow

Thinking radically means breaking away from the present—cutting the intellectual cord that ties us to conventional wisdom. And when those intellectual cords are cut and a writer ventures off beyond the norm, what he or she writes may seem outrageous. In this essay, Simon Benlow escapes the conventional wisdom of his own generation and imagines life beyond it. Notice that the most mundane daily activities, those we'd not otherwise examine, are under investigation.

Writing Strategies

Addresses the reader directly ("you") as someone in the future.

Thesis: We owe future generations an apology, though it cannot really suffice.

(The argument = Benlow's generation is guilty of spoiling the world for the future.)

Evidence for the argument = specific examples.

Using paragraphs as separate reasons for apology.

Exploring Ideas

We can't see ourselves as well as others will see us later.

Apology is not enough.

Personal extravagance and luxury.

We judge previous generations while letting our own generation off the hook.

By now, you certainly know us better than we knew ourselves. You have shaken your heads in amazement. You have, no doubt, wondered at our disregard for you. You know how opulently we lived, how we gorged ourselves daily, how we lived beyond the means of ourselves and of following generations. You know that our desires extended in every direction in time and space, that our capacity to take was monstrous, and our restraint absent. Because we lived in our time, but irreparably harmed the world for those beyond it, I offer this unsatisfactory apology:

- For believing in a world of unlimited resources. We lived as though the water, the land, and the air would perpetually support our fetish with luxury items. We demanded personal extravagances of every imaginable (and entirely unimaginable) kind. Nearly every person of every town had his or her own internal combustion engine lawn mower, leaf blower, snow blower, hedge trimmer. Nearly every home and vehicle had air conditioners. And beyond these "utilities," we had hordes of trinkets, recreational instruments, and pleasure devices that all, eventually, had to lie in waste somewhere when our fickle appetites refocused on the new faster-smoother-quicker-shinier-more-interactive-more-believable gadget. We jet-skied, water-crafted, golf-carted, dune- and moon-buggied, sports-carred, and otherwise spark-plugged ourselves into a frenzy. We became enamored with the movement of machines and the repose of our own bodies.

- For allowing ourselves to be comforted by our own story of progress. The histories of our time kept us self-righteous. We looked back at the waste and pollution of the late nineteenth century—at the dawn of the industrial age. We sighed at the crass industrialists who unknowingly set out to run the entire world on fossil fuels. We denounced the bygone twentieth century leaders who promoted hate and genocide. But, as you know, our crimes of utter disinterest and self-absorption compete with even the most flagrant atrocities of our past.

- For ignoring our scientists who warned repeatedly that our way of life would have dire consequences. Even though we celebrated the role of science in our culture (that is, when it served our longing for increased convenience), we managed to dismiss an entire scientific community when it insisted that our hyper-consumptive lifestyle would ultimately damage the world around us. We branded them political zealots, and conjured up a pseudo anti-mainstream conspiracy so we could complacently dismiss their findings and promote the image of an apolitical, moderate (hence reasonable) population. Once such scientists were assigned to a political agenda (on the "Left"), the masses could be comforted in ignoring their warnings.

We celebrate science yet ignore scientists who call for restraint.

Our intellectual comfort helps create extreme materialism.

The first phrase (stylistic fragment?) is always short.

- For casting away criticisms of our lifestyle and foreign policies. While many peoples of the world (often the most destitute) insisted that our foreign policies promoted obscene degrees of inequity, we demonized or dismissed them. We ignored the lessons from eighteenth- and nineteenth-century revolutions: that absurd degrees of opulence coexist with (or even depend upon) equally absurd degrees of poverty, and even more importantly, that flagrant inequity eventually results in bloody retaliation.

Voice seems formal. (This is a formal apology!)

- For celebrating the most opulent and decadent figures of our time. Our most honored people were those who flaunted their own degrees of comfort and disregard. Their homes, huge monuments to themselves, stretched over acres of private land and, for the most part, sat empty. In the race to mimic the wildly successful, our middle classes, everyday working men and women, sought to build inordinately large homes—with vaulted ceilings and multiple levels. We considered it normal for two adults to occupy vast domestic quarters with numerous empty rooms for storage or show. For holidays, we increased our parade of domestic performances by stringing thousands of electric lights inside and outside of

We celebrate decadence. Our homes are large. Why? Are we out of control?

Provides evidence as support: Middle class sought to build large homes "with vaulted ceilings" and strung "thousands of electric lights" inside and out.

our gargantuan homes and keeping them on for countless hours and days. In short, we measured our success and celebrated our piety with costly ornamentation.

The repetition of the opening structure creates formality.

- For fawning over our children and steeping them in layers of idle comfort, while ignoring, even crudely dismissing, the lives of their children's children. We bought them rooms full of trinkets to occupy their energy, and in so doing, we taught them to treasure petty extravagances that could be easily discarded in favor of new and more sophisticated ones. But we never considered the heaping mounds of discarded, out-of-favor junk—certificates of belonging in our age. We never considered how our self-indulgence would breed a nationalistic capriciousness—a total disregard for others beyond our fenced-in, manicured, up-to-date, polished existence.

Metaphor: "certificates of belonging."

Capriciousness = erratic, impulsive, flighty, inconstant behavior.

- For spreading into every last corner of every last region. We sought out the most pastoral, the most "untouched" land and infiltrated with no remorse. We occupied expanses of natural (what we called "virgin") areas, and transformed them from "undeveloped" terrain into overdeveloped sprawl. And we did it with utmost speed. We saw the land change before our own eyes. We watched our cities smear themselves into outlying rural areas; we saw wetlands, woods, and river flood plains blanketed by pavement, but drove happily over them. We said nothing when our fast-food chains (large corporate entities that sold a homogenous type of ready-to-consume "food") built locations in every remote corner of the map. We felt a comfortable familiarity in encountering the same foods, the same logos, the same containers, the same glowing buildings and signs throughout our land—and the world. And it was not only the corporate entities plowing and paving into virgin terrain. The average citizens cheerily built new, and increasingly bigger, homes despite the shrinking undeveloped space. In fact, we built homes faster than we could fill them—and left old empty ones in our wake.

The constant use of "we" creates public resonance— but also involves the reader in the guilt.

Metaphor

"We" say nothing. Who is "we"? The majority?

Benlow is pointing to the most common parts of our culture—food, homes, cars, toys.

- For perilously ignoring the deep connections among our lifestyles, our foreign policies, our governmental regulations, the environment, and other peoples of the world.

Kind of a summary of all the above?

Metaphor: "breathing the exhaust fumes of our disregard."

I imagine that you are breathing the exhaust fumes of our disregard. If large metropolitan areas are still inhabitable, your citizens must certainly deal with a plague of airborne toxins (brought on by

Urban areas are probably uninhabitable.

war, pollution, or both). Perhaps you wear masks. Perhaps you figured out how to purify the air. Perhaps most of your income goes to such causes. (Perhaps you cannot even imagine what it is like to assume nothing about the air . . . to *not* consider it as daily routine.) I imagine that, in your time, the environment is a daily concern, and that you know the names and effects of toxins that only our most advanced scientists understood. No doubt, you must regard even the most basic food ingredients with scrutiny. I imagine that the sun is no longer personified in children's drawings with a gentle smile and happy radiant beams, but is, instead, something to avoid at all costs. (I imagine that you cannot possibly imagine how we once "bathed" in sun rays for recreation.)

He's not certain of the future—but assumes it'll be rough. (Qualifying here?)

Use of description to paint a picture.

I imagine that your everyday lives are filled with the consequences of our political naïveté. Perhaps the countries that provided our laborers, those we so boldly referred to as "Third World," have by now demanded a change in the world order. Perhaps they are now capable of responding to years of exploitation; perhaps they have escaped the economic imperialism of the twentieth century; or, perhaps their numbers ultimately afforded them the ability to resist their tyrants—who served them up as objects to our "globally minded" leaders. Or perhaps our greed for oil became so great that we no longer concealed our desire to control entire regions of the world. Perhaps, the hidden global tensions of the late twentieth and early twenty-first centuries came to full realization, and you are living in the aftermath.

International policies/politics figure in, too.

Every age has its dissonant voices. But as it shrinks into the past, its internal tensions and dissonant voices fade, and the telescopic lens of history sees it as a unity. And certainly, this fate will befall our time. The material conditions created by our time will frame us all as guilty, as complicit in the deterioration of a socially and environmentally uninhabitable world. And this is no defense of our dissonant voices—those who tried to warn us. They too enjoyed our opulence. As a collective mass of consumers, we all created the conditions that you presently endure—whatever they may be.

Concession: Dissonant voices (such as Benlow) enjoyed opulence, too.

We are all guilty. Even those who object to the current lifestyle contribute to it, participate in it. We must be a part of our culture while at the same time resisting it.

5   Although it is probably impossible, I hope you do not look back and characterize us as purely self-serving and wicked, but as trapped in our own enterprise. We were a young culture with no parents. In fact, we stumbled over ourselves to appear perpetually immature and restless. We packaged restlessness, and sold it in the form of hair dyes, fake breasts, and sexual stimulants. Like a mass of delirious adolescents, we made ourselves increasingly giddy, posing for ourselves and for one another, posing in every aspect of our

Figurative language: "we stumbled over ourselves"

Examples supporting the argument.

We are a young culture. America is a country like a child, without parental control. Our parents are children. Our leaders are like children in the world. As a country, we lack discipline and foresight.

lives: our homes, travel, clothes, food, water, and vacations. It was a mammoth parade of teenage delirium that began in New York, wormed through every tiny town of the Midwest, and wrapped around itself in dizzying perpetual circles on the beaches of California. As it came through every town, no one could resist it. It banged and clamored and woke everyone from dreamy isolation, and so even the most ascetic types found themselves playing along in some small way.

We grew outward and consumed everything because we told ourselves that we could, because our parents said we could, and because their parents said we should. Relentless growth was part of our mythology. It was hard-wired into our daily lives and our nightly dreams. Perhaps it was our conflated notion of private property that eclipsed our potential concern for those outside our fences or beyond our calendar years. Perhaps it was our bloated pride at overcoming nature; we were utterly smitten by the idea that nature could rarely infringe on our desires to move whimsically about the world. Perhaps it was some instinctual drive to outdo others—to surpass the luxuries of past generations. Perhaps it was all of these that blurred our collective vision of the future. Had we been able to look beyond our giant, ballooned notions of self, property, and progress, perhaps we would have been able to foresee something or someone out there in the distance.

Although you cannot possibly imagine it, we were, generally, an agreeable people: We knew how to celebrate, how to have a parade, how to draw a crowd, how to break seating capacity records. And if you could return to our time, I would make a dubious wager that you, too, would find it difficult to resist the lure of our lifestyle, the attraction of our conveniences. And if we had been able to imagine you as real people, even as our own distant progeny, rather than a simple euphemism ("the future"), we certainly would have acted differently. Although we probably would not have relented in our give-it-to-me-now race for more, we would have taken a solemn moment to raise a toast and drink to your hardship.

Margin notes:

"Perhaps" shows Benlow's exploration of the issue.

Very formal language—seems like a funeral.

Conclusion: Any humans tempted by our times would be likely to go along, too.

We are guilty, but nice, people.

. . . we're also ridiculous.

Writing Strategies

1. Evaluate Benlow's introduction. How does or doesn't it invite the reader into the essay?

2. Benlow organizes his essay by dividing his apology into several major sections. What is the purpose of each major section?

3. Describe Benlow's voice as a writer, and refer to several passages to support your description.

4. If workshopping Benlow's essay, what would you tell him? What do you like most about his apology? What one suggestion would you make?

5. Discuss your workshopping ideas (from #4 above) with several classmates. How are your ideas similar to or different from your classmates' ideas?

Exploring Ideas

1. In a paragraph or two, describe how Benlow sees contemporary American culture.

2. How is the way that you see contemporary American culture similar to or different from the way Benlow sees it?

3. Consider your initial reactions to Benlow's essay. What points did you most agree or disagree with? What ideas did you not understand?

4. Ask others if they feel future generations deserve an apology and, if so, for what. Record their responses and compare them to Benlow's essay. How are their views similar to or different from Benlow's and your own?

Ideas for Writing

1. Imagine that Benlow's essay and one of yours will be read by future generations. What would you like to say to future generations?

2. What idea of Benlow's might you expand on?

If responding to one of these ideas, go to the **Analysis** section of this chapter to begin developing ideas for your essay.

Group Minds

Doris Lessing

Radical thinkers go beyond conventional wisdom, and sometimes they speak directly to it. They call out common thinking, name it, poke at it, and explain its harm. In this short essay, Doris Lessing, a novelist and essayist, critiques the way European and American societies ("the West") characterize identity. Although the essay deals with an abstract notion (a critique of identity), Lessing makes the idea concrete, makes it appear realistic, graspable, and vital. At the end of the essay, she even invites us to imagine her critique of identity being applied to education.

People living in the West, in societies that we describe as Western, or as the free world, may be educated in many different ways, but they will all emerge with an idea about themselves that goes something like this: I am a citizen of a free society, and that means I am an individual, making individual choices. My mind is my own, my opinions are chosen by me, I am free to do as I will, and at the worst the pressures on me are economic, that is, I may be too poor to do as I want.

This set of ideas may sound something like a caricature, but it is not so far off from how we see ourselves. It is a portrait that may not have been acquired consciously, but is part of a general atmosphere or set of assumptions that influence our ideas about ourselves.

People in the West therefore may go through their entire lives never thinking to analyze this very flattering picture, and as a result are helpless against all kinds of pressures on them to conform in many kinds of ways.

The fact is that we all live our lives in groups—the family, work groups, social, religious, and political groups. Very few people indeed are happy as solitaries, and they tend to be seen by their neighbors as peculiar or selfish or worse. Most people cannot stand being alone for long. They are always seeking groups to belong to, and if one group dissolves, they look for another. We are group animals still, and there is noth-

ing wrong with that. But what is dangerous is not the belonging to a group, or groups, but not understanding the social laws that govern groups and govern us.

5   When we're in a group, we tend to think as that group does: We may even have joined the group to find "like-minded" people. But we also find our thinking changing because we belong to a group. It is the hardest thing in the world to maintain an individual dissident opinion, as a member of a group.

It seems to me that this is something we have all experienced—something we take for granted, may never have thought about it. But a great deal of experimentation has gone on among psychologists and sociologists on this very theme. If I describe an experiment or two, then anyone listening who may be a sociologist or psychologist will groan, oh God not again—for they will have heard of these classic experiments far too often. My guess is that the rest of the people will never have heard of these experiments, never have had these ideas presented to them. If my guess is true, then it aptly illustrates my general thesis, and the general idea behind these talks, that we (the human race) are now in possession of a great deal of hard information about ourselves, but we do not use it to improve our institutions and therefore our lives.

A typical test, or experiment, on this theme goes like this. A group of people are taken into the researcher's confidence. A minority of one or two are left in the dark. Some situation demanding measurement or assessment is chosen. For instance, comparing lengths of wood that differ only a little from each other, but enough to be perceptible, or shapes that are almost the same size. The majority in the group—according to instruction—will assert stubbornly that these two shapes or lengths are the same length, or size, while the solitary individual, or the couple, who have not been so instructed will assert that pieces of wood or whatever are different. But the majority will continue to insist—speaking metaphorically—that black is white, and after a period of exasperation, irritation, even anger, certainly incomprehension, the minority will fall into line. Not always, but nearly always. There are indeed glorious individuals who stubbornly insist on telling the truth as they see it, but most give in to the majority opinion, obey the atmosphere.

When put as badly, as unflatteringly, as this, reactions tend to be incredulous: "I certainly wouldn't give in, I speak my mind . . ." But would you?

People who have experienced a lot of groups, who perhaps have observed their own behavior, may agree that the hardest thing in the world is to stand out against one's groups, a group of one's peers. Many agree that among our most shameful memories is this: how often we said black was white because other people were saying it.

10   In other words, we know that this is true of human behavior, but how do we know it? It is one thing to admit it, in a vague uncomfortable sort of way (which probably includes the hope that one will never again be in such a testing situation) but quite another to make that cool step into a kind of objectivity, where one may say, "Right, if that's what human beings are like, myself included, then let's admit it, examine and organize our attitudes accordingly."

This mechanism, of obedience to the group, does not only mean obedience or submission to a small group, or one that is sharply determined, like a religious or political party. It means, too, conforming to those large, vague, ill-defined collections of people who may never think of themselves as having a collective mind because they are aware of differences of opinion—but which, to people from outside, from another culture, seem very minor. The underlying assumptions and assertions that govern the group are never discussed,

"Suppose this kind of thing were taught in schools."

never challenged, probably never noticed, the main one being precisely this: That it is a group mind, intensely resistant to change, equipped with sacred assumptions about which there can be no discussion.

But suppose this kind of thing were taught in schools?

Let us just suppose it, for a moment. . . . But at once the nub of the problem is laid bare.

Imagine us saying to children, "In the last fifty or so years, the human race has become aware of a great deal of information about its mechanisms; how it behaves, how it must behave under certain circumstances. If this is to be useful, you must learn to contemplate these rules calmly, dispassionately, disinterestedly, without emotion. It is information that will set people free from blind loyalties, obedience to slogans, rhetoric, leaders, group emotions." Well, there it is.

Writing Strategies

1. How does Lessing's opening paragraph set up the rest of her essay?

2. What does Lessing conclude should be taught in schools but isn't?

3. What type of support does Lessing rely upon most?

4. What additional type of support might Lessing have used, and why?

5. How does Lessing interact with the reader? Identify several specific instances that illustrate Lessing's particular treatment of the reader.

6. Identify an important counterargument, qualifier, or concession in Lessing's argument. Or, suggest one that she does not make, but that would have strengthened her argument.

Exploring Ideas

1. In her opening paragraph, Lessing says most Westerners have the following idea of themselves: "I am a citizen of a free society, and that means I am an individual, making individual choices. My mind is my own, my opinions are chosen by me, I am free to do as I will, and at the worst the pressures on me are economic; that is, I may be too poor to do as I want." What does Lessing think is wrong with this self-image?

2. How has joining and conforming to a particular group changed your thinking?

3. Summarize Lessing's main idea about what should be, but isn't, taught in schools. Then ask others why they agree or disagree with Lessing. What reasons do others give for their agreeing or disagreeing?

4. Lessing states: "This mechanism, of obedience to the group, does not only mean obedience or submission to a small group, or one that is sharply determined, like a religious or political party. It means, too, conforming to those large, vague, ill-defined collections of people who may never think of themselves as having a collective mind because they are aware of differences of opinion — but which, to people from outside, from another culture, seem very minor" (¶ 11). In a small group, come up with several examples that support Lessing's point.

Ideas for Writing

1. What are many people helpless against because they never think to analyze a flattering picture they have of themselves?

2. Why don't we improve our institutions and therefore our lives, even though we now possess a great deal of hard information about ourselves?

If responding to one of these ideas, go to the **Analysis** section of this chapter to begin developing ideas for your essay.

Outside Reading

Find a written text that you believe illustrates radical thinking, and make a copy or print it out. While radical thinking sometimes appears in popular or general readership publications (*Time, Newsweek*, the *New York Times*, and so on), such periodicals usually appeal to conventional thinking. You might have better luck exploring less mainstream sources, such as academic journals in art, science, communication, religion, political science, and so on. To conduct an electronic search of journals and magazines, go to your library's periodical database or to InfoTrac College Edition (http://infotrac.galegroup.com/itweb/). For your library database, perform a keyword search, or for InfoTrac College Edition, go to the main search box and choose "keywords." Enter word combinations such as *radical and ideas and science, innovative and business and ideas, revolutionary and medical and health, avant-garde and physics* (or any topic combined with synonyms for *radical*). (When performing keyword searches, avoid using phrases or articles such as *a, an, the;* instead, use nouns separated by *and*.) The search results will yield lists of journal and magazine articles.

You can also search the Internet. Try the search engine Lycos.com. Like most Internet search engines, Lycos.com combines words using *and*. In the search box, try various combinations, such as those above. Unlike periodical databases, the Internet search results will contain sources that are selling products and services. Be cautious of such sites.

As you will see, writers in many disciplines write and think on the edge of conventional wisdom and, as you will probably discover, any topic can be approached radically. Writing that transcends conventional thought varies widely in tone, style, length, and strategy. As you read through this chapter, keep the text you have discovered and notice the elements and strategies the writer uses. Depending on your instructor's suggestions, do one or more of the following:

1. Notice how the writer employs various rhetorical strategies. On the hard copy or photocopy:

   - Highlight the thesis if it is stated. If the thesis is implied, write it in your own words.

   - Highlight the most radical claims.

   - Highlight any passages in which the writer attempts to bridge conventional wisdom with radical thinking.

   - Identify any counterarguments (passages in which the writer anticipates and refutes opposition) or concessions (passages in which the writer grants value to another position).

2. Analyze the strategies employed by the writer. The following questions may be helpful:

   - In what ways does the writer transcend or challenge conventional thinking?

   - How does the writer persuade the reader to see his or her vision?

   - Who is the audience for this text?

   - How does the audience impact the kinds of things said in the argument?

   - How would you describe the writer's voice?

3. Write at least three "Writing Strategies" questions for the text that you found.

4. Write at least three "Exploring Ideas" questions for the text you found.

5. Write two "Ideas for Writing," such as the ones following the essays in this book, for the text that you found.

INVENTION

"Uncertainty can be your guiding light."

—U2

On the one hand, the focus of this chapter may seem rather abstract; we are, after all, attempting to imagine new intellectual ground. On the other hand, these ideas can have their beginnings in familiar, everyday terrain. While the goal may be to extend thinking beyond familiar ideas, we can still start with everyday life.

For this chapter, nothing is more important than the act of invention. As in previous chapters, the writer should attempt to discover something particularly interesting or valuable — or even bizarre. Unlike previous chapters, the ultimate goal is to escape conventional thinking and to imagine something entirely outside of common intellectual activity. The following sections are designed to help you through this process: specifically, to discover a topic (in **Point of Contact**), to develop particular points about the topic (in **Analysis**), to make it relevant to a community of readers (in **Public Resonance**), to invent a focused position (in **Thesis**), and to develop support (in **Rhetorical Tools**). Use the Invention questions in each section to explore further. Good luck!

POINT OF CONTACT

The prompts on this page are designed to generate possible writing topics. Fill in the blanks with as many possibilities as you can until you find an engaging topic. As you explore each category, you might imagine particular situations or people to help you start exploring ideas. But do not confine yourself to practical situations or personal experiences. Imagine the possibilities beyond your experiences.

Imagining new connections We are taught (directly and indirectly) to see some things as inherently related and others as entirely disconnected. But radical thinkers can see connections that are not normally seen. Radical thinkers might see an important connection between the economy and nature, oceans and people, or music and politics. Imagine various possibilities, and fill in the blanks to the following statements:

> Most people do not see the connection between _____ and _____.

> Even though it is not apparent, _____ and _____ are deeply connected.

Imagining different possibilities The policies and procedures of society often blind us to alternatives. Imagining those alternatives might reveal a new way to live. For example, someone might imagine something even better than democracy, or a new way to fund college, or an alternative to war. Fill in the blanks with possible ideas:

> Presently, most people _____, but they could _____.

> Presently, the law requires that people must _____, but the law could state that _____.

Questioning common sense Living in a society means participating in common practices and beliefs. But a common belief is not always the best belief. Imagine possibilities for the following and fill in the blanks:

> Most people in my community want _____ without examining the underlying meaning.

> I have always been taught to think _____, but now see a different way.

Exploring the past and future A radical vision is one that sees beyond the confines of the present. A radical thinker might imagine what the world would be like if the American Revolution had not occurred, or how work in America will be defined in 50 years. As you imagine time beyond the present, fill in the blanks for the following:

> In the past, people's perspective of _____ was fundamentally different from our present understanding.

> In the future, people will probably understand _____ differently than we do.

Going to the root The term *radical* comes from the Latin *radix,* which means *root* or *source.* Radical thinking might be seen as a process of finding the root or essence. For example, someone might explore the essence of womanhood or manhood, the true meaning of growing old, or the essence of education. Fill in the blanks to the following questions:

> What is the essence of _____?

> What is the most fundamental quality of _____?

ACTIVITY

Now go beyond these questions. In a small group, use the categories in this section to ask more questions. After generating more questions within these categories, try to create more categories, and then create several questions for each category. Do not stop generating questions until everyone participating has encountered a potential topic.

ANALYSIS

The intellectual activity in this chapter involves *theory*—reasoning that is divorced from practical or physical particulars. When people theorize, they explore the realm of ideas and assumptions and make generalized claims. For example, when Sigmund Freud theorized about the nature of the unconscious, he was not making guesses about his own mind, but that of the *human* mind. He theorized that psychological ailments emerge from childhood crises. His theory, like all theories, could be applied to particular situations; he used the general notion to help cure problems within specific patients.

Everyone has theories (general accounts or concepts that inform how we receive ideas and act on the world), but theories are usually not discussed openly. They most often lie undetected in our minds. For instance, people may have a theory about knowledge acquisition; that is, they may have a general account of how people come to know things. This theory may be fairly complicated and may involve memory, experience, and language use—but rarely do people examine such theories closely and ask hard questions: *How does language acquisition relate to knowledge acquisition?* Doing theory, then, is the act of examining and developing our concepts. As you can imagine, theorists take little for granted. They are not willing to accept the answers they have been given, but look around them and imagine what other answers may be possible.

ACTIVITY

Group Theory

Doing theory requires a degree of intellectual play, as well as some deliberate and constructive probing. With several peers (online or in the classroom), choose one of the following topics:

- The difference between men and women
- When a child becomes an adult
- The relationship between individual and community
- The relationship between humans and nature

Each participant should explain his or her theory about the topic in one minute—or one paragraph if using e-mail. After each participant has a turn, start again: Everyone should take another turn and build upon or speak back to particular points made in the previous round. After the second round, start again. After several rounds, each participant should write a brief paragraph explaining how the theory session changed, developed, confirmed, expanded, or highlighted his or her ideas.

Theorists discuss what others avoid . . . or ignore.

Now, *theorize* about your topic: The strategy here is to explore freely, beyond prior assumptions or quick answers. (Ponder your topic for as long as possible before coming to any conclusions. Perhaps keep a notepad with you for a day or for several days, while you continue to rethink your ideas. Record even the most offbeat or seemingly irrelevant notions.)

The following questions may help you discover meaning or make connections:

- What is the basic or essential quality of the topic?
- How does the topic affect or influence thinking?
- How does conventional thought or practice keep people from a radical perspective on this topic?
- What is the origin of the topic?
- What do people normally not consider about the topic?

INVENTION WORKSHOP

Make certain to extend your thinking when answering these questions. In fact, you might not *answer* the questions at all, but begin a process of exploration that could continue in your writing. For example, Linda, a business major, has chosen to explore the *essence of business*. In a discussion with peers, she begins a true exploration of the topic:

What is the basic or essential quality of the topic?

Linda: Well, I wonder if this topic can even be thought about radically, but let's try it: I think the basic quality of business is competition.

Marcus: Competition with other people?

Linda: Yes . . . I think so. Other people or companies—or even countries.

Marcus: For that matter, what about towns and communities?

Linda: Yeah, I guess so. Towns and communities do compete for customers, for market, for tourism dollars.

Diana: So are all these people and communities competing for money?

Linda: Ultimately, yes. But at first, they are competing for more customers or clients.

Marcus: So . . . is it always about more customers? More money?

Linda: Well, I'd think so. Certainly, for retail stores, the daily goal is getting more people through the doors and to the cash register than the store across the street.

Diana: What if we looked at it like the companies are living organisms. I just saw something about bears on the Discovery Channel: every summer and fall, before hibernation, the bears try to consume as much food as possible. But they also need to conserve their strength. They don't want to exert a lot of energy while trying to eat all this food. The ultimate goal isn't the amount of food. It's survival. The bears are competing for food, like salmon, but the essence of their competing is survival.

Linda: So . . . back to business . . . companies are not necessarily competing for just money; they're competing for survival, for life.

Marcus: That makes a lot of sense. Surviving in business involves making a lot of money (more than others), but it also involves conserving. Think about it: Companies that are out just to make a lot of money go down quickly because they didn't conserve.

The important moment here is Diana's brave reference to the Discovery Channel. While bears and business have little in common, Diana is thinking about the essence of things—how entities stay alive. Her inventive connection makes the group rethink the essence of business. And now Linda's thoughts on the essence of business are beginning to take flight. She is going beyond the quick, easy response and exploring some hidden dynamics of business. If she continues developing these ideas, she could transcend conventional wisdom and make valuable discoveries.

THINKING FURTHER

Everyday language is filled with sayings that suggest indisputable truths. They are often widely used but unexamined, and so often conceal more truth than they communicate. These sayings, sometimes called *clichés,* might even misguide our thinking. Consider the following: *What doesn't hurt you only makes you stronger. Bigger is better. Back to the basics. Boys will be boys.* Such clichés might get in the way of exploring your own topic.

The following questions may help you work around conventional thinking:

- Can you think of any clichés related to your topic?
- How do they limit thinking?
- Might the opposite of the cliché be true?

ACTIVITY

In a small group, share topic ideas. Then list the common sayings, assertions, and opinions related to each topic. In this collective brainstorm, try to capture all the conventional wisdom associated with each topic. What do people normally think, feel, and say about each? What are the common opinions, complaints, and hopes? The goal is to give each writer a clear sense of the conventional so that he or she can think beyond it.

INVENTION WRITING

In his invention writing about the future, Simon Benlow explores the present:

What do people normally not consider about the topic?

People do not normally consider pollution and the future because nothing in our popular culture invites us to, unless it's some silly movie inviting us to imagine a post–world war future. In general, we're not asked to consider how our present wants will influence anyone beyond ourselves. The presiding language of our culture is filled with provocations to be fulfilled, to be happy (i.e., buy lots of things and drive a new car). We keep building/buying bigger and bigger vehicles, and consider our actions only (only!) when gas prices go up. In other words, the general trend in buying goods is to wrap ourselves in as much luxury as our wallets allow.

Benlow then goes further when he thinks about the language we use in everyday life. He tries to get beyond the common phrases (such as "the future") that hide complexity:

Can you think of any clichés related to your topic?

Maybe "the future" itself is a cliché. If a cliché hides or glosses over complexity, that phrase ("the future") hides something. It hides the people out there in the distance . . . the real people who'll no doubt have to deal with our wants! When we say "the future" or "posterity" or "our children," we're just glossing over the real people who'll be living with policies and laws and practices that emerge from our overindulgence. "Make sure to wear your air mask, Connor." "Oh, I left it at school yesterday." And then, of course, if anyone today brings up things like breathing nontoxic air or drinking clean water, they get deemed "environmentalists," "tree huggers," "liberals," etc. These terms are ways of dismissing the present and the future . . . real humans with real lungs and kidneys. We've become a culture of lunatics.

Clichés are intellectual bubbles. Pop them, and there's nothing there.

PUBLIC RESONANCE

A topic that has public resonance taps into the concerns of many or makes a connection to public conditions or interests. In one sense, your topic may already have public resonance. Because you are theorizing (exploring more general ideas rather than particular situations), your topic may easily connect to others. However, radical thinking always runs the risk of alienating others. When a writer transcends conventional wisdom, he or she must also do the work of inviting others into the new vision, which is no small task (consider Galileo's fate!).

Use the following questions to help connect your ideas to your readers' concerns:

- What is conventional thought on the topic?
- What nonconventional claims have been made about the topic?
- What keeps people from understanding the thing/idea in nonconventional ways?
- How would a new understanding of the topic help people? (Who, particularly, would a new understanding help?)

"Everything that can be invented has been invented."

—Charles H. Duell. Commissioner, U.S. Office of Patents, 1899.

INVENTION WRITING

In his invention, Simon Benlow goes beyond naming "conventional thought." He tries to explain the nature of present thinking, how it works, how it is limited:

What is conventional thought on the topic?
The thing is . . . there is no conventional thought on this matter. People do not genuinely think about the future—in the specific and local sense. They don't imagine their lives affecting their grandchildren's world. People have been lulled into a present-tense-only mentality. Sure, most parents try to provide for their children . . . but they don't imagine how their lives (outside of creating a savings account) will affect the world that their children (and their children's children's children) will inhabit. In general, people in America spend most of their time thinking about their own *financial existence,* and the *future earning power* of their children. But they do not think about the air, the land, the water of the world 50 years, or 100 years, from now . . . and they don't imagine how present global politics might impact the future.

PUBLIC RESONANCE IN CHAPTER READINGS

Writers who make radical (or new) claims cannot simply dismiss the beliefs of others; they must build an intellectual bridge between conventional thought and new thought. In a sense, this is the primary objective of the writing in this chapter. For example, in her essay, Christiane Northrup makes some radical claims about the biological processes of women's bodies, but she also acknowledges the possible gap between her understanding and more conventional views:

The ebb and flow of dreams, creativity, and hormones associated with different parts of the [menstrual] cycle offer us a profound opportunity to deepen our connection with our inner knowing. This is a gradual process for most women, one that involves unearthing our personal history and then, day by day, thinking differently about our cycles and living with them in a new way. (571)

In this passage Northrup hopes to illustrate a "profound opportunity" for her audience, but she also acknowledges the gradual progression toward such an understanding.

When making adventurous claims, it is especially important to make the connections, so your ideas have genuine significance and are more than vague abstractions. Notice how Michael Moore makes a connection to his readers:

> I think it's time we applied the same attitudes we have about crack to corporate downsizing. It's simple: If it hurts our citizens, it should be illegal. We live in a democracy. We enact laws based on what we believe is right and wrong. Murder? Wrong, so we pass a law making it illegal. Burglary? Wrong, and we attempt to prosecute those who commit it. (569)

Moore's broader point, about the injurious consequences of corporate downsizing, could be presented in abstract terms—and very few people would be engaged. But Moore attempts to make the issue about Americans, about people who live and work in this democracy.

Writers like Moore and Northrup (and all the other writers in this text) work to make a connection between their readers and the bigger social/political/natural world. When that connection is made, the writing gains a sense of purpose and significance.

RESEARCH

Exploring what has been said about your topic may be helpful in creating public resonance. Reading others' ideas on the topic can help to extend or complicate your initial thoughts, help to place your thoughts in a broader context, and/or help to show how your thoughts transcend convention. Finding interesting texts on your topic, however, may be challenging, especially if you are attempting to discover a novel connection. (See Chapter 13, Research & Writing, for guidance in finding sources. Specifically, see What Is Inventive Research? on page 612.)

THESIS

Remember that a thesis provides focus for both writer and reader. For the kind of writing done in this chapter, a thesis is especially important. Since the ideas are potentially abstract and far-reaching, a strong focus will keep the text from wandering. (While the goal may be to invite readers to wonder, a writer should keep readers from wandering.)

The following statements all work to transcend or speak back to conventional thinking. Each focuses on a particular topic, acknowledges or suggests a conventional view, and offers an alternative way of seeing:

- Behind our desire to drive bigger vehicles and own bigger homes lurks more than an attraction to personal success; it is, rather, a deep hostility toward other people and the environment.

- While a glass ceiling may prevent women from climbing the ladder of success, women and men both would have a better quality of life if they participated on the lower rungs only.

- Though *Jeopardy* is often perceived as a test of intelligence, it is really a test of knowledge. A better test of intelligence is *Survivor* or *The Amazing Race*, which requires more analytical thinking skills.

- More gunfights and car crashes actually make a movie duller, not more exciting.

- Because people have come to believe it is the ultimate power, modern medicine has ironically done more harm than good in most people's lives.

- It is commonly thought that the North defeated the South in the Civil War. In fact, the South now controls the American government.

- Even just a cursory look at one's own life will turn up evidence that every American's primary function these days is to consume.

- While the American school system prepares citizens for employment, it allows (and perhaps encourages) them to be helpless against propaganda.

- Farmers or dogcatchers as politicians would serve the people better than professional politicians do.

- A president who doesn't understand why terrorists might fly planes into buildings is ultimately far more dangerous than the terrorists are.

- The poor are better off than the wealthy.

- Had the electric guitar not been invented, the accordion would have continued its reign as the most popular instrument among American youth.

- Although students should feel comfortable in a college classroom, the uneasiness some students feel is necessary to learning.

- All animals, not just humans, should be given the right to life, liberty, and the pursuit of happiness.

- Because of credit and debt, most Americans today are unknowing slaves to the wealthy.

- College professors aren't any smarter than the average Joe.

- Eggs are more valuable than gold.

- Mundane tasks, like weeding a garden or doing the dishes, are a form of meditation that most Americans should indulge in more often and more earnestly.

- The way that Americans communicate with each other is a bigger threat than terrorism.

ACTIVITY

Choose five of the statements on this page. Describe how each statement is or is not radical. Does it transcend or speak back to some particular conventional way of thinking? Does it reveal something usually overlooked or dismissed? How does the wording and construction of each sentence help the reader to see something new?

EVOLUTION OF A THESIS

Do not be in a hurry to solidify your thesis. As you write and think, ideas will evolve—and the *evolution* of ideas is the goal of academic writers. In the following example, Linda's ideas transform over a period of time. She started trying to discover the essence or root of business. In her early discussion with peers (see the Analysis section, page 591), she made a big leap and discovered an alternative way of thinking, as illustrated in the move from the first and second statements. More focused and inventive thinking led her to the final statement.

Linda begins with a widely held understanding of her topic:

- The essence of business is making money.

She develops a position different from conventional thinking:

- Like any organism, the essence of business is survival.

Linda shapes the idea as she writes:

- Beneath the everyday affairs of making money, the essence of business is survival, which involves consuming and conserving.

Because this chapter invites you beyond your initial opinion, you might be wondering: *Am I supposed to give my opinion, or what?* This is a fair question. A radical statement is an opinion insofar as a single writer is offering a new way to see a topic. But it is more than a personal opinion. It is a writer's attempt at rethinking something—and a writer's invitation to others to rethink something.

> Remember that thesis statements often suffer from common problems. See Chapter 6 (page 281) for reminders and guidance.

REVISION

How do you know that your opinion is speaking back to conventional views? How do you know that you've gone far enough in your thinking? To answer these questions, you might enlist the help of others in reevaluating your thesis. In a small group, present your topic. Have the group describe all the conventional opinions they can imagine. Then present your thesis and explain why you think it responds to or transcends conventional thinking. The group members should then ask:

- Does the thesis uncover something new?
- Does it offer a new way of seeing the topic?
- If not, what is holding it back?

RHETORICAL TOOLS

"Adventure is worthwhile in itself."

—Amelia Earhart

The primary objective for this writing is to communicate a new vision on your topic. This will take some sound explaining tactics. But you will also need to persuade your reader that your vision, your adventurous new way of thinking, is valuable, and this will take a broad range of tools.

Using Narration

Narration draws readers into a set of events. A narrative or story can help writers illustrate a broader point; and when making adventurous claims, a narrative can help bridge the gap between conventional and radical ideas. You might also consider anecdotes or testimonials (brief and often personal accounts) to illustrate points. Notice Northrup's use of narration:

> Indeed, my experience of my own menstrual cycle began to change after I noticed that my most meaningful insights about myself, my life, and my writing came on the day or two just before my period. In my mid-thirties, I began to look forward to my periods, understanding them to be a sacred time that our culture didn't honor. When I am premenstrual, the things that make me feel teary are the things that are most important to me, things that I know tune me into my power and my deepest truths. (575)

Using Description

Writers making adventurous or radical claims must consider the intellectual positions of their audience. Because readers may have no mental pictures of the ideas being put forth, it is up to the writer to sufficiently describe or characterize ideas. Notice Benlow's description, which helps the reader to see evidence of his claims:

> Nearly every person of every town had his or her own internal combustion engine lawn mower, leaf blower, snow blower, hedge trimmer. Nearly every home and vehicle had air conditioners. And beyond these "utilities," we had hordes of trinkets, recreational instruments, and pleasure devices that all, eventually, had to lie in waste somewhere when our fickle appetites refocused on the new faster-smoother-quicker-shinier-more-interactive-more-believable gadget. (577)

Using Figurative Language

Literal description is sometimes insufficient to communicate the depth of an idea. This is when writers turn to figurative language, such as similes and metaphors, which help to represent complex or particularly abstract ideas. Notice Benlow's simile, which develops into a metaphor:

> Like a mass of delirious adolescents, we made ourselves increasingly giddy, posing for ourselves and for one another, posing in every aspect of our lives: our homes, travel, clothes, food, water, and vacations. It was a mammoth parade of teenage delirium that

began in New York, wormed through every tiny town of the Midwest, and wrapped around itself in dizzying perpetual circles on the beaches of California. As it came through every town, no one could resist it. It banged and clamored and woke everyone from dreamy isolation, and so even the most ascetic types found themselves playing along in some small way. (580–581)

Using Definitions

Although radical thinking does not depend on dictionary definitions, writers can use definitions to communicate complex ideas. In fact, defining and redefining terms is at the heart of radical thinking. In Moore's essay, he indirectly defines "democracy" and then applies that definition to his argument:

> We live in a democracy. We enact laws based on what we believe is right and wrong. Murder? Wrong, so we pass a law making it illegal. Burglary? Wrong, and we attempt to prosecute those who commit it. . . .
>
> As a society, we have a right to protect ourselves from harm. As a democracy, we have a responsibility to legislate measures to protect us from harm. (569)

Argumentative Support

When making adventurous claims, writers must possess a broad range of support strategies.

Evidence

- **Statistics:** Information (often given in numerical value) collected through experimentation, surveys, polls, and research.
- **Authorities:** References to published (usually written) sources.
- **Facts:** Agreed-upon events or truths.
- **Examples:** Specific cases or illustrations of a phenomenon.

- **Allusions:** References to history, news events, films, television shows, science, nature, or literary texts.
- **Personal Testimonies/Anecdotes:** Individual accounts or experiences.
- **Scenarios:** Hypothetical or fictionalized accounts.

Appeals

- **Appeal to Logic:** Relates the argument to the audience's sense of reason.
- **Appeal to Emotion:** Relates the argument to the audience's emotional state, or attempts to create a particular emotional state in the audience.
- **Appeal of Character:** Relates the argument to a quality of the author or speaker.
- **Appeal to Need:** Relates the argument to people's needs (spiritual, economic, physical, sexual, familial, political, etc.).
- **Appeal to Value:** Relates the argument to people's values (judgments about right and wrong, success, discipline, selflessness, moderation, honesty, chastity, modesty, self-expression, etc.).

In "Why Doesn't GM Sell Crack?" Michael Moore relies on several appeals:

- **Appeal to Logic:** If a company must do "whatever is necessary to create the biggest profit possible," and selling drugs like crack makes a big profit, then companies should just sell crack.
- **Appeal to Logic:** Crack is illegal because it harms lives and destroys communities. Likewise, removing a major employer, for the sake of profit, harms communities. Therefore, removing a major employer for the sake of profit should be illegal.
- **Appeal to Value (fairness or moderation):** CEO salaries shouldn't be more than 30 times that of the workers.
- **Appeal to Value:** If workers lose jobs, CEOs shouldn't prosper.

Counterargument

Counterarguments anticipate and refute opposing claims or positions. Especially when their claims are nonconventional or challenging, writers must anticipate and account for positions outside of or opposed to their own. Because the writer has a whole set of intellectual conventions to contend with, counterargument is an important part of radical thinking. Wendell Berry, for example, uses counterargument throughout his essay. In a turnabout paragraph, Berry points to the opposing side, and then refutes the ideas, showing support for his position:

> The people who benefit from this state of affairs have been at pains to convince us that the agricultural practices and policies that have almost annihilated the farming population have greatly benefited the population of food consumers. But more and more consumers are now becoming aware that our supposed abundance of cheap and healthful food is to a considerable extent illusory. They are beginning to see that the social, ecological, and even the economic costs of such "cheap food" are, in fact, great. (565)

Depending on the position being taken and the kind of claims being put forth, some writers may need to counter many points. For example, we might say that Michael Moore is counterarguing throughout his essay. He is speaking directly back to the claim that corporations should be able to do whatever they deem necessary to generate profit.

Concession

While counterarguments refute objections, concessions acknowledge the value of others' positions or claims. Even though a text making radical claims may not be openly argumentative, by definition it seeks to overturn conventional ideas. For this reason, concessions can be essential to engaging potentially apprehensive readers. Notice Benlow's concession below. Most of Benlow's essay condemns his own generation, but he offers this small note, suggesting that people were more weak than evil. Without such a concession, readers might reject Benlow's ideas as purely antagonistic:

> Although it is probably impossible, I hope you do not look back and characterize us as purely self-serving and wicked, but as trapped in our own enterprise. We were a young culture with no parents. (580)

Toulminian Analysis

Stephen Toulmin's framework for analyzing arguments (claim, warrant, grounds) may be valuable for revealing the shortcomings of conventional thought. (See a more detailed explanation of Toulminian analysis on pages 341–343.) The first step of revolutionary thinkers often is to critique the logic of widely held beliefs. And Toulminian analysis allows writers to show previously unexamined assumptions. For example, Michael Moore's analysis reveals the assumptions (or what he calls "attitudes") beneath the laws of our society. Once he discovers that the basic motivation for enacting laws is to protect society from harm, he can apply that to corporate behavior:

> I think it's time we applied the same attitudes we have about crack to corporate downsizing. It's simple: If it hurts our citizens, it should be illegal. We live in a democracy. We enact laws based on what we believe is right and wrong. Murder? Wrong, so we pass a law making it illegal. Burglary? Wrong, and we attempt to prosecute those who commit it. . . .
>
> As a society, we have a right to protect ourselves from harm. As a democracy, we have a responsibility to legislate measures to protect us from harm. (569)

Outside Sources

Radical or adventurous claims do not exist in a vacuum; they exist alongside other similar claims and discoveries. Notice Northrup's use of outside sources: She begins her writing with the words of Judith Duerk, and later refers to other doctors' work to illustrate her points:

> An astounding study done in the 1930s supports my observations. The psychoanalyst Dr. Therese Benedek studied the psychotherapy records of a group of patients, while her colleague Dr. Boris Rubenstein studied the ovarian hormonal cycles of the same women. By looking at a woman's emotional content, Dr. Benedek was able to predict where she was in her menstrual cycle with incredible accuracy. (574)

Northrup points to other voices not only to support her ideas but also to imply that her own unconventional understanding of the menstrual cycle resonates with others' discoveries.

Remember that the primary goal is to bring potential readers into your new vision, not to leave them behind.

RESEARCH VS. MESEARCH

It is often easy to find outside sources that confirm our positions and support our worldviews. But such work, what we might call *mesearch,* misses the spirit and goal of *research,* which is to explore beyond our own initial suppositions, to read and re-think topics. Researching can be an inventive process—one that catapults us beyond initial ideas.

Avoid:
- Collecting statistics without questioning them, reflecting on them, evaluating their significance.
- Limiting your exploration to sources that share your opinion or perspective.
- Merely "proving" your position with others' words.

Try:
- Gathering perspectives from a variety of sources.
- Closely examining writers who oppose your perspective or who see the world differently.
- Directly addressing the unstated assumptions and values in the sources. Try to discover what the writers value, hope for, or dismiss. What is their basic view of the world and how does that influence their approach to the topic?

ORGANIZATIONAL STRATEGIES

How Should I Begin?

The important point to remember in this chapter is that the writing must move the readers outside of their comfortable intellectual positions. Readers tend to associate highly conventional writing structure with conventional thinking. So if writers want to move readers beyond conventional thinking, they might do well to explore alternative introduction strategies.

Following are some strategies for introductions. Consider an introductory strategy you would not typically use.

- **Anecdote** A brief personal story can illustrate something significant and related to the topic.

- **Scenario** If you have not directly experienced something related to your topic, you can use a hypothetical or fictional situation that illustrates something significant and related to the topic.

- **Allusion** A reference to history, news, popular culture, or literature can create a powerful connection with your readers.

- **Figurative language** A metaphor or simile that sheds new light on the topic can take the reader beyond conventional thinking.

- **Question** An intense question, one that is impossibly difficult to answer or one that is seemingly easy to answer, can get your readers' attention.

For any of these introduction strategies, remember that an opening paragraph should not only establish the tone of a text; it should also create an intellectual climate that is developed throughout the text.

> Examine the essays in this chapter, and decide if or how the introductions help to invite the readers into a new way of thinking.

How Should I Make Connections to Conventional Thinking?

Conventional ideas are those you are trying to transcend or challenge. You might treat them as you would treat opposing arguments, using paragraphs to distinguish between conventional and radical ideas in the same way as you would for counterargument (see page 600).

Conventional thinking ¶
New radical thinking ¶
Conventional thinking ¶
New radical thinking ¶

Or you might use the turnabout paragraph (see page 293). For example, consider Linda's topic (in the Analysis section), the essence of business. In making a connection to conventional thinking, she could use a paragraph that shifts to her new ideas. Notice the turnabout in the middle of the paragraph, where the direction shifts and the new way of thinking is introduced:

> Money seems to be the thing that drives business. It seems to be the ultimate goal, the bottom line, the thing that is pursued every hour of every day. We might even say that money itself is the essence of business. It is, after all, the life source of every business enterprise, from the major international retail chain to the small-town Ma and Pa restaurant. However, money is merely the engine—the thing that sustains and develops business. It is not the essence. The essence of business is the same as the essence of a living organism: the struggle for survival. And when survival is the root of business, an exaggerated focus on money can actually put the nail in the coffin.

How Should I Conclude?

Apprehensive readers might see radical claims as irrelevant, even dangerous, so writers must be vigilant about connecting to readers. Conclusions are especially important places for making those connections and for making the claims in the text relevant and valuable to the world shared by the writer and readers. You might say that a conclusion is where the writer uses *the most dramatic or direct means for connecting the idea to the reader*. Notice, for instance, Benlow's conclusion; he offers a scenario and an image that reinforce the main idea of the essay:

> And if you could return to our time, I would make a dubious wager that you, too, would find it difficult to resist the lure of our lifestyle, the attraction of our conveniences. And if we had been able to imagine you as real people, even as our own distant progeny, rather than a simple euphemism ("the future"), we certainly would have acted differently. Although we probably would not have relented in our give-it-to-me-now race for more, we would have taken a solemn moment to raise a toast and drink to your hardship. (581)

> Examine the conclusions of the other essays in this chapter. Decide how each conclusion creates a connection to the shared world of the writer and reader.

A conclusion is where the writer uses the most dramatic and direct means for connecting the idea to the reader.

For more on harsh description, see page 295.

WRITER'S VOICE

Inviting the Reader

No matter how radical or challenging the ideas, a writer should attempt to bring the reader into a new vision. Even if the writer wants to overtly condemn conventional wisdom (and sometimes such a move is necessary), he or she should craft a voice that invites a reader into the ideas. Notice, too, that writers sometimes condemn *ideas* or *actions*, but are less inclined to attack *people*. After all, people should not necessarily be blamed because they think conventionally. (And attacking people creates a harsh voice, which prompts readers to dismiss writers' ideas.)

Moore, for instance, condemns conventional wisdom, but avoids antagonizing or belittling the reader. He speaks to a collective *we,* presumably Americans who participate in democracy. Notice that he does not condemn people for allowing corporations to "downsize"; instead, he argues for what can be done: "Here's what I think we should do to protect ourselves." He invites readers into his hopes rather than condemning us for believing a particular way.

Writers can invite readers by making direct connections to their shared world. While Northrup makes rather adventurous claims, she also shows how her *ideas* give meaning to readers. She uses first-person plural pronouns (*we* and *us*), and connects her *ideas* to her readers.

> Given our cultural heritage and beliefs about illness in general and the menstrual cycle in particular, it is not difficult to understand how women have come to see their premenstrual phase not as a time for reflection and renewal but as a disease or a curse. (574)

Even though Northrup's primary audience is women, men are not necessarily excluded. That is, men can easily read and engage the argument—that is, if they are willing to learn more about women's lives.

Similarly, Doris Lessing consistently uses the first person pronoun *we* to help the reader feel a connection to the issue—and even to Lessing herself. Although Lessing paints an unflattering picture of common behavior, she includes herself in that behavior:

> When we're in a group, we tend to think as that group does: We may even have joined the group to find "like-minded" people. But we also find our thinking changing because we belong to a group. It is the hardest thing in the world to maintain an individual dissident opinion, as a member of a group.
>
> It seems to me that this is something we have all experienced—something we take for granted, may never have thought about it. (583)

Considering Formality

While some writers tend toward a formal, sober tone, others use comedy or informality to connect with readers. While Northrup is more formal, more traditionally "academic" sounding, Moore is informal. His voice is appropriate because he does not usually write for an exclusively academic crowd. Instead, Moore attempts to engage large, mainstream audiences. He creates an informal tone with subtle jokes:

> If I had a nickel for every time I heard some guy in a suit tell me that "a company must do whatever is necessary to create the biggest profit possible," I would have a very big bottom line right now. (568)

He also draws attention to himself:

> Two really big hairy guys from Gingrich's office pummel me after they read this book? Five to ten in Sing Sing. (569)

And Moore addresses the audience directly, a move not usually made in more formal writing:

> For those of you free-marketers who disagree with these modest suggestions and may end up on a plane sitting next to me, screaming, "You can't tell a business how it can operate!"—I have this to say: Oh, yes, we can! (570)

As you consider your own voice, remember to stay consistent throughout your text. If you are wondering about the degree to which you can explore levels of formality, ask your instructor about the range he or she deems appropriate.

Projecting Wonder

While writers need to create a sense of authority and credibility, they also need to project wonder or curiosity. If a writer is curious about the world and about the topic at hand, the reader will be inclined to explore with an open mind. Writers can invite exploration by suggesting possibilities, rather than forcing absolute statements or fixed answers. Northrup's introduction is a call to, even a celebration of, what could be: a deeper understanding of "inner knowing." The claims themselves provide wonder and an engaging writerly presence:

> The ebb and flow of dreams, creativity, and hormones associated with different parts of the [menstrual] cycle offer us a profound opportunity to deepen our connection with our inner knowing. This is a gradual process for most women, one that involves unearthing our personal history and then, day by day, thinking differently about our cycles and living with them in a new way. (571)

This is a powerful lesson for all writers: Drawing attention to the extraordinary creates interesting writing—and interesting writers!

Writers can also project wonder more directly—by encouraging readers to transcend intellectual conventions. Toward the end of her essay, Lessing calls on us to imagine what's possible:

> This mechanism, of obedience to the group, does not only mean obedience or submission to a small group, or one that is sharply determined, like a religious or political party. It means, too, conforming to those large, vague, ill-defined collections of people who may never think of themselves as having a collective mind because they are aware of differences of opinion—but which, to people from outside, from another culture, seem very minor. The underlying assumptions and assertions that govern the group are never discussed, never challenged, probably never noticed, the main one being precisely this: That it is a group mind, intensely resistant to change, equipped with sacred assumptions about which there can be no discussion.
>
> But suppose this kind of thing were taught in schools?
>
> Let us just suppose it, for a moment . . . But at once the nub of the problem is laid bare. (584)

Draw attention to the extraordinary.

VITALITY

Creating vitality in writing means creating life—making language feel lively and real to the humans who engage it. (Remember, readers are real humans who are swirling around in their own messy lives. When language is intensive enough, it draws us inward to the ideas.) Consider the following strategies, which may fall outside the normal or "safe" academic sentence patterns.

Try the Stylistic Fragment

Sentence fragments are grammatical errors. They occur when a writer punctuates a phrase or dependent clause as though it were a full sentence. Here are some examples of sentence fragments:

Fragment errors

- By writing on the sidewalk in colored chalk and then hiring an airplane to write the message in the sky.

- Because the grand opening of the hotel coincided with the holiday parade and the community's main fundraising festival.

- Just when Marvin flummoxed the toss and flailed wildly at Herdie's aunt, who was then experiencing an intestinal expression.

None of the above can stand alone as full sentences. This is not because of the content, but because of the grammatical structure. None of them are independent clauses.

But some writers venture into fragments intentionally. They deliberately craft fragments because breaking the conventions calls the reader out of a comfortable intellectual pattern. Notice the (underlined) stylistic fragments in the following passages.

Stylistic fragments

- At some point in its life cycle, business must conserve. Like a lion or a bear. Like any organism.

- Sooner, rather than later, evaluating performance will not be the enterprise of faculty. It'll be the work of outside corporations. Profit hounds. Performance peddlers.

- When everything seems broken. When nothing seems fixable. When persistent crisis looms. These are the conditions that make political parties comfortable. Then, they can further etch their agendas into the masses by detailing the wrongs of the other party.

The underlined fragments are technically incorrect. But the writers decided to use the unconventional to help create vitality and intensity.

Deliberately Break Some Other Rule

Grammar is a set of conventions—a code agreed upon and supported by institutions within a culture. But all codes are toyed with. People who know the codes of a culture well intentionally tamper . . . for one of several reasons:

- They want to explore the limits of language and not simply use it.

- They want to assert some sense of individuality—something beyond their complicity in rules.

- They want readers to share in a brief moment of non-conformity.

And, believe it or not, academia is a perfect place for intellectual rule breaking. In fact, many would argue that the job of academia is to make certain that students know the rules so well that they can break them with grace and purpose. Playing with the conventions of language helps us to better understand what's possible, intellectually speaking. Keep in mind that rule breaking should not be a mere game of self-indulgence. It should increase the vitality of the text and increase the reader's understanding of your ideas.

As you look over your writing, consider some sentence-level rule. Break it. Make certain you explore this option with your instructor. Also make certain you understand your own motives!

Share a brief moment of nonconformity with your readers.

PEER REVIEW

Exchange drafts with at least one other writer. Before passing your draft to others, underline the thesis, or write it above your essay. This way, reviewers will get traction as they read.

As a reviewer, use the following questions to guide your response.

1. Does the thesis offer a new way of thinking about the topic? Why or why not?

2. In what sense does this essay transcend or speak back to conventional thinking?

3. Where is the writing most descriptive and specific? Where could the writer be more specific? Remember that it is easy, but less valuable, to remain entirely abstract and general. If the writer makes a general statement (about business, students, women, and so on), it must be exemplified. As a reader, you should come away from the essay with some specific image or impression imprinted on your thoughts. Have you?

4. Where does the writer use appeals to logic? Can you follow the line of reasoning? If not, at what point does it break down? (See appeals to logic, page 283.)

5. Play devil's advocate for a moment: What points seem entirely ungrounded or unreasonable? Why? What could the writer do to make the point more reasonable?

6. Suggest specific points that the writer should concede or qualify. For instance, the writer's position might seem too extreme; the claims might include too many people or include a large, diverse group without making any distinctions. Point out such claims, and help the writer to see the need to acknowledge subtlety, complexity, and exceptions.

7. Does the writer do anything unconventional or especially engaging with the organization? Is the introduction especially intense? The conclusion? Where does the writer seem to rely on old standard strategies?

8. Consider the writer's voice. (See pages 604–605.)

   a. Describe how it invites you into the ideas. Do any passages seem uninviting? Why?

   b. Describe the level of formality. Is it appropriate for the topic, the writer's approach, the assignment?

   c. Does the writer create wonder? Point to a passage that makes you, as a reader, wonder about the ideas. Why is the passage successful?

9. What is the most engaging passage in the draft so far? Why?

10. Check for sentence vitality.

    a. Offer a strategy for a stylistic fragment.

    b. Consider vitality strategies from other chapters:

    • If you encounter any noun clusters, suggest a revision of the sentence.

    • When possible, change nouns (such as in *make a decision*) to verbs *(decide)*.

    • Circle any unnecessary modifiers (*very, really, certainly,* and so on).

    • Where can the writer avoid drawing attention to *I* and *you*?

    • Where can the writer change linking verbs to active verbs?

    • Point to expletives (such as *there are* and *it is*).

    • Help the writer change passive verbs to active verbs for more vitality.

Questions for Research

If the writer used outside sources:

• Where must he or she include in-text citations? (See page 650.)

• Are quotations blended smoothly into the argument and punctuated correctly? (See pages 642–648.)

• Where could more direct textual cues or transitions help the reader? (See pages 641–643.)

• Is the Works Cited page formatted properly? (See pages 652–675.)

DELIVERY

When the *9/11 Commission Report* came out in the summer of 2004, it sold millions of copies. Americans wanted to know the findings: How could 9/11 have occurred? The report pointed to various gaps in communication and governmental oversight, but the panel consistently announced that the successful attacks illustrated a "failure of imagination." The people charged with protecting American interests had been trained *not* to imagine *what could be.* They could only follow rules and make speculations based on what had always occurred. They could only think in conventional ways—while the terrorists had imagined something unimaginable. The *Report* has made millions rethink formal education—what we mean by *educated* individuals, what we value in the process, and what we should assess.

As part of the American educational system, as someone who is charged with exploring new intellectual terrain, how did you do in this chapter? How does your essay transcend the intellectual norm and reveal a new pattern of thinking?

Beyond the Essay

Conventional thinking can be challenged in a variety of ways: images, posters, even bumper stickers.

Combine several images to create a visual essay that challenges common thinking.

RESEARCH & WRITING: GATHERING AND USING INFORMATION FROM SOURCES

Chapter Contents

CHAPTER 13

BASIC CONCEPTS

Issues to Consider and Discuss

- When and why do people refer to sources in everyday life?
- How might sources contribute to a writer's credibility?
- Why should information gained from a source be documented?
- When is informal documentation acceptable?
- How can a researcher evaluate the reliability of information from a source?

Why Get Information from Sources?

How do you know what you know? Where did you learn it? In everyday life, we pick up information, use it, and pass it along to others when we think they might benefit from it. For example, we might tell a friend that we think she would enjoy seeing a certain movie or art exhibit, and to convince her of it we might provide some evidence for our claim. The evidence would not be formally documented: We might informally refer to an article we had just read about it, or we might pass on anecdotal evidence based on personal experience. We are basing our claim (our assertion or opinion) on something—and we can call that something *a source of information.*

In college and workplace writing, sources are used in the same basic way as in everyday life. While we use them in our writing to support claims, a source does not always have to agree with our opinion. Instead, a writer might provide information from a source and then respond to it, or counterargue, by showing how he or she thinks the information is wrong. (See Counterarguing Sources on page 641.) Or the writer might use the source in a variety of other ways—such as to provide necessary background information or to illustrate another interesting way of thinking about the matter.

When to Get Information from Sources

Writers may do research throughout the writing process. For example, getting information from sources is helpful for exploring the topic early in the process, as well as late in the process for developing certain points. Toward the end of the writing process, finding statistics, an appropriate quotation, or some other type of evidence to insert into the right place can be just the thing needed to "top off" part of your essay. But sources are also helpful—more helpful, probably—early in the writing process when exploring an idea. (See "What Is Inventive Research?" below.) Sources provide valuable new information that is likely to alter a writer/reader's early ideas about a topic and raise new and interesting questions. Many academic and workplace assignments require significant research *prior to any serious drafting.*

What Is Inventive Research?

Inventive research is a discovery process in which the researcher is open to a wide range of sources and ideas. Inventive researchers are adventurous. Rather than only reading the most accessible source (say, the first on a database list), they read others that at first may seem irrelevant. Rather than seeking only those sources that are in line with their initial thinking, inventive researchers explore articles that may be opposed to their original positions. They go after essays with strange titles; they crack open dusty books and surf obscure websites. Inventive researchers take a particular posture as they encounter sources. They do more than simply read or listen. They also look beneath the meaning of each keyword or phrase; they go back in history to find the origin of words, attitudes, and beliefs related to the topic; they imagine how their topic resonates with some broader set of rules or earlier cases; they make comparisons to other situations or topics while reading and researching; they read for hidden arguments.

Where to Get Information from Sources

A source can be an interview, a TV show, a movie, a newspaper, a magazine, a scholarly article in a professional journal, a book, and so on. Sources can be thought of as (1) primary, or firsthand accounts, and (2) secondary, or information from another, often primary, source of information. While primary sources (an interview; an experiment, survey, or study; a historical document; correspondence) are often useful and/or necessary, secondary sources save writers the trouble of going out and conducting interviews or experiments (often a time-consuming and expensive process) when others have already done so. Using secondary sources means wisely taking advantage of research other people have done. (See more about finding sources on pages 624–629. And also see Primary Research on pages 615–622 and Secondary Research on pages 623–648.)

What Is Plagiarism?

Plagiarism—failing to acknowledge, or give credit to, a source of information—is literary theft. It involves using either (1) an idea or (2) the manner of expression of another person as if it is the writer's own idea or manner of expression.

Plagiarism can take many forms and may be either intentional or unintentional. For example, knowingly turning in another person's paper and claiming it as one's own work is a serious form of academic dishonesty likely to have a severe consequence, such as damage to one's reputation and expulsion from school. Other times, however, writers plagiarize accidentally because they are unaware of the rules. They do not know, for example, that the ideas taken from a source, even if not quoted directly, must be documented.

Just as it is every driver's responsibility to know and obey the rules of the road (for his or her own benefit as well as for the benefit of others), it is every writer's responsibility to know the rules of documentation. To avoid plagiarism,

you must acknowledge your source (also referred to as "citing" or "crediting" the source) whenever you express someone else's idea, opinion, or theory, or whenever you provide information such as a fact or statistic that is not common knowledge. If you use the exact words of the source, you must indicate that by putting them within quotation marks—and also by crediting the source (using quotation marks alone does not count as crediting the source). If you use information from a source but express it in your own words (called *paraphrasing* or *summarizing*), you should not put the information inside quotation marks, but you still must credit the source. (See more about plagiarism on page 639.)

Why Document Sources?

There are at least three good reasons for documenting sources:

- To be honest. When presenting others' opinions, research, or manner of expression, writers give credit to, or acknowledge, their sources.

- To gain credibility. If a source is credible (see Evaluating Sources, pages 630–634), then the writer's claims gain credibility. Many times writers are not experts on their subject matter; however, they can write confidently about their subjects as a result of sources. Also, writers are taken more seriously if they appear well-informed, having "done their research."

- To provide readers with more information. Listing sources provides readers access to more information. This allows readers to explore the subject matter further.

What's a Good Research Topic?

Using research in a writing project should not change some fundamental principles: The project should still be focused and revelatory. Like any academic writing project, a research essay should develop a new topic or offer a new insight on a familiar topic. It may be tempting to choose a familiar issue (such as abortion) and then report what many others have said. But most often, the job of the researcher is not to *compile* outside sources but to *use* particular insights or information from sources. (This is a big difference.)

Sometimes, a writer may begin a research project and discover very little information or that much of the research does not support his or her initial opinion. But a lack of information is not a bad sign. In fact, it offers writers an opportunity to ask interesting questions and make valuable intellectual connections. Instead of dumping the topic or shifting focus, the writer can:

- Explore what has been said about similar topics and make a comparison in his or her essay.

- Use opposing positions to create counterarguments in his or her own writing.

- Research the history of the topic to see how people's opinions evolved.

- Research the cultural context (the popular, institutional, religious, and scientific activities surrounding the topic itself) and ask: *Why have people not written much about it?*

It might be helpful to think not of *research* topics but of *writing* topics. When a writer generates a topic from a particular situation or intellectual place (a particular point of contact), then he or she can move outward from there—searching out sources that help create public resonance or an historical perspective.

Formal versus Informal Documentation

In academic and professional writing, information from sources may be documented formally or informally, depending upon the situation. Some writing requires in-text documentation that corresponds with a Works Cited page; other writing does not. "My mother said it is raining," is an example of informal documentation. The information from the source is that *it's raining*. The source is *my mother*. In-text documentation and a Works Cited page are unnecessary here. But more formal writing situations require more formal documentation.

Research is another form of invention.

PRIMARY RESEARCH

OBSERVATION, INTERVIEWS, SURVEYS

Academic writers do both *primary* and *secondary* research. In primary research, information is gathered firsthand by the researcher. That is, the researcher interacts directly with the subject(s) and is engaged in the activities and behavior of the thing being studied. A writer doing primary, or field, research makes observations or does experiments, interviews, and surveys. He or she participates in the original actions of gathering data.

Observation

In *detached observation,* the researcher attempts to stay removed or distant from the subject(s). In other words, the researcher tries to remain uninvolved so that his or her conclusions are not influenced by personal attachment to the subject(s). In detached, or what is sometimes called *scientific,* observation, researchers attempt to generate conclusions that others would also generate under the same conditions in the same situation. Findings generated from detached observation usually do not involve the researcher's personal situation or perspective; therefore, the first-person pronouns *I* and *we* are usually absent from the writing.

In *participant observation,* on the other hand, the researcher interacts with the subject(s). The researcher acknowledges, and even draws attention to, the interaction and how it influences the information gathered. Here, the conclusions may depend on the presence of the researcher. Annie Dillard's essay "Living Like Weasels" depends upon her interaction with the subject. What Dillard learns and ultimately communicates about weasels is a result of her brief participation in the weasel's existence:

> The weasel was stunned into stillness as he was emerging from beneath an enormous shaggy wild rose bush four feet away. I was stunned into stillness twisted backward on the tree trunk. Our eyes locked, and someone threw away the key. (99)

Participant observation, however, must be carried out with a consideration for the subjects involved. A researcher must not attempt to change or adversely affect the subjects or the environment.

Examine Jane Goodall's essay "Gombe" (in Chapter 3). Does the essay signal detached or participant observation?

FIELD NOTES

Regardless of the type of observation, whether participant or detached, nothing is more important than good field notes. Good researchers do not rely on memory. After the initial observation, field notes become the primary source of interaction. Because researchers cannot return to the particular time and place of the observation and cannot re-live the experience itself, they must rely on ample notes that capture all possible details, nuances, and impressions. Field notes can be taken in a variety of ways, which may depend on the researcher and the research situation. Notice the range of details in the excerpts from field notes below. Also notice the observers' focus—and strategies for making connections between elements:

> The Apartment
> Second Fl.
> June 1, 2002
>
> The thermostat in the apartment reads 84 degrees (at 11 P.M.). The air conditioner is on, but produces only cool—not cold or air-conditioned— air. If turned on high, the air conditioner eventually blows a fuse. But if on high, it still only produces cool, not cold, air. Needs freon. A 20-inch box fan blows warm air around, not really cooling the place off much. If on medium or high, it makes too much noise. On low, as it is now, it is quiet, yet not very helpful. The television is loud, in order to be heard over the fan and air conditioner. Windows are closed. If open, street noise becomes a problem. Outside on the ground, it is much cooler, comfortable even, but this is a second-floor apartment with a poor, at best, air conditioner.
>
> Sam's Diner
> Palmer Street
> May 18, 2002
>
> At Sam's, the cooks (two men) are fully visible to the customers in the seating area. The grills, the cutting boards, the prep tables, the refrigerators, canisters, and utensils are all in plain view of customers. One of the two cooks, with a dark beard, is slicing meat (what appears to be ham), and the other is frying a sandwich. They are talking and laughing.
> There are three servers, all women. One (wearing blue jeans) is standing behind the counter, by the cash register, occasionally joining in the conversation with the cooks, and also filling ketchup bottles. Another (with a long ponytail) is talking with a table of customers. She seems acquainted with them and the three customers are all engaged in the conversation with her. The other server (with round glasses) is getting drinks for another table of customers (of four people). She is the only one of the staff moving throughout the diner. At 11:24 A.M., three tables are full. The remaining tables are empty.

Between 11:30 and 12:10 the dining area fills. All but two tables are taken by customers. The workers, servers, and cooks have stopped talking among themselves and are focused on different jobs.

12:14: Twelve tables are full and five people are seated at the counter. The first server (in blue jeans) attends to them, and seems to be exclusively in charge of the cash register. The other two (ponytail and round glasses) are now both moving quickly from tables to the kitchen area.

The cooks are both at grills, their backs turned away from the customers (and servers) for long periods of time. (They only turn around quickly to place a finished plate on pickup counter—and are not talking.)

Field notes allow the writer to return to the scene and find new connections or see meaning he or she did not see initially. Without field notes, an observer can only return to mental pictures. Because the human mind remembers selectively, those pictures will hold only details that initially had meaning, so the observer is left exploring a narrow and selective list of details—essentially, exploring his or her own memory. This significantly narrows the chances of discovering something new. The surprising and valuable connections that can be made through observation occur because the observer notices a subtle connection or a hidden pattern—and these connections and patterns do not necessarily exist in an observer's selective memory.

Interviews

At a basic level, interviewing involves gathering information from a single person. But it can mean a great deal more. Good interviewers seek to engage interviewees in intensive conversations. They probe for knowledge and ideas, but they also allow interviewees to explore and develop ideas. A good interview, like a good essay, goes beyond basic knowledge; it provides insight.

ASKING THE RIGHT QUESTIONS

Good interview questions create focus, yet allow interviewees to explore. While they may seek out specific information (data, facts, dates), interview questions should go beyond collecting basic knowledge. (In fact, asking interviewees basic information that can be retrieved through print sources undermines the interview process.) A more valuable strategy is to prompt interviewees to reflect on the meaning of issues or to make connections between ideas. Notice the difference between the following:

What's it like being a doctor?

How has working in the medical field influenced your personal life?

The first question does not focus attention on any particular issue; the interviewee could talk about anything related to the profession. The second question, however, draws attention to a particular issue, asking the interviewee to consider a particular relationship. It is more specific than the first question, but still calls for a certain degree of exploration.

ASKING FOLLOW-UP QUESTIONS

Following up on answers is the interviewer's most powerful research tool. While a survey can only ask a list of preformulated questions, an interview can follow a line of thought that comes from an interviewee's response.

Imagine the following scenario, in which a researcher is interviewing a civil engineer:

Interviewer:	Is being a civil engineer interesting?
Engineer:	Sure. I get to deal with all kinds of people and very real situations.
Interviewer:	Is being a civil engineer hard?
Engineer:	Well, some of the work can be difficult. Trying to figure in all the variables in a given project can be a mathematical nightmare.
Interviewer:	What would you tell someone who wants to become a civil engineer?

Here, the interviewer comes up short in several ways. First, the questions are mundane. As worded here, such questions would probably not yield focused and insightful answers; they prompt the engineer to respond in general terms. They are surface questions (the kind one might ask at a party), which yield short and uncomplicated answers. Also, the interviewer passes up opportunities to follow up. After the engineer's first responses, the interviewer could have asked about the "very real situations" or the "mathematical nightmare" but leaves both ideas and, instead, moves to the next question. This interview does not probe for insight or engage the thoughts of the interviewee, but merely poses a list of unrelated questions. However, notice the following example:

Interviewer:	How is a civil engineer important to society?
Engineer:	Well, civil engineers conceptualize living space for the public. They envision what it might be like to live in particular place, say, a downtown area, and then lay out plans to make a park, an intersection, even an entire downtown livable— and they do it all while considering how an area will grow and how people's needs may change.
Interviewer:	So, civil engineers have to be visionaries?
Engineer:	Yes! They are not simply figuring formulas about buildings and zones and land; they are imagining what it might be like to live and work within a given area in the present and future.
Interviewer:	And they do all this while accommodating the demands of city officials?

Planning an Interview

When setting up an interview, be sure to respect the interviewee's position and accommodate his or her schedule. Researchers should never impose themselves on potential interviewees. Use the following hints and strategies:

- Always request an interview well in advance of your own deadlines.

- When making a request, introduce yourself and the reason for the interview: Explain the nature of your research and how the interview will be integrated.

- Beforehand, negotiate a reasonable amount of time for the interview (such as 30 minutes)—and stick to it so as not to impinge on the interviewee's time.

- Plan out the method of recording responses—writing, audiotaping, or videotaping. Ask the interviewee if his or her answers can be recorded, and if his or her name can be used in the research.

- At the end of the interview, thank the interviewee for his or her time, and leave promptly.

Here, the interviewer starts with a more insightful question. While the first interviewer depends on a vague concept ("interesting"), the second interviewer seeks out the meaning of a potential relationship (between civil engineers and society), and consequently receives an insightful response. Also, the interviewer in the second scenario springboards from the engineer's answers ("So, civil engineers have to be visionaries?"), thereby extending initial thoughts. The second interview evolves, even within a short amount of time.

USING INTERVIEWS

Ideas from an interview can be incorporated into various writing situations and purposes. An interview can be used to support claims made in argument, to help explain an idea, or even to help explain the history or significance of some topic. In the following example, notice how the information helps support an idea:

> Most often the water sewers can withstand the runoff from storms, but the past season has illustrated the inadequacy of the current sewer system. According to Harold Johnston, Director of Utilities, the sewer system was overwhelmed twice in the past three and a half months, and the result was that untreated sewage flowed out into Silver Lake. When an overflow occurs and untreated water spills into the natural water system, the high amounts of bacteria affect the wildlife and jeopardize the health of swimmers and water enthusiasts. In essence, anyone or anything in the lake for days after an overflow is swimming in sewage.

Here, the writer is trying to persuade readers that the water treatment system in her town is inadequate. The claim made by the Director of Utilities supports the idea. Although the writer probably collected extensive information about the treatment system, she only used one particular point in this paragraph because it directly supports the main idea. (Other information might be used in different passages.)

Surveys

While an interview is based on an individual's ideas and knowledge, a survey attempts to find public opinion on a topic. An interview is driven, in part, by the interviewee; his or her insights may influence the direction or emphasis of the interview. But with surveys, the researcher prearranges the direction and emphasis with carefully formulated questions.

GENERATING QUESTIONS

In generating survey questions, a researcher should consider three points.

1. Questions should not lead the respondent to an answer. Good survey questions avoid influencing the respondents' thinking about the issue. For instance, a question that asks *Is our current president completely out of touch with public opinion?* leads the respondent toward a negative evaluation of the president. Such questions prompt respondents to take up a certain position even before answering. A better approach is to state the question without leading the respondent; for example: *Is the current president in touch with labor issues in America?*

2. Questions should narrow the focus of the respondents on a particular topic. While good survey questions should not influence the respondents' thinking on an issue, questions should create a particular focus. For instance, a question that asks *Has the president taken an appropriate stance on international trade?* is more focused than *Do you like our current president?*

3. Questions should use common or unspecialized language. Because survey respondents may come from different walks of life, survey questions should avoid technical jargon or specialized terminology.

CHOOSING RESPONDENTS

Surveyors must consider the demographics (or particular characteristics) of their potential respondents.

> What is the age range in the respondent group?
>
> What is the racial makeup of the respondent group?
>
> What is the gender makeup of the respondent group?
>
> What is the occupational makeup of the respondent group?
>
> What is the geographical origin of the respondent group?

People's occupations, gender, ethnicity, age, and geography impact their understanding of the world—and how they are likely to respond to any particular issue. For instance, imagine a survey about college life: If all the respondents are college instructors, the answers will probably reflect certain biases and assumptions—which may be entirely different than those of students or people not associated with college life.

Working Hours Survey

Please respond to the following questions. Use the back if you need more space.

1. Do you currently hold a full-time or part-time job? If so, what is the nature of the work?

2. If you work part-time, how many hours per week?

3. How many hours per week are you contracted to work? (Or how many hours per week are you supposed to work, according to the job description?)

4. How many hours per week do you normally work (at or away from the job site)? Do you work weekends?

5. How much time do you spend preparing for and/or traveling to and from work? (Feel free to give specifics.)

6. Is overtime mandatory or voluntary at your job? (What kinds of incentive are offered for overtime?)

7. Do you feel sufficiently compensated for the work you do? Why or why not?

RECORDING RESPONSES

Responses can be recorded in a variety of ways. Perhaps the easiest means is to elicit written responses by asking the respondents to write or check off their answers. But if that is not possible, the researcher must do the recording by writing or taping. (If you plan to tape answers, either on video or audio equipment, you must always ask the respondents' permission.)

USING RESPONSES

Survey responses are most often used to show public opinion about a topic or to illustrate common trends in everyday life. A writer researching work issues among students at her college might discover important trends:

> While many students take a full course load, they also work late on weeknights and throughout the weekends. In an informal survey, 24 of 35 respondents reported that they work at least 25 hours each week—and 21 of those 35 work over 30 hours each week. One student explained her situation bluntly: "No one told me that a full load of classes would compete with my work schedule. I thought I could do both, but it's nearly impossible."

Notice that the writer uses the information from the survey to enhance the significance, or the public resonance, of her topic. She sets up the idea in her first sentence, and then plugs in the information from the survey.

This survey offers room for the respondents to write in answers and to develop their thoughts. You could imagine someone responding to this survey fairly quickly because the questions are limited in number and fairly simple. While it could offer some valuable insights about working hours, it is also limited in its scope, like all surveys. Because this survey does not ask for personal information from the respondents (age, sex, education, etc.), the researcher should be careful not to make broad statements about salary and job satisfaction in America, but stay focused on the time people dedicate to their jobs.

SECONDARY RESEARCH

Major Steps in Using Secondary Sources:

1. Finding sources
2. Evaluating sources
3. Gathering and processing ideas
4. Integrating sources
5. Documenting sources

PRINT AND ELECTRONIC SOURCES

In secondary research, the researcher explores the thoughts, theories, or findings of others, in print and electronic sources. Whether a writer is arguing, explaining, or evaluating, sources can give depth and sophistication. However, sources should not replace other means of support and development (anecdotes, allusions, scenarios, appeals, examples, and so on). They should work in conjunction with these other strategies. Print and electronic sources should be thought of as another set of writerly tools for inventing, developing, and delivering ideas.

The research process can be broken into five major steps: *finding sources, evaluating sources, gathering and processing ideas, integrating sources,* and *documenting sources.* This might seem like an easy chronological path, but the entire research process should be seen as an act of invention. Good writers do *inventive research,* approaching the process as an archeological journey in which each source is a potential link to some idea, some springboard, that might further develop their understanding and stance on a subject. They see each text, whether a book, newspaper, or website, as a hypertextual connection to another idea. Inventive researchers do not simply scan sources looking for information that fits into a particular subject; instead, they read with the thought of broadening their perspectives, of expanding their ideas, of changing their opinions. Sources help to educate a writer about his or her particular subject and to develop a stance regarding that subject.

Finding Sources

The first rule of finding secondary sources is: *Don't give up.* Many writers are surprised to find how much information is out there. No matter how esoteric a topic, chances are that a great deal has been written about it. The key to doing research is finding the right path—or paths—to the information. And because of interconnected library resources, print reference guides, and electronic networks, the paths are many.

Books, periodicals, newspapers, government documents, reference books (such as dictionaries and encyclopedias), audiovisual materials, and websites can all be valuable sources of information, and all of these sources can be found by searching a library's catalog of holdings and/or the Internet. Knowing how to navigate through library catalogs and cyberspace is the first step in finding relevant, reliable, timely, and diverse sources.

THE LIBRARY

You might begin by getting familiar with your library's website. Most likely, it will explain all the library's resources, and it may provide links to other useful websites and databases.

When searching your library's catalog, you may be given the options of doing *an author search, a title search, a subject search,* or *a keyword search.* Do an *author search* if looking for works by a particular author; do a *title search* if you already know the title of the specific work. *Subject searches* are organized by headings (such as *agriculture, government, gender*), and will usually produce many sources for a particular topic. *Keyword searches* can be used to focus a search. For example, the keyword search for "weight" on one library's online catalog produced 804 entries. But narrowing the search by typing "weight and body" produced only 146 entries. Thus, if you know you are looking for information about weight and the body, "weight and body" allows you to find the relevant sources without having to sort through all the others—the computer does the sorting for you. Typing "weight *or* body" produced 3,993 entries. And typing "weight and body and media" produced just one entry. Typing "body weight" produced 93, and typing "bodyweight" produced none.

Searches can be made more efficient by using the following words (what are called *Boolean operators*):

Using *and* between words narrows a search by finding documents containing multiple words—*weight and body.*

Using *or* between words broadens a search by finding documents with either word in a multiword search—*weight or body.*

Using *and not* between words finds documents excluding the word or phrase following "and not"—*weight and not body* (that is, *weight* only, without any references to *body*).

Using *near* between words finds documents containing both words or phrases that are near, but not necessarily next to, each other—*weight near body.*

You may also want to become familiar with the physical layout of your library building before you use it. Many libraries offer tours; some tours are even online. Most libraries have online catalogs, which list resources they physically hold (such as Northwestern Michigan College's WebCat). Most libraries also have databases for finding articles beyond their walls—such as InfoTrac and EBSCOhost.

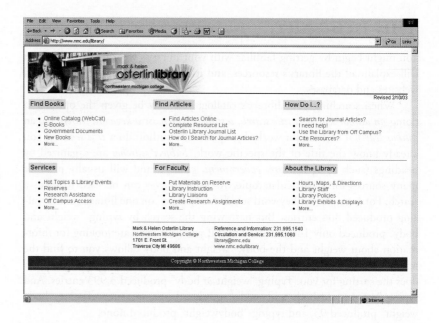

THE INTERNET

The Internet is an electronic communications network that connects computer networks and organizational computer facilities around the world. The World Wide Web is "a part of the Internet designed to allow for easier navigation of the network through the use of graphical user interfaces and hypertext links between different addresses" (Merriam-Webster's Online Dictionary). The World Wide Web, or Web, is made up of many websites created and maintained by all types of organizations and individuals. Your school has a website, for example, as does your school's library, as may you. A home page, which greets the user upon arriving at a website, usually contains links to the other pages of that site or to other sites outside of it. Websites can be found by (1) typing in the known address (or URL) of the site (such as www.whitehouse.gov) or (2) doing a subject or keyword search.

Searching or surfing the Web basically means skimming through different websites using search engines. A search engine works like a keyword search on a library database. That is, you type in a word or phrase and the engine scans the World Wide Web for related sites. All search engines are not the same. Some, for example, attempt to be faster while others attempt to be more comprehensive. To read more about what search engines are and how they work, try doing a keyword search, or type in the following URL: http://www.monash.com/spidap.html. *The Composition of Everyday Life* website (http://english.wadsworth.com/maukmetz_2) has links to major search engines, including the following:

http://www.google.com

http://www.altavista.com

http://www.allonesearch.com

http://dogpile.com

http://goto.com

http://www.monstercrawler.com

http://search.aol.com/

http://www.askjeeves.com/

http://www.ezgov.com/

http://yahoo.com

http://lawcrawler.lp.findlaw.com

http://www.lycos.com

http://www.webcrawler.com

SOURCES OF INFORMATION

Secondary sources include books, periodicals (which are journals, magazines, and newspapers), government documents, reference books (such as dictionaries and encyclopedias), audiovisual materials, and websites. They give a researcher a broader understanding of a topic. In many ways, the process of reading and analyzing secondary sources is a process of invention: The writer is generating new ideas and perspectives, which, in turn, make writing more interesting and engaging (for both writer and reader).

When exploring a topic, it is helpful to use different types of sources—not just books, not just websites. For example, books, although they contain a lot of information and are easy to find, can contain too much information to sort through, thus taking up a lot of the researcher's time. Books can also be outdated; a journal or magazine article might be shorter, more current, and more focused on your particular topic. Websites, too, are easy to find but are not always the most helpful source and may not always be up to date. An online article found through a library database can be more relevant and reliable even though it may take a bit more effort to find.

Books are found by searching a library's catalog. While most libraries have electronic catalogs (which allow for author, title, subject, or keyword searches), many academic libraries also have catalogs that are linked to other libraries, so people can check titles not only at that particular location but also in all other connected libraries. Through such services, library users can then order books to be delivered to a desired location.

When you have obtained a promising book, the best strategy is to read through the introductory and concluding chapters. (Introductions and conclusions most often give a broad understanding of the main argument and ideas of the text.) Also, consider edited books (a collection of chapters or articles by different authors) in your search. Edited books, which are very common in academia, often cover a very specific topic and offer many different perspectives from various authors.

Online catalogs can be easier to search by keeping some points in mind. Adding words narrows a search, while using fewer words broadens the scope. For instance, "economics" by itself tells the catalog to find any and all works with "economics" in the title or description. (At Northwestern Michigan College, this search yielded 1,387 works.) "Economics and consumers" narrows the search (and yielded 9 works—a much more reasonable number to browse.)

Indicates status or availability and the location (a particular section in the library).

The call number.

The title of the book.

The author.

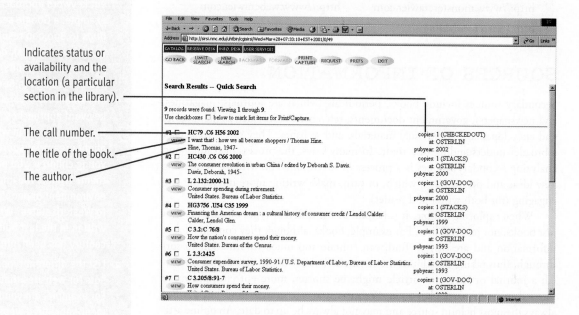

Periodicals include magazines (for a general audience) or journals (for a specialized audience). (Some periodicals, such as *Ladies Home Journal* and the *Wall Street Journal,* are called journals, but are, in fact, magazines or newspapers.) Popular magazines, such as *People* or *Rolling Stone,* offer information about mainstream news or popular culture events but rarely provide in-depth analysis of issues, and even more rarely deal with issues outside of major social and political topics.

Scholarly journals, which are usually specific to one discipline (such as English, writing, business, marketing, and so on), offer very detailed analyses and well-developed opinions on a seemingly endless range of topics. The writing in academic journals is most often well-researched and documented, so it tends to be more reliable than that of popular magazines.

Periodicals are listed on electronic databases, which are often available at public and academic libraries. Use searches (described above) to find articles by particular authors, about particular subjects, or in specific periodicals.

Newspapers are most valuable for highly publicized topics—those which are or have been visible to the public eye such as political events, public figures, national or local disasters, and significant cultural events. Most academic and public libraries have newspaper databases (with access to past editions). Major newspapers also have websites. *USA Today*, for example, can be accessed online through a simple keyword search *(USA Today)* or by entering the URL www.usatoday.com. Explore local newspapers for regional and local events, and national newspapers such as the following for national or world events: *Afro American, American Banker, Amsterdam News, Atlanta Constitution, Atlanta Journal, Boston Globe, Chicago Tribune, Christian Science Monitor, Denver Post, Detroit News, Houston Chronicle, Houston Post, Los Angeles Times, Muslim Journal, New York Times, San Francisco Chronicle, Sentinel* [Los Angeles], *St. Louis Post Dispatch, Times-Picayune, USA Today, Wall Street Journal, Washington Post.*

Government documents include reports, transcripts, pamphlets, articles, speeches, books, maps, films, and more. While the U.S. government is the nation's largest publisher, state and city governments publish as well. Such documents, which can be of great value in one's research, can be found online with keyword searches, or by going directly to the Government Printing Office (GPO) website at www.access.gpo.gov.

Reference books such as dictionaries, encyclopedias, and almanacs can be helpful, but should not be relied upon as one's only sources for a college research paper. (Doing so may indicate a researcher's inability to find a range of sources.) Reference materials are usually found in a library's reference room or reference area and often cannot be checked out. They can be located, as with other library materials, by searching the library's catalog of holdings or by asking the reference librarian.

Audiovisual materials include videos, CDs, DVDs, films, photographs, cassettes, records, microfilm, and microfiche, and are often used to supplement text resources. For example, for a project on fly-fishing, a video might supplement other sources such as books and magazine articles. Or, for a project on a poet, a CD or cassette of the poet reading his or her work could be helpful. These materials are usually kept in a separate part of the library and can be found by searching the library's card catalog.

Websites, as discussed earlier, can be found by typing in the website address (URL) or by doing a keyword search using your favorite search engine, such as Google, Yahoo!, or Dogpile. Worthwhile information can be found on websites, yet researchers must beware. Because of the open nature of the Web, much information is likely to be unreliable. Thus, good evaluating skills (discussed in the next section) are essential. Also, remember that a simple keyword search can turn up thousands of websites. Narrowing one's focus by typing "weight and body and media," for example, will eliminate irrelevant sites found by typing just "weight."

Sources should not replace other means of support: allusions, scenarios, appeals, etc.

Evaluating Sources

Sources should be reliable, relevant, timely, and diverse. Weak or unreliable sources introduce weakness or unreliability into a writing project. Thus, evaluating sources before using them is key.

RELEVANCE

A source that is relevant is appropriately related to the writer's particular topic. A writer's first inclination may be to find those sources that directly support his or her thesis statement; that is, sources that speak directly about the writer's particular subject and that espouse his or her particular stance on it. However, this is very limiting—especially since the research process might develop or change how a writer thinks about a subject. Sources do much more than back up someone's opinion. They might help to explain the complexities of the subject; explain the history of the subject; explain the writer's position; support the writer's position; show claims that oppose the writer's; show claims that are different from the writer's.

Because sources can be used in a variety of ways, a source that seems only remotely related to your project might, in fact, be extremely valuable in the long run. Consider the following example: A writer is researching voting practices in his community and wants to make a claim about low voter turnouts in recent elections. He finds a newspaper article about a local school, scheduled for demolition, that had previously been used as a voting location. This article at first might seem unhelpful. After all, how does this particular school relate to voting trends in the community? It may, in fact, suggest a great deal about voting. That is, one of the factors in voter turnout is proximity to voting locations. This article might therefore show a trend in declining number of voting locations. The same writer might find a government Web page about the history of voting in his state. At first this source may not seem valuable because the writer is primarily concerned with recent voter activity. However, the history may provide some clues about the system itself, about the reasons for establishing Tuesdays as election days, about the number of constituents in a given area—all potentially valuable factors in understanding the complexities of recent voter turnout.

Consider the following questions for the sources you find:

- Does the source speak directly to my specific topic?
- How does the source help to clarify some broader or related point?
- How does the source help to explain the history or complexities of the topic?

RELIABILITY

Reliability refers to the quality of information in the source. A reliable source uses verifiable information and helps readers to trace the sources of information. The most reliable sources document the information they offer. (That's why academic audiences value some type of formal documentation, such as in-text citations and a bibliographical list.) In effect, formal documentation says to readers, "Here is the path to relevant research."

For published books and academic journal articles, reliability may not be an issue because such sources endure a process of critical peer review. However, many publications do not have peer reviews. Most magazines and newspapers also do not have room to include formal documentation. Their editorial policies exclude in-text documentation and Works Cited lists.

But there are other ways for writers to signal reliability, such as an appositive phrase. In the following examples, the underlined appositive phrases lend some reliability to the information. Even though the passages lack formal documentation (a formal link to a particular text), they give the reader specific cues about the nature of the source:

> Kalle Lasn, <u>a co-founder of the Canadian media criticism and environmentalist magazine *Adbusters*,</u> explains how dependence on television first occurred and continues today each time we turn on our sets:

> Deirdre Mahoney, <u>a professor of writing at Northwestern Michigan College and a scholar of rhetoric,</u> argues that online courses are significantly more challenging for college students than traditional face-to-face courses.

Notice that the information after the name indicates the source's credentials. When a formal Works Cited list is not possible, writers in many publications use such phrases to document the reliability of their information.

Consider the following questions for each source you find:

- Does the source offer formal documentation? Do other sources check out? Are they available?
- If there is no formal documentation, does the source acknowledge authorities with related credentials or qualifications?
- What about the source itself? Is it published by a reputable organization?

Remember that most popular magazines are guided by a primary force: money. Editorial policies are driven by the need to make information attractive to consumers. Therefore claims may be inflated, mitigating details may be excluded, and generalizations are common. Also remember that magazines are funded in large part by corporate advertising and so are not apt to publish articles that might compromise relationships with those advertisers. For these reasons, researchers should always be cautious about quoting popular magazines (or even news magazines) as unbiased truth.

CREDIBILITY

Credibility refers to the internal logic of the information presented in the source. A credible source does not attempt to hide its biases or its argument. It makes logical claims and helps the reader to follow its logic. If the source offers an argument, it makes its position clear and reveals its biases. (Of course, it is free of logical fallacies.) If the source attempts to inform rather than persuade, it does not spin information or conceal its biases.

The question of credibility may also involve the source's author. Some authors have more credentials than others. However, a book or article by a well-known author should not necessarily outweigh one by a less familiar writer. Many academic and professional writers are not necessarily big names in popular media but are well respected within small communities because they have spent years researching a particularly focused issue. For instance, Patricia Limerick, a highly respected scholar in history, has written a great deal about the American West. Although her name is not recognizable to the general public, it is often noted in history scholarship.

Use the following questions to check the credibility of sources you find:

- Does the source make an argument? If so, are the claims well supported and well reasoned?

- Do you sense any logical fallacies?

- Does the source attempt to conceal its biases?

- Do you have reason to question the author's credibility? (If so, do a quick Web or database search to see if he or she has written for or is referenced in other publications.)

- Is your reason for questioning the author's credibility reasonable? (Are you unnecessarily suspicious?)

TIMELINESS

A significant concern in academic research is the date of the sources. It is important that claims are supported with sources that are not obsolete or behind the times. But this criterion depends upon the issue and the claim being made. Some claims require very current sources. For example, a writer making a claim about the state of cloning in America would be wise to consider sources published only within two to three years of her research. (Because the science of biotechnology evolves so rapidly and because each new advancement prompts significant public debate, claims that are ten years old would probably be antiquated.) However, that same writer might also want to discuss the role of science in human development and discover a valuable text by a 19th-century philosopher about the role of machines in the evolution of the modern consciousness. In this case, the writer would use current texts to support claims about time-sensitive topics, and would refer to an older source to express an issue that stretches beyond a particular era.

Consider the following questions for the sources you find:

- Is this a time-sensitive topic?
- If this is a time-sensitive topic, why might the information in the source be either timely or out of date?

DIVERSITY

Diversity refers to the variety of different sources a writer uses. Good writers seek to develop their projects and their perspectives with a variety of voices and media. Writers develop their views on a subject from a range of sources—much in the same way that we develop our views on religion or marriage or education from taking in and making sense of information from various sources. For example, our religious beliefs may have been influenced primarily by our parents, but other sources, such as childhood friends, books, movies, and music, also influence us. Even views that oppose our own are important, because they help us to define the borders of our beliefs. This process, building our own ideas from a variety of sources, is called *synthesis,* and it is what writers do when researching their topics.

Writers need to consider and synthesize various sources about their topics; otherwise, their perspectives, and ultimately their positions, will be limited. Primarily, this means that writers should explore different *perspectives,* not necessarily different types of sources. In other words, all your information need not come from different types of sources (journals, websites, books, and so on), but exploring a variety helps give a sense of different value systems and beliefs. A scholarly community (which tends to write in academic journals or scholarly books) is likely to see a topic differently than a popular or mainstream perspective (which might be represented in a popular magazine).

Consider the following questions for the sources you find:

- Do my sources represent a variety (or more than one) viewpoint?
- How do the sources represent different value or belief systems?

> Synthesis is the process of building ideas from a variety of sources.

Evaluating Electronic Sources

Writers should be especially careful when evaluating websites; a particularly important criterion for a website is reliability. Anyone with a computer (or access to a computer) can publish a website and make any claim he or she wishes. In other words, much information on the World Wide Web is potentially bogus.

Bias also must be considered, because the purpose of many sites is to sell something—so they may provide information that is slanted. Of course, bias in itself is not bad. It is only negative when it is concealed. If a source is trying to sell something, its claims should not be accepted as unbiased truth.

If the source asks for personal information, it may have an alternative agenda. Although some online sources (such as newspapers) require you to register to enter the site, many other sources may ask for personal information so they can market products or services to you. Be very cautious about giving personal information (especially credit card or social security numbers!) to websites.

Websites should also be scrutinized for timeliness. Many sites have been abandoned by their creators, and although the content may appear recent, it may have been uploaded long ago. Reliable sites are updated regularly and have "last updated" notes toward the top or bottom of the homepage.

To evaluate the content of websites, ask the following questions:

- Who sponsors this site, and what credibility do they have for posting the information?

- Is the site attempting to sell something? If so, how might that impact the nature of the information?

- Does the site ask for personal information? (Does it state the purpose of this request?)

- Are statistics/data supported with appropriately documented sources?

- Is the information presented up to date? (When was the site last updated?)

Gathering and Processing Ideas from Sources

As you read through sources, remain open to ideas and collect those that not only confirm your own opinions but also extend or even oppose your perspective. Remember that sources can serve many purposes in a research project. They can help to:

- explain the complexities of the subject
- explain the history of the subject
- explain the writer's position
- support the writer's position
- show claims that oppose the writer's
- show claims that are different from the writer's

USING NOTE CARDS

It may be tempting to photocopy or print out sources, and then underline or highlight the information you need. This strategy works best when using just a little information from a source or two, but taking notes in a journal or on note cards is a more efficient strategy, especially for a project involving several sources. The note-taking process gives the writer a chance to process information and consider how it relates to the goals of the project. Taking notes, then, is an early part of the writing process: The ideas crafted during the note-taking process can be transferred directly into a formal text. So, as you take notes, imagine how that information might appear in your text.

While writing down ideas on note cards is initially more time-consuming than highlighting or underlining, the extra time spent can pay off by saving *more* time later, in the writing stage. For example, if you write down ideas on index or note cards, you can then arrange those cards in the appropriate order and write without having to sift through your many pages of highlighted text. Photocopying entire articles and printing out entire Web pages for an idea or two can create paperwork confusion.

Note cards contain three pieces of information besides the note: (1) the source, (2) the page number, (3) the topic.

Working with Note Cards

- Each note card contains one idea.

- The source is indicated, either by a few key words or by a symbol (such as A, B, C) that refers to a keyed list of sources.

- Sources are properly paraphrased, summarized, or quoted.

- The page number, if available, is listed.

- A topic heading helps the writer organize the information into logical sections.

- Note cards are put in the order in which information will appear in the text.

- Additional notes are taken on cards to fill in gaps in the argument.

- The writer develops a draft, referring to the note cards at hand.

The source Any time information from a source is used (summarized, paraphrased, or quoted) in a text, that source must be cited (acknowledged within the passage). Instead of going back later and having to find the source information (or worse, making it up, which is a form of plagiarism!) writing it down on the note card will save the time and trouble of having to go looking for it later. You need not write down complete bibliographic information, such as:

King, Martin Luther, Jr. "Letter from Birmingham Jail." <u>A World of Ideas: Essential Readings for College Writers</u>. Ed. Lee A. Jacobus. Boston: St. Martin's, 1994. 121–37.

Instead, just write "King" or "Letter from Birmingham Jail" and make certain that you have recorded the complete bibliographic information for this source where you can easily find it, such as in a notebook with other sources.

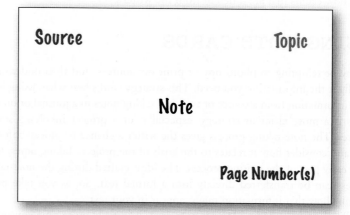

The page number When sources are used in academic writing, the page numbers are included in the documentation.

The topic Researchers also record the topic the source covers, or the way the source contributes to the overall project (*Cause of the Problem, Solutions, Taking Individual Action,* and so on). This is especially valuable in bigger projects, which may deal with many sources and various points because you can shuffle the cards about to determine what sections your final text will have. Once you group the cards in general sections (background, problem, solution #1, solution #2, and so on), you can place each card within a section in order. Arranging each note card in the order it will appear in your text helps in two ways: (1) It allows you to arrive at an organization based on the ideas you discovered through your research, and (2) it allows the drafting process to go more smoothly because the ideas are laid out in front of you.

Sample Note Cards

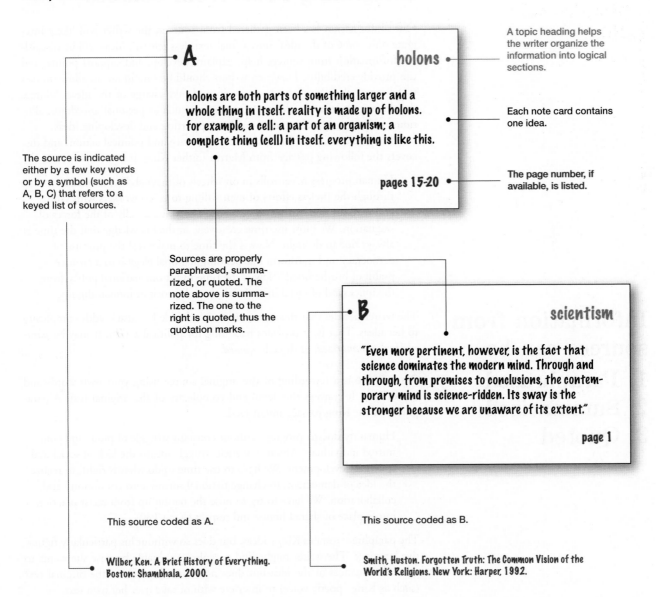

A topic heading helps the writer organize the information into logical sections.

Each note card contains one idea.

The page number, if available, is listed.

The source is indicated either by a few key words or by a symbol (such as A, B, C) that refers to a keyed list of sources.

Sources are properly paraphrased, summarized, or quoted. The note above is summarized. The one to the right is quoted, thus the quotation marks.

A   holons

holons are both parts of something larger and a whole thing in itself. reality is made up of holons. for example, a cell: a part of an organism; a complete thing (cell) in itself. everything is like this.

pages 15-20

B   scientism

"Even more pertinent, however, is the fact that science dominates the modern mind. Through and through, from premises to conclusions, the contemporary mind is science-ridden. Its sway is the stronger because we are unaware of its extent."

page 1

This source coded as A.

This source coded as B.

Wilber, Ken. A Brief History of Everything. Boston: Shambhala, 2000.

Smith, Huston. Forgotten Truth: The Common Vision of the World's Religions. New York: Harper, 1992.

Integrating Ideas from Sources

Once information has been gathered from sources, the writer will likely integrate only some of the ideas into a final text; less relevant ideas will be discarded. Information from sources helps explain, develop, and support points, and can provide credibility. However, writers should be careful not to allow sources to take over their writing—to move in and take charge of the ideas. Sources should be part of a broader set of strategies (such as personal anecdotes, allusions, scenarios, appeals, and so on) for supporting and developing ideas.

Imagine a writer is doing research on justice and political action, and discovers the following passage from Martin Luther King, Jr.:

> Human progress never rolls in on wheels of inevitability; it comes through the tireless efforts of men willing to be co-workers with God, and without this hard work, time itself becomes an ally of the forces of stagnation. We must use time creatively, in the knowledge that the time is always ripe to do right. Now is the time to make real the promise of democracy and transform our pending national elegy into a creative psalm of brotherhood. Now is the time to lift our national policy from the quicksand of racial injustice to the solid rock of human dignity.

The writer decides that this information is valuable because it adds complexity to her ideas. That is, it provides reasoning for political action. It may be *paraphrased, summarized,* or directly *quoted.*

Paraphrase is a rewording of the original source using your own words and expressions. It conveys the detail and complexity of the original text. A paraphrase of the King passage might read:

> Humanity doesn't progress without constant struggle of pious and committed individuals. Absence of such struggle means the lack of social and spiritual development. We have to use time to do what is right, to realize the idea of democracy, to change national sorrow into community and collaboration. We have to try to raise the nation up from racist practices into a place of shared honor and respect (King 130).

The paraphrase restates King's ideas, but does so without his particularly figurative language. The writer might find paraphrase valuable because she wants to share the nuances of the idea but does not want the tone of the original text (such as King's poetic voice) to interfere with or take over her own text.

Information from sources can be

1. Paraphrased
2. Summarized
3. Quoted

Paraphrasing does not involve merely changing a word or two, or shifting around sentence parts. Inappropriate or lazy paraphrasing leads to *plagiarism:* taking others' ideas or words without attributing proper credit. In the following example, the writer does not rephrase the ideas, but merely shifts some words around and replaces others. If the following appeared in a text, it would be plagiarism:

> Human progress never rolls in on tires of inevitability; it comes by way of the tireless efforts of men willing to be co-workers with God, and without this hard work, time itself becomes an ally of the forces of stagnation. In the knowledge that the time is always ripe to do right, we must use time creatively (King 130).

Notice that in the first sentence, the note taker has only substituted one word for another here and there. In the second sentence, the note taker has just shifted sentence parts around. This is plagiarism rather than paraphrasing because the note retains the original flavor and expression of the author.

Plagiarism often results from faulty paraphrasing.

A Note about Plagiarism

Most often, plagiarism occurs because writers are simply not going far enough in their paraphrasing. That is, they are not sufficiently rewording the ideas from the original source. A good paraphrase avoids using the same subjects and verbs as in the original text. To avoid this, read the original passage closely, but rather than writing down the ideas immediately, talk through them first. Remember that any one idea can be phrased in infinite ways.

Writers sometimes plagiarize intentionally because they are desperate to complete an assignment or pass a class. They set out to steal (or buy) others' ideas. In this age of technology, students can easily download text from an online source, and they can even buy college essays from websites and online databases. However, such essays are prepackaged, the topics are generalized, and the writing mundane—essentially, they are the opposite of what most college instructors want, and are contrary to the **Invention** strategies suggested throughout this book. Also, as websites featuring prewritten essays increase, so does the ability of instructors to detect plagiarism.

The consequences of plagiarism are more far-reaching and destructive than what some students may assume. Besides failing an assignment, failing an entire class, or being expelled, students who plagiarize fail to learn essential writing and thinking skills—or even when and how to ask for help. They also establish a low standard for themselves, which is perhaps the worst result of plagiarizing.

Summary, like paraphrasing, involves expressing a source's ideas in your own words instead of using the words of the source. Unlike paraphrasing, summary removes much of the detail while still dealing with the complexity of the idea. A writer may summarize because he or she simply wants to illustrate a point (made by the original text) and then move on to another idea. Usually, a summarized point is used to support a broader claim or to illustrate a stance, and the writer has several other strategies for illustrating the claim or making the stance clear to the reader. Consider this summary note of the original King passage. Notice that the idea of the passage is still represented, but it has been shortened:

> Humanity progresses only by the struggle of spiritually motivated people, and those people must use time for social change and raise the country from racist oppression to shared honor and respect (King 130).

Since summary leaves out detail while capturing the main idea, accuracy is essential. Be careful not to misinterpret the source, as the following summary does:

> Only people who go to church regularly can make the world a better place. Racism will thrive without their timely efforts (King 130).

Quotation, using the exact words of a source, puts a spotlight on another writer's language. It allows writers to integrate especially important phrasing or passages. The key, however, is to carefully select what ideas and manners of expression are *worth* quoting. Generally, writers avoid quoting more than 15 percent of their texts, though certain situations may call for more. When writing down quotes, keep in mind two points:

1. Quote sparingly. Quote only when a passage is particularly striking, AND quote only the striking part. For example, do not quote an entire paragraph if you can quote just a sentence; do not quote an entire sentence if you can quote only three words from that sentence.

2. Put others' words within quotation marks. Consider the following well-taken quotation from the original King passage:

> According to Martin Luther King Jr., "Human progress never rolls in on wheels of inevitability; it comes through the tireless efforts of men willing to be co-workers with God, and without this hard work, time itself becomes an ally of the forces of stagnation" (130).

Quotation puts a spotlight on other writers' language

SPECIAL CONSIDERATIONS
FOR ORGANIZING SOURCES

Organizing a text with sources may seem more difficult than organizing a text that is based exclusively on personal insights. However, the same principles apply to both: Paragraphs must be coherent, and transitions must be made between points. Whether information is paraphrased, summarized, or directly quoted, it should be blended smoothly into the text so that the reader (1) understands its relationship to the writer's own ideas and (2) knows where the information came from. The challenge is to maintain coherence and flow while integrating other voices and opinions. The best way to achieve coherence and flow is to develop an overall plan for your text without using outside sources. That is, develop a general strategy for your organization, and then decide how the sources can help complete that plan. Perhaps the biggest mistake that writers make in working with sources is allowing the other texts, especially quotations, to take over the project. This can be avoided by making a general framework and using the sources to help fill in the points.

Counterarguing sources Writers sometimes directly refer to sources because the sources oppose their own claims. That is, they counter the claims made in a source. (See Counterargument, pages 286–287.) In these cases, the writers first refer to the source (by paraphrasing, summarizing, or quoting), and then respond directly to the idea. This can be done with a turnabout paragraph or by splitting the source's ideas from the writer's with a paragraph break. (See page 293 in Chapter 6, Making Arguments.)

Textual cues Whatever organizational strategy you use, make certain that you distinguish your own ideas and claims from those of others so the reader can tell whose ideas are being explained or asserted. Also, make certain you show the relationships between and among sources. In other words, be sure to use appropriate *textual cues* (sentences, words, and phrases that explain the relationship between ideas, sources, or points in the paper) for the reader.

> Most music critics, *such as Smith, Castella, and Sanchez,* see the latest alternative genre as a collective response to the grunge scene of the early '90s.

Here, the critics listed have been discussed prior to this sentence, and the writer simply reminds the reader about these voices and how they relate to the present point being made. Simple phrases *(such as* or *for example)* cue the reader to make connections between passages in the text.

> Jones's ideas are often seen as radical. Alberta Slavik, *for example,* casts Jones aside as a "hyper-liberal" journalist: "William Jones has gone too far, simply parading his politics at the cost of facts" (76).

Paragraph transitions Integrating outside sources can make a text more sophisticated, but it can also create confusion if the writer does not make clear connections between points. Because outside sources often increase the complexity of a text, *paragraph transitions* (sentences and phrases that join the content of paragraphs and show the logical connections) become vital to a coherent paper. Transition statements usually begin paragraphs and act as bridges from one paragraph to the next. The following sentences, which all begin paragraphs, act as bridges from previous points:

Not all farmers, however, agree with Johnson's strategy.

Despite this overwhelming amount of evidence, some teachers refuse to acknowledge the way gender and race figure into the classroom.

But all of the discussion on war distracts voters from significant domestic issues that will impact everyday life in the present and future.

Because of Smith's recent book, many researchers have begun focusing their attention on the ways technology will change our ability to communicate.

BLENDING INFORMATION FROM A SOURCE INTO YOUR TEXT

In the following paragraph, notice how Daniel Bruno blends together, or integrates, what he thinks and what his source says. He (1) states his main idea *(Sacks illustrates that all of today's college students cannot just be thrown in the same big barrel),* (2) directs the reader to the source *(he spends; he says; he mentions),* (3) provides the information from the source that supports or explains his idea (in this paragraph, Bruno both quotes and summarizes the source), and (4) concludes by commenting on the information. Writers need not include these four steps every time they use information from a source, but it can be helpful to frequently rely on these four elements: (1) the writer's main idea, (2) reference to the source, (3) information from the source, (4) the writer's commentary.

In *Generation X Goes to College,* Peter Sacks illustrates that all of today's college students cannot just be thrown in the same big barrel. In describing the modern/post-modern clash in education, he spends the majority of his time talking about those students who are underprepared, who lack the basic study skills required in academic work, and who demonstrate little real commitment to their own education. Yet, he does not discuss this problem in isolation. He also mentions another type of student. For example, he introduces the reader to Marissa and Carol: "As very good students, [their views] were virtually excluded by The College in order to accommodate the whiners and complainers" (61). And he says they "suffered not only educationally" (63). In addition to discussing specific good students, an entire chapter presents survey results about students' attitudes toward education. While he makes claims such as "nearly a quarter of the students . . . harbored a disproportionate sense of entitlement," this very statement tells the reader that a full three quarters (that is, three out of four) students *do not* "harbor a disproportionate sense of entitlement" (54–59). He wraps up the book by focusing on another student, Andie, who he describes as "a good student, constantly picking [his] brain for information and feedback on her work" (186–87). His final paragraph, before the Epilogue, says, "Let's create a system that encourages people like Andie at least as much as the ones who don't give a damn" (187). Thus, Sacks shows that today's students are a more diverse group—in skill level, background, and attitude toward education—than has ever before been gathered together in the college classroom.

Notice how the references to sources cue the reader that the text is moving to an idea from a source. Writers use cues, also called *attributive phrases* (such as *according to, says, explains,* etc.), to help readers see when ideas are from a source. Notice Ann Marie Paulin's strategies. She first makes a point about diets—they don't work. And then she offers a source and a quotation to support that point. In this case, the reader knows why the quotation is offered: to give credence to her claim about diets:

> And most diets don't work. Psychologist Mary Pipher, in her book *Hunger Pains: The Modern Woman's Quest for Thinness,* cites a 1994 study which found that "90 percent of dieters regain all the weight they lost within five years" (32). The evidence is beginning to pile up out there that being fat may not be nearly as bad for a person's health as the crazy things people inflict upon their bodies to lose weight.

Planting a Tree

You might think of integrating sources as planting a tree. First, the hole should be dug. (One cannot simply plop a tree onto the ground.) Then, after the hole is prepared, the tree can be dropped into place. But the job is not done! The planter must fill in the hole, pack good dirt back into that space, and water, making certain that the roots of the tree are nestled into the new soil. Likewise, a writer must first set up the idea— not simply plop the ideas from a source into a paragraph. Then, the information (summary, paraphrase, quotation) can be integrated smoothly into the writer's own language. Finally, the writer should then consider how to fill in and reinforce the connectedness of the source and his or her own points.

PUNCTUATING QUOTATIONS

Learning the three basic ways of punctuating quotations will be helpful when integrating the exact words of others into your text. Since readers are used to seeing quotations punctuated this way, if you follow these conventions your readers will more easily understand the relationship between your words and the words of your source.

1) Quotation marks only

And he says they "suffered not only educationally" (Sacks 63).

Emphasizing her point, Miller demands that "it is now time for something drastic to change here on campus" (43).

When the quoted matter blends directly into your sentence without a speaking verb (such as *say, says, said, exclaims, proclaims, states,* etc.) indicating a change in voice, no punctuation is required before the quotation. The sentence may be punctuated just as it would be if there were no quotation marks—*And he says they suffered not only educationally.*

2) Speaking verb followed by a comma

His final paragraph, before the epilogue, says, "Let's create a system that encourages people like Andie at least as much as the ones who don't give a damn" (Sacks 187).

Emphasizing her point, Miller suggests, "it is now time for something drastic to change here on campus" (43).

As Martin Luther King, Jr., explains, in his "Letter from Birmingham Jail," "One day the South will know that when these disinherited children of God sat down at lunch counters, they were in reality standing up for what is best in the American dream."

Speaking verbs (such as *say, says, suggests, exclaims, states,* etc.) indicate a shift in voice from your voice to the voice of your source. In the third example above, explains (a speaking verb) tells the reader that the text is going to shift from the writer's voice to the voice of the source. A comma follows the speaking verb and precedes the quotation.

A speaking verb combined with a noun creates an attributive phrase that can be placed at the beginning, in the middle, or at the end of a sentence. Quoting involves crafting sentences carefully to create clear and natural-sounding connections between the writer's own ideas and the words of the source. Here are some standard strategies:

Quotation at the beginning of a sentence

"All voting is a sort of gaming, like checkers or backgammon, with a slight moral tinge to it," explains Henry David Thoreau (56).

Quotation in the middle of a sentence

As Thoreau points out, "all voting is a sort of gaming, like checkers or backgammon, with a slight moral tinge to it" (56), and it is this moral issue that is often overemphasized on ballots.

Quotation at the end of a sentence

Henry David Thoreau claims that "voting is a sort of gaming, like checkers or backgammon, with a slight moral tinge to it" (56).

Quotation divided by your own words

"All voting," explains Thoreau, "is a sort of gaming" (56).

3) Sentence followed by a colon

For example, he introduced the reader to Marissa and Carol: "As very good students, [their views] were virtually excluded by The College in order to accommodate the whiners and complainers" (Sacks 61).

As George Williams notes, protection of white privilege is critical to patterns of discrimination: "Whenever a number of persons within a society have enjoyed for a considerable period of time certain opportunities for getting wealth, for exercising power and authority, and for successfully claiming prestige and social deference, there is strong tendency for these people to feel that these benefits are theirs by 'right'" (727).

When the words to the left of a quotation (a list or explanation) are a complete thought consisting of an independent clause—that is, when those words alone could be followed by a period—a colon is used to connect the quotation (list or explanation) to the complete thought introducing it.

If an entire sentence is a quotation—that is, if it begins and ends with a quotation mark and contains no reference to the source in between—consider (1) connecting the quote, if appropriate, to the preceding sentence with a colon, or (2) adding a cue, or transition, as an introduction to the quote.

Quote connected with a colon

For example, Sacks introduced the reader to Marissa and Carol: "As very good students, [their views] were virtually excluded by The College in order to accommodate the whiners and complainers" (Sacks 61).

Helpful Verbs for Attributing Quotes

says	considers
argues	shows
explains	demands
suggests	teaches
emphasizes	describes
insists	tells
offers	informs
claims	instructs
points out	

Quote connected with a cue or transitional expression

For example, Sacks introduced the reader to Marissa and Carol. He said, "As very good students, [their views] were virtually excluded by The College in order to accommodate the whiners and complainers" (Sacks 61).

SPECIAL CONDITIONS IN QUOTING

To integrate quotes smoothly into a text, writers sometimes find it helpful to omit or add certain words for clarity or cohesion. Standard guidelines exist for letting the reader know how the writer has altered a quotation. Of course, the writer must be absolutely certain that he or she has not changed the source's intended meaning. Note also the standard approach to using long quotations.

Omitting words Occasionally, writers want to quote a passage but to leave out words or phrases. This is done with ellipses (. . .). They tell the reader that words have been taken out of the original passage. Notice how one might quote a passage from David Crabtree's essay:

> **Original:** The world is changing at a bewildering pace. Anyone who owns a computer and tries to keep up with the developments in hardware, software, and the accompanying incompatibilities is all too aware of the speed of change. This rapid change, especially technological change, has extremely important implications for the job market. In the past, it was possible to look at the nation's work force, determine which of the existing occupations was most desirable in terms of pay and working conditions, and pick one to prepare for. But the rapid rate of change is clouding the crystal ball. How do we know that a high-paying job today will be high-paying tomorrow? (255)

> **Quotation:** According to David Crabtree, "The world is changing at a bewildering pace . . . . This rapid change, especially technological change, has extremely important implications for the job market."

The ellipses indicate the missing sentence from the quotation. The same strategy can be applied to cut any amount of text from a passage. For instance, in the sentence below, a few words have been cut from Crabtree's passage:

> **Quotation:** According to David Crabtree, "This rapid change . . . has extremely important implications for the job market."

Adding words Sometimes it is valuable to add a note or comment within a quote. In this case, writers use square brackets to set off their own words. For example, a writer may insert a word in a quoted passage to clarify a vague pronoun or to give a brief explanation:

> **Original:** After months of exhausting research, they had finally come to understand the problem with their design.

> **Quotation:** "After months of exhausting research, [the nuclear scientists] had finally come to understand the problem with their design" (Smith 82).

Here, the writer substitutes the actual noun for the pronoun *they*. Without the noun, the reader may not understand the meaning of the quotation. As in this example, inserting bracketed comments within quotes can clear up any potentially confusing information within a quote while maintaining the flow of the sentence.

Noting an error If a quotation is grammatically or syntactically flawed, a writer cannot simply change it. In such cases, the quotation must remain intact, and the writer must use square brackets and the three-letter word *sic* directly after the error. Otherwise, a reader might assume that the error is on the part of the writer.

Using lengthy quotes When writers quote more than four lines, they must use a block quote. As in this passage from Ann Marie Paulin's essay, writers often use a colon before block quotes:

> Another example of this bullying someone thin comes from Pipher's book *Hunger Pains: The Modern Woman's Tragic Quest for Thinness*. Pipher recounts a conversation she overheard one day in a dress shop:
>
> > I overheard a mother talking to her daughter, who was trying on party dresses. She put on each dress and then asked her mother how she looked. Time after time, her mother responded by saying, "You look just awful in that, Kathy. You're so fat nothing fits you right." The mother's voice dripped with disgust and soon Kathy was crying. (89)

Pipher goes on to suggest that Kathy's mother is a victim of the culture, too, because she realizes how hard the world will be on her fat daughter. Unfortunately, what she doesn't realize is how much better her daughter's quality of life would be if she felt loved by her mother. Any person surrounded by loving family members at home is much better equipped to deal with whatever the cruel world outside throws at her or him.

Sic is Latin for *thus* or *so*. It is used after an error to tell readers that the passage is as quoted *as it is*.

ACTIVITY

The following passage appears in Ann Marie Paulin's essay in Chapter 6, Making Arguments.

> For example, in one commercial for Slim Fast, the woman on the ad is prattling on about how she had gained weight when she was pregnant (seems to me, if you make a person, you ought to be entitled to an extra ten pounds) and how awful she felt. Then there is a shot of this woman months later as a thin person with her toddler in her yard. She joyously proclaims that Slim Fast is "the best thing that ever happened to me!" The best thing that ever happened to her?! I thought I heard wrong. What about that little child romping by her heels? Presumably, there is a daddy somewhere for that little cherub. What about his role in her life? The thought that losing that weight is the most important thing that ever occurred in her life is sad and terrifying. (261)

Divide the class into four groups, and assign each group one of the following "special conditions": omitting words, adding words, using lengthy quotes, and double quotes. Each group should write a new passage that uses the Paulin quote and the assigned special condition. The groups then should share their passages with the class.

Double quotes Occasionally, writers quote a passage that contains a quotation or is itself a quotation. In this case, single quotation marks are used inside the double quotation marks:

> As Maria Gallagher has argued, "it is time that we turn the corner on the road of national energy policies and begin to take 'alternative energy' seriously" (23).

Using Sources in Brief

Information can come from primary or secondary sources.

- Primary research is gathered firsthand: observation, interviews, surveys.
- Secondary research explores others' published ideas, conclusions, and theories.

Sources should be evaluated for:

- Relevance—appropriately related to your particular topic.
- Reliability—verifiable and trustworthy.
- Credibility—reasonable and logical.
- Timeliness—not outdated or behind the times.
- Diversity—providing different viewpoints.

Information from sources can be:

- Paraphrased—expressed in your own words.
- Summarized—expressed in your own words, but with fewer details.
- Quoted—repeated exactly from the source.

DOCUMENTING SOURCES

MLA STYLE

Different disciplines rely on different styles of documentation. The two most common styles are MLA (Modern Language Association) and APA (American Psychological Association). English and humanities use MLA. Like other documentation styles, MLA depends on two basic components: (1) an in-text citation of a work and (2) a list of works cited at the end of the text. These two components function in the following ways:

- In-text citations let a reader know that particular ideas come from a particular source.
- In-text documentation corresponds to the complete bibliographic information provided at the end of the text.
- In-text citations lead the reader directly to the corresponding Works Cited page.
- Done correctly, the in-text reference lists the first word(s)—whether it be the author's last name or the article title—plus the page reference of the citation on the alphabetized Works Cited page. This allows the reader to easily locate the source in the list of works.
- The Works Cited page provides complete information for finding all formal sources.
- This complete information is provided only once and comes at the end of the entire text so that it doesn't interfere with ease of reading.

In-Text Citation

In-text documentation involves referencing the original text in parentheses within the actual sentences of your text; because it uses parentheses, it is sometimes called *parenthetical citation*. In general, for MLA style, in-text citations should include the author's last name (unless it is given within the sentence) and page number of the source from which the cited material is taken (unless the source is electronic and lacks page numbers).

> **An in-text citation must occur whenever a writer:**
> - Quotes directly from a source.
> - Paraphrases ideas from a source.
> - Summarizes ideas from a source.
> - References statistics or data from a source.

"After months of exhausting research, they had finally come to understand the problem with their design" (Smith 82).

A space separates the name and the page number. ⌐

The end punctuation comes after the citation. ⌐

If the author is referred to in the sentence, his or her name can be omitted from the citation.

> Emphasizing her point, Miller demands that "it is now time for something drastic to change here on campus" (43).

If the source has no author, use the first word or phrase of the source's title and punctuate accordingly (quotation marks for an article and underlining for books).

> The oil had spread over much of the shoreline and had "already begun its death grip on a vast array of wildlife" ("Black Death" 54).

If the source has two or three authors, use the last name of all authors.

> (Lunsford, Olin, and Ede 158)

If you have more than one work by the same author, insert the title of the work after the author name, followed by the page number.

> (Faigley, <u>Fragments of Rationality</u> 43)

If you are citing material that is already quoted in the source, cite the source in which you found the quotation and add "qtd. in" before the author's name or title.

> (qtd. in Smith 82)

If you want to acknowledge more than one source for the same information, use a semicolon between citations within one set of parentheses.

> (Lunsford and Ede 78; Smith 82)

If you have an electronic source with no page numbers, simply exclude the page number from the citation. Do not add page numbers, and do not use those that a computer printer assigns.

> According to Martha Smith, "untold numbers of children are negatively affected by the proficiency test craze."

Works Cited

Works Cited pages list the sources that are directly cited in the text. (Bibliographies or Works Consulted pages, on the other hand, list all the sources that a writer may have read and digested in the process of researching the project.) Entries in Works Cited pages must follow strict formatting guidelines, but the process is easy if you know the formulas involved. In general, the first piece of information in the Works Cited entry should correspond directly with the in-text citation. For example, notice the relationship between the in-text citation for King, below, and the entire bibliographic information in the Works Cited page:

People must create change because "progress never rolls in on wheels of inevitability" (**King** 130).

Smith 4

Works Cited

King, Martin Luther, Jr. "Letter from Birmingham Jail." A World of Ideas: Essential Readings for College Writers. Ed. Lee A. Jacobus. Boston: St. Martin's, 1994. 121–37.

The in-text reference refers the reader to the Works Cited page at the end of the essay, where complete bibliographic information allows the reader to locate the source.

CONSISTENT RULES FOR ALL SOURCES

- Author name(s) comes first and is inverted (last name first) with a comma between last and first names.

- Title of the work comes directly after author name. All words in titles are capitalized except prepositions (such as *on, in, between*), articles *(a, an, the)*, coordinating conjunctions *(and, but, for, nor, or, so, yet)*, and *to* in infinitives (such as *to run, to go*).

- If no author is listed, the title comes first.

- Article titles are in quotation marks, while the sources in which they appear, newspapers, books, journals, and magazines, are underlined.

- Publication information follows the title of the source.

- Copyright or publication dates come last. But if the source is an article, then page numbers come last. If the source is electronic, the date of access and URL come last.

- Periods come after names of people (authors, editors, translators), after titles, the year of publication, and at the end of all entries.

> Bibliographic information for books is contained on the title page and the copyright page (the back side of the title page). The title page contains the full title of the book, the author(s), the publishing company, and the city of publication. The copyright page contains date(s) and any edition numbers. Go to the title and copyright pages of this text, and find all the information you would need to cite it as a source.

BOOKS

Single author

Author's name:
As for all sources in MLA format, single author names are inverted.

The title:
Book titles are underlined.

Cook, Claire Kehrwald. Line by Line: How to Improve Your Own Writing. Boston: Houghton, 1995.

City of publication:
If multiple cities are listed on the title page of the book, give only the first.

Publishing company:
Publishing companies are always found on the title page of the book. List them in shortened form, directly after the city. A colon separates the city of publication and the publisher.

Date of publication:
The date usually appears on the copyright page, which is the back side of the title page in a book. Always use the most recent date listed. Use a comma between the publishing company and the date of publication.

Two or more authors

Vasta, Ross, Marshall M. Haith, and Scott A. Miller. <u>Child Psychology: The Modern Science</u>. New York: Wiley, 1995.

For more than three authors, you may avoid listing all the names and simply add *et al.*, Latin for "and others" after the first name.

Johansen, Sturla, et al.

Corporate author or government publication

American Automobile Association. <u>Tour Book: New Jersey and Pennsylvania</u>. Heathrow: AAA, 2001.

If an author is not given for a government publication, list the name of the government first, followed by the agency. The title follows, and then the publication information. Many federal publications are published by the Government Printing Office (GPO).

United States. Office of Consumer Affairs. <u>2003 Consumer's Resource Handbook</u>. Washington: GPO, 2003.

Subsequent editions

Wicks-Nelson, Rita, and Allen C. Israel. <u>Behavior Disorders of Childhood</u>. 3rd ed. Upper Saddle River: Prentice, 1997.

Find the edition information on the title page of the book, and place the information in the entry directly after the title or the editor, if there is one. Use the abbreviations *2nd ed.*, *3rd ed.*, and so on, or *Rev. ed.* for "Revised edition," depending on what the title page says.

Republished book

Tolkien, J. R. R. <u>The Hobbit</u>. 1937. New York: Ballantine, 1982.

Older books may be published by a company different than the original publishers, or a hardcover book may be republished in paperback. In this case, insert the original publication date after the title, and then give the recent publisher and date.

Edited book

Foucault, Michel. <u>The Foucault Reader</u>. Ed. Paul Rabinow. New
York: Pantheon, 1984.

Add *Ed.* after the title of the book, followed by the editor's name, not inverted. Since *Ed.* here means "Edited by," not "Editor," it should never appear as "Eds." even if there is more than one editor.

Translated book

Bakhtin, Mikhail. <u>Problems of Dostoevsky's Poetics</u>. Trans. Caryl
Emerson. Minneapolis: U of Minnesota P, 1984.

Add *Trans.* after the tile of the book followed by the translator's name, not inverted.

ARTICLES

Articles appear in newspapers and periodicals (journals or magazines). While newspapers are usually published daily, magazines are usually published weekly or monthly, and journals are published quarterly or even biannually.

Article in magazine

Author name:
Regardless of the type of source, the author name is inverted. The same rules apply for all sources.

Article title:
Article titles are always in quotation marks.

Ellison, Harlan. "Strangers in a Strange Land." <u>Newsweek</u>
7 Apr. 1997: 49–53.

Publication date:
For weekly or biweekly magazines, include the date (day, month, and year) directly after the title of the publication. (For all types of sources, abbreviate all months except May, June, and July.) For monthly magazines, give the month or months (e.g., *Sept.–Oct.*) and year.

Page numbers:
End with the specific page number(s) on which the article appears. If the article covers consecutive pages, include the range (such as *52–75*). If the page numbers are not consecutive, include the first page number, immediately followed by a plus sign (such as *64+*). Place a colon after the date and before the page numbers.

Periodical title:
The title of the magazine, journal, or newspaper is underlined.

Article in a journal paginated by volume

Crow, Angela. "What's Age Got to Do with It? Teaching Older Students in the Computer-Aided Classrooms." <u>Teaching English in the Two-Year College</u> 27 (2000): 400–15.

Most academic journals number the pages of each issue continuously through a volume. The second issue does not begin with page 1, but with the number after the last page of the previous issue. For these sources, the volume number comes directly after the title. The year is in parentheses, followed by a colon and the inclusive page numbers.

ACTIVITIES

Decide which type of periodical (magazine or journal) may have published the following articles, and in groups or as a class, discuss the reasoning behind your decisions:

"Heading for the Mountains: An Exciting Getaway for the Whole Family"

"Climactic Shifts in the Mountain Region"

"Coach Fired, Team Responds"

"Enzymes, Nutrition, and Aging: A Twenty-Year Study"

"The Latest in Deep Water Bait"

"Re-inventing the Microscope"

"The Epistemology of Literature: Reading and Knowing"

Is It a Journal or a Magazine?

At first glance, journals and magazines may look a lot alike. But closer inspection will reveal significant differences. Generally, journals are written for academic or highly specialized readers, and the articles put forward new theories or practices in a particular field of study (sociology, psychology, nursing, English, chemistry, history, etc.). Magazines are written for general readers, who may have a particular interest (cycling, running, gardening, and so on). If you are not certain what kind of periodical you have, use the following criteria:

Journals
- Seek to advance knowledge in a *field of study*.
- Deal with principles, theories, or core practices in an academic discipline.
- Are associated with a particular discipline or field of academic study.
- Have few advertisements, which usually appear only at the beginning and end (not between or among articles).
- Have few colors and flashy pictures (unless they are related to a study or article)

Magazines
- Report information/news or offer how-to advice.
- Offer the latest technique in a hobby or sport.
- May appeal to readers with a particular *interest*.
- Have advertisements throughout the pages, even interrupting articles.
- Tend to have more colors and pictures.

Article in a newspaper

"Bush: Shift Superfund Costs to Taxpayers." <u>Blade</u> [Toledo] 24
    Feb. 2002: A7.

After the author, if one appears, list the title of the article and the publication information.
Exclude introductory articles *(A, An, The)* from publication titles. Add the city name in square
brackets if it does not appear in the title of the newspaper and the newspaper is local. Add
section letters before the page numbers. As with magazine articles, if the page numbers are
not consecutive, list the first page number, immediately followed by a plus sign.

Scholarly article reprinted in an anthology
(such as a college textbook)

Faigley, Lester. "Judging Writing, Judging Selves." <u>College
    Composition and Communication</u> 40 (1989): 395–412.
    Rpt. in <u>Landmark Essays on Voice and Writing</u>. Ed. Peter
    Elbow. Davis: Hermagoras, 1994. 107–20.

First use the basic article format with the information of the original publication. Then add *Rpt.
in* (abbreviation for "Reprinted in") and include the information for the anthology. End with the
page numbers on which the article appears.

Encyclopedia article

Esposito, Vincent J. "World War II: The Diplomatic History of
    the War and Post-War Period." <u>Encyclopedia Americana</u>.
    Intl. ed. 2000.

Like all sources, begin with an author name (inverted) if one is given. (Check for author names
at the beginning or end of the article.) Put the title of the article in quotation marks, and
underline the encyclopedia title. End with the edition and year.

OTHER SOURCES

Brochure

Masonic Information Center. <u>A Response to Critics of
Freemasonry</u>. Silver Spring: Masonic Services Assn.: n.d.

Give information in the same format as a book. Use abbreviations to indicate missing publication information: *n.p.* (no publisher or no place), *n.d.* (no date of publication), and *n. pag.* (no page numbers).

Personal interview

Jackson, Lynn. Personal interview. 4 Mar. 2002.

Begin with the name of the interviewee, inverted. End with the interview date.

Personal letter or memo

Bosley, Cindy. Letter to author. 15 Nov. 2004.

Like all sources, begin with the author name (inverted). Then give the title or description of the letter. End with the date.

Published letter

Tolkien, J. R. R. "To Christopher Tolkien." 18 Jan. 1944. Letter
55 of <u>The Letters of J. R. R. Tolkien</u>. Ed. Humphrey
Carpenter and Christopher Tolkien. New York: Houghton,
2000. 67–68.

After the date of the letter, give the number of the letter, if available. List the information of the source in which the letter was published, according to the correct format for the source. (In other words, if the letter is published in a book, as above, follow the book format.)

Television program

"A Streetcar Named Marge." <u>The Simpsons</u>. FOX. WAGA,

Atlanta. 10 Oct. 1992.

Begin with the title of the episode or segment (in quotation marks). Underline the title of the program. Name the creator, producer, director, narrator, performer, or writer (if known), network, call letters, and city of the television station (if appropriate and available). End with the broadcast date.

Film

<u>Monty Python's The Meaning of Life</u>. Dir. Terry Jones. 1983.

DVD. Celandine, 2004.

After the title (underlined), list the director, the year of original release (if relevant), the type of medium on which you viewed the film (such as *DVD* or *Videocassette*), the distributor, and the year of release or re-release.

Musical composition

Strauss, Johann. <u>Tales from the Vienna Woods</u>, waltz op. 325.

Begin with the composer's name (inverted). Underline the title of the work. Do not underline the form, number, or key of the work.

Sound recording

Radiohead. "Karma Police." <u>OK Computer</u>. Capitol, 1997.

Begin with the artist's name. Then list the title of a particular song or section (in quotation marks), the collection title (underlined), the recording company, and the year of release. All of this information is available on the product sleeve or insert. If the recording is not on compact disc, list the medium *(Audiocassette, Audiotape, LP)*, followed by a period, before the recording company.

Lecture or speech

Harkin, Patricia. "What's Wrong with This Picture? Teaching
English in the Corporate Academy." Thirty-Third Annual
CEA Conf. Coll. English Assn. Westin Hotel, Cincinnati.
6 Apr. 2002.

Begin with the speaker's name (inverted). Then list the title of the presentation (in quotation
marks), the name of the meeting and sponsoring organization (if applicable), the location of
the lecture or speech, and the date.

Advertisement

ShopForChange.com. Advertisement. <u>Utne Reader</u>. July–Aug.
1999: 34.

Begin with the company or product name, followed by *Advertisement*. Then list the relevant
publication information. For instance, if the ad appears in a periodical, list the information in
the appropriate format and end with the page number.

Work of art (painting, sculpture, photograph)

O'Keeffe, Georgia. <u>Evening Star No. VI</u>. Georgia O'Keeffe
Museum, Santa Fe.

Include the artist's name (inverted), the title of the work (underlined), the collector or
institution that houses it, and the city where it is held.

Performance

<u>A Christmas Carol</u>. By Charles Dickens. Perf. Nebraska
Theatre Caravan. Corson Auditorium, Interlochen, MI.
19 Nov. 2002.

Begin with the title (if applicable), the author of the performed work (if applicable), the
director, the performers, the site of the performance, and the date.

ELECTRONIC SOURCES

Often, websites do not list authors. But when they do, author names should be documented as they are for print sources (inverted at the beginning of the entry). Like print sources, websites also have publication information, but it is different in nature: While a book, for instance, has a publishing company, a website is sponsored by an institution or organization (unless the site is a personal home page). Website entries should include: the title of the site (underlined), the date of publication or the date of the most recent update (if available), the name of the sponsoring institution or organization, the date when the researcher accessed the site, and the Uniform Resource Locator (URL), or the Internet address.

URLs can be excessively long and cumbersome. Rather than reproduce a URL that bleeds onto several lines of text, give the URL for the previous page in your search, so the reader can easily access the document by typing in the title or the author name. (When adding the URL to your citation, break it only after a slash [/] and do not add hyphens.) And with electronic sources especially, remember the basic principle behind documentation: *to provide a guide for finding the sources you used.*

> The purpose of citing sources: To provide a guide for finding the sources you used.

Official website

Robin Flies Again: Letters Written by Women of Goucher
College, Class of 1903. Ed. Sarah Pinsker. 1999.
Goucher Coll. 20 Mar. 2005 <http://goucher.edu/library/
robin>.

Begin with the title of the site (underlined). If the site has no title, offer a description, such as *Home page* (not underlined) in its place. Next, give the name of the site's editor (if available), the date of electronic publication or the latest update (if available), and the name of any sponsoring or supporting institution or organization. Always end with the date that you accessed the site and the URL.

Personal home page

Good, Melissa. Merwolf's Cave. 10 Apr. 2005. 14 Apr. 2005
<http://www.merwolf.com/>.

Begin with the creator's name, followed by the title (or *Home page* if no title is given), the most recent update, the date of access, and the URL.

Document from website (author and date stated)

Harris, Tom. "How Urban Legends Work." <u>HowStuffWorks</u>.
    2005. HowStuffWorks. 12 Apr. 2005 <http://
    science.howstuffworks.com/urban-legend.htm>.

Begin with the author name, followed by the title of the particular document (in quotation marks), the title of the entire site (underlined), the date of last update or publication (if given), the hosting organization, the date of access, and the URL.

Document from website (no author or date stated)

"CCC Interactive." <u>CCC Online</u>. National Council of Teachers
    of English. 19 Mar. 2005 <http://archive.ncte.org/ccc/
    front.html>.

Begin with the title of the particular document (or article), and follow the same rules as the previous entry.

Magazine or journal article retrieved from a database

Stanglin, Douglas, and Amy Bernstein. "Making the Grade."
    <u>U.S. News and World Report</u>. 4 Nov. 1996: 18. <u>Academic</u>
    <u>Search Elite</u>. EBSCOhost. Northwestern Michigan Coll.,
    Osterlin Lib. 4 June 2005 <http://www.epnet.com/>.

Clifford, Edwards H. "Grade Inflation: The Effects on
    Educational Quality and Personal Well-Being." <u>Education</u>.
    120 (2000): 538– . <u>Academic Search Elite</u>. EBSCOhost.
    Northwestern Michigan Coll., Osterlin Lib. 4 June 2005
    <http://www.epnet.com/>.

First cite as a print article. Then list the name of the database, the name of the publishing service (if known), the name of the library, the city and state if useful, the date of access, and the URL. (Use a direct link to the article if possible. Otherwise, use the URL of the database's home page.) Notice that databases do not always list the entire page range of an article. In that case, list the initial page number, followed by a hyphen, a space, and a period.

Article in online journal

Silva, Mary Cipriano, and Ruth Ludwick. "Interstate Nursing
Practice and Regulation: Ethical Issues for the 21st
Century." Online Journal of Issues in Nursing. 2 July 1999.
16 May 2005 <http://www.nursingworld.org/ojin/ethicol/
ethics_1.htm>.

Follow the format for print articles. After the date of publication, give the range of pages or
paragraphs (abbreviated as *pars.*) if they are numbered in the article. At the end of the entry,
add the date of access and the URL.

Online book

Shaw, Bernard. Pygmalion. New York, 1916. Bartelby.com: Great
Books Online. 9 Feb. 2005 <http://bartleby.com/138/
index.html>.

Follow the format for print books. Underline the title of the website. If the book is part of an
online scholarly project, which is often the case, include the sponsoring institution. At the end
of the entry, add the date of access and URL.

Abstract

Barton, Ellen. "Resources for Discourse Analysis in Composition
Studies." Style 36.4 (2002): 575–95. Abstract. InfoTrac
College Edition. InfoTrac. 10 July 2005 <http://
infotrac.thomsonlearning.com>.

Use the format approriate for the type of source (book, article, etc.) and add the descriptor
Abstract before the title of the database, date of access, and URL.

E-mail

Miller, Maria. "Changes to Physics Dept." E-mail to Dennis
Suarez. 23 Nov. 2005.

Begin with the author, followed by the title (the word or phrase from the subject line of the
e-mail) in quotation marks, the descriptor *E-mail to,* and the recipient's name. If you were the
e-mail's recipient, insert *E-mail to author.* End with the e-mail's date.

E-mail/listserver posting

Brandywine, Jacob. "Raising Standards." Online posting. 21 Apr. 2005. Writing Program Forum. 4 May 2005 <http:// writingforum@nmc.edu>.

Follow the format for e-mail, but use the descriptor *Online posting*. Then give the date of the posting, the name of the listserver or forum, the date of access, and the electronic address of the listserver (if known) or the e-mail address of the moderator (in angled brackets).

CD-ROM

The Trigonometry Explorer. CD-ROM. Chevy Chase: Cognitive Technologies, 1996.

If no author is given, use the editor, compiler, or translator's name, with the abbreviation *(ed., comp., trans.)*. If none of these are listed, begin with the title, followed by the descriptor *CD-ROM*. End with publication information (city, publishing company, date).

Part of CD-ROM

Allen Edmonds Shoes. Advertisement. Comp21: Composition in the 21st Century, The Composition of Everyday Life. CD-ROM. Boston: Wadsworth, 2006.

If citing a portion of a CD-ROM, begin with the author of that particular section (if one is listed), the title of the section, and then follow the format for a CD-ROM entry.

Online encyclopedia

"India." Columbia Encyclopedia. 2003. Yahoo!. 5 June 2005. Path: Reference; Encyclopedia; Columbia Encyclopedia; India; India History.

As with a print encyclopedia, begin with the title of the article if no author is available. Then list the title of the encyclopedia, the publication date (if available), the name of the online service, and the date of access. If you found the source through a sequence of related topics, add *Path:* and give the words in your search sequence, separated by semicolons.

Sample Research Essay

Ben Wetherbee wrote this essay for his English 112 class (a second-semester composition course). As you read, take note of the strategies Wetherbee uses to integrate sources into his argument.

Wetherbee 1

Ben Wetherbee
Professor Mauk
English 112
23 April 2005

Branded

Often we recall the days of knights in shining armor, those men forever etched into history within their majestic shells of war. The bravery, the nobility, the selflessness of these radiant warriors—we recall that. But why shining armor? Yes, it undoubtedly had practical merit, but it acted as more than a protective casing: It was gleaming, curving, accompanied by luminous plumes and banners. Why the extravagance?

Easy! Medieval folks expected their knights to come in shining armor. Hulking, thick breastplates; glistening chain mail; colorful, intricate crests displayed upon great shields of iron—all indications of the times. The outfit—as much as the man, even—made a knight a knight. A knight without his armor, his shield, his weaponry, or his colors would pass only as an indistinct and vulnerable man, a commoner. In this spectacle-oriented world, the heart of a knight is insufficient; one must look the part to appear in the history textbook.

The result: Dress reflects cultural identity. Victorian women ruthlessly layered themselves in constricting attire certainly not for the sake of practicality or comfort, but because that's how women dressed; a woman improperly outfitted was scarcely a woman. Young men sported Beatles haircuts in the early '60s because the Beatles exemplified rock 'n' roll, rebellion, and freedom. The anti-Vietnam War movement displayed the peace

Historical allusion: gives a familiar reference to the reader.

More historical allusions make the point: dress reflects cultural identity.

sign not because it was geometrically pleasing, but because it symbolized peace. Exposed chest hair, gold medallions, and white bellbottoms symbolized the disco movement. Eyeliner, tattoos, and uncouth, black-dyed hair symbolized the punk movement. Every hairstyle, makeup job, pair of jeans, white undershirt, and piece of jewelry means something—always! A glance at a person's garments, lipstick, or hairdo invariably offers a small insight to his/her cultural identity.

The flip side, of course, is that dress reflects individual identity, too. A knight's colors, crest, or specific style of armor might have represented what specific sort of knight he was—his family, cause, or place of origin. Personal modifications are easily applicable to disco attire, hippie attire, punk attire—a personally significant emblem on a medallion, a jean jacket encrusted with handpicked embroidered patches, a tattoo reflecting an event in one's life. Personal expression even seeps from the cracks of the army, a place one would assume does its utmost to stifle individuality; recall Stanley Kubrick's Vietnam War film <u>Full Metal Jacket</u>—the protagonist's helmet sports both the peace symbol and the phrase "born to kill." Even officers' insignias convey a level of individuality by symbolizing personal accomplishment. Individual expression completes the duality of physical self-presentation, allowing great insight in the examination of identity.

So in the interest of argument, let's examine my identity. I typically wear loose-fitting jeans or khakis, often with side "cargo" pockets. My shirts vary from button-up to softball-style to basic t-shirts, but they're all simple, often exhibiting deep tones of blue, green, and grey. My shoes are simple, black, rugged, and masculine. I have no piercings, no tattoos. I wear a fleece jacket in the spring and fall, a wool peacoat and knit scarf in winter. No hats, usually. Trendy metal watch with a blue face. Two trendy necklaces with earthy beads. These observations may fail to offer any insights into my soul, but I am certainly a visible product of the '90s and '00s. I look normal for one born in 1985, one who became a teenager in 1998—normal except for one thing . . .

Focusing the point on individual identity.

Cultural allusions and reference to a popular film support the main idea so far.

Testimony and an appeal to character. (The writer is part of a cultural trend.)

Wetherbee 3

What's missing? Give up?

Here's where the individual identity comes in—no corporate logos. I wear no corporate logos. My backpack displays the Eastpack emblem, but this one exception I've masked with political buttons. It's nearly impossible to buy decent shoes that don't display a logo these days, but I've succeeded even in this field. I ardently exercise my right not to wear corporate logos, which is a monumental deviation from the trend of my generation.

Why? Here's why: The way my generation wears corporate logos scares the hell out of me.

Especially among middle- and high-schoolers, corporate logos appear rampantly. One can hardly set foot in a public school's hallway without drowning under a barrage of geometric homage to capitalism—the sleek meanness of the Nike swoosh, the catchy asymmetry of the Adidas stripes, the pseudo-heart insignia of Roxy, the many bubbly fonts of Billabong. Also appearing in mass: Polo Jeans' patriotic display, Tommy Hilfiger's boldly shaded rectangular tapestry, and the ultramodern Reebok regalia—to name a few. Shoes, jeans, sweatshirts, t-shirts, socks, hats, and even jewelry exhibit the plentiful etchings of a *laissez-faire* dream.

And while secondary schools provide their most overstated presence, the corporate-clad appear ubiquitously, even in the most seemingly unlikely settings. Political columnist Kirsten Anderberg, for example, even recalls the omnipresence of corporate logos at an anti-war rally:

> As my son put it, "The Anti-War Movement, brought to you by Banana Republic!" . . . People were pulling anti-war fliers out of Swatch bags and wearing Old Navy shirts! The corporate logos on the umbrellas in the crowd were representative of this new population also. We saw a man with an umbrella that said "Telecommunications Systems" and he was holding up a sign that said "No Iraq Attack."

Appeal to character: the writer chooses not to be "branded."

Specific examples prove the point about his generation.

The source, Anderberg, helps make the point that is already expressed.

The block quotation is connected with a textual cue, "for example," and the content is set up.

Wetherbee 4

The writer comments on Anderberg's point.

One might expect an anti-war protest to be consistent with the notion of hippie amaterialism, but no. Not in this age. Amazingly, the Nike swoosh and the peace symbol may traverse hand in hand.

Not surprisingly, corporations deliberately capitalize the public's willingness to wear their logos—it's a fantastic form of advertising! Brand consultant Jim Knutsen, in his appropriately titled article "Making Your Mark," discusses the value of "distinctiveness and consistency" in corporate labels: "The visual identities of the best brands trigger recognition and response, having been pounded into our subconscious over long periods of time" (56). Clothing offers a delicious means of exhibiting corporate "distinctiveness and consistency"—nothing like a succinct blurb of imagery on the breast of a hooded sweatshirt to help trigger the ol' "recognition and response." Because clothing is worn by people, and people are mobile, brand-name apparel presents a pervasive and inescapable means of advertisement. The eagerness of brands to create and distribute clothing-friendly logos melds in complete harmony with—and contributes to—the abundance of willful walking advertisements.

The in-text citation requires only the page number because the author is given in the set up.

A transition sentence brings us from the idea in the previous paragraph.

In addition to the more-than-enthusiastic support of the brands themselves, the logo-wearing phenomenon owes much of its endurance to good old-fashioned conformity. People love to conform. A glance at any human society from any time will reveal this; it's what enables trends in the first place. Furthermore, numerous psychological investigations (Zimbardo's mock prison and the famous Milgram experiment, for example); have scientifically established the willingness—eagerness, even—of the individual to bow to group expectations. As renowned author Doris Lessing sums up the matter, "When we're in a group, we tend to think as that group does: we may even have joined the group to find 'like-minded' people. But we also find our thinking changing because we belong to a group. It is the hardest thing in the world to maintain an individual dissident opinion, as a member of a group" (48). So, once the trend of logo-wearing sets in (which it has), it

The quotation reinforces the point made by the allusions to Milgram and Zimbardo.

Wetherbee 5

escalates. To use a cliché, "monkey see, monkey do." Humans <u>are</u> primates, after all—in Lessing's words, "we are group animals"—so humans mimic popular behavior (48). Once a trend gains popularity, social pressure colossally adds to its momentum; it's that simple. For my own example (this was before I became rebelliously anti-logo), I recall the desire to wear Airwalk shoes as a middle-schooler, the longing for miniature insignias to dot my socks just above the ankles. These things were cool. Social pressure—there's no avoiding it.

But enough with the how of the matter—corporate enthusiasm and the psychology of conformity explain that simply enough. The more pressing question is why? Why did the phenomenon of logo-wearing appear in the first place? Logos on employee attire and company-owned vehicles—sure, those make complete sense. Nobody's questioning those who wear logos to advertise their own businesses. But what prompted the pioneers of the logo-wearing movement to plaster other people's logos across their backpacks, sweatshirts, and jeans?

The answer is frightening: If clothing reflects cultural identity, and my generation wears corporate logos on its clothing, then my generation must identify with corporations. I, therefore, am a member of the Corporate Generation. How precisely did we come to identify with corporations? That's a difficult question with particularly elusive details. However, one can hardly ignore the correlation between the logo-wearing phenomenon and the general rise of corporate America—the symbiotic existence of Washington and big business, the sweeping deployment of Wal-Marts against local enterprises. Corporate America has engraved its mark on this nation, including this nation's youth. My generation, we have been branded.

What's scarier, though, is how well we have adapted to our brands. To best describe my generation's passion for corporate logos, one must employ a word that evades the dictionary. The extraordinary novelist Kurt Vonnegut, in his book <u>Cat's Cradle</u>, first introduced the much-needed term *granfalloon*. *Granfalloon* describes a group of people

The writer follows the quotation with personal testimony—wrapping the outside sources into his own argument.

Transition paragraph—to a more "frightening" insight.

All the support, thus far, leads here: the "corporate generation."

Wetherbee 6

bound by a hollow cause, who have nothing genuinely significant in common—"a seeming team that [is] meaningless in ways God gets things done," as Vonnegut puts it (91). "Hazel's obsession with Hoosiers around the world was a textbook example of a . . . granfalloon," Vonnegut elaborates. "Other examples of granfalloons are the Communist party, the Daughters of the American Revolution, the General Electric Company, the International Order of Odd Fellows—and any nation, anytime, anywhere" (91–92). With this in mind, one could aptly accuse my generation of assembling itself into a brand-based granfalloon.

I try to like my generation—sometimes successfully. But this is too much. First, the premise uniting my generation's granfalloon is positively ludicrous. Much worse than Vonnegut's examples, our cause has no deep and philosophical criticism. No, ours is blatantly nutty: We willingly advertise corporations with which we have no affiliation whatsoever. Furthermore, brand-name attire is usually more costly than "plain" clothes, clothes that don't advertise—and we buy it anyway! We financially go out of our way to advertise other people's corporations. It's borderline insanity! Don't we realize we're doing their work for them? Don't we get it?—we're advertising for them; they should be paying us!

And it goes deeper. Recall that clothing also reflects individual identity. The Corporate Generation's members still seek to express their individual identities, but even this is often achieved through logo-wearing. Some wish to show off their wealth by wearing pricey brands. Some wish to boast their acute tastes in fashion. Some think the Nike swoosh just looks so damn cool. So, the Corporate Generation has broken itself into sub-granfalloons: the Nike-wearers, the Abercrombie-wearers, etc. And this is our individual expression—brand selection. On marches the rich kids' granfalloon, wearing its seventy-dollar Tommy Hilfiger jeans. On marches the in-crowd girls' granfalloon, signifying its lofty social altitude with Roxy sweatshirts and pink Adidas shoes. And on

Even literature helps to make the point. (Good writers find the connections between culture, literature, history, film, and their secondary sources.)

The writer maintains a strong but playful voice—even among the sources and allusions.

The writer intensifies the point by using the terms from his sources.

Wetherbee 7

marches the wannabe jocks' granfalloon, t-shirts and warm-up pants plastered with any number of athletically oriented logos. This is my generation.

We don't use the symbol the way other generations have. Symbols are wildly effective in triggering ideas—the two-fingered V, the black armband, the holy cross. Past generations have used symbols effectively to represent specific movements and ideas; they have personalized symbols. The peace sign, for example, originally stood specifically for nuclear disarmament, its design very possibly inspired by the semaphore code positions for N and D (Liungman 253). The anti-Vietnam War movement personalized the emblem in the late '60s—its meaning was slightly altered to fit a new cause. But our emblems still mean "Nike," "Adidas," and "Reebok". The matter would vastly change if we were to use corporate logos against corporations—protesters have adopted this ironic spirit by wearing old army jackets to anti-war rallies. But irony is not our intention. We provide good publicity.

And let us take a moment to consider what we're publicizing. By and large, these corporations we advertise fall short of refined virtue; their methods are often questionable, to say the least. Nike, for example—undoubtedly among the worst offenders—remains a long-time target of human rights groups. A report from 2000 entitled Sweatshops Behind the Swoosh alleges that "Nike [factory] workers in China . . . put in 12-hour days and seven-day weeks and earn $1.50 for every pair of shoes they turn out—which Nike sells for $80–$120" (qtd. in "The Swoosh"). Furthermore, the report directly asserts that "the deplorable conditions in Nike factories are Nike's fault. In a global economy with no rules that protect workers, it is companies such as Nike [that] direct the global sweatshop in industries such as clothing and footwear" (qtd. in "The Swoosh"). Ouch! So Nike is not quite a monument to morality and good will toward men, and other corporations face similar charges. Names like Adidas, Gap, Reebok, and many more can also be associated with the third-world sweatshop, and it doesn't even end there. Abercrombie,

The source helps to prove a small supporting point.

He follows the info from the source with a direct response—which resonates with his voice.

Wetherbee 8

for instance, faces accusations of racial discrimination in its hiring policies. Do we really want to pay top dollar to advertise for the Abercrombies and Nikes of the world, to essentially do their work for them? If it isn't absurd enough to willingly advertise other people's companies in the first place, we're advertising companies with distinctly sinister backgrounds.

In all fairness, however, Nike and other corporations have undertaken efforts to improve working conditions since 2000. But this hardly justifies the small fortunes we pay to do their advertising work for them. It seems unlikely, anyway, that these sweatshop-based corporations would have taken any virtuous steps in the absence of scalding pressure from humanitarian groups. They have no excuses. They exploited their impoverished workers.

My generation, let us not reward such exploiters, even if they have shown a little progress. At the very least, let them do their own advertising.

I have to give my generation a bit of credit, though—not every company logo worn may directly reflect a granfalloon. Paintball enthusiasts, for instance, may wear the logo of a certain paintball equipment company—thus the logo reflects their identities as paintballers. And wearing the Atari logo may be a genuine expression of proud nerdiness, though even this logo has been trivialized by widespread popularity. These groups may qualify as granfalloons, too, by Vonnegut's standards, but at least their status is debatable. The Nike-wearers, the Roxy-wearers, the Adidas-wearers, the Abercrombie-wearers, though—they're only expressing their membership in the Corporate Generation, a certain granfalloon among granfalloons.

Indeed, Aldous Huxley may have foreseen the Corporate Generation in his 1932 novel Brave New World, a depiction of an ultra-consumerist future in which *Ford* has replaced God: "Ford! Ford! it was too revolting . . ." (91). Had Huxley only lived to witness the upsurge of Nike and its compatriots, perhaps he'd have found a more

The source ("The Swoosh") prompts several paragraphs of writer's commentary.

Speaking directly to his generation makes the essay slightly informal.

He consistently points to corporate logo examples.

Wetherbee 9

contemporary replacement for Ford—"[Nike! Nike!] it was too revolting . . ." Or perhaps

"Adidas! Adidas!" or "Reebok! Reebok!" After all, we have taken our logo-wearing

perilously near a religious status. Perhaps we're out to make Huxley a prophet, to attain

the dystopia of his vision. It's a farfetched notion, but here we are—marching steadfastly

onward, proudly adorned by our favorite corporate insignias. This is my generation.

And to you, my generation, I offer this challenge: We can do better. We're still the

young generation; we're supposed to rebel against the machine. We're supposed to rally

against the aged fat cats who watch us from lofty offices—cigars dangling from their lips;

disgusted, aghast, and mortified by our presence. We're supposed to strike blows for

humanity. We're supposed to be out to change the world.

Rather, we're blithely buying into the schemes of those aged conservatives in their

towering office buildings. Some youth of the nation we are.

So what happened to the creativity of youth? Look at how the hippie kids dressed.

It may have been eccentrically colorful and a little too LSD-inspired, but at least it was

their style. Look at how the '70s kids dressed. Brown and orange may be a thoroughly

nasty color combination, but at least it was theirs. Look at how the original punks

dressed. They may have been crude, vulgar, and downright revolting, but at least it was

their crudeness. At least it was their vulgarity, their downright revoltingness.

These corporate logos—they aren't ours. They belong to old men in grey suits,

sweatshop-perpetuators, violators of human rights, crushers of the little guy. Our

adornment of these logos plainly exposes our shortcoming as the young generation.

We aren't even trying. We actually wear the mark of the enemy—all that the young

generation, by definition, is supposed to oppose. Nike is not ours. Adidas is not ours.

Reebok is not ours. Billabong is not ours. Roxy is not ours. Abercrombie is not ours.

No corporate entities are ours.

So let's be damn sure we aren't theirs.

Another novel helps illustrate the point. And the writer helps make the connection between the fictional and the real.

The historical allusions now contrast with the present generation.

Wetherbee 10

Works Cited

Anderberg, Kirsten. "Corporate Logos and Protest Signs." <u>Eat the State!</u> 26 Feb. 2003.

    20 Apr. 2005 <http://www.eatthestate.org/07-13/CorporateLogosProtest.htm>.

Huxley, Aldous. <u>Brave New World</u>. New York: Harper, 1969.

Knutsen, Jim. "Making Your Mark." <u>Searcher</u> 12 (2004): 56. <u>Academic Search Elite</u>.

    EBSCOhost. Northwestern Michigan Coll., Osterlin Lib. 24 Apr. 2005

    <http://www.epnet.com/>.

Lessing, Doris. "Group Minds." <u>Prisons We Choose to Live Inside</u>. New York: Harper,

    1988. 47–62.

Liungman, Carl G. <u>Dictionary of Symbols</u>. New York: Norton, 1991.

"The Swoosh and the Sweats." <u>Nation</u>. 22 May 2000: 7. <u>General Reference Center Gold</u>.

    InfoTrac. Northwestern Michigan Coll., Osterlin Lib. 30 Apr. 2005 <http://

    infotrac.galegroup.com/>.

Vonnegut, Kurt. <u>Cat's Cradle</u>. New York: Delta, 1998.

The first element in each
entry (usually the last
name of the author)
appears in the text.

APA STYLE

The American Psychological Association (APA) documentation style is used in psychology, nursing, education, and related fields. But while the format is somewhat different from MLA, the strategies for finding, evaluating, and integrating sources remain the same. And even the basic principles of documentation remain the same across styles: The information in the in-text citation should correspond directly with the References page (the APA equivalent of a Works Cited page).

- In-text (or parenthetical) citations provide unobtrusive documentation of specific information.

- In-text citation lets a reader know that particular ideas come from a particular source.

- In-text citation corresponds to the complete bibliographic information provided at the end of the text.

- In-text citations lead the reader directly to the corresponding References page.

- Done correctly, the in-text citation is the first word(s)—whether it be the author's last name or the article title—plus year of publication and the page number of the citation on the alphabetized References page. This allows the reader to easily find the appropriate source on the References page.

- The References page provides complete information for finding the source.

- This complete information is provided only once and comes at the end of the entire text so that it doesn't interfere with ease of reading.

- This complete information should allow the reader to find the source easily.

In-Text Citation

Like MLA style, in-text documentation for APA involves referencing the original text in parentheses within the actual sentences of your text. An in-text citation must occur whenever a writer:

- Quotes directly from a source.
- Paraphrases ideas from a source.
- Summarizes ideas from a source.
- References statistics or data from a source.

For direct quotes, APA in-text citations should include the author name, date (year only) of the source, and page number from which the cited material is taken. Include the author name in the citation unless it is given within the sentence.

"After months of exhausting research, they had finally come to understand the problem with their design" (Smith, 1998, p. 82).

p. or *pp.* comes before the actual page number(s).

End punctuation comes after the parenthetical citation.

Commas separate elements within the parentheses.

Writers using APA style often include the date directly after the author's name in the sentence.

Emphasizing her point, Miller (2000) demands that "it is now time for something drastic to change here on campus" (p. 43).

If the source has no author, use the first word or phrase of the source title and punctuate the title accordingly (either with quotation marks or italics).

> "Even though most of the nation's coastal shorelines can no longer sustain a full range of sea life, the vast majority of Americans seem unconcerned" ("Dead Seas," 2001, p. 27).

If the source has two authors, use the last name of both authors. (Notice that APA style uses &, an ampersand, for in-text citations and the References page.)

> (Lunsford & Ede, 1984, p. 158)

If the cited material is quoted in another source, cite the source in which you found the quotation and add *as cited in* before the author name or title.

> (as cited in Smith, 1998)

If you want to acknowledge more than one source for the same information, use a semicolon between citations within one set of parentheses. The sources should be listed in alphabetical order.

> (Lunsford & Ede, 1984; Smith, 1998)

Electronic Sources: Many electronic sources (Web pages, for instance) do not have page numbers, but page numbers may appear on the hard copy. Unless the original source has page numbers, omit them from the in-text citation. Instead, either use the paragraph number (with ¶ or *para.*), if provided, or, if the source has headings, use the heading plus the paragraph number of the source. Electronic texts (especially Web pages) may lack authors; in that case, follow the same formula as with print sources and use the title of the source in the citation.

> (Vince, 2005, Blood to Brain section, para. 2)

References

In general, the rule for in-text citation is that the information given should align with the first piece of information in the References list. The References list gives sources that are directly cited in the text. (Bibliographies, on the other hand, list all the sources that a writer may have read and digested in the process of researching the project.) Entries in a References list must follow strict formatting guidelines, but the process is easy if you know the formulas involved.

The most basic idea in referencing sources is that the information in the in-text citation should correspond with the first piece of information given in the References list. For example, notice how the citation from Stremlow's essay (on page 688) corresponds with the entry from her References list:

> Some 91.2 million people choose to make a New Year's resolution each year (**Wrightson,** 1992, p. 19).

> Vultures 9
>
> References
>
> **Wrightson,** C. (1992, November/December). Vital statistics. *Health, 6* (6), 19. Retrieved December 6, 2004, from EBSCOhost database.

The following pages show specific formatting for different types of sources, but the following rules apply for all sources:

- Author names come first. Last name first, followed by first initial of first name (and first initial of middle name, if given).
- The date comes in parentheses directly after the author names.
- Title of the work comes directly after the date. Article titles are always in regular type, while the sources in which they appear—newspapers, magazines, and journals—are italicized. (Only the first letter of the title or subtitle is capitalized unless there are proper nouns.)
- If no author appears, the title comes first.
- Publication information follows the title of the source.
- If the source is an article, page numbers come last. If the source is electronic, the date of access and URL come last.

BOOKS

All of the necessary information for books can usually be found on the title page, which is inside the front cover.

General format for books

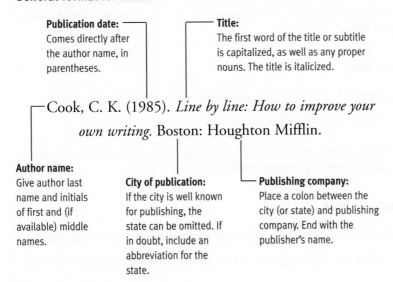

Publication date:
Comes directly after the author name, in parentheses.

Title:
The first word of the title or subtitle is capitalized, as well as any proper nouns. The title is italicized.

Cook, C. K. (1985). *Line by line: How to improve your own writing.* Boston: Houghton Mifflin.

Author name:
Give author last name and initials of first and (if available) middle names.

City of publication:
If the city is well known for publishing, the state can be omitted. If in doubt, include an abbreviation for the state.

Publishing company:
Place a colon between the city (or state) and publishing company. End with the publisher's name.

Two or more authors

Vasta, R., Haith, M. M., & Miller, S. A. (1995). *Child psychology: The modern science.* New York: Wiley.

Add all additional author names, also inverted, before the title. Use an ampersand (&), not *and,* between the names.

Corporate author

American Automobile Association. (2001). *Tour book: New Jersey and Pennsylvania.* Heathrow, FL: Author.

Use the name of the corporation for the author name. If the corporate author also published the text, write *Author* for the publisher.

Subsequent editions

Lauwers, J., & Shinskie, D. (2004). *Counseling the nursing mother* (4th ed.). Sudbury, MA: Jones and Bartlett.

Find the edition information on the title page of the book, and place the information in parentheses directly after the title. Use abbreviations: *2nd ed., 3rd ed.,* etc., or use *Rev. ed.* for "Revised edition."

Edited book

Foucault, M. (1984). *The Foucault reader* (P. Rabinow, Ed.). New York: Pantheon.

After the title, add the editor's name (first initial and last name) and *Ed.* (for "editor"). Use *Eds.* (for "editors") if the book has more than one editor.

Translated book

Bakhtin, M. (1984). *Problems of Dostoevsky's poetics* (C. Emerson, Trans.). Minneapolis, MN: University of Minnesota Press.

Add the translator's name (first initial and last name) and *Trans.* (all in parentheses) after the title of the book.

ARTICLES

Articles appear in newspapers and periodicals (journals or magazines). While newspapers are usually published daily, magazines are usually published weekly or monthly, and journals are published quarterly or even biannually.

Article in a magazine

Buchanan, M. (2004, November 20). A billion brains are better than one. *New Scientist, 184,* 34–37.

Include the date (year, month, day) directly after the author name. Do not abbreviate months. Give the volume number in italics after the magazine title.

Article in a newspaper

Bush: Shift superfund costs to taxpayers. (2002, February 24).
The Blade, p. A7.

If no author appears, give the title of the article first, followed by the date. After the title of the newspaper, add section letters before the page numbers.

Article in a journal paginated by volume

Crow, A. (2003). Risky behavior among youth: A study of
American teens. *American Psychologist, 58,* 400–415.

Most academic journals number the pages of each issue continuously through a volume. The second issue does not begin with page 1, but with the number after the last page of the previous issue. For these journal articles, place the volume number in italics directly after the journal title, and before the page numbers.

Article or chapter in an edited book

Mickelson, R. A., & Smith, S. S. (1991). Education and the
struggle against race, class, and gender inequality. In E.
Disch (Ed.), *Reconstructing gender: A multicultural anthology*
(pp. 303–317). Mountain View, CA: Mayfield.

After the author and date, give the title of the article or chapter. Then write *In* and the first initial and last name of the editor(s). The abbreviation *Ed.* or *Eds.* (in parentheses) should follow the editor(s). End with the title of the book, the page numbers in which the article appears, and the publication information.

Encyclopedia article

Esposito, V. J. (2000). World War II: The diplomatic history of
the war and post-war period. In *Encyclopedia Americana*
(9th ed., Vol. 29, pp. 364–367). Danbury, CT: Grolier.

Begin with the author (if given) and date. Then give the title of the article. The name of the encyclopedia (after *In*) should be in italics. The edition number, volume number, and page number(s) should be in parentheses.

OTHER SOURCES

Brochure

Masonic Information Center. (n.d.). *A response to critics of freemasonry* [Brochure]. Silver Spring, MD: Masonic Services Association.

Use *n.d.* to indicate no date, which is often necessary for brochures. After the title, add the descriptor *Brochure* in brackets before the publication information.

Personal interview or letter

(L. Jackson, personal communication, March 4, 2002)

APA style recommends citing personal communications only with an in-text citation—not in the References list. In the in-text citation, give the name of the interviewee, the title *personal communication*, and the date.

Television program

Martin, J. (Writer), & Moore, R. (Director). (1992). A streetcar named Marge [Television series episode]. In A. Jean & M. Reiss (Producers), *The Simpsons.* Los Angeles: Twentieth Century Fox.

Begin with the name and title of the scriptwriter, then the name and title of the director and the date. Give the title of the episode or segment followed by the producer and the title of the program (italicized). End with the location of the broadcasting company and the company name.

Government publication

U.S. Census Bureau. (2002). *Statistical abstract of the United States* (122nd ed.). Washington, DC: U.S. Government Printing Office.

If no author is given, use the government agency as the author, followed by the date, the title (in italics), and the publication information that appears on the title page. If no publication information appears and the publication is a federal document, you can assume that it was published by the Government Printing Office in Washington, D.C.

ELECTRONIC SOURCES

As for print sources, citations for electronic sources require author(s), date, title, and publication information. Authors and titles are formatted in the same manner as print sources. The difference occurs with publication information. The primary difference is that all entries for electronic sources require the date of access (date on which you retrieved the information) and a URL or database name. After publication information, add *Retrieved,* the date, *from,* and the URL, or the name of the database. (When adding the URL to your citation, break it only after slashes [/] and do not add hyphens.) Especially with electronic sources, remember the basic principle behind citing sources: *to provide a guide for finding the sources you used.* Therefore, the most direct route to the source should always be used in the entry.

In APA format, the word *Retrieved* always precedes the date of access and the word *from* always precedes the name of the source or its URL.

Website

Pinsker, S. (Ed.). (1999). *Robin flies again: Letters written by women of Goucher College, class of 1903.* Retrieved March 17, 2005, from Goucher College, Julia Rogers Library Web site: http://goucher.edu/library/robin

As with all sources, begin with the author's or editor's name(s) (inverted), if available, and the date of electronic publication. Give the title of the site (italicized). Write *Retrieved* and then the date of access, followed by *from* and the name of the source or its URL. If the site has a sponsoring institution or organization, include the name and then a colon before the URL.

Document from website (author and date stated)

Harris, T. (2005). How urban legends work. *HowStuffWorks.* Retrieved April 12, 2005, from http:// science.howstuffworks.com/urban-legend.htm

Begin with the author name (normal APA format), followed by the date (in parentheses), the title of the specific document, the title of the website (in italics), the word *Retrieved* and the access date, and finally *from* and the URL.

Document from website (no author or date stated)

CCC interactive. (n.d.). *CCC online.* Retrieved March 19, 2005, from http://archive.ncte.org/ccc/front.html

Begin with the title. In place of the date, write *n.d.* in parentheses for "no date." Then, give the title of the specific document, the title of the website in italics, *Retrieved* and the access date, and finally *from* and the URL.

Personal home page

Good, M. (2005, April). *Merwolf's cave.* Retrieved April 25, 2005, from http://www.merwolf.com/

Begin with the creator's name, followed by the date of the most recent update, the title, *Retrieved,* the date of access, *from* and the URL.

Journal or magazine article retrieved from a database

Boyd, Nancy G. (2002). Mentoring dilemmas: Developmental relationships within multicultural organizations. *Journal of Occupational & Organizational Psychology, 18,* 123–125. Retrieved August 16, 2004, from Ohiolink database.

First cite as a print article. Then write *Retrieved* and the date of access, then *from* and the name of the database.

Article in an online journal

If the online journal is exactly the same as the print version (which is most common for academic journals), then follow the format for print articles, but after the article title, add the label *[Electronic version]* in brackets:

Crow, A. (2000). What's age got to do with it? Teaching older students in the computer-aided classrooms [Electronic version]. *Teaching English in the Two-Year College, 27,* 400–415.

If it varies at all (format, no page numbers, etc.), do not use *[Electronic version]*. Instead, list the retrieval date and the URL or database:

Silva, M. C., & Ludwick, R. (1999, July 2). Interstate nursing practice and regulation: Ethical issues for the 21st century. *Online Journal of Issues in Nursing.* Retrieved March 20, 2005, from http://www.nursingworld.org/ojin/ethicol/ethics_1.htm

Document within a scholarly database

Hay, R. *Archive for the history of economic thought.* Hamilton, Ontario: McMaster University. Retrieved January 8, 2005, from http://socserv2.socsci.mcmaster.ca/~econ/ugcm/3ll3/

Begin with the author (if one is listed), followed by the title, the city, and the institution that sponsors the database. End with the date of access and URL.

Online book

Shaw, B. (1916). *Pygmalion.* [Online]. Bartleby.com: Great books online. Retrieved February 9, 2005, from http://bartleby.com/ 138/index.html

Follow the format for print books, but exclude the original print publication information. After the title, insert *[Online]* and the sponsoring organization or institution. End with date of access and the URL.

Abstract

Barton, E. (2002). Resources for discourse analysis in composition studies. *Style, 36*(4), 575–595. Abstract retrieved July 10, 2004, from http://infotrac.thomsonlearning.com

Use the format appropriate for the type of source (book, journal, etc.) and add the descriptor *Abstract retrieved* before the date of access and URL.

Part of CD-ROM

Guffey, M. E. (2005). Essentials of Business Communication (Enhanced Version 6th Edition) [Computer software]. Mason, OH: Thomson South-Western.

Begin with the author (if one is listed), the date (in parentheses), the complete title. For the title in this case, use standard capitalization. After the title, add the descriptor *Computer software* in brackets, followed by the city of publication and the publishing company name.

Sample Research Essay

Amanda Stremlow wrote this essay for her English 112 class, a second-semester composition course. As you read, notice how Stremlow uses sources to develop ideas.

The title page includes the title of the essay, the student's name, the course number, the instructor's name, and the date. This information may be arranged as shown or centered at the top half of the page. (For more information, ask your instructor.) Also, notice that a shortened form of the title and the page number appear at the top of the title page and on all subsequent pages.

Vultures 1

1/2" from top
shortened title and page number

Vultures

Amanda Stremlow

English 112

Dr. Johnathon Mauk

December 13, 2004

Title centered and double-spaced if longer than one line

Your name, in the center of the page both vertically and horizontally

Course title, instructor's name, and date (double-spaced)

Vultures 2

Vultures

"5, 4, 3, 2 . . . 1! I am going to lose weight this year." How many people recited these words last New Year's Eve? Probably more than anyone thinks! Some 91.2 million people choose to make a New Year's resolution each year (Wrightson, 1992, p. 19). New Year's celebrations almost always lead to the infamous resolution. With all the fun of New Year's Eve, it is doubtful that many of us ever wonder why we even made a resolution in the first place. Most would say that is a part of our culture, something we are taught. But ask this: Are we taught that it has to be to lose weight, eat healthy, or quit smoking at the beginning of each year?

No one ever told me that I needed to resolve to lose weight, but still for the last three years I have told myself: "I am going to lose weight this year." The first year I bought diet pills I had heard about on a commercial. Needless to say, they don't magically "melt away the pounds." So, one whole year later, there I sat making the same resolution: "I am going to lose weight this year." But after wasting a couple hundred dollars on a gym membership, I still hadn't lost any weight. Why waste my time making a resolution I was unable to keep? That's exactly what I was thinking last year on December 31st. Still at the stroke of midnight, I uttered those same words, but to avail because here I sit approaching the New Year with those same ten pounds (and probably more) to lose. Why did I feel the need to lose weight every year? The rest of the year I am happy with the way I look and I never think about it.

More than likely, most people have a story that follows these same lines. An amazing 91.2 million people make resolutions and, more importantly, there is a "top 10 resolutions" as most of us make the same resolutions every year (Wrightson, 1992, p. 19). One has to wonder why, but most consumers probably don't. Let's be honest: People don't like to question things they don't see clear answers to. However, it is possible that the sheer number and collective similarities of New Year's resolutions in our society are directly

The statistic requires an in-text citation.

Testimony—the writer's own experience illustrates the point.

The writer quotes only key words or phrases when appropriate.

Vultures 3

related to marketing strategies that prey on consumers' vulnerabilities during the holiday season. There is a reason why we don't make Fourth of July resolutions or Groundhog Day resolutions. Instead of ignore it, I suggest that we analyze the reasons and delegate responsibility where it is due.

Latent elements of our consciousness may allow us to overlook the impact marketing strategies could have on New Year's resolutions. Embedded in our minds, a distinct ideology prevents us from grasping the concept of market control. In "Group Minds," Doris Lessing (1988) reveals valuable information about people and the way we view ourselves. Lessing insists that we operate under the ideology: "I am a citizen of a free society, and that means I am an individual, making individual choices" (p. 47). This ideology allows consumers to overlook the possibility of market control. As educated individuals, Americans would like to believe that, if we make decisions about self-improvement and actually resolve to change our own lives, it is a matter of free will. The claim that marketing strategies can control our resolutions is unnerving and, therefore, questionable simply because of this ideology. However, consumers must be willing to investigate how and why companies have an ability to control our choices.

An enterprise that controls collective trends should be monitored closely because it impact people's finances—and personal desires. As American consumers, our lives revolve around our money; so paying close attention to the mechanisms that control our purchases is invaluable. The way we spend our money determines how much of it we need, which in turn affects the way we live. Clearly, our money and the issues that surround our spending should be scrutinized. (Again, remember it is our money that the diet industry, or any industry, is after. Our purchases determine their profit.)

Consumers must see the forms of control at work. If 91.2 million people chose to wear the same hat on the same day, we would immediately wonder. If 91.2 million people choose to make a resolution at the same time (and sometimes, more importantly, the

She first sets up the idea, then gives a brief summary of the source before giving the quotation.

She follows the quotation with further explanation.

A line of reasoning.

The statistic from the intro is used throughout the argument.

Vultures 4

same one), we must question the cause. Making a resolution is not an instinct; it is not a means of survival and no gene in our body codes for resolutions. With those causes out of the equation, consumers must look outside ourselves for some influence. This is where specifically designed marketing comes into play—a type of marketing that probably starts in late November and preys on consumers' vulnerabilities during the holiday season.

Counterarguing.

Some consumers may say that the holiday season is no different than any other time of the year. However, there are distinct cultural traditions that make us more vulnerable to holiday marketing. This is why we make New Year's resolutions and not Groundhog Day resolutions. First off, the holidays are a time for reflection; we spend time with our close family and friends. This type of interaction allows us to closely compare ourselves with our peers and our family. For me, I sit and compare aspects of my life to those of three female cousins my age. And close inspection always seems to turn up inadequacies no matter what the situation is.

Secondly, consumers have preconceptions surrounding the New Year; specifically, it is a chance for rebirth. It is the most drastic change our calendar makes, a whole new year, a chance to change the most undesirable aspects about ourselves. If we can be shown that we need to change, we easily *know* that this is the time to do it. We feel a looming sense of rebirth as the calendar year shifts. According to a publication from Indiana University (2004), resolutions are "a ritualized way of reviewing the past and looking toward the future." Universally, the New Year is "an opportunity to clean house." Symbolically, we can "clean house" by changing our lives *(New)*.

The quotation reinforces the point expressed at the beginning of the paragraph.

The difference between the holiday season and other seasons, and the vulnerabilities we encounter during the New Year, make resolutions an excellent opportunity for companies to increase their profit. Writing in the *Journal of Health Communication,* Michael Basil, Debra Basil, and Caroline Schooler (2001) insist that the basic principle of "consumer behavior is that marketing and advertising are most effective when they target an

Vultures 5

existing need." Consequently, by preying on the vulnerabilities of consumers (the existing need for self-improvement or change), companies spawn increased sales of the product. Basil et al. also assert that an awareness of "psychological needs is the most important device available to marketers." They proclaim that the "needs that consumers actually feel reveal the type of products that are generally easiest to sell to them and the time it is easiest to sell them." These basic tenets of marketing explain how and why companies prey on consumers' vulnerabilities during the holiday season.

Marketing strategies prey on these vulnerabilities by forcing us to see what we must change: to see the extra weight, the debt, the smoking. If they can simply make us want to change something, we will pick the night of December 31st to change. Upon making the resolutions, we will more than likely employ the products or services of the company in order to uphold them. Whether or not we keep our resolutions isn't their concern. Simply making a resolution that entails the purchase of their product is enough to promote their profits.

Let's imagine a girl, Sarah, in her late twenties. She has gained a few pounds every year, but for the most part she is a beautiful person with a lot of potential. She spends time with her family during all their get-togethers for Thanksgiving, Christmas, and the New Year. Looking around at her family, she notices a slight difference. All but her uncle look thinner than her. Feeling a little larger in last year's red dress, she throws on a cardigan over it and thinks nothing more of her inadequacies. Then, later that night an ad on the TV screams, "Finally, a diet pill that melts the pounds away" as a "newly transformed" beautiful blonde women blabs on and on about her new life. The line of reasoning behind the ad: Sarah can have a new life if she just takes the pills. Mixed with the inadequacy she felt at the Christmas party, this commercial is enough to prompt the subsequent resolution: to lose weight this year. BOOM . . . the company just made a profit.

No page number is given because the source was retrieved from a database. (The writer cannot know the actual page number for the quotation.)

A scenario illustrates the point.

Analysis of the advertising strategy reveals a hidden line of reasoning.

Vultures 6

This is how it works: By exploiting our vulnerabilities during the holiday season and forcing faulty reasoning on us, the company makes money. Preying on our intellectual immobility, these companies force an oversimplified line of reasoning on consumers. Like most commercials, they proclaim that doing this one thing will solve all of our problems. They control our consciousness, creating the desire for a product that we ignored previously.

Even with ample research to support this point, many consumers chose to ignore it. They continue to operate under the ideology Doris Lessing explains: "I am a citizen of a free country, an individual making individual choices" (1988, p. 47). Of course, we are comfortable living within this box, but unfortunately it cannot be true. If companies can justify spending billions of dollars on advertising, it must serve a purpose. In a capitalistic society, the goal is profit and that which doesn't serve that single goal is abandoned. If advertising didn't serve that goal, companies would have found a better means of controlling their profit.

Companies track their advertising budgets. If consumers could even fathom the amount of these budgets, we would understand what the companies plan to gain back from the investment. This money is only gained if the company can persuade an individual, who wouldn't have, to buy their product or service. Many companies' advertising budgets increase during and directly after the holiday season, to impact New Year's resolution making. The diet/health industry and smoking cessation companies, whose advertising budgets increase during these months, prey on consumers' engrained vulnerabilities.

The frozen food companies, like Lean Cuisine, manipulate their market by increasing their advertising budget during the holiday season. According to Betsy Spethmann (1995), Stouffer Foods was to spend an estimated 8 to 10 million dollars by March to "extend the lift diet foods get from consumers' New Year's resolutions" (p. 1). If the company spent this much money between November and March, they spent 2 to 2.5 million dollars a month on advertising during and directly after the holiday season. Preying on

She returns to key lines from her sources.

The statistics support the initial statement of the paragraph.

consumers' vulnerability, they make an increased profit off the propagation of New Year's resolutions. The continuous marketing of their "health lifestyles" culture with its subtle cues about the value of thinness and the lifestyle it *creates* controls the conscious thoughts of its audience with faulty reasoning.

Similarly, according to Ian Murphy, the Healthy Choice food product line "'typically sees a double-digits sales increase' from January promotions" (1997, p. 12). Also they doubled first-quarter advertising and promotions, spending just over 3 million dollars a month on advertising directly after the holiday season (Murphy, p. 12). Their method preys on consumers' internal thoughts about inadequacy and worth, specifically the ones that surround the holidays. Knowing that this is the most fertile time in which to implant this faulty reasoning, they increase their budgets and, in turn, succeed in creating a customer that they previously didn't have. This type of strategic marketing is not exclusive to the diet/health industry but it is probably the most obvious to the average consumer. Clearly, strategic marketing that preys on our existing vulnerability (or need) during the holiday season promotes great profit.

Even the tobacco industry recognizes and reacts to the trends of New Year's resolutions in our society by increasing their marketing during the months of January and February (Basil et al., 2000). But they aren't trying to increase profit; clearly, one can infer that their marketing seeks to counter the impact of smoking cessation during the New Year. In an article from *Advertising Age,* Mercedes Cardona (1998) outlines how SmithKline Beecham, the company in charge of NicoDerm and Nicorette, is "following the dieter's recipe" by taking "advantage of a tendency among smokers to choose the beginning of the year as the kick off for their attempts at quitting" (1998). According to a Gallup poll, half of the smokers who aim to quit begin their attempts on New Year's Day (as cited in Cardona). Smoking cessation companies increase their advertisements in an attempt to maximize their profit by exploiting this tendency.

Paragraphs 14–17 all work to support the same point about money, advertising, and the strategic marketing.

The references to sources always give information about the writer's identity or the publication. This boosts reliability.

Vultures 8

A concession paragraph.

This is not to say that companies should not cater to our needs during the season, but they shouldn't have to create them. As in the above scenario, Sarah doesn't have the best confidence in herself, but she can ignore her inadequacies until they are thrown in her face by the diet industry. This is how advertising works; this is its purpose. In our capitalistic society, competition is key and an edge on the market is the best way to increase profit.

The conclusion avoids mere summary—and offers a new way to think about our own attitudes.

Maybe consumers can't stop advertising from affecting us, but we can tip the balance by at least understanding and accepting its power to do so. We, the consumers, push this art of advertising forward by participating in the process. Looking at our clothes, our houses, our cars, our refrigerators, and our lifestyles we must accept the effects of advertising and level with them. As Doris Lessing argues, "It is one thing to admit it, in a vague uncomfortable way . . . but quite another to make that cool step into a kind of objectivity" where consumers can say, "'let's admit it, examine and organize our attitudes accordingly'" (1998, p. 50). Think about that on New Year's and choose wisely at the stroke of midnight.

Vultures 9

References

Basil, M. D., Basil, D. Z., & Schooler, C. (2000). Cigarette advertising to counter New Year's resolutions. *Journal of Health Communication, 5,* 161–174. Retrieved November 17, 2004, from EBSCOhost database.

Cardona, M. M. (1998, December 21). Nicorette, Nicoderm CQ ads tied to New Year's resolutions. *Advertising Age, 69*(51), 4. Retrieved November 17, 2004, from EBSCOhost database.

Lessing, D. (1988). Group minds. *Prisons we choose to live inside* (pp. 47–62). New York: HarperCollins.

Murphy, I. P. (1997, February 3). Marketers help consumers to keep their resolutions. *Marketing News, 31*(3), 12–13. Retrieved December 7, 2004, from EBSCOhost database.

New Year's resolutions: Why do we make them when we usually don't keep them? (2004, February 17). Retrieved December 6, 2004, from Indiana University, Media Relations Web site: http://newsinfo.iu.edu/news/page/normal/1206.html

Spethmann, B. (1995, November 6). Lean mean New Year. *Brandweek, 36*(42), 1. Retrieved November 17, 2004, from EBSCOhost database.

Wrightson, C. (1992, November/December). Vital statistics. *Health, 6*(6), 19. Retrieved December 6, 2004, from EBSCOhost database.

The sources are listed in alphabetical order—each corresponding to the appropriate format. (Pages 679–686 show APA formatting for articles, books, and so on.)

Frequently Asked Questions

WHAT IF I DON'T KNOW WHAT TYPE OF SOURCE I HAVE?

This question often comes up when researching electronic sources. Most online research methods lead to either periodicals (journals, magazines, and newspapers) or websites. (Online books are generally not in the same search paths as periodicals.) If you have an electronic source and are not sure if it is a website or a periodical, check the top of the first page for publication information. If the text has a volume, an issue, or date information, it is most likely a periodical. Also, an electronic article most often contains the title of the magazine or journal at the top of the first page.

HOW DO I TELL THE DIFFERENCE BETWEEN A JOURNAL AND A MAGAZINE?

In general, a magazine is published more often than a journal. Magazines are published every week *(Time, Newsweek)*, every other week, or even every month. Magazines are written for nonspecialized, or *general,* readership, whereas journals are written for readers with a specialized field of knowledge (such as nursing, engineering, or pharmacology). While magazines attempt to inform or entertain the public about various (sometimes even eccentric) topics, journals attempt to investigate particular ideas, theories, or situations within a discipline or field of study. Check the publication information to see how often the periodical is published, and look at the table of contents to see if the articles are written for general or specialized readers. (See page 656.)

HOW DO I FIND THE PUBLICATION INFORMATION?

Publication information for books can be found on the title page. The front of the title page has the full title, the publisher, and the city of publication, and the reverse (or copyright page) includes the copyright dates and any edition information. For periodicals, the volume and issue number usually appear at the bottom of each page and are often printed on the first page inside the cover along with the table of contents. (However, some periodicals fill the first few pages with advertisements.) Websites can be more tricky. If the author, last update, or sponsoring institution does not appear on the opening (or home) page, scroll down to the bottom of the page (or look on the menu for *Information* or *About Us*).

HOW DO I KNOW THE PAGE NUMBERS OF AN ELECTRONIC SOURCE?

Generally, electronic sources do not have page numbers—and documentation styles do not require page numbers for websites or online journal articles. Sometimes, however, a print source will republish its contents electronically and retain page numbers. (In other words, the source appears online exactly as it does in print.) In that case, simply use the page numbers as they appear.

SHOULD I USE APA OR MLA OR WHAT?

MLA (or Modern Language Association) style is used by writers in the humanities and literature (such as English and communications). APA (or American Psychological Association) style is used by writers in the medical field, education, and, of course, psychology. CMS (or Chicago Manual of Style) is used by writers in humanities fields, such as religion, history, and philosophy. The sciences (such as physics and chemistry) have particular styles as well. When writing for an academic audience, you should always ask what style to use. Some instructors want their students to use a particular style, regardless of their major or field of study.

WHY ARE THERE DIFFERENT DOCUMENTATION STYLES?

The different styles have emerged over the course of years. They have developed because different research techniques sometimes call for a particular type of documentation. As academic fields grow, they develop and reward particular research strategies—and one documentation style cannot always account for those strategies.

Standard Abbreviations

MLA	APA	
ed.	Ed.	= Editor or Edited by
eds.	Eds.	= Editors
ed.	ed.	= Edition, usually associated with a number (4th ed.)
Rev. ed.	Rev. ed.	= Revised edition
n.d.	n.d.	= No date
n.p.	n.p.	= No publisher or no place
n. pag.	n. pag.	= No page numbers
trans.	Trans.	= Translator
p.	p.	= Page number
pp.	pp.	= Page numbers
no.	No.	= Number
pars.	para.	= Paragraphs
vol.	Vol.	= Volume

EVERYDAY RHETORIC

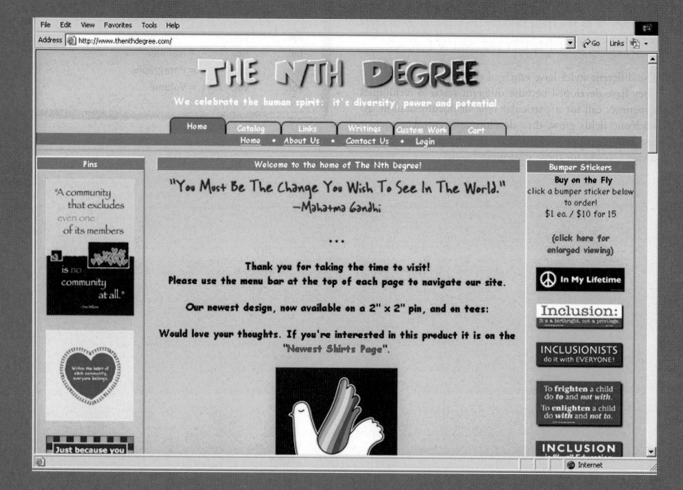

CHAPTER 14

Portraits, such as this one of President Ronald Reagan, are not objective photographs or paintings. They create and communicate an idea about the person. What ideas does this photograph of Reagan communicate? What specific elements (framing, lighting, composition, and so on) are most important?

"If I had a voice, hey, this is what I'd sing."

—Randall Bramblett

Rhetoric is everywhere—not only in essays. Anytime someone uses any form of language to influence others, rhetoric is at work. Think about the following pages as a small sampling of the everyday rhetoric that surrounds, bombards, and overwhelms us daily. While we fail to see much of it, or learn to tune it out, intensive and sophisticated rhetoric operates in every corner of everyday life. And once we start to notice it, once we focus in, we can ask important questions: How does this text influence people? Why did someone choose this particular image and not another? What's the motive driving such language? What's the hidden meaning or subtext of the language? What types of appeals are working in such language?

This professional letter is based on the invention strategies Therese Cherry used to write her essay in Chapter 6.

205 West 5th Street
Kenmore, OH 46904
(213) 555-9086
April 22, 2005

Ruth Weisheit, Public Affairs Specialist
Brunswick Resident Post
Food and Drug Administration
3820 Center Road
Brunswick, OH 44212

Dear Ms. Weisheit:

As a concerned citizen and patient, I have become very alarmed at the growing addiction to prescription drugs in the United States. Though the medical advancements of our time are to be applauded, it seems that stricter regulations on the marketing and prescribing of these drugs may be in order to help ensure public health.

According to the United Nations International Narcotics Control Board, advanced countries are overdosing on quick fix pills to ease non-medical problems like fat and stress. The INCB also reported that mood-altering drugs are often prescribed for social problems, such as unemployment or relationship problems. Not only are many of these drugs being pre-scribed unnecessarily, they are increasingly dangerous. According to Steven Pomper's May 2000 article "Drug Rush" in the *Washington Monthly Online,* toxic reactions to marketed drugs are estimated to cost more than 30 billion dollars per year and to be among the ten leading causes of death in the U.S. Six new drugs approved since mid 1996 have been pulled off the market, and 150 deaths were linked to these drugs before they were pulled.

Although part of the problem involves unnecessary prescriptions being written, the aggres-sive marketing of these drugs appears to play a key role in this addiction issue. "Drug Rush" also reported that in 1997, the FDA loosened restrictions on the marketing of pharmaceuti-cal companies, due in large part to heavy pressure from the pharmaceutical industry. This

2

made it possible for drug companies to advertise on T.V. without spending huge chunks of time describing risks and side effects. And the 2000 *Journal of the AMA* has researched and shown findings that doctors are influenced to prescribe drugs that are marketed more heavily. Recent studies in *Health Magazine* stated that three-quarters of the respondents who saw one of these ads on T.V. and asked their doctors to prescribe it were successful.

Apparently, many factors have contributed to this growing epidemic, but none so fully or irresponsibly as the marketing companies that are pushing these drugs. The INCB stated in its 2000 report that there was a "continuing existence of aggressive sales methods and even some cases of financial support to various advocacy groups to foster sales" and appealed to the pharmaceutical industry to demonstrate social responsibility and voluntary cooperation. Even people in the industry will concede off the record that groups acting as advertising agents for manufacturers should be subject to FDA regulations. Since this voluntary cooperation does not seem likely, I would like to know what actions the FDA, as well as other organizations, are taking to curb the aggressive sales tactics of these pharmaceutical drugs.

The growing use of new and heavily marketed drugs for the ease of social conditions is not going to just go away. I am concerned about this issue and would like to learn how I can get involved with organizations that understand the importance of placing stronger restrictions on advertisers. Thank you for taking the time to address my concerns and I would appreciate any information you can send me.

Sincerely,

Therese Cherry

Therese Cherry

1. How does Cherry support her main idea?
2. Describe Cherry's writer's voice, using several sentences from her letter to support your description.
3. Give some examples of good sentence vitality in Cherry's letter.

Scott Stewart (VP, Managing Director of Sales) wrote this e-mail to sales associates at Thomson Learning. His purpose was to promote a particular mindset for the sales team during a critical time of year.

From: Stewart, Scott
Sent: Tuesday, August 16, 2005 12:52 AM
To: _TL HE Social Sciences Reps Only; _TL HE Humanities Reps Only;
    _TL HE Hardside Reps Only
Cc: Zlotnick, Stephen
Subject: Mrs. Sparkman

Hello All,

We all have people in our past that—even though we only spent a brief period of time with them—made a truly huge difference in our lives. There are a quite a few of them in my life, but very few are more important than my sixth-grade history teacher, Mrs. Sparkman. Up until 6th grade, the only thing that mattered to me was playing sports: my life's priorities consisted of coming home from school so I could go play football and baseball.

Then I walked into Mrs. Sparkman's class and she opened my eyes to ancient history and cultures that I knew nothing about. Once she started lecturing us, I could not get enough of what she had to say. She spent a great deal of that year on Greek history and I was totally fascinated with the cultures of places like Athens and Corinth. And even though I consider myself a pacifist, the whole concept of Sparta simply got to me. (That does not mean I am not the most uber-competitive person you will ever meet—and while I respected the Athenians for their ideals, I respected the Spartans for their work ethic.) Although they were a small "city state" by comparison, to the Spartans, they were all about honor, code, courage, and being warriors. They lived by one simple credo: to "come back from battle either carrying your shield or being carried upon it." Quite simply, it was all about giving your very best effort each and every day—in both life and work, even in the face of long odds.

By now I am sure that many of you are thinking, "Where in the world is he going this time?"

Everywhere I go, it is really "hot" right now and there are so many moving parts. And everyone that I talk to is working hard to get their orders shipped, complete the CRMS project, give FCIS presentations, bundle clickers, complete the T-3 program, and finish the various and sundry issues that all of you are dealing with. Consequently, we get up every morning having to coach ourselves up just to start the day in the face of a huge "to do" list. However, to finally get to the point, the more hard work we do now and in the next 3 weeks prior to the more traditional start of the fall selling period, the better off each and every one of us will be.

Remaining diligent and patient in working with Customer Service, Custom, "the clicker folks," and all other principal players to get all of your orders shipped will make a real difference. Entering reliable and detailed information into CRMS so we can work as a team to close big adoptions going forward will make a real difference. Completing all of your FCIS presentations to increase sell-through will make a real difference as will completing the T-3 program. Most important, being in those bookstores pushing for reorders as a collective team (B&E, Science & Math, Social Sciences, and Humanities) can and will make a huge difference when we get to the end of the year. That extra effort (heavy lifting) we do right now can determine if you make your sales goal in 2005, and/or how just how big your bonus check is going to be.

Also, while I am asking each of you to push yourselves in the next few weeks, that does not mean the work will lessen once we get to early September as we turn our energies toward closing Q4 business. However, the days will then be cool and crisp, and the beautiful long shadows of late fall afternoons will be upon us as we make our way across campus.

Finally, as you reach the end of each workday and you have given your very best; do make sure that you separate from work. Work and life are a delicate balance and if you give one the upper hand, then the other one will suffer from lack of attention. Therefore, be sure you laugh early and often; do not take it all so seriously. Life and work are both journeys, and it is the sights we see and the experiences we live while traveling these paths that provide us with substance, meaning, and a feeling of accomplishment in our lives. So yes, even though you do work very hard every day, there will still be some days where you did not feel like you made a positive difference. When that does happen, put your work anxiety aside and live a little life for the moment. The very next day, get up in the morning, have faith in yourself, and simply plan on making a positive difference at work. If your aim is true, chances are that will happen more often than not.

Back in the 6th grade, Mrs. Sparkman made a real difference in my life.

The rest was up to me.

Scott

What rhetorical strategies support Stewart's purpose?

This letter to the editor is based on the invention strategies Daniel Bruno used to write his essay in Chapter 7.

—In Your Opinion—

Entitlement Education

The American education system is failing. But why? Today's student has what Peter Sacks, in his book *Generation X Goes to College,* calls a "sense of entitlement." Today's students, or many of today's students, think showing up entitles them to not just a passing grade, but to a B or better. And many parents support their children in this belief.

What these students and their parents need to know is that many other students do not expect A's and B's for just showing up, for putting forth a minimal effort, or for paying tuition. Instead they work hard and develop good attitudes and skills that prepare them for a competitive future. The students who feel entitled are the ones getting cheated because the gap between the more motivated and the less motivated students grows wider.

By the time they both graduate from college, the less motivated students are at a greater disadvantage than when they began college.

There is plenty of blame to go around. And, unfortunately, implementing the solution on a large scale seems impossible. Entire systems, educational and otherwise, are difficult to change. But a solution is possible: For their own benefit, the individual student and the individual parent must take action before it is too late. They must understand the reality of the situation. Yes, students can get good grades quite easily, but so what? Feeling entitled and sliding by can leave them severely disadvantaged. The entitlement mentality must be discouraged early in a child's life, or else by the time a student reaches college, it might be too late.

Daniel Bruno
Perrysburg

Read two different letters to the editor, preferably from different publications. Consider the following for each letter:

1. How might someone think or act differently after reading the letter?
2. To what degree does each letter go beyond the common beliefs of the reader?
3. What support strategies are most effective?
4. How is the writer's voice inviting or alienating?
5. What makes the reader want to read on?

Research how a particular symbol, such as a yellow ribbon, came to represent an idea.

Manhole Cover

Check out several websites dedicated to manhole covers, and ask yourself: What do manhole covers say? Do they use rhetoric? What strategies do manhole covers use to communicate?

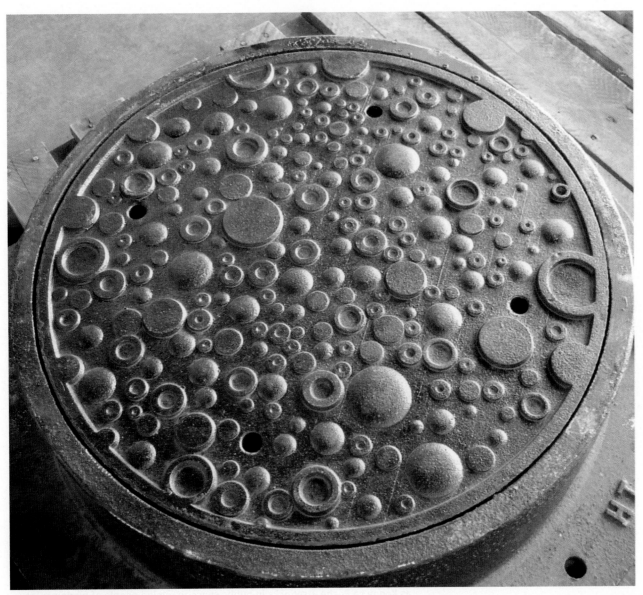

Jen Weih's winning design

1. The city of Vancouver, British Columbia, had a contest to design a manhole cover. Why would a city government sponsor such a contest?
2. How might such a contest be judged? What criteria might be used to select the winning design? For example, is it attractive; does it communicate clearly; does it express something positive about the community; how might citizens react; and so on.

Public Art

Public art expresses the sprit and values of a community. Many individual public works of art (which include manhole covers, street lights, and boulevards, not just statues, fountains, and murals) combine to celebrate the community—to remember, honor, acknowledge, and imagine what the community was, is, and can be. Someone designed each work, and the individual pieces interact to create a bigger picture. Public art is often functional, ornamental, AND interesting.

1. What is the relationship between art and community?
2. What works of art in your community express that relationship?
3. What work of art could your community use?

This work appears in a park in northern Michigan. The artists, a collective known as Kenny La Roche, use rocks in public space to remind people of fundamental principles in the world around them.

This statue stands in Boston Common, one of the oldest public parks in the country. The dome of the State House, designed by Charles Bullfinch, can be seen in the background.

Explore the possibilities for meaning in these photos.

This memo is based on the invention strategies that Therese Cherry used to write her essay in Chapter 6.

MEMORANDUM
National Council of Medical Practitioners

TO: Michael Toth, V.P. of Health Care Administration,
                        Midwest Region
FROM: Therese Cherry, Assistant to the Secretary of Public Health
SUBJECT: Aggressive Marketing of Pharmaceutical Drugs
DATE: April 23, 2002

The United Nations International Narcotics Control Board (INBC) recently stated that advanced countries are overdosing on quick fix pills to ease "non-medical" problems like fat and stress. It also reported that mood-altering drugs are often prescribed for social problems, such as unemployment or relationship problems.

These facts are not unknown to the NCMP, and due to the growing concern in the field of health care professionals, it is time to address this issue and determine any possible solutions.

Risks of Overprescribed Drugs

Not only are a rising number of patients taking prescription drugs to cure the normal stress that goes along with everyday life, the danger to public health is climbing too.

1. Toxic reactions to marketed drugs are estimated to cost more than 30 billion dollars per year and to be among the ten leading causes of death in the U.S.
2. Six new drugs approved since mid 1996 have been pulled off the market, and 150 deaths were linked to these drugs before they were pulled.

Aggressive Marketing Partly to Blame

Pharmaceutical drugs are being advertised more widely and more frequently than ever before. The 2000 *Journal of the AMA* has shown findings that doctors are influenced to prescribe drugs that are marketed more heavily. And with all new drugs, there are some side effects and under-studied long-term results that are unknown.

1. In 1997, the FDA caved to heavy pressure from the industry and loosened restrictions, making it possible for drug companies to advertise on TV without spending huge chunks of time describing risks and side effects.
2. As a result, recent studies in *Health Magazine* reported that three-quarters of the respondents who saw one of these incomplete ads on television and asked their doctors to prescribe it were successful.

Obviously, patients should have every possible benefit and opportunity to improve their health, but it is unethical and a disservice to say that an informed decision can be based solely on these ads. The fact is, some of the side effects of the newer drugs are unknown even to physicians.

A Call for Responsibility

The most obvious way to cope with this growing epidemic would be to leave health care between the physicians and their patients, and to advertise these pharmaceutical drugs with full disclosure. Unfortunately, marketing companies are in the business of selling products to make the money, not to cure the disease.

1. The INBC stated in its 2000 report that there was a "continuing existence of aggressive sales methods and even some cases of financial support to various advocacy groups to foster sales" and appealed to the pharmaceutical industry to demonstrate social responsibility and voluntary cooperation.
2. "Even people in the industry will concede off the record that groups acting as advertising agents for manufacturers should be subject to FDA regulations."

Although the FDA has allowed restrictions to be lifted, physicians still bear the responsibility of the care of their patients and the prescription of medication. When prescribing these drugs, responsible physicians fully disclose all possible risks to the patient, including what is unknown. Along with more responsible dispensing of these drugs, the NCMP supports a lobby to the FDA to apply stronger restrictions on the marketing of pharmaceutical drugs.

As health care professionals, we must regard this crisis with utmost importance, and the Secretary of Health encourages and welcomes any insights or suggestions from you and your staff. Thank you for your time and concern for this important issue. Any questions or comments can be e-mailed to tcNCMP@publichealth.com, or you can call me directly at (216) 555-4351 ext. 366.

Compare this memo to Cherry's essay in Chapter 6, and describe differences in her use of rhetorical tools, organizational strategies, and writer's voice.

This memo is based on the invention and delivery strategies that Daniel Bruno used to write his essay for Chapter 7.

To: All Faculty
From: Daniel Bruno, Vice-President for Academic Affairs
Re: Faculty Discussion on Entitlement Education
Date: August 20, 2005

Welcome back, Faculty. As we begin another academic year, I would like to encourage discussion regarding our responsibility to incoming and continuing students, particularly regarding what Peter Sacks describes in his book *Generation X Goes to College* as the students' "sense of entitlement."

Our first of several planned discussions will be Tuesday, September 10th at 10:30 a.m. in College Hall, Room 12.

We will begin our discussion by considering this question: Can students in today's American education system graduate from high school and some colleges with minimal effort and minimal learning? We will openly discuss this question, whether this happens at State College, and what might be the consequences for students and the community overall.

A particular concern of mine is that such students would ultimately find themselves severely disadvantaged because so many other students do not possess an entitlement mentality. These students grow and develop a great deal during their time at college. If this is true, the gap between the more-motivated and the less-motivated students grows even wider, leaving some college-educated students at a greater disadvantage than when they entered college.

What is our responsibility as faculty and what action can we take to best serve our students? I hope you can join me to discuss these important issues. If you have any questions or comments before September 10th, you can reach me at 555-5151 or at dbruno@ statecollege.edu.

What rhetorical tools does Bruno use most effectively?

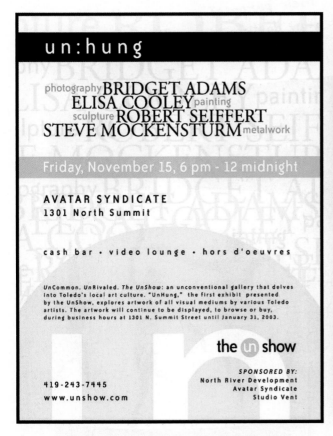

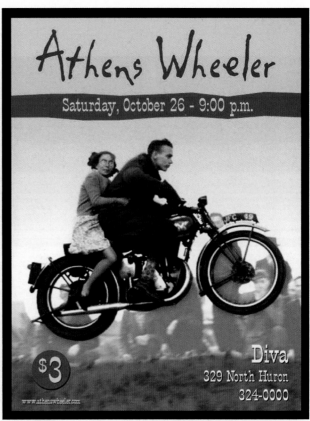

As you consider how visuals such as the posters above communicate, ask the following questions:

- What argument does the image make?
- How is the argument supported?
- What values and beliefs does it appeal to?
- How does it make the appeal?

Labels

The rhetoric of labels: What is their purpose? How do they communicate?

Other Everyday Ways of Communicating

LETTERS

Perhaps the most significant difference between writing an essay and writing a letter is the relationship between the reader and the writer. The more general audience of an essay is usually replaced in letter writing by a more specific reader who has different expectations.

Idea for Writing

Write a letter or use one you have written in the past. Consider, but don't limit yourself to, the following situations:

- to thank someone who has helped you
- to suggest a better way of doing something
- to solve a problem
- to assure someone that you are doing well

Then consider the following:

- What is the letter's thesis?
- What strategies are used to support the thesis?
- Does the letter include any counterarguments? Concessions? Qualifiers?
- Does the letter include any logical fallacies?
- How is the letter organized?
- How would you describe the writer's voice? Support your description with several specific examples.
- Provide several examples of good sentence vitality.

MEMOS

Memos—short for "memorandums"—are a common type of workplace communication. While letters are most often used to communicate with people outside of one's organization, memos are used among workers within an organization.

- Memos vary in their degree of formality. Factors such as the seriousness of the subject matter and the relationship between the reader and the writer will determine the degree of formality.

- Memos are written to quickly convey essential workplace information. A memo may use headings, bulleted lists, and other techniques that allow the reader to locate and take in the most relevant information.

Memo Format The memo format serves a purpose: to help communicate important workplace information quickly. In addition to setting up the memo with *To, From, Subject,* and *Date* headings, the text of the memo should be easy to read and understand.

WEBSITES

Find a website you think is effective. How are rhetorical tools, organizational strategies, writer's voice, and visual design used to achieve the site's purpose?

Find a website you think is ineffective, and answer the same question.

E-MAIL

Rewrite an old e-mail you have sent. What improvements did you make in terms of rhetorical tools, organizational strategies, and writer's voice?

Why should you carefully edit each e-mail you send?

SPEECHES

Write and deliver a short speech. Consider, but don't limit yourself to the following occasions: paying tribute to someone; informing others of an important issue; calling others to take action; announcing a change.

POSTERS

Choose one of the posters in this chapter and explain how it argues.

Websites often rely on intensive rhetoric—strong appeals to value, emotion, character, and need. This home page for Sojo.net relies on graphics and text in its appeals to humanistic values. Notice how the calls to action rely on values such as fairness, peace, equality, kindness, goodwill.

1. How do the advertisements in the left column relate to the rhetoric in the main column?
2. What particular values operate in the articles?
3. What values can you detect in the headlines (article titles)?
4. How do the images strengthen or reinforce the appeals in the articles or article titles?

The Weekly Standard relies on a group of well-known political commentators who forward their opinions on a variety of social and governmental issues. However, the site is far more than a stage for opinion; it gives voice to a collective political vision.

1. How does the Weekly Standard's website differ from Sojourner's? How are the appeals to value and emotion different? What other appeals operate in the Weekly Standard?
2. How does the Weekly Standard's website use personal desire to forward political ideas?
3. How do the caricatures (the cartoonish drawings of the contributors) influence the voice of the site? (If possible, visit the site and read one or more of the articles.)
4. How does the voice of the opening page relate to the nature of the articles?

The Gettysburg Address

Abraham Lincoln

More than 51,000 soldiers were wounded, missing, or dead after the Battle of Gettysburg. Seventeen acres of land were acquired in Gettysburg and dedicated as a national cemetery on November 19, 1863. As part of the ceremony, President Abraham Lincoln delivered the Gettysburg Address. His remarks speak to the larger significance of the war and its relationship to the nation. He focuses the listener not just on what happened, but on what should happen next.

Fourscore and seven years ago our fathers brought forth on this continent a new nation, conceived in liberty and dedicated to the proposition that all men are created equal.

Now we are engaged in a great civil war, testing whether that nation or any nation so conceived and so dedicated can long endure. We are met on a great battlefield of that war. We have come to dedicate a portion of it as a final resting place for those who died here that the nation might live. This we may, in all propriety do. But in a larger sense, we cannot dedicate, we cannot consecrate, we cannot hallow this ground. The brave men, living and dead who struggled here have hallowed it far above our poor power to add or detract. The world will little note nor long remember what we say here, but it can never forget what they did here.

It is rather for us the living, we here be dedicated to the great task remaining before us—that from these honored dead we take increased devotion to that cause for which they here gave the last full measure of devotion—that we here highly resolve that these dead shall not have died in vain, that this nation shall have a new birth of freedom, and that government of the people, by the people, for the people shall not perish from the earth.

1. Lincoln's famous speech moves people toward particular ideas about life, country, war, sacrifice, and death. In your own words, what are those ideas?
2. What appeals does Lincoln rely on?
3. How would you describe Lincoln's voice?

Surrender Speech

Chief Joseph

In 1877, instead of moving to a reservation in Idaho as ordered, Chief Joseph and a band of Nez Perce retreated 1,400 miles across Idaho and Montana, pursued by General Oliver Otis Howard and the U.S. Army. Along the way they fought several battles. The Nez Perce were finally stopped forty miles from Canada, and on October 5, 1877, at Bears Paw, Chief Joseph, known by his people as Hin-mah-too Yah-lat-kekt (Thunder Rolling in the Mountains), made this surrender speech.

Tell General Howard that I know his heart. What he told me before I have in my heart. I am tired of fighting. Our chiefs are killed. Looking Glass is dead, Tu-hul-hil-sote is dead. The old men are all dead. It is the young men who now say yes or no. He who led the young men [Joseph's brother Alikut] is dead. It is cold and we have no blankets. The little children are freezing to death. My people—some of them have run away to the hills and have no blankets and no food. No one knows where they are—perhaps freezing to death. I want to have time to look for my children and see how many of them I can find. Maybe I shall find them among the dead. Hear me, my chiefs, my heart is sick and sad. From where the sun now stands I will fight no more against the white man.

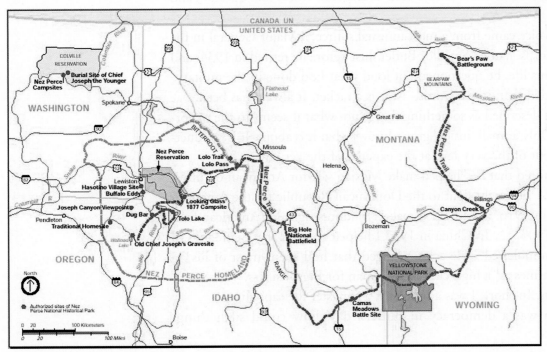

Map of the Nez Perce Trail

Research Chief Joseph and the Nez Perce trail. How does the context provided by additional background information, or knowledge, help develop your understanding of the speech?

Do We Live in a Democracy?

Mike Ferner

Mike Ferner delivered "Do We Live in a Democracy?" at the Democracy Rising rally held in Toledo, Ohio, on December 15, 2001.

With your permission tonight I would like to provoke us with this question: Do we live in a democracy? Do "we the people," listed right up front in our Constitution's preamble, really form the basis of government power and policy?

"Well, of course," you might say. After all, we are taught that from our earliest days in school. Millions of advertising images equate freedom with everything from 7-11 stores to Calvin Klein jeans. And of course President Bush repeats daily that we are fighting the terrorist foes of democracy and freedom.

Even though the media and every aspect of our dominant culture daily reinforce the notion that America is a democracy—that we always fight on the side of the angels—there have always been courageous voices that question and challenge.

One such voice came from a most unusual source, a Major General in the U.S. Marine Corps, named Smedley Butler. Just before he retired in 1934, and for the rest of his life, he questioned out loud what he'd done in the military.

He concluded that, in his words, "War is a racket. It always has been. . . . A racket is best described as something that is not what it seems to the majority of people. Only a small 'inside' group knows what it is about. It is conducted for the benefit of the very few, at the expense of the very many."

Butler admitted that he "helped make Mexico safe for American oil interests in 1914. . . . I brought light to the Dominican Republic for the American sugar interests in 1916. . . . I helped make Honduras right for American fruit companies in 1903. . . . In China in 1927 I helped see to it that Standard Oil went its way unmolested." He acknowledged that he'd spent most of his 33 years in the Marines as "a high-class muscle man for Big Business, Wall Street, and the bankers. In short, I was a racketeer, a gangster for capitalism."

If America was a democracy in Butler's day, how could such things happen?

If we live in a democracy today, how could our government get away with bombing one of the poorest nations on earth, killing thousands of civilians who had absolutely nothing to do with the criminal, inexcusable attacks of September 11?

If we live in a democracy, how is it that UNOCAL Corp. executives are counting the days until, as General Butler might say, Afghanistan is made safe for American oil interests?

If we live in a democracy, where "we the people" are sovereign citizens from whom all political power flows, by what authority does Daimler-Chrysler Corporation extort $89 million dollars in tax abatements, and then our elected school board submits a funding request to the company's foundation for a technical training school?

If we live in a democracy, by what authority do our elected officials impoverish our sacred democratic institutions, like our public schools, and force them to beg for corporate charity?

If we live in a democracy, why do our school officials implore the Coca-Cola Co. to please cut back on how many hours a day its machines beckon to students, creating lifelong "brand loyalty," and rotting their health?

Do we in fact live in a democracy, or is it more accurately a plutocracy, defined by *Webster's* as "a government in which the wealthy class rules"? Or as Smedley Butler put it, a "racket . . . conducted for the benefit of the very few, at the expense of the very many"?

Brothers and sisters, we don't have unlimited time to use our humanity and our hearts to build a democratic society, and with its power create a world where we are at peace with ourselves, other species, and the planet. Tonight we are privileged to be here with hundreds of our fellow citizens who care deeply. In a few minutes we will hear from Ralph Nader, one of America's most stalwart believers in the power of people. This is a golden opportunity. Let us make the most of it.

1. What about Ferner's text suggests that it was a speech?
2. What is his main idea, and how does he support it?
3. What values does the speech appeal to?
4. Describe Ferner's voice.

The Flag Code

Title 4, United States Code, Chapter 1

§ 8. Respect for flag

No disrespect should be shown to the flag of the United States of America; the flag should not be dipped to any person or thing. Regimental colors, State flags, and organization or institutional flags are to be dipped as a mark of honor.

(a) The flag should never be displayed with the union down, except as a signal of dire distress in instances of extreme danger to life or property.

(b) The flag should never touch anything beneath it, such as the ground, the floor, water, or merchandise.

(c) The flag should never be carried flat or horizontally, but always aloft and free.

(d) The flag should never be used as wearing apparel, bedding, or drapery. It should never be festooned, drawn back, nor up, in folds, but always allowed to fall free. Bunting of blue, white, and red, always arranged with the blue above, the white in the middle, and the red below, should be used for covering a speaker's desk, draping the front of the platform, and for decoration in general.

(e) The flag should never be fastened, displayed, used, or stored in such a manner as to permit it to be easily torn, soiled, or damaged in any way.

(f) The flag should never be used as a covering for a ceiling.

(g) The flag should never have placed upon it, nor on any part of it, nor attached to it any mark, insignia, letter, word, figure, design, picture, or drawing of any nature.

(h) The flag should never be used as a receptacle for receiving, holding, carrying, or delivering anything.

(i) The flag should never be used for advertising purposes in any manner whatsoever. It should not be embroidered on such articles as cushions or handkerchiefs and the like, printed or otherwise impressed on paper napkins or boxes or anything that is designed for temporary use and discard. Advertising signs should not be fastened to a staff or halyard from which the flag is flown.

(j) No part of the flag should ever be used as a costume or athletic uniform. However, a flag patch may be affixed to the uniform of military personnel, firemen, policemen, and members of patriotic organizations. The flag represents a living country and is itself considered a living thing. Therefore, the lapel flag pin being a replica, should be worn on the left lapel near the heart.

(k) The flag, when it is in such condition that it is no longer a fitting emblem for display, should be destroyed in a dignified way, preferably by burning.

1. Is a flag rhetorical? How?
2. Why such reverence and awe over a piece of cloth?
3. How do Americans typically violate Title 4?

Briefings

Briefings are short, often informal speeches that concisely convey only the most relevant information. The speaker may draw conclusions and make recommendations, or just report information. Because a briefing focuses on main ideas, questions that probe into specifics are likely to follow. Briefings may be carefully planned and somewhat formal, or they can be impromptu. Heads of government and business routinely receive briefings, as do lower-level employees. One never knows when a coworker or teacher might ask for a briefing on a particular situation.

To help you explore the role briefings play, consider the following:

1. Recall an everyday briefing you delivered. What did you brief someone on? Was the briefing requested, or did you initiate it? How long was the briefing? What was its result? Was there a question-and-answer period afterward?

2. Prepare a briefing for a situation in your everyday life. For example, you might have to update a professor on a class project, inform your boss about your schedule, or explain to a customer how a product works.

3. Prepare three briefings of an essay you wrote: thirty seconds, one minute, and two minutes long.

This briefing, given by White House Press Secretary Ari Fleischer to reporters aboard Air Force One, is from September 11, 2001. It is followed by questions from the press, along with Mr. Fleischer's responses.

5:30 P.M. EDT

MR. FLEISCHER: The President will address the nation tonight, upon his return to the White House. He met this afternoon for one hour and five minutes with his national security team via live tele-conference from Offutt Air Force Base in Nebraska.

Among the things the President said were, "We will find these people and they will suffer the consequence of taking on this nation. We will do what it takes," and, he continued, "No one is going to diminish the spirit of this country."

The President has also heard today from countless world leaders either who are calling to—back to Washington or have sent him directly communiqués. He's heard from Britain, France, Germany, Russia—a host of nations, all of whom have expressed their outrage at this attack, and who have assured the American people that the international community stands with America.

That's what I've got.

Q: The message tonight, do you know how soon after he gets back to the White House he'll be able to do that?

MR. FLEISCHER: Can't indicate yet.

Q: And when he does, the message is to the American people, as he said earlier, and to foreign countries?

MR. FLEISCHER: It will be a message of resolve and reassurance. It will be a reassuring message that our nation has been tested before, our nation has always prevailed.

Q: Does the President have any information about the source of the violence and the mastermind behind it?

MR. FLEISCHER: I'm not going to discuss any of the intelligence information that's been provided to the President.

Q: Can you give us some idea of why the stops that we made today were made? I understand the nature of the tragedy that we're dealing with, but why these particular locations?

MR. FLEISCHER: For security purposes that involve the President.

(To read the additional questions and answers that followed, go to the White House website.)

1. What is the purpose of the briefing?
2. What values does the briefing appeal to?

How would Jesus drive?

This bumper sticker provides a rich study in rhetoric. On the surface, it speaks to drivers and suggests that drivers in general and the reader in particular might consider driving differently. It alludes to the teachings of Jesus and as Jesus taught stops short of judging others instead asking them to consider their own actions. (Imagine a bumper sticker that said, *"Hey! You oughta drive like Jesus, you stupid jerk!"*) And it prompts readers to apply a philosophy (a belief system or a religious principle) to the way they treat other drivers (other people)—and themselves. (Are they relaxed, angry, at peace, stressed out?) So at a deeper level, the sticker connects the present act of driving and an overriding philosophy or approach to life.

Of course, to some people the bumper sticker may simply be amusing. To others, it may be offensive or make no sense at all. And to some, it may serve as an important reminder, helping them to better live what they believe. Someone reading the bumper sticker might feel that it convicts him or her of bad or inconsiderate driving. Or the reader might think it is a critique of other drivers. Or both.

While on one level the bumper sticker is talking about operating a motor vehicle, referencing Jesus, especially for certain readers, elevates the question—particularly the meaning of the word "drive." Those who are used to reading religious texts on different levels are bound to extend their thinking outward, to other aspects of their lives. (How would Jesus drive on the highway? How would Jesus drive through life?)

The decision to place a bumper sticker on a car and to drive around with it, parking in parking lots, speeding down the highway, or pulling into your own driveway, involves considering all the rhetorical issues above—and more.

How would Buddha drive?

How would Lao Tzu drive?

How would Moses drive?

How would Muhammad drive?

_____?

Discussion

Discussion is common in all walks of life. It involves two things: responding and listening. In good discussion, when we *listen* and *respond,* we do it in a way that *adds* to the discussion. You might, for example, contribute a strong point; ask a question that helps the group to probe the issue further; provide an example to illustrate what someone else has said; or keep quiet, listening to others who have a lot to say about the topic, then contribute an important point at just the right moment. The best discussers don't necessarily say or write the most.

The first four discussions that follow lack focus and intensity. In the final discussion, the participants explore complexity. They make specific rhetorical decisions that help keep focus; they create and use a line of reasoning.

Discussion (n)
1. Consideration of a subject by a group; an earnest conversation
2. A formal discourse on a topic; an exposition

—*The American Heritage College Dictionary*

DISCUSSION 1

LINDA: What is the significance of a tattoo?

MARCUS: The significance is just whatever people think it is.

DISCUSSION 2

LINDA: What is the significance of a tattoo?

DIANA: Well, it depends on the actual tattoo, doesn't it? A flower has different significance than a skull.

LINDA: Maybe. But why do people get any tattoo?

DIANA: They just want to. Everybody has their own reasons.

DISCUSSION 3

LINDA: What is the significance of a tattoo?

JACK: What do you mean?

LINDA: What do tattoos mean, what's the meaning behind inscribing ink permanently onto the skin?

JACK: My cousin has this huge tattoo on his back.

DISCUSSION 4

LINDA: What is the significance of a tattoo?

MARCUS: What does that mean, "significance"?

LINDA: You know, what's the fundamental meaning of a tattoo? What's the *meaning* behind inscribing ink permanently onto the skin?

DIANA: I think it's gross, myself. I mean, don't get me wrong, people can do whatever they want with their own bodies, but it's really disgusting to me.

DISCUSSION 5

LINDA: What is the significance of a tattoo?

MARCUS: What does that mean, "significance"?

LINDA: You know, what's the fundamental meaning of a tattoo? What's the *meaning* behind inscribing ink permanently onto the skin?

DIANA: Well, when people get a tattoo, they're doing something permanent to themselves—or at least they assume they are.

MARCUS: They're making a statement of some kind.

DIANA: A statement that has permanence.

JACK: Yeah, that's gotta mean something. People must want to have something about themselves, on themselves, that is not going to go away. It must feel . . . sorta . . . important, ritualistic, big, you know . . .

LINDA: So people long for permanence. That's interesting. And a tattoo is a little (maybe tiny) way of establishing that . . . on their own bodies.

MARCUS: It's also something that is totally personal. I mean, you can have a tattoo of anything and it's all your own.

DIANA: Yeah, that's why people get tattoos of their loved ones' names.

JACK: My brother has a tattoo of his old girlfriend's name.

DIANA: Yeah, my dad has a tattoo of some kind that doesn't really mean anything and he won't even tell us what it's from. He got it when he was a teenager.

LINDA: OK. But what do those examples show? Tattoos are still there, but their lives go on.

MARCUS: Well, life is change. You can't escape change.

LINDA: And tattoos are a way of resisting change? A way of marking the present on one's body—storing it, keeping it with you.

MARCUS: Right! That's the significance.

You know you are truly discussing if you are trying to understand or find truth in what other people are saying. If you learn something, think differently, change your mind, or seriously consider a different point of view, the discussion can be considered fruitful.

1. What rhetorical decisions derail the first four discussions?
2. What rhetorical decisions propel the discussion in #5?

Letter from Birmingham Jail

Martin Luther King, Jr.

AUTHOR'S NOTE: This response to a published statement by eight fellow clergymen from Alabama (Bishop C. C. J. Carpenter, Bishop Joseph A. Durick, Rabbi Hilton L. Grafman, Bishop Paul Hardin, Bishop Holan B. Harmon, the Reverend George M. Murray, the Reverend Edward V. Ramage and the Reverend Earl Stallings) was composed under somewhat constricting circumstance. Begun on the margins of the newspaper in which the statement appeared while I was in jail, the letter was continued on scraps of writing paper supplied by a friendly Negro trusty, and concluded on a pad my attorneys were eventually permitted to leave me. Although the text remains in substance unaltered, I have indulged in the author's prerogative of polishing it for publication.

April 16, 1963

MY DEAR FELLOW CLERGYMEN:

While confined here in the Birmingham city jail, I came across your recent statement calling my present activities "unwise and untimely." Seldom do I pause to answer criticism of my work and ideas. If I sought to answer all the criticisms that cross my desk, my secretaries would have little time for anything other than such correspondence in the course of the day, and I would have no time for constructive work. But since I feel that you are men of genuine good will and that your criticisms are sincerely set forth, I want to try to answer your statement in what I hope will be patient and reasonable terms.

I think I should indicate why I am here in Birmingham, since you have been influenced by the view which argues against "outsiders coming in." I have the honor of serving as president of the Southern Christian Leadership Conference, an organization operating in every southern state, with headquarters in Atlanta, Georgia. We have some eighty-five affiliated organizations across the South, and one of them is the Alabama Christian Movement for Human Rights. Frequently we share staff, educational and financial resources with our affiliates. Several months ago the affiliate here in Birmingham asked us to be on call to engage in a nonviolent direct-action program if such were deemed necessary. We readily consented, and when the hour came we lived up to our promise. So I, along with several members of my staff, am here because I was invited here. I am here because I have organizational ties here.

But more basically, I am in Birmingham because injustice is here. Just as the prophets of the eighth century B.C. left their villages and carried their "thus saith the Lord" far beyond the boundaries of their home towns, and just as the Apostle Paul left his village of Tarsus and carried the gospel of Jesus Christ to the far corners of the Greco-Roman world, so am I compelled to carry the gospel of freedom beyond my own home town. Like Paul, I must constantly respond to the Macedonian call for aid.

Moreover, I am cognizant of the interrelatedness of all communities and states. I cannot sit idly by in Atlanta and not be concerned about what happens in Birmingham. Injustice anywhere is a threat to justice everywhere. We are caught in an inescapable network of mutuality, tied in a single garment of destiny. Whatever affects one directly, affects all indirectly. Never again can we afford to live with the narrow, provincial "outside agitator" idea. Anyone who lives inside the United States can never be considered an outsider anywhere within its bounds.

You deplore the demonstrations taking place in Birmingham. But your statement, I am sorry to say, fails to express a similar concern for the conditions that brought about the demonstrations. I am sure that none of you would want to rest content with the superficial kind of social analysis that deals merely with effects and does not grapple with underlying causes. It is unfortunate that demonstrations are taking place in Birmingham, but it is even more unfortunate that the city's white power structure left the Negro community with no alternative.

In any nonviolent campaign there are four basic steps: collection of the facts to determine whether injustices exist; negotiation; self-purification; and direct action. We have gone through all these steps in Birmingham. There can be no gainsaying the fact that racial injustice engulfs this community. Birmingham is probably the most thoroughly segregated city in the United States. Its ugly record of brutality is widely known. Negroes have experienced grossly unjust treatment in the courts. There have been more unsolved bombings of Negro homes and churches in Birmingham than in any other city in the nation. These are the hard, brutal facts of the case. On the basis of these conditions, Negro leaders sought to negotiate with the city fathers. But the latter consistently refused to engage in good-faith negotiation.

Then, last September, came the opportunity to talk with leaders of Birmingham's economic community. In the course of the negotiations, certain promises were made by the merchants—for example, to remove the stores' humiliating racial signs. On the basis of these promises, the Reverend Fred Shuttlesworth and the leaders of the Alabama Christian Movement for Human Rights agreed to a moratorium on all demonstrations. As the weeks and months went by, we realized that we were the victims of a broken promise. A few signs, briefly removed, returned; the others remained.

As in so many past experiences, our hopes had been blasted, and the shadow of deep disappointment settled upon us. We had no alternative except to prepare for direct action, whereby we would present our very bodies as a means of laying our case before the conscience of the local and the national community. Mindful of the difficulties involved, we decided to undertake a process of self-purification. We began a series of workshops on nonviolence, and we repeatedly asked ourselves: "Are you able to accept blows without retaliating?" "Are you able to endure the ordeal of jail?" We decided to schedule our direct-action program for the Easter season, realizing that except for Christmas, this is the main shopping period of the year. Knowing that a strong economic-withdrawl program would be the by-product of direct action, we felt that this would be the best time to bring pressure to bear on the merchants for the needed change.

Then it occurred to us that Birmingham's mayoral election was coming up in March, and we speedily decided to postpone action until after election day. When we discovered that the Commissioner of Public Safety, Eugene "Bull" Connor, had piled up enough votes to be in the run-off we decided again to postpone action until the day after the run-off so that the demonstrations could not be used to cloud the issues. Like many others, we waited to see Mr. Connor defeated, and to this end we endured postponement after postponement. Having aided in this community need, we felt that our direct-action program could be delayed no longer.

You may well ask: "Why direct action? Why sit-ins, marches and so forth? Isn't negotiation a better path?" You are quite right in calling for negotiation. Indeed, this is the very purpose of direct action. Nonviolent direct action seeks to create such a crisis and foster such a tension that a community which has constantly refused to negotiate is forced to confront the issue. It seeks so to dramatize the issue that it can no longer be ignored. My citing the creation of tension as part of the work of the nonviolent-resister may sound rather shocking. But I must confess that I am not afraid of the word "tension." I have earnestly opposed violent tension, but there is a type of constructive, nonviolent tension which is necessary for growth. Just as Socrates felt that it was necessary to create a tension in the mind so that individuals could rise from the bondage of myths and half-truths to the unfettered realm of creative analysis and objective appraisal, so must we see the need for nonviolent gadflies to create the kind of tension in society that will help men rise from the dark depths of prejudice and racism to the majestic heights of understanding and brotherhood.

The purpose of our direct-action program is to create a situation so crisis-packed that it will inevitably open the door to negotiation. I therefore concur with you in your call for negotiation. Too long has our beloved Southland been bogged down in a tragic effort to live in monologue rather than dialogue.

One of the basic points in your statement is that the action that I and my associates have taken in Birmingham is untimely. Some have asked: "Why didn't you give the new city administration time to act?" The only answer that I can give to this query is that the new Birmingham administration must be prodded about as much as the outgoing one, before it will act. We are sadly mistaken if we feel that the election of Albert Boutwell as mayor will bring the millennium to Birmingham. While Mr. Boutwell is a much more gentle person than Mr. Connor, they are both segregationists, dedicated to maintenance of the status quo. I have hope that Mr. Boutwell will be reasonable enough to see the futility of massive resistance to desegregation. But he will not see this without pressure from devotees of civil rights. My friends, I must say to you that we have not made a single gain for civil rights without determined legal and nonviolent pressure. Lamentably, it is an historical fact that privileged groups seldom give up their privileges voluntarily. Individuals may see the moral light and voluntarily give up their unjust posture; but, as Reinhold Niebuhr has reminded us, groups tend to be more immoral than individuals.

We know through painful experience that freedom is never voluntarily given by the oppressor; it must be demanded by the oppressed. Frankly, I have yet to engage in a direct-action campaign that was "well timed" in the view of those who have not suffered unduly from the disease of segregation. For years now I have heard the word "Wait!" It rings in the ear of every Negro with piercing familiarity. This "Wait" has almost always meant "Never." We must come to see, with one of our distinguished jurists, that "justice too long delayed is justice denied."

We have waited for more than 340 years for our constitutional and God-given rights. The nations of Asia and Africa are moving with jetlike speed toward gaining political independence, but we still creep at horse-and-buggy pace toward gaining a cup of coffee at a lunch counter. Perhaps it is easy for those who have never felt the stinging darts of segregation to say, "Wait." But when you have seen vicious mobs lynch your mothers and fathers at will and drown your sisters and brothers at whim; when you have seen hate-filled policemen curse, kick and even kill your black brothers and sisters; when you see the vast majority of your twenty million Negro brothers smothering in an air-tight cage of poverty in the midst of an affluent society; when you suddenly find your tongue twisted and your speech stammering as you seek to explain to your six-year-old daughter why she can't go to the public amusement park that has just been advertised on television, and see tears welling up in her eyes when she is told that Funtown is closed to colored children, and see ominous clouds of inferiority beginning to form in her little mental sky, and see her beginning to distort her personality by developing an unconscious bitterness toward white people; when you have to concoct an answer for a five-year-old son who is asking: "Daddy, why do white people treat colored people so mean?"; when you take a cross-county drive and find it necessary to sleep night after night in the uncomfortable corners of your automobile because no motel will accept you; when you are humiliated day in and day out by nagging signs reading "white" and "colored"; when your first name becomes "nigger," your middle name becomes "boy" (however old you are) and your last name becomes "John," and your wife and mother are never given the respected title "Mrs."; when you are harried by day and haunted by night by the fact that you are a Negro, living constantly at tiptoe stance, never quite knowing what to expect next, and are plagued with inner fears and outer resentments; when you are forever fighting a degenerating sense of "nobodiness" then you will understand why we find it difficult to wait. There comes a time when the cup of endurance runs over, and men are no longer willing to be plunged into the abyss of despair. I hope, sirs, you can understand our legitimate and unavoidable impatience.

You express a great deal of anxiety over our willingness to break laws. This is certainly a legitimate concern. Since we so diligently urge people to obey the Supreme Court's decision of 1954 outlawing segregation in the public schools, at first glance it may seem rather paradoxical for us consciously to break laws. One may well ask: "How can you advocate breaking some laws and obeying others?" The answer lies in the fact that there are two types of laws: just and unjust. I would be the first to advocate obeying just laws. One has not only a legal but a moral responsibility to obey just laws. Conversely, one has a moral responsibility to disobey unjust laws. I would agree with St. Augustine that "an unjust law is no law at all."

Now, what is the difference between the two? How does one determine whether a law is just or unjust? A just law is a man-made code that squares with the moral law or the law of God. An unjust law is a code that is out of harmony with the moral law. To put it in the terms of St. Thomas Aquinas: An unjust law is a human law that is not rooted in eternal law and natural law. Any law that uplifts human personality is just. Any law that degrades human personality is unjust. All segregation statutes are unjust because segregation distorts the soul and damages the personality. It gives the segregator a false sense of superiority and the segregated a false sense of inferiority. Segregation, to use the terminology of the Jewish philosopher Martin Buber, substitutes an "I-it" relationship for an "I-thou" relationship and ends up relegating persons to the status of things. Hence segregation is not only politically, economically and sociologically unsound, it is morally wrong and sinful. Paul Tillich has said that sin is separation. Is not segregation an existential expression of man's tragic separation, his awful estrangement, his terrible sinfulness? Thus it is that I can urge men to obey the 1954 decision of the Supreme Court, for it is morally right; and I can urge them to disobey segregation ordinances, for they are morally wrong.

Let us consider a more concrete example of just and unjust laws. An unjust law is a code that a numerical or power majority group compels a minority group to obey but does not make binding on itself. This is *difference* made legal. By the same token, a just law is a code that a majority compels a minority to follow and that it is willing to follow itself. This is *sameness* made legal.

Let me give another explanation. A law is unjust if it is inflicted on a minority that, as a result of being denied the right to vote, had no part in enacting or devising the law. Who can say that the legislature of Alabama which set up that state's segregation laws was democratically elected? Throughout Alabama all sorts of devious methods are used to prevent Negroes from becoming registered voters, and there are some counties in which, even though Negroes constitute a majority of the population, not a single Negro is registered. Can any law enacted under such circumstances be considered democratically structured?

Sometimes a law is just on its face and unjust in its application. For instance, I have been arrested on a charge of parading without a permit. Now, there is nothing wrong in having an ordinance which requires a permit for a parade. But such an ordinance becomes unjust when it is used to maintain segregation and to deny citizens the First Amendment privilege of peaceful assembly and protest.

I hope you are able to see the distinction I am trying to point out. In no sense do I advocate evading or defying the law, as would the rabid segregationist. That would lead to anarchy. One who breaks an unjust law must do so openly, lovingly, and with a willingness to accept the penalty. I submit that an individual who breaks a law that conscience tells him is unjust and who willingly accepts the penalty of imprisonment in order to arouse the conscience of the community over its injustice, is in reality expressing the highest respect for law.

Of course, there is nothing new about this kind of civil disobedience. It was evidenced sublimely in the refusal of Shadrach, Meshach and Abednego to obey the laws of Nebuchadnezzar, on the ground that a higher moral law was at stake. It was practiced superbly by the early Christians, who were willing to face hungry lions and the excruciating pain of chopping blocks rather than submit to certain unjust laws of the Roman Empire. To a degree, academic freedom is a reality today because Socrates practiced civil disobedience.

In our own nation, the Boston Tea Party represented a massive act of civil disobedience.

We should never forget that everything Adolf Hitler did in Germany was "legal" and everything the Hungarian freedom fighters did in Hungary was "illegal." It was "illegal" to aid and comfort a Jew in Hitler's Germany. Even so, I am sure that, had I lived in Germany at the time, I would have aided and comforted my Jewish brothers. If today I lived in a Communist country where certain principles dear to the Christian faith are suppressed, I would openly advocate disobeying that country's antireligious laws.

I must make two honest confessions to you, my Christian and Jewish brothers. First, I must confess that over the past few years I have been gravely disappointed with the white moderate. I have almost reached the regrettable conclusion that the Negro's great stumbling block in his stride toward freedom is not the White Citizen's Counciler or the Ku Klux Klanner, but the white moderate, who is more devoted to "order" than to justice; who prefers a negative peace which is the absence of tension to a positive peace which is the presence of justice; who constantly says: "I agree with you in the goal you seek, but I cannot agree with your methods of direct action"; who paternalistically believes he can set the timetable for another man's freedom; who lives by a mythical concept of time and who constantly advises the Negro to wait for a "more convenient season." Shallow understanding from people of good will is more frustrating than absolute misunderstanding from people of ill will. Lukewarm acceptance is much more bewildering than outright rejection.

I had hoped that the white moderate would understand that law and order exist for the purpose of establishing justice and that when they fail in this purpose they become the dangerously structured dams that block the flow of social progress. I had hoped that the white moderate would understand that the present tension in the South is a necessary phase of the transition from an obnoxious negative peace, in which the Negro passively accepted his unjust plight, to a substantive and positive peace, in which all men will respect the dignity and worth of human personality. Actually, we who engage in nonviolent direct action are not the creators of tension. We merely bring to the surface the hidden tension that is already alive. We bring it out in the open, where it can be seen and dealt with. Like a boil that can never be cured so long as it is covered up but must be opened with all its ugliness to the natural medicines of air and light, injustice must be exposed, with all the tension its exposure creates, to the light of human conscience and the air of national opinion before it can be cured.

In your statement you assert that our actions, even though peaceful, must be condemned because they precipitate violence. But is this a logical assertion? Isn't this like condemning a robbed man because his possession of money precipitated the evil act of robbery? Isn't this like condemning Socrates because his unswerving commitment to truth and his philosophical inquiries precipitated the act by the misguided populace in which they made him drink hemlock? Isn't this like condemning Jesus because his unique God-consciousness and never-ceasing devotion to God's will precipitated the evil act of crucifixion? We must come to see that, as the federal courts have consistently affirmed, it is wrong to urge an individual to cease his efforts to gain his basic constitutional rights because the quest may precipitate violence. Society must protect the robbed and punish the robber.

I had also hoped that the white moderate would reject the myth concerning time in relation to the struggle for freedom. I have just received a letter from a white brother in Texas. He writes: "All Christians know that the colored people will receive equal rights eventually, but it is possible that you are in too great a religious hurry. It has taken Christianity almost two thousand years to accomplish what it has. The teachings of Christ take time to come to earth." Such an attitude stems from a tragic misconception of time, from the strangely rational notion that there is something in the very flow of time that will inevitably cure all ills. Actually, time itself is neutral; it can be used either destructively or constructively. More and more I feel that the people of ill will have used time much more effectively than have the people of good will. We will have to repent in this generation not merely for the hateful words and actions of the bad people but for the appalling silence of the good people. Human progress never rolls in on wheels of inevitability; it comes through the tireless efforts of men willing to be co-workers with God, and without this hard work, time itself becomes an ally of the forces of social stagnation. We must use time creatively, in the knowledge that the time is always ripe to do right. Now is the time to make real the promise of democracy and transform our pending national elegy into a creative psalm of brotherhood. Now is the time to lift our national policy from the quicksand of racial injustice to the solid rock of human dignity.

You speak of our activity in Birmingham as extreme. At first I was rather disappointed that fellow clergymen would see my nonviolent efforts as those of an extremist. I began thinking about the fact that I stand in the middle of two opposing forces in the Negro community. One is a force of complacency, made up in part of Negroes who, as a result of long years of oppression, are so drained of self-respect and a sense of "somebodiness" that they have adjusted to segregation; and in part of a few middle class Negroes who, because of a degree of academic and economic security and because in some ways they profit by segregation, have become insensitive to the problems of the masses. The other force is one of bitterness and hatred, and it comes perilously close to advocating violence. It is expressed in the various black nationalist groups that are springing up across the nation, the largest and best-known being Elijah Muhammad's Muslim movement. Nourished by the Negro's frustration over the continued existence of racial discrimination, this movement is made up of people who have lost faith in America, who have absolutely repudiated Christianity, and who have concluded that the white man is an incorrigible "devil."

I have tried to stand between these two forces, saying that we need emulate neither the "do-nothingism" of the complacent nor the hatred and despair of the black nationalist. For there is the more excellent way of love and nonviolent protest. I am grateful to God that, through the influence of the Negro church, the way of nonviolence became an integral part of our struggle.

If this philosophy had not emerged, by now many streets of the South would, I am convinced, be flowing with blood. And I am further convinced that if our white brothers dismiss as "rabble-rousers" and "outside agitators" those of us who employ nonviolent direct action, and if they refuse to support our nonviolent efforts, millions of Negroes will, out of frustration and despair, seek solace and security in black-nationalist ideologies, a development that would inevitably lead to a frightening racial nightmare.

Oppressed people cannot remain oppressed forever. The yearning for freedom eventually manifests itself, and that is what has happened to the American Negro. Something within has reminded him of his birthright of freedom, and something without has reminded him that it can be gained. Consciously or unconsciously, he has been caught up by the Zeitgeist, and with his black brothers of Africa and his brown and yellow brothers of Asia, South America and the Caribbean, the United States Negro is moving with a sense of great urgency toward the promised land of racial justice. If one recognizes this vital urge that has engulfed the Negro community, one should readily understand why public demonstrations are taking place. The Negro has many pent-up resentments and latent frustrations, and he must release them. So let him march; let him make prayer pilgrimages to the city hall; let him go on freedom rides—and try to understand why he must do so. If his repressed emotions are not released in nonviolent ways, they will seek expression through violence; this is not a threat but a fact of history. So I have not said to my people: "Get rid of your discontent." Rather, I have tried to say that this normal and healthy discontent can be channeled into the creative outlet of nonviolent direct action. And now this approach is being termed extremist.

But though I was initially disappointed at being categorized as an extremist, as I continued to think about the matter I gradually gained a measure of satisfaction from the label. Was not Jesus an extremist for love: "Love your enemies, bless them that curse you, do good to them that hate you, and pray for them which despitefully use you, and persecute you." Was not Amos an extremist for justice: "Let justice roll down like waters and righteousness like an ever-flowing stream." Was not Paul an extremist for the Christian gospel: "I bear in my body the marks of the Lord Jesus." Was not Martin Luther an extremist: "Here I stand; I cannot do otherwise, so help me God." And John Bunyan: "I will stay in jail to the end of my days before I make a butchery of my conscience." And Abraham Lincoln: "This nation cannot survive half slave and half free." And Thomas Jefferson: "We hold these truths to be self-evident, that all men are created equal. . . ." So the question is not whether we will be extremists, but what kind of extremists we will be. Will we be extremists for hate or for love? Will we be extremists for the preservation of injustice or for the extension of justice? In that dramatic scene on Calvary's hill three men were crucified. We must never forget that all three were crucified for the same crime—the crime of extremism. Two were extremists for immorality, and thus fell below their

environment. The other, Jesus Christ, was an extremist for love, truth and goodness, and thereby rose above his environment. Perhaps the South, the nation, and the world are in dire need of creative extremists.

I had hoped that the white moderate would see this need. Perhaps I was too optimistic; perhaps I expected too much. I suppose I should have realized that few members of the oppressor race can understand the deep groans and passionate yearnings of the oppressed race, and still fewer have the vision to see that injustice must be rooted out by strong, persistent and determined action. I am thankful, however, that some of our white brothers in the South have grasped the meaning of this social revolution and committed themselves to it. They are still too few in quantity, but they are big in quality. Some—such as Ralph McGill, Lillian Smith, Harry Golden, James McBride Dabbs, Ann Braden and Sarah Patton Boyle—have written about our struggle in eloquent and prophetic terms. Others have marched with us down nameless streets of the South. They have languished in filthy, roach-infested jails, suffering the abuse and brutality of policemen who view them as "dirty nigger lovers." Unlike so many of their moderate brothers and sisters, they have recognized the urgency of the moment and sensed the need for powerful "action" antidotes to combat the disease of segregation.

Let me take note of my other major disappointment. I have been so greatly disappointed with the white church and its leadership. Of course, there are some notable exceptions. I am not unmindful of the fact that each of you has taken some significant stands on this issue. I commend you, Reverend Stallings, for your Christian stand on this past Sunday, in welcoming Negroes to your worship service on a nonsegregated basis. I commend the Catholic leaders of this state for integrating Spring Hill College several years ago.

But despite these notable exceptions, I must honestly reiterate that I have been disappointed with the church. I do not say this as one of those negative critics who can always find something wrong with the church. I say this as a minister of the gospel, who loves the church; who was nurtured in its bosom; who has been sustained by its spiritual blessings and who will remain true to it as long as the cord of life shall lengthen.

When I was suddenly catapulted into the leadership of the bus protest in Montgomery, Alabama, a few years ago,

I felt we would be supported by the white church, felt that the white ministers, priests, and rabbis of the South would be among our strongest allies. Instead, some have been outright opponents, refusing to understand the freedom movement and misrepresenting its leaders; all too many others have been more cautious than courageous and have remained silent behind the anesthetizing security of stained-glass windows.

In spite of my shattered dreams, I came to Birmingham with the hope that the white religious leadership of this community would see the justice of our cause and, with deep moral concern, would serve as the channel through which our just grievances could reach the power structure. I had hoped that each of you would understand. But again I have been disappointed.

I have heard numerous southern religious leaders admonish their worshipers to comply with a desegregation decision because it is the law, but I have longed to hear white ministers declare: "Follow this decree because integration is morally right and because the Negro is your brother." In the midst of blatant injustices inflicted upon the Negro, I have watched white churchmen stand on the sideline and mouth pious irrelevancies and sanctimonious trivialities. In the midst of a mighty struggle to rid our nation of racial and economic injustice, I have heard many ministers say: "Those are social issues, with which the gospel has no real concern." And I have watched many churches commit themselves to a completely other-worldly religion which makes a strange, un-Biblical distinction between body and soul, between the sacred and the secular.

I have traveled the length and breadth of Alabama, Mississippi and all the other southern states. On sweltering summer days and crisp autumn mornings I have looked at the South's beautiful churches with their lofty spires pointing heavenward. I have beheld the impressive outlines of her massive religious-education buildings. Over and over I have found myself asking: "What kind of people worship here? Who is their God? Where were their voices when the lips of Governor Barnett dripped with words of interposition and nullification? Where were they when Governor Wallace gave a clarion call for defiance and hatred? Where were their voices of support when bruised and weary Negro men and women decided to rise from the dark dungeons of complacency to the bright hills of creative protest?"

Yes, these questions are still in my mind. In deep disappointment I have wept over the laxity of the church. But be assured that my tears have been tears of love. There can be no deep disappointment where there is not deep love. Yes, I love the church. How could I do otherwise? I am in the rather unique position of being the son, the grandson and the great-grandson of preachers. Yes, I see the church as the body of Christ. But, oh! How we have blemished and scarred that body through social neglect and through fear of being nonconformists.

There was a time when the church was very powerful—in the time when the early Christians rejoiced at being deemed worthy to suffer for what they believed. In those days the church was not merely a thermometer that recorded the ideas and principles of popular opinion; it was a thermostat that transformed the mores of society. Whenever the early Christians entered a town, the people in power became disturbed and immediately sought to convict the Christians for being "disturbers of the peace" and "outside agitators." But the Christians pressed on, in the conviction that they were "a colony of heaven," called to obey God rather than man. Small in number, they were big in commitment. They were too God intoxicated to be "astronomically intimidated." By their effort and example they brought an end to such ancient evils as infanticide and gladiatorial contests.

Things are different now. So often the contemporary church is a weak, ineffectual voice with an uncertain sound. So often it is an archdefender of the status quo. Far from being disturbed by the presence of the church, the power structure of the average community is consoled by the church's silent and often even vocal sanction of things as they are.

But the judgment of God is upon the church as never before. If today's church does not recapture the sacrificial spirit of the early church, it will lose its authenticity, forfeit the loyalty of millions, and be dismissed as an irrelevant social club with no meaning for the twentieth century. Every day I meet young people whose disappointment with the church has turned into outright disgust.

Perhaps I have once again been too optimistic. Is organized religion too inextricably bound to the status quo to save our nation and the world? Perhaps I must turn my faith to the inner spiritual church, the church within the church, as the true ekklesia and the hope of the world. But again I am thankful to God that some noble souls from the ranks of organized religion have broken loose from the paralyzing chains of conformity and joined us as active partners in the struggle for freedom. They have left their secure congregations and walked the streets of Albany, Georgia, with us. They have gone down the highways of the South on tortuous rides for freedom. Yes, they have gone to jail with us. Some have been dismissed from their churches, have lost the support of their bishops and fellow ministers. But they have acted in the faith that right defeated is stronger than evil triumphant. Their witness has been the spiritual salt that has preserved the true meaning of the gospel in these troubled times. They have carved a tunnel of hope through the dark mountain of disappointment.

I hope the church as a whole will meet the challenge of this decisive hour. But even if the church does not come to the aid of justice, I have no despair about the future. I have no fear about the outcome of our struggle in Birmingham, even if our motives are at present misunderstood. We will reach the goal of freedom in Birmingham, and all over the nation, because the goal of America is freedom. Abused and scorned though we may be, our destiny is tied up with America's destiny. Before the pilgrims landed at Plymouth, we were here. Before the pen of Jefferson etched the majestic words of the Declaration of Independence across the pages of history, we were here. For more than two centuries our forebears labored in this country without wages; they made cotton king; they built the homes of their masters while suffering gross injustice and shameful humiliation—and yet out of a bottomless vitality they continued to thrive and develop. If the inexpressible cruelties of slavery could not stop us, the opposition we now face will surely fail. We will win our freedom because the sacred heritage of our nation and the eternal will of God are embodied in our echoing demands.

Before closing I feel impelled to mention one other point in your statement that has troubled me profoundly. You warmly commended the Birmingham police force for keeping "order" and "preventing violence." I doubt that you would have so warmly commended the police force if you had seen its dogs sinking their teeth into unarmed, nonviolent Negroes. I doubt that you would so quickly commend the policemen if you were to observe their ugly and inhumane treatment of Negroes here in the city jail; if you were

to watch them push and curse old Negro women and young Negro girls; if you were to see them slap and kick old Negro men and young boys; if you were to observe them, as they did on two occasions, refuse to give us food because we wanted to sing our grace together. I cannot join you in your praise of the Birmingham police department.

It is true that the police have exercised a degree of discipline in handing the demonstrators. In this sense they have conducted themselves rather "nonviolently" in pubic. But for what purpose? To preserve the evil system of segregation. Over the past few years I have consistently preached that nonviolence demands that the means we use must be as pure as the ends we seek. I have tried to make clear that it is wrong to use immoral means to attain moral ends. But now I must affirm that it is just as wrong, or perhaps even more so, to use moral means to preserve immoral ends. Perhaps Mr. Connor and his policemen have been rather nonviolent in public, as was Chief Pritchett in Albany, Georgia, but they have used the moral means of nonviolence to maintain the immoral end of racial injustice. As T. S. Eliot has said: "The last temptation is the greatest treason: To do the right deed for the wrong reason."

I wish you had commended the Negro sit-inners and demonstrators of Birmingham for their sublime courage, their willingness to suffer and their amazing discipline in the midst of great provocation. One day the South will recognize its real heroes. They will be the James Merediths, with the noble sense of purpose that enables them to face jeering and hostile mobs, and with the agonizing loneliness that characterizes the life of the pioneer. They will be old, oppressed, battered Negro women, symbolized in a seventy-two-year-old woman in Montgomery, Alabama, who rose up with a sense of dignity and with her people decided not to ride segregated buses, and who responded with ungrammatical profundity to one who inquired about her weariness: "My feets is tired, but my soul is at rest." They will be the young high school and college students, the young ministers of the gospel and a host of their elders, courageously and nonviolently sitting in at lunch counters and willingly going to jail for conscience's sake. One day the South will know that when these disinherited children of God sat down at lunch counters, they were in reality standing up for what is best in the American dream and for the most sacred values in our Judaeo-Christian heritage, thereby bringing our nation back to those great wells of democracy which were dug deep by the founding fathers in their formulation of the Constitution and the Declaration of Independence.

Never before have I written so long a letter. I'm afraid it is much too long to take your precious time. I can assure you that it would have been much shorter if I had been writing from a comfortable desk, but what else can one do when he is alone in a narrow jail cell, other than write long letters, think long thoughts and pray long prayers?

If I have said anything in this letter that overstates the truth and indicates an unreasonable impatience, I beg you to forgive me. If I have said anything that understates the truth and indicates my having a patience that allows me to settle for anything less than brotherhood, I beg God to forgive me.

I hope this letter finds you strong in the faith. I also hope that circumstances will soon make it possible for me to meet each of you, not as an integrationist or a civil rights leader but as a fellow clergyman and a Christian brother. Let us all hope that the dark clouds of racial prejudice will soon pass away and the deep fog of misunderstanding will be lifted from our fear-drenched communities, and in some not too distant tomorrow the radiant stars of love and brotherhood will shine over our great nation with all their scintillating beauty.

Yours for the cause of
Peace and Brotherhood,

MARTIN LUTHER KING, JR.

1. King addresses eight fellow clergy members, but his letter is also written for a broader audience. How does the open letter format impact the arguments he offers?

2. Identify specific uses of counterargument and concession in King's letter. (See Chapter 6, pages 286–288.) How do they affect King's argument?

3. King addresses a specific set of circumstances and laws in the 1960s, but he also makes several points about right and wrong, about patriotism, moderation, and law. What points extend beyond the situation of the 1960s? How does King's rhetoric help you to make a connection between then and now?

RHETORICAL HANDBOOK

Chapter Contents

CHAPTER 15

Where to Find It

ORGANIZATION

Every essay has a structure, or organization. Like word choice, content, voice, and so on, organization is determined by considering one's purpose in writing, the reader, and the overall writing situation. It is also determined by the ideas being presented.

Controlling Idea An essay (like any piece of writing) is organized around a main (or controlling) idea. The main idea of an essay is also referred to as a thesis. Shorter pieces, such as the ones often written in college writing courses, benefit from having a narrow focus. Since those pieces are relatively short, there isn't enough time or space to deal with a broad topic. Longer writings may have a broader main idea, though even they benefit from a narrow focus. Whether the thesis is stated or implied, the support for the main idea (the rest of the essay) is carefully arranged to help the reader accept the main idea.

Beginning, Middle, and End An essay (letter, report, etc.) has a beginning, middle, and end. The beginning (or introduction) leads the reader into the meat of the essay. The bulk of an essay supports the main idea. (The essays in this text illustrate the various strategies that can be used.) The ending (or conclusion) of the essay brings it to a close in one of various ways. While a conclusion could just summarize the main points, this summary is often unnecessary. Instead, a strong conclusion might suggest or emphasize the public resonance of the essay, create a strong and lasting image, call the reader to action, and so on (see pages 752–753). Conclusions lead the reader out of the essay and back to the larger world. They try to answer the reader's main question: "So what? What is the point of this essay?" They (often subtly) encourage the reader to think or act differently. Finally, introductions and conclusions are not necessarily one paragraph each. They can bleed into several paragraphs—blurring the boundaries between beginning, middle, and end.

> You should not feel that you must figure out the <u>right</u> organization, but instead that you must figure out an organization that engages readers, directs them through your ideas, and leaves them reflective in the end.

Controlling idea, main idea, and thesis all mean the same thing.

ACTIVITY

Study the organization of several essays in this text. What is each paragraph about, and how does it function in the overall scheme of the essay? How do the introduction and conclusion lead the reader into and out of the essay?

The Five-Paragraph Essay

One typical organization, often helpful but ultimately limiting, is the five-paragraph essay. It includes a brief introduction, three supporting paragraphs (each developing a different point), and a conclusion (usually one fairly brief paragraph).

Because it is simple, the five-paragraph essay allows a better understanding of the basics of organization. Five-paragraph essays contain a clear beginning, middle, and end: The main idea is often stated in the beginning; three distinct, though related, ideas support or develop the main idea; and a conclusion follows.

Notice in the example below how each supporting paragraph will develop or support a clearly stated main idea. Notice also how key terms from the controlling idea are repeated, word for word or with synonyms, in the topic sentences (or main ideas for the supporting paragraphs):

Controlling Idea: Myrtle Beach is a great place to go on vacation.

Supporting Paragraph #1: Myrtle Beach has a lot of nice golf courses.
Supporting Paragraph #2: Myrtle Beach has a beautiful long beach.
Supporting Paragraph #3: Myrtle Beach has plenty of good nightlife.

Concluding Paragraph

BEYOND THE FIVE-PARAGRAPH ESSAY

These characteristics of essay organization should be kept in mind without becoming limiting. There is a lot of potential for going beyond the five-paragraph essay in the above example. By narrowing the essay's focus, dealing with counterarguments and concessions, or establishing a purpose beyond merely describing some positive aspects of Myrtle Beach, the writer would naturally require a more complex (and less limiting) essay organization.

Instead of explaining three nice things about Myrtle Beach, a writer might show why Myrtle Beach is preferable to Daytona Beach, Panama City, Acapulco, or the New Jersey shore. This approach would likely include making counterarguments and concessions. Or the writer might narrow his or her focus to *just the beach*. Such an approach might deal briefly with the region's golf courses, night life, and other matters in the introduction or elsewhere, then focus more specifically on the virtues of the beach. Going beyond the five-paragraph approach requires more analysis and will produce a more engaging essay.

Caution: The five-paragraph essay can have more than five paragraphs—and still be limiting. The problem is not with the number of points or paragraphs, but with the lack of exploration and discovery. Often, the writer using the five-paragraph strategy avoids asking hard questions, dissecting points, analyzing assumptions—all the strategies that create an engaging essay.

ACTIVITIES

1. To make sure you understand your own essay's organization, summarize each paragraph. You might (1) state the paragraph's main idea and/or (2) explain how the paragraph functions. This involves not just stating its main idea, but also explaining the paragraph's main idea in relationship to the overall piece—not just describing a spark plug, but explaining its role in the running of the automobile.

2. Make two lists, one naming the advantages of the five-paragraph essay structure, and one naming the disadvantages. Then, consider your relationship as a writer to the five-paragraph essay. When does it suit your needs? When doesn't it? Can you benefit at this point in your career from learning the five-paragraph approach, from using aspects of it, or from avoiding it altogether?

PARAGRAPHS

Paragraphs serve different purposes. Some introduce the main idea of an essay; others support that idea; and others bring the essay to a satisfying conclusion. In longer writings, an introduction or conclusion may take several paragraphs, and one supporting point may require more than just one paragraph.

Three important qualities of paragraphs (and essays) are unity, development, and coherence.

Unity means that each paragraph is about one thing; that is, it has a purpose and it goes about achieving that purpose without significant digression.

Development means that each paragraph is sufficiently thorough. This can only be determined by considering each paragraph's purpose and what must be done to achieve that purpose.

Coherence means that the relationship between ideas is clear to the reader—that the writing flows. The writer assists the reader by arranging ideas in an appropriate order and by providing transitions, repeating key terms, and following conventions of grammar.

> When revising, working toward a more unified, developed, and coherent essay will help create more readable writing.

Supporting Paragraphs

Writers think about (1) how each paragraph functions within the overall essay and (2) how each paragraph is organized within itself. Read through several essays in this book, and notice how their paragraphs function and are organized. Paragraphs are often organized deductively—stating the main idea first, then supporting it. They also can be organized inductively—giving support first, then the main idea. Some paragraphs (called "turnabout paragraphs" in this text) begin with a point and then pivot, or move, the reader a related point. And other paragraphs serve as transitions between the preceding and following paragraphs or sections of text.

Deductive If information is organized deductively, the main idea is presented first and the support for that idea follows. Stating the main idea first often helps the reader to understand the point of the paragraph more readily.

> Sadly, the gap between these two groups grows even wider. The motivated student with good study skills (the one who has had at least an adequate high school education) attends class, takes notes, understands reading assignments, follows instructions, develops even better habits of mind, gains even more knowledge, and learns ways of making that knowledge work for her and his fellow humans. But in a system where B's are average

and C's might indicate that although a student "tried" she did not demonstrate understanding or skill, the poorer students continue to advance through the system while remaining trapped at the bottom. Their level of thinking does not change much, while that of their better-prepared peers does.

The opening sentence of the preceding paragraph expresses a main idea: The gap between two groups of students grows wider. The rest of the paragraph explains *why*.

Inductive If information is organized inductively, the main idea is presented following the support. The deductive paragraph above can be reorganized by placing the main idea last.

The motivated student with good study skills (the one who has had at least an adequate high school education) attends class, takes notes, understands reading assignments, follows instructions, develops even better habits of mind, gains even more knowledge, and learns ways of making that knowledge work for her and his fellow humans. But in a system where B's are average and C's might indicate that although a student "tried" she did not demonstrate understanding or skill, the poorer students continue to advance through the system while remaining trapped at the bottom. Their level of thinking does not change much, while that of their better-prepared peers does. Sadly, the gap between these two groups grows even wider.

Turnabout Writers often find it helpful to pivot from one idea to another within the same paragraph—the second idea being a major point that plays off of the first idea. The pivot, or turnabout, is usually signaled by a transition word or expression such as *but, however, on the other hand, still, yet,* and so on.

In his book *Generation X Goes to College,* Peter Sacks describes, among other things, the sense of entitlement that some students in today's consumerist culture have toward a college education. One entire chapter explores this issue alone, providing examples of this "sense" and looking into its "humble beginnings." Sacks shows how consumerism has invaded education, leading some students to expect good grades for little effort. But he fails, it seems, to emphasize enough a most harmful effect of this sense of entitlement. The biggest problem, as I see it, is that although students are able to graduate from high school (and even some colleges) with minimal effort, those students may find themselves cheated in the long run.

Notice how the above paragraph turns on the word *But,* thus building on the previous point and moving in a different, yet appropriate, direction. The first part of the paragraph tells what Peter Sacks describes; the second part turns on *but* and tells what he *doesn't* do.

Transition Some paragraphs, especially in longer pieces, function as transitions that take the reader from one idea (usually a section of an essay) to another idea (another section of the essay).

> True enough, these are all ways that students who are allowed to just slide by end up getting cheated. But another way (and one less talked about) strikes me as being far more offensive. This reason hinges on the fact that many students are not just sliding by.

The above paragraph moves the reader from the previously mentioned ways that students are cheated to a far more offensive way that students are cheated. Then the rest of the essay develops this point.

Opening and Closing Paragraphs

Shorter essays often have an opening paragraph, several supporting paragraphs, and a closing paragraph. Opening paragraphs bring the reader into the essay, introducing the subject and setting the tone. Closing paragraphs take the reader out of the essay, back to the outside world. The ways of beginning and ending essays are unlimited. But readers respond well to introductions that open a door to a new way of thinking and conclusions that emphasize the most important idea in the essay.

STRATEGIES FOR INTRODUCTIONS

1. Begin with a statistic, quotation, or anecdote.
2. Ask a question.
3. Create a strong visual image.
4. Provide necessary background.
5. Make a comparison.
6. Briefly explain what the essay is responding to.
7. Allude to the public resonance of the essay.
8. Create a tone for the essay.

Test the approach: Will the introduction invite the reader into a new way of thinking?

STRATEGIES FOR CONCLUSIONS

1. Suggest or emphasize the public resonance.
2. State and explain the main idea.
3. Create a strong image.
4. Ask an important question.
5. Relate back to a point from the introduction.
6. Call the reader to thought or action.
7. Make a recommendation.
8. Suggest a consequence.

Test the approach: Will the conclusion reinforce a new way of thinking . . . or just repeat what the reader might have already considered?

ACTIVITIES

1. Read one essay in this book, and study its paragraphs. Note each paragraph's organization (deductive, inductive, turnabout) and function (transition, support). Do you think each paragraph is unified, developed, and coherent? Explain why or why not.

2. Revise one of your essays by writing out a main idea for each paragraph. Try moving the main idea to different places.

3. Read just the introductions of several essays in this book. How do they work? Do they fit into one of the strategies listed to the left, or do they use a different strategy? How does each introduction introduce the main idea and engage the reader?

4. Read just the conclusions of several essays. (Keep in mind that some may be more than one paragraph long.) How do they work? Do they leave the reader with something to ponder?

5. Analyze one introduction and one conclusion, either from an essay in this book or elsewhere. How did the introduction attempt to engage the reader? How did it introduce the topic? Was it successful? How did the conclusion emphasize the main point of the essay? Why was or wasn't it successful?

6. Rewrite your introduction with an eye towards getting into the essay more quickly. Cut anything that unnecessarily delays getting to main points or that takes away from the essay's forward momentum.

WRITING STYLE

Style is the way a writer treats his or her readers.

Style is a term that characterizes the words and phrases that a writer decides to use in communicating with readers. Many different styles can be considered good writing. But an effective style in one situation may not work as well in another (for example, writing a letter to a friend vs. writing a college essay; writing an initial response to a movie vs. writing a research paper; writing a thank-you note vs. writing a letter to the college newspaper). Consider Daniel Bruno's writing style in "Entitlement Education." He writes:

> In our competitive world, the sad truth is that even some of the very good students, though their college dreams were to be doctors and lawyers and pharmacists and engineers, will be waiting tables. (324)

In an e-mail to a friend—a less formal writing situation—Bruno might have written:

> Wake up! It's a dog-eat-dog world. Even a lot of good students won't get the job they're after.

Writing style is influenced by a variety of factors, including word choice, sentence structure, paragraph length, punctuation, figurative expressions, and writing purpose. For example, deciding to elevate one's vocabulary, use fewer commas, or make the reader laugh will affect a writer's style.

Problems with Style

Appropriate writing style helps a writer communicate with the reader. Inappropriate styles can interfere with the communication of ideas. For example, some writers stretching to sound educated or professional dress up simple ideas in unnecessarily complex or fancy language. This can make reading more difficult. Writing style should be focused on clearly expressing the ideas of the writer without drawing much attention to the writing style itself. Style that does not call attention to itself (but that instead focuses on the ideas being expressed) is usually the most effective. Consider the following passage from Daniel Bruno's essay "Entitlement Education."

> The problem, of course, is that the two students have entered college on different academic levels and the one on the higher level has graduated on an *even higher* level while the one on the lower level has remained pretty much the same. (323)

Bruno could have expressed the same idea in various ways, some of which might sound too elevated or too chatty to his audience, as the examples on the next page demonstrate.

Elevated

Upon careful study it appears that the problem, per se, is at the time of matriculation two collegians embarked upon higher education at dissimilar academic levels and the first such student ultimately graduated on a higher academic level of learning whereas the second such student continually resided upon the lower of the two academic levels.

Too Chatty

Well, the problem is two students go off to college and one is already better off school-wise than the other. And the better-off one graduates even better off, and the other one doesn't do so hot.

Not Thoughtful

Simply put, smart students learn a lot and dumb ones don't.

Wishy-Washy

It seems to me that perhaps the problem might be that two students could have entered college on different academic levels and, in my opinion, the one on the higher level might graduate on an even higher level while the one on the lower level might possibly not have learned as much.

Pig-Headed

Wake up! The problem is so simple I can't imagine why no one has done anything about it. Obviously, two students have entered college on different academic levels and the one on the higher level is bound to graduate on an even higher level. The one on the lower level gets what he deserves. Got it?

Formulaic

The problem is two students have entered college on different academic levels. The one on the higher level has graduated on an even higher level. The lower one has remained the same.

> # Writing style should not make a topic sound more complex than it actually is.

If the style of a college textbook or scholarly article sounds elevated, it could be that the subject matter is complex and requires a more technical vocabulary and complex sentence structure. Or it could be that the style is unnecessarily elevated.

Because language is shared and because our purpose in writing is to communicate information from one person to another, we can judge writing by the degree to which it achieves its purpose.

The Circle of Good Writing

The shared nature of language requires that a writer's style will fall within a certain area in most writing situations. We can call this area the Circle of Good Writing. Your writing need not be the same as your instructor's or anyone else's. In fact, it couldn't be exactly the same. But it should not vary significantly from the usual conventions that others—such as professors, employers, and clients—employ in their writing.

Circle of Good Writing

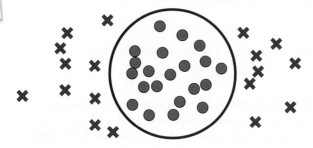

ACTIVITIES

1. Create or find three examples of different writing styles. Explain why each does or does not fall within the Circle of Good Writing. Explain in what situation each might or might not be appropriate.

2. Describe your own writing style. It may help to read through old essays, letters, e-mails, and so on. How does your writing style vary from one situation to another? How would you describe the writing style you use for college essays, and why do you use that style?

SENTENCE VITALITY

Vitality is liveliness. It is not a matter of right and wrong, correct and incorrect, but a matter of degree. Good writers persistently work at increasing the liveliness of their sentences. Whether sentences are short, long, or very long, they can often be livelier. Consider the following sentences. Which ones seem more alive—and why?

> The Gods, they say, give breath, and they take it away. But the same could be said—could it not?—of the humble comma. (Pico Iyer)

> Once he stamped so hard on my head that my neck was nearly broken. (Jane Goodall)

> Still, the city creeps closer, day by day. (Edward Abbey)

> Sadly, the gap between these two groups grows even wider. (Daniel Bruno)

> So here's what I don't understand: if profit is supreme, why doesn't a company like General Motors sell crack? (Michael Moore)

> I imagine that you are breathing the exhaust fumes of our disregard. (Simon Benlow)

> The menstrual cycle itself mirrors how consciousness becomes matter and how thought creates reality. (Christiane Northrup)

> Situated on a lake, the Sea World I visited featured a water show with ski jumps and corny skits. (Jayme Stayer)

Sentence vitality is not about checking grammar, creating over-dramatic phrases, or puffing up language. Instead, it involves a range of strategies for making sentences more focused, cleaner, and more concentrated.

1. RELY ON ACTIVE (NOT PASSIVE) SENTENCES

While both active and passive sentences are useful, active sentences tend to express ideas more directly and thus contribute to sentence vitality. In an active sentence, the grammatical subject does the action; in a passive sentence, the grammatical subject is acted upon. Consider how these two sentences both express the same idea:

> The farmer milked the cow.

> The cow was milked by the farmer.

> Vitality is the peculiarity distinguishing the living from the nonliving.

The first sentence is active because the grammatical subject—*the farmer*—is doing the action. The second sentence is passive because the grammatical subject—*the cow*—is being acted upon. To recognize passive sentences, look for the following: (1) the grammatical subject is being acted upon, (2) the verb requires a helping word (*was milked,* for example, instead of *milked*), (3) the noun doing the action is expressed in a prepositional phrase beginning with *by,* and (4) this *by* phrase could be eliminated from the sentence. Consider two more sentences (one active and one passive). Each could be used to express the same idea.

> The CEO made millions while employees lost their life savings.

> Millions were made by the CEO while their life savings was lost by the employees.

The first sentence consists of two clauses: (1) *The CEO* (subject) *made* (verb) and (2) *while* (subordinating conjunction) *employees* (subject) *lost* (verb). Both clauses are active because the grammatical subject is doing the action. The second sentence expresses the same idea but with a passive construction. The *by* phrases and the verb forms make the second sentence more wordy and cumbersome.

When to Use the Passive Voice   Both active and passive sentences are important in writing. If focusing on the cow, the passive construction—*The cow was milked by the farmer*—may be more appropriate than the active sentence that features the farmer. Similarly, the newspaper headline *Kennedy Shot* is passive, yet more appropriate than an active expression of the same idea: *Oswald Shoots.* And in certain situations, it may be appropriate to avoid placing blame (or seeking praise) by saying *Millions were made* or *The cow was milked.*

2. ELIMINATE WORDINESS

Early drafts tend to contain unnecessary words that slow the pace of the reading and distract the reader. Writers weed sentences of unnecessary words the way a gardener removes unwanted plants from a flower garden, thus featuring the flowers. Notice the following concise and lively sentences and the fabricated wordier versions a writer might find in a rough draft.

> <u>Concise:</u> Still, the city creeps closer, day by day. (Edward Abbey)
> <u>Wordy:</u> In the final analysis, the city is still creeping a little bit closer each and every day.

> <u>Concise:</u> Sadly, the gap between these two groups grows even wider. (Daniel Bruno)
> <u>Wordy:</u> It is sad that the gap between the first group of students and the second group of students continues to grow wider and wider.

Concise: So here's what I don't understand: if profit is supreme, why
doesn't a company like General Motors sell crack? (Michael Moore)
Wordy: I'm a little puzzled about something. If profit is really what is
supreme, why wouldn't General Motors decide to sell something like
crack instead of selling cars, trucks, SUVs, etc.?

3. AVOID UNNECESSARY EXPLETIVES

Expletives, phrases such as *there are* or *it is,* slow down sentences. They often take over as the main subject and verb of a sentence. They function like subjects and verbs—but contain no content. While expletives are sometimes helpful and even necessary, eliminating some expletives can add to sentence vitality. Consider the following two ways of expressing the same idea:

Idea expressed using an expletive:
There are laws that we can enact that will prevent companies from doing anything to hurt us.

Michael Moore's actual statement without the expletive:
We can enact laws to prevent companies from doing anything to hurt us.

In the first sentence above, the expletive construction seems unnecessary and requires the sentence to be wordy. The writer could (1) simply eliminate the expletive, (2) eliminate the word *that,* and then (3) make a few adjustments to the rest of the sentence. The result is that the subject *(we)* and the verb *(can enact)* have been moved to the front of the sentence, and a few unhelpful words have been deleted. Similar revision could be done in the following sentence:

It was Joe who paid for the tickets.

Eliminating the expletive *(it was)* allows the writer to eliminate the relative pronoun *who* and create a more concise sentence:

Joe paid for the tickets.

Not all expletives are so easy to avoid, and not all expletives should be avoided. In many cases, instead of rewriting a single sentence, the writer will be able to combine several sentences, thus being even more concise.

4. EXPLORE THE STRATEGIES IN THE VITALITY SECTIONS IN CHAPTERS 1-12

Chapter 1

- Combine Sentences
- Repeat Structures
- Intensify Verbs

Chapter 2

- Avoid *Be* Verbs When Possible
- Turn Clauses to Phrases
- Turn Phrases to Words

Chapter 3

- Experiment with Length
- Experiment with Brevity
- Change Out Vague Nouns

Chapter 4

- Avoid Clichés
- Avoid Stilted Language

Chapter 5

- Avoid Blueprinting
- Avoid Vague Pronouns

Chapter 6

- Avoid Unnecessary Attention to *I*
- Avoid Unnecessary Attention to *You*
- Vitalize with Verbs

Chapter 7

- Avoid Over-Embedding
- Clean Up Attributive Phrases
- Try Absolutes!

Chapter 8

- Avoid Unnecessary Interruption
- Repeat Clause or Phrase Patterns
- Condense Wordy Phrases

Chapter 9

- Avoid Strings of Phrases
- Intensify with a Series

Chapter 10

- Avoid the Obvious Content
- Get Rid of Obvious Padding
- Call a Fool a Fool

Chapter 11

- Break Apart Noun Clusters
- Change Nouns to Verbs
- Avoid Unnecessary Modifiers

Chapter 12

- Try the Stylistic Fragment
- Deliberately Break Some Other Rule
- Try Writing Hard and Fast

COHERENCE AND CONCISENESS

Sentences, paragraphs, and essays (as well as letters, reports, and other writing) should be coherent and concise. **Coherence** involves connecting ideas in a systematic and logical way. If a piece of writing is coherent, it is logically or aesthetically arranged to help make its ideas clear and understandable. **Conciseness** involves expressing an idea without unnecessary words, sentences, or paragraphs. Concise writing is free of ornamentation and superfluous details. It makes its point economically, with little waste. A variety of concerns, ranging from purpose in writing to in-text documentation, contribute to coherence and conciseness. Notice how the following strategies combine to create coherence and conciseness in the sample essay "Entitlement Education" (page 762):

- A title that expresses the focus of the essay
- Purposeful writing
- A purposeful introduction that moves steadily toward a main point
- Accurate word choice
- Sentence vitality (eliminating expletives, wordiness, etc.)
- Explicit statements (including statements of main ideas and statements of support)
- Summary of appropriate information
- Consistent verb tense
- Conventional punctuation (commas, colons, quotation marks, etc.)
- Transitional words, expressions, sentences, and paragraphs
- Pronouns
- Pronoun/antecedent agreement
- Subject/verb agreement
- Parallelism
- Parenthetical information
- Subordination/coordination
- Relevant use of sources
- Integration of borrowed material
- In-text documentation and a corresponding Works Cited page

Daniel Bruno
Composition I
Dr. Fritz Strisky
November 5, 2005

Title provides coherence by providing the reader with an overall focus.

Entitlement Education

In his book <u>Generation X Goes to College</u>, Peter Sacks describes, among other things, the sense of entitlement that some students in today's consumerist culture have toward a college education. One entire chapter explores this issue alone, providing examples of this "sense" and looking into its "humble beginnings." Sacks shows how consumerism has invaded education, leading some students to expect good grades for little effort. But he fails, it seems, to emphasize enough a most harmful effect of this sense of entitlement. The biggest problem, as I see it, is that although students are able to graduate from high school (and even some colleges) with minimal effort, those students may find themselves cheated in the long run.

Clear reference to Sacks's book provides coherence—the rest of the essay is about this.

Consistent verb tense—present—provides coherence.

How might they be cheated? One might argue that students get cheated because entitlement doesn't go on forever. At some point it stops. For example, a college graduate with a marketing degree, but especially weak thinking or writing skills, may find himself disadvantaged on the job. It is not that his boss puts her foot down; instead, the job does. Our student finds himself not well prepared for it. He gets cheated because he is disadvantaged at his job—a job that he paid money to learn how to do. Of course the point isn't about marketing majors. The same is true of students in any field. (Marketing is just what came to mind.)

Transitional expressions such as "for example" provide coherence by clarifying the relationship between ideas.

One might also claim that students will be cheated because their lives will somehow *be less*. This argument claims that a person's intelligence contributes to his quality of life. Here we must remember that "intelligence" is not just "knowledge." Instead, it is being able to use knowledge, to make connections and figure things out, to see causes and solve problems. A person may have much knowledge—that is, he may have accumulated a lot of facts—but not have much intelligence . . . or so the argument goes. As one goes from first grade to twelfth, from twelfth grade to college, and from freshman to senior, education shifts focus from mere accumulation of information (knowledge) to application of information (intelligence). And while we may accumulate more knowledge as a senior in college than we did as a senior in high school, the focus in college has (or should have) shifted from mere knowledge to intelligence—that is, to the ability to make good use of one's knowledge.

"Also" indicates a relationship between this claim and the previous one.

Pronouns such as "this" provide coherence by connecting ideas.

Parallelism provides coherence (to use; to make; to see OR may have much knowledge; but not have much intelligence).

Other standard arguments claim other ways students might be cheated. For example, we might feel sorry for someone who doesn't get a joke—or a reference. Allusions to literature, history, philosophy and so on allow us to say much in few words. But does the listener understand? If a person is unaware of common references—the Battle of the Bulge, Normandy, Existentialism, T. S. Eliot, World War I, Rasputin, John the Baptist, Gandhi, apartheid, Jonas Salk, Johnny Appleseed, Lewis and Clark, the Trail of Tears,

"Other," "for example," "but," "of course," and "and" show the relationship between ideas.

slavery, the Donner Party, and so on—he misses out on conversations, on meaning, on connecting with his fellow inmates. Of course, here one might counter that you don't need to know all of these things. And, I agree, you don't. People tend to hang out with people who have similar interests and tastes.

5   One more argument claims that because we live in a democracy, we must be well-educated. Since all the citizens are responsible for the government, our forefathers promoted public education so that all citizens—not just the wealthy and elite—would know how to read and write. Thomas Jefferson wrote,

> I know no safe depository of the ultimate powers of society but the people them-selves; and if we think them not enlightened enough to exercise their control with a wholesome discretion, the remedy is not to take it from them, but to inform their discretion by education. This is the true corrective of abuses of constitutional power. (278)

In what ways can educated citizens correct abuses in a democracy? A person's way of life, his purchases and activities—not just a person's vote or protest march—is part of the responsibility. Thus, consumers and neighbors and co-workers and so on should behave responsibly and think intelligently. It is our responsibility as citizens of a democracy.

True enough, these are all ways that students who are allowed to just slide by end up getting cheated. But another way (and one less talked about) strikes me as being far more offensive. This reason hinges on the fact that many students are not just sliding by. In Generation X Goes to College, Peter Sacks illustrates that all of today's college students cannot just be thrown in the same big barrel. In describing the modern/post-modern clash in education, he spends the majority of his time talking about those students who are underprepared, who lack the basic study skills required in academic work, and who demonstrate little real commitment to their own education. Yet, he does not discuss this problem in isolation. He also mentions another type of student. For example, he introduces the reader to Marissa and Carol: "As very good students, [their views] were virtually excluded by The College in order to accommodate the whiners and complain-ers" (61). And he says they "suffered not only educationally" (63). In addition to dis-cussing specific good students, an entire chapter presents survey results about students' attitudes toward education. While he makes claims such as "nearly a quarter of the students . . . harbored a disproportionate sense of entitlement," this very statement tells the reader that a full three-quarters (that is, three out of four) students *do not* "harbor a disproportionate sense of entitlement" (54–59). He wraps up the book by focusing on another student, Andie, who he describes as "a good student, constantly picking [his] brain for information and feedback on her work" (186–87). His final paragraph, before the Epilogue, says, "Let's create a system that encourages people like Andie at least as much as the ones who don't give a damn" (187). Thus, Sacks shows that today's students are a more diverse group—in skill level, background, and attitude toward education—than has ever before been gathered together in the college classroom.

Items in a series (on con-versations, on meaning, on connecting) expressed in parallel grammatical form contribute to coherence.

Explicit statements of main ideas, followed with sup-port for that idea, con-tribute to coherence.

Smoothly integrating appropriate outside infor-mation and documenting correctly contribute to coherence.

The quoted material is dis-cussed.

This entire paragraph pro-vides coherence between two sections by taking the reader from the previous ideas to "another way."

Main ideas at the beginning of paragraphs provide coherence by letting the reader know the reason for the information that follows.

A properly used colon—to introduce a quote with words that could be punc-tuated as a sentence— pro-vides coherence. The reader knows immediately the relationship of the words on the left and right of the colon. Quotation marks pro-vide coherence by making clear that the words inside them are from a source.

In-text documentation that corresponds to a Works Cited page provides coher-ence by being inobtrusive while at the same time pro-viding important informa-tion.

Works Cited

"Almanac." <u>The Chronicle of Higher Education</u>. 18 Oct. 2000. <http://chronicle.com/free/almanac/2000/almanac.htm>.

Jefferson, Thomas. <u>The Writings of Thomas Jefferson</u>. Ed. Andrew Adgate Lipscomb and Albert Ellery Bergh. Vol. 15. Washington, DC: Thomas Jefferson Memorial Assn., 1903-04.

Sacks, Peter. <u>Generation X Goes to College</u>. Open Court: Chicago, 1996.

ACTIVITIES

1. Check your own essay for coherence and conciseness by referring to the strategies in Bruno's essay. For example, how does the title help focus the reader on the main idea, or how does your purpose in writing help to make the essay coherent and concise?

2. Weed your writing of unnecessary words. Then, if your essay fails to meet a length requirement for the assignment, return to the appropriate invention section in the text and explore your topic further, developing interesting ideas worth discussing in your essay.

3. Examine the table of contents of this book. What strategies do authors seem to use when titling their essays? Which titles are most intriguing, and why? Which ones do you want to read based on just the title? Describe how a few successful titles help to focus the reader on the writer's purpose in writing.

COMPLETE SENTENCES

Writers and readers share ideas about what constitutes a sentence or a part of a sentence. In academic and professional written English, sentences generally contain at least one independent clause (a group of related words with a subject and verb). Sometimes they contain more than one independent clause. Consider the following sentence basics:

- A group of words lacking an independent clause is a **sentence fragment.**
- A group of words made up of two independent clauses not connected by either a coordinating conjunction *(and, or, nor, for, yet, but, so)* or a semicolon is a **run-on sentence.**
- There are two kinds of run-on sentences: a **fused sentence** and a **comma splice.**

Sentence Fragment

A sentence fragment, since it contains no independent clause, can be a single word, a phrase, a dependent clause, or any combination of the three *without an independent clause.* Writers sometimes use fragments purposely, for effect. Such as here. This strategy is acceptable and can be effective if used sparingly, although fragments should not creep into one's writing by accident.

Phrases are not complete sentences.

> Falling off his horse and getting right back on it.
>
> The neighbor's new Siamese kitten, Lorenzo.

Dependent clauses are not complete sentences.

> When Joe passed his algebra test.
>
> As long as you and Susie are going to the game.

Combinations of phrases and dependent clauses are not complete sentences.

> Running to catch the bus so I won't be late for class.
>
> George Washington who was the first president of the United States and general of the Continental Army.

Run-On Sentence

In a run-on sentence, the two independent clauses are "run together," either with a comma (a comma splice) or with no punctuation at all (a fused sentence).

Comma splice

I went home, she stayed at the party.

I am tired of reading, I am going to bed now.

Joe flew the 767, he had never landed a plane before.

There is a mouse in the closet, we need a better mousetrap.

Fused sentence

I went home she stayed at the party.

I am tired of reading I am going to bed now.

Joe flew the 767 he had never landed a plane before.

There is a mouse in the closet we need a better mousetrap.

HOW TO IDENTIFY SENTENCE FRAGMENTS AND RUN-ON SENTENCES

To identify sentence fragments and run-on sentences in your writing, you must take a grammatical approach. Vague, non-grammatical approaches can be unhelpful. For example, fragments are not just incomplete thoughts. Run-on sentences are not just long sentences or sentences with a lot of ideas in them. And comma splices are not just the misuse of a comma. For example, all sentences are somewhat incomplete when it comes to meaning. *He was there* doesn't say who he is or where he is. Thus, its meaning is not complete, even though it is a grammatically complete sentence. *I went she stayed* is a run-on sentence even though it is short and contains only a few ideas. (And a much longer sentence—even one hundred words—can be a complete sentence, not a run-on sentence.) *I, went, and, she, stayed* is not a comma splice, even though commas are misused in the sentence. Feeling like a sentence might be a fragment or run-on is a starting place, but to be certain, you must take the following grammatical approach to the problem:

1. Identify the independent clauses in your sentence.
   - If there are no independent clauses, the sentence is a fragment.
   - If there is only one independent clause, the sentence is a complete sentence.
   - If there are two or more independent clauses, go to step 2.

2. If you found two or more independent clauses, how are they connected?
   - If with a coordinating conjunction (*and, or, nor, for, yet, but, so*), you have a complete sentence.

A sentence is not a complete thought.

- If with a semicolon, you have a complete sentence.
- If with a comma, you have a comma splice.
- If with no punctuation, you have a fused sentence.

3. If you have a fragment, comma splice, or a fused sentence, you may revise your sentence in several ways.

HOW TO REVISE FRAGMENTS

Some writers use fragments sparingly to achieve a desired effect. But fragments should not occur by accident. Most sentence fragments should be identified and revised to read as complete sentences. While this can be done in various ways, the objective is always to either (1) attach the fragment to an independent clause, (2) add an independent clause to the fragment, or (3) restructure the sentence to create an independent clause.

Revising fragments that are phrases

(A phrase is a group of related words without a subject and a verb.)

Falling off his horse and getting right back on it.

a fragment because it is a phrase and has no independent clause

Joe fell off his horse and got right back on it.

a complete sentence because an independent clause—*Joe* (subject) *fell* and *got* (verb)— has been added

Falling off his horse and getting right back on it, Joe joined the posse and captured the bandits.

a complete sentence because the phrase has been connected to an independent clause—*Joe* (subject) *joined* and *captured* (verb)

Revising fragments that are dependent clauses

(A dependent clause is a clause preceded by a subordinating conjunction.)

When Joe passed his algebra test.

a fragment because it is a dependent clause and has no independent clause

Joe passed his algebra test.

a complete sentence because the subordinating conjunction—*when*—has been eliminated, thus creating an independent clause

When Joe passed his algebra test, he let out a sigh of relief.

a complete sentence because the dependent clause has been attached to an independent clause

AGREEMENT

Agreement—the grammatical relationship between a subject and a verb or between a pronoun and its antecedent—contributes to coherence, or the way a piece of writing flows smoothly from one idea to another. For example, a writer will decide to write in a particular tense—such as past or present—and then stick to that tense until there is a good reason to change. Unnecessary shifts in tense can be confusing and distracting. In the sentence below, the verbs do not agree in tense. The sentence shifts from present tense *(contributes)* to past tense *(was)*. The shift is unnecessary and distracting:

> One thing that contributes to coherence—or the way a piece of writing flows smoothly from one idea to another—was agreement.

Verb Tense Agreement

A piece of writing generally has one controlling tense—in other words, most of the verb tenses are the same. However, verb tense may shift to indicate a change in time:

> Liz **left** the football game early and **went** to a movie. She **is** not a big fan of the game. I **doubt** that she **will** ever **enjoy** football.

The first sentence above uses past-tense verbs (*left* and *went*). But the follow-up sentence is written in present tense because Liz still *is* not a fan of the game. The third sentence uses a present tense verb *(doubt)* and a future tense verb *(will enjoy)*. These shifts in tense accurately express the time relationship among several ideas; thus, there is a good reason to change tense. Some shifts, however, are less purposeful and are confusing or distracting:

> Liz **left** the football game early and **goes** to a movie.

This shift is unnecessary. It is hard to imagine why the writer shifts from past tense *(left)* to present tense *(goes)*. While the meaning still seems clear, the shift is distracting. If further unnecessary shifts were to occur or if the passage were to deal with a more complex concept, the reader would eventually become confused.

Unnecessary tense shifts sometimes occur when the writer changes unexpectedly to the present tense after beginning in the past tense. This often occurs when narrating. Consider the following example:

> When I first **got** off the plane in Belgrade, I **noticed** how cool and crisp the air felt. I **see** the mountains in the distance and **want** to drive out to them and begin climbing.

The verb *see* in the second sentence marks an unnecessary shift from past tense to present. Because the verb tense is not consistent and because the change does not express an actual change in time, the shift is likely to distract the reader.

Shifts in Person

The passage below shifts not only from past tense to present, but also from first person to second—from *I* to *you*. An unnecessary shift in person may distract or confuse the reader.

> When **I** first got off the plane in Belgrade, **I** noticed how cool and crisp the air felt. **You** see the mountains in the distance and want to drive out to them and begin climbing.

Pronouns can be first, second, or third person. First-person pronouns refer to the person speaking *(I, me, mine; we, our, ours)*; second-person pronouns refer to the person being spoken to *(you, your, yours)*; and third-person pronouns refer to the person or thing being talked about *(he, him, his; she, her, hers; it, its; they, them, theirs)*. In the example above, the writer refers to himself in the first person *(I)*, then shifts unnecessarily to the second person *(you)*. The passage below is consistent in tense (past) and person (first).

> When **I** first **got** off the plane in Belgrade, **I noticed** how cool and crisp the air felt. **I saw** the mountains in the distance and **wanted** to drive out to them and begin climbing.

Pronoun/Antecedent Agreement

Pronouns take the place of (or refer back to) nouns; the nouns they replace (or refer back to) are called their antecedents. For example, in the sentence below, *her* takes the place of *the little girl*—that is, it allows the writer to not repeat *the little girl*. Since *girl* is (1) singular, (2) feminine, and (3) in the third person, so is the pronoun that replaces it.

> The little **girl** enjoyed **her** ride on the giant Ferris wheel.

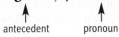

Pronoun/antecedent agreement can be tricky in sentences more complex than the one above. When several sentences work together to form a paragraph or several paragraphs, more vigilance is required to make sure pronouns and antecedents agree. In the following example, Daniel Bruno consistently uses the third-person plural pronoun *they* because the passage begins with the plural noun *students:*

> Students would do well to look around **them,** at the room full of fellow classmates. **They** should imagine that many of those students will be graduating one day. And **they** should imagine the students in the classroom next door and across the hall and in all the other buildings on campus. **They** will be graduating, too. (323)

Third-person singular Pronouns and antecedents require special attention when it comes to the third-person singular. In the example below, Bruno decides to use the feminine pronoun *she* to refer to both men and women.

> The injustice, then, has been done to the students (as Sacks says, the students are the victims). **While the student** has happily skipped (or unhappily slogged) along through sixteen years of formal education, **she** is allowed, if **she** wants, to come away with very little in terms of education. **She** is allowed, unfortunately, to escape practically unscathed by learning. (323)

The use of a feminine pronoun to refer to both men and women might be considered unusual. In the past, *he* was commonly used this way. Although the singular pronoun (*he* or *she*) may be correct in number (matching the antecedent), it does not accurately represent the reality beyond grammar—the real men and women who are students. (For more discussion, see Gender Bias and Sensitivity in Language, page 776.) Generally, third-person singular situations such as this one provide the writer with a difficult decision. Writers can avoid the pronoun problem by changing singular antecedents (such as *student*) to the plural (*students*) and using *they* as the pronoun.

Subject/Verb Agreement

In addition to indicating tense (past, present, future), verbs indicate number—they can be singular or plural. Nouns, too, indicate number (*dog* is singular; *dogs* is plural). Singular nouns take singular verbs; and plural nouns take plural verbs.

> My **sister takes** the train to work.
> My **sisters take** the train to work.

A singular noun *(sister)* with a plural verb *(take)* conveys the same meaning as when the subject and verb agree. But in academic and professional written English, subjects and verbs agree in number. Consider the following questions:

- How important is it that subjects and verbs agree?
- In what situations would you consider *My sister take the train to work* to be acceptable? Unacceptable?
- How might an employer, colleague, classmate, teacher, English teacher, client, boyfriend, or girlfriend react to sentences in which subjects and verbs do not agree?
- How might an English teacher react in different situations, such as in the classroom, at the supermarket, at home?

OTHER SUBJECT/VERB AGREEMENT ISSUES

Phrases or clauses that act as subjects take singular verbs.

Having a kennel full of hungry puppies and no dog food is Marcia's biggest fear.

In academic and professional written English, collective nouns take singular verbs.

The government is taxing the citizens more now than in previous years.

(Other collective nouns to look for include *team, class, congress, orchestra,* and *administration.*)

Compound subjects joined by *and* take a plural verb; some other compound subjects take plural or singular verbs, depending upon the meaning.

Bob and Sue share a common interest in painting. (*share* is plural—two people *share*)

Bob shares a common interest with Sue. (*shares* is singular—one person *shares*)

Either Bob or Sue shares a common interest with Sally. (*shares* is singular—one or the other *shares*)

Neither Bob nor Sue shares a common interest with Sally. (*shares* is singular—not one or the other *shares*)

Indefinite pronouns, such as *everyone, everybody, all,* and *anybody,* usually take a singular verb and singular pronoun.

Everyone in our family goes to the annual ice cream social at the volunteer fire department.

ACTIVITIES

1. Write a paragraph that changes verb tense to indicate different times. What is the controlling tense of your paragraph? Did you use any tenses besides simple past, present, and future? That is, did you use a perfect or progressive tense?

2. Write a paragraph with a controlling tense. Then try to distract and confuse the reader by shifting verb tenses unnecessarily.

3. Before turning in your next essay, check your pronoun/antecedent agreement carefully. First, go through what you have written and circle every *they, their,* and *them.* Then identify the word to which the pronoun refers (draw a line from the circled word to the word it replaces). Since *they, their,* and *them* are plural, the antecedent must also be plural. If it is not, revise the sentence accordingly.

PARALLELISM

Parallelism (like agreement) contributes to the coherence of a piece of writing, or to how it flows. Parallel structure means using the same grammatical form (noun, verb, participial phrase, etc.) to help indicate that ideas are related. In the following, the first sentence is parallel; the second is not:

> Herbert **ate** a big dinner, **sat down** in his favorite chair, and **put on** his slippers.
>
> We see that Herbert did three things. Each is expressed by the same grammatical form—a verb phrase.

> Herbert **ate** a big dinner, **sat down** in his favorite chair, and **putting on** his slippers.
>
> Here, the third thing, *putting on his slippers,* is expressed in a different grammatical form—a participial phrase instead of a verb.

Parallel items are related in two ways:
1. grammatical form
2. meaning

COORDINATING CONJUNCTIONS

One way to ensure better parallelism is to identify all coordinating conjunctions *(and, or, nor, for, yet, but, so)* and then to make sure the sentence parts they connect are grammatically equal. For example, since *and* connects parallel (or coordinate) sentence parts, the words, phrases, or clauses connected by *and* should take the same grammatical form. This helps the reader to pick up on the relationship between the ideas more easily.

> Bob <u>went</u> fishing **and** <u>fell</u> into the lake.
>
> *And* connects two verbs—*went* and *fell.*

> The <u>man</u> in the green hat **and** the <u>woman</u> with the umbrella are old friends.
>
> *And* connects two nouns—*man* and *woman.*

> I went <u>to the market</u> **and** <u>to the bookstore</u> before it rained.
>
> *And* connects two prepositional phrases—*to the market* and *to the bookstore.*

> <u>The doctor was two hours behind schedule</u>, **and** <u>all the patients had to wait</u>.
>
> *And* connects two independent clauses—*The doctor was . . .* and *all the patients had. . . .*

<u>It was raining</u>, **yet** <u>everyone had fun</u>.

Yet connects two independent clauses—*It was raining* and *everyone had fun.*

We finished cleaning <u>the garage</u>, **but** not <u>the basement</u>.

But connects two nouns—*the garage* and *the basement.*

SEMICOLONS

Semicolons express a coordinate relationship, just as coordinating conjunctions do. The sentence parts connected by a semicolon should be grammatically equal because that's what a semicolon does: It connects sentence parts that are grammatically equal. In the sentence below, the semicolons connect independent clauses: (1) *Engineers will build defective bridges;* (2) *doctors will botch their operations;* (3) *marketers will have no clue how to market.*

> For example, one might argue that students find themselves cheated because upon graduation they will not be prepared to do their jobs: Engineers will build defective bridges**;** doctors will botch their operations**;** and marketers will have no clue how to market.

COMPARISONS/CONTRASTS

The parallel grammatical structure of comparison/contrast helps the reader to more easily notice the relationship between the ideas. A comparison/contrast relationship is indicated through parallelism: *the one on the higher level* and *the one on the lower level.*

> The problem, of course, is that the two students have entered college on different academic levels and **the one on the higher level** <u>has graduated on an *even higher* level</u> while **the one on the lower level** <u>has remained pretty much the same</u>. (323)

LISTS

A grocery list provides a good example of how meaning and grammatical form work together. When meaning is parallel or equal (all things we can pick up at a grocery store) then form tends also to be parallel or equal (all nouns).

> eggs, cheese, butter, bagels, cookies, sauce, milk, bread, beans, soap, light bulbs

Notice that the listed items below are all nouns and are expressed in parallel terms:

> We bought eggs, cheese, butter, and milk.

The following items in the list are verb phrases:

> They have at least three options: (1) take advantage of the easy system and learn a little along the way; (2) motivate themselves, working harder (and learning more) than the system requires them to; and (3) attend a more academically rigorous school (of course, such schools still exist, though they are likely to cost more to attend). (322)

HEADINGS

Notice the parallel structure of the headings in Paul Roberts's essay, "How to Say Nothing in 500 Words." They are all imperative statements. But headings need not be imperative statements. Any grammatical form can be used.

Headings from "How to Say Nothing in 500 Words" are imperative statements.

> Avoid the Obvious Content
> Take the Less Usual Side
> Slip Out of Abstraction
> Get Rid of Obvious Padding

ACTIVITIES

1. Before turning in an essay, check for parallel structure.

   a. Identify all coordinating conjunctions (*and, or, nor, for, yet, but, so*) and make sure that the words or group of words they connect are the same grammatical form. This includes items in a series, such as *bread, cheese, butter, and milk*. (Note: The word *for* most often functions as a prepositional phrase and not a coordinating conjunction.)

   b. Find semicolons, and make sure that the words or group of words they connect have the same grammatical form.

2. Exchange essays with a classmate and check for parallel structure.

WORD CHOICE

The right word will be accurate and appropriate for the audience. To choose the right word, writers consider their purpose in writing, the reader, and the overall writing situation.

Accurate

Accuracy in word choice begins with understanding language as something that is shared. For example, people generally agree on what a cat is, and on what to call it. Thus, the word *cat* accurately expresses the idea *cat* (which corresponds to the material reality of a cat). This simple example illustrates how we share language. What I call a cat, you, too, call a cat. And we not only share the word *cat*—we also share the concept *cat*. Other, more abstract concepts—such as *patriotism, honesty, love, service,* and so on—can vary more in meaning from one person to another. As humans, we share not only words but categories of thoughts. We group various animals into *cats, dogs, rabbits,* or various people into *holy, heathen, pagan,* or *successful, struggling, washed up.* When we refer to a category of thought *(cat, love, rest, white, struggling)*, we try to choose a word that will accurately express our thought to others—and thus allow us to be heard by them.

When choosing words, consider the following questions:

- Am I using this word in the way that it is usually understood?
- If I am using this word in an unusual sense, will my reader understand it? Should I define the word and/or illustrate it with an example?
- Could I replace this word with one that more accurately expresses my meaning?
- Have I used unusual words in an attempt to impress my reader with my vocabulary? If so, should I replace these words with plain, straightforward language?
- Am I comfortable with my word choice? How does it make me sound?

Appropriate

If writers are not attentive to their readers, the language can be accurate but not appropriate. For example, word choice might be too casual or too formal for a particular writing situation; it might be gender-biased, overly technical, insensitive, or archaic. Writers determine whether or not words are appropriate by sizing up each writing situation and considering how their word choice is likely to influence the reader. (See the Writer's Voice sections in Chapters 1–12 as you develop your writing.)

> The difference between the almost right word & the right word is really a large matter—it's the difference between the lightning bug and the lightning.
>
> —Mark Twain

Imagine the Reader
Imagine how your reader is likely to understand a particular term.

Imagine the Reader Imagining You
When you write, you come across to the reader in a certain way. Ask yourself: How do I want to sound to my reader?

Level of Formality Formality in word choice varies, depending upon the writing situation. An e-mail to a friend would probably be casual, a scientific report formal. As Chapter 3 explains, the expected level of formality varies in different essay writing situations. For more information about level of formality, refer to the discussion on pages 134–135.

- Slang can be used effectively in an essay; but slang used indiscriminately often indicates a lack of serious thought or a lack of sensitivity for the reader.

- Archaic (old and outdated) language strikes some modern readers as insincere, and thus should be used cautiously, if at all.

- Flowery writing draws attention to itself, not to the ideas being expressed. This type of writing can make for slow and difficult reading.

Gender Bias and Sensitivity in Language Writers must be aware of the consequences of gender-biased language. A job ad that states "the candidate must own his own tools" appears to be excluding women candidates. Thus, third-person singular pronouns (such as *he, she, he/she, s/he,* etc.) should be chosen carefully. Words once common, such as *congressman, policeman, chairman,* have been replaced with gender-neutral terms, such as *representative, police officer, chair.* Nurses are not assumed to be women, and CEOs are not assumed to be men. Showing awareness and sensitivity through one's choice of words invites the reader to listen—whereas showing insensitivity gives the reader a reason for tuning out. Also see Third-Person Singular (page 770).

Jargon The technical language of a field (jargon) must be used carefully with an audience that is not expert in that field. Technical language should be replaced with more common terms or defined. Experts use jargon to talk shop, but non-experts do not share the same language. Some readers will become suspicious of technical vocabulary, wondering why the writer cannot explain the idea more simply and directly. Using technical jargon is a matter of audience awareness. Will your audience understand the jargon or not? Good communicators are able to explain complex ideas in plain language.

General and Specific Language When choosing the right word, the writer must decide upon the appropriate level of abstraction. Some words are specific, or concrete, while other words are general, or abstract—that is, they express general qualities but do not provide specific detail about those qualities.

Every time a writer moves to a more specific term, possibilities of meaning are eliminated. For example, *farm animals* includes cows, pigs, mules, goats, sheep, ducks, chickens, and geese. But *fowl* eliminates cows, pigs, mules, and goats. *Fowl* can mean ducks, chickens, or geese—but *rooster* eliminates ducks and geese. Jim, our rooster, is specific. He is one particular rooster—though we can refer to "Jim" either *generally* over the course of his life or more *specifically,* such as "Jim when he was a chick," "Jim the day we got him," or "Jim the day he died."

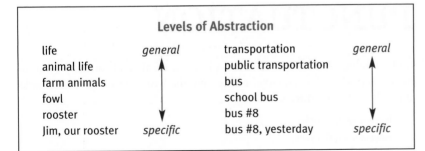

Writers must consider what level of abstraction to use. When we refer to examples and statistics and colors, we are being specific. But specifics are not always desirable; the reader can get bogged down in too much detail or sidetracked by irrelevant detail. A more specific word choice can be more accurate, but at times you will want to speak more generally. It is good to keep in mind two tips about using abstraction:

- Move back and forth between general and specific information
- Consider replacing general language with more specific language

Notice how the following paragraph from Pico Iyer's "In Praise of the Humble Comma" provides the reader with an appropriate balance of general and specific information.

> Punctuation thus becomes the signature of cultures. The hot-blooded Spaniard seems to be revealed in the passion and urgency of his doubled exclamation points and question marks ("¡Caramba! ¿Quién sabe?"), while the impassive Chinese traditionally added to his so-called inscrutability by omitting all directions from his ideograms. The anarchy and commotion of the sixties were given voice in the exploding exclamation marks, riotous capital letters, and Day-Glo italics of Tom Wolfe's spray-paint prose; and in Communist societies, where the State is absolute, the dignity—and divinity—of capital letters is reserved for Ministries, Subcommittees, and Secretariats. (146–147)

This paragraph states a general idea first, and then develops that idea with specific information. Iyer supports his general claim that "punctuation thus becomes the signature of cultures" by providing specific examples (Spanish and Chinese punctuation, Tom Wolfe's "spray-paint prose," and capitalization in Communist societies). Notice how other writers throughout this text move back and forth from general ideas to specific support.

ACTIVITIES

1. Read through some of your own writing, and identify words that may be inaccurate. How might a different word choice allow the reader a better chance of understanding what you meant?

2. Read through some of your own writing, and identify words that may be accurate yet inappropriate. Explain why the word choice might be inappropriate and how a different word choice might be better.

3. Take one paragraph from your own writing, and rewrite it two different ways: (1) using more formal diction and (2) using less formal diction. Do not make your changes too drastic—instead, experiment with fine adjustments in your writer's voice.

4. Find three paragraphs in this book that include both general and specific information. How many levels of abstraction can you identify? How does the writer move from one level to another?

5. Study one essay in this book to see how it presents general and abstract information. Consider highlighting general statements with one color and specific information with another color. Describe how the writer moves back and forth throughout the essay from general to specific.

PUNCTUATION

Understanding punctuation allows you to more clearly and concisely communicate your ideas. For example, notice how the basic end punctuation marks affect the following three sentences:

> Have a seat, George.
>
> Have a seat, George!
>
> Have a seat, George?

Because of punctuation, each sentence speaks to you differently. The same point could be illustrated by looking at how commas, dashes, and parentheses can be used to set off a sentence part.

> Notice how, because of punctuation, each sentence speaks to you differently.
>
> Notice how—because of punctuation—each sentence speaks to you differently.
>
> Notice how (because of punctuation) each sentence speaks to you differently.

Each of these sentences speaks to you differently, perhaps with a very slight difference, because of their punctuation. Setting off a sentence part with dashes (—) means something different than setting off a sentence part with parentheses ( ). Just as knowing what words mean (or what words suggest) allows you to communicate with others more effectively, knowing what different forms of punctuation mean (or suggest) does the same. Many readers know that when a writer places ideas within dashes, he or she means to emphasize those ideas and that ideas placed within parentheses are thought to be less important. Understanding these subtleties, which can be learned through reading about punctuation rules as well as by being attentive to how others punctuate, can help you as both a writer and a reader.

Commas

Commas separate certain parts of a sentence, and by doing so help to indicate the relationship between the parts of a sentence.

> While I was talking on the phone, I was watering my plants.

The comma above separates the two main parts of the sentence: *While I was talking on the phone* (a dependent clause) and *I was watering my plants* (an independent clause).

> Mike Easler, left-handed power hitter for the Pirates, slugged one out of the park.

The two commas in this example, like bookends, stand at the beginning and ending of a sentence part *(a left-handed power hitter for the Pirates)*. That sentence part interrupts the main part of the sentence *(Mike Easler slugged one out of the park)*. The interrupting part, an appositive, restates the noun that it follows (Mike Easler = left-handed power hitter for the Pirates). Commas separate ideas for the reader, who quickly makes sense of the relationship.

Quick Guide to Commas

1. Commas come after introductory clauses or phrases:

   After the party at Jake's house, we sang Calypso songs for days.

   Although they were tired from hunting, the hounds chased the children around the backyard.

2. Commas are generally used to separate items in a series:

   Alice gave Ralph a necktie, a bottle of cologne, and some chocolates.

   We ate good food, drank some tasty apple cider, and sang songs around the campfire.

   The Big Reds were moving the ball down the field, scoring touchdowns, and taking all the fun out of the game for the Spartans.

3. Commas are generally used between coordinate modifiers:

   Suzette is a lovely, intelligent girl.

   Some large, purple birds swooped down from above.

4. Commas are generally used to set off an interrupting element:

   The rest of our group, for example, is going home tomorrow.

   The parking on campus, though it doesn't bother me, has become a hot topic.

   Ella Fitzgerald, the famous jazz singer, was born in Newport News, Virginia.

5. Commas are also used in dates, addresses, place names, and long numbers:

   We drove through Whitley City, Kentucky, on August 16, 1972.

   John's truck has 124,618 miles on it.

   Please mail my refund to 35 Flarton Place, Burton, Maine 00178.

6. Commas are also used when a quotation follows a speaking verb:

   She said, "Are you coming?"

   After it rained for three days straight, Mrs. Merriweather asked, "Who wants to mop up all this water?"

Commas are often used in the following ways:

Before independent (or main) clauses

Notice the comma after
the Introductory clause

Whenever an introductory phrase, word, or clause begins a sentence, a comma comes directly after it. The comma helps separate the introductory material from the main part of the sentence:

> Going down the road, the truck stopped to pick up the hitchhiker.
>
> introductory phrase

> While I was talking on the phone, I was watering my plants.
> introductory clause

> Sadly, the Comets came out flat for the second half.
> introductory word

Before coordinating conjunctions when they join two independent clauses

Commas usually appear before coordinating conjunctions connecting two independent clauses. But when coordinating conjunctions connect two dependent clauses, phrases, or words, commas are not used.

> The fire was burning brightly, and the rain was still falling gently.
>
> *and* connects two independent clauses ⟍

> The Rangers were sitting around and talking.
>
> *and* connects two participles—
> *sitting around* and *talking* ⟍

> Herbert felt awful after the firefighters' cookout and called his sister for advice.
>
> *and* connects two verbs—*felt* and *called* ⟍

Not before dependent (or subordinate) clauses

Commas don't usually precede subordinating conjunctions (*because, since, although,* etc.) the way they do coordinating conjunctions *(and, or, nor, for, yet, but, so)*. The sentence parts (an independent clause and a dependent clause) are distinct because of the subordinating conjunction and thus don't require a comma. At times, however, a comma may be used to build an even stronger distinction between the two clauses. For example, S. I. Hayakawa writes, "All new ideas sound foolish at first, because they are new." Writers size up the situation and decide whether or not inserting a comma before a dependent clause will help the reader to better see the intended relationship between ideas.

To set off interrupting elements

Some sentence parts interrupt. For example, *The dog, as you know, barked at the biker* can be viewed as having two parts: the main clause *(The dog barked at the biker)* and an interrupting element *(as you know)*. Interrupting elements can be one word, a phrase, or a clause.

> French fries, although I haven't had any for a while, sure do taste good.
>
> French fries, an American classic, are sold all around the world.
>
> French fries, yum, are my favorite kind of potatoes.

Notice how the interrupting elements are punctuated in the following sentences:

> A sadder truth, I am afraid, is that because of skills and attitudes developed in high school, for some students the reality of genuine learning (as opposed to just getting by) might already be too late. (Daniel Bruno)
>
> Soon, I predict, they and other companies will not be able to sell us out. (Michael Moore)
>
> I crouched low to avoid destroying a jewelled spider's web that stretched, exquisite and fragile, across the trail. (Jane Goodall)

Interrupting elements can also be set off with parentheses or dashes. In general, parentheses suggest that the inserted information is somehow less important compared to the main point being made. Yet, because this information is included, it is still important and interesting. Dashes—unlike parentheses—draw attention to the interrupting bit of information. Dashes and parentheses are stronger separators than the comma. Read more about dashes and parentheses on pages 784–785.

To separate items in a series

Placing a comma between each item in a series helps the reader know where one item stops and another begins. Thus, we punctuate the following sentence this way: *As individuals in a society, we conform to laws, clothing styles, hairstyles, and even culinary tastes (most Americans like French fries but not raw oysters)*. Not punctuating the list *laws clothing styles hairstyles and even culinary tastes* would have been, at the least, distracting to the reader.

> Just go to any pet store and look at the vast array of foods, toys, beds, and treats, not to mention the shampoos and skin treatments. (David Hawes)
>
> If a person is unaware of common references—the Battle of the Bulge, Normandy, Existentialism, T. S. Eliot, World War I, Rasputin, John the Baptist, Gandhi, apartheid, Jonas Salk, Johnny Appleseed, Lewis and Clark, the Trail of Tears, slavery, the Donner Party, and so on—he misses out on conversations, *on meaning, on connecting with his fellow inmates*. (Daniel Bruno)
>
> Three, four, sometimes five times a month, I spend the day in bed with a migraine headache, insensible to the world around me. (Joan Didion)

To separate coordinate modifiers

When side-by-side modifiers modify the same word independently of each other, the modifiers are usually separated with a comma.

>the big, black dog

Each modifier (*big* and *black*) modifies the dog independently of the other. The dog is big. And the dog is black. Notice the use of coordinate modifiers *(black, brown, white carpet)* in the following passage:

>What happened was that I took a bite of honey and then I joined my sister and brother, two and ten years younger, watching Saturday morning cartoons together on the black, brown, white carpet, patterned in such a wild way that it was quickly making my head ache. (63)

Another type of modifier, the compound modifier, is punctuated with a hyphen. See Hyphens on page 784.

ACTIVITIES

1. Scan the essays in this book, noticing how commas are used. Find at least three examples of the following: (1) a comma before a main clause (or setting off an introductory element), (2) two commas setting off an interrupting element, (3) a comma between items in a series, (4) a comma between coordinate modifiers.

2. Scan your own writing—an essay, letter, e-mail—and notice how commas are used. Find at least three examples of the following: (1) a comma before a main clause (or setting off an introductory element), (2) two commas setting off an interrupting element, (3) a comma between items in a series, (4) a comma between coordinate modifiers.

Colons

Colons are useful for connecting a list, explanation, or quotation to the statement introducing it. Properly used colons can save time while connecting ideas clearly.

>So here's what I don't understand: if profit is supreme, why doesn't a company like General Motors sell crack? (Michael Moore)

>It was a long time before I began thinking mechanistically enough to accept migraine for what it was: something with which I would be living, the way some people live with diabetes. (Joan Didion)

>Punctuation, one is taught, has a point: to keep up law and order. (Pico Iyer)

Semicolons

Semicolons are stronger than commas and weaker than periods. They are used to connect sentence parts that are equal grammatically, such as two independent clauses, two dependent clauses, two phrases, or two words. They are not used to connect sentence parts that aren't grammatically equal, such as a clause and a phrase or an independent clause and a dependent clause.

> Ovulation represents mental and emotional creativity at its peak; the FSH-LH surge that accompanies ovulation may be the biological basis for this. (Christiane Northrup)

> The sky is clear and blue; however, the game has been postponed.

> Last summer I drove through Bangor, Maine; Hanover, New Hampshire; and Halifax, Nova Scotia.

In the first two examples above, the semicolon is used to connect two independent clauses. Notice that in the second example, the conjunctive adverb *however* is also used. Semicolons precede conjunctive adverbs when they connect two independent clauses. In the third example, the semicolons are used to connect (or separate) locations: Bangor, Maine; Hanover, New Hampshire; and Halifax, Nova Scotia. Semicolons are used because the sentence already contains commas between the cities and states.

ACTIVITIES

Commas

1. Create a comma quiz for your peers by removing the commas from one page of your recent writing. Allow your peers ten minutes to punctuate the text, and then discuss how their punctuation compares to the original.

2. Find or create at least one example of the following: (1) a sentence that is clearer to the reader because it is punctuated one way instead of another, (2) a sentence that is clear but distracting to the reader because it is punctuated one way instead of another.

Colons and Semicolons

3. Scan the essays in this book, noticing how colons and semicolons are used. Carefully study several examples of each. How is the colon or semicolon used? What two sentence parts are being connected?

Hyphens

Hyphens are used to connect compound modifiers. A compound modifier is two or more words combined to function as one modifier.

> We had thirty-five minutes to write an in-class essay.

The words *in* and *class* combine to modify *essay*. Each word alone is unable to modify *essay*. It is not an *in* essay or a *class* essay. It is an *in-class* essay. Thus, *in-class* is hyphenated. Notice also that numbers from twenty-one through ninety-nine are hyphenated. Consider these additional examples of compound modifiers: *give-it-to-me-now race for more, water-covered land:*

> Although we probably would not have relented in our give-it-to-me-now race for more, we would have taken a solemn moment to raise a toast and drink to your hardship. (Simon Benlow)

> One of the largest land-holding families in California took its richest holdings by a trick: By law a man could take up all the swamp or water-covered land he wanted. (John Steinbeck)

Coordinate modifiers (page 782) are punctuated with a comma—not a hyphen.

Dashes

Dashes—like this—are used to set off interrupting elements. As discussed on page 781, interrupting elements can be set off with commas, parentheses, or dashes. In general, dashes draw attention to the interrupting information, while parentheses suggest that the information is somehow less important compared to the main point being made.

> Given time—time not in years but in millennia—life adjusts, and a balance has been reached. (Rachel Carson)

> The Gods, they say, give breath, and they take it away. But the same could be said—could it not?—of the humble comma. (Pico Iyer)

Parentheses

Parentheses (like this) are used to set off interrupting elements. As discussed on page 781, interrupting elements can be set off with commas, parentheses, or dashes. Parentheses suggest that the information is somehow less important compared to the main point being made. Yet, because this information is still included it is somehow important and interesting.

> After my mother's never-subtle hints that if I'd just lose 20 pounds boys would like me and I might even win a beauty contest, it was my friend Bridget who wanted us to enter the Ottumwa (pronounced Uh-TUM-wuh) Junior Miss Pageant together. (Cindy Bosley)

> Doubtless, my sense of education at that time (as well as my sense of what constituted good writing) was more than mildly seasoned by huges dose of the Beats—Allen Ginsburg, Gregory Corso, William Burroughs, Kenneth Patchen, LeRoi Jones, and, of course, Jack Kerouac. (Leonard Kress)

> When I am in a migraine aura (for some people the aura lasts fifteen minutes, for others several hours), I will drive through red lights, lose the house keys, spill whatever I am holding, lose the ability to focus my eyes or frame coherent sentences, and generally give the appearance of being on drugs, or drunk. (Joan Didion)

What is grammar? Why is it important?

HOW SENTENCES WORK: A LOOK AT BASIC GRAMMAR

Every sentence is made up of words that cluster into related groups. If a group has a subject and a verb, it is called a *clause*. (If it doesn't, it is called a *phrase*.) When a noun (such as *dog*) and a verb (such as *sleeps* or *eats* or *barks* or *bites*) group together, a sort of reaction occurs. Other words group together around *dog* and *sleeps* to fill in the story. Some words describe the dog *(big, black, furry, stray)*, while others describe the sleeping *(soundly, restlessly, peacefully)*. Still other words connect, explaining the relationship between one word or word group and another. And, as you know, words change their forms to express number and time, so that instead of "one dog sleeps" we can say "two dogs slept" or "two big dogs slept soundly" and so on. The brief explanation of words, phrases, and clauses that follows is basically how that reaction works.

How Sentences Work (in Brief)

WORDS—PARTS OF SPEECH

1. **Noun**—A noun names a person, place, or thing.
2. **Pronoun**—A pronoun takes the place of a noun.
3. **Verb**—A verb expresses an action or a state of being.
4. **Adjective**—An adjective modifies a noun or pronoun.
5. **Adverb**—An adverb modifies a verb, adjective, or adverb.
6. **Conjunction**—A conjunction connects words, phrases, and clauses and shows a relationship.
7. **Preposition**—A preposition, placed before a noun and its modifiers, creates a modifying phrase.
8. **Interjection**—An interjection expresses surprise or strong emotion.

Words (parts of speech) are combined into phrases and clauses to create sentences (see next page).

PHRASES

1. **Prepositional**—Consisting of a preposition, modifiers, and a noun, the prepositional phrase functions most often as an adjective or adverb.

2. **Participial**—Consisting of a participle, modifiers, and a noun, the participial phrase functions as an adjective.

3. **Gerund**—Consisting of a gerund, modifiers, and a noun, the gerund phrase functions as a noun.

4. **Infinitive**—Consisting of an infinitive, modifiers, and a noun, the infinitive phrase functions as a noun, adjective, or adverb.

5. **Appositive**—An appositive (which may also be a single noun) describes or restates a noun.

6. **Absolute**—Consisting of a noun, modifiers, and often a participle, the absolute phrase modifies an entire clause.

CLAUSES

1. **Independent**—An independent clause (main clause) contains a subject and a verb, and is not preceded by a subordinating conjunction.

2. **Dependent**—A dependent clause (subordinate clause) contains a subject and a verb and is preceded by a subordinating conjunction or a relative pronoun.

   - **Noun clause**—Noun clauses function as subjects, objects, or complements.

   - **Adjective clause**—Adjective clauses modify nouns or pronouns.

   - **Adverb clause**—Adverb clauses modify verbs, adjectives, or adverbs.

SENTENCES—CLASSIFIED BY STRUCTURE

1. **Simple**—A simple sentence contains one independent clause.

2. **Compound**—A compound sentence contains two independent clauses.

3. **Complex**—A complex sentence contains one independent and one dependent clause.

4. **Compound-complex**—A compound-complex sentence contains at least two independent clauses and at least one dependent clause.

HOW PARTS OF SPEECH FUNCTION IN A SENTENCE

Words may function in different ways in a sentence. For example, *fish* can be a noun or a verb. *(Fish are fun to watch. I fish at my grandma's lake.)* Parts of speech may also function in different ways in a sentence. For example, a noun—such as *fish*—may be the subject of a sentence or the object of a sentence. *(Fish are fun to watch. I saw a fish.)*

1. **Subject**—The subject of a sentence is a noun (or noun phrase, noun clause, or pronoun). It normally precedes the verb (predicate), and it names who or what the sentence is about.

2. **Verb (Predicate)**—The predicate of a sentence (a verb and the words that complete its meaning) usually follows the subject and expresses what the subject does, what it is, or what has been done to it.

3. **Object**—Objects are nouns (or noun phrases, noun clauses, or pronouns), usually follow the verb and can be direct objects or indirect objects.

4. **Complement**—Complements are nouns (or noun phrases, noun clauses, or pronouns) but can also be adjectives (or adjective phrases). They usually follow a subject, verb, and any objects, and they can be subject complements, object complements, predicate nouns, or predicate adjectives.

5. **Adverbials**—Adverbials are adverbs (or adverb phrases or adverb clauses) that refer to the verb.

SENTENCES—CLASSIFIED BY PURPOSE

1. **Declarative**—A sentence that makes a statement and ends with a period.

2. **Imperative**—A sentence that expresses a command.

3. **Interrogative**—A sentence that asks a question.

4. **Exclamatory**—A sentence that expresses an emphatic statement and ends with an exclamation mark.

NINE WAYS OF COMBINING SIMPLE SENTENCES (INDEPENDENT CLAUSES)

1. Subject + verb. Subject + verb.

2. Subject + verb; subject + verb.

3. Subject + verb, coordinating conjunction subject + verb.

4. Subject + verb; conjunctive adverb, subject + verb.

5. Subject + verb subordinating conjunction subject + verb.

6. Subordinating conjunction subject + verb, subject + verb.

7. Subject + relative clause (relative pronoun + verb) + verb.

8. Subject + verb + verb.

9. Phrase, subject + verb.

How Sentences Work (Expanded)

WORDS—PARTS OF SPEECH

Noun

A noun names a person, place, thing, idea, quantity, or condition. Nouns can be proper, common, collective, abstract, or concrete.

Proper nouns name specific people, places, and things. They are always capitalized.

Jane	Zaire
Eatonton, Georgia	the Red Cross
John Kenneth Galbraith	Mexican American
Gutenberg College	English
Star Wars	the Middle East

Common nouns name people, places, and things by general type. They are not capitalized.

woman	nation
town	organization
economist	people
college	language
movie	region

Collective nouns name groups of people or things and are treated as singular, not plural.

jury	band
congress	public
committee	

Abstract nouns name ideas, qualities, and conditions.

patriotism	despair
hatred	freedom
love	perfection
integrity	respect
joy	

Concrete nouns name things or qualities that are perceptible by the senses.

reporter	book
ball	hot dog
cricket	flower
letter	bed
check	

Pronoun

A pronoun takes the place of a noun. Pronouns can be personal, possessive, reflexive, interrogative, demonstrative, indefinite, or relative.

Personal pronouns refer to specific persons or things.

	Subject Form		**Object Form**	
	Singular	*Plural*	*Singular*	*Plural*
first person	I	we	me	us
second person	you	you	you	you
third person	he		him	
	she	they	her	them
	it		it	

Possessive pronouns indicate ownership.

	Singular	*Plural*
first person	my, mine	our, ours
second person	your, yours	your, yours
third person	his, his	
	her, hers	their, theirs
	its, its	

Reflexive pronouns show that someone or something is acting for or on itself.

	Singular	*Plural*
first person	myself	ourselves
second person	yourself	yourselves
third person	himself	
	herself	themselves
	itself	

Interrogative pronouns are used to ask questions.

Subject	*Object*	*Other*
who / whoever	whom / whomever	what / which / whose

Demonstrative pronouns point out particular persons or things.

Singular	*Plural*
this / that	these / those

Indefinite pronouns serve as general subjects or objects in a sentence.

Singular	*Plural*
another / any* / anybody / anyone / anything	all* / both / few
each / either / everybody / everyone / everything	many / several
neither / nobody / no one / nothing / one	some*
somebody / someone / something	

*Some indefinite pronouns can be either singular or plural: singular if they refer to a unit or quantity and plural if they refer to individuals. For example, "Some of my friends **are** leaving" (plural); "Some of the money **is** gone" (singular).

Relative pronouns connect adjective clauses to nouns or pronouns.

Refer to People	*Refer to Things*	*Refer to People or Things*
who / whom	that / what / whatever	that / whose
whoever / whomever	which / whichever	

Verb

A verb expresses an action or a state of being. The three types of verbs are *action, linking,* and *auxiliary.* Verbs can take other forms and become *verbals*—words formed from verbs that do not function as verbs. (See "Verbals" at the end of this section.)

Action verbs express action, either physical or mental. Action verbs are either transitive or intransitive.

Transitive verbs require direct objects to complete their meaning.

Joe sold . . .

subject   verb

Joe sold the boat.

The direct object names whom or what is directly acted upon.

Joe finally sold Tom the old sailboat in the backyard.

An indirect object names who was indirectly affected by the action of the verb. *Finally* modifies *sold. Old* modifies *sailboat,* as does the prepositional phrase *in the backyard.*

I love . . .

subject   verb

I love baseball.

The direct object names whom or what is directly acted upon.

I still love baseball after all these years.

Other words fill out the sentence. *Still* modifies *love,* as does the prepositional phrase *after all these years.*

Intransitive verbs do not require direct objects to complete their meaning.

The ship sank.

Chelsea skipped.

Scott flipped.

Other words—such as modifiers—can be added to the sentences, but as long as no object is required, the verb is considered to be intransitive.

The ship sank off the coast of South America.

Off the coast of South America is two prepositional phrases.

Chelsea, the little girl next door, skipped down the sidewalk.

The little girl next door is an appositive that describes *Chelsea; down the sidewalk* is a prepositional phrase.

Scott flipped. (intransitive)

Scott flipped a pancake. (transitive)

If Scott did a flip, then *flipped* requires no object and is intransitive. But if Scott flipped a pancake, then *flipped* has a direct object, *a pancake,* and the verb is therefore transitive. Thus, the same verb can be intransitive or transitive, depending upon whether or not an object is required to complete its meaning.

Linking verbs express a state of being or a condition, not an action.

The consumer <u>is</u> king. (Juliet Schor)

We <u>were</u> a young culture with no parents. (Simon Benlow)

The biggest problem as I see it <u>is</u> that although students <u>are</u> able to graduate from high school (and even some colleges) with minimal effort, those students may find themselves cheated in the long run. (Daniel Bruno)

Common Linking Verbs—Forms of *to be*

is	am	are	was
were	be	being	been

Common Linking Verbs—Other Forms

appear	feel	grow	look	become
make	seem	smell	taste	sound

Auxiliary verbs (also called helping verbs) work with other verbs to create verb tenses or form questions.

> As Albert Schweitzer has said, "Man can hardly even recognize the devils of his own creation." (Rachel Carson)
>
> The verb consists of two words: *has* (a helping verb) and *said* (a past participle).

> If parents are entitled to put their needs and interests before those of their own children, why should they or any other adults feel an obligation to help somebody else's children? (Barbara Dafoe Whitehead)
>
> The verb consists of two words: *are* (a helping verb) and *entitled* (a past participle).

Common Auxiliary Verbs—Forms of *to be*

is	am	are	was
were	being	been	

Common Auxiliary Verbs—Other Forms

can	do	has	might	should	would
could	does	have	must	will	
did	had	may	ought to		

Verb forms

Verbs take different forms that can be categorized as infinitive, third-person singular present, past, present participle, and past participle.

Infinitive: The base form of a verb, often used with the word *to*, the infinitive (the form one would look up in the dictionary) indicates action that occurs in the present, occurs habitually, or is generally true.

Third-person singular present: Frequently ending in *-s* or *-es*, the third-person singular indicates action that occurs in the present, occurs habitually, or is generally true.

Past: Ending in *-d* or *-ed* (except in irregular verbs), the past tense indicates that something happened before now.

Present participle: Ending in *-ing,* the present participle with an auxiliary forms a verb; without an auxiliary verb, it functions as an adjective or a noun.

Past participle: Usually ending in *-d* or *-ed* (the same as the past tense except in irregular verbs), the past participle with an auxiliary forms a verb; without an auxiliary, it functions as an adjective.

infinitive	(I, you, we) walk	say, sing, care
third-person		
singular present	(he, she, it) walks	says, sings, cares
past	(I, she, they) walked	said, sang, cared
present participle	(am, was) walking	saying, singing, caring
past participle	(have, has, was) walked	said, sung, cared

Many common English verbs are irregular and form their past tense and participle forms in unpredictable ways. Below is a partial list.

	Infinitive	*Past Tense*	*Past Participle*
Regular Verbs (most verbs in English are regular verbs)			
	walk	walked	walked
	jump	jumped	jumped
	follow	followed	followed
Irregular Verbs (many verbs in English are irregular verbs)			
	be	was/were	been
	begin	began	begun
	bite	bit	bitten
	blow	blew	blown
	break	broke	broken
	come	came	come
	cost	cost	cost
	do	did	done
	draw	drew	drawn
	drink	drank	drunk
	drive	drove	driven
	eat	ate	eaten
	fly	flew	flown
	freeze	froze	frozen
	give	gave	given
	go	went	gone
	read	read	read
	ring	rang	rung
	see	saw	seen

Verb Talk

- **Action verbs** express action, either physical or mental.
- **Intransitive verbs** show action that is limited to the subject.
- **Transitive verbs** transfer the action from an actor to a direct object.
- **Linking verbs** allow the word or words following them to complete the meaning of the subject.
- **Auxiliary,** or **helping, verbs** combine with the base or a participle form of another verb to create tense, mood, and voice (active or passive).
- **Verbals** are formed from verbs and act as adjectives, adverbs, and nouns.
- **Verb tense** indicates when an action or state of being occurs.
- **Verb mood** expresses whether the speaker considers a thing to be a fact, a command, or an unreal or hypothetical condition contrary to fact.
- **Voice** can be active or passive, depending upon whether the grammatical subject is doing the action or being acted upon.

	Infinitive	Past Tense	Past Participle
(continued)	shoot	shot	shot
	spring	sprang	sprung
	swear	swore	sworn
	swim	swam	swum
	take	took	taken
	tear	tore	torn
	throw	threw	thrown
	wear	wore	worn
	write	wrote	written

Verbals

Verbals are formed from verbs but do not function as verbs. There are three types: *participles* (verbals that function as modifiers or as part of the verb), *gerunds* (verbals that function as nouns), and *infinitives* (verbals that function as nouns or modifiers). Notice how a verb, such as *fish,* can be used as a participle, gerund, or infinitive.

I fish with cousin Dan.

Fish is a verb in this sentence. We might have used any other action verb: *swim, work, play, argue, eat,* etc.

Participles look like verbs and are formed from verbs but cannot function as verbs in a sentence. Participles can be present or past (present participles end in *-ing,* and past participles end in *-ed* or an irregular past tense form). Participles are used (1) in participial phrases that modify other sentence parts, (2) as modifying words, or (3) with a helping word or words to create a verb.

Participial phrase

Fishing with cousin Dan, I lost my wallet.
While fishing with cousin Dan, I lost my wallet.
I lost my wallet fishing with cousin Dan.

Participle as modifier

Cousin Dan is my fishing guru.
I am cousin Dan's favorite fishing partner.
Cousin Dan and I both enjoy the fishing life.

Participle as part of a verb

I go fishing with cousin Dan.
I am fishing with cousin Dan.
I have never been fishing with cousin Dan.

Gerunds are verbals that act as nouns.

Fishing is fun.
No one likes fishing like I do.
You can watch TV shows about cooking, painting, hunting, and fishing.

Infinitives, like gerunds, can act as nouns.

To fish is fun.
No one likes to fish like I do.

Verb tense

Tense indicates time. Verbs have three simple tenses (present, past, and future) along with three perfect tenses (present perfect, past perfect, and future perfect) and six progressive tenses, one corresponding to each simple and perfect tense.

present	I dance. She sings.
past	I danced. She sang.
future	I will dance. She will sing.
present perfect	I have danced. She has sung.
past perfect	I had danced. She had sung.
future perfect	I will have danced. She will have sung.
present progressive	I am dancing. She is singing.
past progressive	I was dancing. She was singing.
future progressive	I will be dancing. She will be singing.
present perfect progressive	I have been dancing. She has been singing.
past perfect progressive	I had been dancing. She had been singing.
future perfect progressive	I will have been dancing. She will have been singing.

Tenses are indicated by the form of the main verb (*dance* and *sing* in the examples above) and the auxiliary verbs. Notice that *dance* is a regular verb: *dance, danced, danced.* And *sing* is an irregular verb: *sing, sang, sung.*

Verb mood

Mood reflects a writer's attitude towards a statement.

Indicative mood expresses a declarative statement or question.

> The whole process of spraying seems caught up in an endless spiral.
> (Rachel Carson)
>
> I crouched low to avoid destroying a jewelled spider's web that stretched,
> exquisite and fragile, across the trail. (Jane Goodall)

Imperative mood expresses a command or a direct request.

> Vote.
>
> Help yourself to another burger.
>
> Take the less usual side. (Paul Roberts)

Subjunctive mood expresses a conditional situation, a hypothetical, a wish, or some statement contrary to fact.

> If I were the president, I would make some changes around here.
>
> I wish I were the president.

Adjective

An adjective modifies a noun or pronoun. The three articles—*a, an,* and *the*—mark, or precede, certain nouns and, therefore, function as a special type of adjective. An adjective answers one of the following questions:

What kind?	How many?
Which one?	Whose?

Adjectives modifying nouns

red balloon	Orwellian partyspeak
big river	skulking rhetoric
little women	bright, doomed city
recent layoffs	endless, obsessive preoccupation
practical goal	pure elation
blatant manipulation	everyday lives
amusing instance	simple euphemism

Adverb

An adverb modifies a verb, adjective, or adverb. Adverbs frequently end in *-ly* and answer the following questions:

How?	How often?
When?	To what extent?
Where?	

Adverbs modifying verbs

clearly said	reluctantly explained
jump quickly	suddenly stopped
constantly sang	replied sheepishly
will happily move	land smoothly
willingly applauded	dropped instantly

Interjection

An interjection expresses surprise or strong emotion.

Hey!	Wow! This cheesecake is delicious.
Oh!	Hey! Let's go to the coffeehouse and
Okay!	get a bagel.
Wow!	

Good and Well

In casual, everyday speech, people often use the adjective *good* instead of the adverb *well*. For example:

"I did good at bowling last night." OR "I bowled good."

Or, if asked, "How did you bowl?" someone might respond,

"I did good."

Or someone might just say,

"Good."

Yet *good* is an adjective, and *well* is an adverb; adjectives modify nouns and pronouns while adverbs modify verbs, adjectives, and adverbs.

1. Do you consider *good* to be incorrect in the sentences above? Why or why not?

2. Why should, or shouldn't, you avoid using *good* as an adverb?

3. Interview several classmates and others outside of class to get their views on using *good* and *well* correctly.

4. Consider the following sentences. Would you say *good* or *well*, and why?

   Lisa does _____ at whatever she does.

   She hasn't felt _____ about New England since she left.

Lorenzo is _____ at playing the spoons.

Diamonds don't look _____ in that ring.

I don't feel _____.

5. *Bad* and *badly* pose a similar problem. Which word would you use in the sentences below, and why?

   Martha golfed _____.

   I have never done so _____ on a math test.

   The _____ thing about it is the grinding sound.

   Dan is _____ at being on time.

   I feel _____ when it rains.

6. What word would you use below? Did you use an adjective or adverb? Why?

   Jefferson _____ explained his reason for leaving early.

   Georgia told a _____ story that helped me to understand.

   Next month we are _____ driving to Detroit.

   My head was _____ spinning after my second time on the Tilt-a-Whirl.

   Did you hear about the _____ strike at the refinery?

Conjunction

A conjunction connects words, phrases, and clauses and shows a relationship. Conjunctions may be coordinating, subordinating, or correlative.

Coordinating conjunctions link sentence parts of equal grammatical rank. There are only seven coordinating conjunctions.

> I went, <u>and</u> she stayed.
>
> She <u>and</u> I went to dinner <u>and</u> a movie.
>
> We went to a movie <u>but</u> not to dinner.

and   or   nor   for   yet   but   so

Subordinating conjunctions link clauses, making one clause dependent on, or subordinate to, the other. Many words act as subordinating conjunctions.

> Because I went, she stayed.
>
> I went although she stayed.
>
> Even though I went and she stayed, we still had fun.

after	however	that
although	if	though
as	in case	till
as if	in order that	unless
as far as	in that	until
as soon as	no matter how	when
as though	now that	whenever
because	once	where
before	since	wherever
even if	so that	whether
even though	supposing that	while
how	than	why

Correlative conjunctions work in pairs to link sentence parts.

> <u>Whether</u> it rains <u>or</u> not, I am washing my pickup truck tomorrow.
>
> I could go for <u>either</u> a bath <u>or</u> a shower right now.

both . . . and	either . . . or	whether . . . or
neither . . . nor	not only . . . but also	

Preposition

A preposition placed before a noun and its modifiers creates a prepositional phrase. Prepositional phrases function as either adverbs or adjectives.

> Paul left his umbrella <u>by the door</u>.
>
> The woman <u>at the counter</u> said the bus leaves <u>at noon</u>.
>
> Who said the majority <u>of customers in the carryout</u> were buying emergency supplies?

Common One-Word Prepositions

about	by	outside
above	concerning	over
across	despite	past
after	down	since
against	during	through
along	except	throughout
among	for	till
around	from	to
at	in	toward
before	inside	under
behind	into	underneath
below	like	until
beneath	near	up
beside	of	upon
besides	off	with
between	on	within
beyond	onto	without
but	out	

Common Multiple-Word Prepositions

according to	by way of	instead of
ahead of	due to	on account of
along with	except for	out of
apart from	in addition to	up to
as for	in case of	with regard to
as to	in front of	with respect to
as well as	in spite of	with the exception of
because of	inside of	

PHRASES

A phrase is a group of related words without a subject and a verb. Phrases can be categorized as prepositional, participial, gerund, infinitive, appositive, or absolute.

Prepositional: Consisting of a preposition, modifiers, and a noun, the prepositional phrase functions most often as an adjective or adverb.

Barney chased a rabbit <u>under the porch</u>.

The top executives met <u>in the conference room for about two hours</u>.

Participial: Consisting of a participle, modifiers, and a noun, the participial phrase functions as an adjective.

<u>Running after the rabbit</u>, Barney disappeared under the porch.

<u>While meeting in the conference room</u>, the executives voted to study the issue further.

Gerund: Consisting of a gerund, modifiers, and a noun, the gerund phrase functions as a noun.

<u>Running after a rabbit</u> is hard work for a small dog.

<u>Meeting in the conference room</u> is convenient for everyone except Mary.

Infinitive: Consisting of an infinitive, modifiers, and a noun, the infinitive phrase functions as a noun, adjective, or adverb.

<u>To run after a rabbit all day</u> is good exercise.

The most convenient place <u>to meet the new employee</u> is the conference room.

Appositive: An appositive (which may also be a single noun) describes or restates a noun.

Barney, a short-haired terrier, chased a wild rabbit under the porch.

Mary, the only executive with an office across the street, didn't mind meeting in the conference room.

Absolute: Consisting of a noun, modifiers, and often a participle, the absolute phrase modifies an entire clause.

The rabbit hiding under the porch, Barney barked at the screen door.

Mary arrived at the meeting late, her office being across town.

CLAUSES

A clause is a group of words with a subject and a verb (or predicate). The two types of clauses are *independent* (or main) and *dependent* (or subordinate).

Independent: An independent (main) clause contains a subject and a verb not preceded by a subordinating conjunction.

> Joe passed his math test.

> Independent clause: subject *(Joe)* + verb *(passed)*

> To see *Star Wars* again after 20 years is to revisit a place in the mind. (Roger Ebert).

> Independent clause: subject *(To see)* + verb *(is)*

Dependent: A dependent (subordinate) clause contains a subject and a verb and is preceded by a subordinating conjunction or a relative pronoun. Dependent clauses can function as nouns, adjectives, or adverbs.

> Because Joe passed his math test, he ordered a pizza with all the toppings.

> Dependent clause: subordinating conjunction *(because)* + subject *(Joe)* + verb *(passed)*
> Independent clause: subject *(he)* + verb *(ordered)*

> It's possible, however, that as we grow older, we retain the tastes of our earlier selves. (Roger Ebert)

> Dependent clauses: *that we retain* and *as we grow*
> Independent clause: *It's possible*

relative pronoun   verb

> Now it was adults who were the emotionally fragile ones and thus had to be protected against adversity while children were the resilient ones and could take it. (Barbara Dafoe Whitehead)

> The relative clause *who were the emotionally fragile ones and thus had to be protected against adversity* modifies the noun *adults*. (Other relative pronouns include *that* and *which* and are either followed by a subject and a verb or just a verb. In either case, the relative clause modifies the noun before it.)

Examples of Relative Clauses

the lion that roared at Dorothy

. . .

the band that the club owner hired

. . .

the woman who won the marathon

. . .

SENTENCES—CLASSIFIED BY STRUCTURE

Simple: A simple sentence contains one independent clause.

Bobby played the banjo on the back step.

Independent clause: subject *(Bobby)* + verb *(played)*

My daughter doesn't ask for $42 pants from the Gap or $38 shirts from Abercrombie & Fitch.

Independent clause: subject *(daughter)* + verb *(doesn't ask)*

Compound: A compound sentence contains two independent clauses.

Bobby played the banjo on the back step, and he made a musical dent in the night.

Independent clause: subject *(Bobby)* + verb *(played)*
Independent clause: subject *(he)* + verb *(made)*
Because *and* is a coordinating **(not a subordinating)** conjunction, the second clause is independent **(not dependent).**

This bipartisan consensus has been politically expedient but it has taken an enormous toll on our public commitment to children. (Barbara Dafoe Whitehead)

Independent clause: subject *(consensus)* + verb *(has been politically expedient)*
Independent clause: subject *(it)* + verb *(has taken)*
Because *but* is a coordinating **(not a subordinating)** conjunction, the second clause is independent **(not dependent).**

Complex: A complex sentence contains one independent and one dependent clause.

> When Bobby played the banjo on the back step, he made a musical dent in the night.
>
> Dependent clause: subordinating conjunction *(when)* + subject *(Bobby)* + verb *(played)*
> Independent clause: subject *(he)* + verb *(made)*

> If you want the reader to believe that college football is bad for the players, you have to do more than say so. (Paul Roberts)
>
> Dependent clause: subordinating conjunction *(If)* + subject *(you)* + verb *(want)*
> Independent clause: subject *(you)* + verb *(have)*

Compound-complex: A compound-complex sentence contains at least two independent clauses and at least one dependent clause.

> When Bobby played the banjo on the back step, he made a musical dent in the night, and the neighbors complained.
>
> Dependent clause: subordinating conjunction *(when)* + subject *(Bobby)* + verb *(played)*
> Independent clause: subject *(he)* + verb *(made)*
> Independent clause: subject *(neighbors)* + verb *(complained)*

> Now this is a way to go about reaching five hundred words, and if you are content with a "D" grade, it is as good a way as any. (Paul Roberts)
>
> Independent clause: subject *(this)* + verb *(is)*
> Dependent clause: subordinating conjunction *(if)* + subject *(you)* + verb *(are)*
> Independent clause: subject *(it)* + verb *(is)*

HOW PARTS OF SPEECH FUNCTION IN A SENTENCE

Remember, words may function in different ways in a sentence. For example, *fish* can be a noun or a verb. *(Fish are fun to watch. I fish with cousin Dan at Carpenter Lake.)* Parts of speech may also function in different ways in a sentence. For example, a noun—such as *fish*—may be the subject of a sentence or the object of a sentence. *(Fish are fun to watch. I saw a fish.)*

ACTIVITY

Identify the parts of speech, particularly subjects and verbs, in the following sentences.

1. As health care professionals, we must regard this crisis with the utmost importance.
2. I like the story because it is put together so well.
3. As a concerned citizen and patient, I have become very alarmed at the growing addiction to prescription drugs in the United States.
4. At the same time, each fearless and self-sacrificing helper shows each victim a human face, stands for respect for that person's dignity, and is a source of hope for peace and reconciliation.
5. The President will address the nation tonight, upon his return to the White House.

1. **Subject**—The subject of a sentence is a noun (or noun phrase, noun clause, or pronoun). It normally precedes the verb (predicate), and it names who or what the sentence is about.

2. **Verb (Predicate)**—The predicate of a sentence (a verb and the words that complete its meaning) usually follows the subject and expresses what the subject does, what it is, or what has been done to it.

3. **Objects**—Objects are nouns (or noun phrases, noun clauses, or pronouns), usually follow the verb, and can be direct objects or indirect objects.

4. **Complements**—Complements are nouns (or noun phrases, noun clauses, or pronouns) but can also be adjectives (or adjective phrases). They usually follow a subject, verb, and any objects, and can be subject complements, object complements, predicate nouns, or predicate adjectives.

5. **Adverbials**—Adverbials are adverbs (or adverb phrases or adverb clauses) that refer to the verb.

SENTENCES—CLASSIFIED BY PURPOSE

Declarative: A sentence that makes a statement and ends with a period.

> Up in the trees the other chimpanzees of the group were moving about, getting ready for the new day. (Jane Goodall)

> We ourselves may never see this cottonwood reach maturity, probably will never take pleasure in its shade or birds or witness the pale gold of its autumn leaves. (Edward Abbey)

Imperative: A sentence that expresses a command.

> Avoid the Obvious Content. (Paul Roberts)

> Know that it causes real pain and real suffering to real people. (Ward Churchill)

Interrogative: A sentence that asks a question.

> And what is it that Sea World doesn't want its customers to think about? (Jayme Stayer)

> Does he feel like something is missing from his life, but he's not sure what it is? And worst of all, does he blame me for what is missing? (David Hawes)

Exclamatory: A sentence that expresses an emphatic statement and ends with an exclamation mark.

> She was no good! Why did *she win*? What were those judges thinking! (Cindy Bosley)

> If there was a crack house in your neighborhood, what would you do? You would try to get rid of it! (Michael Moore)

Combining sentences sometimes helps the reader see the relationship between ideas. For example, "I went. She stayed." can mean "I went because she stayed" or "I went although she stayed." Combining the sentences with a subordinating conjunction clarifies the relationship. The strategies on the following page can be helpful for combining sentences, and for eliminating fused sentences and comma splices. For example, the comma splice "I went, she stayed." can be rewritten using 1, 2, 3, 4, 5, or 6 on the following pages.

NINE WAYS OF COMBINING SIMPLE SENTENCES (INDEPENDENT CLAUSES)

1. **Subject + verb. Subject + verb. (two simple sentences)**

   Mary was relaxing in the meadow. Mary saw a dragonfly.

   Larry had never flown a plane before. He landed the 747 safely.

   A nickel isn't worth much anymore. George gave Susie a dime.

2. **Subject + verb; subject + verb. (one compound sentence)**

   Mary was relaxing in the meadow; Mary saw a dragonfly.

   Larry had never flown a plane before; he landed the 747 safely.

   A nickel isn't worth much anymore; George gave Susie a dime.

3. **Subject + verb, coordinating conjunction subject + verb. (one compound sentence)**

   Mary was relaxing in the meadow, and she saw a dragonfly.

   Larry had never flown a plane before, yet he landed the 747 safely.

   A nickel isn't worth much anymore, so George gave Susie a dime.

4. **Subject + verb; conjunctive adverb, subject + verb. (one compound sentence)**

   Mary was relaxing in the meadow; therefore, she saw a dragonfly.

   Larry had never flown a plane before; nevertheless, he landed the 747 safely.

   A nickel isn't worth much anymore; hence, George gave Susie a dime.

5. **Subject + verb subordinating conjunction subject + verb. (one complex sentence)**

   Mary was relaxing in the meadow when she saw a dragonfly.

   Larry had never flown a plane before until he landed the 747 safely.

   A nickel isn't worth much anymore though George gave Susie a dime.

6. **Subordinating conjunction subject + verb, subject + verb. (one complex sentence)**

>   Because Mary was relaxing in the meadow, she saw a dragonfly.

>   Although Larry had never flown a plane before, he landed the 747 safely.

>   Now that a nickel isn't worth much anymore, George gave Susie a dime.

7. **Subject + relative clause (relative pronoun + verb) + verb. (one complex sentence)**

>   Mary, who was relaxing in the meadow, saw a dragonfly.

>   Larry, who had never flown a plane before, landed the 747 safely.

>   A nickel isn't worth much anymore. George gave Susie a dime.
>   [A relative clause will not work.]

8. **Subject + verb + verb. (one simple sentence)**

>   Mary was relaxing in the meadow and saw a dragonfly.

>   Larry had never flown a plane before and landed the 747 safely.

>   A nickel isn't worth much anymore. George gave Susie a dime.
>   [A compound verb will not work.]

9. **Phrase, subject + verb. (one simple sentence)**

>   Relaxing in the meadow, Mary saw a dragonfly.

>   Never having flown a plane before, Larry landed the 747 safely.

>   A nickel not being worth much anymore, George gave Susie a dime.

CREDITS

This page constitutes an extension of the copyright page. We have made every effort to trace the ownership of all copyrighted material and to secure permission from copyright holders. In the event of any question arising as to the use of any material, we will be pleased to make the necessary corrections in future printings. Thanks are due to the following authors, publishers, and agents for permission to use the material indicated.

Text Credits

Chapter 1: 20: Samantha Tengelitsch, "The Greatest Gift." Reprinted by permission.

Chapter 2: 54: Copyright 1966 by John Steinbeck, renewed 1984 by Elaine Steinbeck and Thom Steinbeck. Used by permission of Viking Penguin, a division of Penguin Putnam, Inc. **59:** Copyright 2004 by The New York Times Co. Reprinted with permission.

Chapter 3: 98: "Living Like Weasels" from TEACHING A STONE TO TALK: EXPEDITIONS AND ENCOUNTERS by ANNIE DILLARD. Copyright 1982 by Annie Dillard. Reprinted by permission of HarperCollins Publishers, Inc. **102:** "Planting a Tree," from DOWN THE RIVER by Edward Abbey, Copyright 1982 by Edward Abbey. Used by permission of Dutton, a division of Penguin Putnam, Inc. **104:** "Gombe," from THROUGH A WINDOW by Jane Goodall. Copyright 1990 by Soko Publications, Ltd. Reprinted by Permission of Houghton Mifflin Company. All rights reserved. **111:** Royce Flores, "Onward, Gamers, Onward!" Reprinted by permission.

Chapter 4: 146: Copyright 1988 Time Inc. Reprinted by Permission **149:** "What it Means to be Creative" by S.I. Hayakawa from THROUGH THE COMMUNICATION BARRIER. New York: Harper & Row, 1979. **154:** Skye Bass, "In Search of . . . Something." Reprinted by permission.

Chapter 5: 188: Calvin and Hobbes © 1990 Watterson. Distributed by UNIVERSAL PRESS SYNDICATE. Reprinted with permission. All rights reserved. **192:** Reprinted with the permission of The Free Press, a Division of Simon & Schuster Adult Publishing Group, from CAN'T BUY MY LOVE: How Advertising Changes the Way We Think and Feel (previously published as Deadly Persuasion) by Jean Kilbourne. Copyright 1999 by Jean Kilbourne. All rights reserved. **202:** Reprinted with permission from Media&Values #57, 1992 by the Center for Media Literacy/www.medialit.org **207:** Reprinted with permission from Media&Values #20, 1982 by the Center for Media Literacy/www.medialit.org **215:** Reprinted

with permission from Media&Values #57, 1992 by the Center for Media Literacy/www.medialit.org

Chapter 6: 248: "Crimes Against Humanity" by Ward Churchill as appeared in Z Magazine, March 1993. Reprinted by permission of the author. **255:** Reprinted by permission of David W. Crabtree, President, Gutenberg College. **266:** Elizabeth Bohnhorst, "Floppy Disk Fallacies." Reprinted by permission. **266:** Excerpts from Guignon, Anne. "Laptop Computers for Every Student" Education World, 19 Jan. 1998, 28 Apr. 2003.

Chapter 7: 306: Reprinted with the permission of the Free Press, a Division of Simon & Schuster Adult Publishing Group, from THE TYRANNY OF THE MAJORITY: Fundamental Fairness in Representative Democracy by Lani Guinier. Copyright 1994 by Lani Guinier. All rights reserved. **326:** "Response to Juliet Schor," Betsy Taylor. Boston Review-Summer, 1999. **329:** "Is Hunting Ethical?", by Ann F. Causey.

Chapter 8: 362: Taken from the ROGER EBERT column by Roger Ebert, copyright 1999, The Ebert Company. Dist. By UNIVERSAL PRESS SYNDICATE. Reprinted with permission. All rights reserved. **379:** "Rethinking Divorce" by Barbara Dafoe Whitehead from the Boston Globe, 1997. Reprinted by permission of the author.

Chapter 9: 410: Reprinted by permission of the author. **422:** "Sex, Lies and Conversation: Why Is It So Hard for Men and Women to Talk to Each Other?" by Deborah Tannen, The Washington Post, June 24, 1990, copyright Deborah Tannen. Reprinted by permission. This article is adapted in part from the author's book You Just Don't Understand (Quill, 1990) **427:** When Bright Girls Decide Math Is a "Waste of Time" by Susan Jacoby. Copyright 1983 by Susan Jacoby. Used by permission of Geroges Borchardt, Inc.

Chapter 10: 456: "An Obligation to Endure", from SILENT SPRING by Rachel Carson. Copyright 1962 by Rachel Carson, renewed 1990 by Roger Christie. Reprinted by permission of Houghton Mifflin. All rights reserved. **461:** "In Bed" from THE WHITE ALBUM by Joan Didion. Copyright 1979 by Joan Didion. Reprinted by permission of Farrar, Straus and Giroux, LLC. **464:** "How to Say Nothing in Five Hundred Words" from UNDERSTANDING ENGLISH by Paul Roberts. Copyright 1958 by Paul Roberts. Reprinted by permission of Pearson Education, Inc. **474:** Reprinted by permission of International Creative Management, Inc., Copyright by Barbara Ehrenreich

Chapter 11: 507: All pages from "A VERY OLD MAN WITH ENORMOUS WINGS" from LEAF STORM AND OTHER STORIES by GABRIEL GARCIA MARQUEZ. Tranlsated by Gregory Rabassa. Copyright 1971 by Gabriel García Márquez. Reprinted by permission of HarperCollins Publishers. **511:** Reprinted by permission of the author. **513:** "Running to Stand Still" by Paul Hewson, Dave Evans, Adam Clayton, Larry Mullen. Copyright 1986 by Polygram International Music Publishing, B.V. All rights in the United States administered by Universal - Polygram International Publishing/ASCAP. Used by permission. All rights reserved. **514:** Used by permission of Righteous Babe Records. **517:** Reprinted by permission of the author. **528:** Reprinted by permission of the author.

Chapter 12: 564: Copyright 1995 by Wendell Berry. Reprinted by permission of Counterpoint Press, a member of Perseus Books, LLC. **568:** From DOWNSIZE THIS by Michael Moore, copyright 1996 by Michael Moore. Used by permission of Crown Pub-lishers, a division of Random House, Inc. **571:** From WOMEN'S BODIES, WOMEN'S WISDOM by Christiane Northrup, M.D., copyright 1994, 1998 by Christiane Northrup, M.D. Used by per-mission of Bantam Books, a division of Random House, Inc. **577:** Simon Benlow, "An Apology to Future Generations." Reprinted by permission. **583:** "Group Minds" pages 47–62 from PRISONS WE CHOOSE TO LIVE INSIDE by Doris Lessing. Copyright 1988 by Doris Lessing. Reprinted by permission of HarperCollins Publishers.

Chapter 13: 665: Ben Wetherbee, "Branded." Reprinted by permis-sion. **687:** Amanda Stremlow, "Vultures." Reprinted by permission.

Chapter 14: 724: Mike Ferner, copyright 2001, mike.ferner@sbc-global.net **732:** Copyright © 2004 by Houghton Mifflin Compa-ny. Reproduced by permission from The American Heritage College Dictionary, Fourth Edition. **734:** Copyright 1963 Martin Luther King, Jr., copyright renewed 1991 Coretta Scott King.

Photo and Illustration Credits

Chapter Openers and Chapter Introductions: Asphalt and shat-tered glass background images © Ben Cloward. Provided courtesy of Ben Cloward, www.monitorstudios.com/bcloward/index.html.

Chapter 1: 2: © Stuart Whitmore/Morguefile.com; **10:** Used by permission; **22:** © Daniel Wildman/stockxchange; **27:** © Anita Pat-terson/Morguefile.com; *clockwise from upper left:* © Darren Hester/morguefile.com; © Kenn Kiser/morguefile.com; ©McRASTRILLO/morguefilecom; © Malina Welte/morguefile.com; © Anita Patter-son/morguefile.com

Chapter 2: 50: ©Alvaro Prieto/stockxchange; **73:** © Clarita/morguefile.com; *clockwise from upper left:* © Hal Wilson/ stockx-change; © hoodsie/morguefile.com; © Dawn M. Turjner/ morgue-file.com; © Steve Mockensturm/Madhouse; © Jonas Jordan/USACE; **93:** © Valeria Obregon/stockxchange

Chapter 3: 94: Used by permission of the author; **108:** © Bett-mann/Corbis; **114:** © cardsnstuff; **121:** © wanda/aka beata laki/stockxchange; *right, top to bottom:* © Gilbert Tremblay/stock-xchange; © Cris Watk/stockxchange; © Jane Schenker/stock-xchange; **141:** © Steve Mockensturm/Madhouse

Chapter 4: 142: © Ibon San Martin/stockxchange; **155:** © Kenn Kiser/morguefile.com; **161:** Adam Clark/stockxchange; **165:** © phestus/morguefile.com; *clockwise from upper right:* © Caio Cas-soli/stockxchange; © Library of Congress; © Laura Kennedy/stockxchange; © Steve Mockensturm/Madhouse; **168:** © Steve Mockensturm/Madhouse; **172:** © Steve Mockensturm/Madhouse; **187:** © Steve Mockensturm/Madhouse

Chapter 5: 191: Used by permission of the author; **206:** Daimler-Chrysler Maybach; **209:** © Robert Crumb. Used by permission of the Agence Litteraire Lora Fountain & Associates; **222:** *top:* Cour-tesy of Advertising Archives; *bottom:* Reebok Cubist Classic; **223:** *clockwise from top left:* Kabaret poster; © Marcos Weskamp. Used with permission; © 2005 Chin Music Press. Used with permission; © Ron English/Popaganda; © Common Sense for Drug Policy. www.csdp.org; **225:** © Dawn M. Turner/morguefile.com; **226:** *clockwise from top left:* © Nick Cowie/stockxchange; © Rene Schwietzke; © Dawn M. Turner/morguefile.com; © Quentin Houyoux/stockxchange; © Nate Powell/stockxchange; **228:** © National Fluid Milk Processor Promotion Board. Used with per-mission; © Family Theater Productions; **229:** © Haagen Dazs. Used by permission of Dreyer's Grand Ice Cream, Inc.; **230:** *clock-wise from top left:* © EPA/LYDIE/Landov; © Beiot Tessier/Maxppp/Landov; © picturesonwalls.com Used with permission; © Zane Williams/Getty Images

Chapter 6: 244: © Big Pictures Media Corporation/The Kobal Collection; **254:** The Frito Bandito; **275:** © USGS/NASA; *clockwise from top right:* Napster logo and marks reprinted with the permission of Napster, LLC.; © George Zimzores/morguefile.com; © Francie Manning/Index Stock Imagery; **282:** © Steve Mockensturm/Madhouse

Chapter 7: 302: © Keith Syvinski/stockxchange; **325:** © Madhouse; **334:** Used by permission of the author; **339:** © BrookeB/stockxchange; *clockwise from left:* © Petra Giner/stockxchange; © Kevin Connors/morguefile.com; © Barbara Bar/morguefile.com; © Barbara Bar/stockxchange

Chapter 8: 358: © Wilfried/Heider/stockxchange; **363:** © LUCASFILM/20TH CENTURY FOX/THE KOBAL COLLECTION; **375:** © CBS/Landov; **377:** Homer Simpson's Scream; **385:** © Raul Martins Junior/stockxchange; *top to bottom:* © Kay Pat/stockxchange; © Ben Merghart/stockxchange; © Mauro Simonato/stockxchange

Chapter 9: 406: © Tim Dalek/morguefile.com; **421:** © Christopher Wilhelm/Corbis; **428:** © Howard Grey/Photodisc Red; **433:** © Milca Mulders/stockxchange; *clockwise from top left:* © Christopher Scott/morguefile.com; © Adam Ciesielski/stockxchange; © Image After; © Tatiana Tsokolova/morguefile.com; **451:** Used by permission of the author.

Chapter 10: 452: © XianStudio LLC/morguefile.com; **472:** © Tony Freeman/Photoedit; **483:** © Rich Stern/stockxchange; *clockwise from top:* © Ronnie Bergeron/morguefile.com; © Malinda Welte/morguefile.com; © Konrad Prissnitz/stockxchange; **501:** © Steve Mockensturm/Madhouse

Chapter 11: 502: © Dave Gilligan/stockxchange; **516:** © ARS, NY. Train at Night in the Desert. 1916. Watercolor, and pencil on paper, sheet 11 7/8 x 8/7/8. Acquired with matching funds from the Committee on Drawings and the National Endowment for the Arts. The Museum of Modern Art, New York, NY. U.S.A. Digital Image; **530:** Mona Lisa, c.1503-6 (oil on panel), Vinci, Leonardo da (1452–1519)/Louvre, Paris, France. Giraudon/Bridgeman Art Library; **539:** © Juan Romero/stockxchange; *clockwise from top left:* © Paul Fris/stockxchange; © Kevin Connors/morguefile.com; © Michael Connors/morguefile.com; © Kevin Connors/morguefile.com

Chapter 12: 560: Michelin Tweel™ lets the air out of tire performance. Copyright © 2005 Michelin North America, Inc.; **589:** Carlos Paes/morguefile.com; *clockwise from center:* Library of Congress; © Michael Connors/morguefile.com; © Dawn M. Turner/morguefile.com; © Dawn M. Turner/morguefile.com; **609:** *clockwise from top left:* © Carl Dwyer/stockxchange; © Lynsey Addario/Corbis; © Lars Sundstrom/stockxchange

Chapter 13: 626: © Northwestern Michigan College, Mark and Helen Osterlin Library; **637:** © Steve Mockensturm/Madhouse

Chapter 14: 698: © Thenthdegree. Used with permission; **700:** © Tony Korody/Corbis Sygma; **707:** Used by permission of the author; **708:** Used by permission of the author; **709:** Test mold photo courtesy of City of Vancouver and artist Jen Weih. Copyright © 2005, **710:** Courtesy of Kenny La Roche; **711-13:** All used by permission of the author; **717:** © Steve Mockensturm/Madhouse; **720:** © Sojourners, Inc. Used with permission; **721:** The Weekly Standard; **723:** © MIP/Getty Images; **726:** Used by permission of the author; **743:** Library of Congress

INDEX